SUPERMAN
RETURNS

THE MOVIE AND OTHER TALES
OF THE MAN OF STEEL

Dan DiDio Senior VP-Executive Editor

Jaye Gardner, Eddie Berganza, Ivan Cohen
Editors-original series

Tom Palmer, Jr. Associate Editor-original series

Jeanine Schaefer Assistant Editor-original series

Anton Kawasaki Editor-collected edition

Robbin Brosterman Senior Art Director

Paul Levitz President & Publisher

Georg Brewer VP-Design & DC Direct Creative

Richard Bruning Senior VP-Creative Director

Patrick Caldon Executive VP-Finance & Operations

Chris Caramalis VP-Finance

John Cunningham VP-Marketing

Terri Cunningham VP-Managing Editor

Stephanie Fierman Senior VP-Sales & Marketing

Alison Gill VP-Manufacturing

Rich Johnson VP-Book Trade Sales

Hank Kanalz VP-General Manager, WildStorm

Lillian Laserson Senior VP & General Counsel

Jim Lee Editorial Director-WildStorm

Paula Lowitt Senior VP-Business & Legal Affairs

David McKillips VP-Advertising & Custom Publishing

John Nee VP-Business Development

Gregory Noveck Senior VP-Creative Affairs

Cheryl Rubin Senior VP-Brand Management

Bob Wayne VP-Sales

SUPERMAN CREATED BY JERRY SIEGEL AND JOE SHUSTER

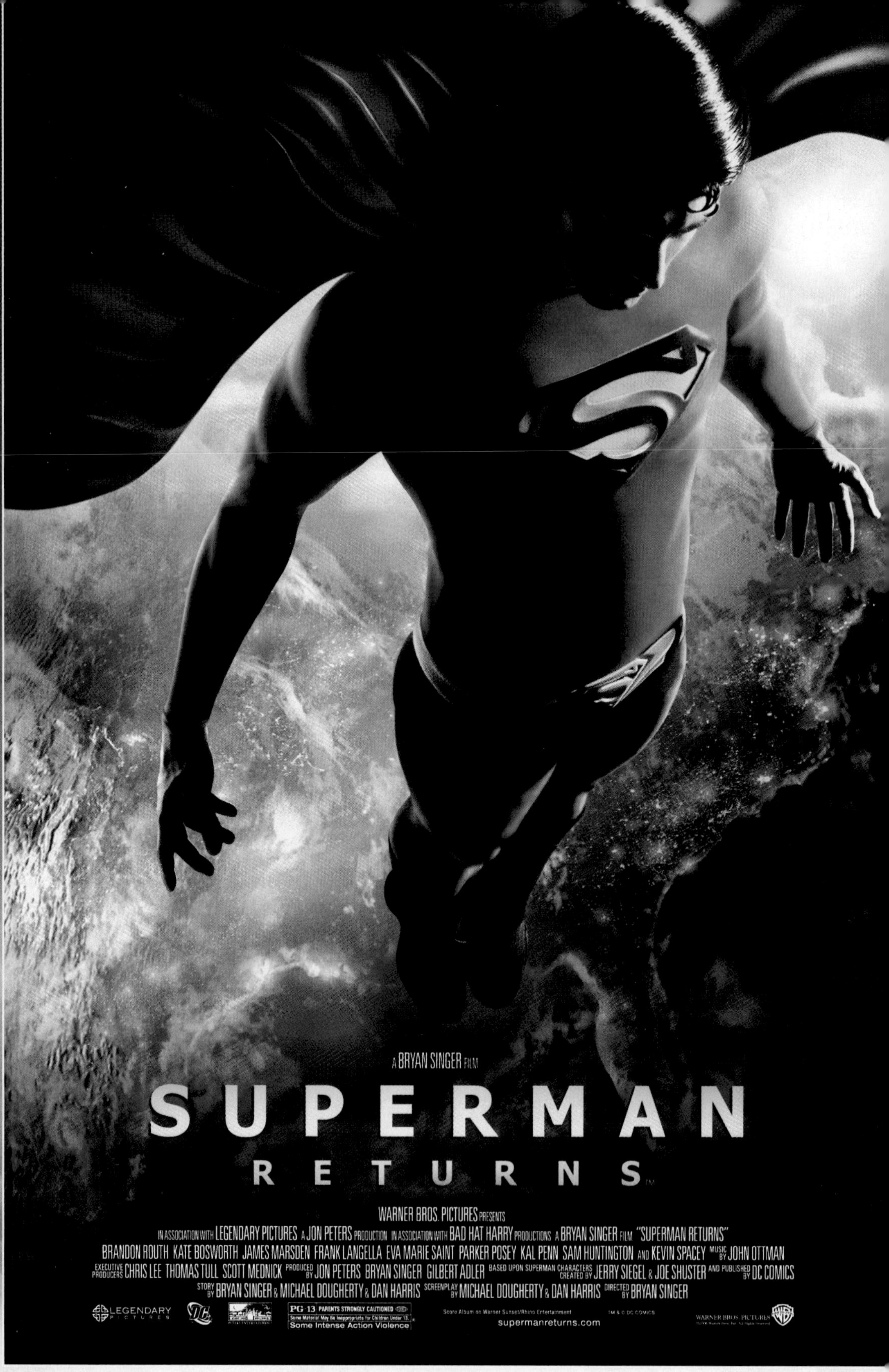
A BRYAN SINGER FILM
SUPERMAN
RETURNS™
WARNER BROS. PICTURES PRESENTS
IN ASSOCIATION WITH LEGENDARY PICTURES A JON PETERS PRODUCTION IN ASSOCIATION WITH BAD HAT HARRY PRODUCTIONS A BRYAN SINGER FILM "SUPERMAN RETURNS"
BRANDON ROUTH KATE BOSWORTH JAMES MARSDEN FRANK LANGELLA EVA MARIE SAINT PARKER POSEY KAL PENN SAM HUNTINGTON AND KEVIN SPACEY MUSIC BY JOHN OTTMAN
EXECUTIVE PRODUCERS CHRIS LEE THOMAS TULL SCOTT MEDNICK PRODUCED BY JON PETERS BRYAN SINGER GILBERT ADLER BASED UPON SUPERMAN CHARACTERS CREATED BY JERRY SIEGEL & JOE SHUSTER AND PUBLISHED BY DC COMICS
STORY BY BRYAN SINGER & MICHAEL DOUGHERTY & DAN HARRIS SCREENPLAY BY MICHAEL DOUGHERTY & DAN HARRIS DIRECTED BY BRYAN SINGER
LEGENDARY PICTURES
PG-13 PARENTS STRONGLY CAUTIONED
Some Material May Be Inappropriate for Children Under 13.
Some Intense Action Violence
Score Album on Warner Sunset/Rhino Entertainment
supermanreturns.com
TM & © DC COMICS
WARNER BROS. PICTURES

SUPERMAN RETURNS: The Movie Adaptatio

MARTIN PASKO writer **MATT HALEY, MIKE COLLINS AND RON RANDALL** pencillers
NATHAN EYRING LARRY MOLINAR colorists **KEN LOPEZ** letterer

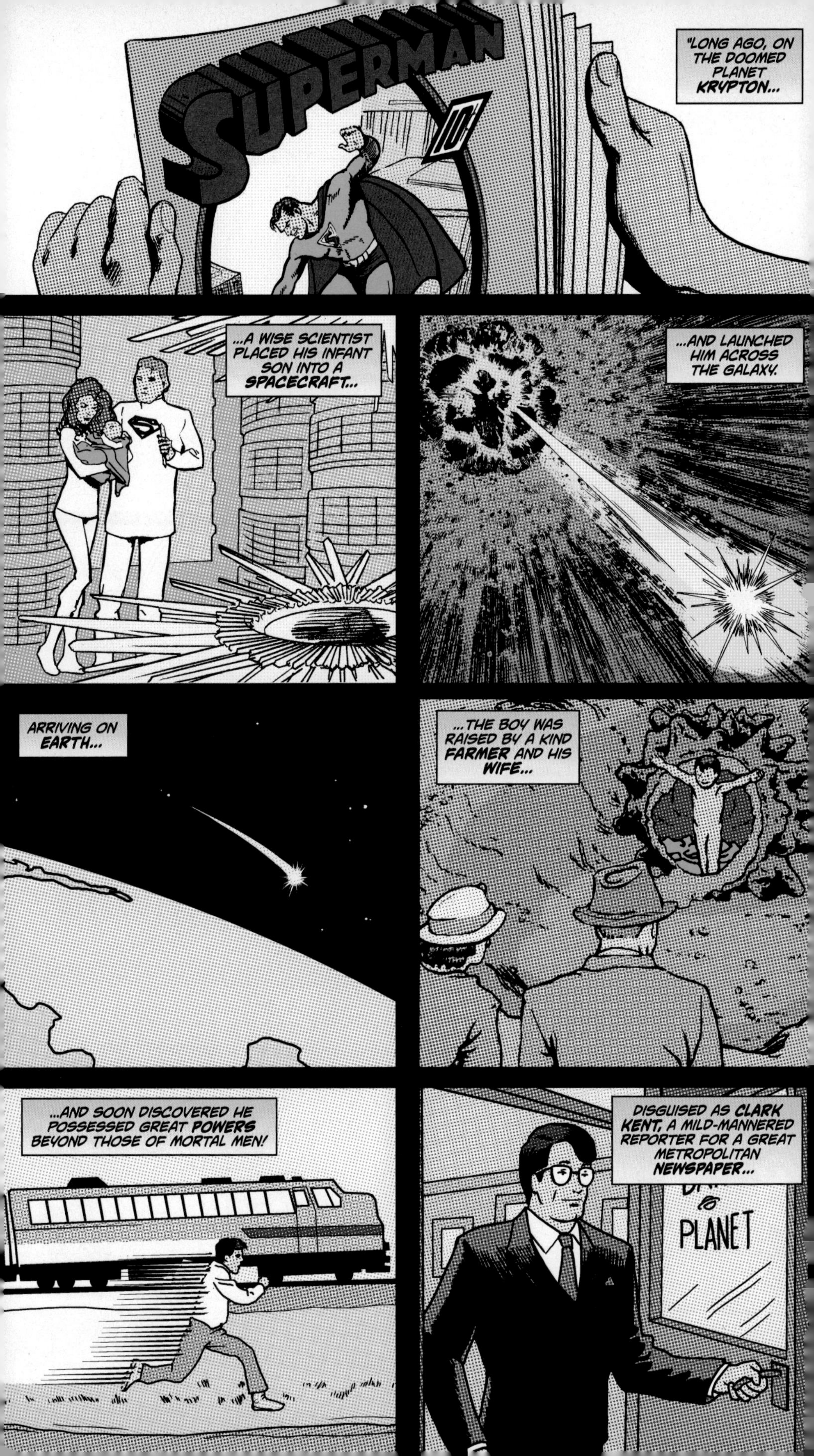
SUPERMAN
10¢
"LONG AGO, ON THE DOOMED PLANET KRYPTON...
...A WISE SCIENTIST PLACED HIS INFANT SON INTO A SPACECRAFT...
...AND LAUNCHED HIM ACROSS THE GALAXY.
ARRIVING ON EARTH...
...THE BOY WAS RAISED BY A KIND FARMER AND HIS WIFE...
...AND SOON DISCOVERED HE POSSESSED GREAT POWERS BEYOND THOSE OF MORTAL MEN!
DISGUISED AS CLARK KENT, A MILD-MANNERED REPORTER FOR A GREAT METROPOLITAN NEWSPAPER...
PLANET

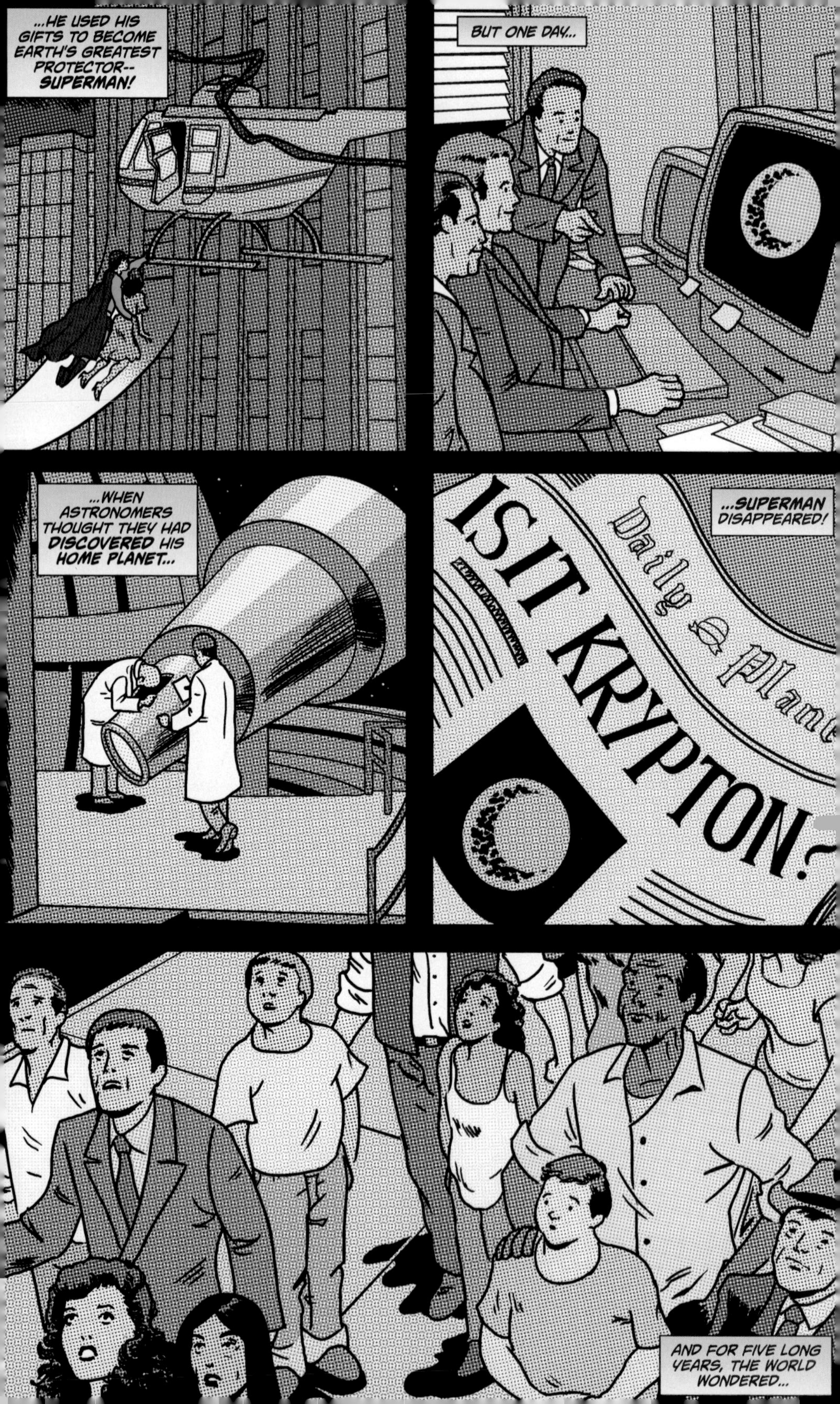
...HE USED HIS GIFTS TO BECOME EARTH'S GREATEST PROTECTOR-- SUPERMAN!
BUT ONE DAY...
...WHEN ASTRONOMERS THOUGHT THEY HAD DISCOVERED HIS HOME PLANET...
Daily Planet
IS IT KRYPTON?
...SUPERMAN DISAPPEARED!
AND FOR FIVE LONG YEARS, THE WORLD WONDERED...

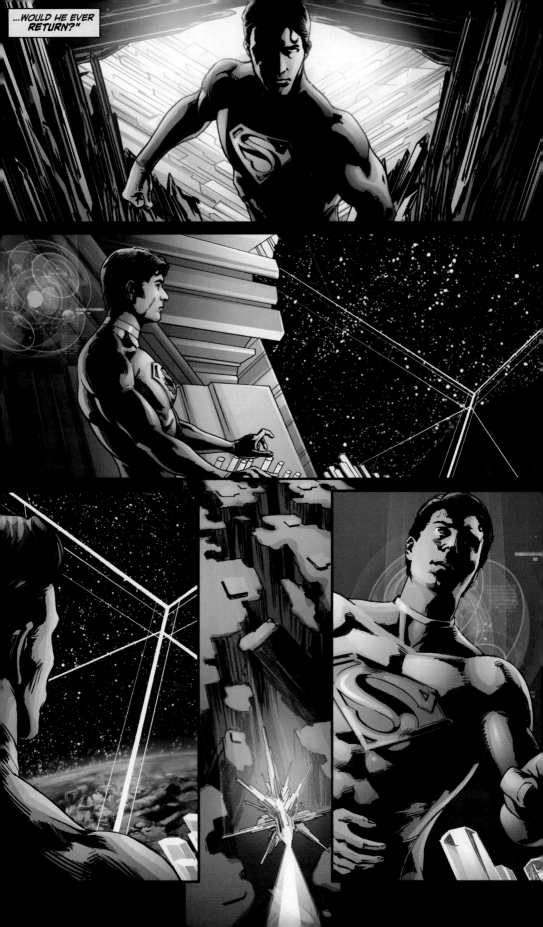

...WOULD HE EVER RETURN?"

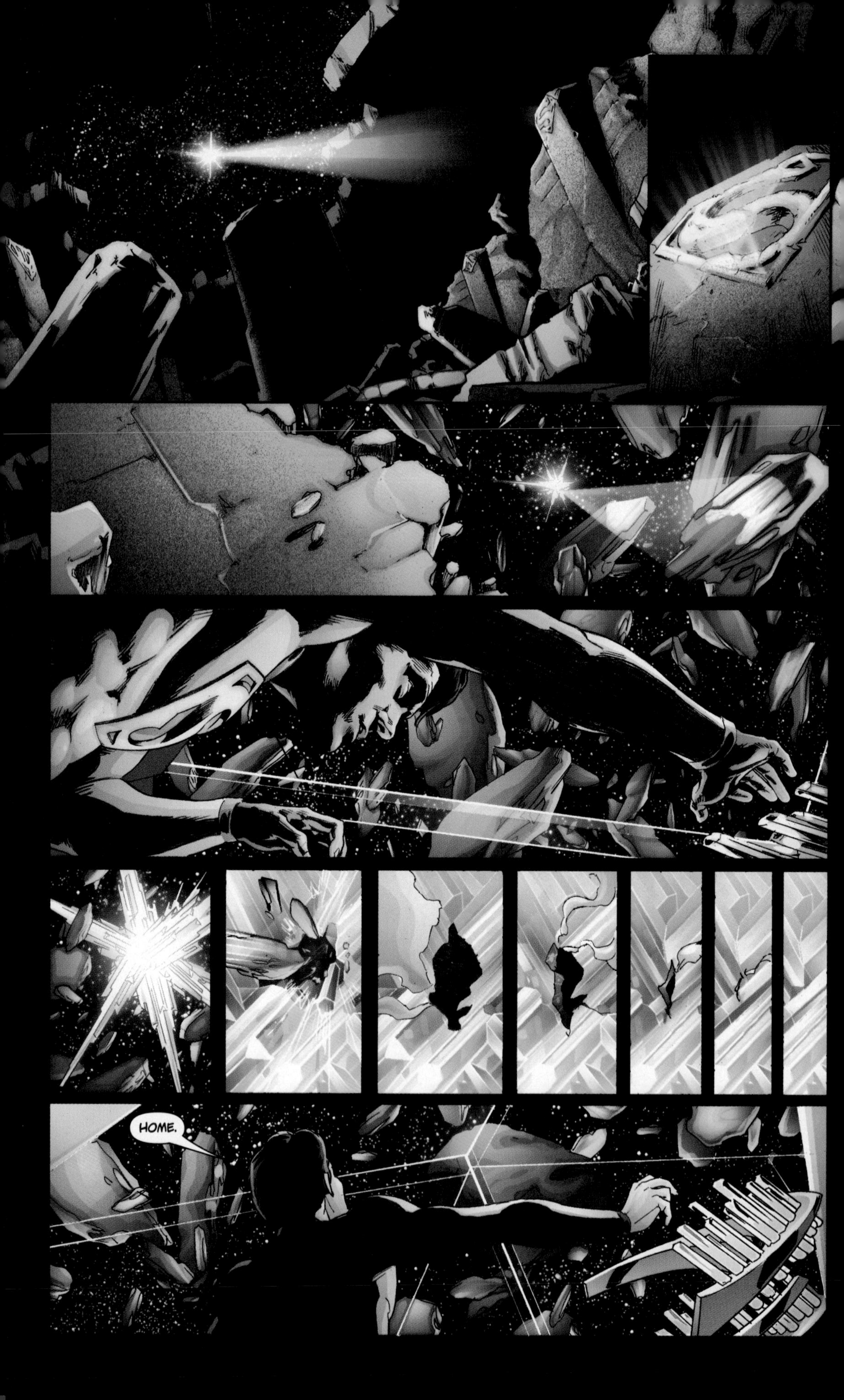
HOME.

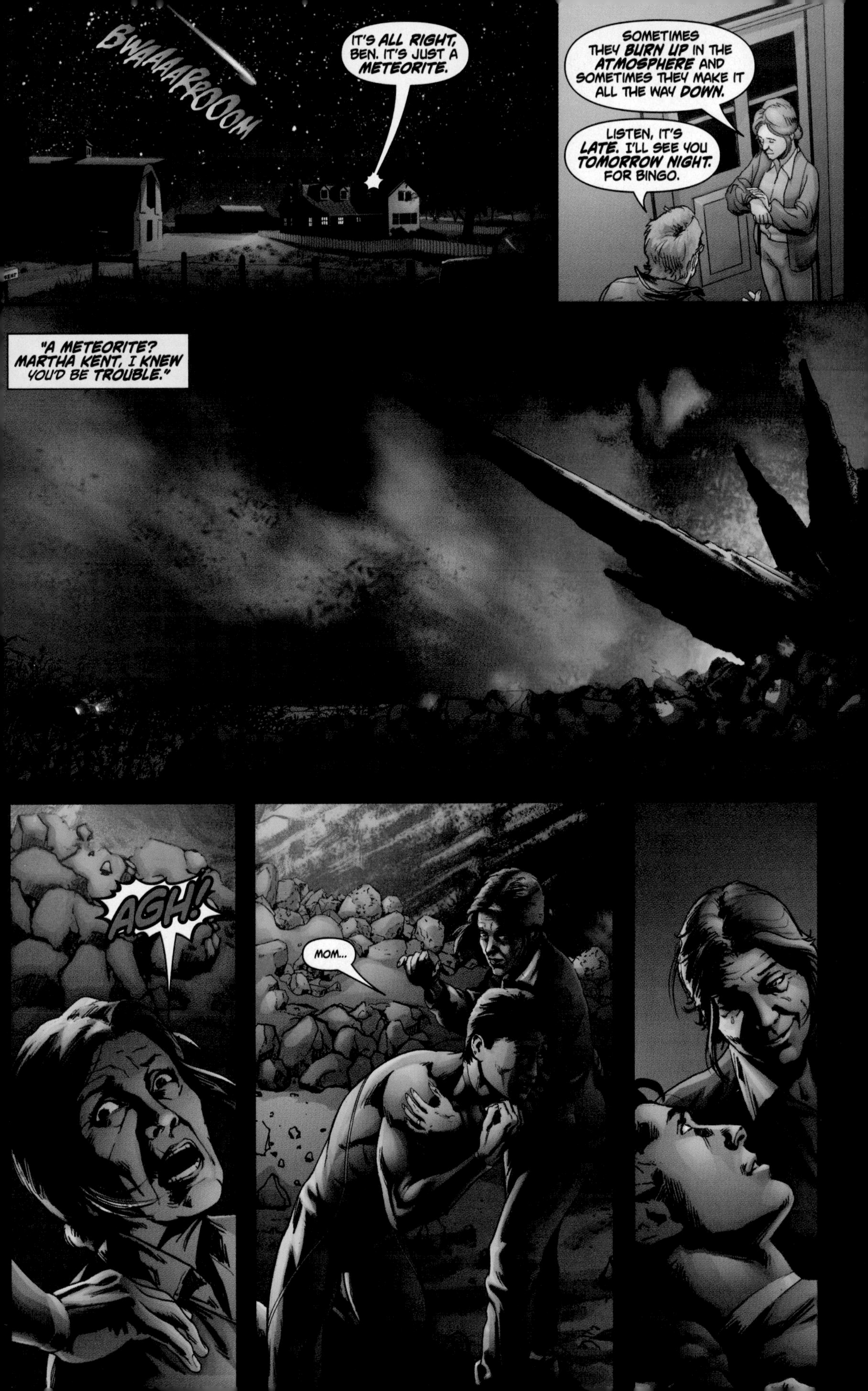
BWAAAARROOOM
IT'S ALL RIGHT, BEN. IT'S JUST A METEORITE.
SOMETIMES THEY BURN UP IN THE ATMOSPHERE AND SOMETIMES THEY MAKE IT ALL THE WAY DOWN.
LISTEN, IT'S LATE. I'LL SEE YOU TOMORROW NIGHT. FOR BINGO.
"A METEORITE? MARTHA KENT, I KNEW YOU'D BE TROUBLE."
AGH!
MOM...

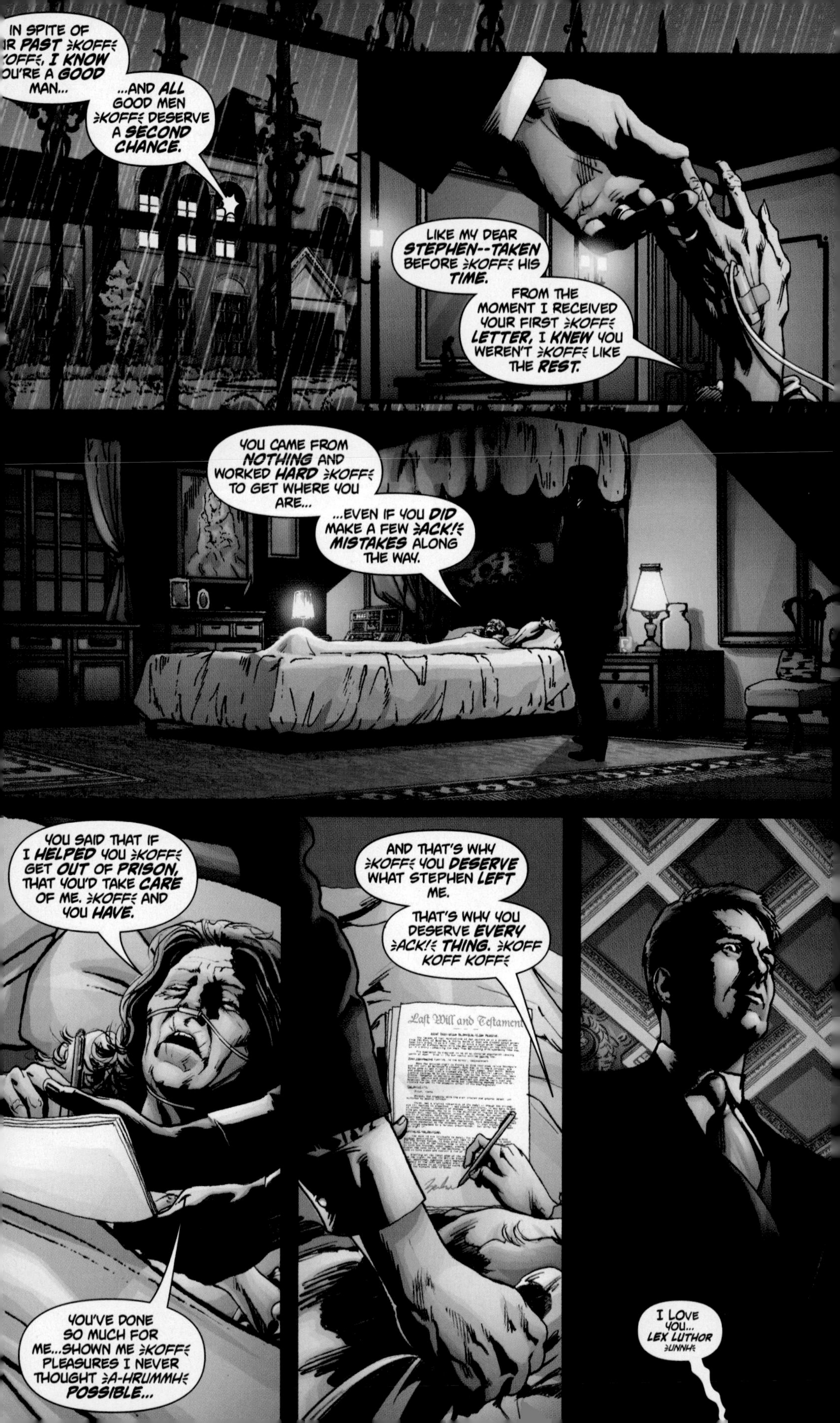
IN SPITE OF R PAST KOFF KOFF, I KNOW OU'RE A GOOD MAN...
...AND ALL GOOD MEN KOFF DESERVE A SECOND CHANCE.
LIKE MY DEAR STEPHEN--TAKEN BEFORE KOFF HIS TIME.
FROM THE MOMENT I RECEIVED YOUR FIRST KOFF LETTER, I KNEW YOU WEREN'T KOFF LIKE THE REST.
YOU CAME FROM NOTHING AND WORKED HARD KOFF TO GET WHERE YOU ARE...
...EVEN IF YOU DID MAKE A FEW ACK! MISTAKES ALONG THE WAY.
YOU SAID THAT IF I HELPED YOU KOFF GET OUT OF PRISON, THAT YOU'D TAKE CARE OF ME. KOFF AND YOU HAVE.
YOU'VE DONE SO MUCH FOR ME...SHOWN ME KOFF PLEASURES I NEVER THOUGHT A-HRUMMH POSSIBLE...
AND THAT'S WHY KOFF YOU DESERVE WHAT STEPHEN LEFT ME.
THAT'S WHY YOU DESERVE EVERY ACK! THING. KOFF KOFF KOFF
Last Will and Testament
I LOVE YOU... LEX LUTHOR UNNH

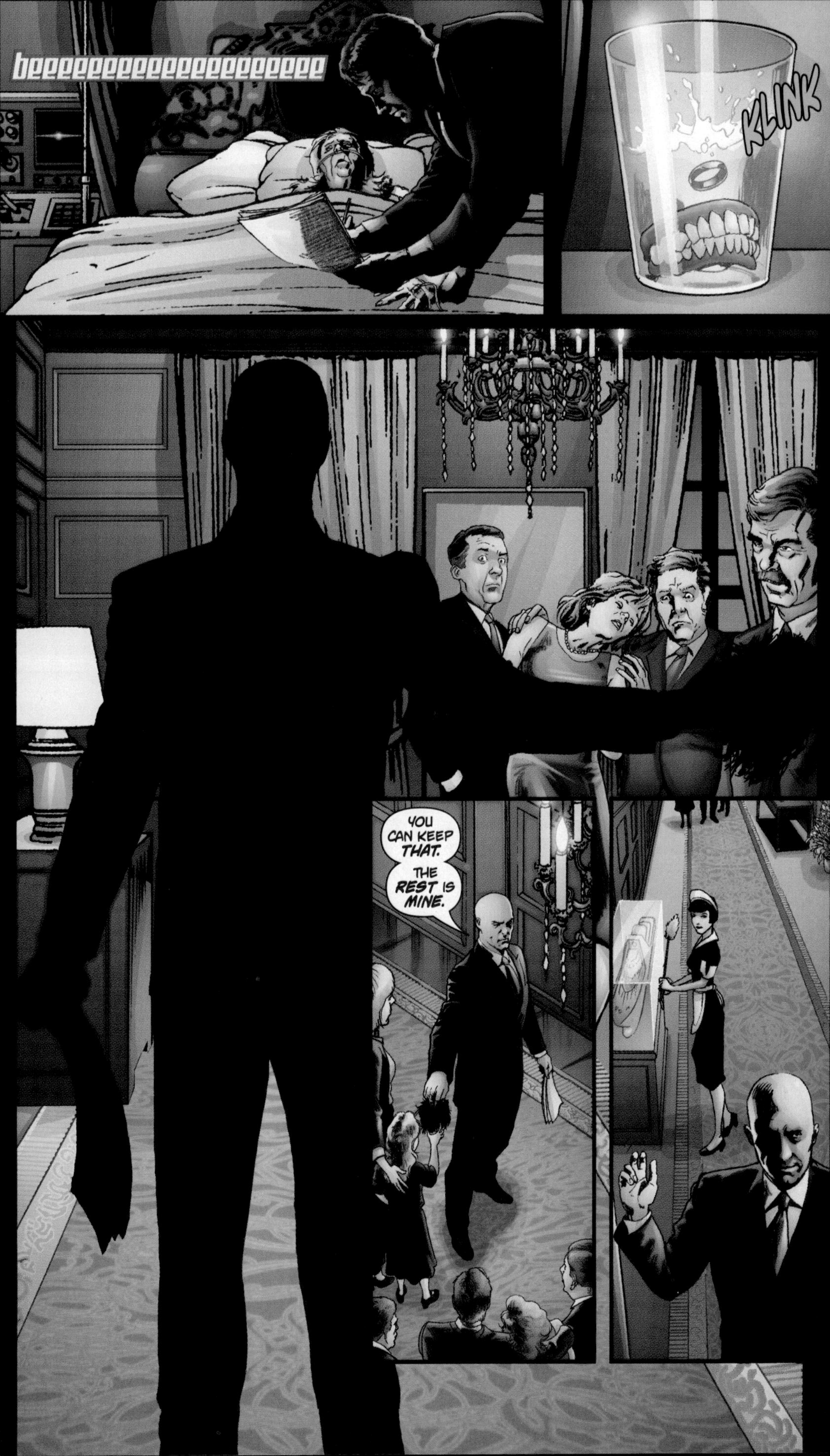
beeeeeeeeeeeeeeeeeeeeeee
KLINK
YOU CAN KEEP THAT. THE REST IS MINE.

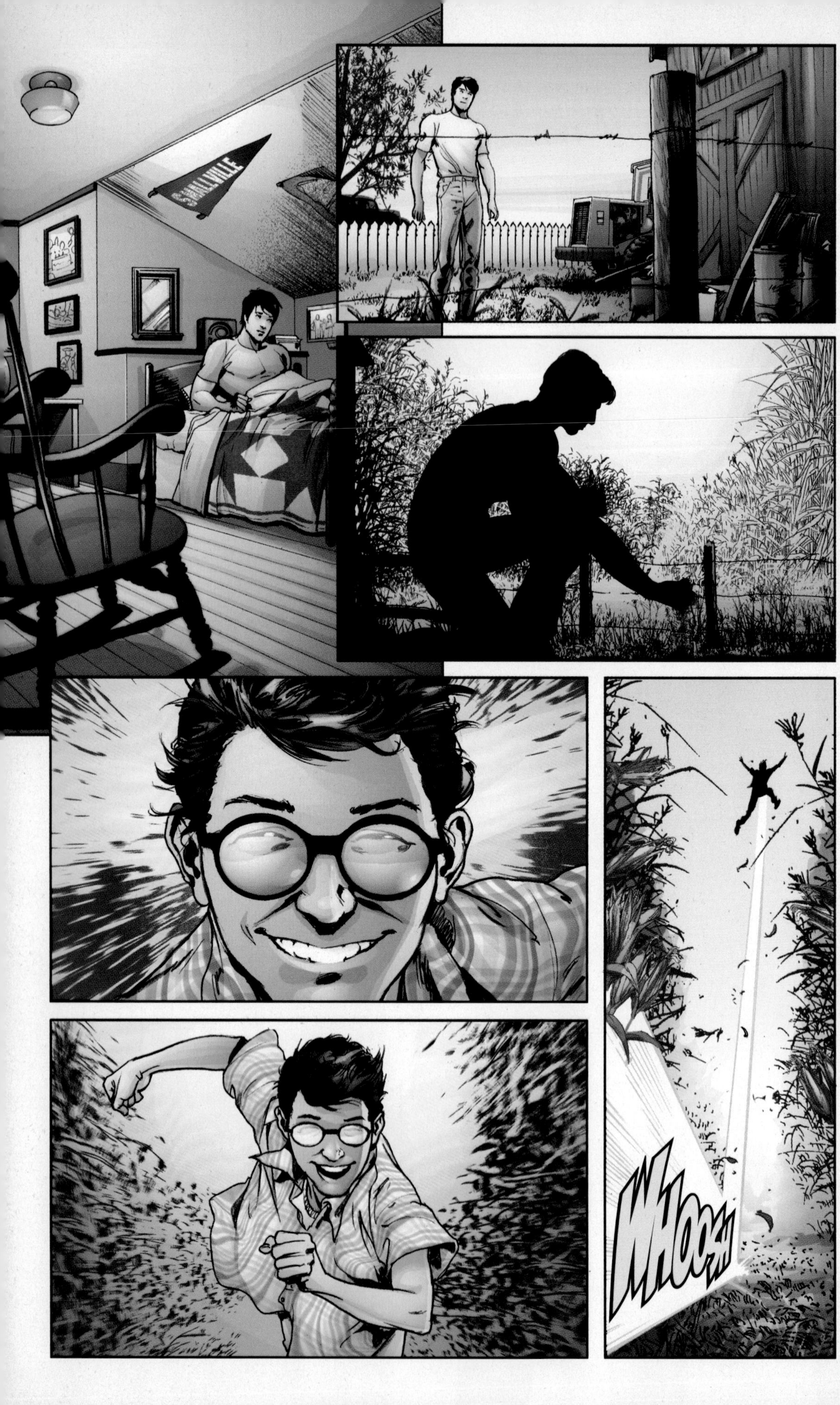
SMALLVILLE
WHOOSH

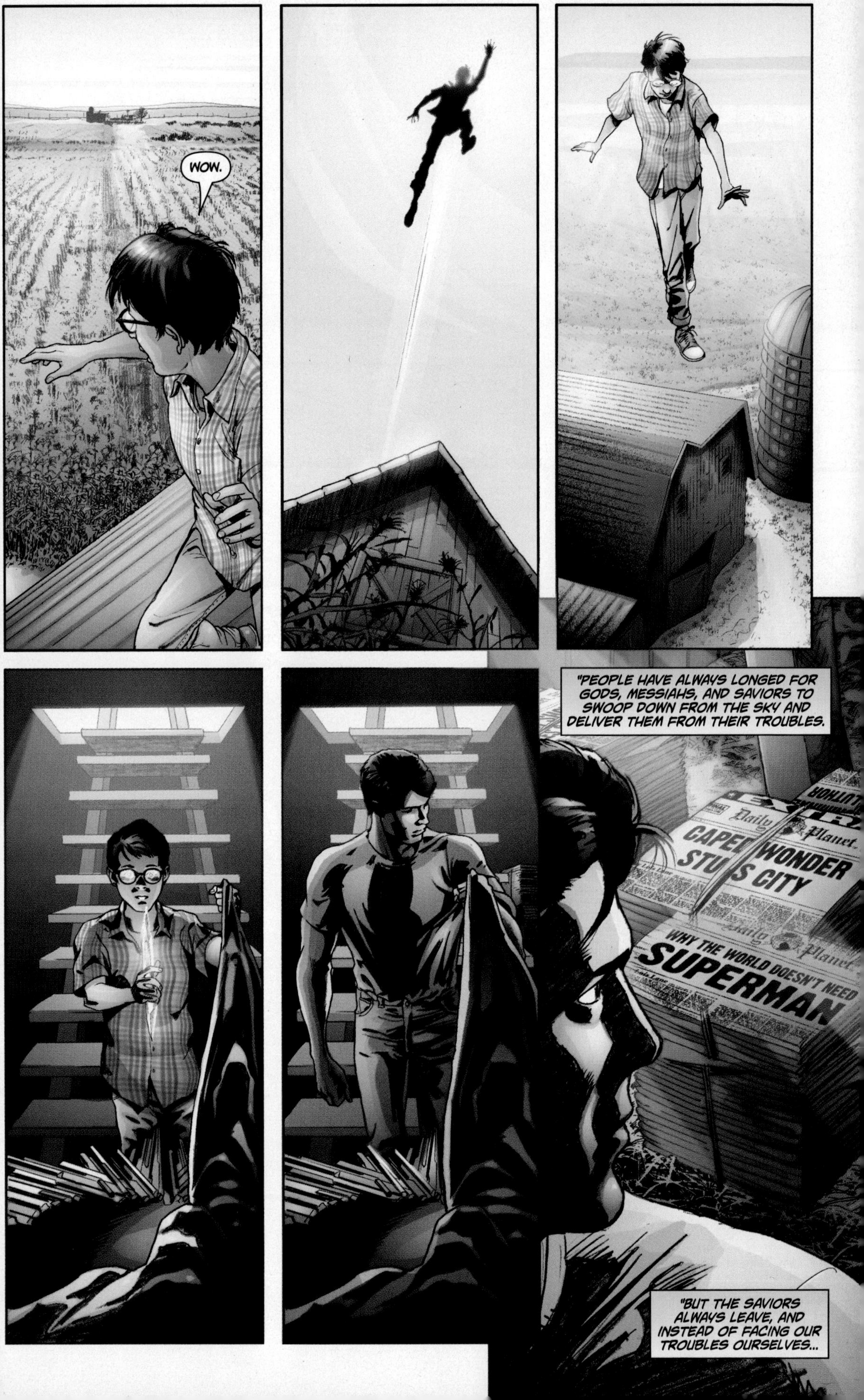
WOW.
"PEOPLE HAVE ALWAYS LONGED FOR GODS, MESSIAHS, AND SAVIORS TO SWOOP DOWN FROM THE SKY AND DELIVER THEM FROM THEIR TROUBLES.
Daily Planet
WHY THE WORLD DOESN'T NEED
SUPERMAN
"BUT THE SAVIORS ALWAYS LEAVE, AND INSTEAD OF FACING OUR TROUBLES OURSELVES...

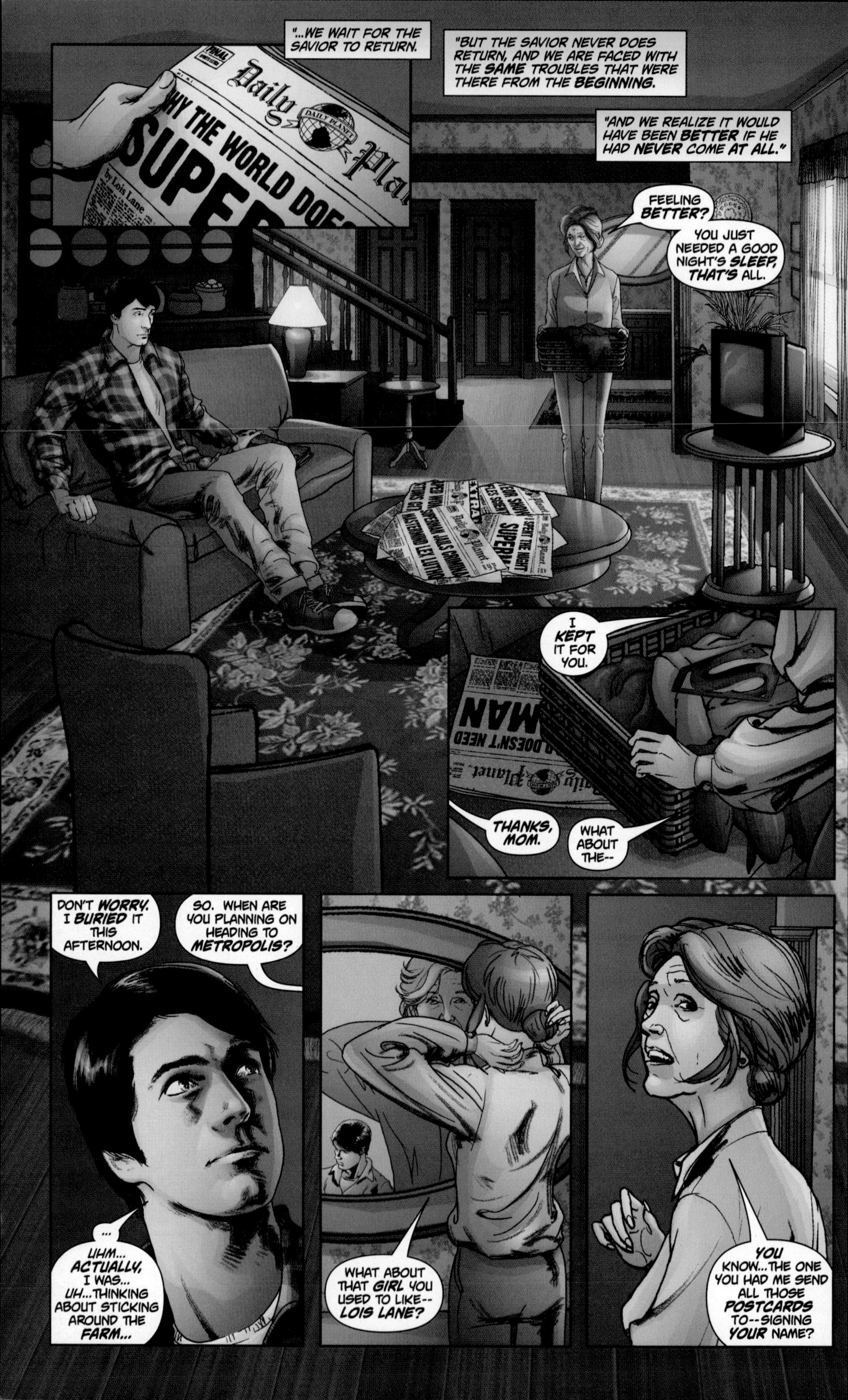
"...WE WAIT FOR THE SAVIOR TO RETURN.
Daily Planet
WHY THE WORLD DOES
SUPER
by Lois Lane
"BUT THE SAVIOR NEVER DOES RETURN, AND WE ARE FACED WITH THE SAME TROUBLES THAT WERE THERE FROM THE BEGINNING.
"AND WE REALIZE IT WOULD HAVE BEEN BETTER IF HE HAD NEVER COME AT ALL."
FEELING BETTER?
YOU JUST NEEDED A GOOD NIGHT'S SLEEP, THAT'S ALL.
I KEPT IT FOR YOU.
THANKS, MOM.
WHAT ABOUT THE--
DON'T WORRY. I BURIED IT THIS AFTERNOON.
SO. WHEN ARE YOU PLANNING ON HEADING TO METROPOLIS?
...
UHM... ACTUALLY, I WAS... UH...THINKING ABOUT STICKING AROUND THE FARM...
WHAT ABOUT THAT GIRL YOU USED TO LIKE-- LOIS LANE?
YOU KNOW...THE ONE YOU HAD ME SEND ALL THOSE POSTCARDS TO--SIGNING YOUR NAME?

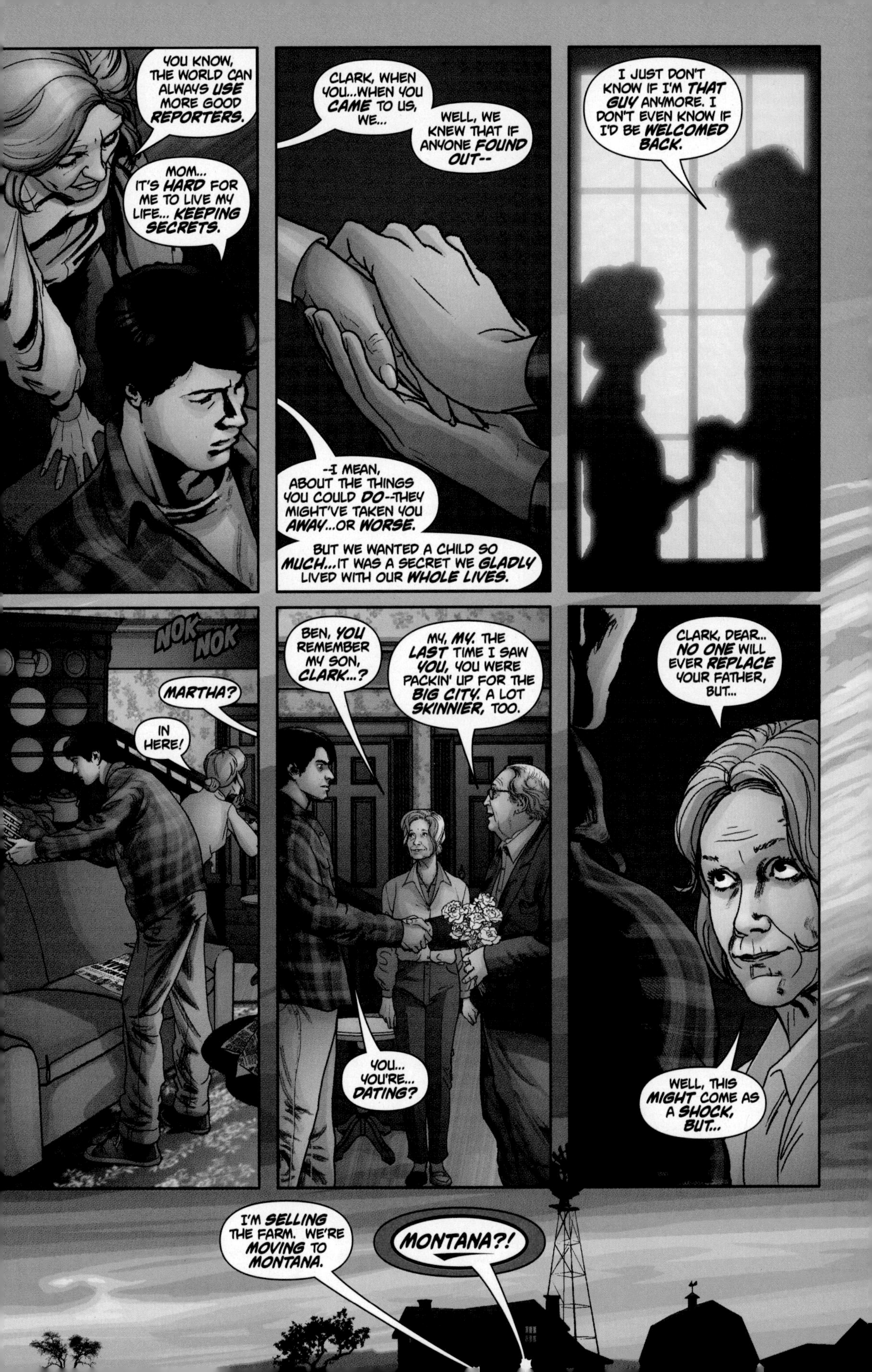
YOU KNOW, THE WORLD CAN ALWAYS USE MORE GOOD REPORTERS.
MOM... IT'S HARD FOR ME TO LIVE MY LIFE... KEEPING SECRETS.
CLARK, WHEN YOU...WHEN YOU CAME TO US, WE...
WELL, WE KNEW THAT IF ANYONE FOUND OUT--
--I MEAN, ABOUT THE THINGS YOU COULD DO--THEY MIGHT'VE TAKEN YOU AWAY...OR WORSE.
BUT WE WANTED A CHILD SO MUCH...IT WAS A SECRET WE GLADLY LIVED WITH OUR WHOLE LIVES.
I JUST DON'T KNOW IF I'M THAT GUY ANYMORE. I DON'T EVEN KNOW IF I'D BE WELCOMED BACK.
NOK NOK
MARTHA?
IN HERE!
BEN, YOU REMEMBER MY SON, CLARK...?
MY, MY. THE LAST TIME I SAW YOU, YOU WERE PACKIN' UP FOR THE BIG CITY. A LOT SKINNIER, TOO.
YOU... YOU'RE... DATING?
CLARK, DEAR... NO ONE WILL EVER REPLACE YOUR FATHER, BUT...
WELL, THIS MIGHT COME AS A SHOCK, BUT...
I'M SELLING THE FARM. WE'RE MOVING TO MONTANA.
MONTANA?!

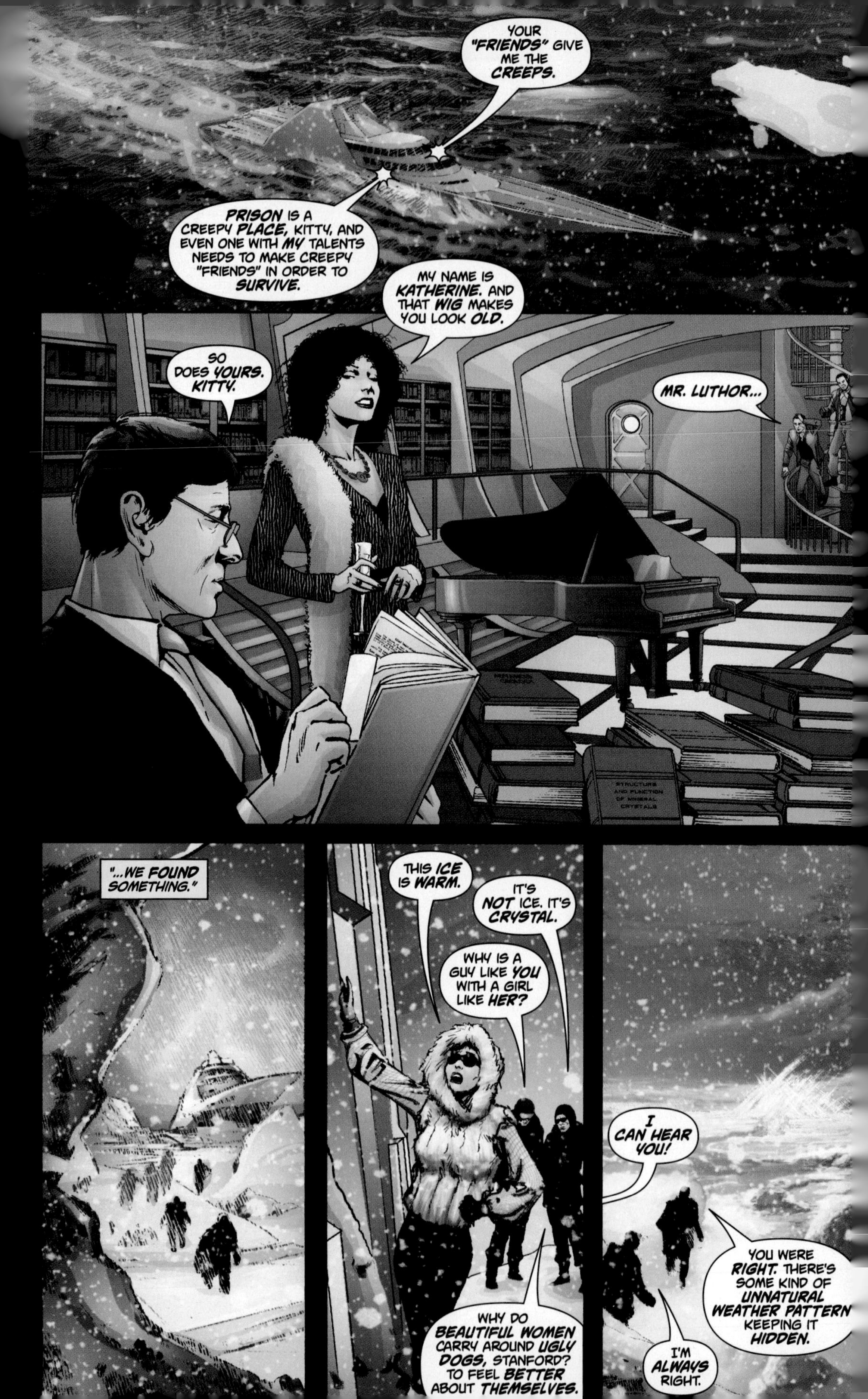
YOUR "FRIENDS" GIVE ME THE CREEPS.
PRISON IS A CREEPY PLACE, KITTY, AND EVEN ONE WITH MY TALENTS NEEDS TO MAKE CREEPY "FRIENDS" IN ORDER TO SURVIVE.
MY NAME IS KATHERINE. AND THAT WIG MAKES YOU LOOK OLD.
SO DOES YOURS. KITTY.
MR. LUTHOR...
STRUCTURES AND FUNCTION OF MINERAL CRYSTALS
"...WE FOUND SOMETHING."
THIS ICE IS WARM.
IT'S NOT ICE. IT'S CRYSTAL.
WHY IS A GUY LIKE YOU WITH A GIRL LIKE HER?
WHY DO BEAUTIFUL WOMEN CARRY AROUND UGLY DOGS, STANFORD? TO FEEL BETTER ABOUT THEMSELVES.
I CAN HEAR YOU!
YOU WERE RIGHT. THERE'S SOME KIND OF UNNATURAL WEATHER PATTERN KEEPING IT HIDDEN.
I'M ALWAYS RIGHT.

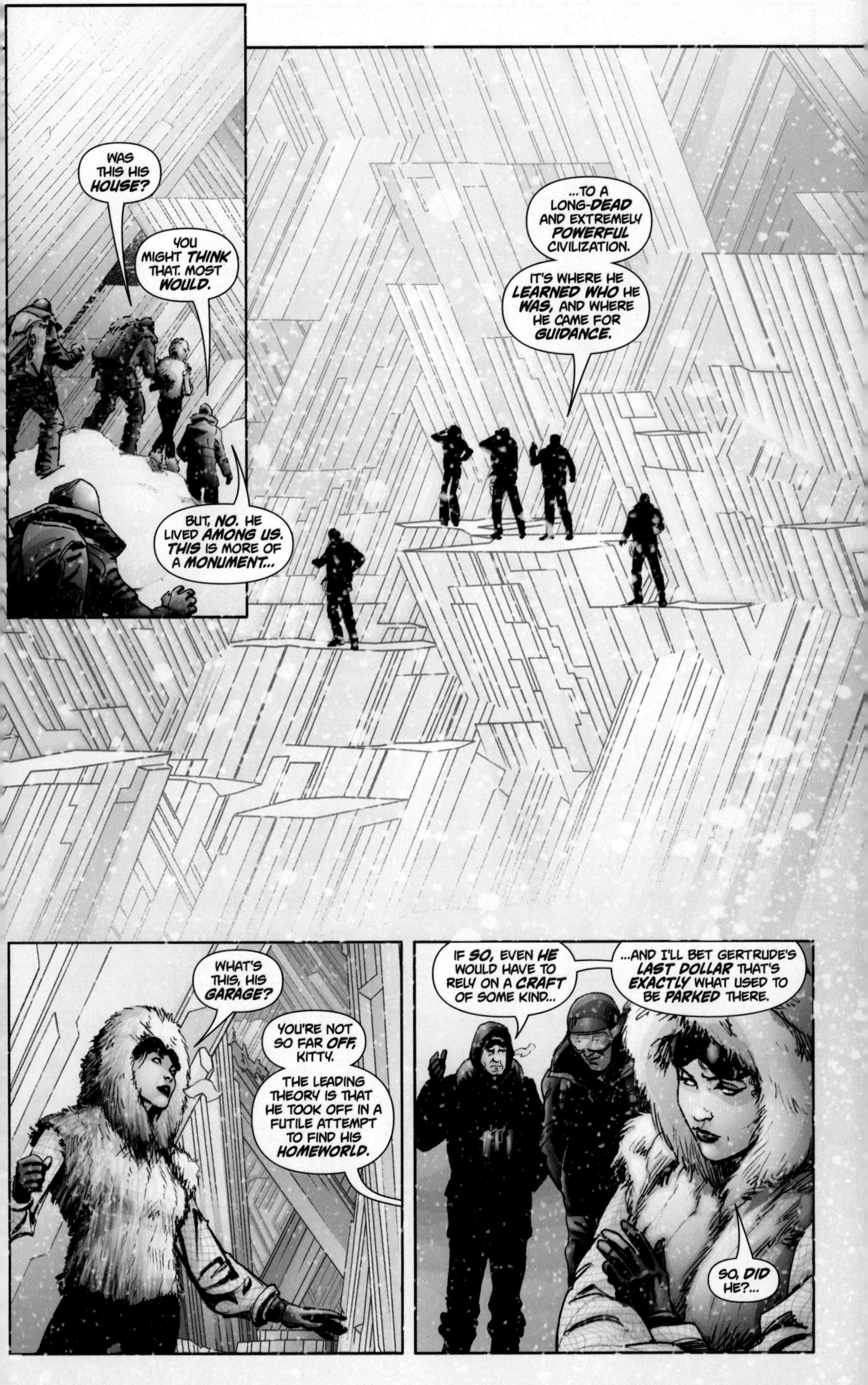

WAS THIS HIS HOUSE?
YOU MIGHT THINK THAT. MOST WOULD.
BUT, NO. HE LIVED AMONG US. THIS IS MORE OF A MONUMENT...
...TO A LONG-DEAD AND EXTREMELY POWERFUL CIVILIZATION.
IT'S WHERE HE LEARNED WHO HE WAS, AND WHERE HE CAME FOR GUIDANCE.
WHAT'S THIS, HIS GARAGE?
YOU'RE NOT SO FAR OFF, KITTY.
THE LEADING THEORY IS THAT HE TOOK OFF IN A FUTILE ATTEMPT TO FIND HIS HOMEWORLD.
IF SO, EVEN HE WOULD HAVE TO RELY ON A CRAFT OF SOME KIND...
...AND I'LL BET GERTRUDE'S LAST DOLLAR THAT'S EXACTLY WHAT USED TO BE PARKED THERE.
SO, DID HE?...

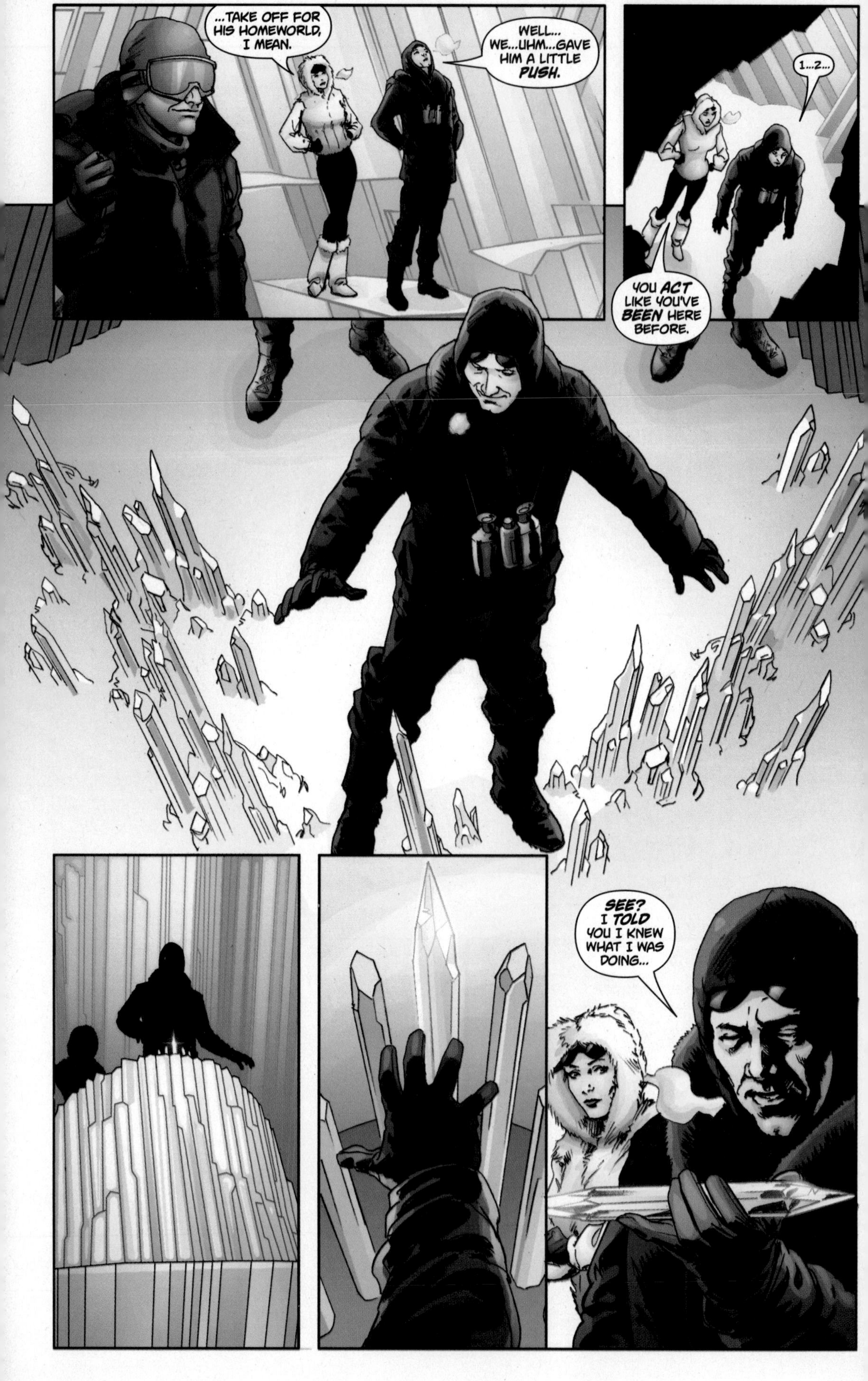
...TAKE OFF FOR HIS HOMEWORLD, I MEAN.
WELL... WE...UHM...GAVE HIM A LITTLE PUSH.
1...2...
YOU ACT LIKE YOU'VE BEEN HERE BEFORE.
SEE? I TOLD YOU I KNEW WHAT I WAS DOING...

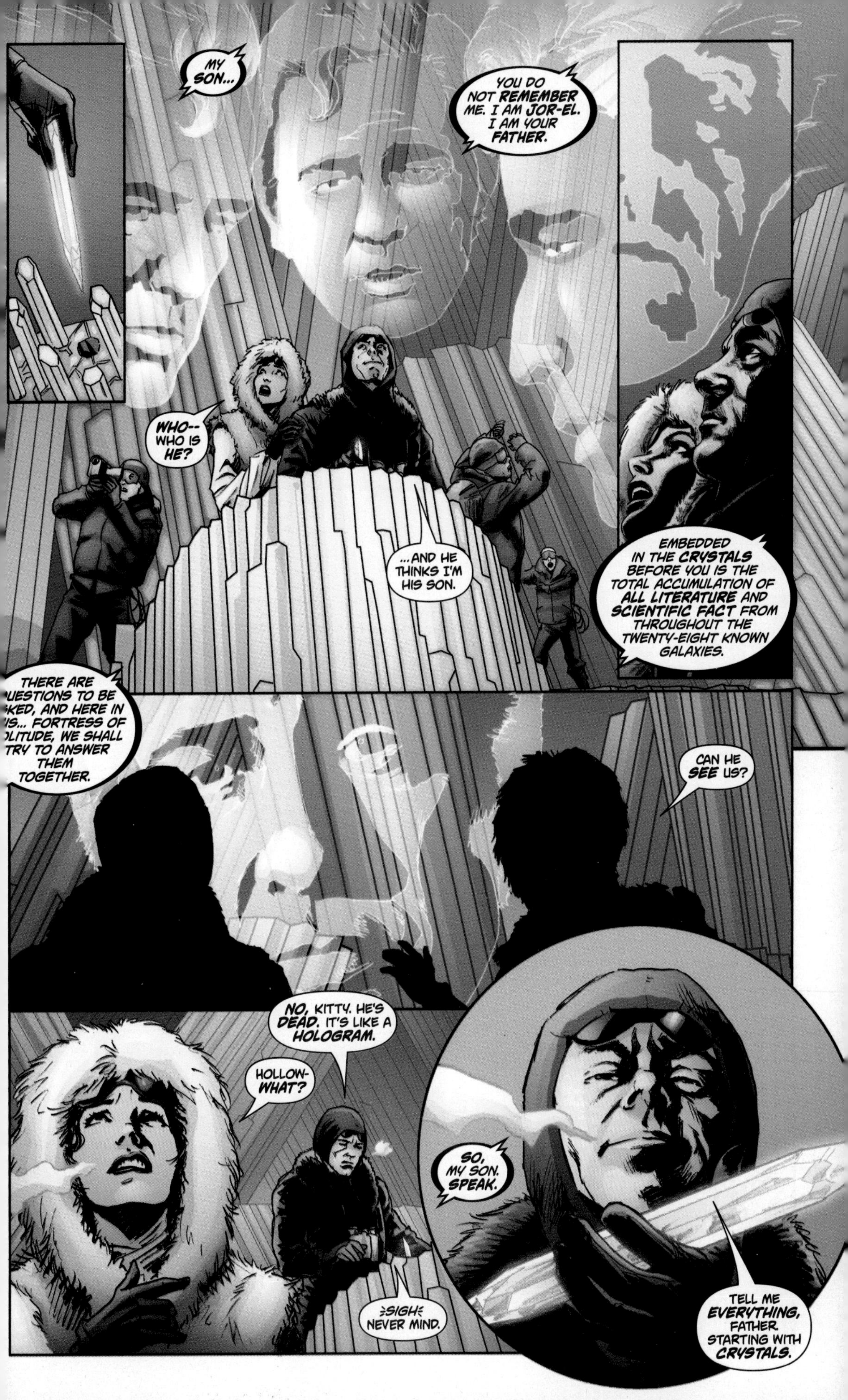
MY SON...
YOU DO NOT REMEMBER ME. I AM JOR-EL. I AM YOUR FATHER.
WHO-- WHO IS HE?
...AND HE THINKS I'M HIS SON.
EMBEDDED IN THE CRYSTALS BEFORE YOU IS THE TOTAL ACCUMULATION OF ALL LITERATURE AND SCIENTIFIC FACT FROM THROUGHOUT THE TWENTY-EIGHT KNOWN GALAXIES.
THERE ARE UESTIONS TO BE KED, AND HERE IN IS... FORTRESS OF OLITUDE, WE SHALL TRY TO ANSWER THEM TOGETHER.
CAN HE SEE US?
NO, KITTY. HE'S DEAD. IT'S LIKE A HOLOGRAM.
HOLLOW-WHAT?
SIGH NEVER MIND.
SO, MY SON. SPEAK.
TELL ME EVERYTHING, FATHER. STARTING WITH CRYSTALS.

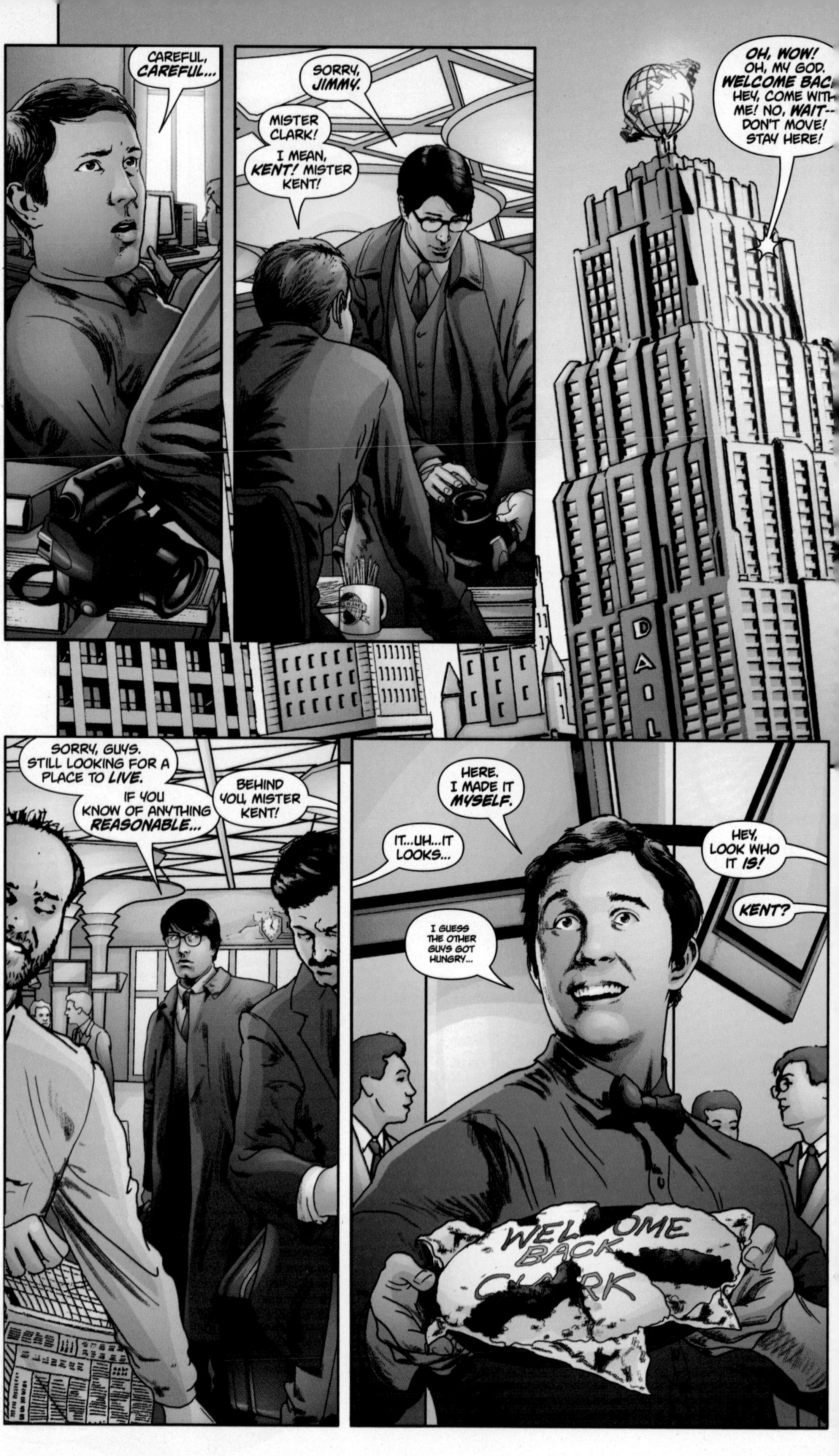
CAREFUL, CAREFUL...
SORRY, JIMMY.
MISTER CLARK!
I MEAN, KENT! MISTER KENT!
OH, WOW! OH, MY GOD. WELCOME BAC
HEY, COME WIT ME! NO, WAIT-- DON'T MOVE! STAY HERE!
DAIL
SORRY, GUYS. STILL LOOKING FOR A PLACE TO LIVE.
IF YOU KNOW OF ANYTHING REASONABLE...
BEHIND YOU, MISTER KENT!
HERE. I MADE IT MYSELF.
IT...UH...IT LOOKS...
HEY, LOOK WHO IT IS!
KENT?
I GUESS THE OTHER GUYS GOT HUNGRY...
WEL OME BACK C ARK

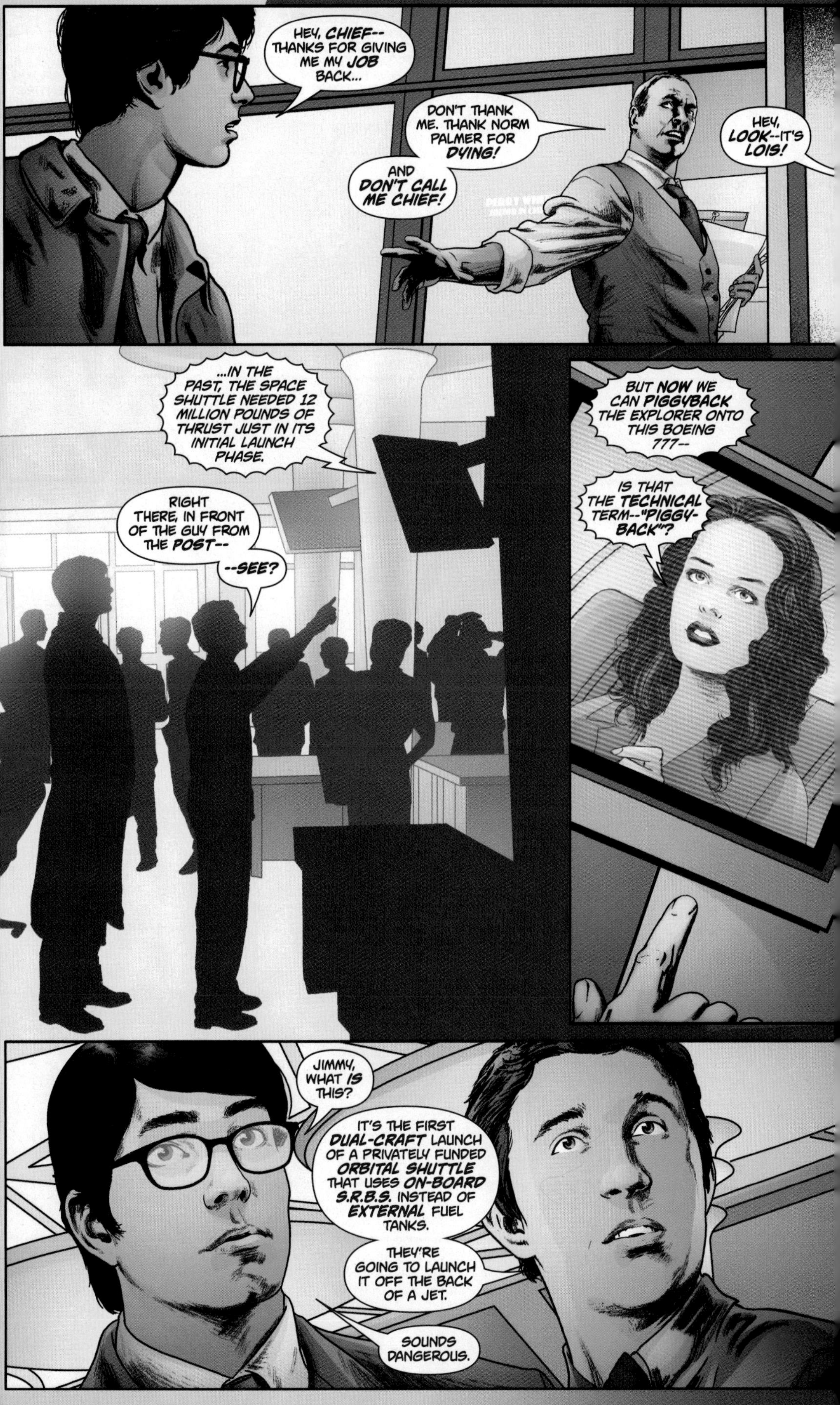
HEY, CHIEF-- THANKS FOR GIVING ME MY JOB BACK...
DON'T THANK ME. THANK NORM PALMER FOR DYING!
AND DON'T CALL ME CHIEF!
HEY, LOOK--IT'S LOIS!
...IN THE PAST, THE SPACE SHUTTLE NEEDED 12 MILLION POUNDS OF THRUST JUST IN ITS INITIAL LAUNCH PHASE.
RIGHT THERE, IN FRONT OF THE GUY FROM THE POST--
--SEE?
BUT NOW WE CAN PIGGYBACK THE EXPLORER ONTO THIS BOEING 777--
IS THAT THE TECHNICAL TERM--"PIGGY-BACK"?
JIMMY, WHAT IS THIS?
IT'S THE FIRST DUAL-CRAFT LAUNCH OF A PRIVATELY FUNDED ORBITAL SHUTTLE THAT USES ON-BOARD S.R.B.S. INSTEAD OF EXTERNAL FUEL TANKS.
THEY'RE GOING TO LAUNCH IT OFF THE BACK OF A JET.
SOUNDS DANGEROUS.

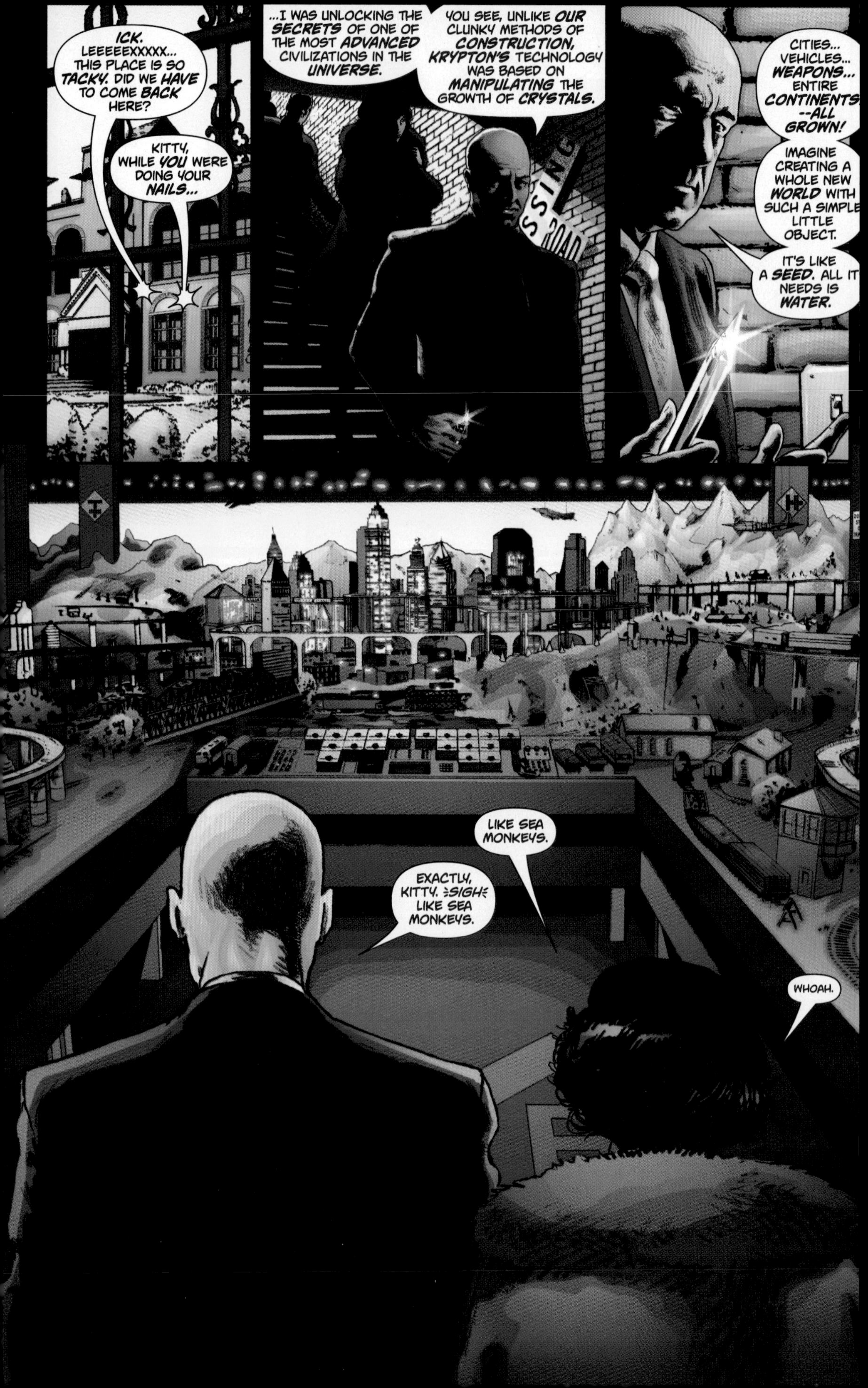
ICK. LEEEEEXXXXX... THIS PLACE IS SO TACKY. DID WE HAVE TO COME BACK HERE?
KITTY, WHILE YOU WERE DOING YOUR NAILS...
...I WAS UNLOCKING THE SECRETS OF ONE OF THE MOST ADVANCED CIVILIZATIONS IN THE UNIVERSE.
YOU SEE, UNLIKE OUR CLUNKY METHODS OF CONSTRUCTION, KRYPTON'S TECHNOLOGY WAS BASED ON MANIPULATING THE GROWTH OF CRYSTALS.
CITIES... VEHICLES... WEAPONS... ENTIRE CONTINENTS! --ALL GROWN!
IMAGINE CREATING A WHOLE NEW WORLD WITH SUCH A SIMPLE LITTLE OBJECT.
IT'S LIKE A SEED. ALL IT NEEDS IS WATER.
LIKE SEA MONKEYS.
EXACTLY, KITTY. ≶SIGH≷ LIKE SEA MONKEYS.
WHOAH.

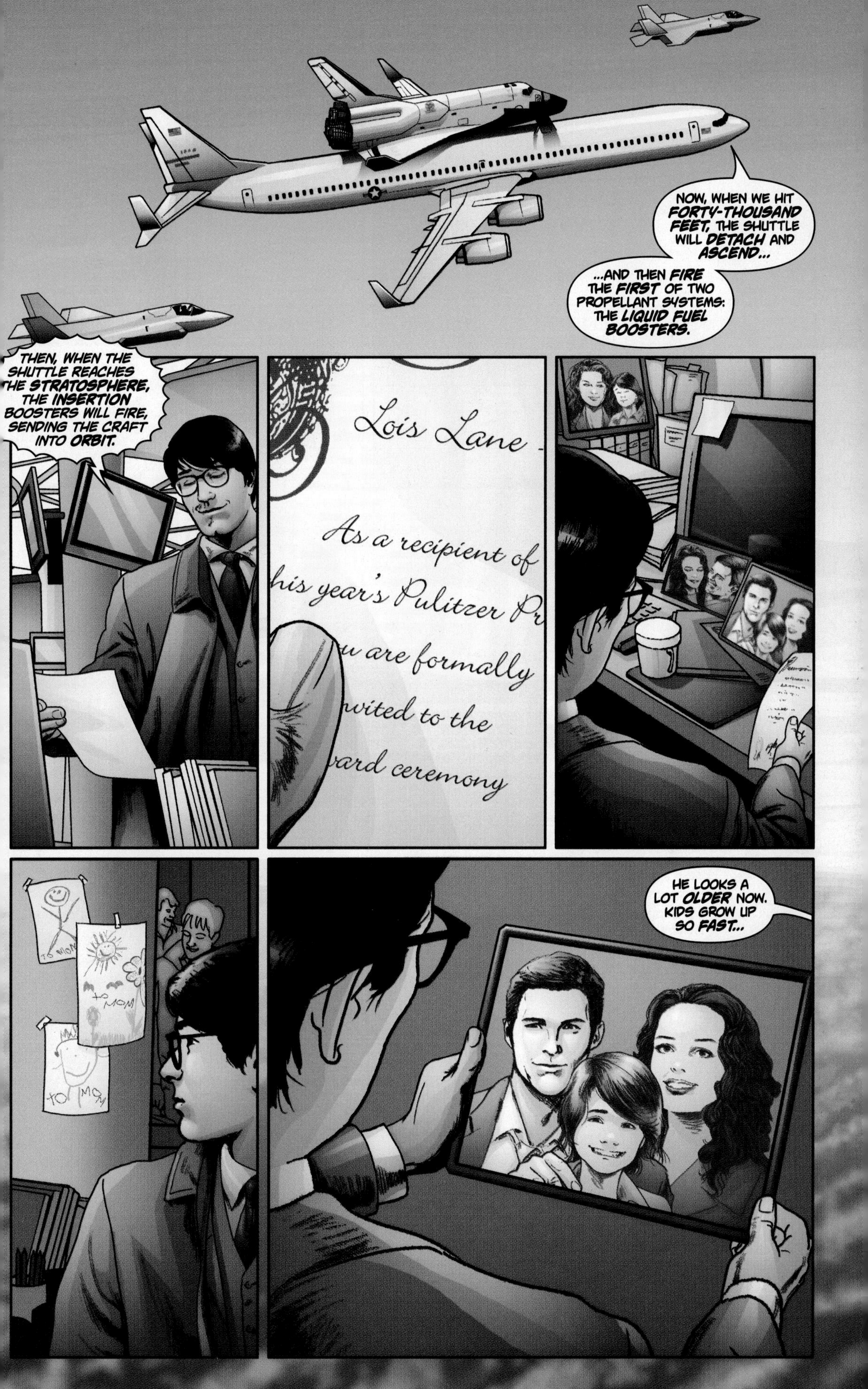
NOW, WHEN WE HIT FORTY-THOUSAND FEET, THE SHUTTLE WILL DETACH AND ASCEND...
...AND THEN FIRE THE FIRST OF TWO PROPELLANT SYSTEMS: THE LIQUID FUEL BOOSTERS.
THEN, WHEN THE SHUTTLE REACHES THE STRATOSPHERE, THE INSERTION BOOSTERS WILL FIRE, SENDING THE CRAFT INTO ORBIT.
Lois Lane
As a recipient of
his year's Pulitzer Pr
u are formally
vited to the
ard ceremony
TO MOM
TO MOM
TO MOM
HE LOOKS A LOT OLDER NOW. KIDS GROW UP SO FAST...

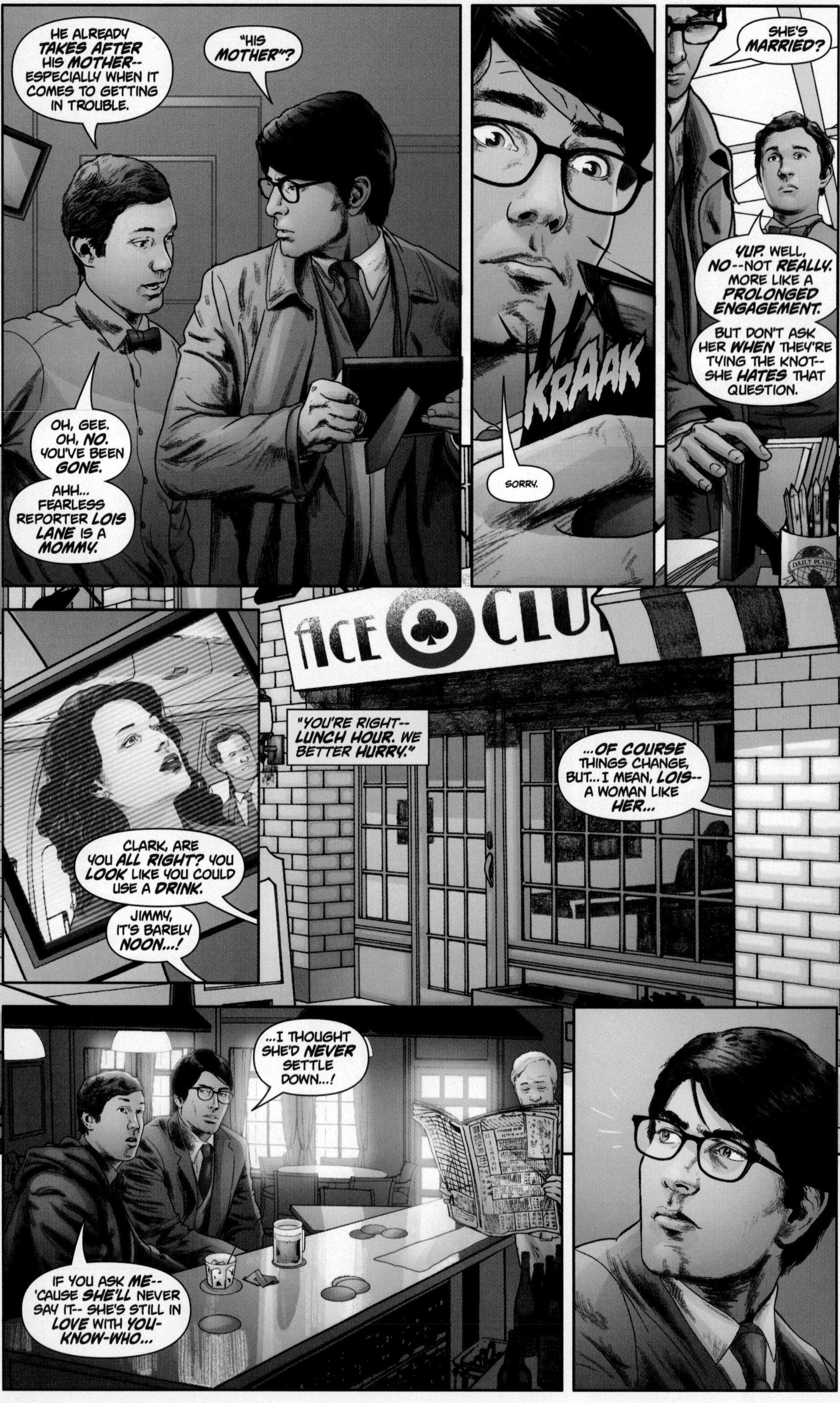
HE ALREADY TAKES AFTER HIS MOTHER-- ESPECIALLY WHEN IT COMES TO GETTING IN TROUBLE.
"HIS MOTHER"?
OH, GEE. OH, NO. YOU'VE BEEN GONE.
AHH... FEARLESS REPORTER LOIS LANE IS A MOMMY.
KRAAK
SORRY.
SHE'S MARRIED?
YUP. WELL, NO--NOT REALLY. MORE LIKE A PROLONGED ENGAGEMENT.
BUT DON'T ASK HER WHEN THEY'RE TYING THE KNOT-- SHE HATES THAT QUESTION.
DAILY PLANET
ACE CLU
CLARK, ARE YOU ALL RIGHT? YOU LOOK LIKE YOU COULD USE A DRINK.
JIMMY, IT'S BARELY NOON...!
"YOU'RE RIGHT-- LUNCH HOUR. WE BETTER HURRY."
...OF COURSE THINGS CHANGE, BUT...I MEAN, LOIS-- A WOMAN LIKE HER...
...I THOUGHT SHE'D NEVER SETTLE DOWN...!
IF YOU ASK ME-- 'CAUSE SHE'LL NEVER SAY IT-- SHE'S STILL IN LOVE WITH YOU-KNOW-WHO...

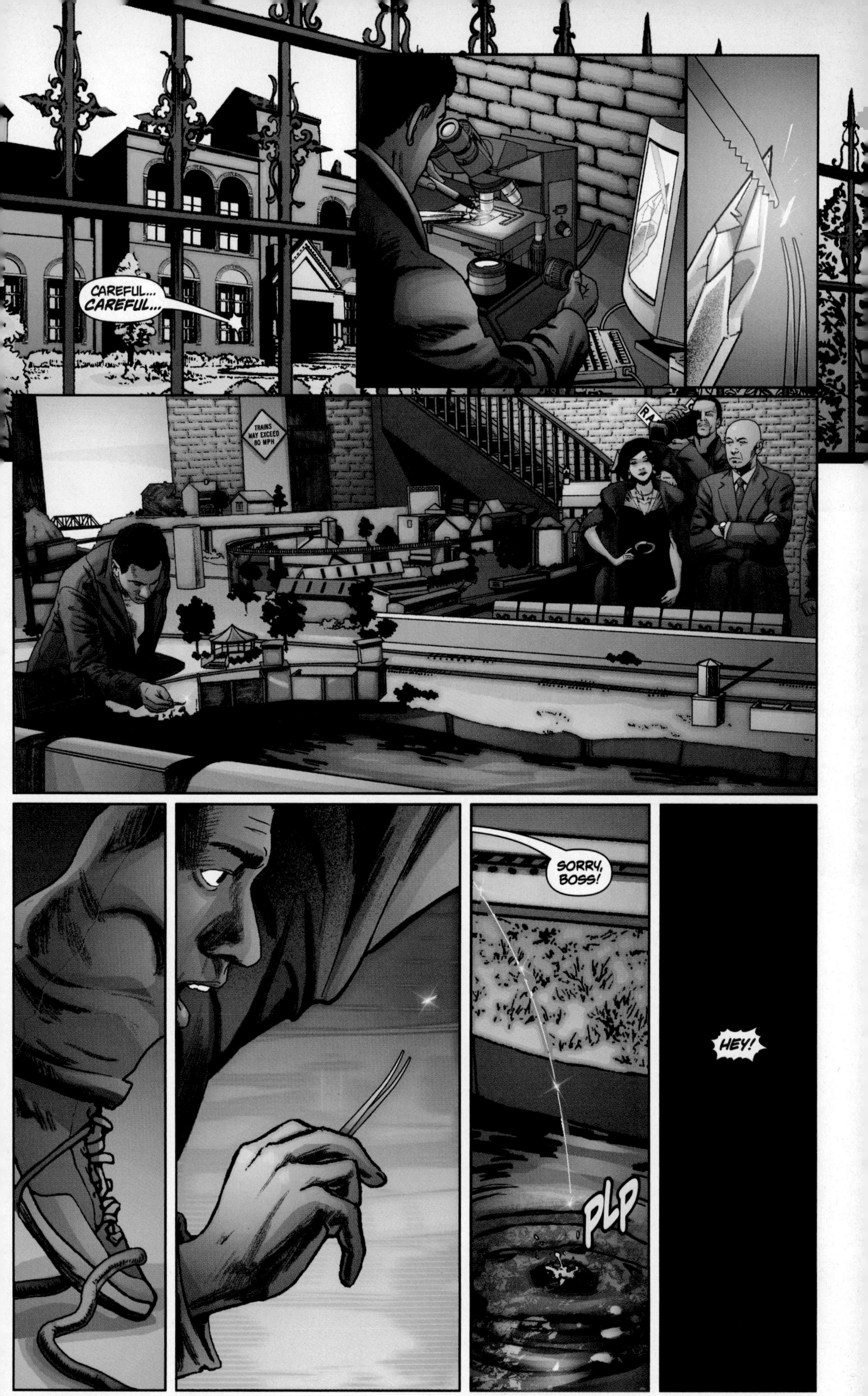

CAREFUL... CAREFUL...
TRAINS MAY EXCEED 80 MPH
SORRY, BOSS!
PLP
HEY!

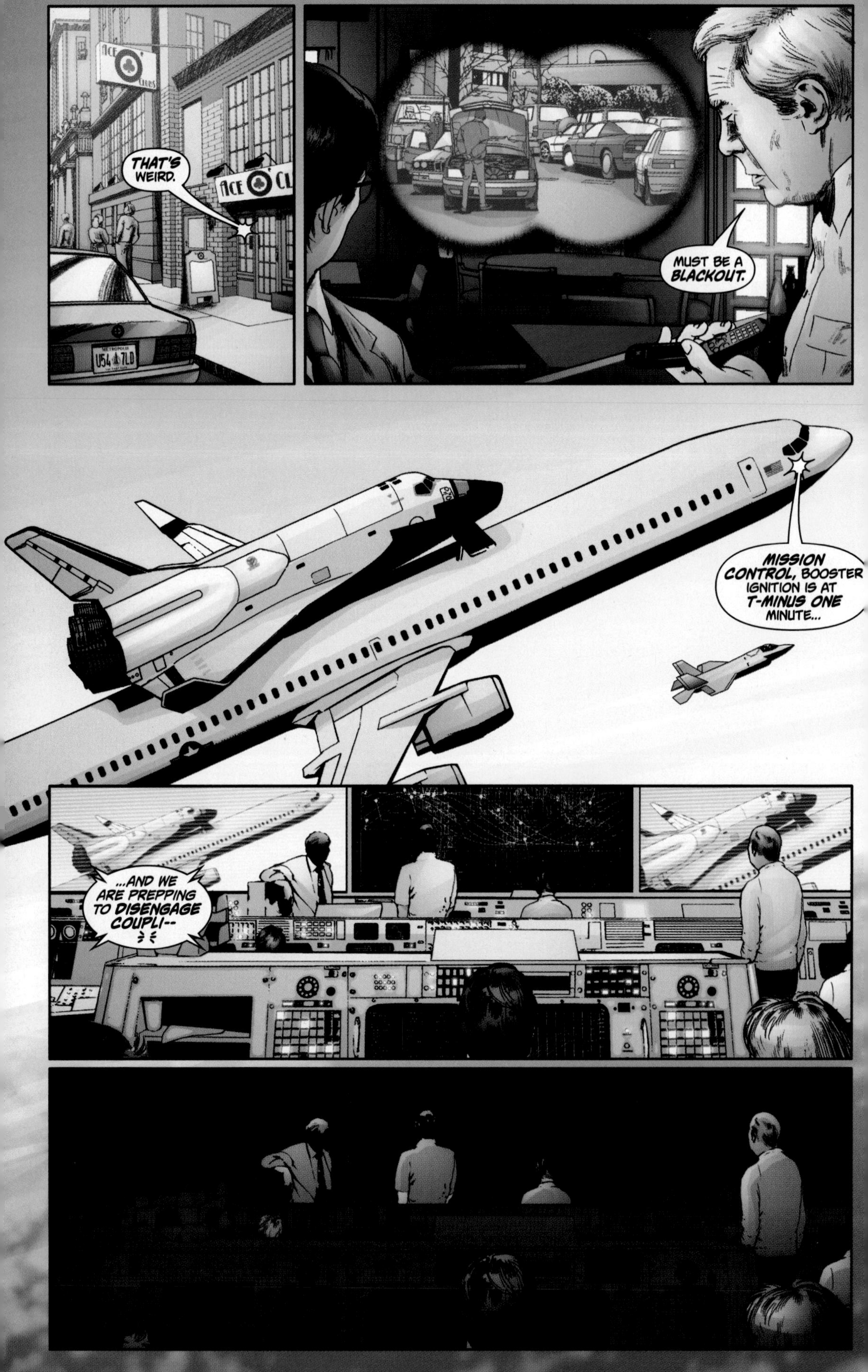
THAT'S WEIRD.
MUST BE A BLACKOUT.
MISSION CONTROL, BOOSTER IGNITION IS AT T-MINUS ONE MINUTE...
...AND WE ARE PREPPING TO DISENGAGE COUPLI--

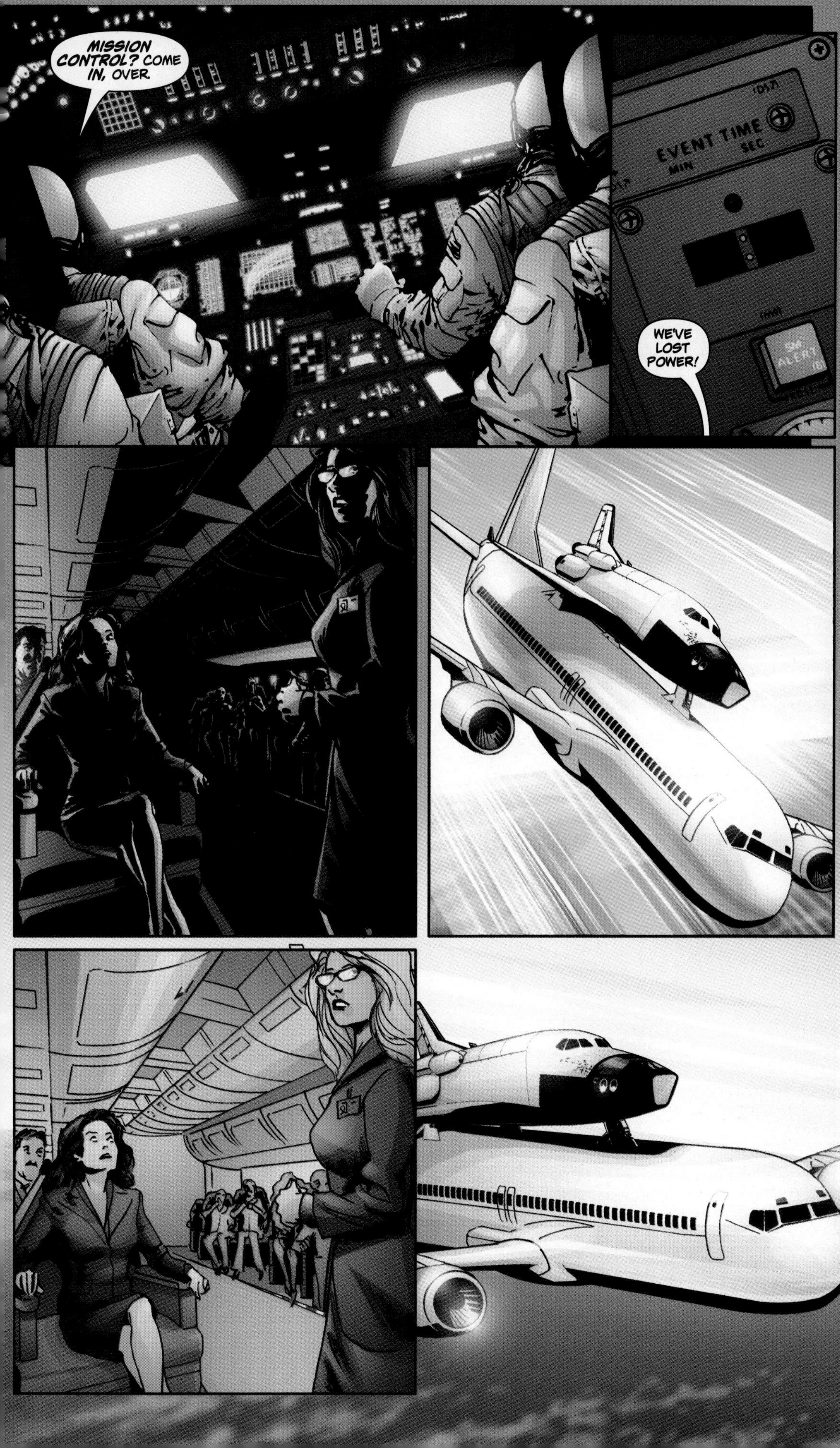
MISSION CONTROL? COME IN, OVER.
EVENT TIME
MIN SEC
SM ALERT (B)
WE'VE LOST POWER!

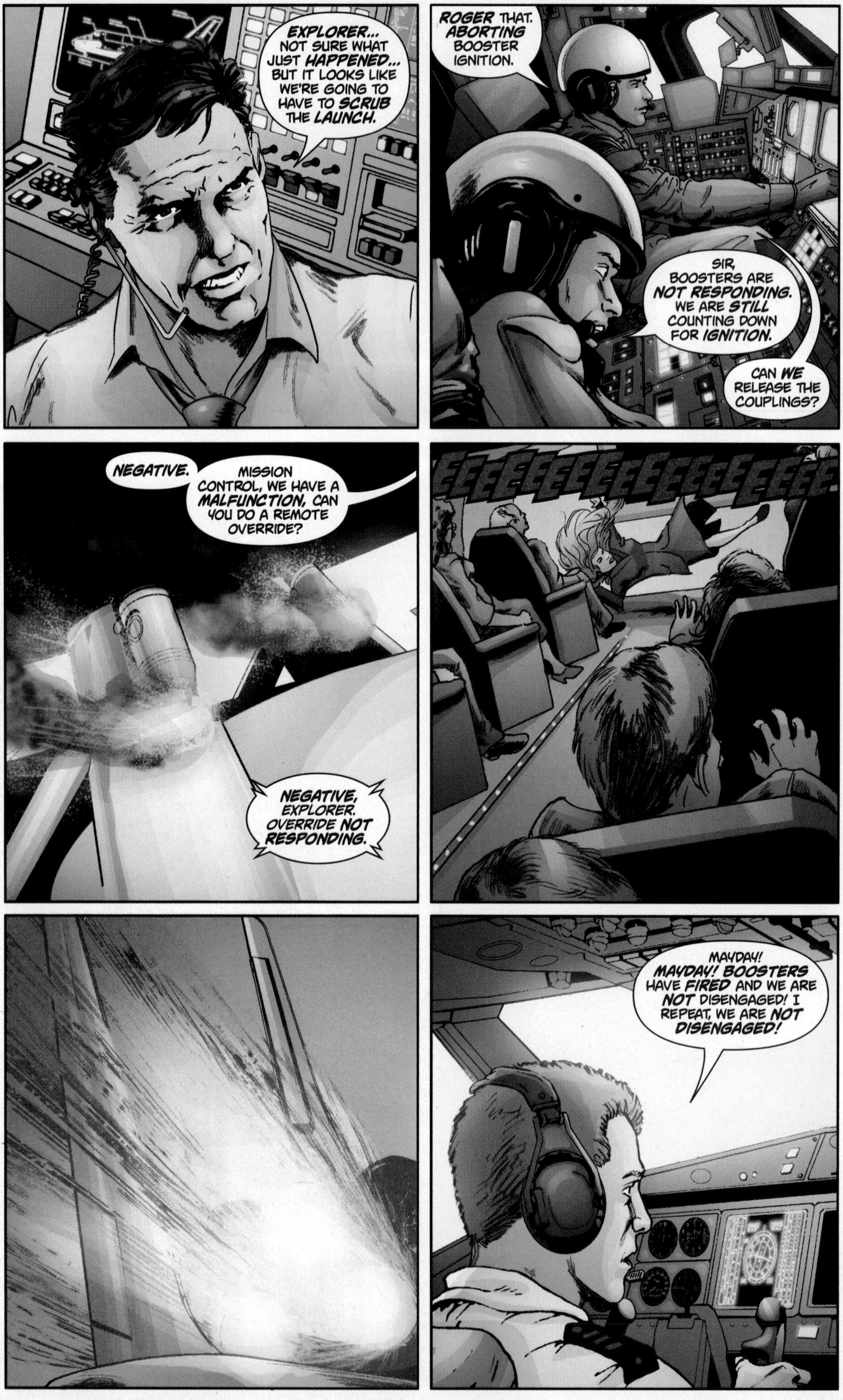
EXPLORER... NOT SURE WHAT JUST HAPPENED... BUT IT LOOKS LIKE WE'RE GOING TO HAVE TO SCRUB THE LAUNCH.
ROGER THAT. ABORTING BOOSTER IGNITION.
SIR, BOOSTERS ARE NOT RESPONDING. WE ARE STILL COUNTING DOWN FOR IGNITION.
CAN WE RELEASE THE COUPLINGS?
NEGATIVE.
MISSION CONTROL, WE HAVE A MALFUNCTION, CAN YOU DO A REMOTE OVERRIDE?
NEGATIVE, EXPLORER. OVERRIDE NOT RESPONDING.
EEEEEEEEEEEEEEEEEE
MAYDAY! MAYDAY! BOOSTERS HAVE FIRED AND WE ARE NOT DISENGAGED! I REPEAT, WE ARE NOT DISENGAGED!

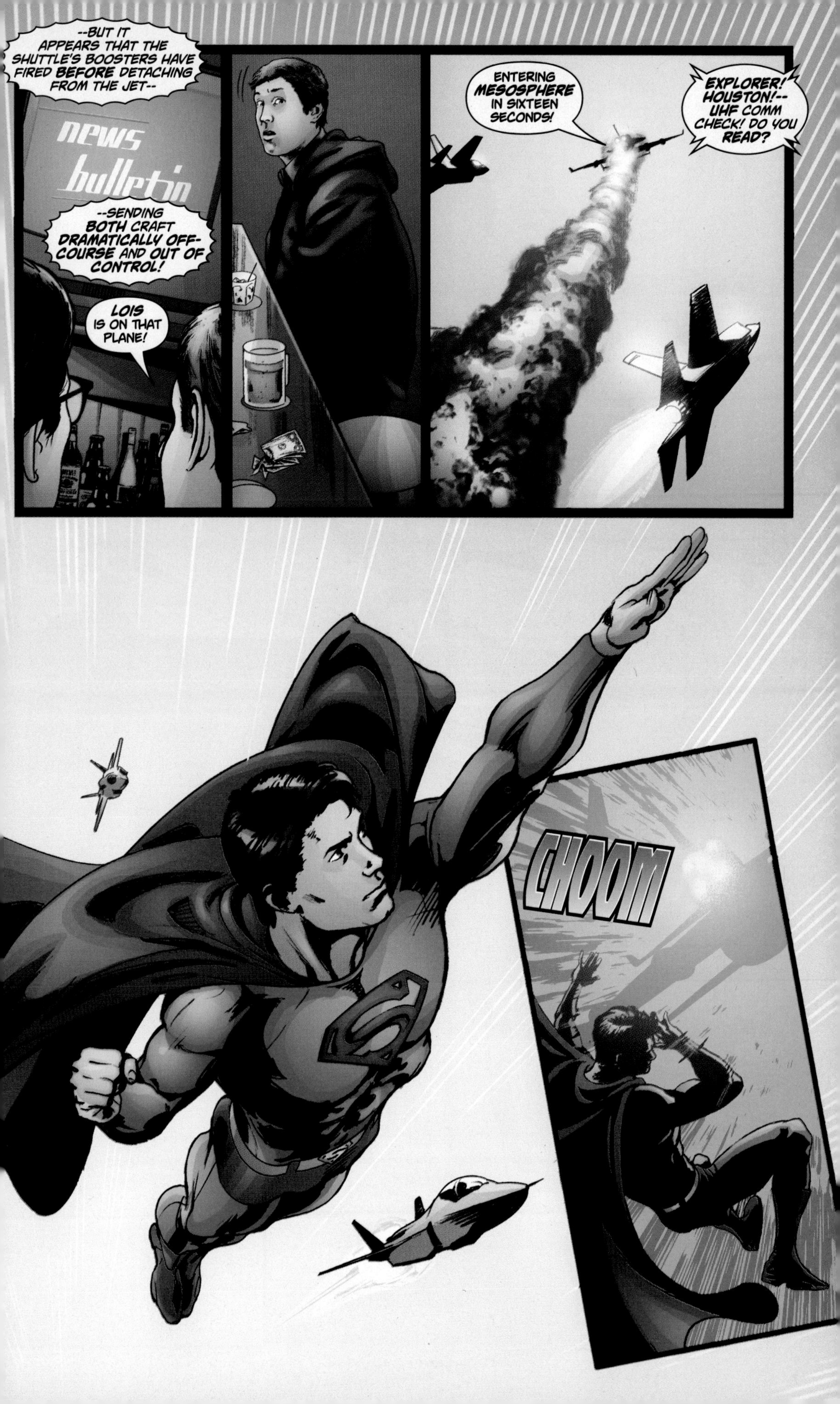
--BUT IT APPEARS THAT THE SHUTTLE'S BOOSTERS HAVE FIRED BEFORE DETACHING FROM THE JET--
news bulletin
--SENDING BOTH CRAFT DRAMATICALLY OFF-COURSE AND OUT OF CONTROL!
LOIS IS ON THAT PLANE!
ENTERING MESOSPHERE IN SIXTEEN SECONDS!
EXPLORER! HOUSTON!-- UHF COMM CHECK! DO YOU READ?
CHOOM

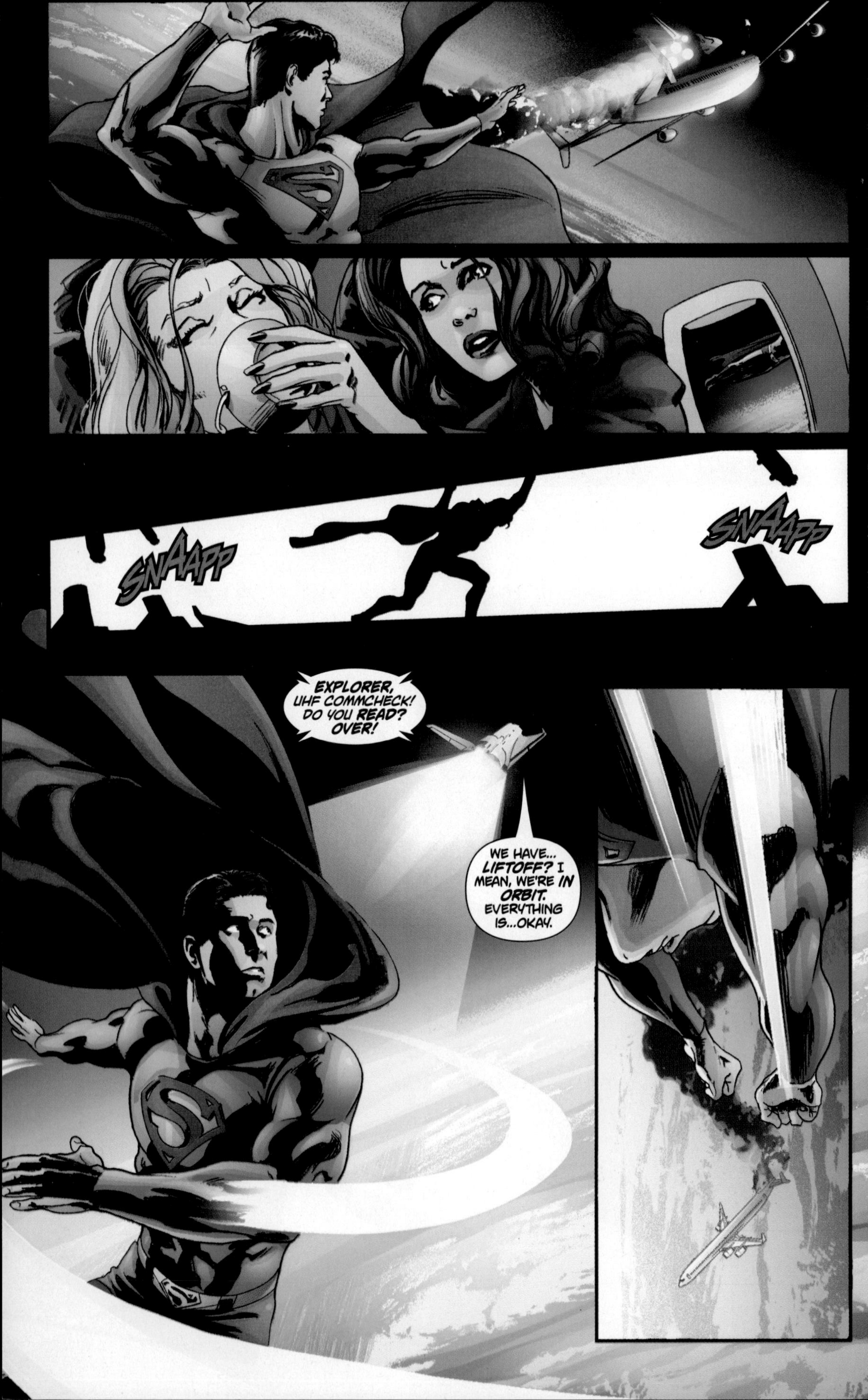
SNAAPP
SNAAPP
EXPLORER, UHF COMMCHECK! DO YOU READ? OVER!
WE HAVE... LIFTOFF? I MEAN, WE'RE IN ORBIT. EVERYTHING IS...OKAY.

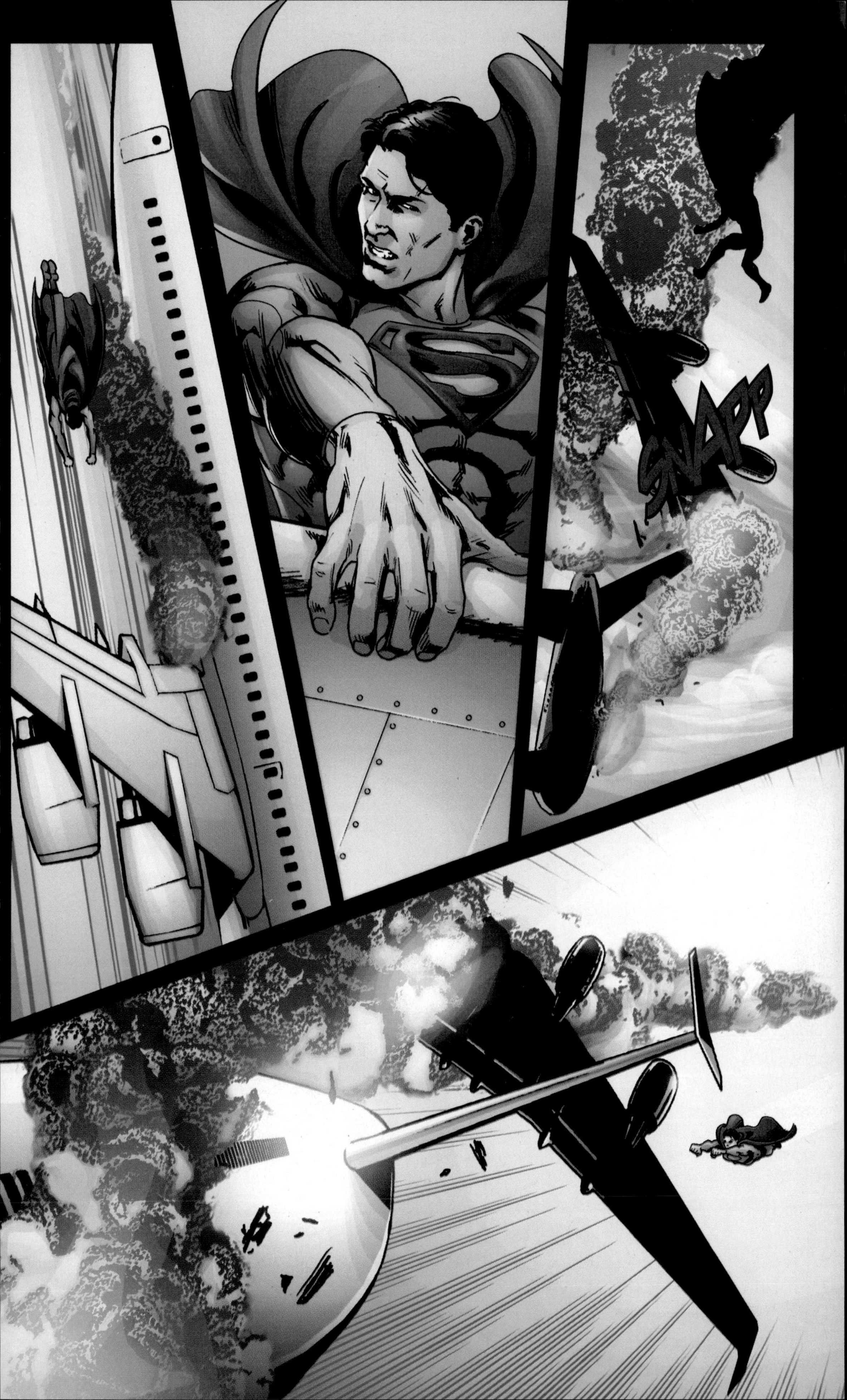
SNAPP

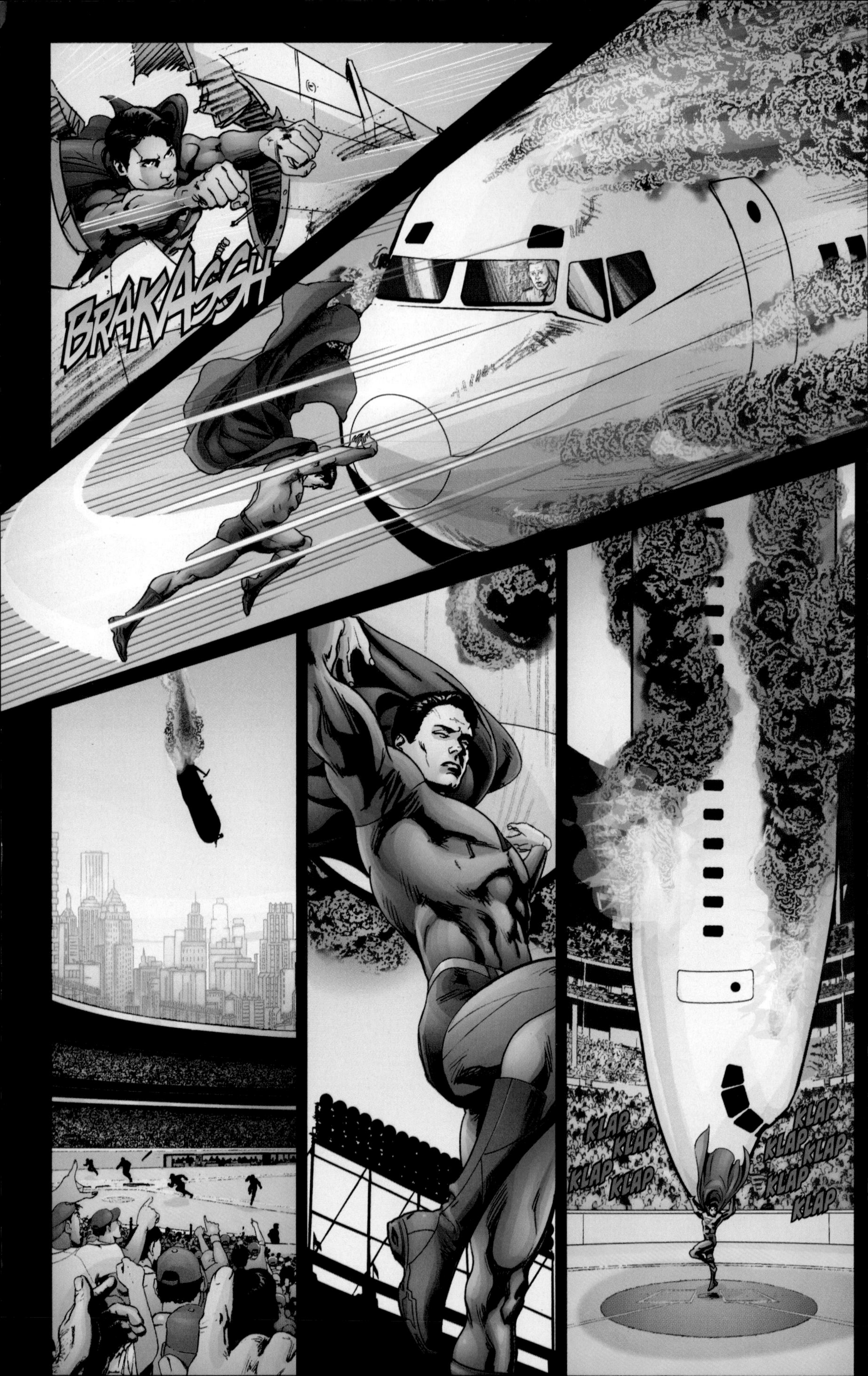
BRAKASSH
KLAP KLAP KLAP KLAP
KLAP KLAP KLAP KLAP KLAP

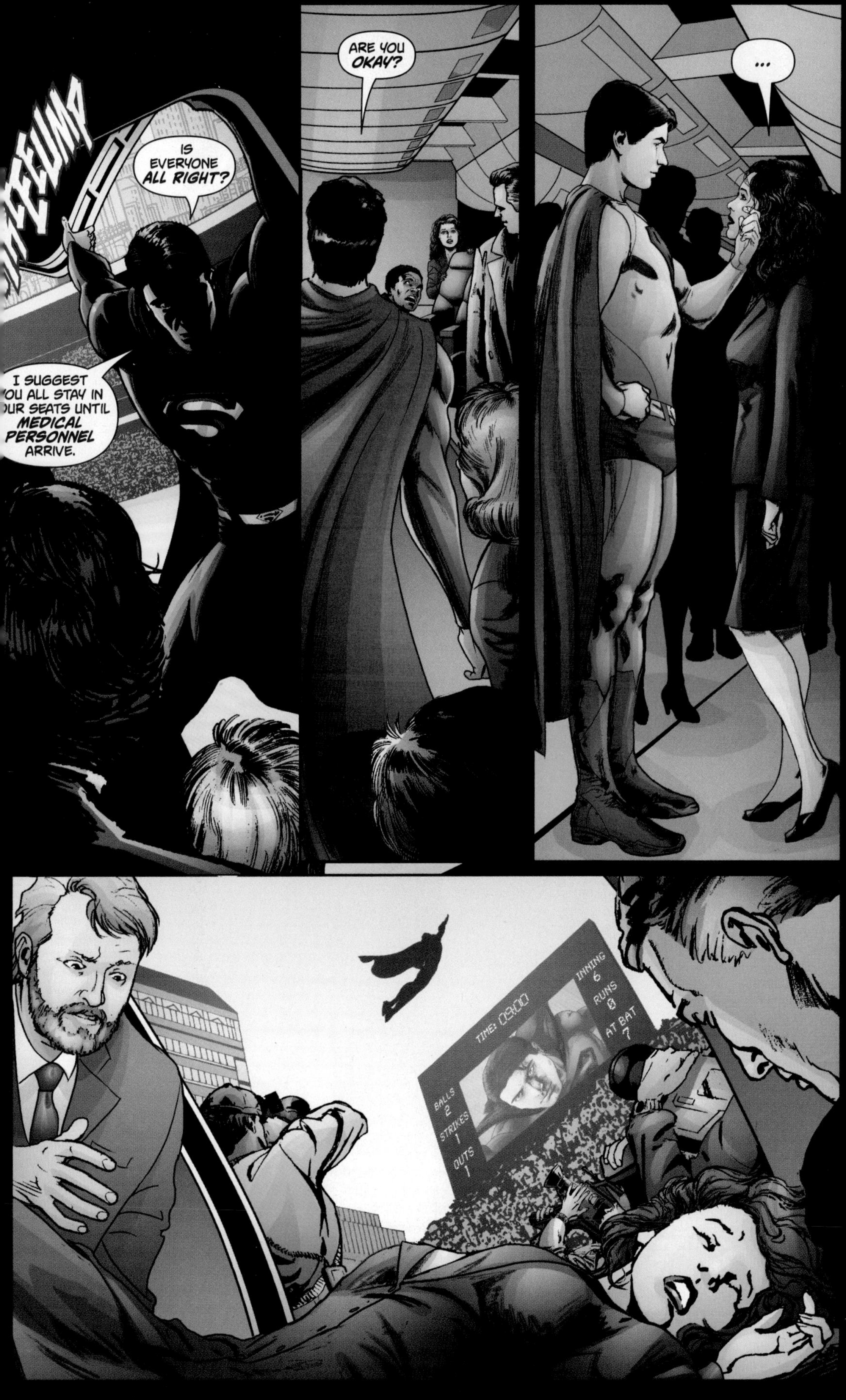
IS EVERYONE ALL RIGHT?
I SUGGEST OU ALL STAY IN UR SEATS UNTIL MEDICAL PERSONNEL ARRIVE.
ARE YOU OKAY?
...
TIME: 08:00
INNING 6
RUNS 0
AT BAT 7
BALLS 2
STRIKES 1
OUTS 1

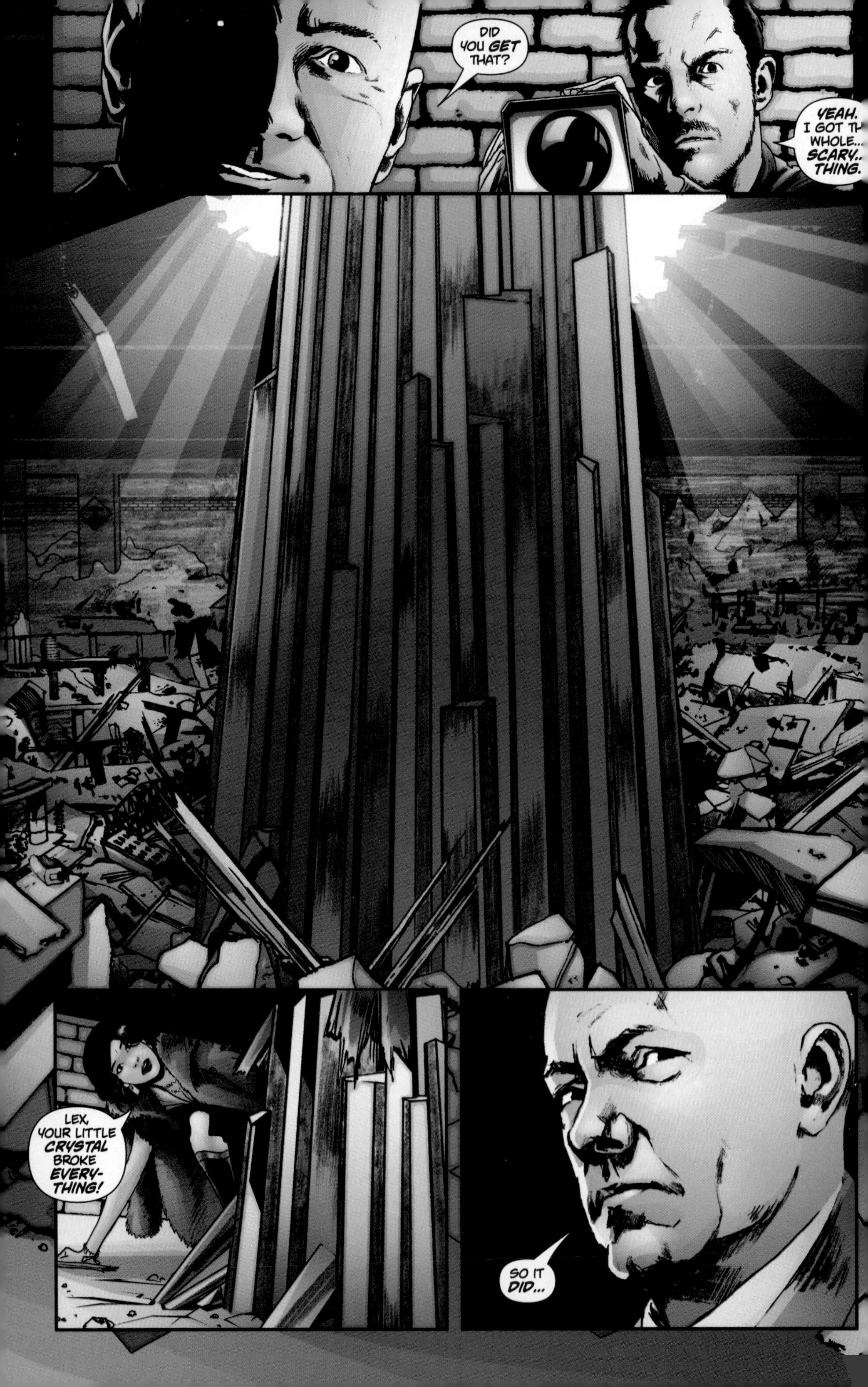
DID YOU GET THAT?
YEAH. I GOT TH WHOLE... SCARY... THING.
LEX, YOUR LITTLE CRYSTAL BROKE EVERY-THING!
SO IT DID...

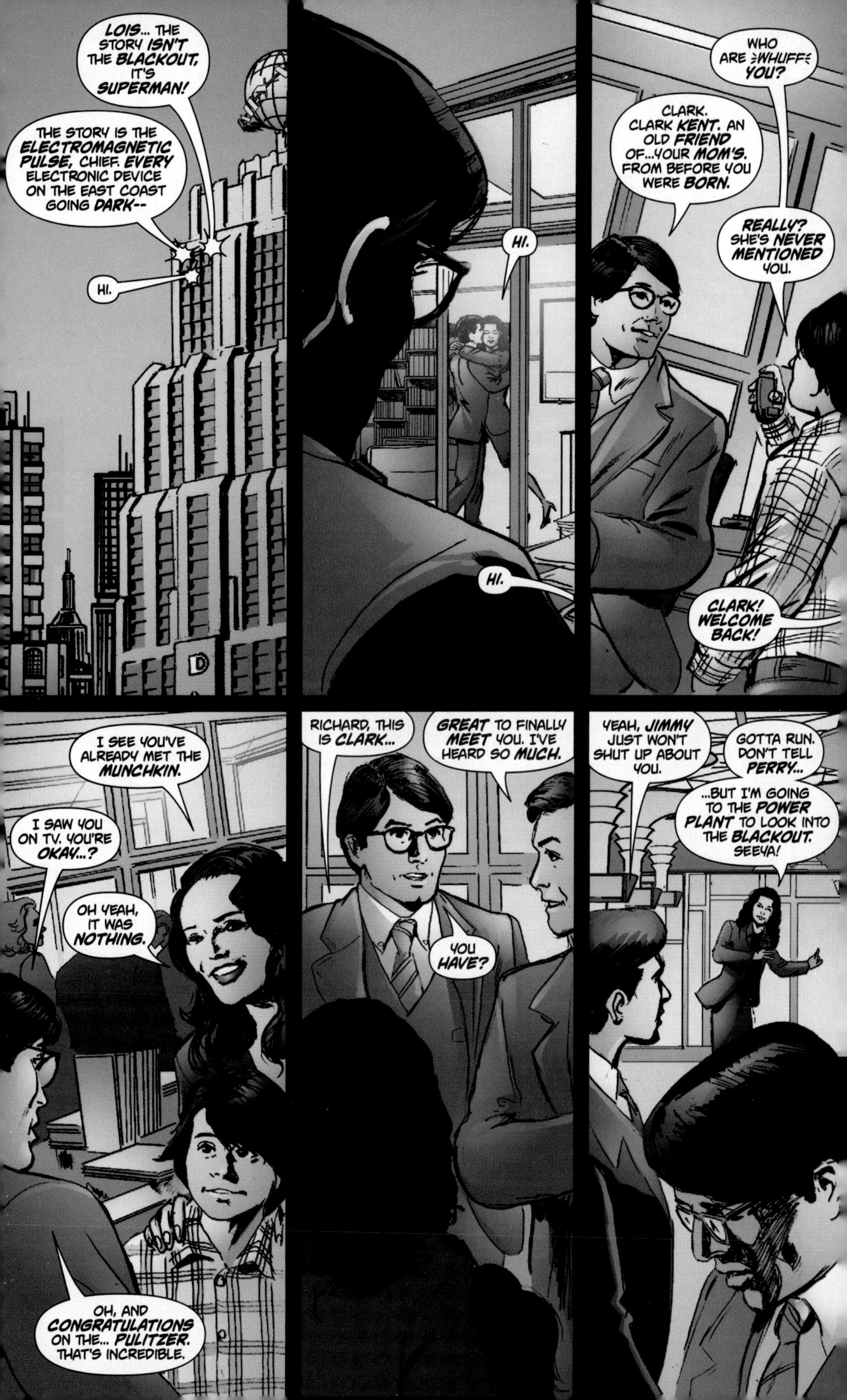
LOIS... THE STORY ISN'T THE BLACKOUT, IT'S SUPERMAN!
THE STORY IS THE ELECTROMAGNETIC PULSE, CHIEF. EVERY ELECTRONIC DEVICE ON THE EAST COAST GOING DARK--
HI.
HI.
HI.
WHO ARE ≷WHUFF≶ YOU?
CLARK. CLARK KENT. AN OLD FRIEND OF...YOUR MOM'S. FROM BEFORE YOU WERE BORN.
REALLY? SHE'S NEVER MENTIONED YOU.
CLARK! WELCOME BACK!
I SEE YOU'VE ALREADY MET THE MUNCHKIN.
I SAW YOU ON TV. YOU'RE OKAY...?
OH YEAH, IT WAS NOTHING.
OH, AND CONGRATULATIONS ON THE... PULITZER. THAT'S INCREDIBLE.
RICHARD, THIS IS CLARK...
GREAT TO FINALLY MEET YOU. I'VE HEARD SO MUCH.
YOU HAVE?
YEAH, JIMMY JUST WON'T SHUT UP ABOUT YOU.
GOTTA RUN. DON'T TELL PERRY...
...BUT I'M GOING TO THE POWER PLANT TO LOOK INTO THE BLACKOUT. SEEYA!

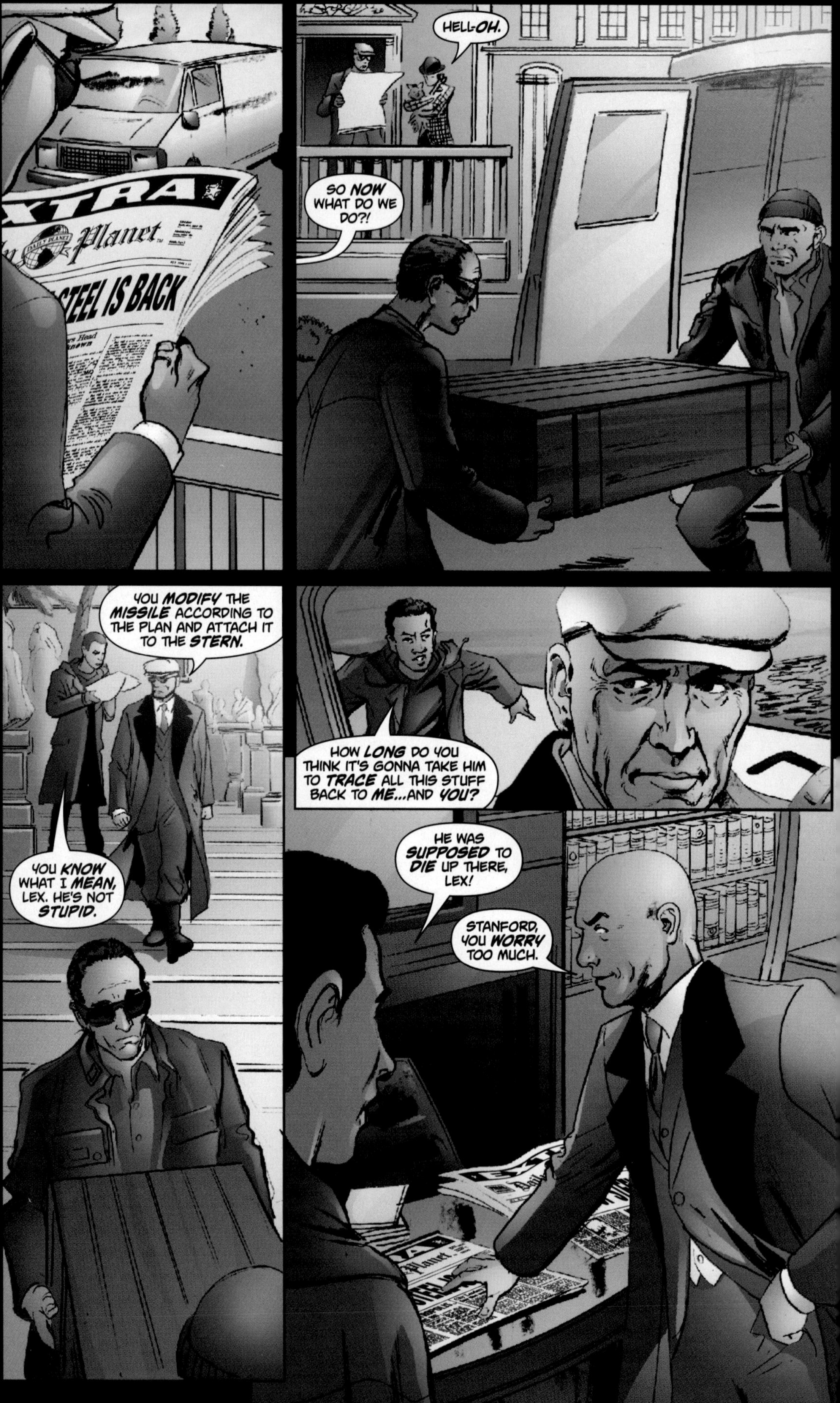
XTRA
Planet
HELL-OH.
SO NOW WHAT DO WE DO?!
YOU MODIFY THE MISSILE ACCORDING TO THE PLAN AND ATTACH IT TO THE STERN.
YOU KNOW WHAT I MEAN, LEX. HE'S NOT STUPID.
HOW LONG DO YOU THINK IT'S GONNA TAKE HIM TO TRACE ALL THIS STUFF BACK TO ME...AND YOU?
HE WAS SUPPOSED TO DIE UP THERE, LEX!
STANFORD, YOU WORRY TOO MUCH.

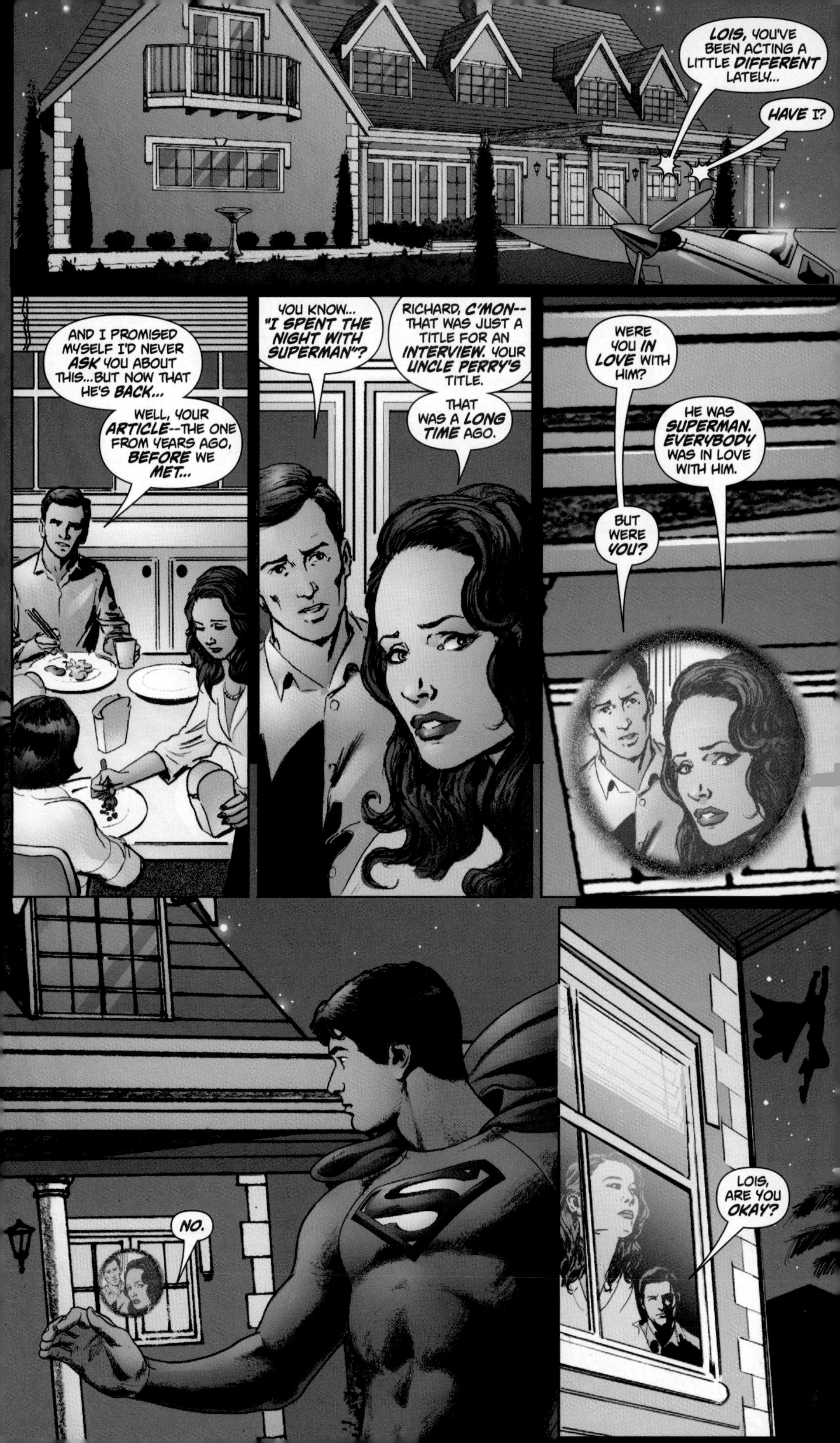

LOIS, YOU'VE BEEN ACTING A LITTLE DIFFERENT LATELY...
HAVE I?
AND I PROMISED MYSELF I'D NEVER ASK YOU ABOUT THIS...BUT NOW THAT HE'S BACK...
WELL, YOUR ARTICLE--THE ONE FROM YEARS AGO, BEFORE WE MET...
YOU KNOW... "I SPENT THE NIGHT WITH SUPERMAN"?
RICHARD, C'MON--THAT WAS JUST A TITLE FOR AN INTERVIEW. YOUR UNCLE PERRY'S TITLE.
THAT WAS A LONG TIME AGO.
WERE YOU IN LOVE WITH HIM?
HE WAS SUPERMAN. EVERYBODY WAS IN LOVE WITH HIM.
BUT WERE YOU?
NO.
LOIS, ARE YOU OKAY?

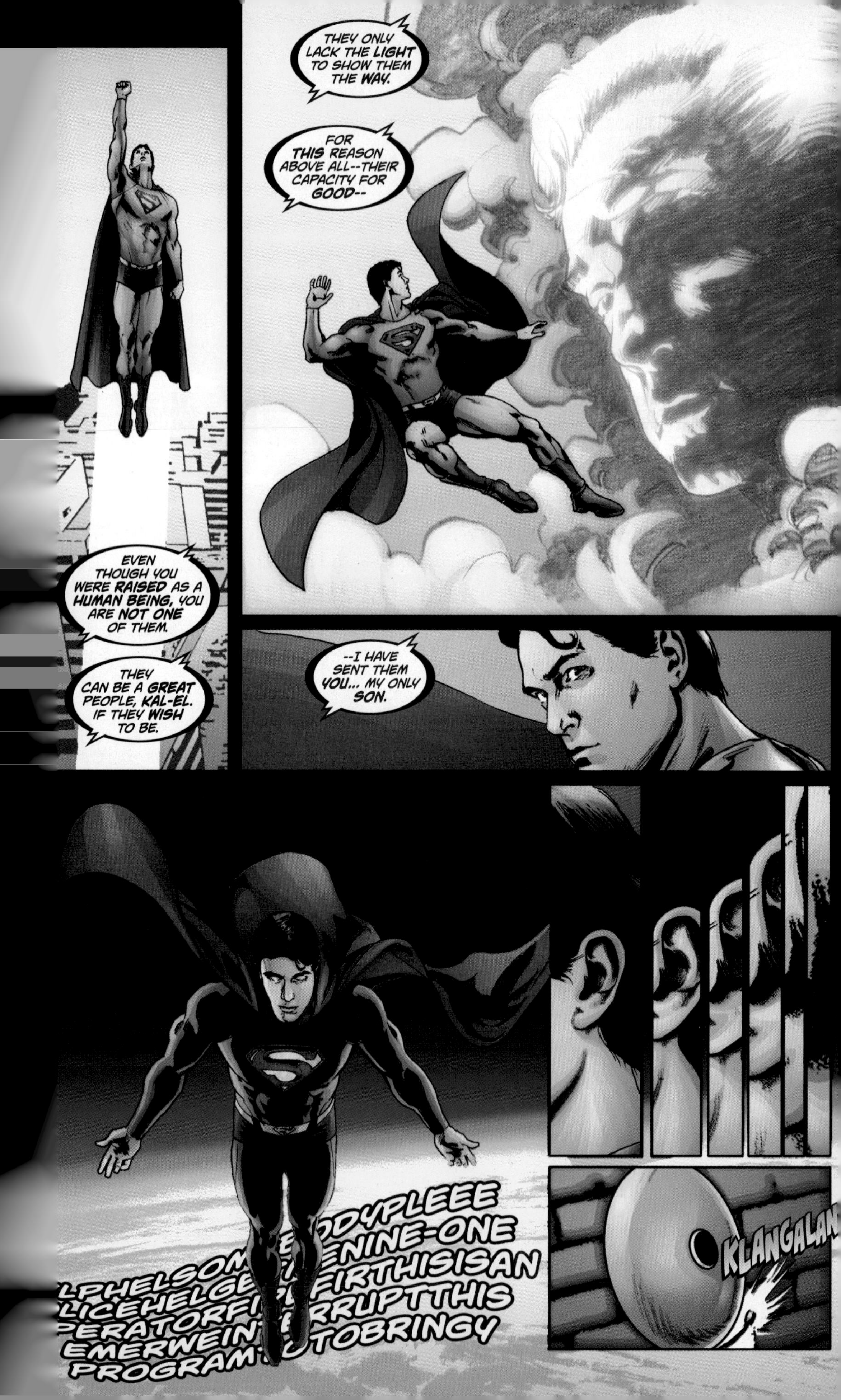
EVEN THOUGH YOU WERE RAISED AS A HUMAN BEING, YOU ARE NOT ONE OF THEM.
THEY CAN BE A GREAT PEOPLE, KAL-EL. IF THEY WISH TO BE.
THEY ONLY LACK THE LIGHT TO SHOW THEM THE WAY.
FOR THIS REASON ABOVE ALL--THEIR CAPACITY FOR GOOD--
--I HAVE SENT THEM YOU... MY ONLY SON.
LPHELSOM ODYPLEEE
LICEHELGE NINE-ONE
PERATORFI FIRTHISISAN
EMERWEIN RRUPTTHIS
PROGRAM TOBRINGY
KLANGALAN

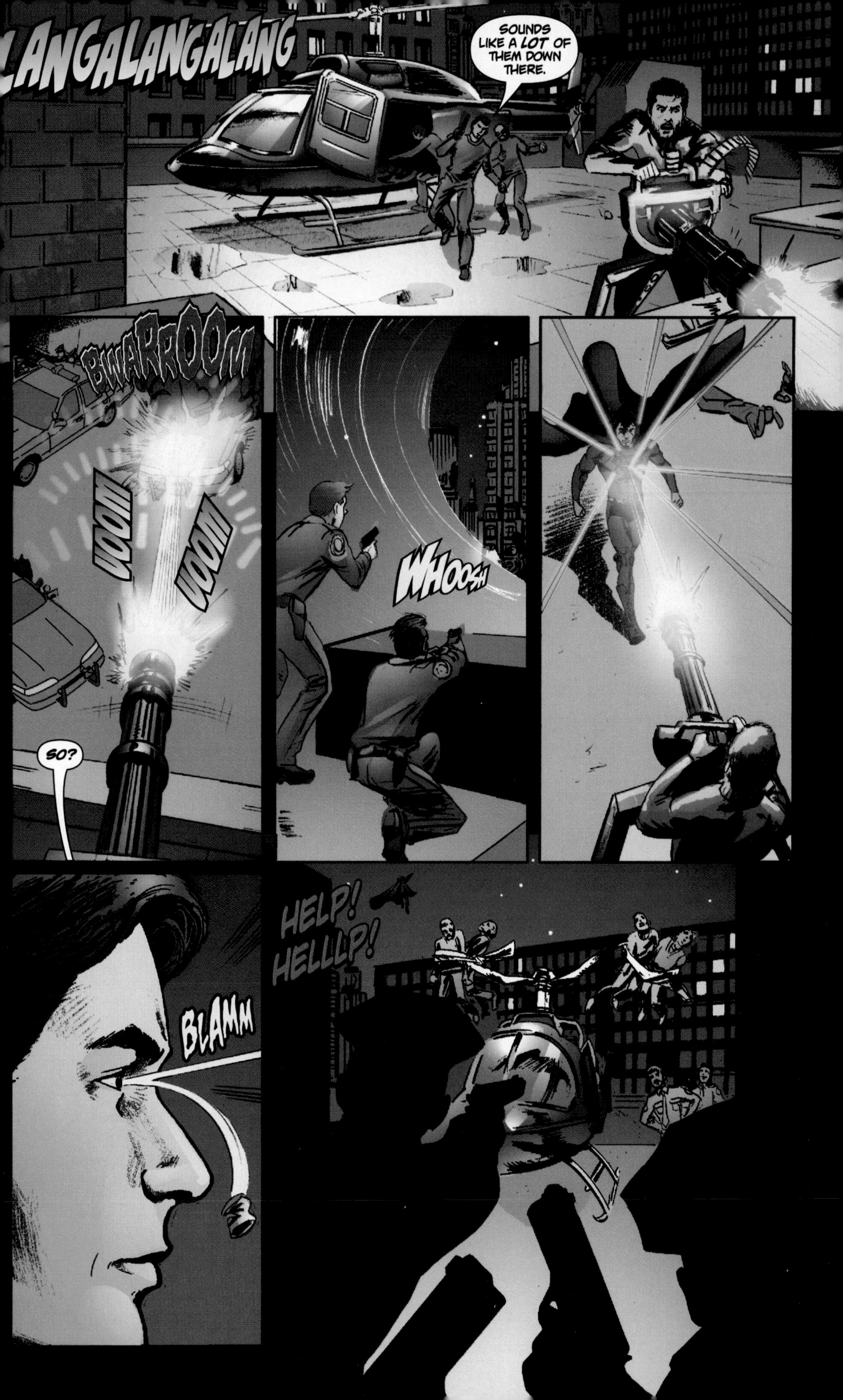
LANGALANGALANG
SOUNDS LIKE A LOT OF THEM DOWN THERE.
BWARROOM
VOOM
VOOM
SO?
WHOOSH
HELP! HELLLP!
BLAMM

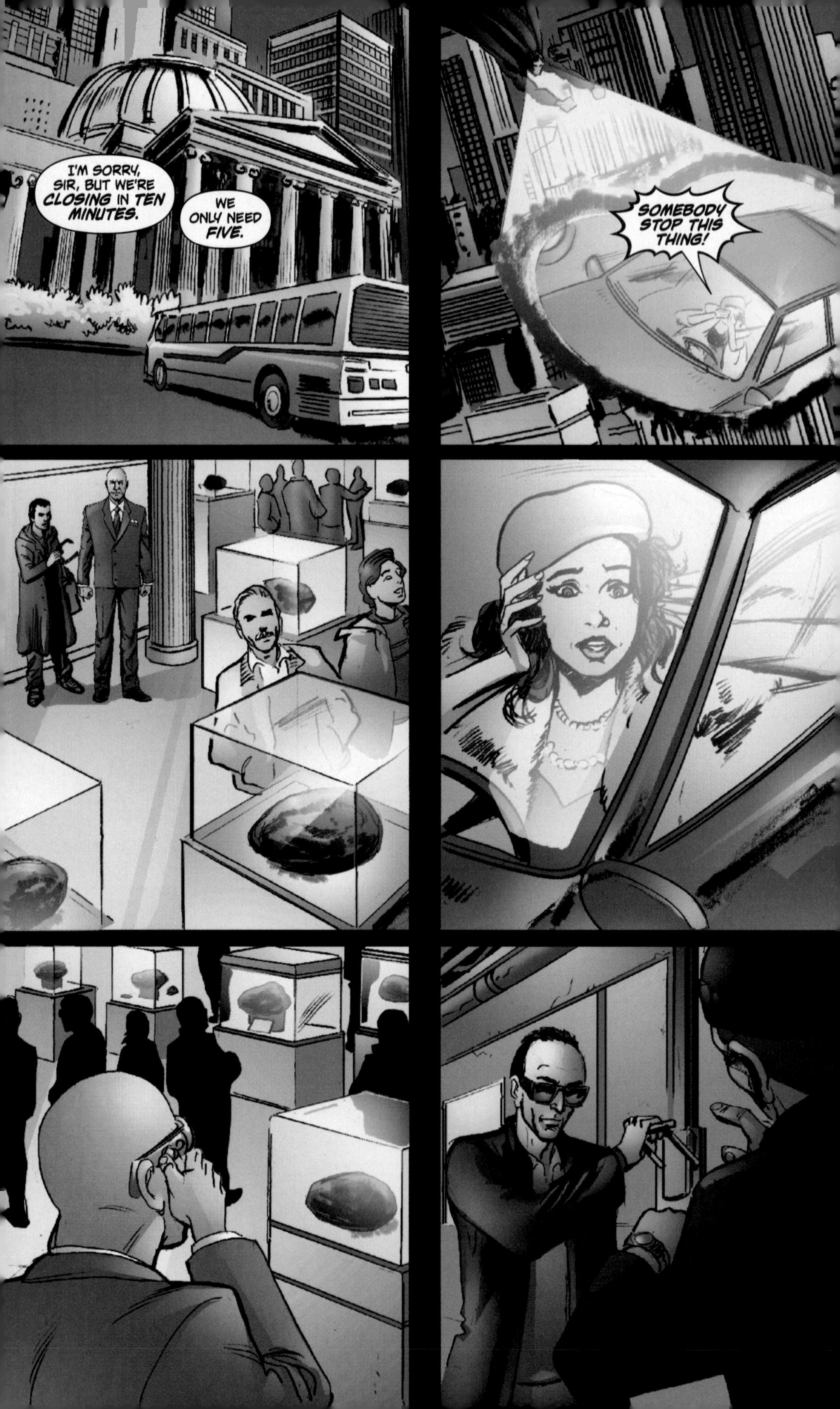
I'M SORRY, SIR, BUT WE'RE CLOSING IN TEN MINUTES.
WE ONLY NEED FIVE.
SOMEBODY STOP THIS THING!

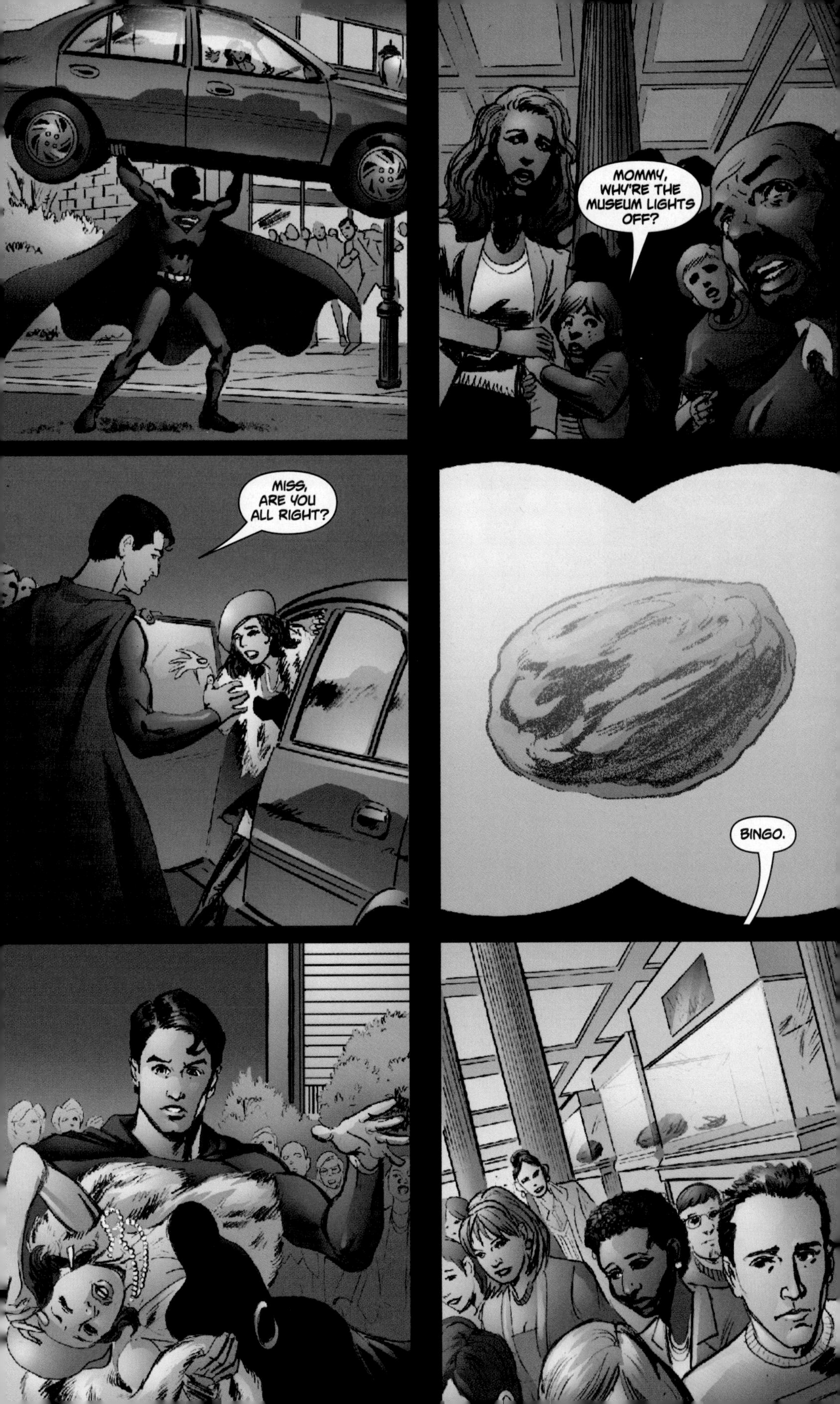
MOMMY, WHY'RE THE MUSEUM LIGHTS OFF?
MISS, ARE YOU ALL RIGHT?
BINGO.

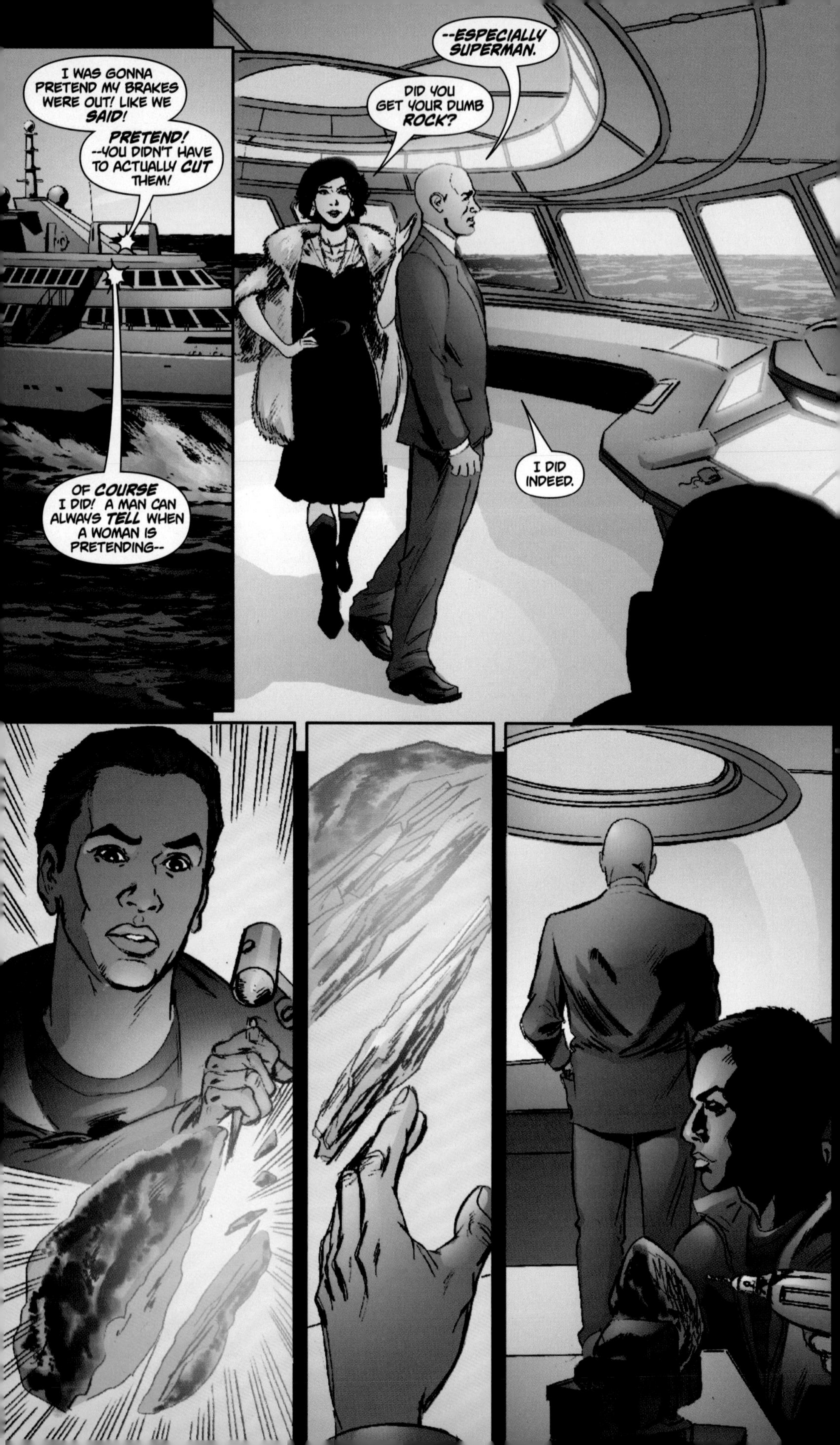

I WAS GONNA PRETEND MY BRAKES WERE OUT! LIKE WE SAID!
PRETEND! --YOU DIDN'T HAVE TO ACTUALLY CUT THEM!
OF COURSE I DID! A MAN CAN ALWAYS TELL WHEN A WOMAN IS PRETENDING--
--ESPECIALLY SUPERMAN.
DID YOU GET YOUR DUMB ROCK?
I DID INDEED.

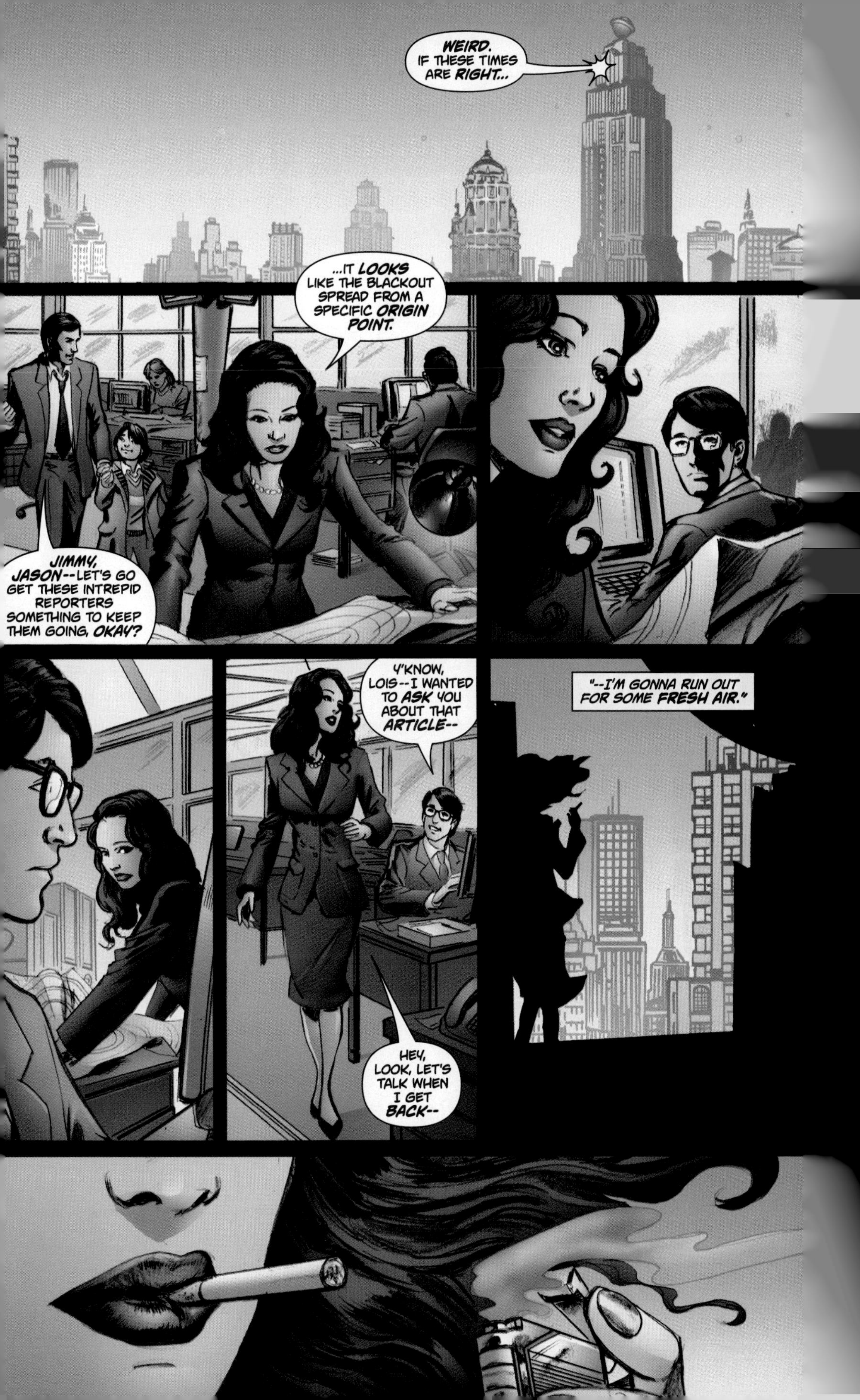

WEIRD. IF THESE TIMES ARE RIGHT...
...IT LOOKS LIKE THE BLACKOUT SPREAD FROM A SPECIFIC ORIGIN POINT.
JIMMY, JASON--LET'S GO GET THESE INTREPID REPORTERS SOMETHING TO KEEP THEM GOING, OKAY?
Y'KNOW, LOIS--I WANTED TO ASK YOU ABOUT THAT ARTICLE--
HEY, LOOK, LET'S TALK WHEN I GET BACK--
"--I'M GONNA RUN OUT FOR SOME FRESH AIR."

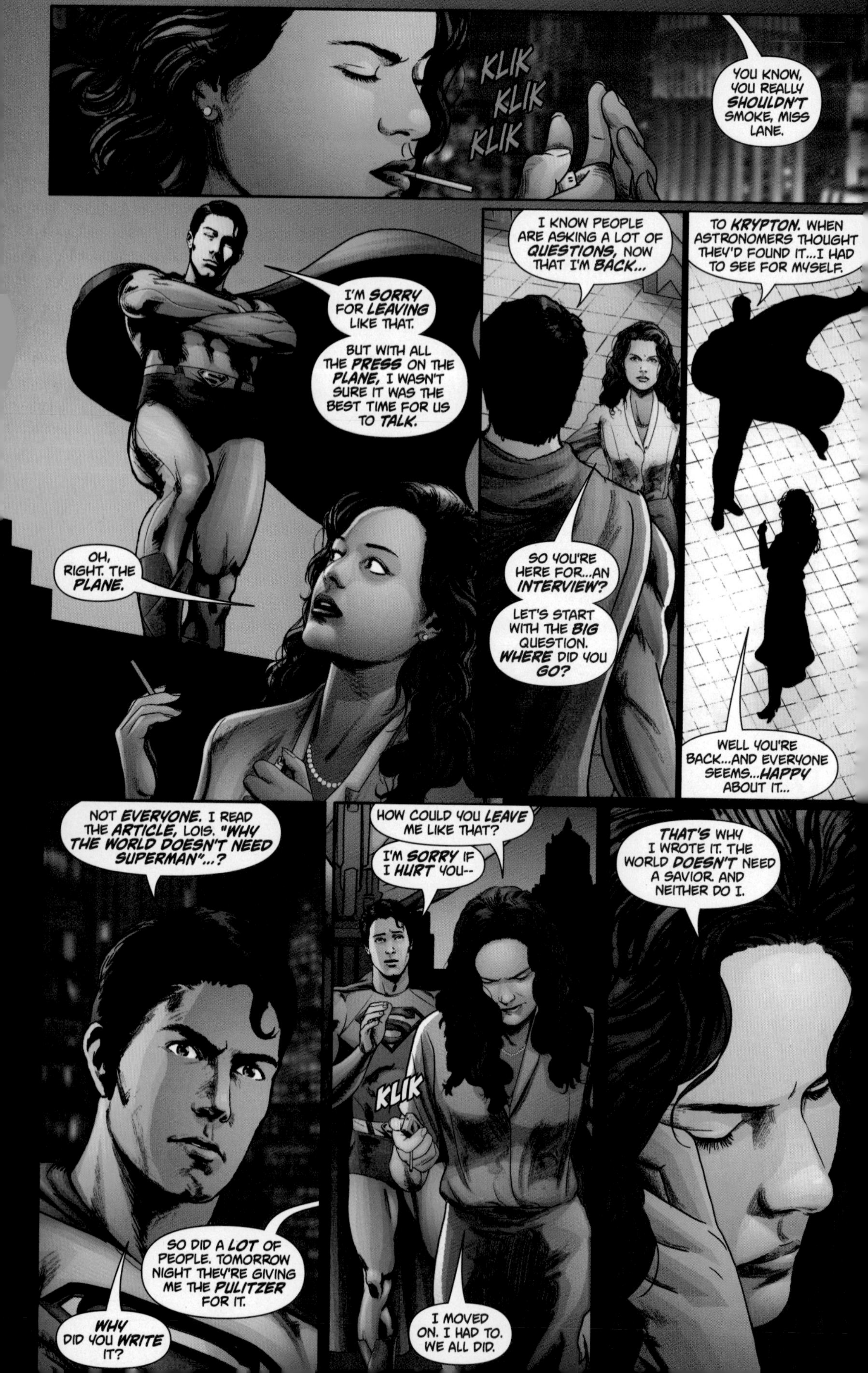
KLIK KLIK KLIK
YOU KNOW, YOU REALLY SHOULDN'T SMOKE, MISS LANE.
I'M SORRY FOR LEAVING LIKE THAT.
BUT WITH ALL THE PRESS ON THE PLANE, I WASN'T SURE IT WAS THE BEST TIME FOR US TO TALK.
OH, RIGHT. THE PLANE.
I KNOW PEOPLE ARE ASKING A LOT OF QUESTIONS, NOW THAT I'M BACK...
SO YOU'RE HERE FOR...AN INTERVIEW?
LET'S START WITH THE BIG QUESTION. WHERE DID YOU GO?
TO KRYPTON. WHEN ASTRONOMERS THOUGHT THEY'D FOUND IT...I HAD TO SEE FOR MYSELF.
WELL YOU'RE BACK...AND EVERYONE SEEMS...HAPPY ABOUT IT...
NOT EVERYONE. I READ THE ARTICLE, LOIS. "WHY THE WORLD DOESN'T NEED SUPERMAN"...?
SO DID A LOT OF PEOPLE. TOMORROW NIGHT THEY'RE GIVING ME THE PULITZER FOR IT.
WHY DID YOU WRITE IT?
HOW COULD YOU LEAVE ME LIKE THAT?
I'M SORRY IF I HURT YOU--
KLIK
I MOVED ON. I HAD TO. WE ALL DID.
THAT'S WHY I WROTE IT. THE WORLD DOESN'T NEED A SAVIOR. AND NEITHER DO I.

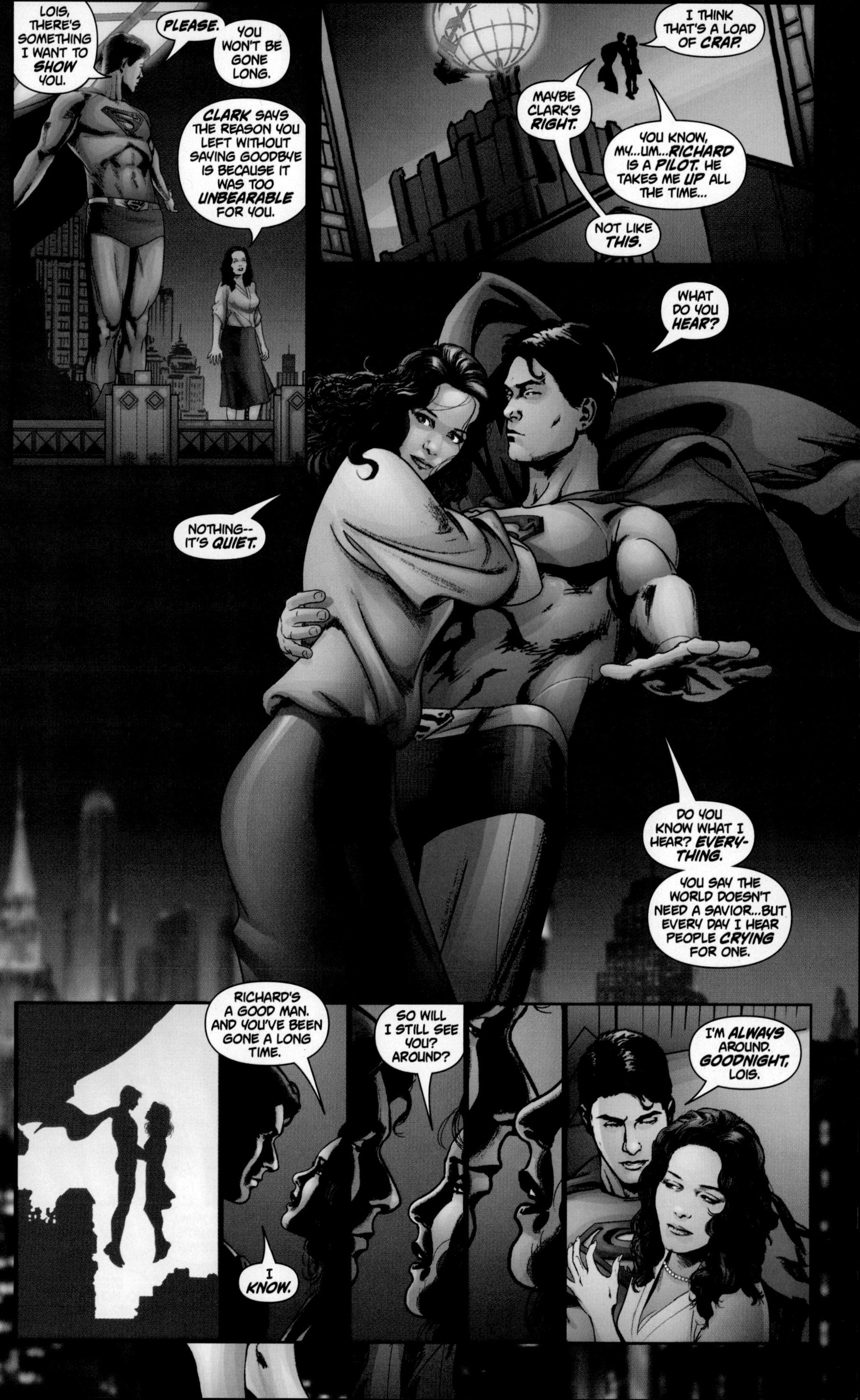
LOIS, THERE'S SOMETHING I WANT TO SHOW YOU.
PLEASE.
YOU WON'T BE GONE LONG.
CLARK SAYS THE REASON YOU LEFT WITHOUT SAYING GOODBYE IS BECAUSE IT WAS TOO UNBEARABLE FOR YOU.
I THINK THAT'S A LOAD OF CRAP.
MAYBE CLARK'S RIGHT.
YOU KNOW, MY...UM...RICHARD IS A PILOT. HE TAKES ME UP ALL THE TIME...
NOT LIKE THIS.
WHAT DO YOU HEAR?
NOTHING-- IT'S QUIET.
DO YOU KNOW WHAT I HEAR? EVERY-THING.
YOU SAY THE WORLD DOESN'T NEED A SAVIOR...BUT EVERY DAY I HEAR PEOPLE CRYING FOR ONE.
RICHARD'S A GOOD MAN. AND YOU'VE BEEN GONE A LONG TIME.
I KNOW.
SO WILL I STILL SEE YOU? AROUND?
I'M ALWAYS AROUND. GOODNIGHT, LOIS.

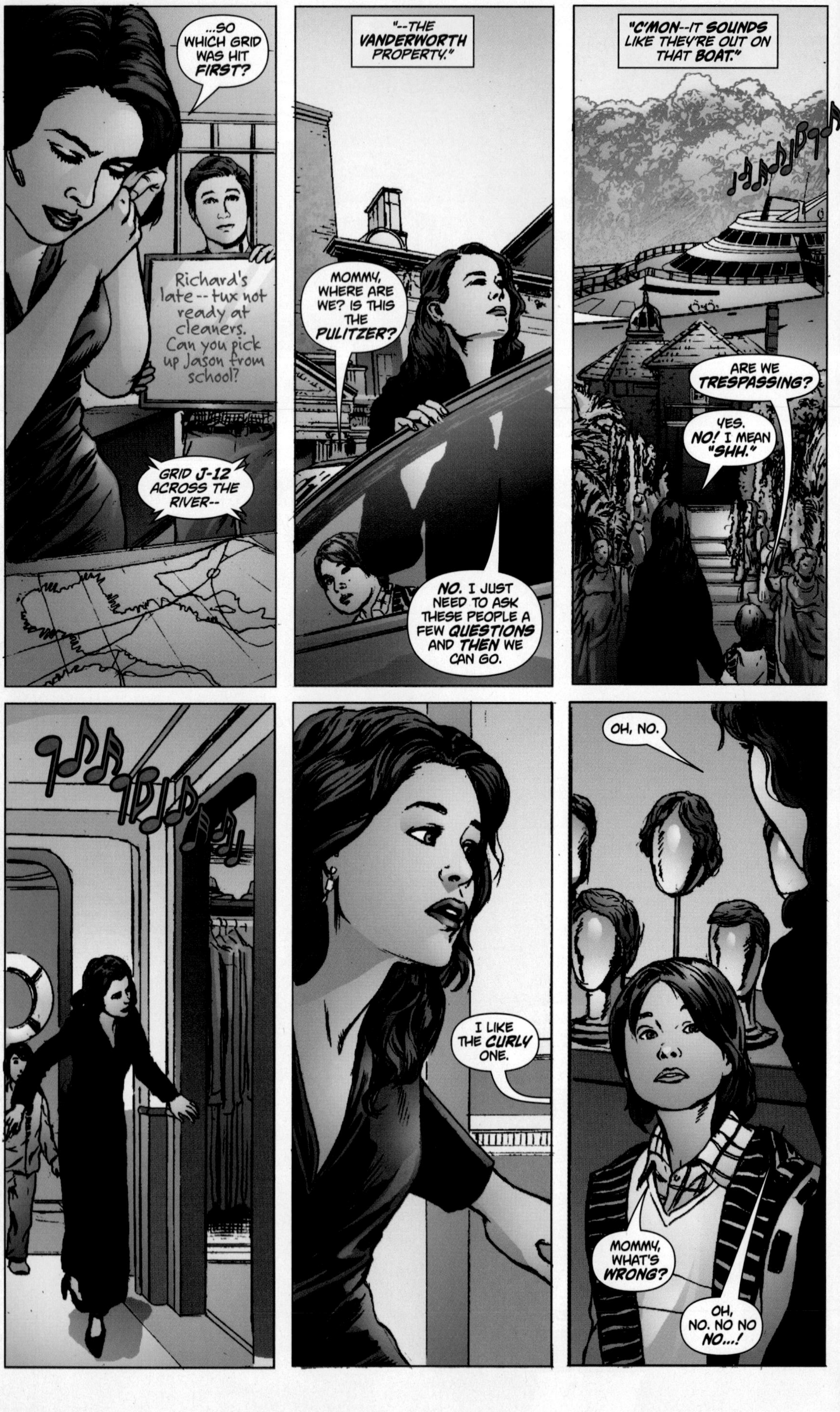
...SO WHICH GRID WAS HIT FIRST?
Richard's late--tux not ready at cleaners. Can you pick up Jason from school?
GRID J-12 ACROSS THE RIVER--
"--THE VANDERWORTH PROPERTY."
MOMMY, WHERE ARE WE? IS THIS THE PULITZER?
NO. I JUST NEED TO ASK THESE PEOPLE A FEW QUESTIONS AND THEN WE CAN GO.
"C'MON--IT SOUNDS LIKE THEY'RE OUT ON THAT BOAT."
ARE WE TRESPASSING?
YES. NO! I MEAN "SHH."
I LIKE THE CURLY ONE.
OH, NO.
MOMMY, WHAT'S WRONG?
OH, NO. NO NO NO...!

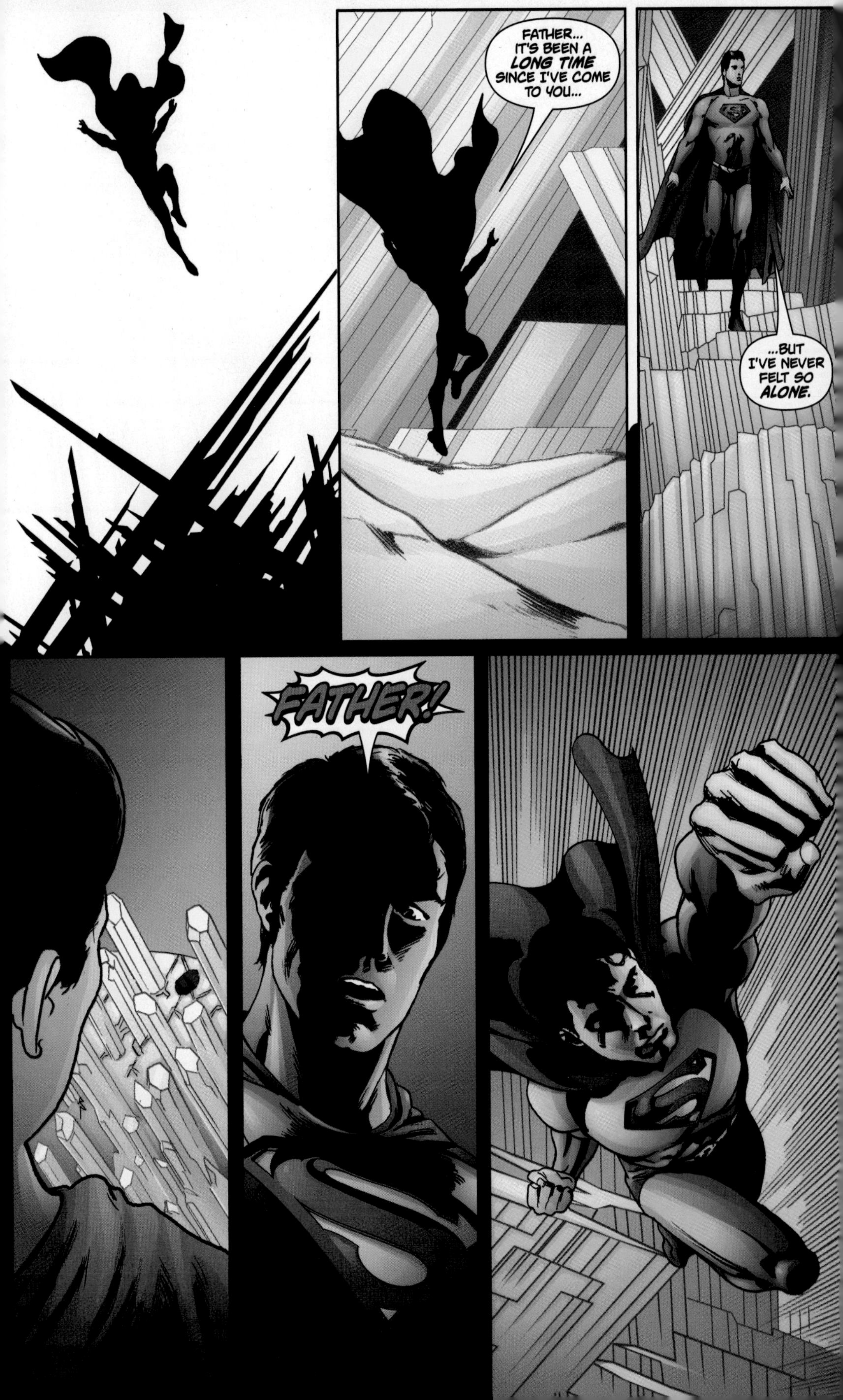
FATHER... IT'S BEEN A LONG TIME SINCE I'VE COME TO YOU...
...BUT I'VE NEVER FELT SO ALONE.
FATHER!

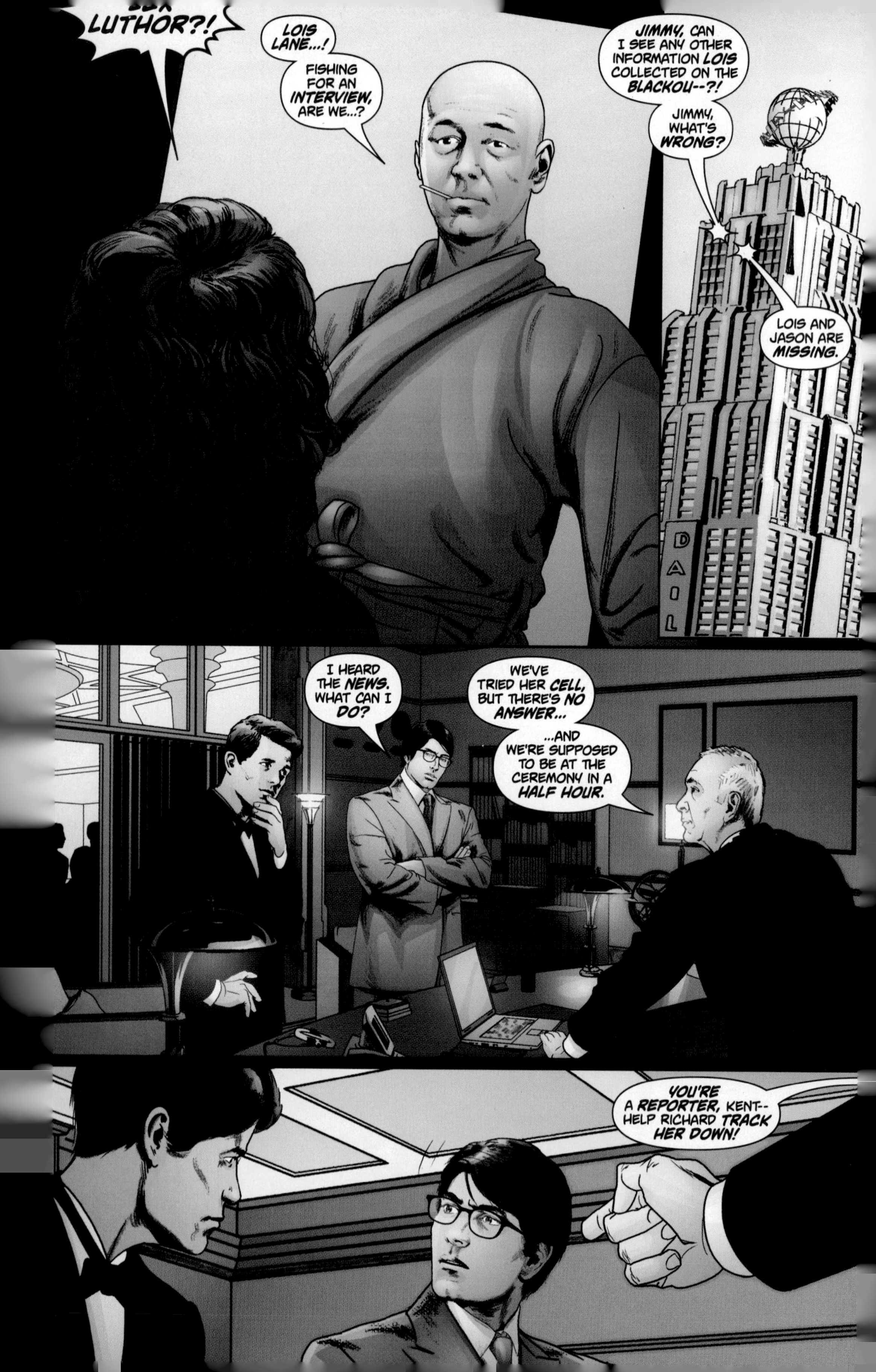
LUTHOR?!
LOIS LANE...!
FISHING FOR AN INTERVIEW, ARE WE...?
JIMMY, CAN I SEE ANY OTHER INFORMATION LOIS COLLECTED ON THE BLACKOU--?!
JIMMY, WHAT'S WRONG?
LOIS AND JASON ARE MISSING.
I HEARD THE NEWS. WHAT CAN I DO?
WE'VE TRIED HER CELL, BUT THERE'S NO ANSWER...
...AND WE'RE SUPPOSED TO BE AT THE CEREMONY IN A HALF HOUR.
YOU'RE A REPORTER, KENT-- HELP RICHARD TRACK HER DOWN!

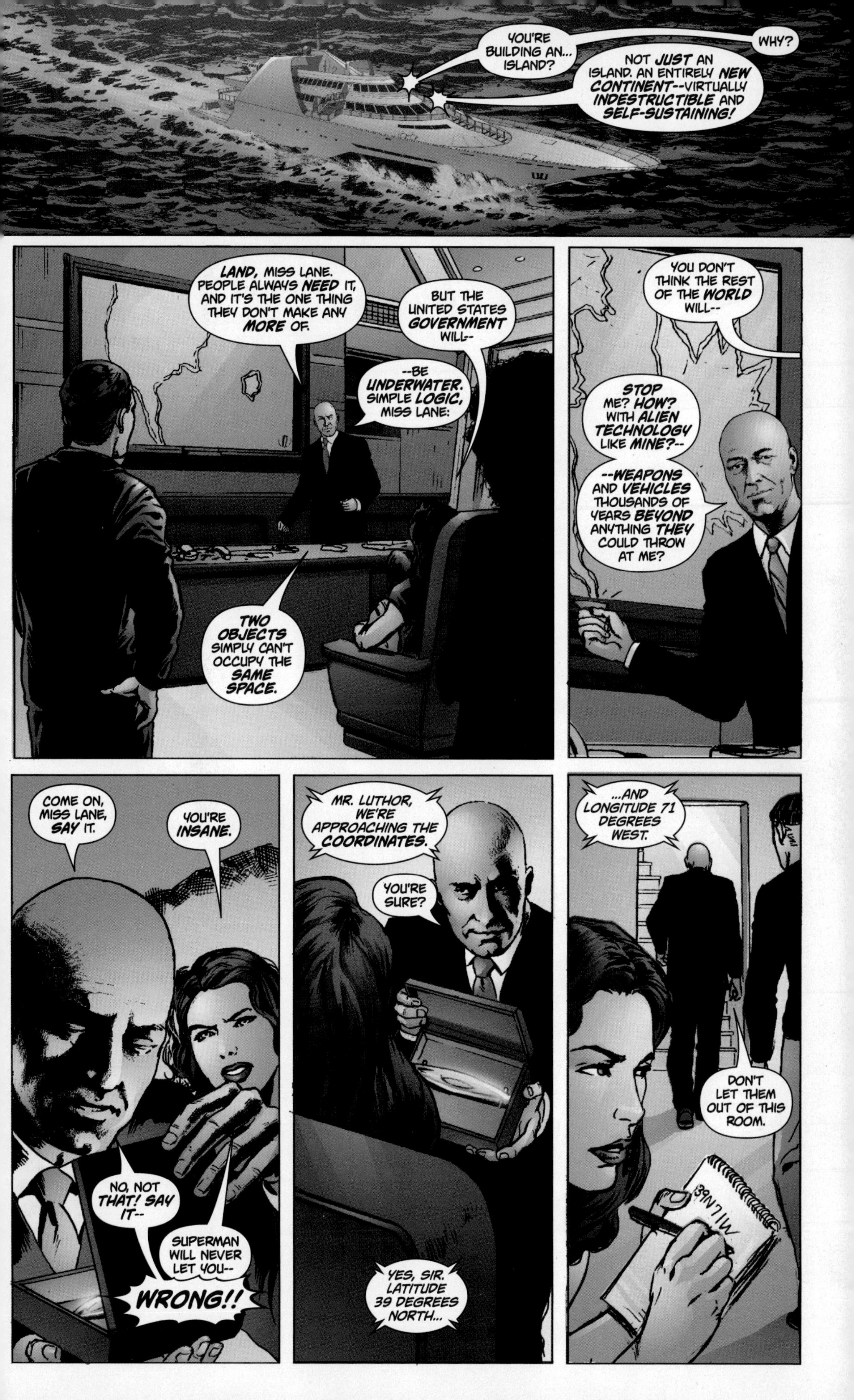
YOU'RE BUILDING AN... ISLAND?
WHY?
NOT JUST AN ISLAND. AN ENTIRELY NEW CONTINENT--VIRTUALLY INDESTRUCTIBLE AND SELF-SUSTAINING!
LAND, MISS LANE. PEOPLE ALWAYS NEED IT, AND IT'S THE ONE THING THEY DON'T MAKE ANY MORE OF.
BUT THE UNITED STATES GOVERNMENT WILL--
--BE UNDERWATER. SIMPLE LOGIC, MISS LANE:
TWO OBJECTS SIMPLY CAN'T OCCUPY THE SAME SPACE.
YOU DON'T THINK THE REST OF THE WORLD WILL--
STOP ME? HOW? WITH ALIEN TECHNOLOGY LIKE MINE?--
--WEAPONS AND VEHICLES THOUSANDS OF YEARS BEYOND ANYTHING THEY COULD THROW AT ME?
COME ON, MISS LANE, SAY IT.
YOU'RE INSANE.
NO, NOT THAT! SAY IT--
SUPERMAN WILL NEVER LET YOU--
WRONG!!
MR. LUTHOR, WE'RE APPROACHING THE COORDINATES.
YOU'RE SURE?
YES, SIR. LATITUDE 39 DEGREES NORTH...
...AND LONGITUDE 71 DEGREES WEST.
DON'T LET THEM OUT OF THIS ROOM.

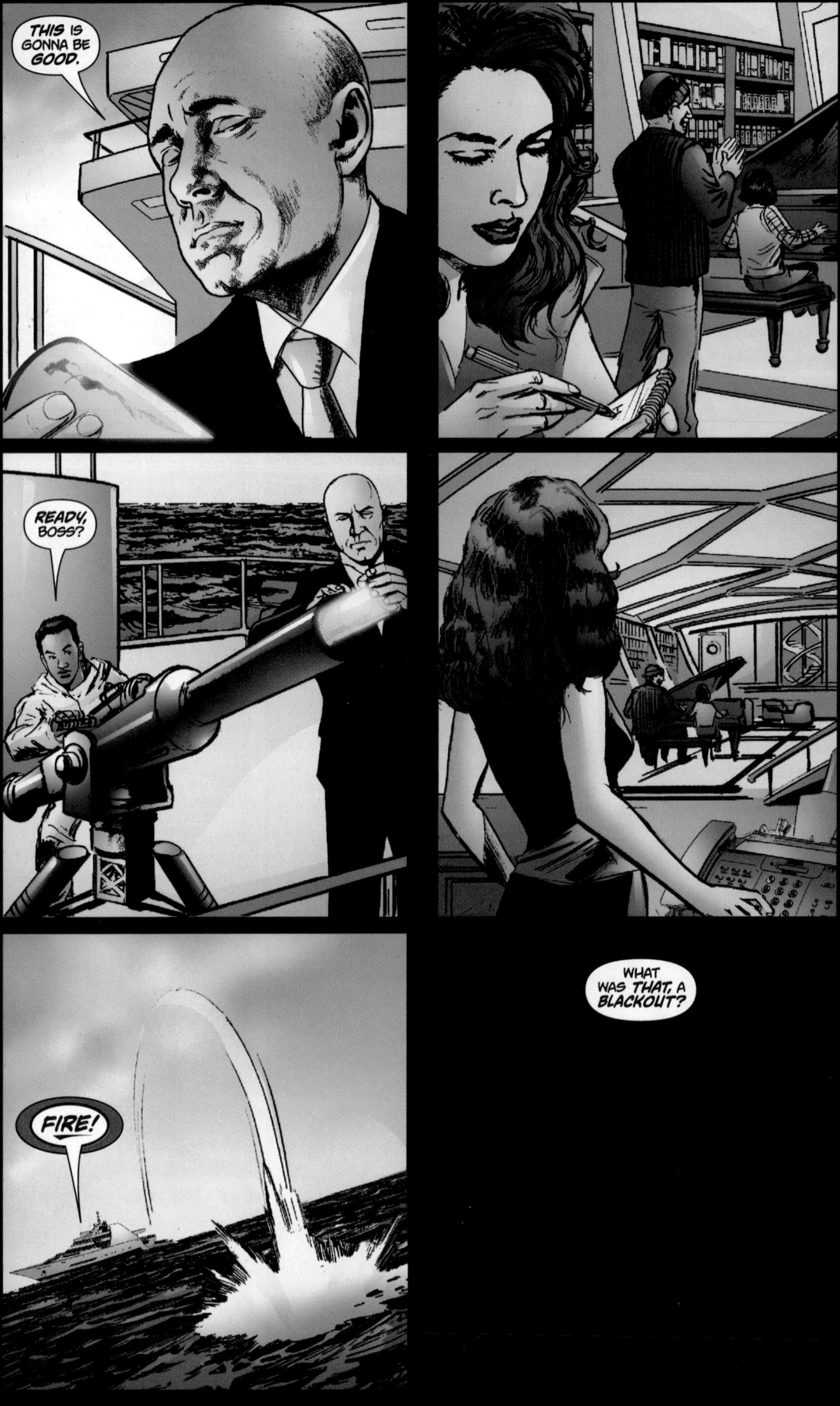
THIS is GONNA BE GOOD.
READY, BOSS?
FIRE!
WHAT WAS THAT, A BLACKOUT?

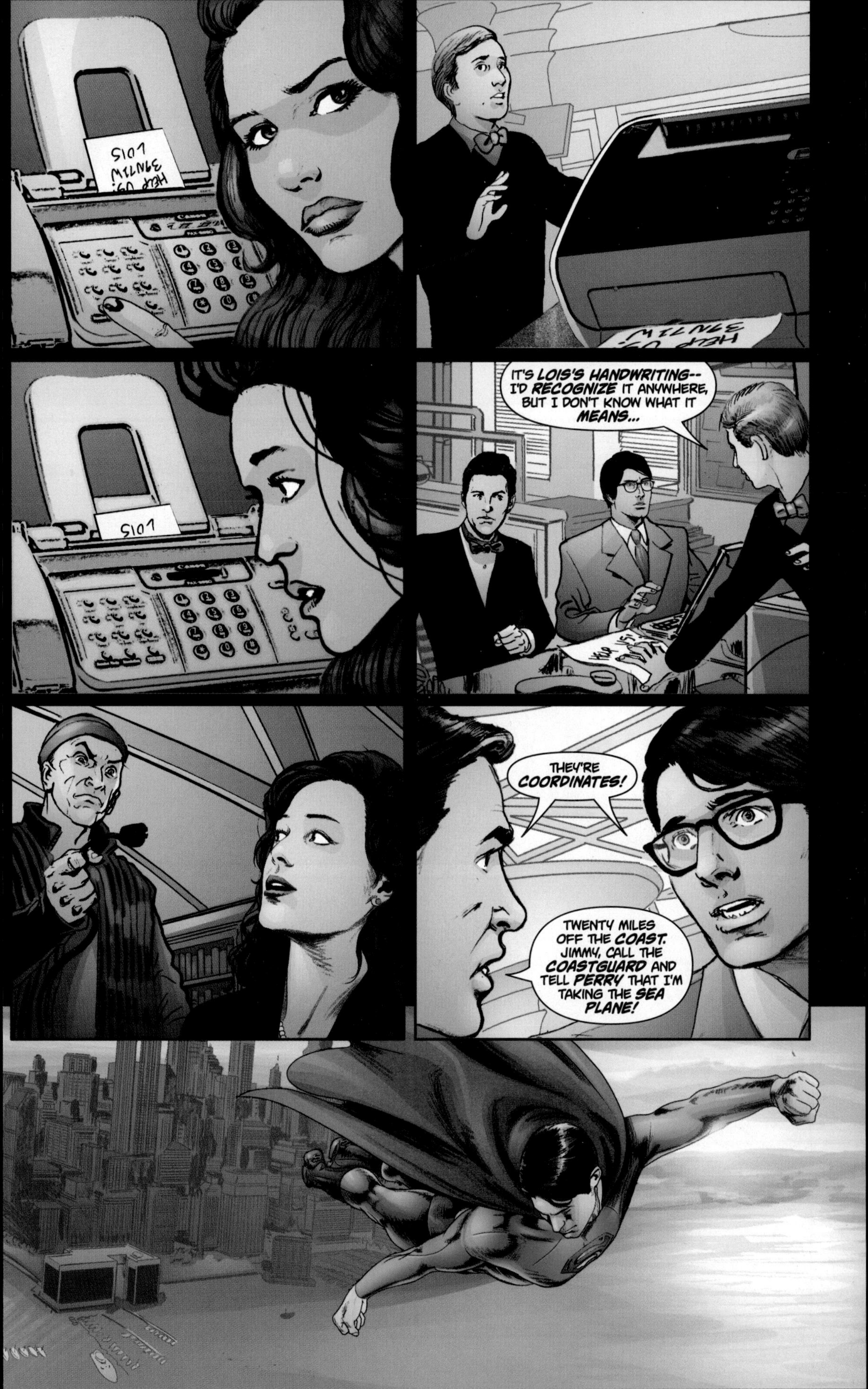
IT'S LOIS'S HANDWRITING-- I'D RECOGNIZE IT ANYWHERE, BUT I DON'T KNOW WHAT IT MEANS...
THEY'RE COORDINATES!
TWENTY MILES OFF THE COAST. JIMMY, CALL THE COASTGUARD AND TELL PERRY THAT I'M TAKING THE SEA PLANE!

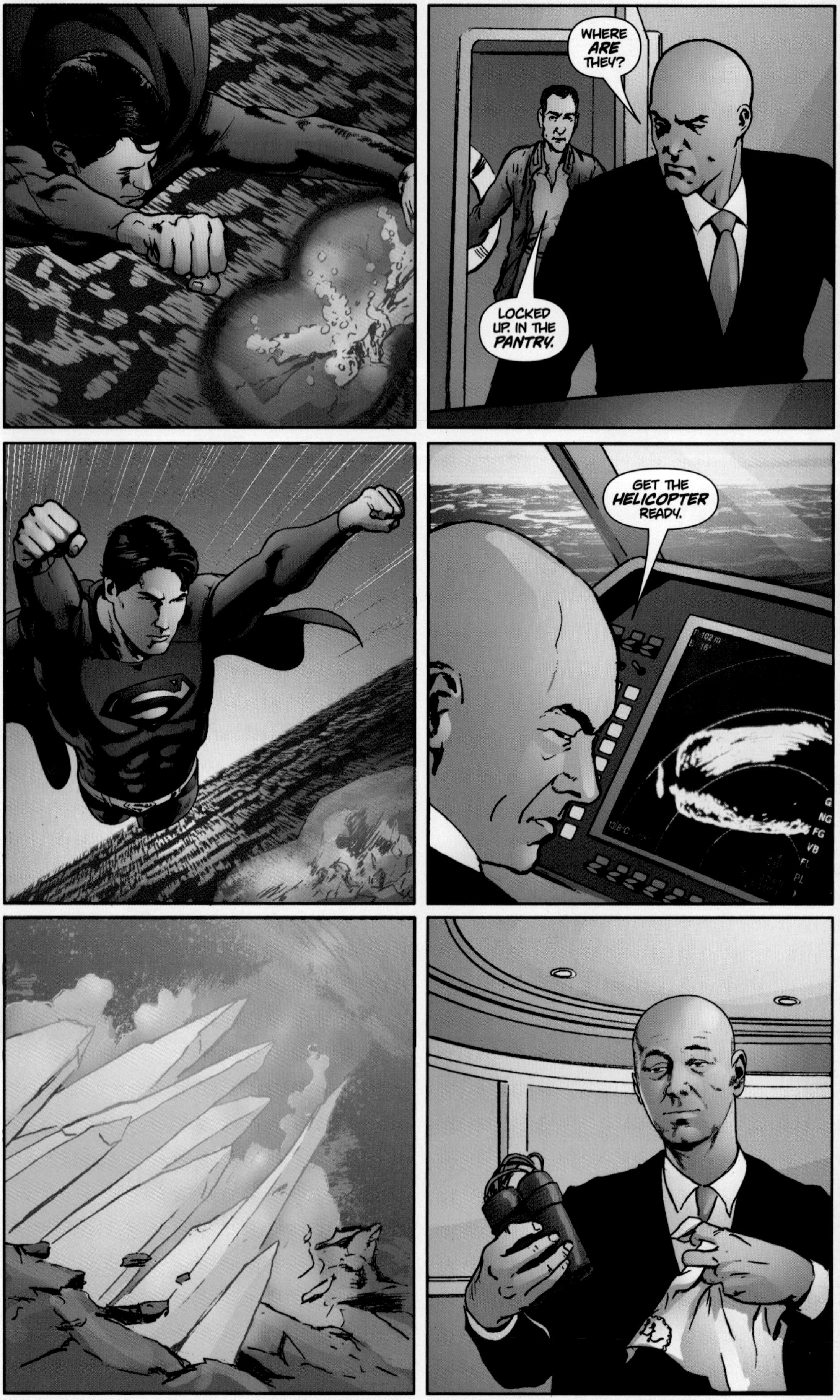
WHERE ARE THEY?
LOCKED UP. IN THE PANTRY.
GET THE HELICOPTER READY.

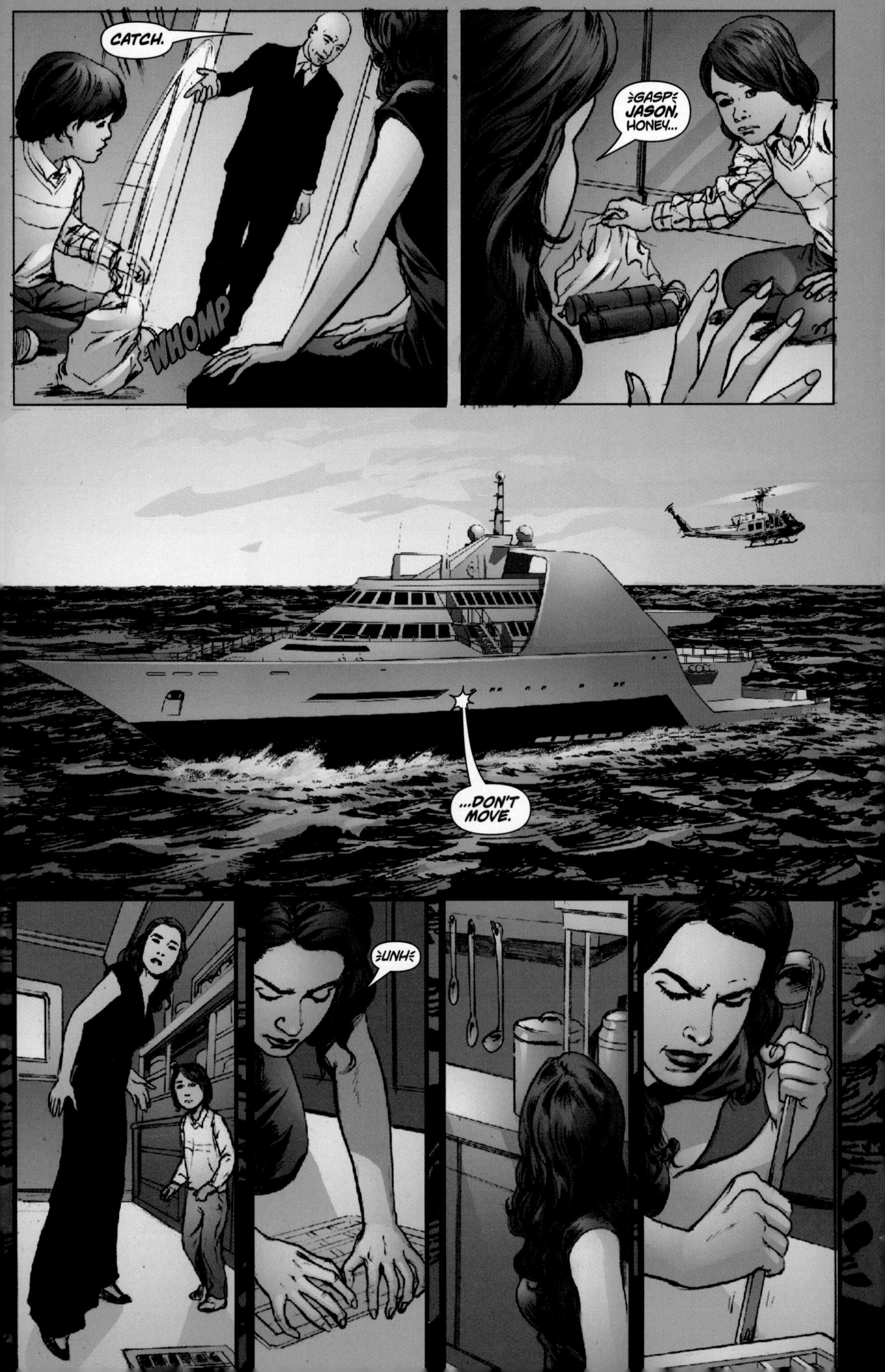
CATCH.
WHOMP
GASP
JASON, HONEY...
...DON'T MOVE.
UNH

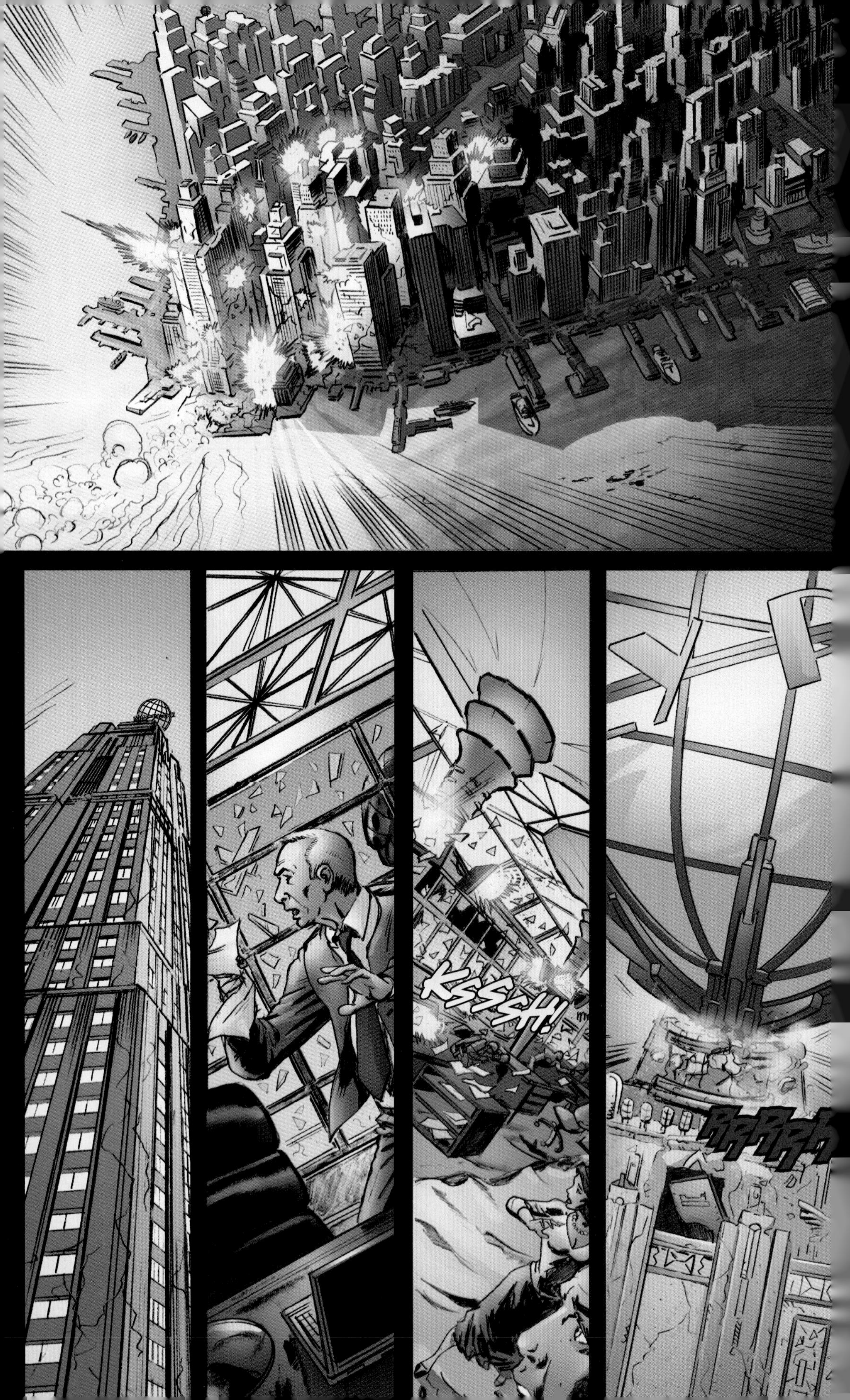
KSSSH!
RRRRRH

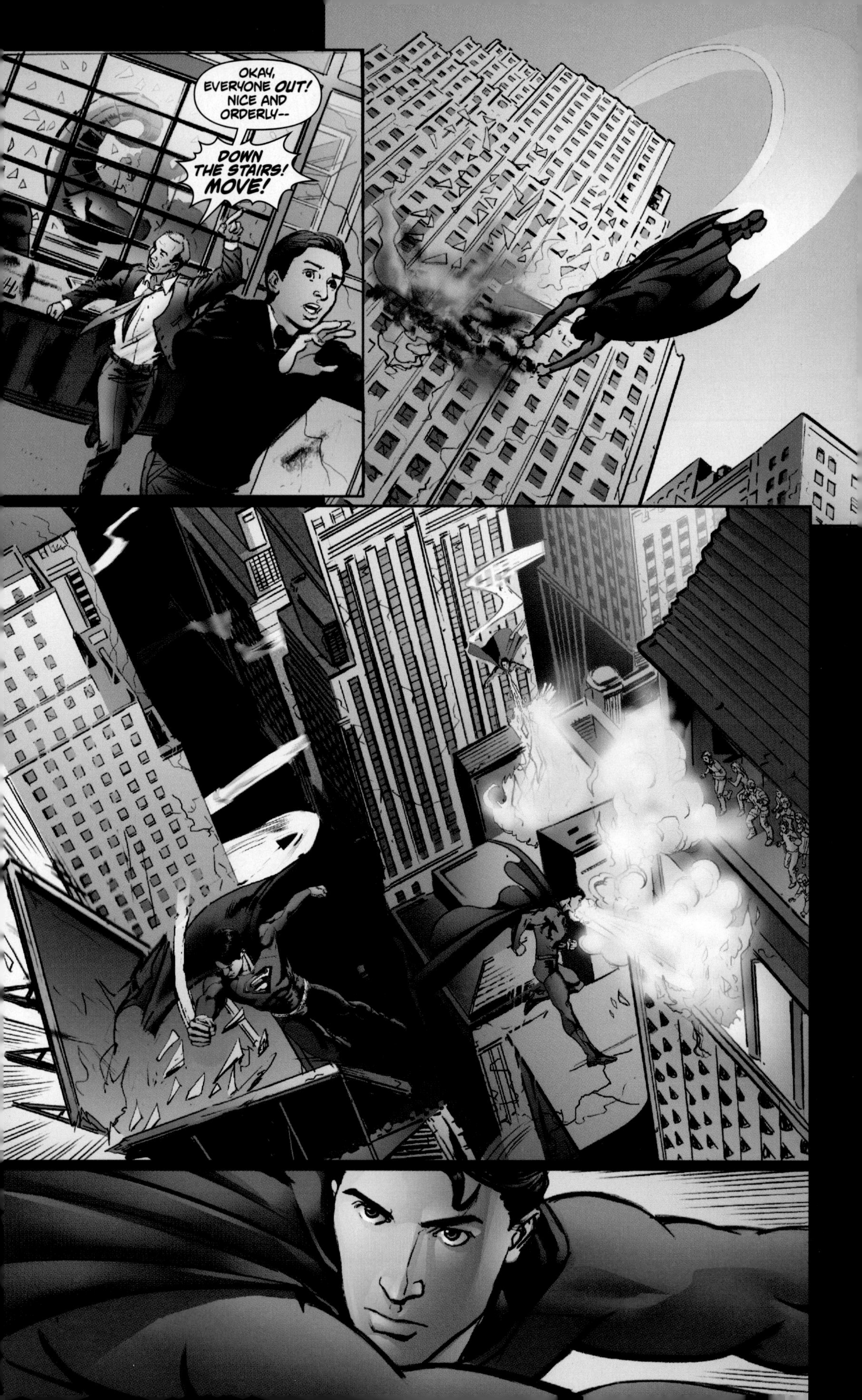
OKAY, EVERYONE OUT! NICE AND ORDERLY--
DOWN THE STAIRS! MOVE!

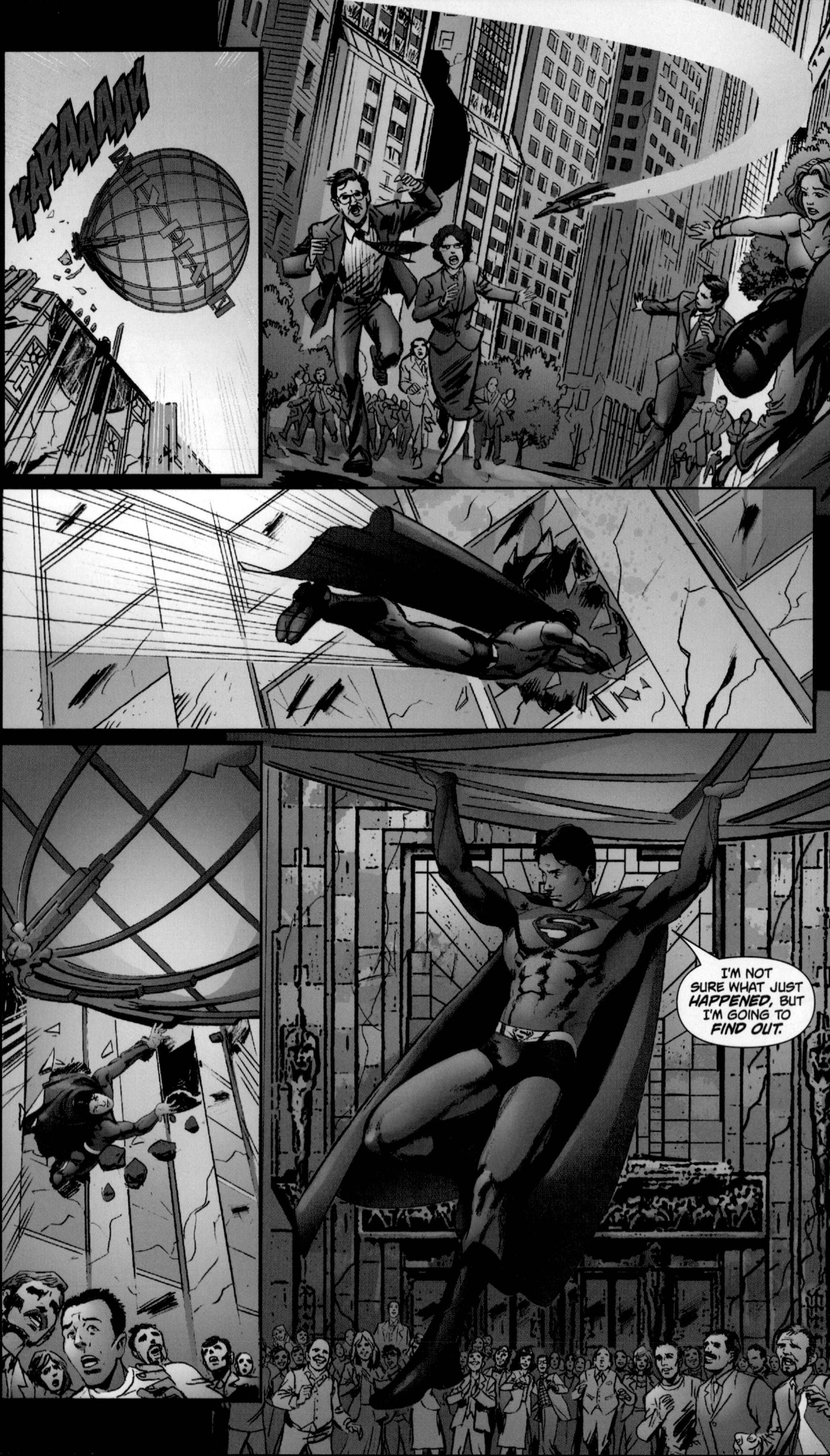
KARAAAK
I'M NOT SURE WHAT JUST *HAPPENED*, BUT I'M GOING TO *FIND OUT*.

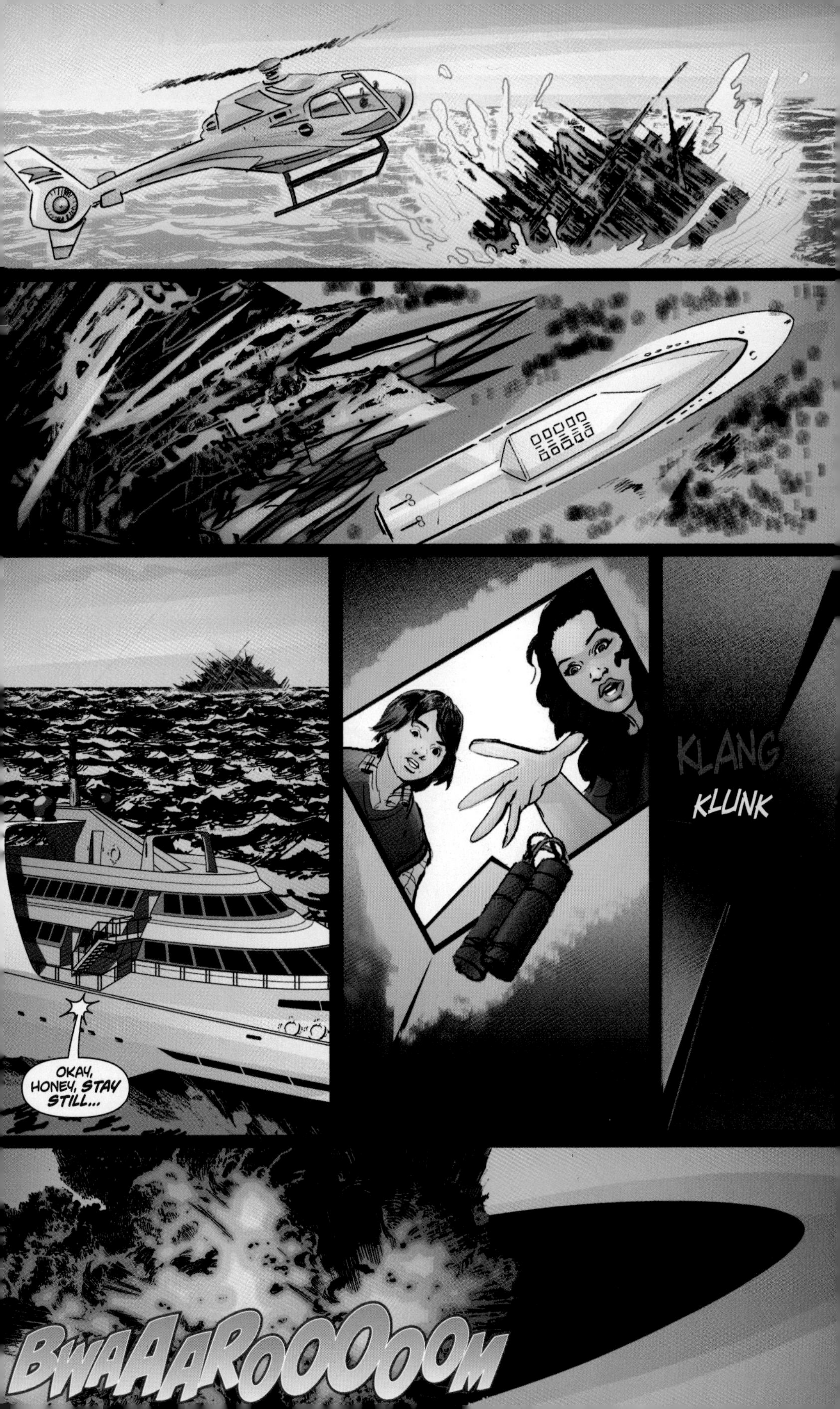
OKAY, HONEY, STAY STILL...
KLANG
KLUNK
BWAAAROOOOOOM

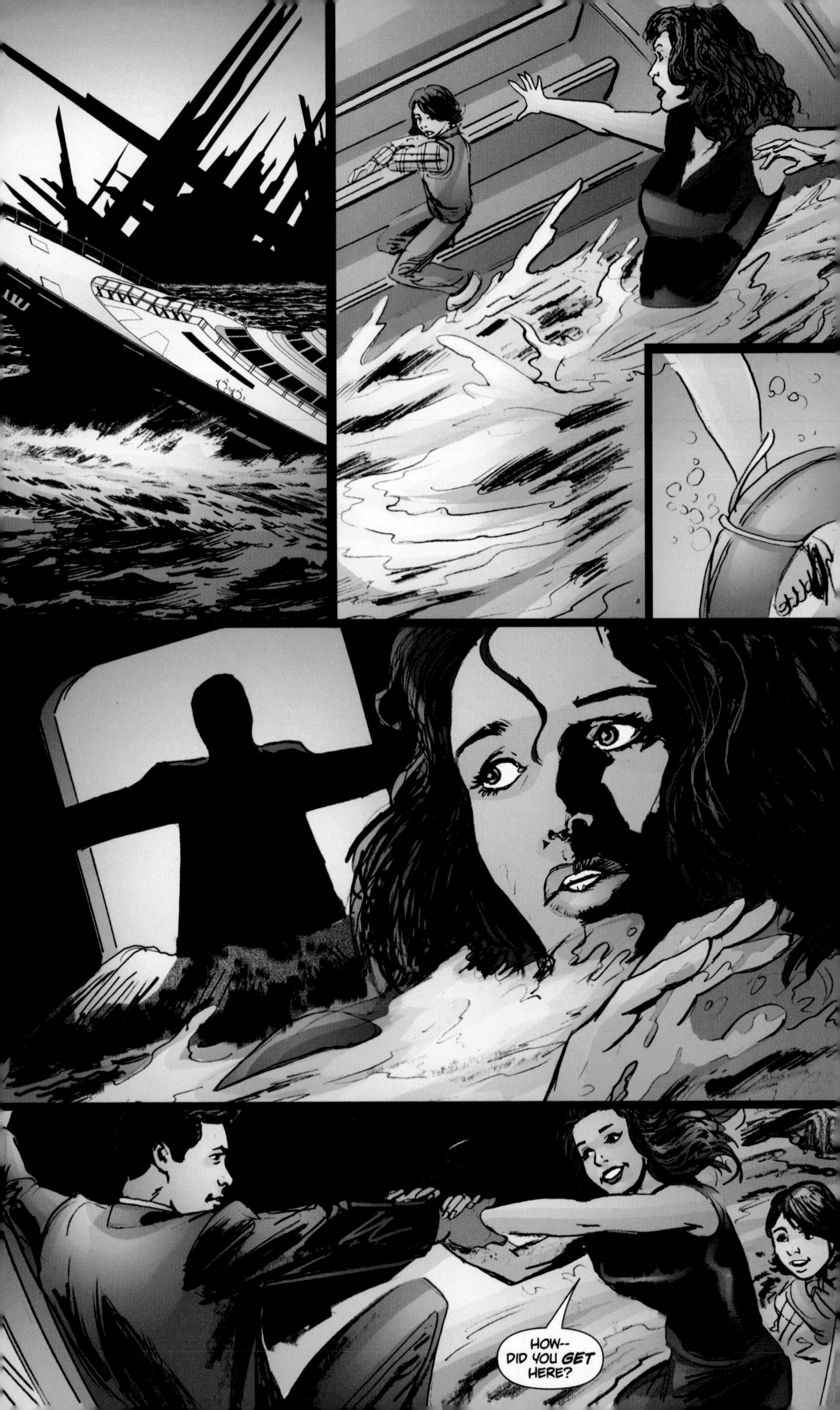
HOW-- DID YOU GET HERE?

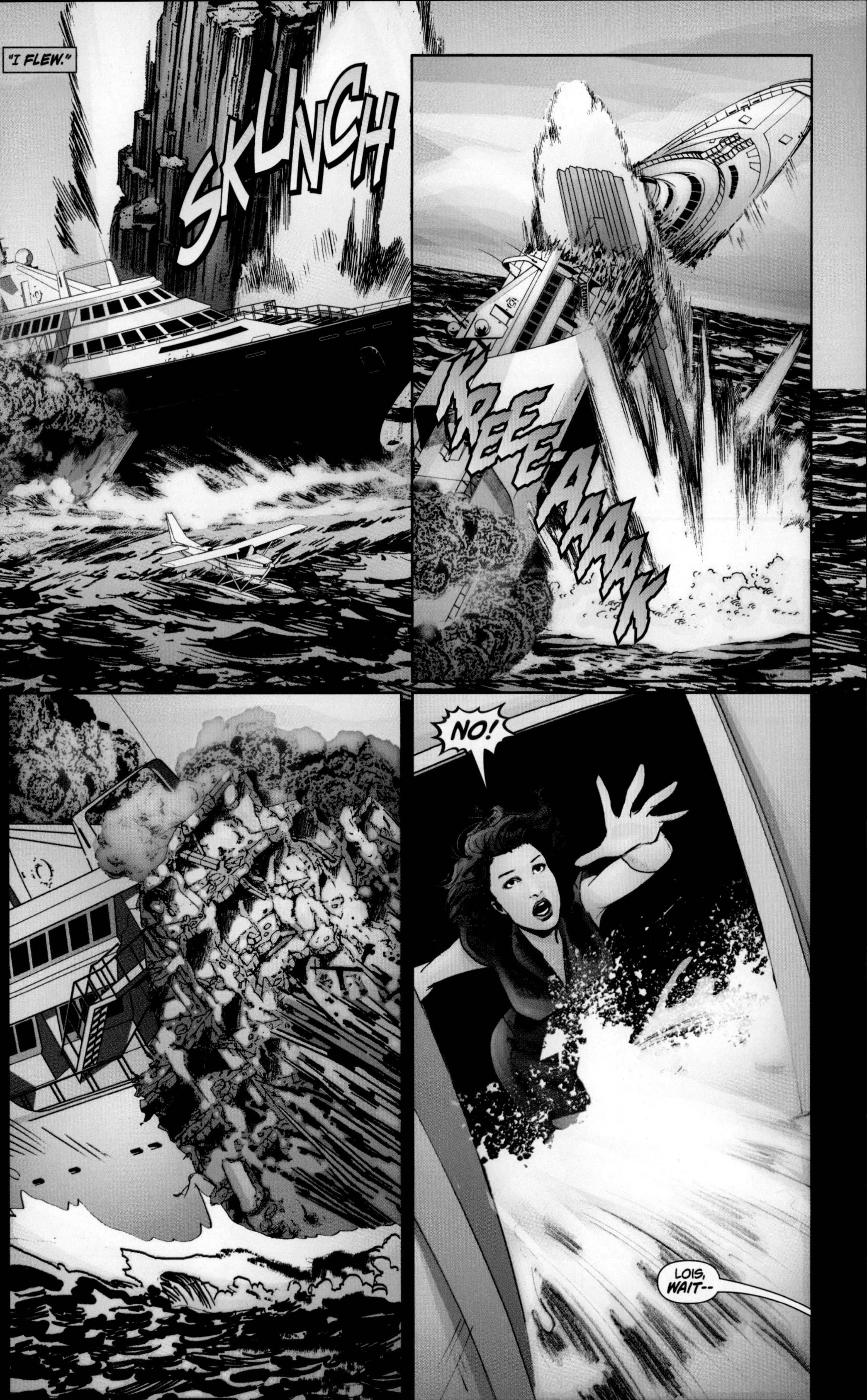
"I FLEW."
SKUNCH
KREEE-AAAAK
NO!
LOIS, WAIT--

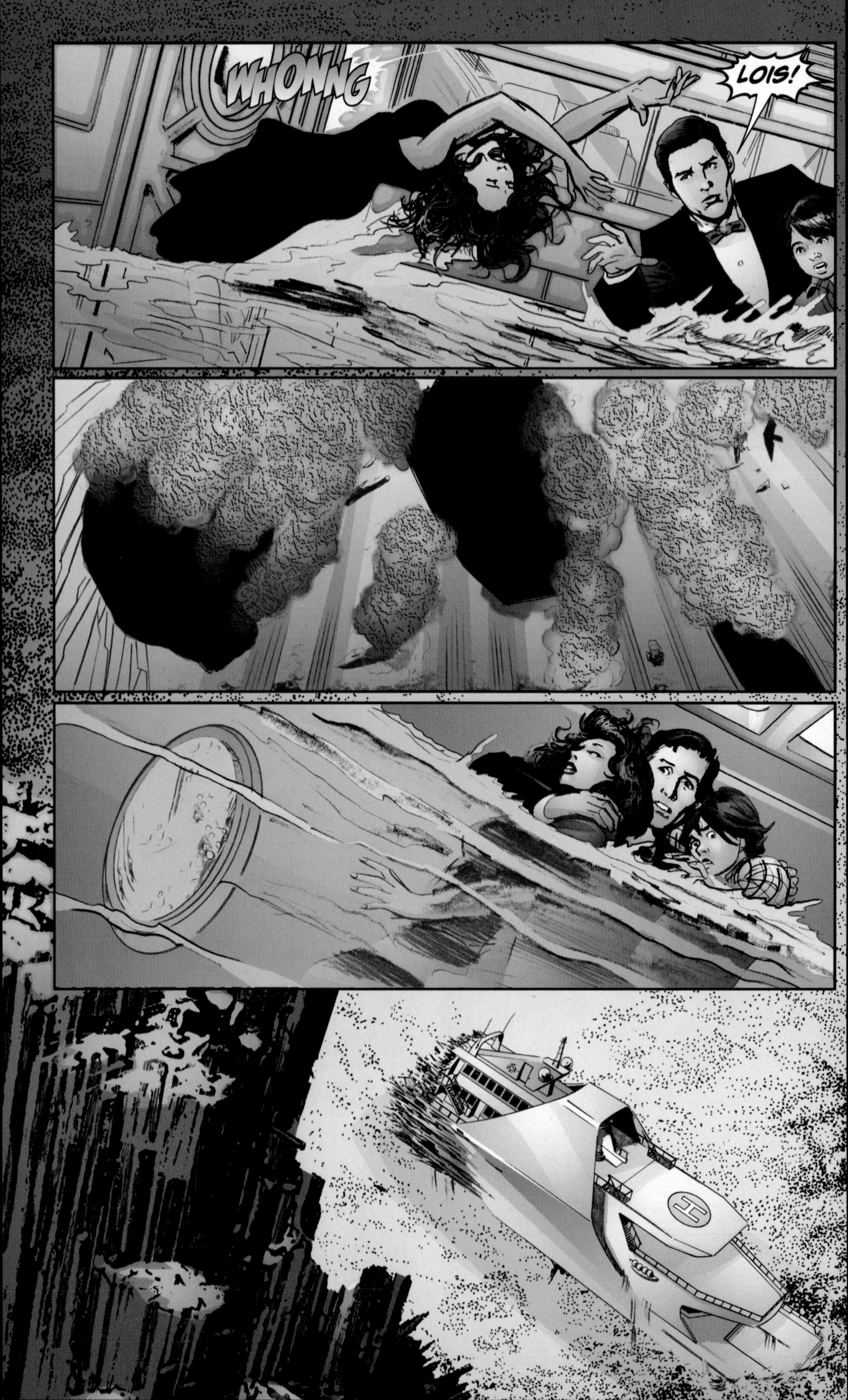
WHONNG
LOIS!

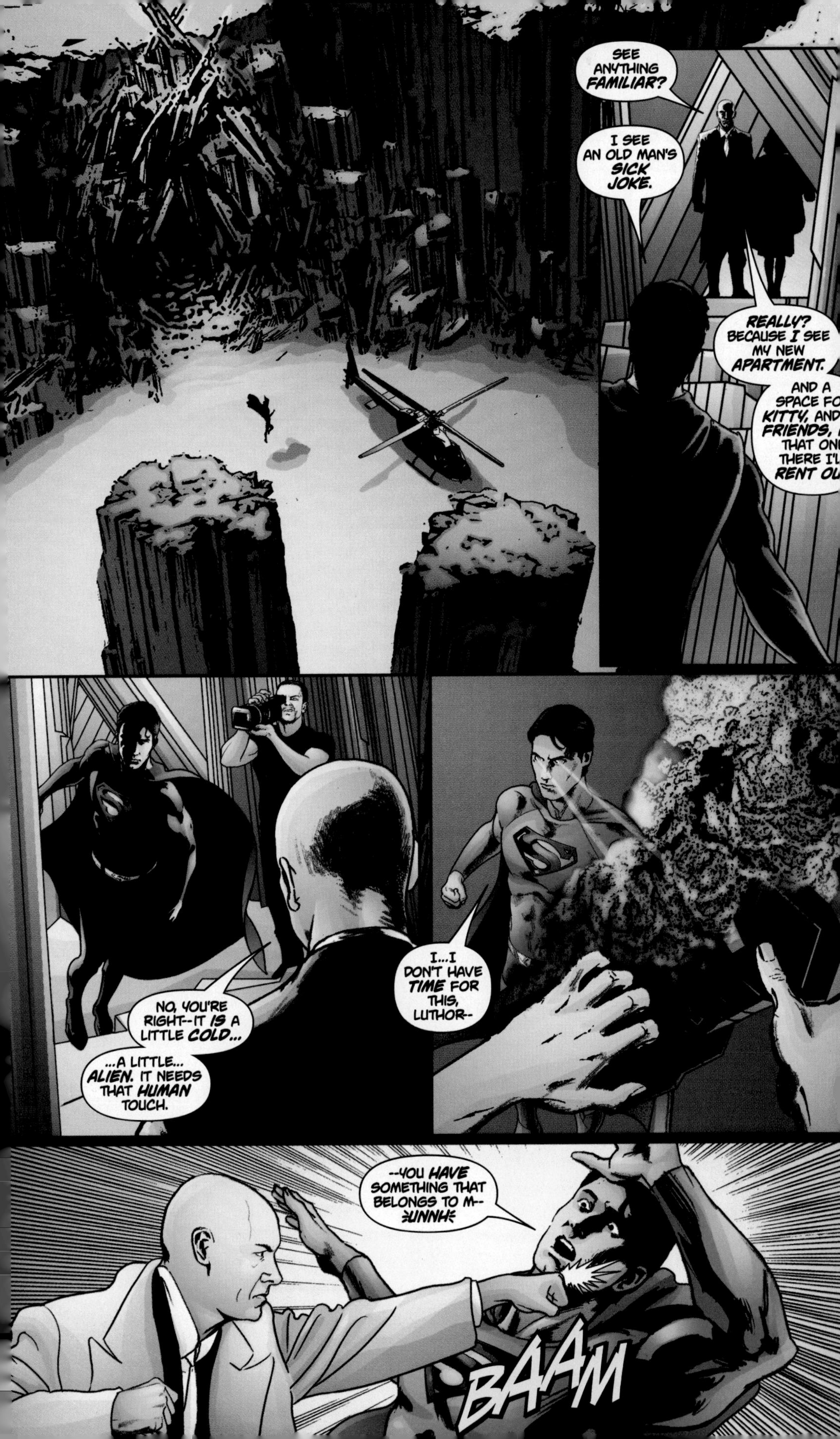
SEE ANYTHING FAMILIAR?
I SEE AN OLD MAN'S SICK JOKE.
REALLY? BECAUSE I SEE MY NEW APARTMENT.
AND A SPACE FO KITTY, AND FRIENDS, THAT ON THERE I'L RENT OU
NO, YOU'RE RIGHT--IT IS A LITTLE COLD...
...A LITTLE... ALIEN. IT NEEDS THAT HUMAN TOUCH.
I...I DON'T HAVE TIME FOR THIS, LUTHOR--
--YOU HAVE SOMETHING THAT BELONGS TO M-- UNNH
BAAM

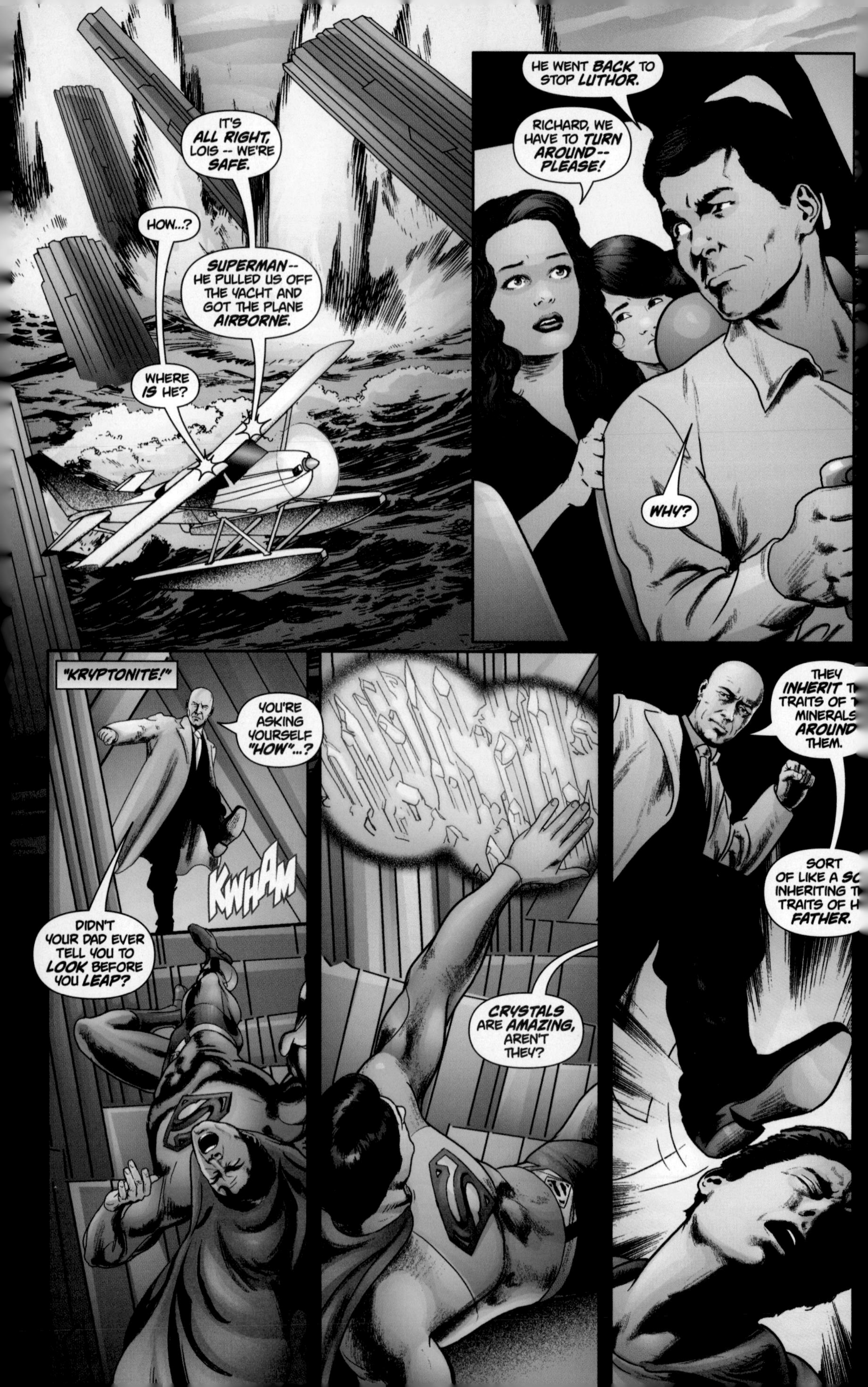
IT'S ALL RIGHT, LOIS -- WE'RE SAFE.
HOW...?
SUPERMAN-- HE PULLED US OFF THE YACHT AND GOT THE PLANE AIRBORNE.
WHERE IS HE?
HE WENT BACK TO STOP LUTHOR.
RICHARD, WE HAVE TO TURN AROUND-- PLEASE!
WHY?
"KRYPTONITE!"
YOU'RE ASKING YOURSELF "HOW"...?
KWHAM
DIDN'T YOUR DAD EVER TELL YOU TO LOOK BEFORE YOU LEAP?
CRYSTALS ARE AMAZING, AREN'T THEY?
THEY INHERIT
TRAITS OF
MINERALS
AROUND
THEM.
SORT
OF LIKE A
INHERITING
TRAITS OF
FATHER.

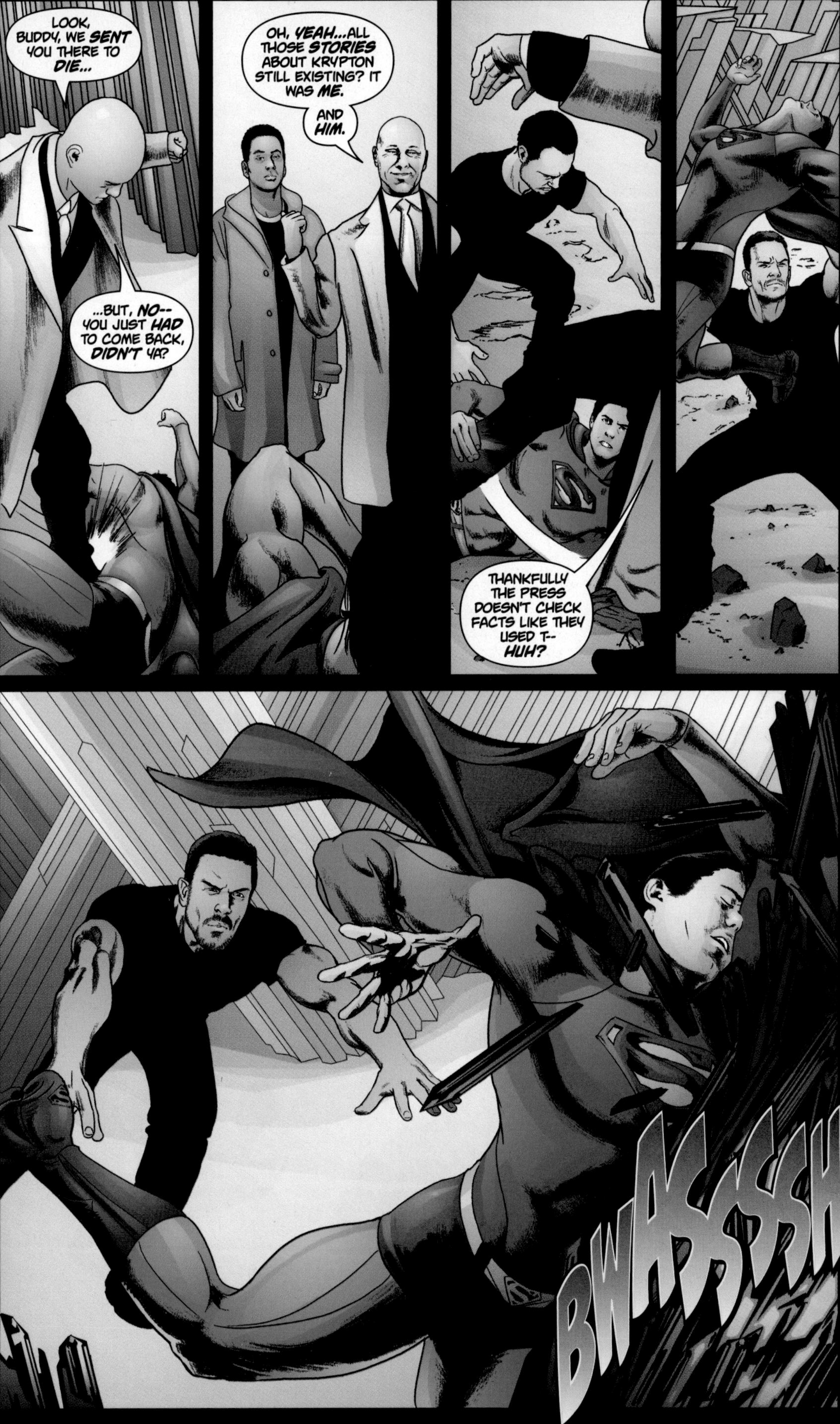
LOOK, BUDDY, WE SENT YOU THERE TO DIE...
...BUT, NO-- YOU JUST HAD TO COME BACK, DIDN'T YA?
OH, YEAH...ALL THOSE STORIES ABOUT KRYPTON STILL EXISTING? IT WAS ME.
AND HIM.
THANKFULLY THE PRESS DOESN'T CHECK FACTS LIKE THEY USED T-- HUH?
BWASSSH

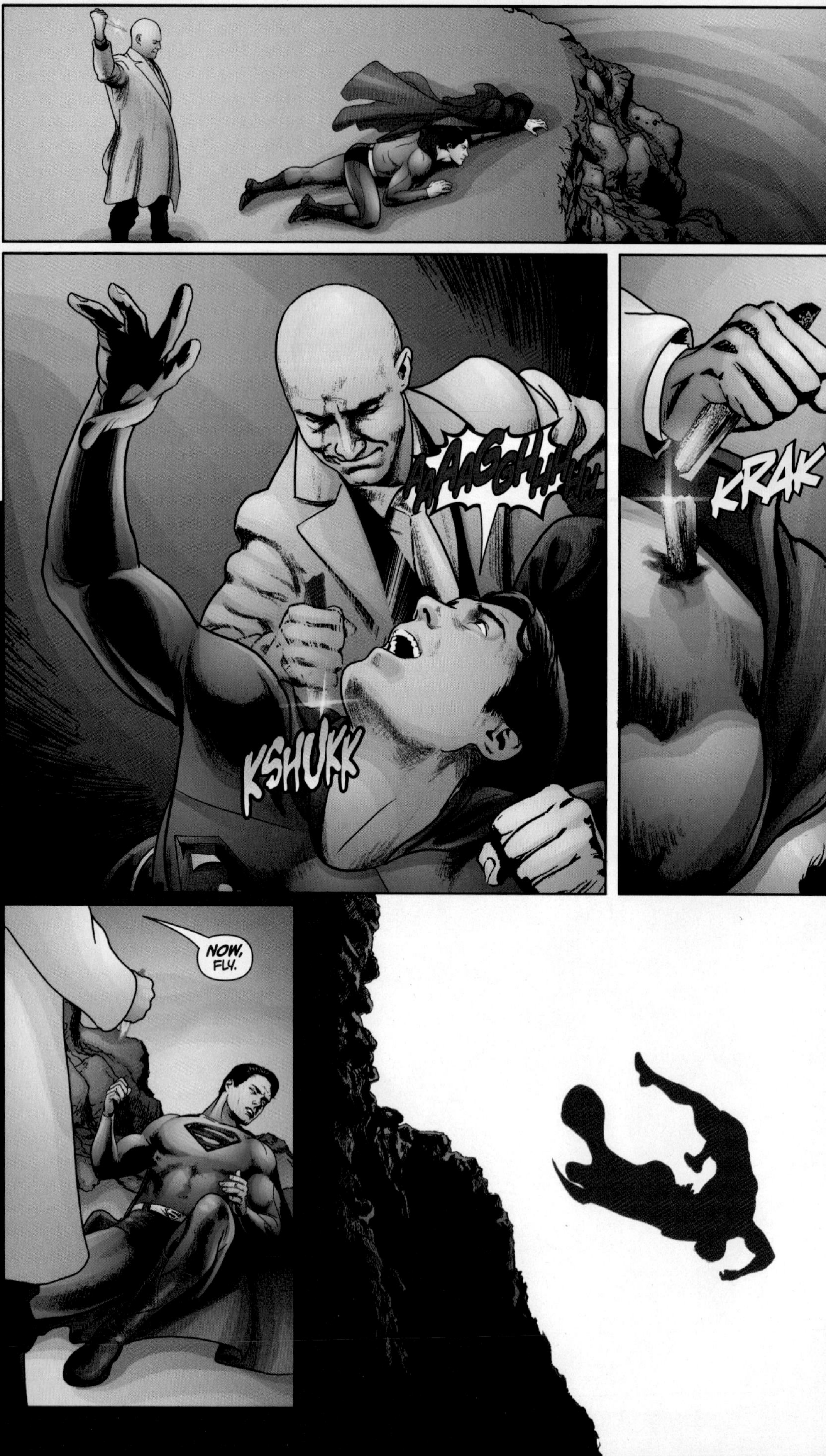
AAAAGGHHHHH
KSHUKK
KRAK
NOW, FLY.

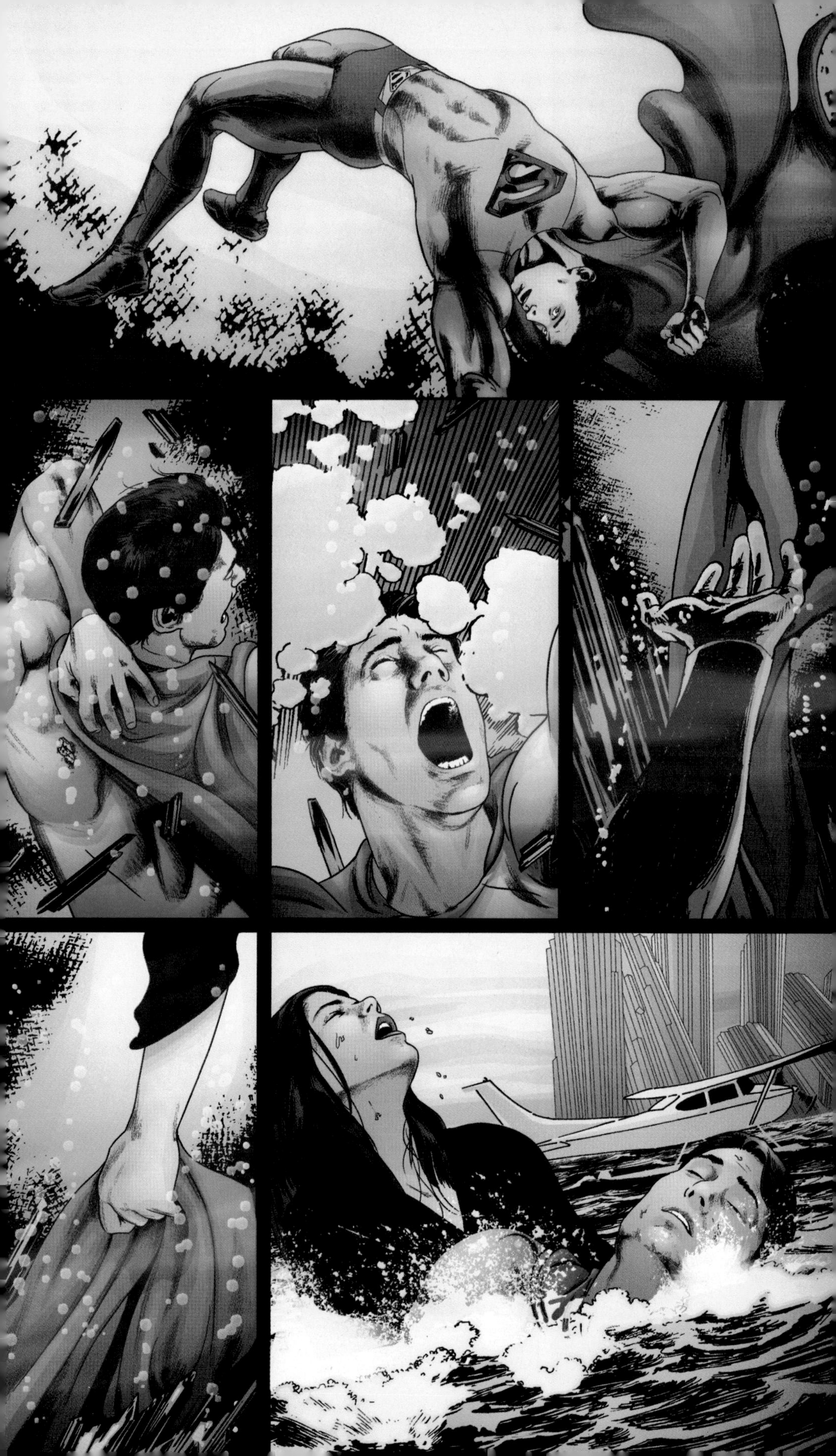

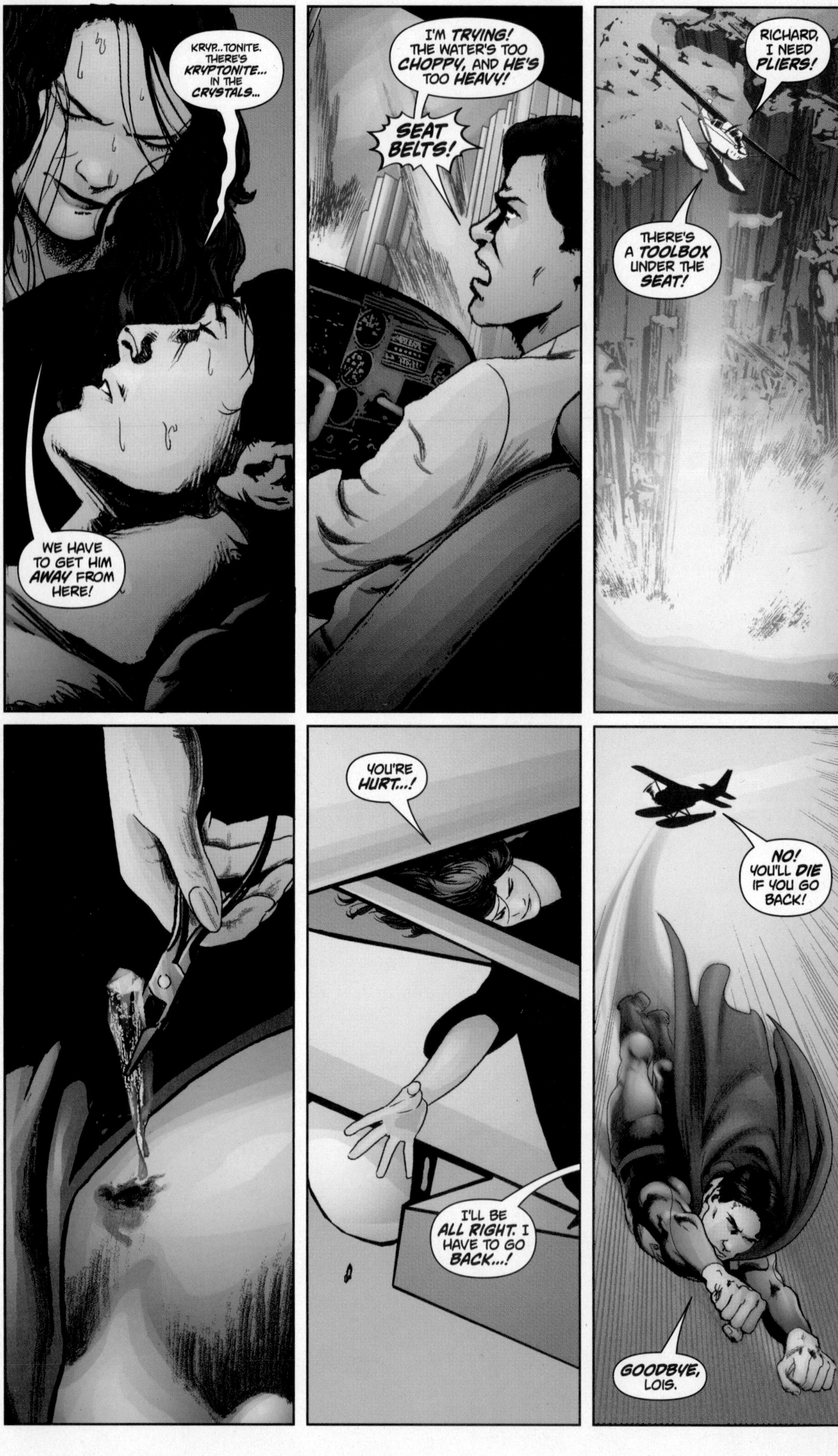
KRYP...TONITE. THERE'S KRYPTONITE... IN THE CRYSTALS...
WE HAVE TO GET HIM AWAY FROM HERE!
I'M TRYING! THE WATER'S TOO CHOPPY, AND HE'S TOO HEAVY!
SEAT BELTS!
RICHARD, I NEED PLIERS!
THERE'S A TOOLBOX UNDER THE SEAT!
YOU'RE HURT...!
I'LL BE ALL RIGHT. I HAVE TO GO BACK...!
NO! YOU'LL DIE IF YOU GO BACK!
GOODBYE, LOIS.

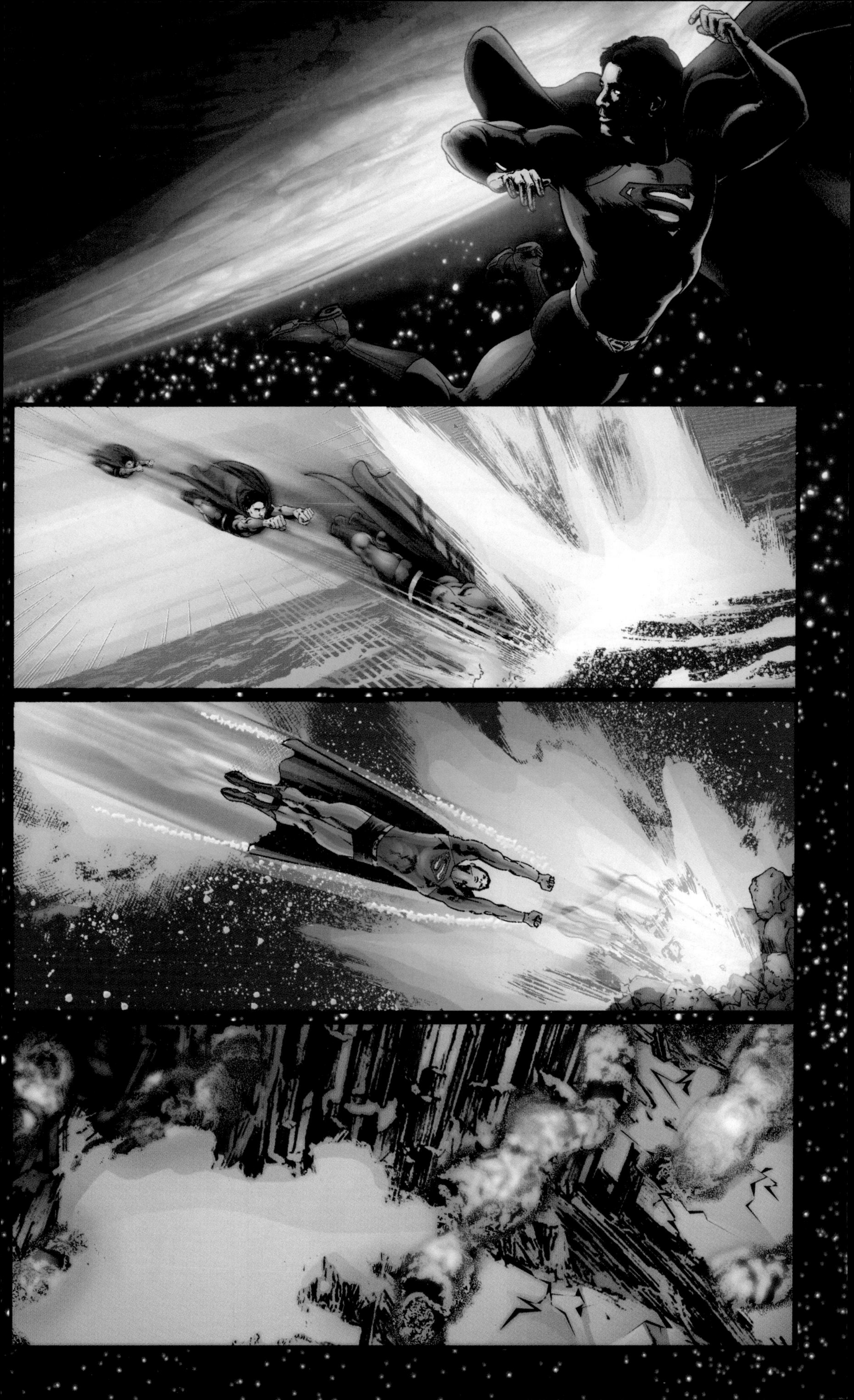

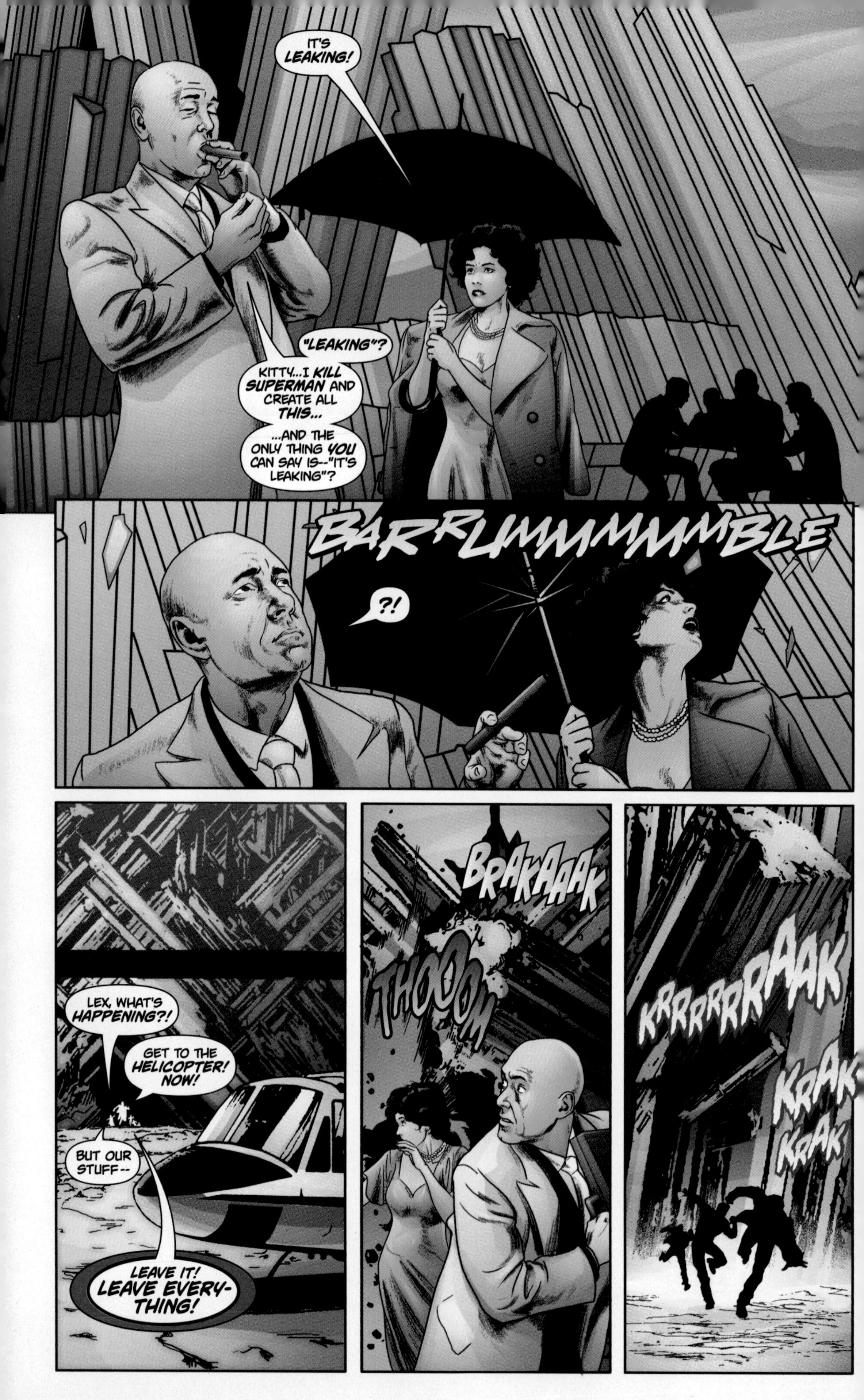
IT'S LEAKING!
"LEAKING"?
KITTY...I KILL SUPERMAN AND CREATE ALL THIS...
...AND THE ONLY THING YOU CAN SAY IS--"IT'S LEAKING"?
BARRUMMMMMMBLE
?!
LEX, WHAT'S HAPPENING?!
GET TO THE HELICOPTER! NOW!
BUT OUR STUFF--
LEAVE IT! LEAVE EVERY-THING!
BRAKAAAK
THOOOM
KRRRRRRAAK
KRAK
KRAK

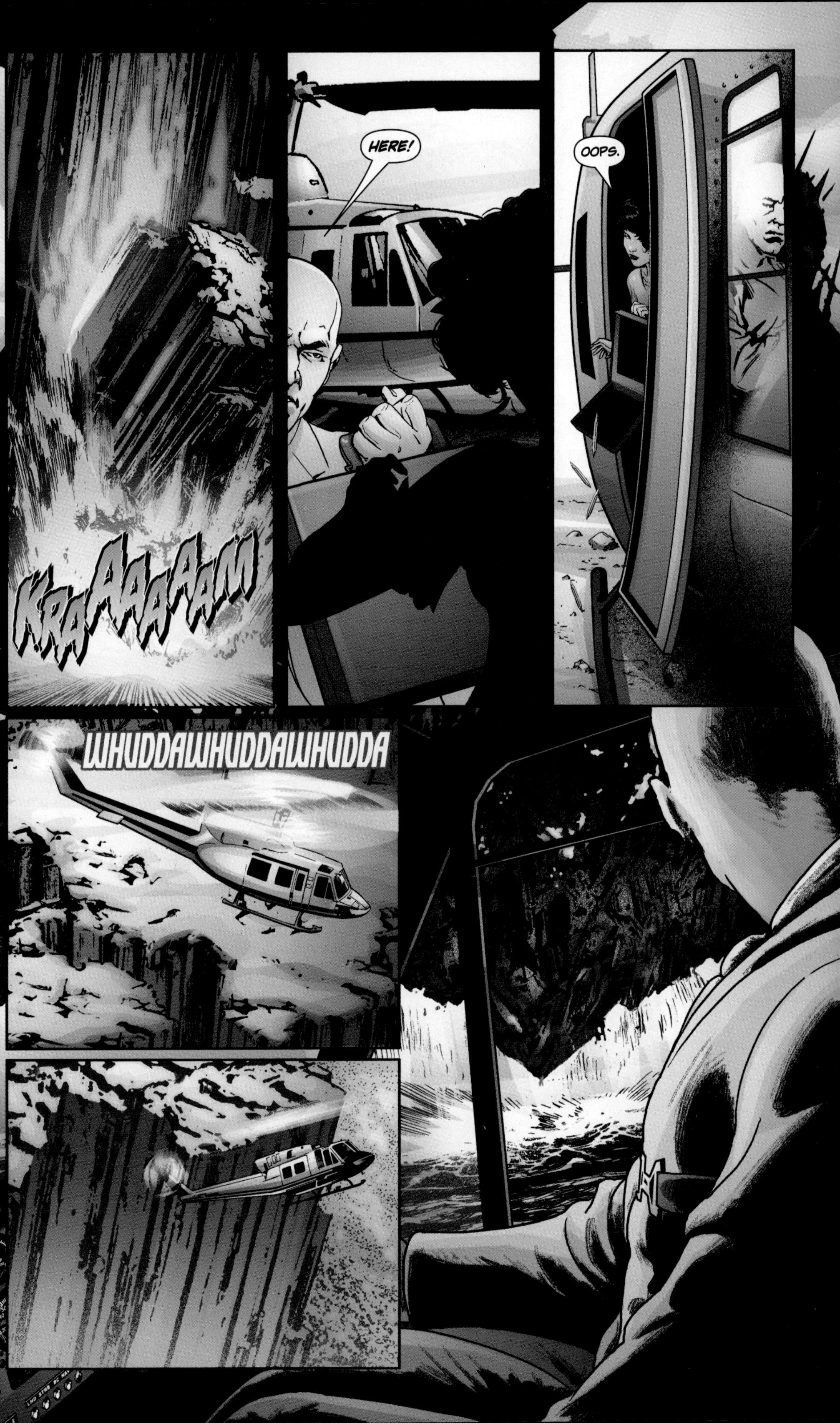
KRAAAAAM
HERE!
OOPS.
WHUDDAWHUDDAWHUDDA

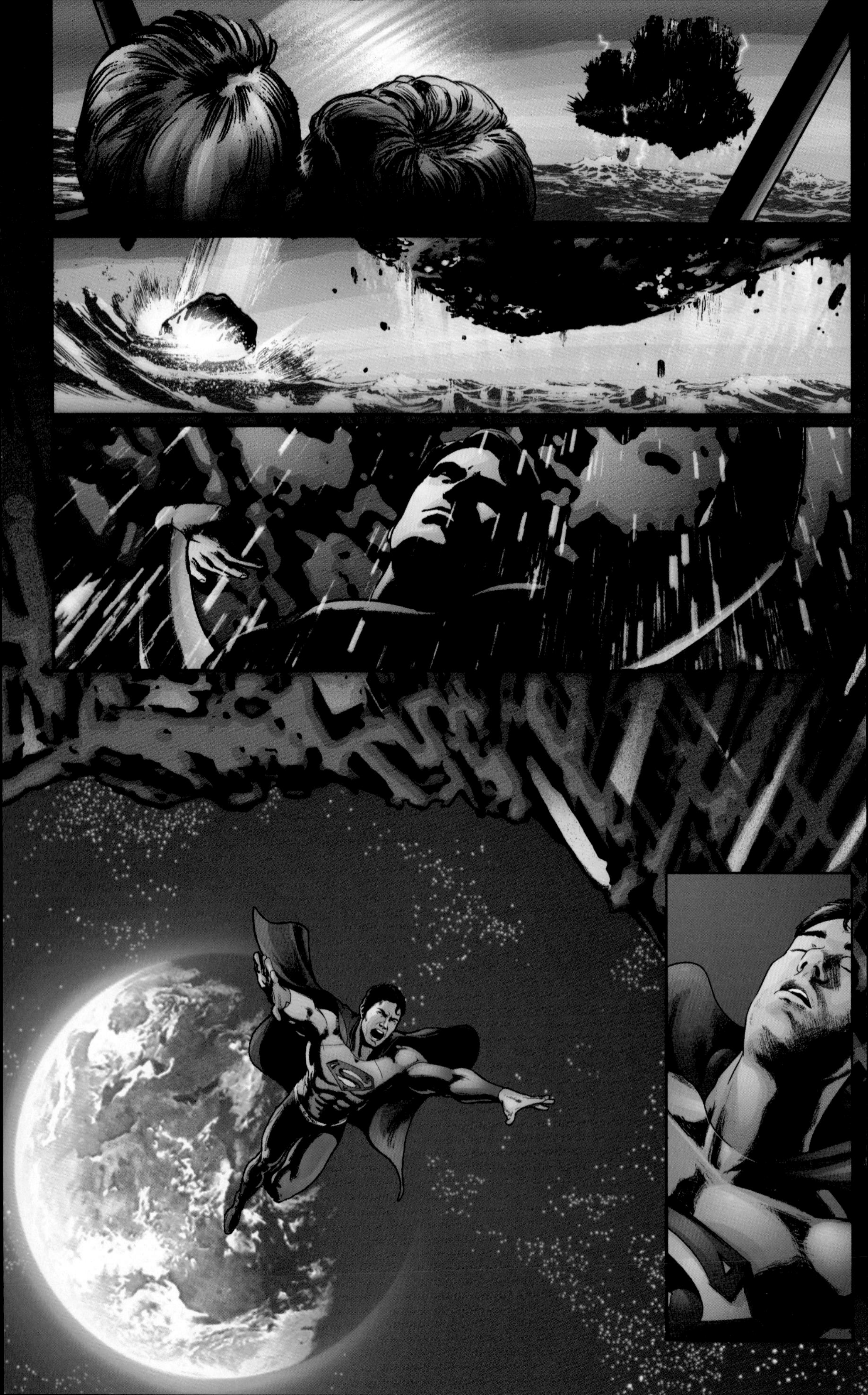

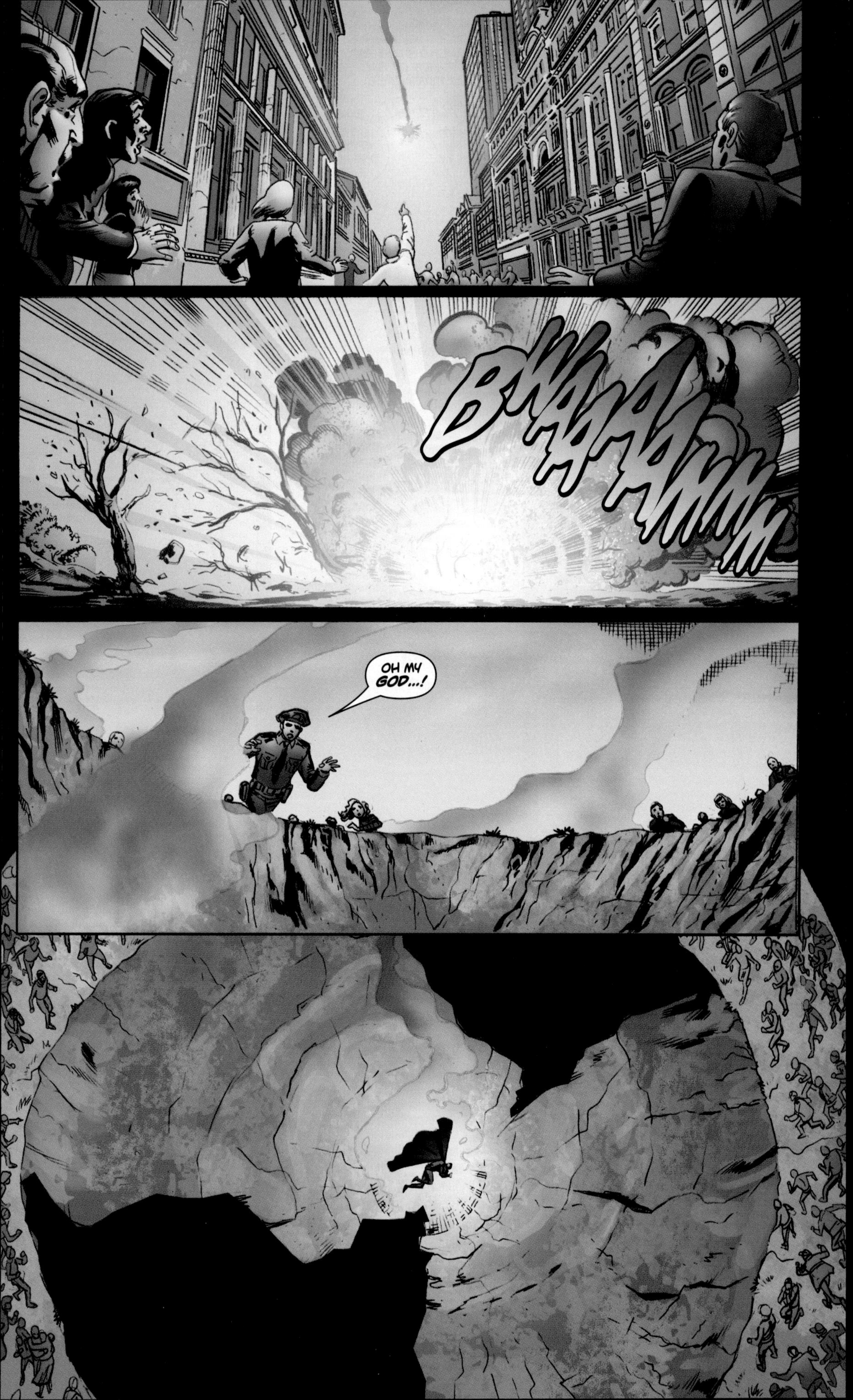
BWAAAAMMM
OH MY GOD...!

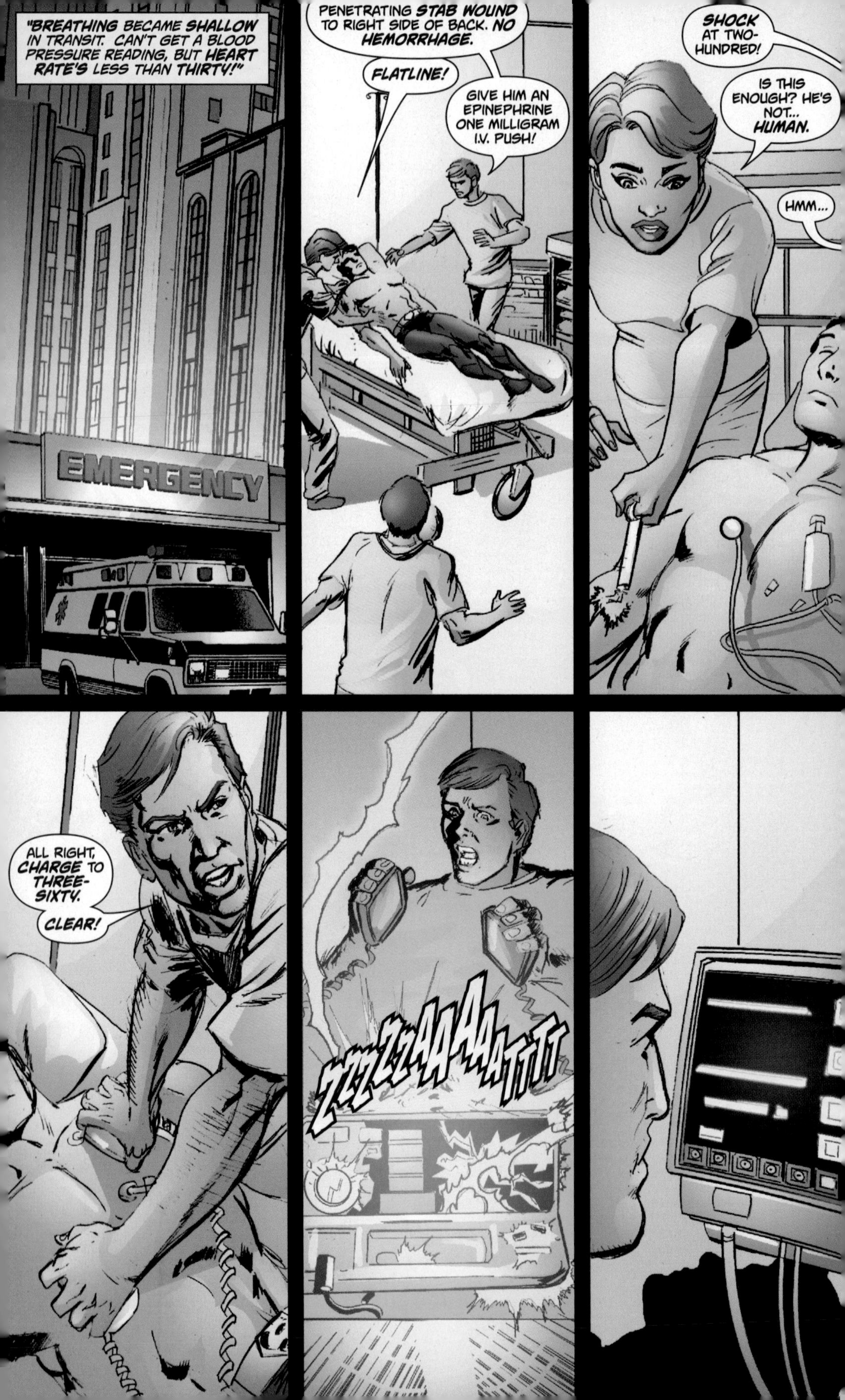
"BREATHING BECAME SHALLOW IN TRANSIT. CAN'T GET A BLOOD PRESSURE READING, BUT HEART RATE'S LESS THAN THIRTY!"
EMERGENCY
PENETRATING STAB WOUND TO RIGHT SIDE OF BACK. NO HEMORRHAGE.
FLATLINE!
GIVE HIM AN EPINEPHRINE ONE MILLIGRAM I.V. PUSH!
SHOCK AT TWO-HUNDRED!
IS THIS ENOUGH? HE'S NOT... HUMAN.
HMM...
ALL RIGHT, CHARGE TO THREE-SIXTY.
CLEAR!
ZZZZZZAAAAAATTTT

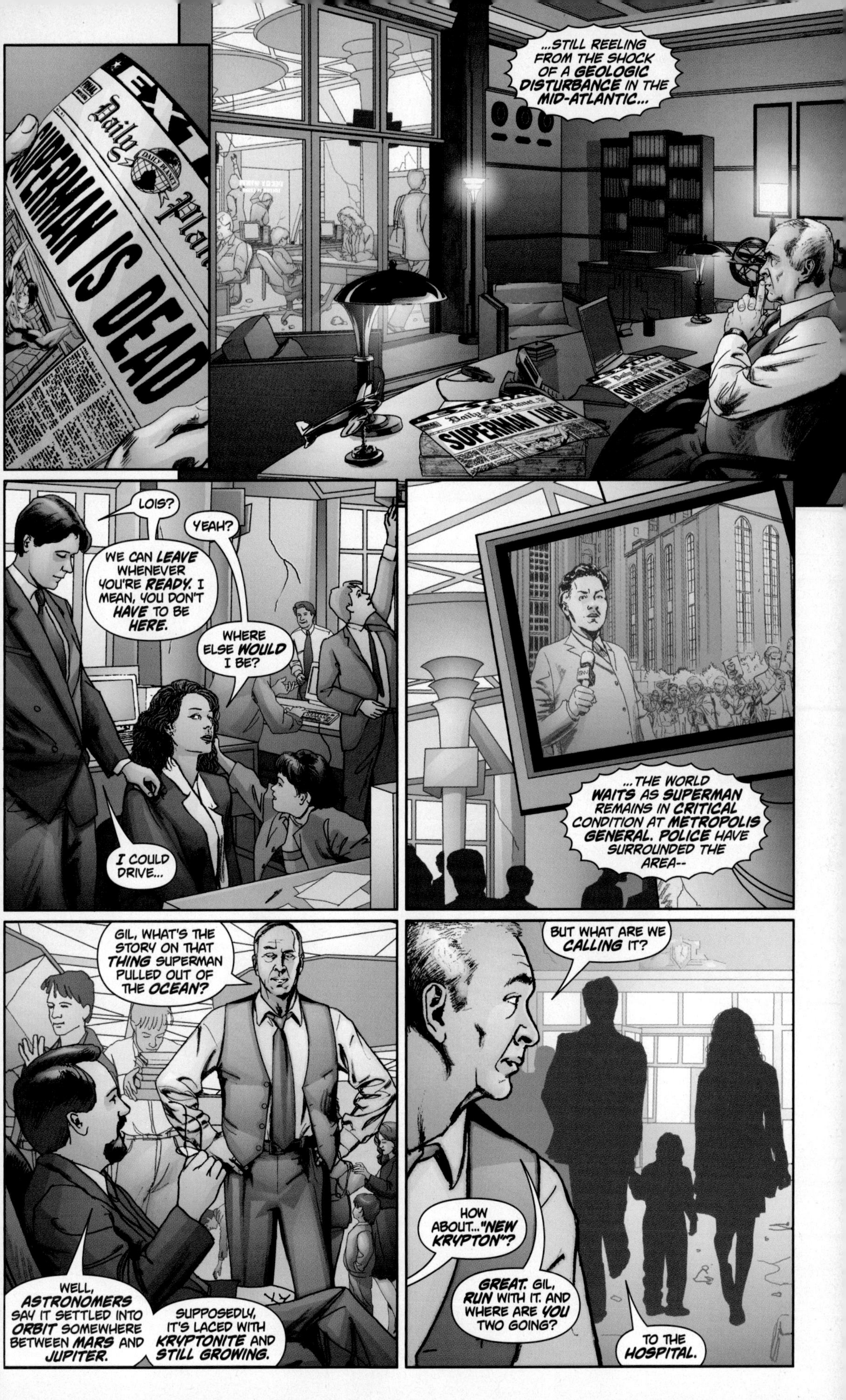

EXTRA
Daily Planet
SUPERMAN IS DEAD
...STILL REELING FROM THE SHOCK OF A GEOLOGIC DISTURBANCE IN THE MID-ATLANTIC...
SUPERMAN IS DEAD
SUPERMAN LIVES
LOIS?
WE CAN LEAVE WHENEVER YOU'RE READY. I MEAN, YOU DON'T HAVE TO BE HERE.
YEAH?
WHERE ELSE WOULD I BE?
I COULD DRIVE...
...THE WORLD WAITS AS SUPERMAN REMAINS IN CRITICAL CONDITION AT METROPOLIS GENERAL. POLICE HAVE SURROUNDED THE AREA--
GIL, WHAT'S THE STORY ON THAT THING SUPERMAN PULLED OUT OF THE OCEAN?
WELL, ASTRONOMERS SAY IT SETTLED INTO ORBIT SOMEWHERE BETWEEN MARS AND JUPITER.
SUPPOSEDLY, IT'S LACED WITH KRYPTONITE AND STILL GROWING.
BUT WHAT ARE WE CALLING IT?
HOW ABOUT..."NEW KRYPTON"?
GREAT. GIL, RUN WITH IT. AND WHERE ARE YOU TWO GOING?
TO THE HOSPITAL.

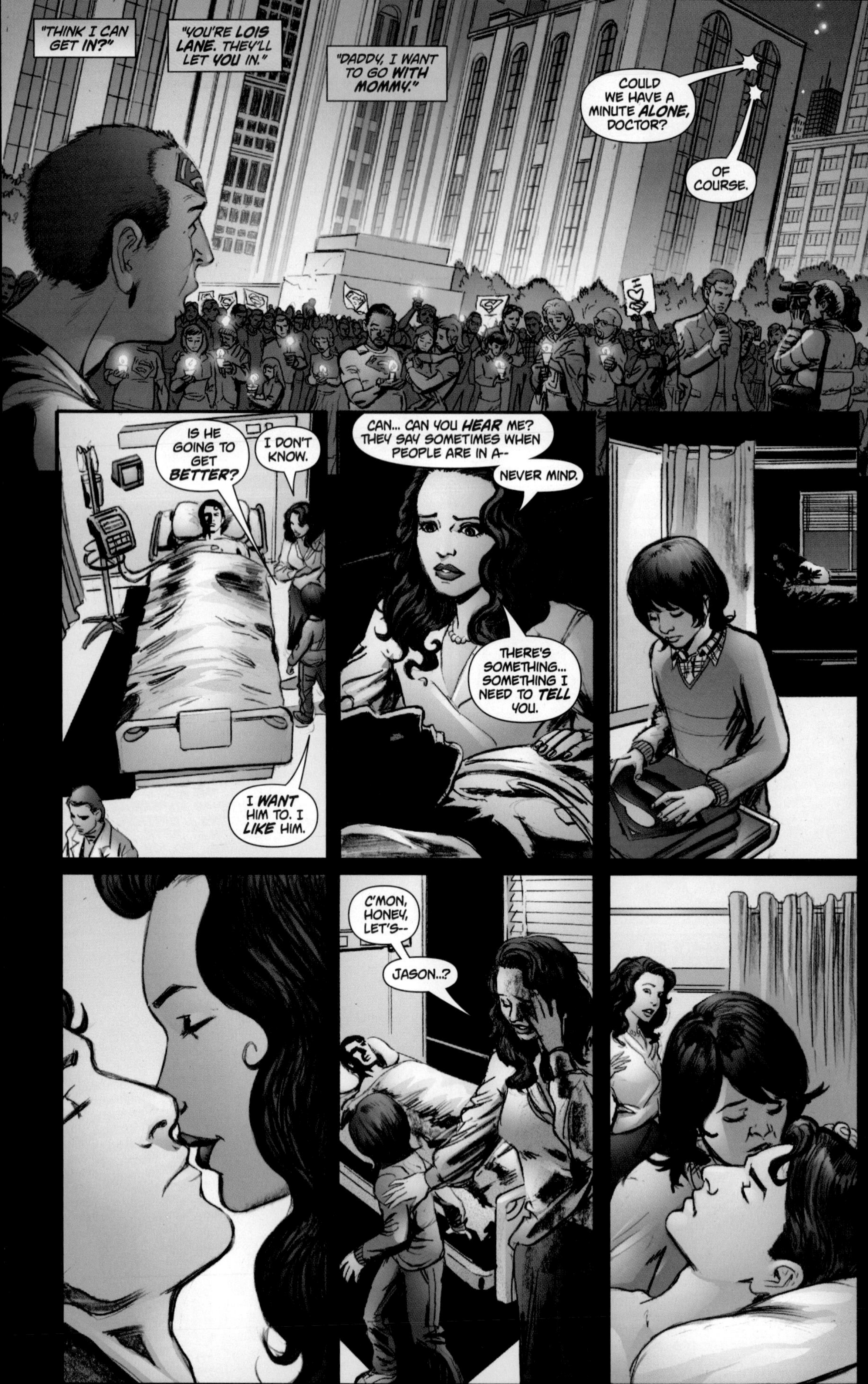
"THINK I CAN GET IN?"
"YOU'RE LOIS LANE. THEY'LL LET YOU IN."
"DADDY, I WANT TO GO WITH MOMMY."
COULD WE HAVE A MINUTE ALONE, DOCTOR?
OF COURSE.
IS HE GOING TO GET BETTER?
I DON'T KNOW.
I WANT HIM TO. I LIKE HIM.
CAN... CAN YOU HEAR ME? THEY SAY SOMETIMES WHEN PEOPLE ARE IN A--
NEVER MIND.
THERE'S SOMETHING... SOMETHING I NEED TO TELL YOU.
C'MON, HONEY, LET'S--
JASON...?

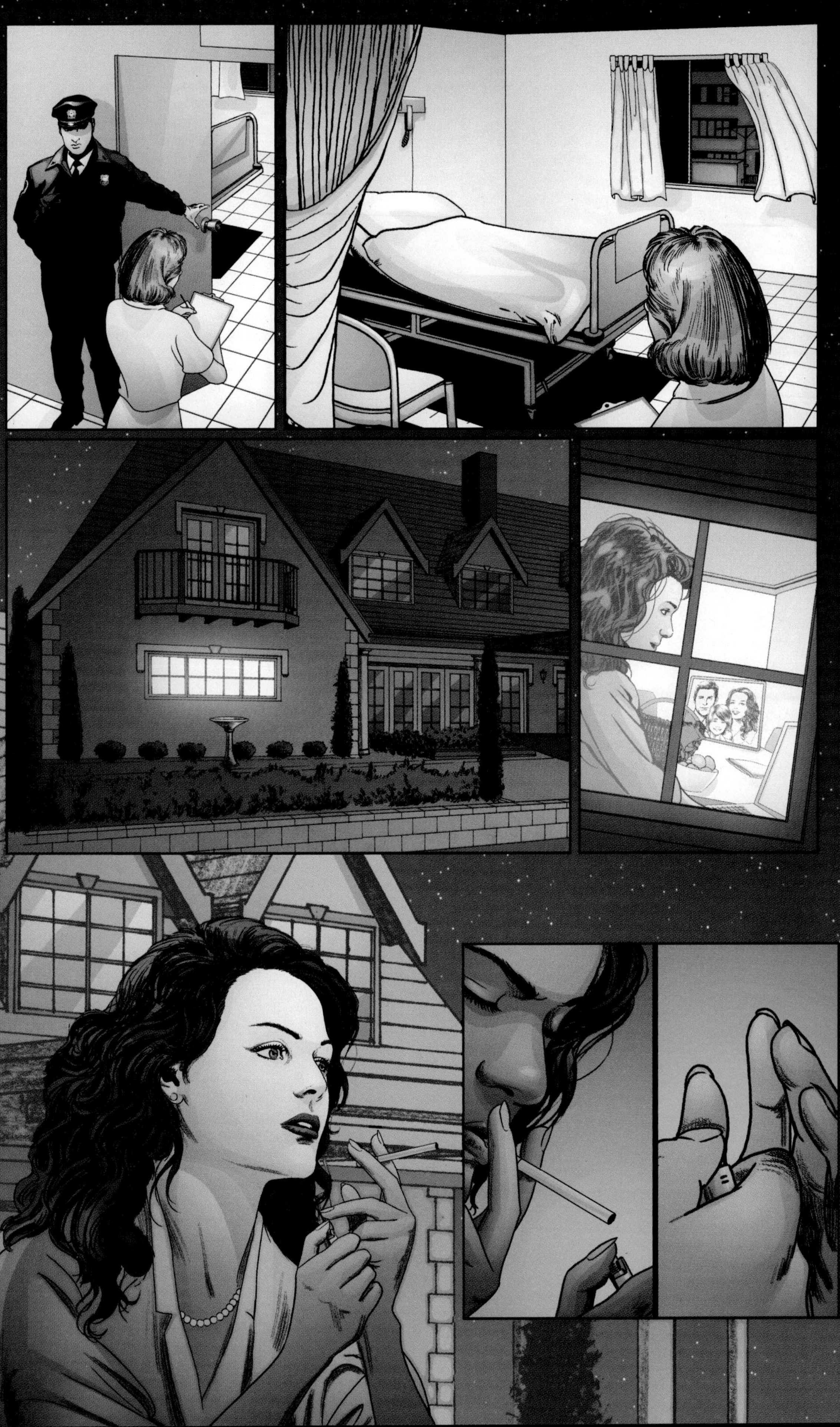

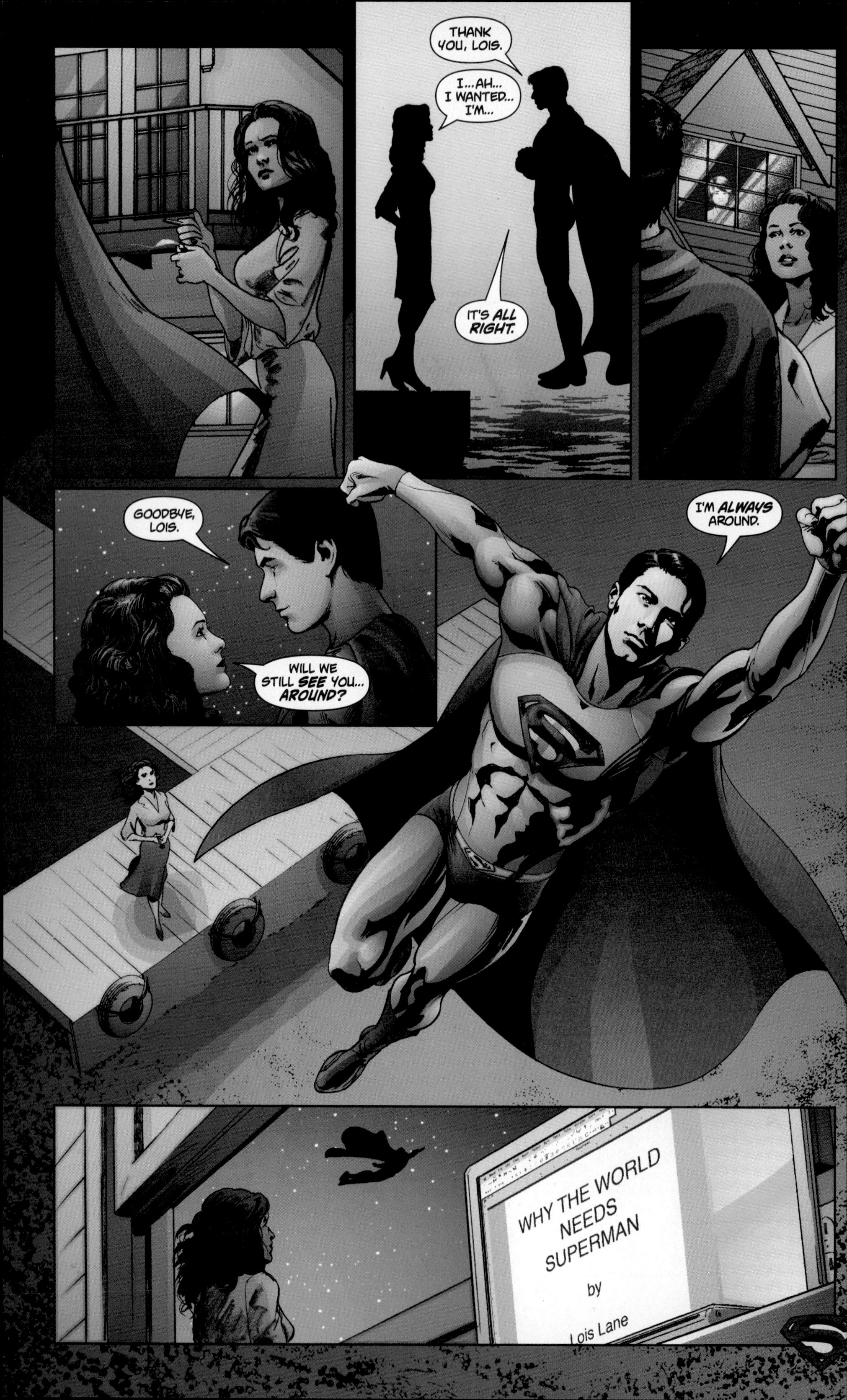
THANK YOU, LOIS.
I...AH... I WANTED... I'M...
IT'S ALL RIGHT.
GOODBYE, LOIS.
WILL WE STILL SEE YOU... AROUND?
I'M ALWAYS AROUND.
WHY THE WORLD NEEDS SUPERMAN
by
Lois Lane

OTHER TALES OF
THE MAN OF STEEL

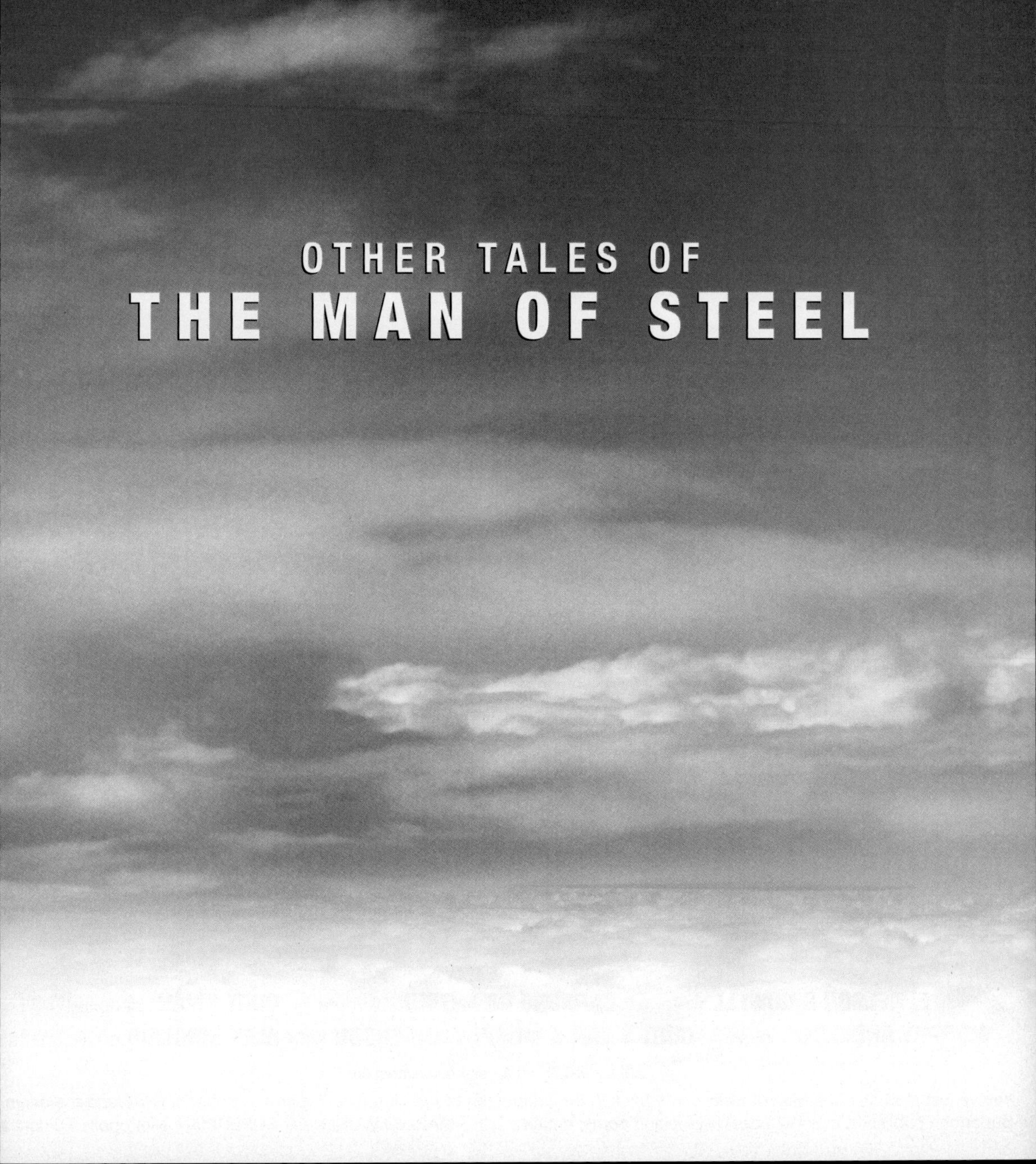

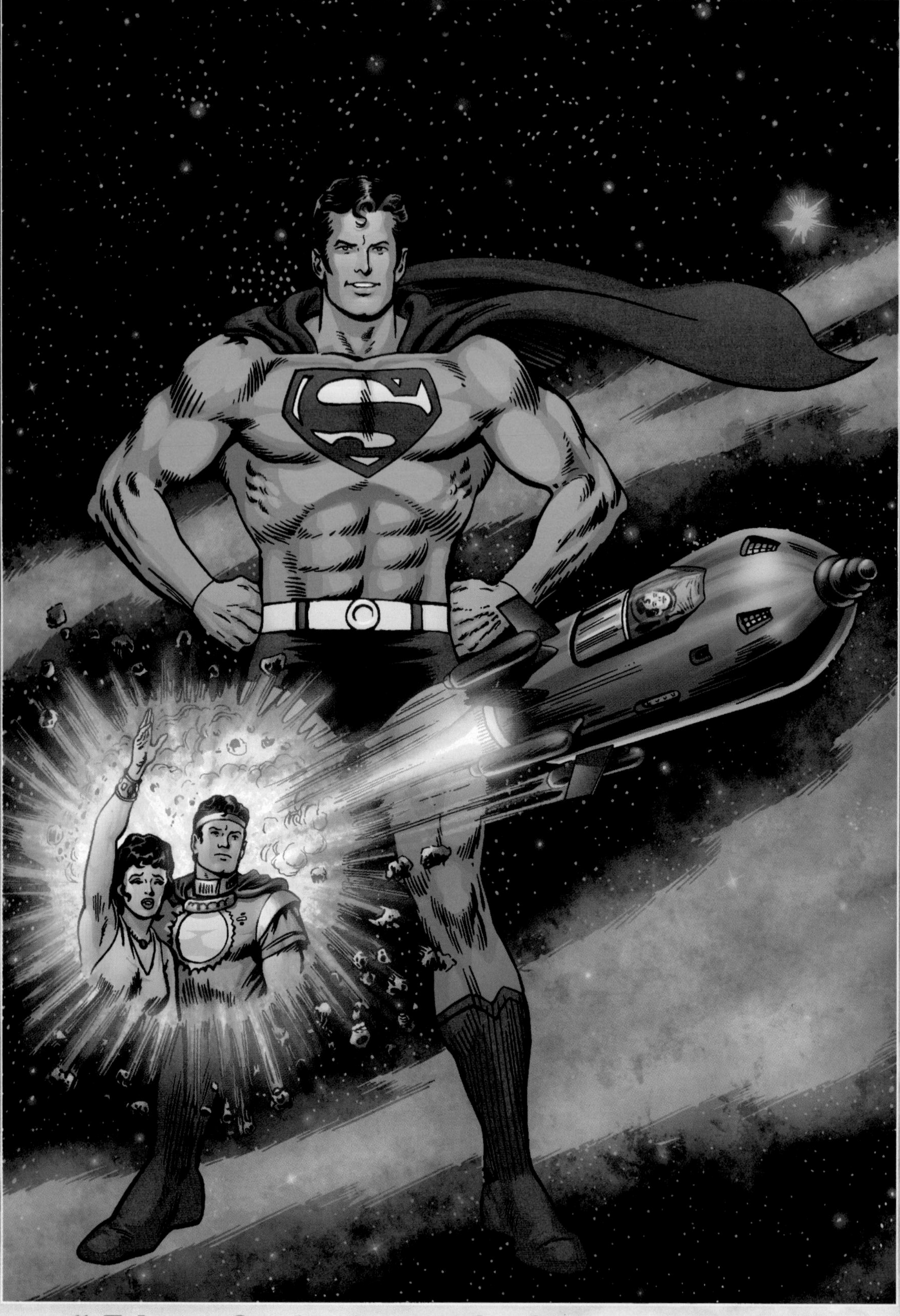

"The Origin of Superman"

E. NELSON BRIDWELL writer **CARMINE INFANTINO** Layouts **CURT SWAN** penciller
MURPHY ANDERSON inker **CURT SWAN & MURPHY ANDERSON WITH ALEX SINCLAIR** cover artists
DALE CRAIN art & color reconstruction

You've just read how the Man of Steel came back in the adaptation of the hit movie Superman Returns. Now read the origin
Superman published in a 1973 treasury-edition comic entitled THE AMAZING WORLD OF SUPERMAN (Metropolis Edition) #

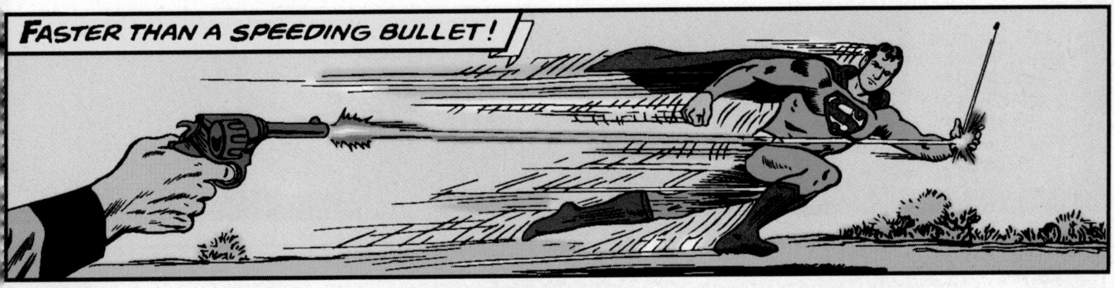
FASTER THAN A SPEEDING BULLET!

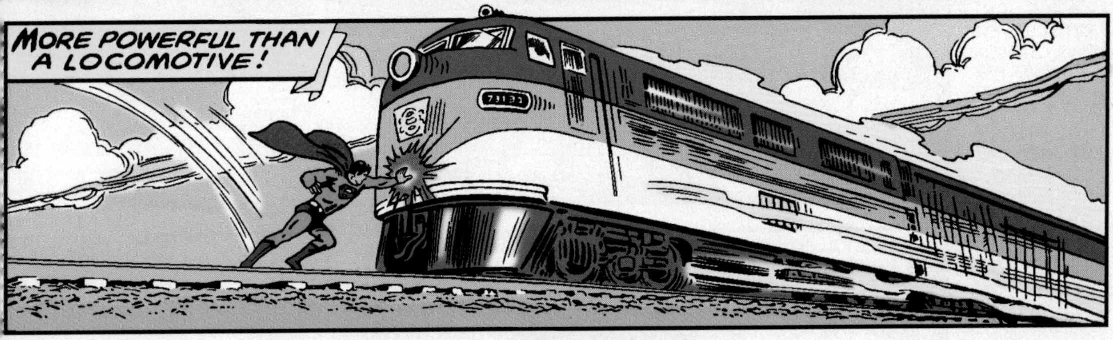
MORE POWERFUL THAN A LOCOMOTIVE!

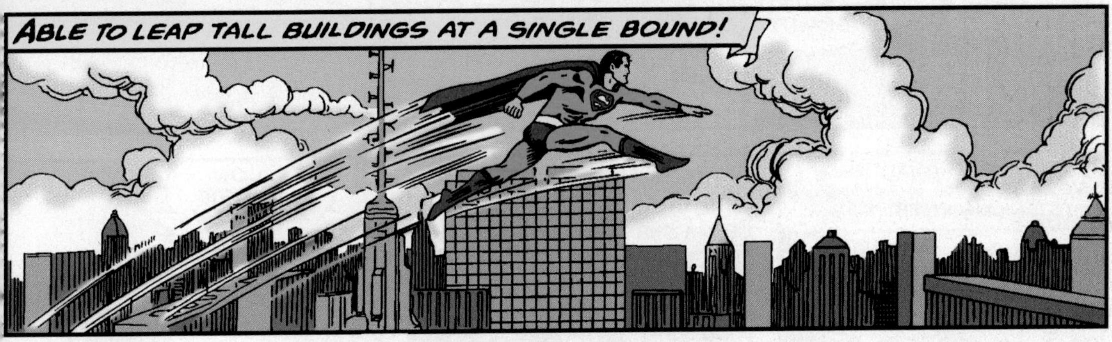
ABLE TO LEAP TALL BUILDINGS AT A SINGLE BOUND!

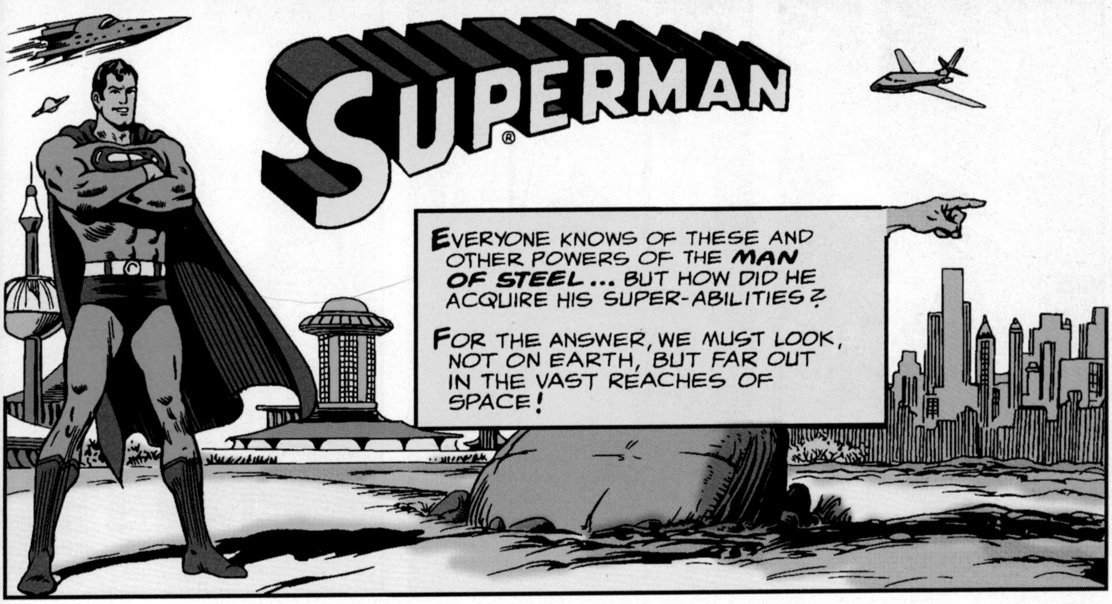
SUPERMAN®
EVERYONE KNOWS OF THESE AND OTHER POWERS OF THE MAN OF STEEL... BUT HOW DID HE ACQUIRE HIS SUPER-ABILITIES?
FOR THE ANSWER, WE MUST LOOK, NOT ON EARTH, BUT FAR OUT IN THE VAST REACHES OF SPACE!

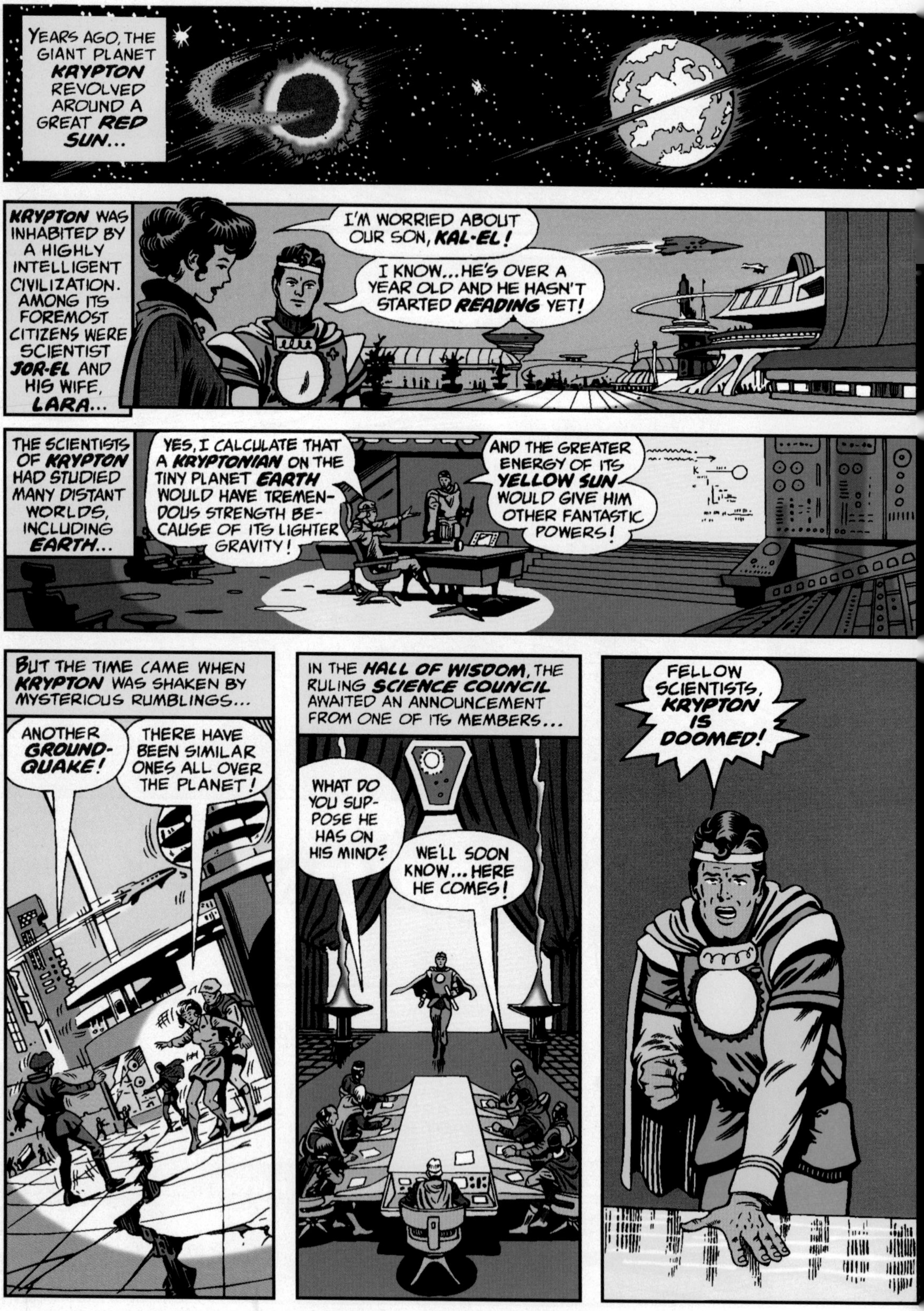

YEARS AGO, THE GIANT PLANET KRYPTON REVOLVED AROUND A GREAT RED SUN...
KRYPTON WAS INHABITED BY A HIGHLY INTELLIGENT CIVILIZATION. AMONG ITS FOREMOST CITIZENS WERE SCIENTIST JOR-EL AND HIS WIFE, LARA...
I'M WORRIED ABOUT OUR SON, KAL-EL!
I KNOW... HE'S OVER A YEAR OLD AND HE HASN'T STARTED READING YET!
THE SCIENTISTS OF KRYPTON HAD STUDIED MANY DISTANT WORLDS, INCLUDING EARTH...
YES, I CALCULATE THAT A KRYPTONIAN ON THE TINY PLANET EARTH WOULD HAVE TREMENDOUS STRENGTH BECAUSE OF ITS LIGHTER GRAVITY!
AND THE GREATER ENERGY OF ITS YELLOW SUN WOULD GIVE HIM OTHER FANTASTIC POWERS!
BUT THE TIME CAME WHEN KRYPTON WAS SHAKEN BY MYSTERIOUS RUMBLINGS...
ANOTHER GROUND-QUAKE!
THERE HAVE BEEN SIMILAR ONES ALL OVER THE PLANET!
IN THE HALL OF WISDOM, THE RULING SCIENCE COUNCIL AWAITED AN ANNOUNCEMENT FROM ONE OF ITS MEMBERS...
WHAT DO YOU SUPPOSE HE HAS ON HIS MIND?
WE'LL SOON KNOW... HERE HE COMES!
FELLOW SCIENTISTS, KRYPTON IS DOOMED!

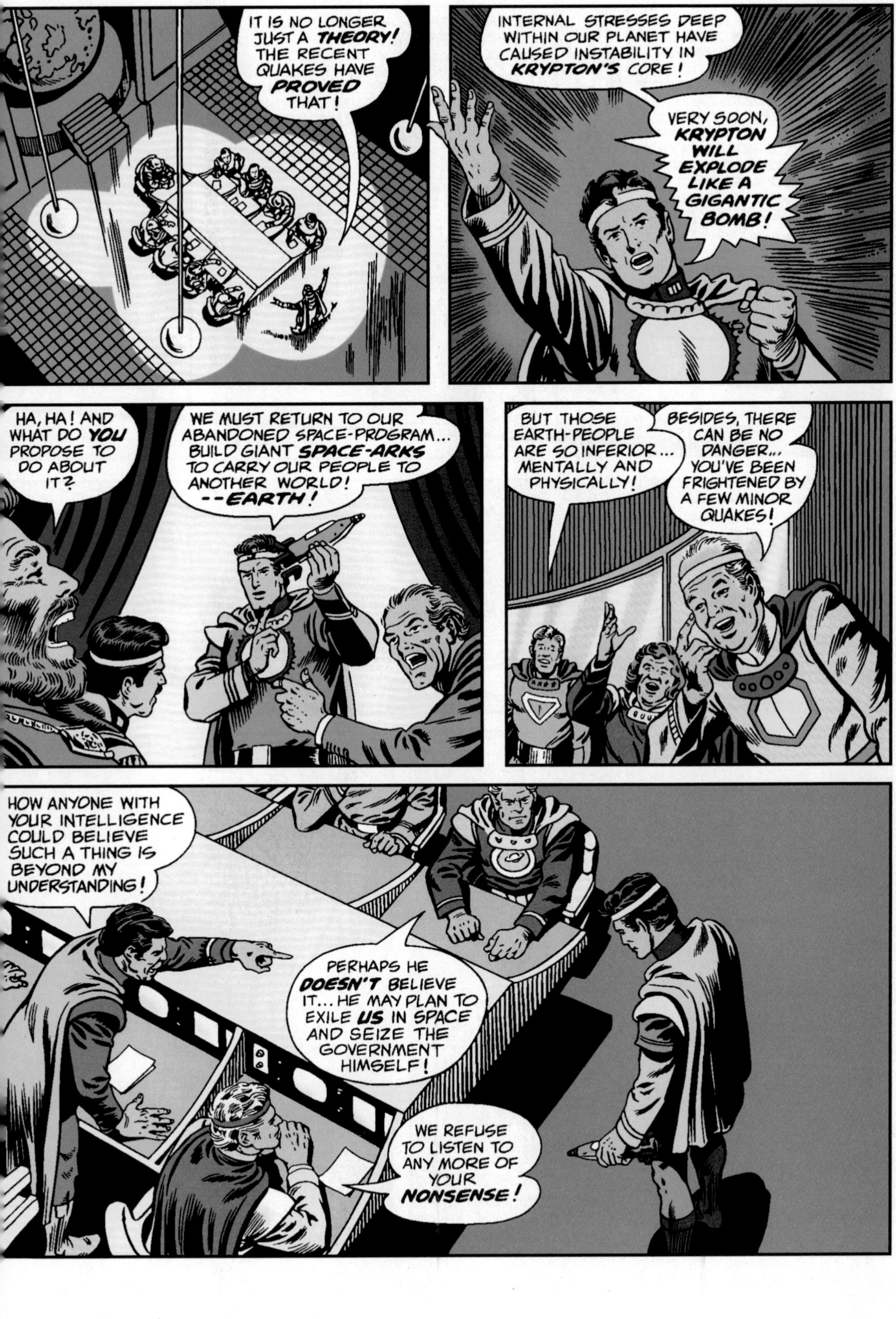
IT IS NO LONGER JUST A THEORY! THE RECENT QUAKES HAVE PROVED THAT!
INTERNAL STRESSES DEEP WITHIN OUR PLANET HAVE CAUSED INSTABILITY IN KRYPTON'S CORE!
VERY SOON, KRYPTON WILL EXPLODE LIKE A GIGANTIC BOMB!
HA, HA! AND WHAT DO YOU PROPOSE TO DO ABOUT IT?
WE MUST RETURN TO OUR ABANDONED SPACE-PROGRAM... BUILD GIANT SPACE-ARKS TO CARRY OUR PEOPLE TO ANOTHER WORLD! --EARTH!
BUT THOSE EARTH-PEOPLE ARE SO INFERIOR... MENTALLY AND PHYSICALLY!
BESIDES, THERE CAN BE NO DANGER... YOU'VE BEEN FRIGHTENED BY A FEW MINOR QUAKES!
HOW ANYONE WITH YOUR INTELLIGENCE COULD BELIEVE SUCH A THING IS BEYOND MY UNDERSTANDING!
PERHAPS HE DOESN'T BELIEVE IT... HE MAY PLAN TO EXILE US IN SPACE AND SEIZE THE GOVERNMENT HIMSELF!
WE REFUSE TO LISTEN TO ANY MORE OF YOUR NONSENSE!

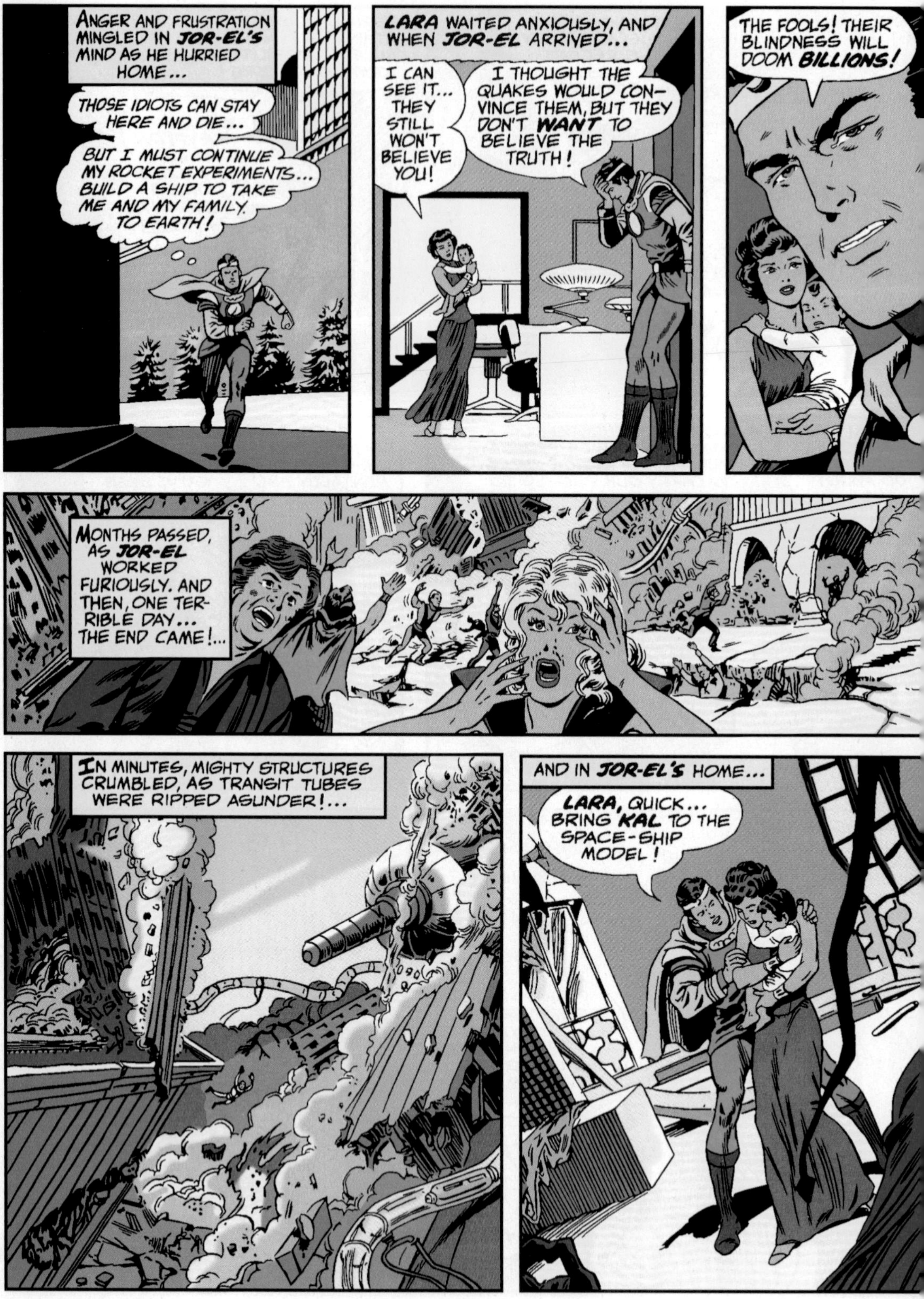
ANGER AND FRUSTRATION MINGLED IN JOR-EL'S MIND AS HE HURRIED HOME...
THOSE IDIOTS CAN STAY HERE AND DIE...
BUT I MUST CONTINUE MY ROCKET EXPERIMENTS... BUILD A SHIP TO TAKE ME AND MY FAMILY TO EARTH!
LARA WAITED ANXIOUSLY, AND WHEN JOR-EL ARRIVED...
I CAN SEE IT... THEY STILL WON'T BELIEVE YOU!
I THOUGHT THE QUAKES WOULD CONVINCE THEM, BUT THEY DON'T WANT TO BELIEVE THE TRUTH!
THE FOOLS! THEIR BLINDNESS WILL DOOM BILLIONS!
MONTHS PASSED, AS JOR-EL WORKED FURIOUSLY. AND THEN, ONE TERRIBLE DAY... THE END CAME!...
IN MINUTES, MIGHTY STRUCTURES CRUMBLED, AS TRANSIT TUBES WERE RIPPED ASUNDER!...
AND IN JOR-EL'S HOME...
LARA, QUICK... BRING KAL TO THE SPACE-SHIP MODEL!

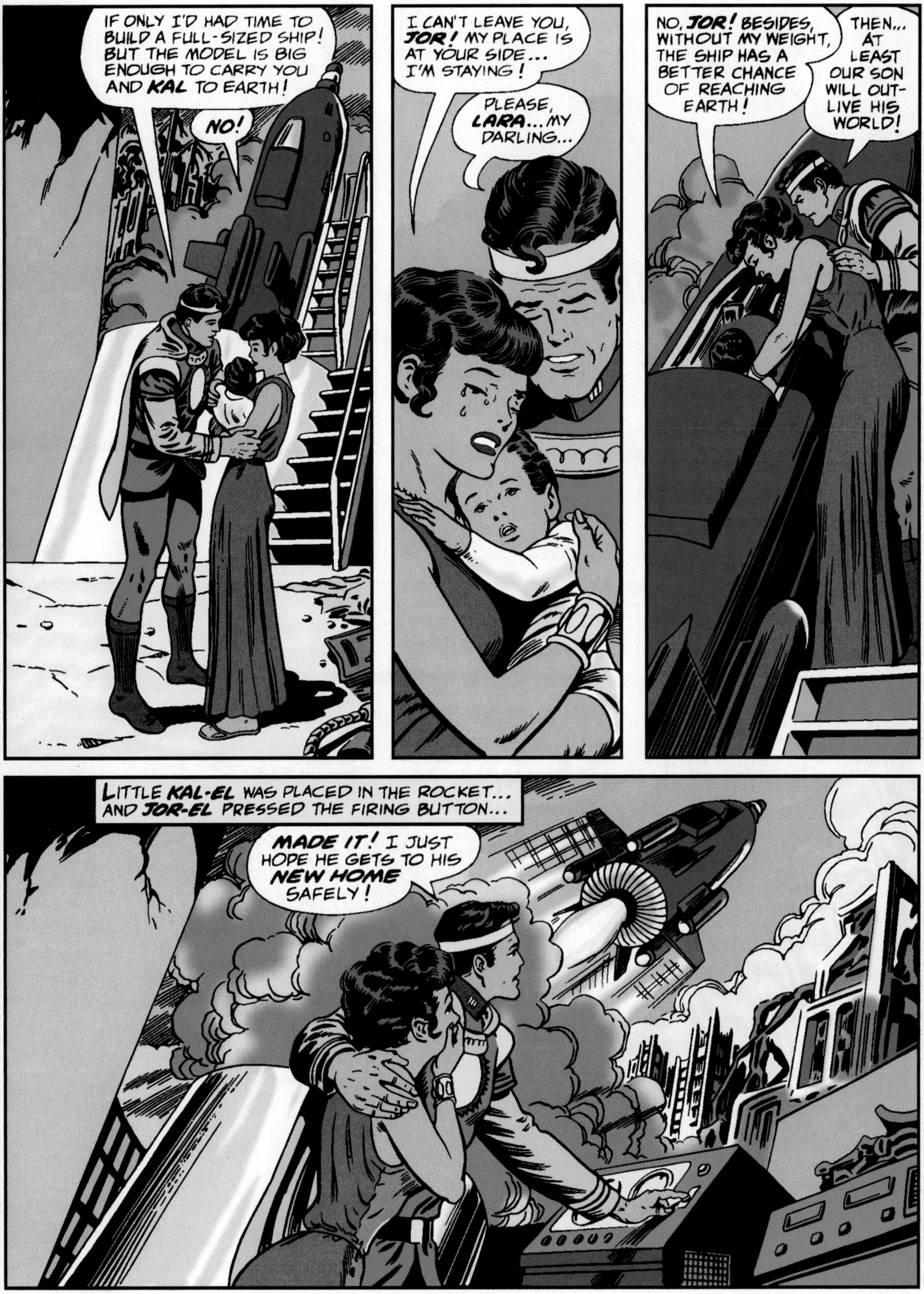
IF ONLY I'D HAD TIME TO BUILD A FULL-SIZED SHIP! BUT THE MODEL IS BIG ENOUGH TO CARRY YOU AND KAL TO EARTH!
NO!
I CAN'T LEAVE YOU, JOR! MY PLACE IS AT YOUR SIDE... I'M STAYING!
PLEASE, LARA... MY DARLING...
NO, JOR! BESIDES, WITHOUT MY WEIGHT, THE SHIP HAS A BETTER CHANCE OF REACHING EARTH!
THEN... AT LEAST OUR SON WILL OUT-LIVE HIS WORLD!
LITTLE KAL-EL WAS PLACED IN THE ROCKET... AND JOR-EL PRESSED THE FIRING BUTTON...
MADE IT! I JUST HOPE HE GETS TO HIS NEW HOME SAFELY!

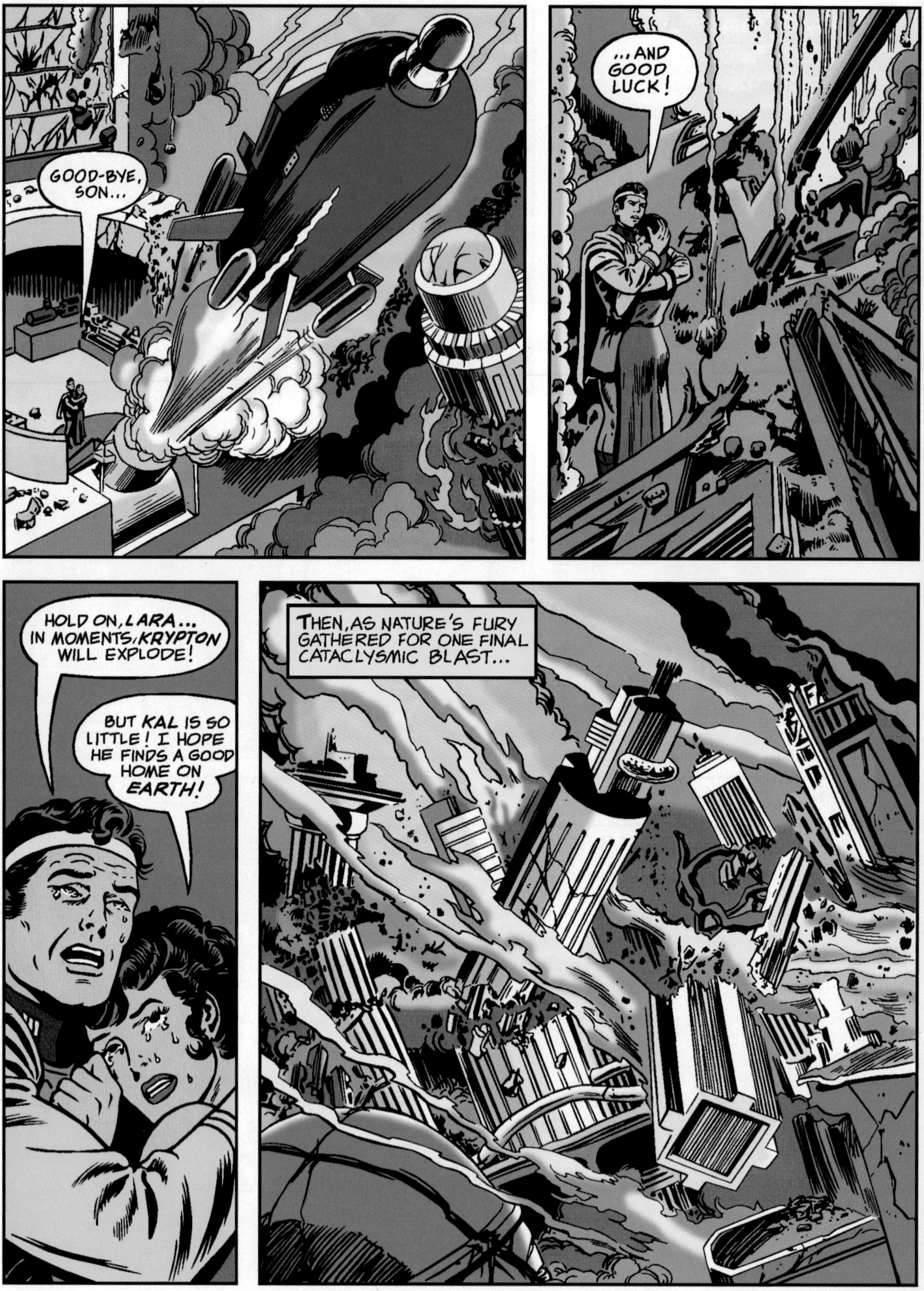
GOOD-BYE, SON...
...AND GOOD LUCK!
HOLD ON, LARA... IN MOMENTS, KRYPTON WILL EXPLODE!
BUT KAL IS SO LITTLE! I HOPE HE FINDS A GOOD HOME ON EARTH!
THEN, AS NATURE'S FURY GATHERED FOR ONE FINAL CATACLYSMIC BLAST...

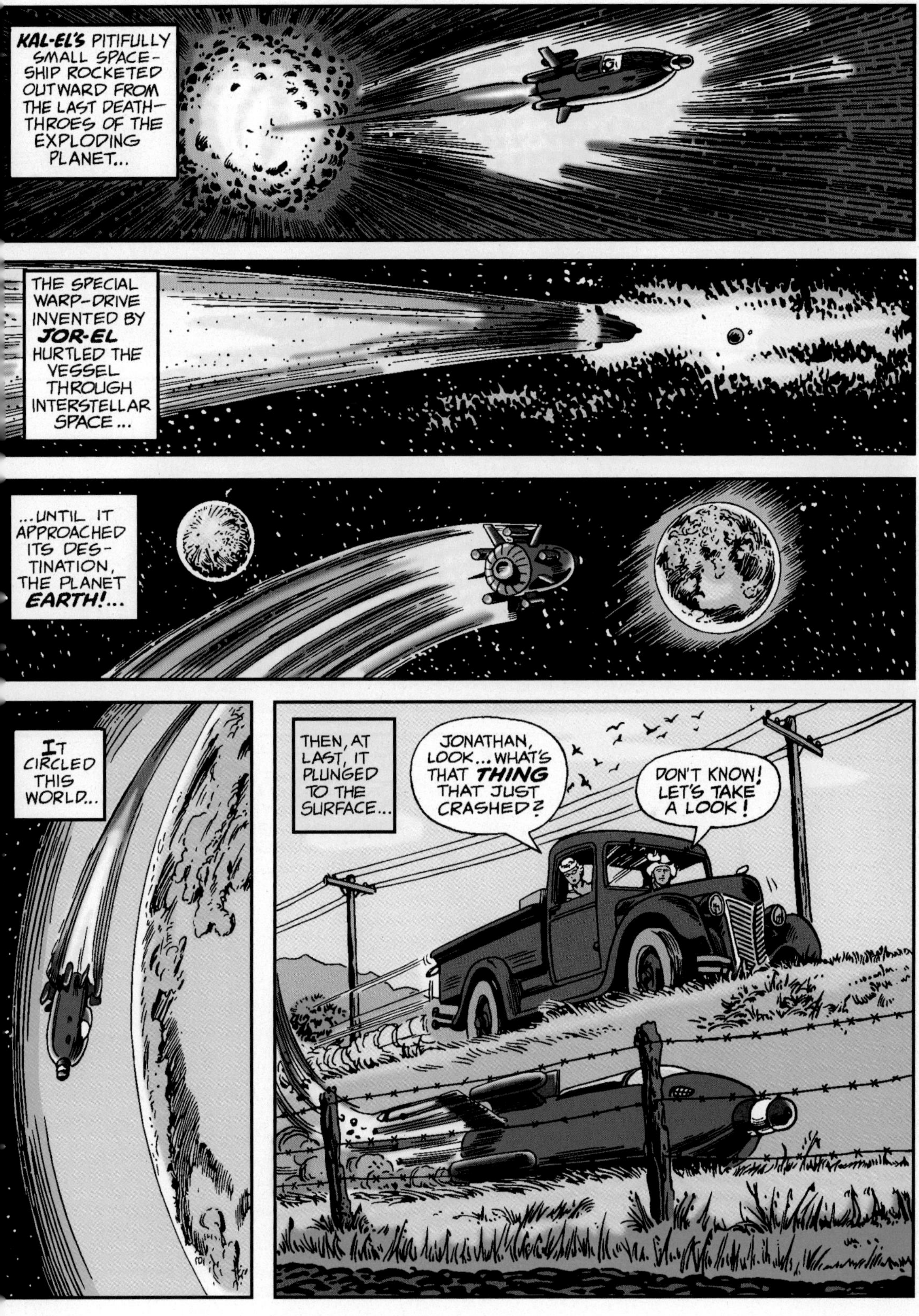
KAL-EL'S PITIFULLY SMALL SPACE-SHIP ROCKETED OUTWARD FROM THE LAST DEATH-THROES OF THE EXPLODING PLANET...
THE SPECIAL WARP-DRIVE INVENTED BY JOR-EL HURTLED THE VESSEL THROUGH INTERSTELLAR SPACE...
...UNTIL IT APPROACHED ITS DESTINATION, THE PLANET EARTH!...
IT CIRCLED THIS WORLD...
THEN, AT LAST, IT PLUNGED TO THE SURFACE...
JONATHAN, LOOK...WHAT'S THAT THING THAT JUST CRASHED?
DON'T KNOW! LET'S TAKE A LOOK!

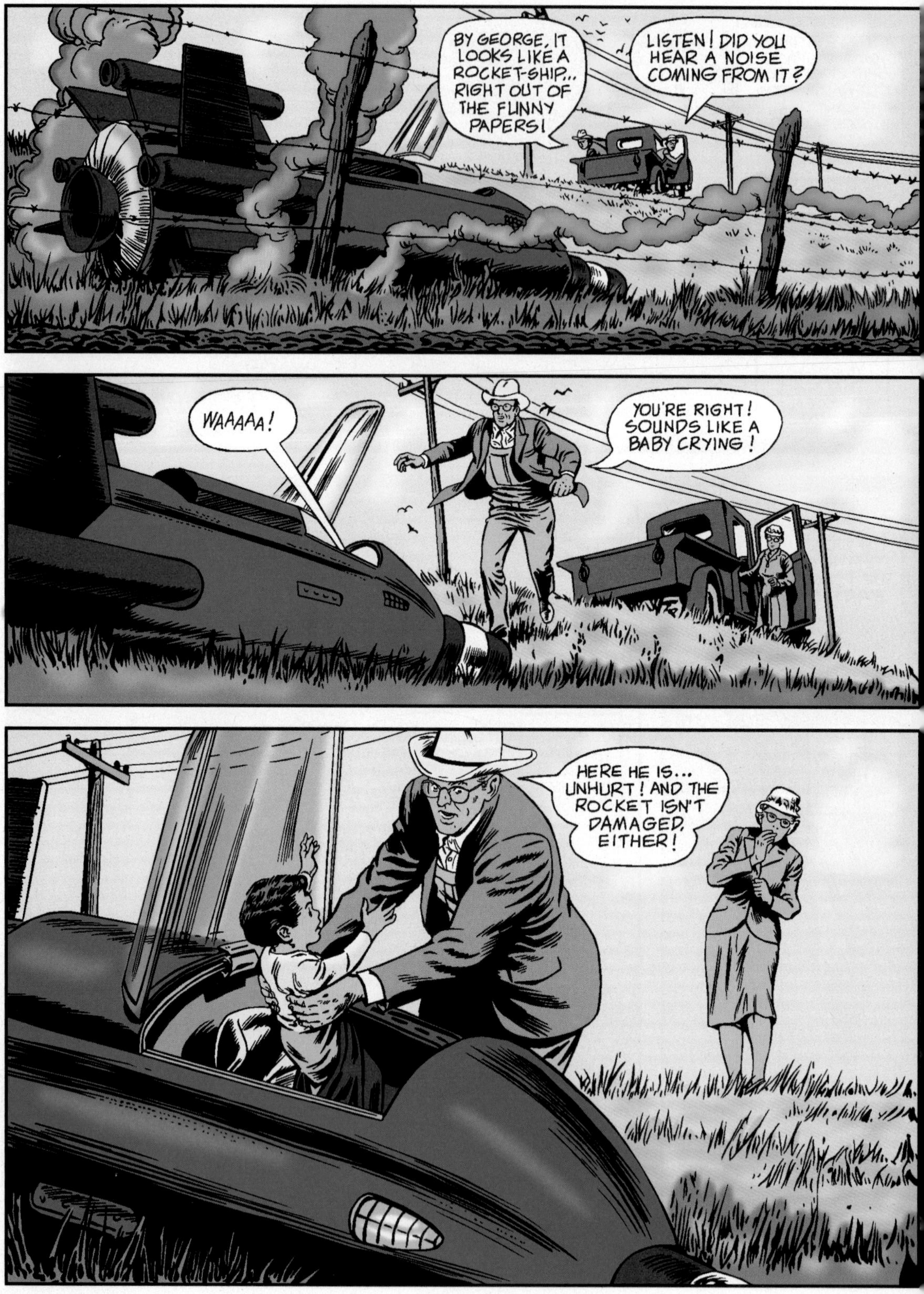
BY GEORGE, IT LOOKS LIKE A ROCKET-SHIP... RIGHT OUT OF THE FUNNY PAPERS!
LISTEN! DID YOU HEAR A NOISE COMING FROM IT?
WAAAAA!
YOU'RE RIGHT! SOUNDS LIKE A BABY CRYING!
HERE HE IS... UNHURT! AND THE ROCKET ISN'T DAMAGED, EITHER!

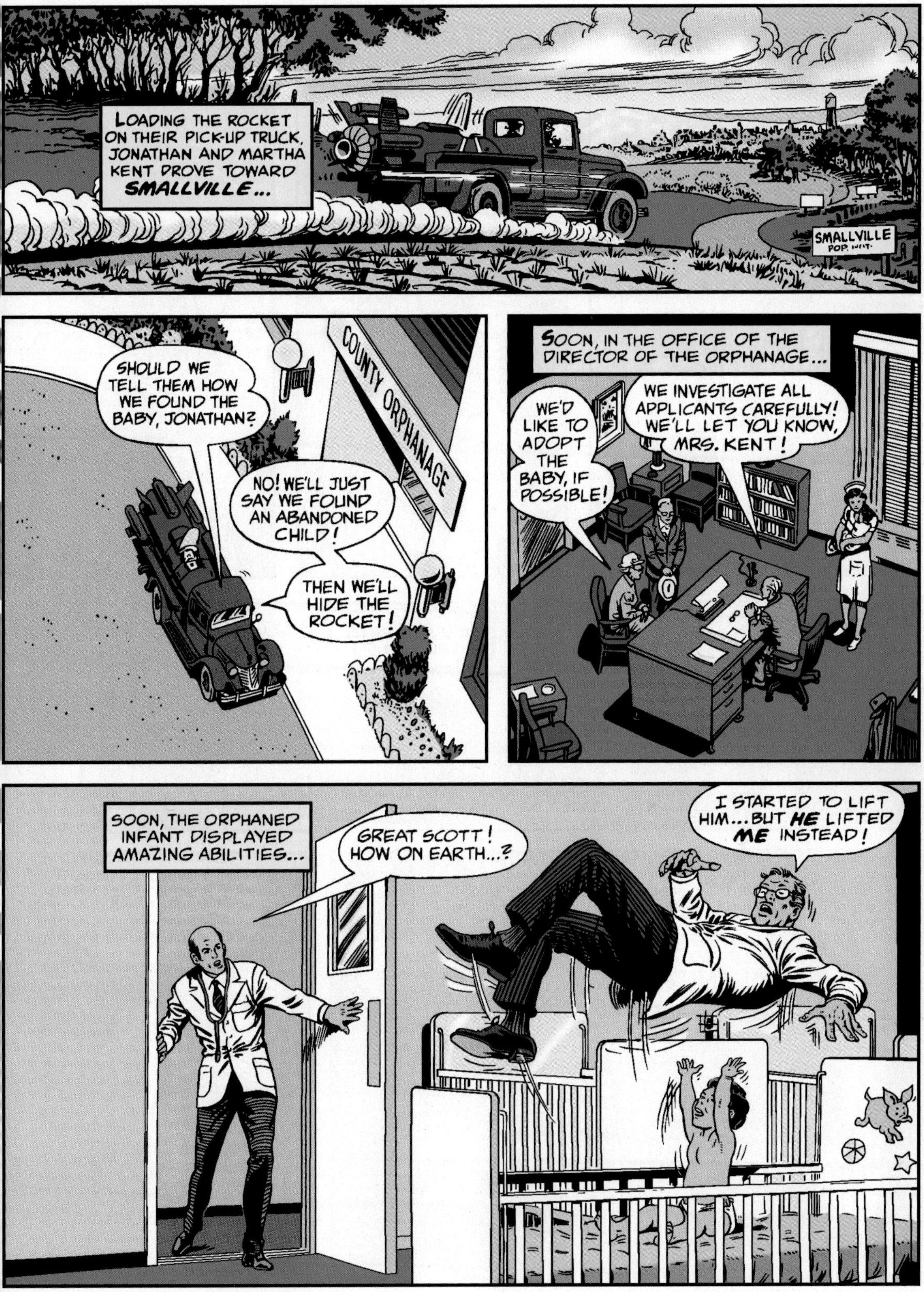
LOADING THE ROCKET ON THEIR PICK-UP TRUCK, JONATHAN AND MARTHA KENT DROVE TOWARD SMALLVILLE...
SMALLVILLE
SHOULD WE TELL THEM HOW WE FOUND THE BABY, JONATHAN?
COUNTY ORPHANAGE
NO! WE'LL JUST SAY WE FOUND AN ABANDONED CHILD!
THEN WE'LL HIDE THE ROCKET!
SOON, IN THE OFFICE OF THE DIRECTOR OF THE ORPHANAGE...
WE'D LIKE TO ADOPT THE BABY, IF POSSIBLE!
WE INVESTIGATE ALL APPLICANTS CAREFULLY! WE'LL LET YOU KNOW, MRS. KENT!
SOON, THE ORPHANED INFANT DISPLAYED AMAZING ABILITIES...
GREAT SCOTT! HOW ON EARTH...?
I STARTED TO LIFT HIM... BUT HE LIFTED ME INSTEAD!

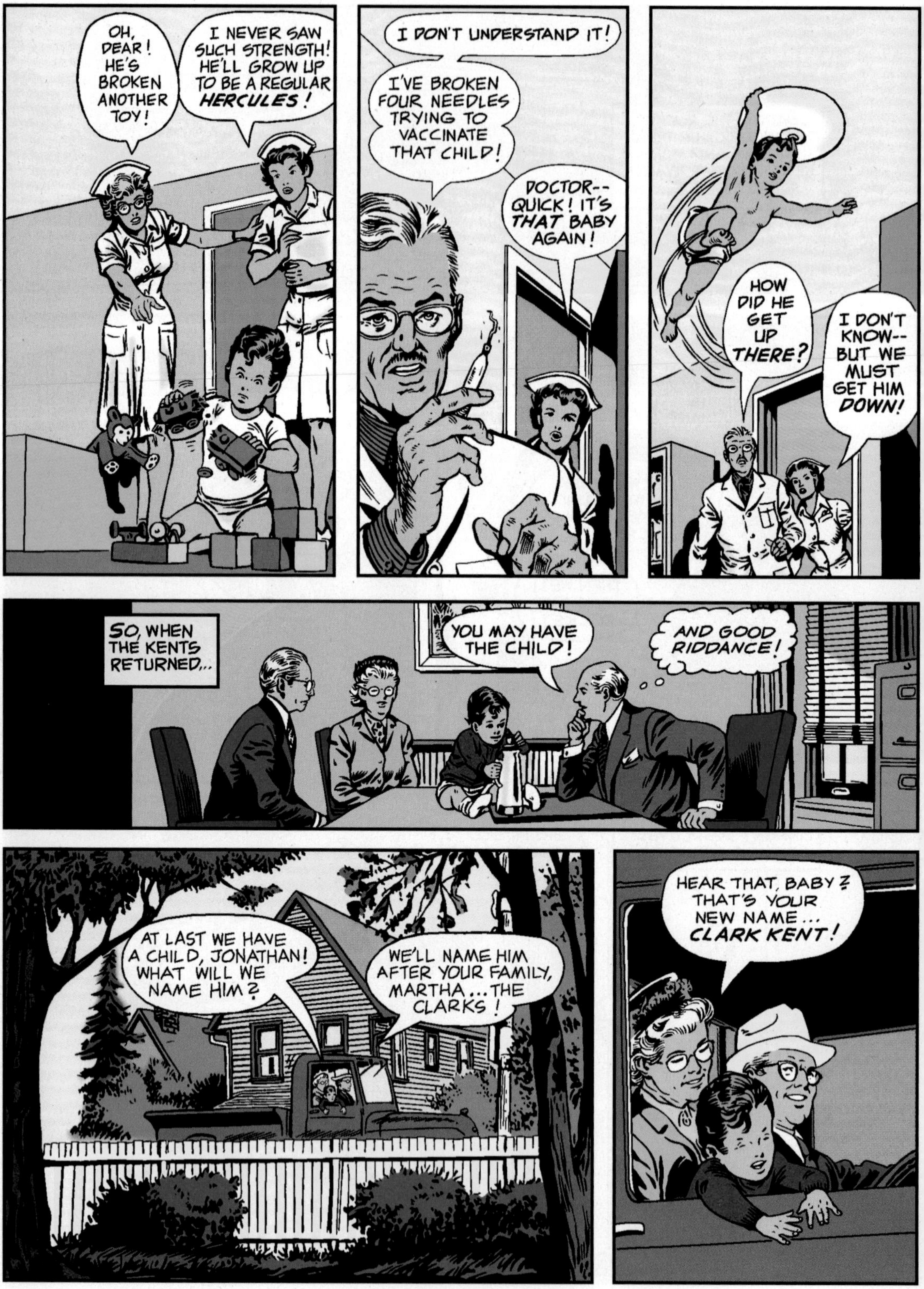
OH, DEAR! HE'S BROKEN ANOTHER TOY!
I NEVER SAW SUCH STRENGTH! HE'LL GROW UP TO BE A REGULAR HERCULES!
I DON'T UNDERSTAND IT!
I'VE BROKEN FOUR NEEDLES TRYING TO VACCINATE THAT CHILD!
DOCTOR-- QUICK! IT'S THAT BABY AGAIN!
HOW DID HE GET UP THERE?
I DON'T KNOW-- BUT WE MUST GET HIM DOWN!
SO, WHEN THE KENTS RETURNED...
YOU MAY HAVE THE CHILD!
AND GOOD RIDDANCE!
AT LAST WE HAVE A CHILD, JONATHAN! WHAT WILL WE NAME HIM?
WE'LL NAME HIM AFTER YOUR FAMILY, MARTHA... THE CLARKS!
HEAR THAT, BABY? THAT'S YOUR NEW NAME... CLARK KENT!

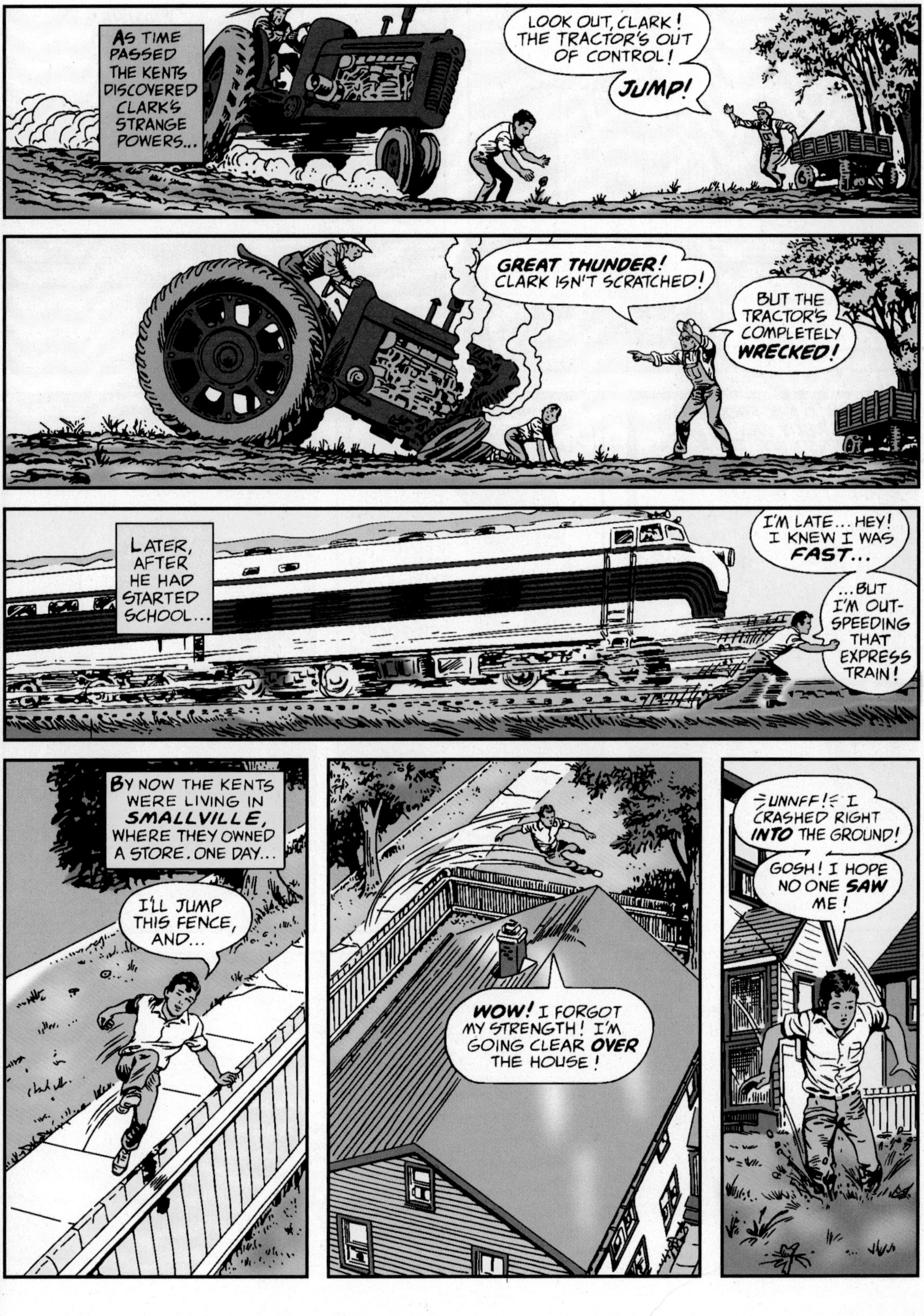
AS TIME PASSED THE KENTS DISCOVERED CLARK'S STRANGE POWERS...
LOOK OUT, CLARK! THE TRACTOR'S OUT OF CONTROL!
JUMP!
GREAT THUNDER! CLARK ISN'T SCRATCHED!
BUT THE TRACTOR'S COMPLETELY WRECKED!
LATER, AFTER HE HAD STARTED SCHOOL...
I'M LATE... HEY! I KNEW I WAS FAST...
...BUT I'M OUT-SPEEDING THAT EXPRESS TRAIN!
BY NOW THE KENTS WERE LIVING IN SMALLVILLE, WHERE THEY OWNED A STORE. ONE DAY...
I'LL JUMP THIS FENCE, AND...
WOW! I FORGOT MY STRENGTH! I'M GOING CLEAR OVER THE HOUSE!
=UNNFF!= I CRASHED RIGHT INTO THE GROUND!
GOSH! I HOPE NO ONE SAW ME!

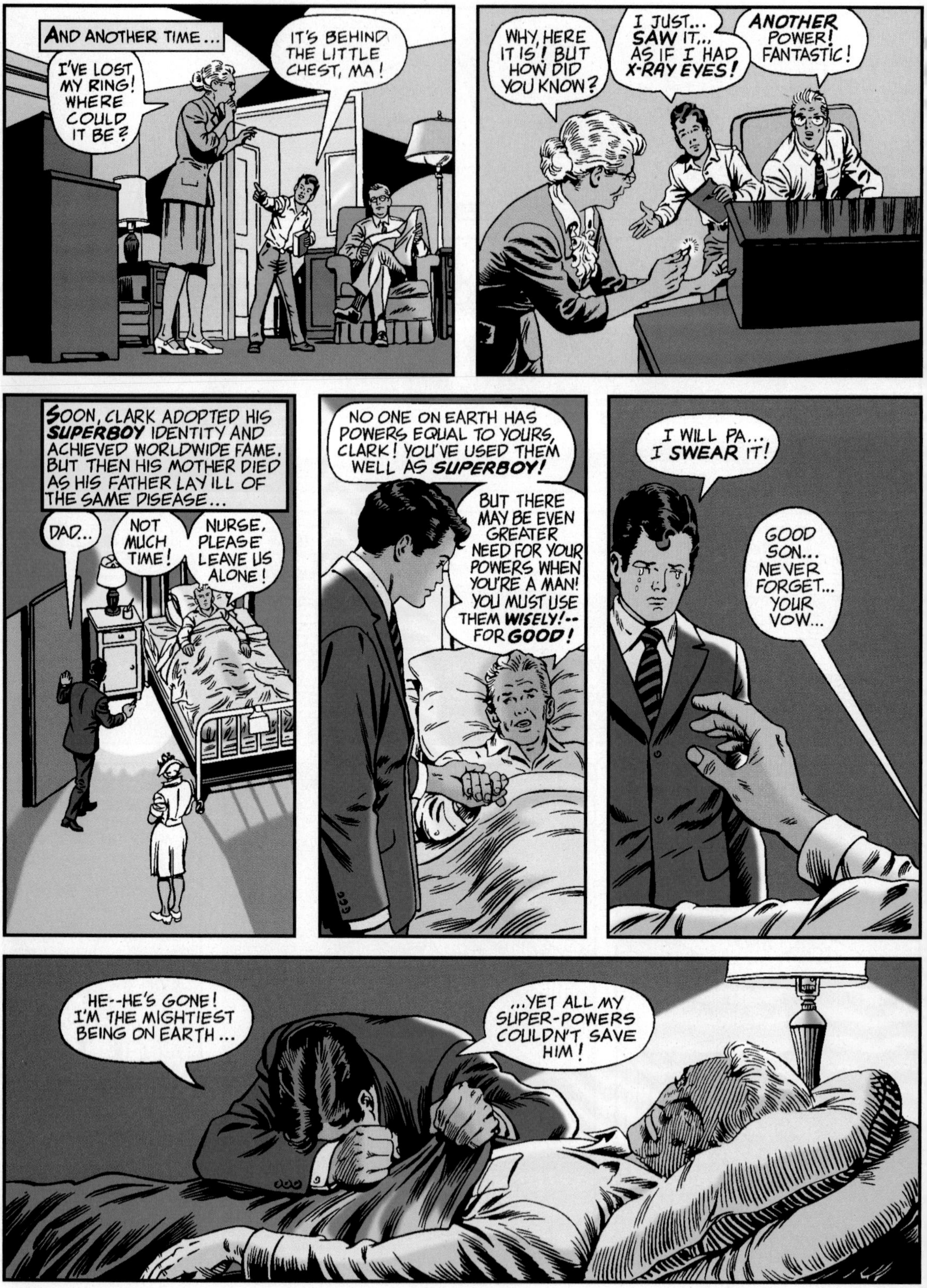
AND ANOTHER TIME...
I'VE LOST MY RING! WHERE COULD IT BE?
IT'S BEHIND THE LITTLE CHEST, MA!
WHY, HERE IT IS! BUT HOW DID YOU KNOW?
I JUST... SAW IT... AS IF I HAD X-RAY EYES!
ANOTHER POWER! FANTASTIC!
SOON, CLARK ADOPTED HIS SUPERBOY IDENTITY AND ACHIEVED WORLDWIDE FAME. BUT THEN HIS MOTHER DIED AS HIS FATHER LAY ILL OF THE SAME DISEASE...
DAD...
NOT MUCH TIME!
NURSE, PLEASE LEAVE US ALONE!
NO ONE ON EARTH HAS POWERS EQUAL TO YOURS, CLARK! YOU'VE USED THEM WELL AS SUPERBOY!
BUT THERE MAY BE EVEN GREATER NEED FOR YOUR POWERS WHEN YOU'RE A MAN! YOU MUST USE THEM WISELY!-- FOR GOOD!
I WILL PA... I SWEAR IT!
GOOD SON... NEVER FORGET... YOUR VOW...
HE--HE'S GONE! I'M THE MIGHTIEST BEING ON EARTH...
...YET ALL MY SUPER-POWERS COULDN'T SAVE HIM!

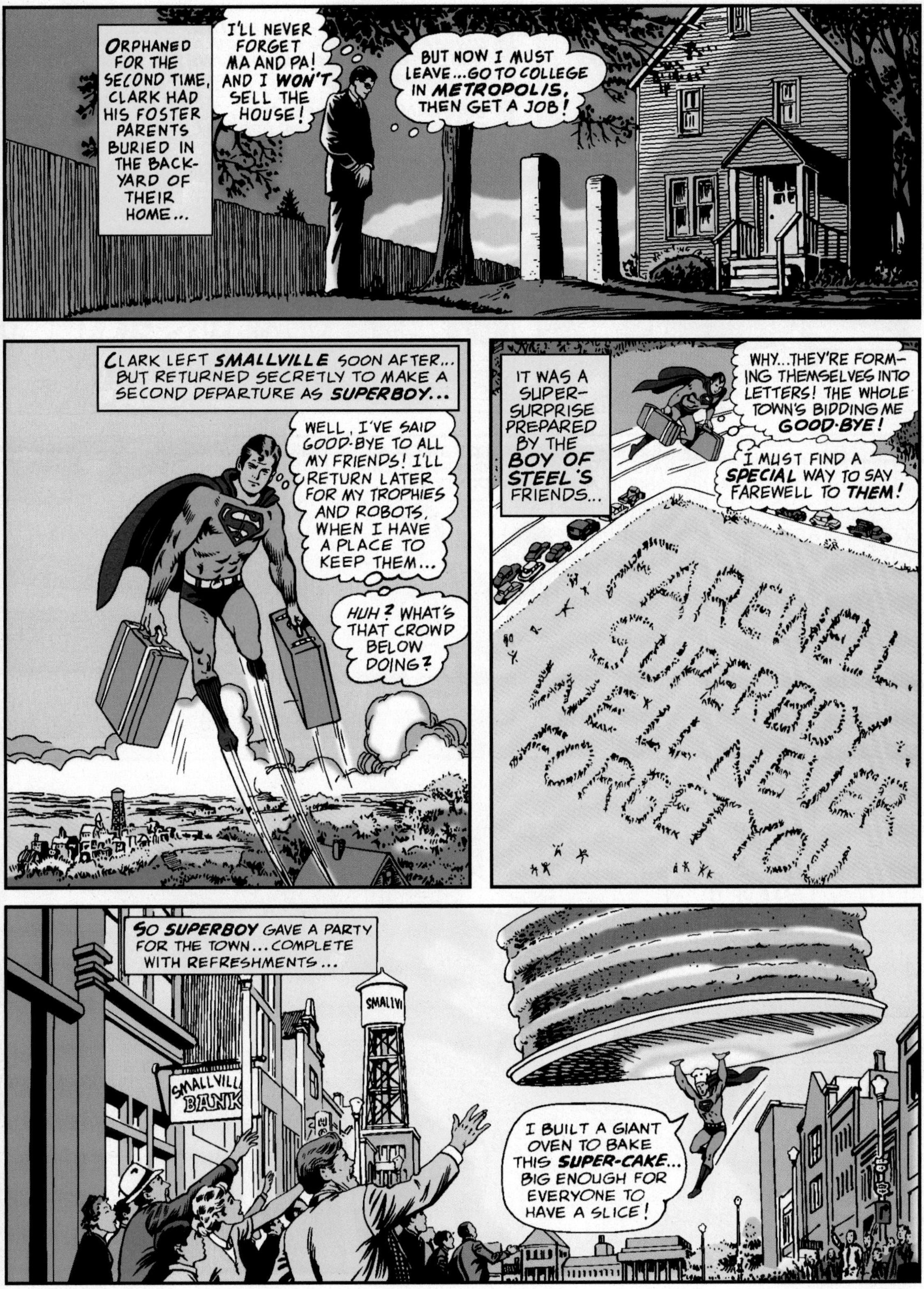
ORPHANED FOR THE SECOND TIME, CLARK HAD HIS FOSTER PARENTS BURIED IN THE BACK-YARD OF THEIR HOME...
I'LL NEVER FORGET MA AND PA! AND I WON'T SELL THE HOUSE!
BUT NOW I MUST LEAVE...GO TO COLLEGE IN METROPOLIS, THEN GET A JOB!
CLARK LEFT SMALLVILLE SOON AFTER... BUT RETURNED SECRETLY TO MAKE A SECOND DEPARTURE AS SUPERBOY...
WELL, I'VE SAID GOOD-BYE TO ALL MY FRIENDS! I'LL RETURN LATER FOR MY TROPHIES AND ROBOTS, WHEN I HAVE A PLACE TO KEEP THEM...
HUH? WHAT'S THAT CROWD BELOW DOING?
IT WAS A SUPER-SURPRISE PREPARED BY THE BOY OF STEEL'S FRIENDS...
WHY...THEY'RE FORMING THEMSELVES INTO LETTERS! THE WHOLE TOWN'S BIDDING ME GOOD-BYE!
I MUST FIND A SPECIAL WAY TO SAY FAREWELL TO THEM!
FAREWELL SUPERBOY WE'LL NEVER FORGET YOU
SO SUPERBOY GAVE A PARTY FOR THE TOWN... COMPLETE WITH REFRESHMENTS...
SMALLVILL BANK
SMALLVI
I BUILT A GIANT OVEN TO BAKE THIS SUPER-CAKE... BIG ENOUGH FOR EVERYONE TO HAVE A SLICE!

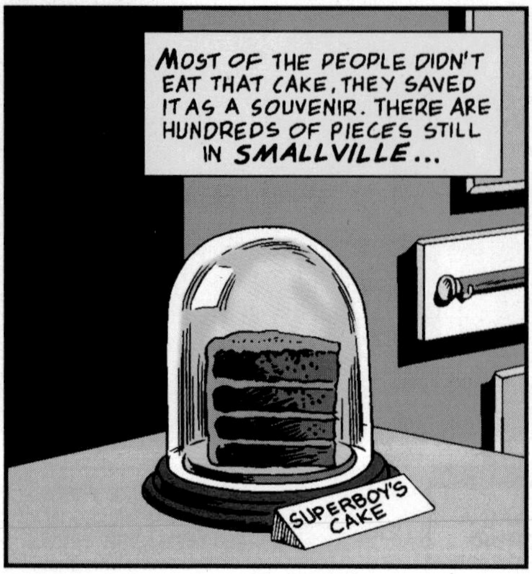
MOST OF THE PEOPLE DIDN'T EAT THAT CAKE. THEY SAVED IT AS A SOUVENIR. THERE ARE HUNDREDS OF PIECES STILL IN SMALLVILLE...
SUPERBOY'S CAKE

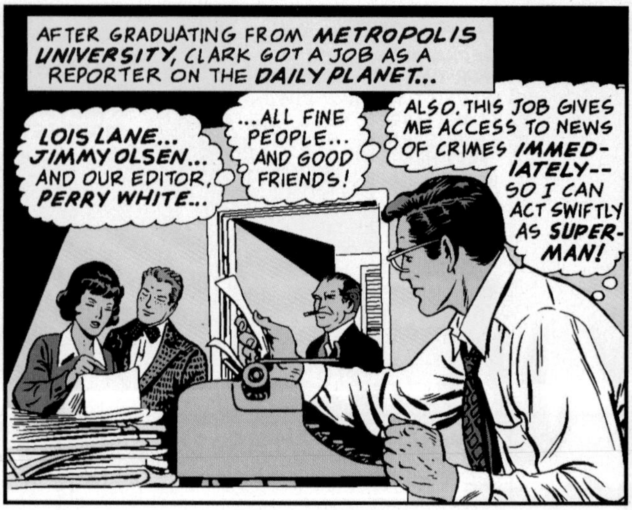
AFTER GRADUATING FROM METROPOLIS UNIVERSITY, CLARK GOT A JOB AS A REPORTER ON THE DAILY PLANET...
LOIS LANE... JIMMY OLSEN... AND OUR EDITOR, PERRY WHITE...
...ALL FINE PEOPLE... AND GOOD FRIENDS!
ALSO, THIS JOB GIVES ME ACCESS TO NEWS OF CRIMES IMMEDIATELY--SO I CAN ACT SWIFTLY AS SUPERMAN!

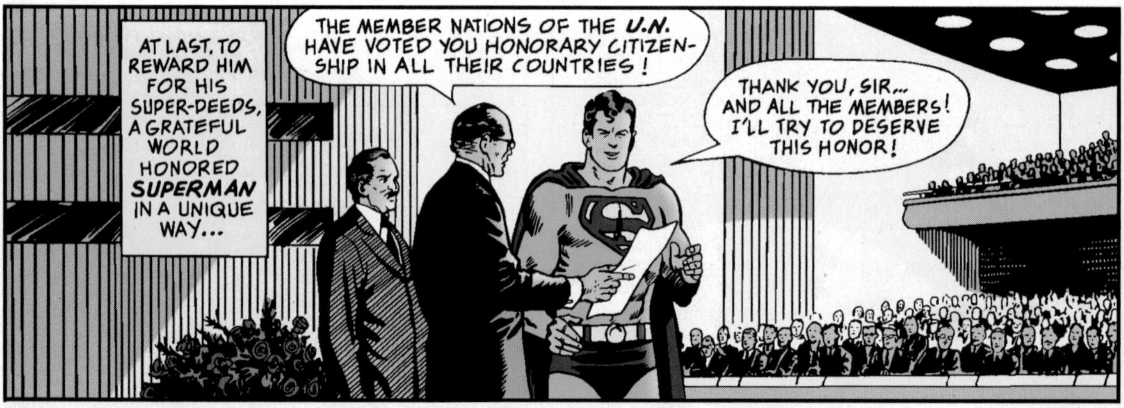
AT LAST, TO REWARD HIM FOR HIS SUPER-DEEDS, A GRATEFUL WORLD HONORED SUPERMAN IN A UNIQUE WAY...
THE MEMBER NATIONS OF THE U.N. HAVE VOTED YOU HONORARY CITIZENSHIP IN ALL THEIR COUNTRIES!
THANK YOU, SIR... AND ALL THE MEMBERS! I'LL TRY TO DESERVE THIS HONOR!

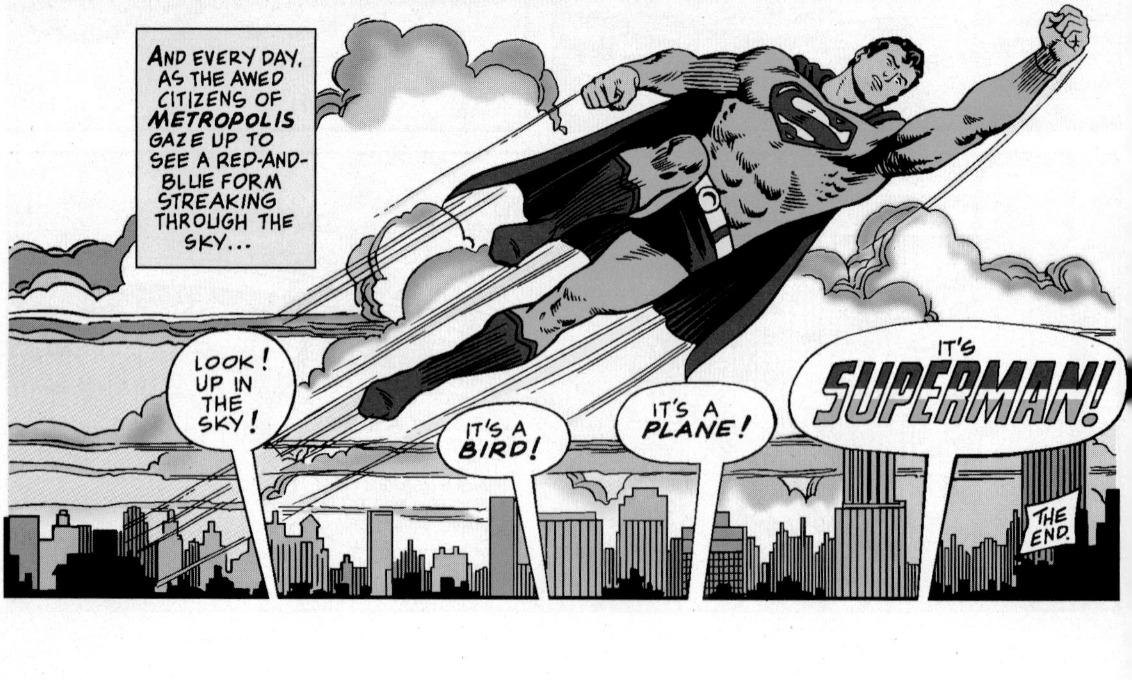
AND EVERY DAY, AS THE AWED CITIZENS OF METROPOLIS GAZE UP TO SEE A RED-AND-BLUE FORM STREAKING THROUGH THE SKY...
LOOK! UP IN THE SKY!
IT'S A BIRD!
IT'S A PLANE!
IT'S SUPERMAN!
THE END.

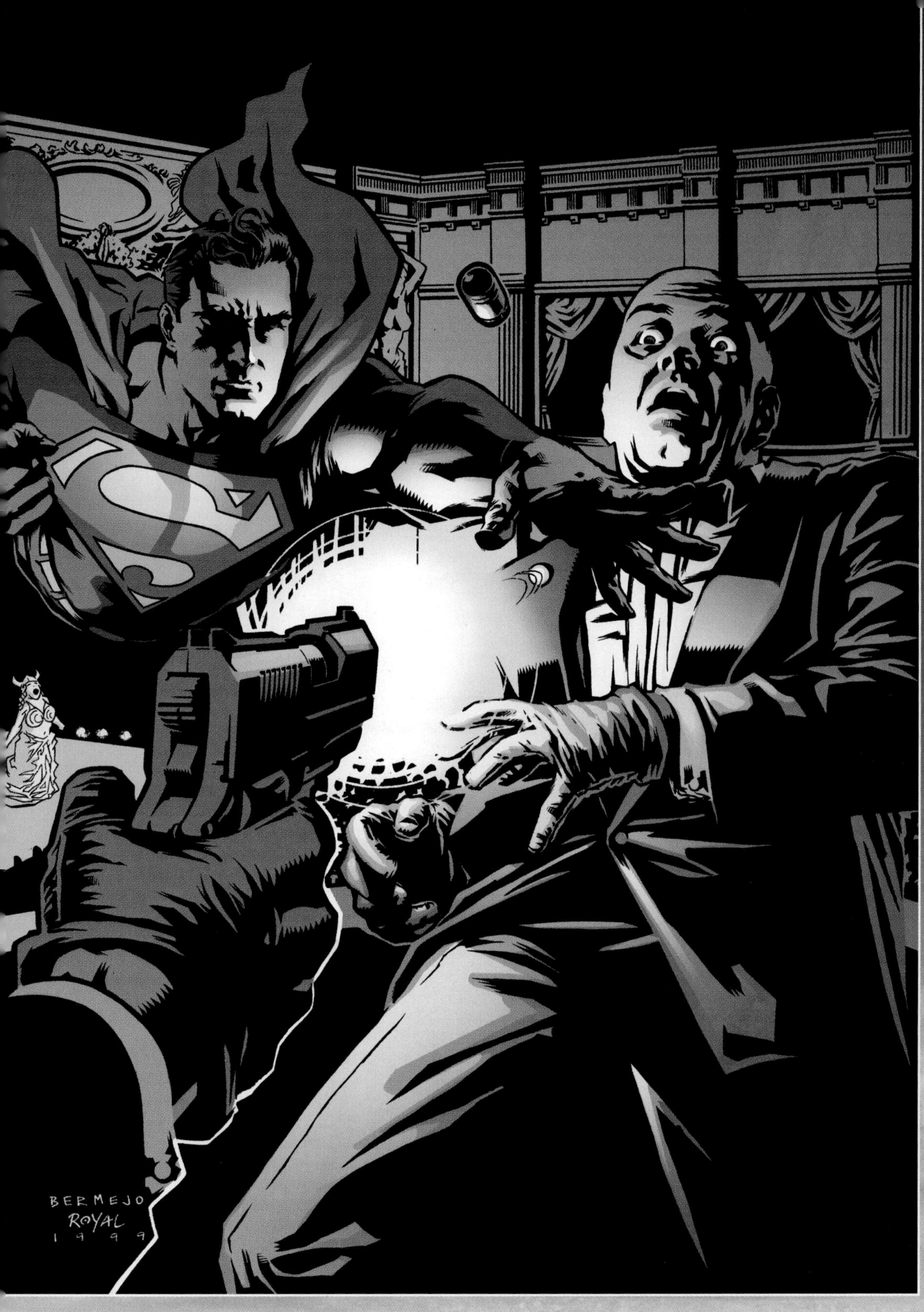
BERMEJO
ROYAL
1999

"A Night at the Opera"

STUART IMMONEN plotter **MARK MILLAR** scripter **YANICK PAQUETTE** penciller
EXTER VINES, RICH FABER & JIM ROYAL inkers **GLENN WHITMORE** colorist **BILL OAKLEY** letterer
LEE BERMEJO & JIM ROYAL WITH LIQUID cover artists

Superman's archnemesis, Lex Luthor, is once again up to no good in this story from THE ADVENTURES OF SUPERMAN.

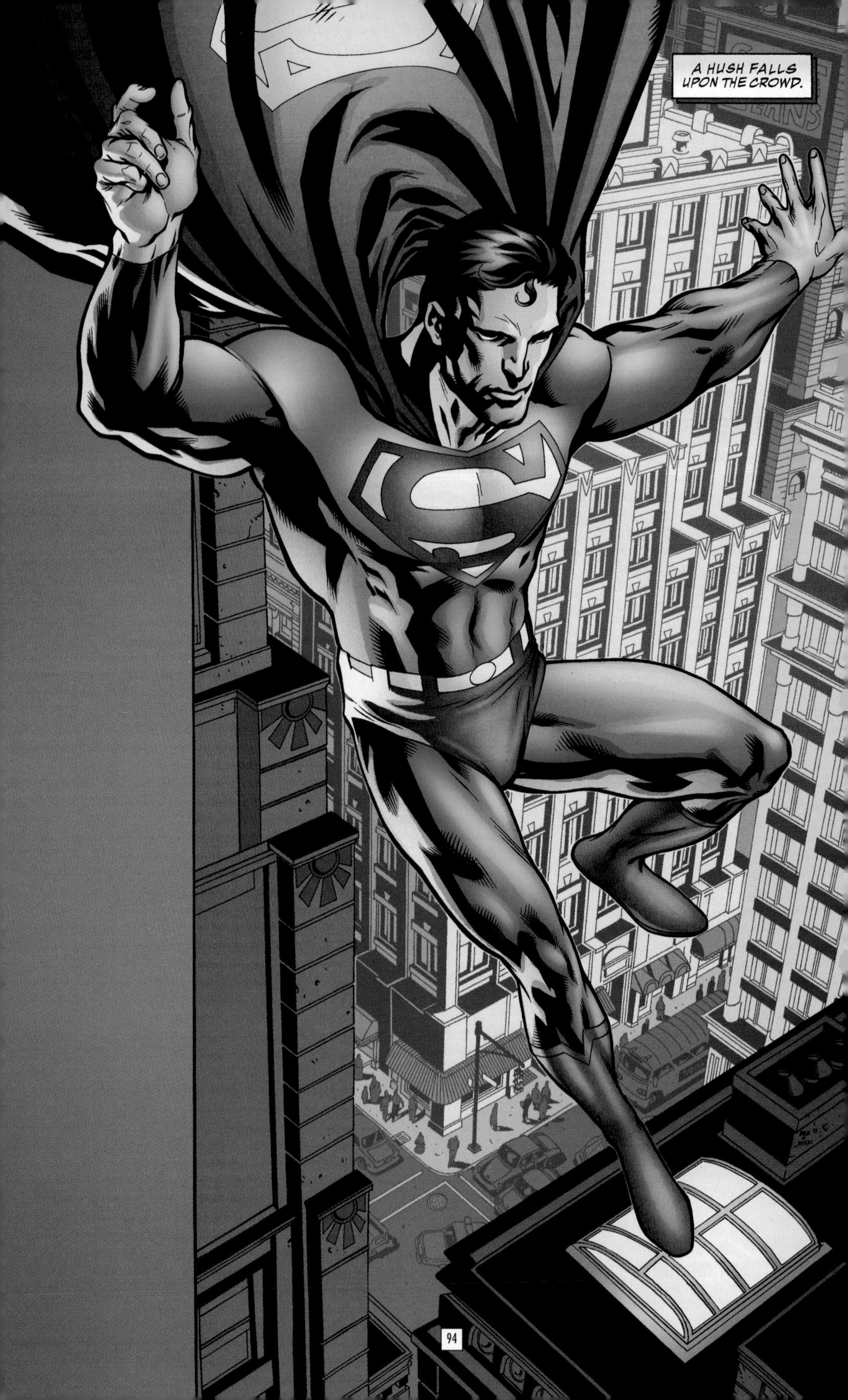
A HUSH FALLS UPON THE CROWD.

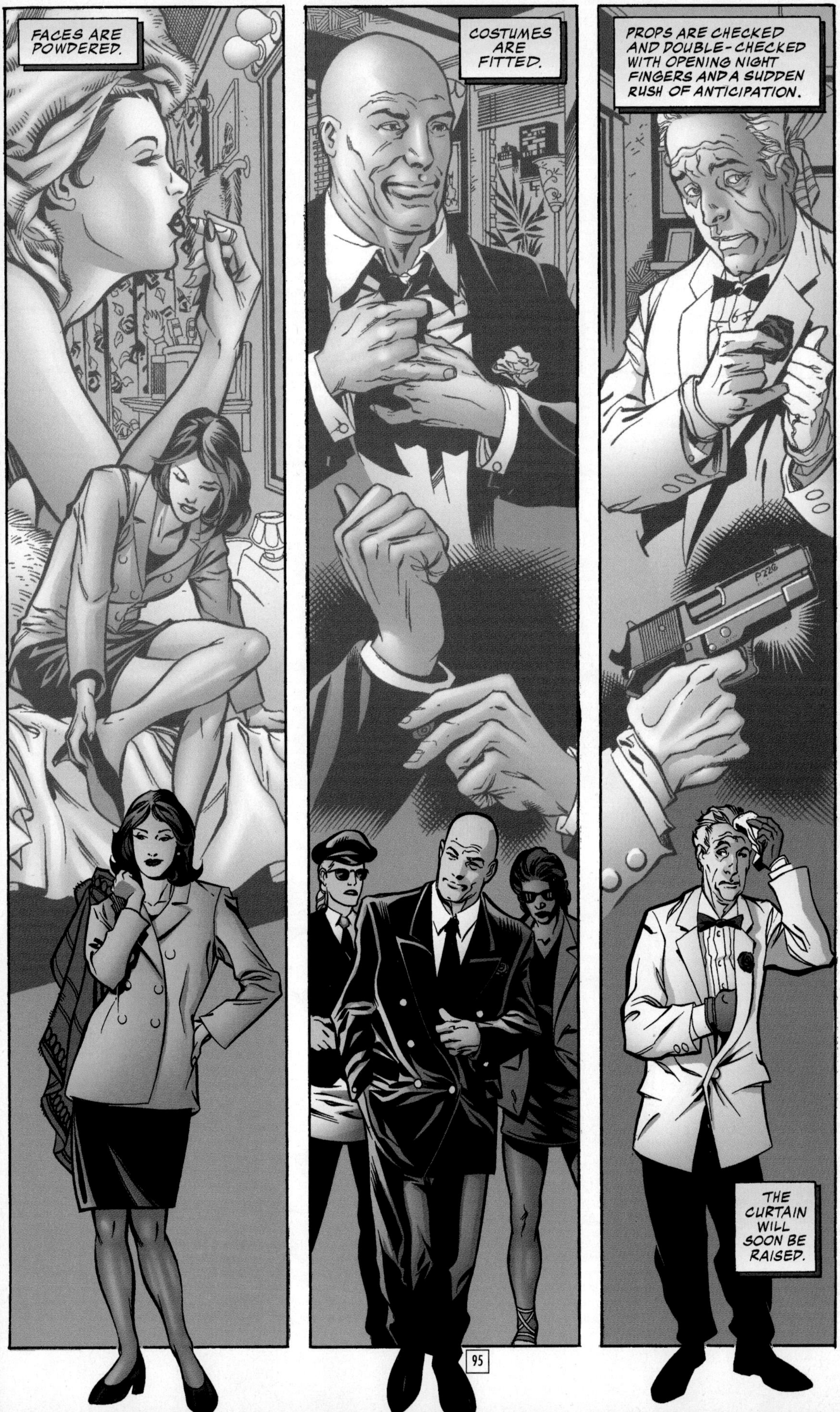
FACES ARE POWDERED.
COSTUMES ARE FITTED.
PROPS ARE CHECKED AND DOUBLE-CHECKED WITH OPENING NIGHT FINGERS AND A SUDDEN RUSH OF ANTICIPATION.
THE CURTAIN WILL SOON BE RAISED.

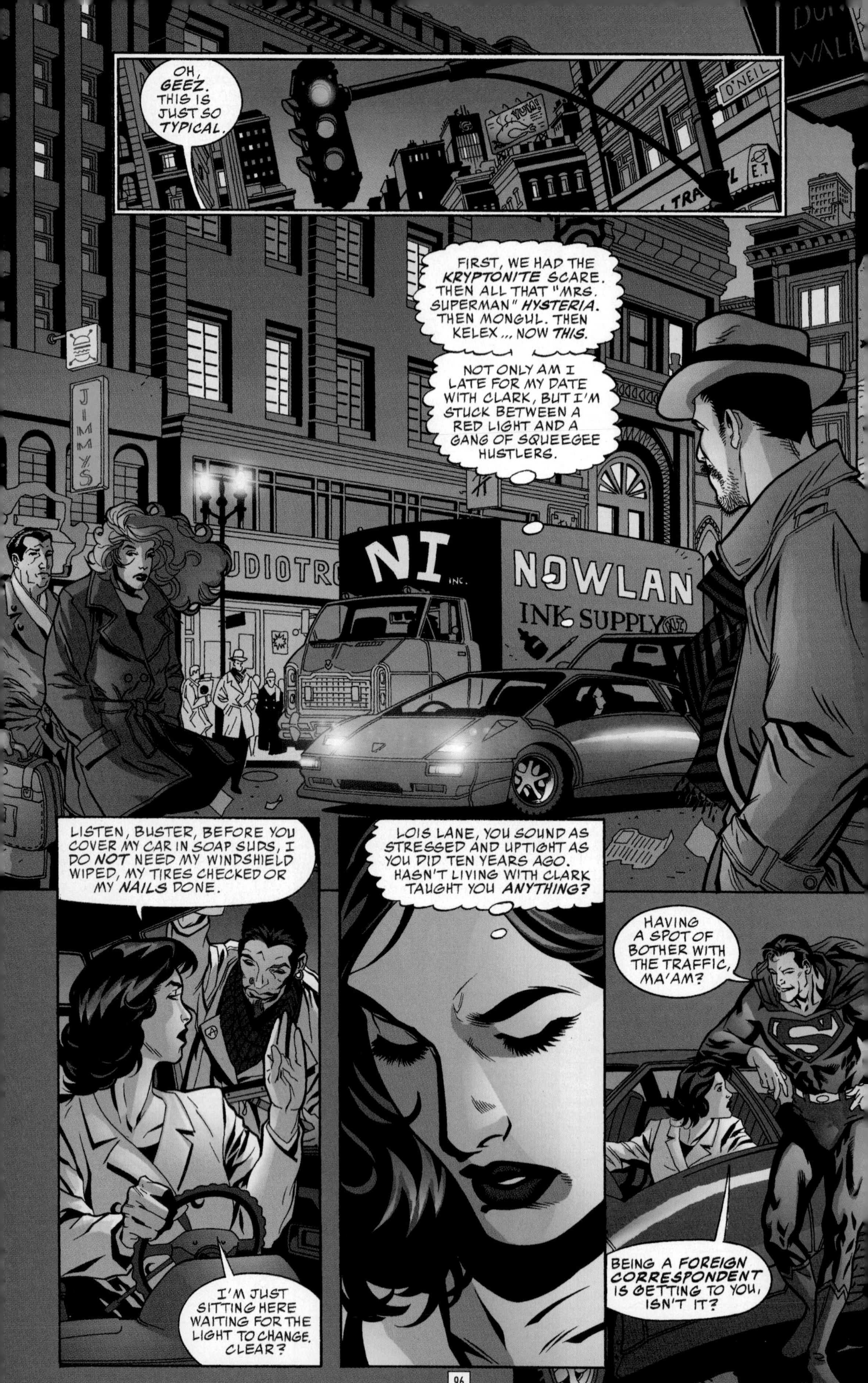
OH, GEEZ. THIS IS JUST SO TYPICAL.
O'NEIL
FIRST, WE HAD THE KRYPTONITE SCARE. THEN ALL THAT "MRS. SUPERMAN" HYSTERIA. THEN MONGUL. THEN KELEX ... NOW THIS.
NOT ONLY AM I LATE FOR MY DATE WITH CLARK, BUT I'M STUCK BETWEEN A RED LIGHT AND A GANG OF SQUEEGEE HUSTLERS.
JIMMY'S
NI INC.
NOWLAN
INK SUPPLY
LISTEN, BUSTER, BEFORE YOU COVER MY CAR IN SOAP SUDS, I DO NOT NEED MY WINDSHIELD WIPED, MY TIRES CHECKED OR MY NAILS DONE.
I'M JUST SITTING HERE WAITING FOR THE LIGHT TO CHANGE. CLEAR?
LOIS LANE, YOU SOUND AS STRESSED AND UPTIGHT AS YOU DID TEN YEARS AGO. HASN'T LIVING WITH CLARK TAUGHT YOU ANYTHING?
HAVING A SPOT OF BOTHER WITH THE TRAFFIC, MA'AM?
BEING A FOREIGN CORRESPONDENT IS GETTING TO YOU, ISN'T IT?

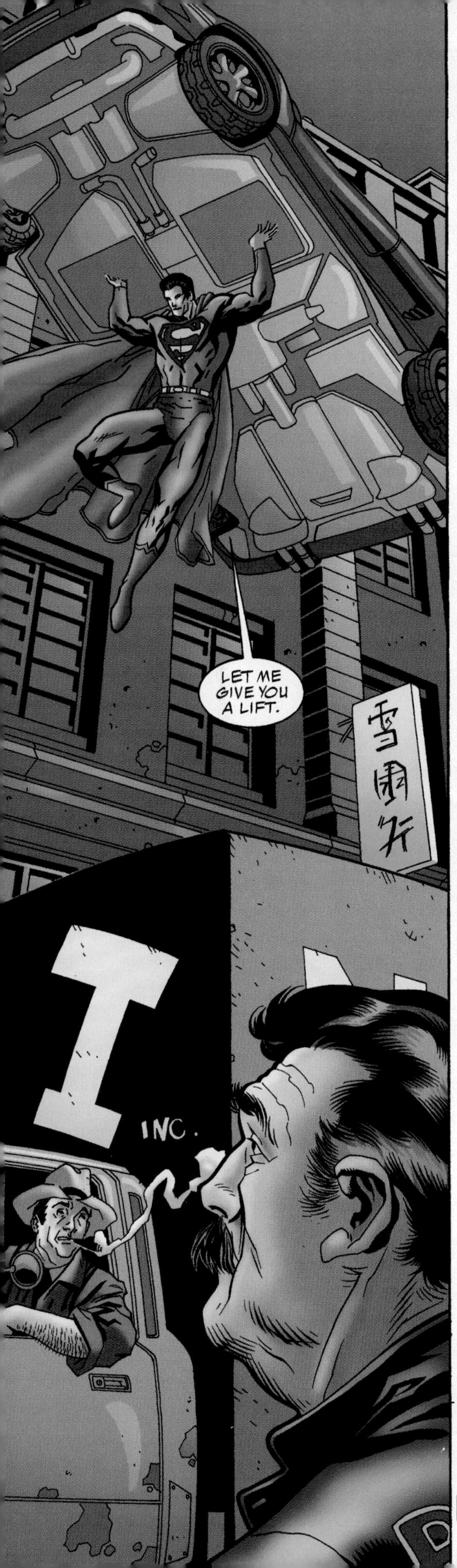
LET ME GIVE YOU A LIFT.
INC.

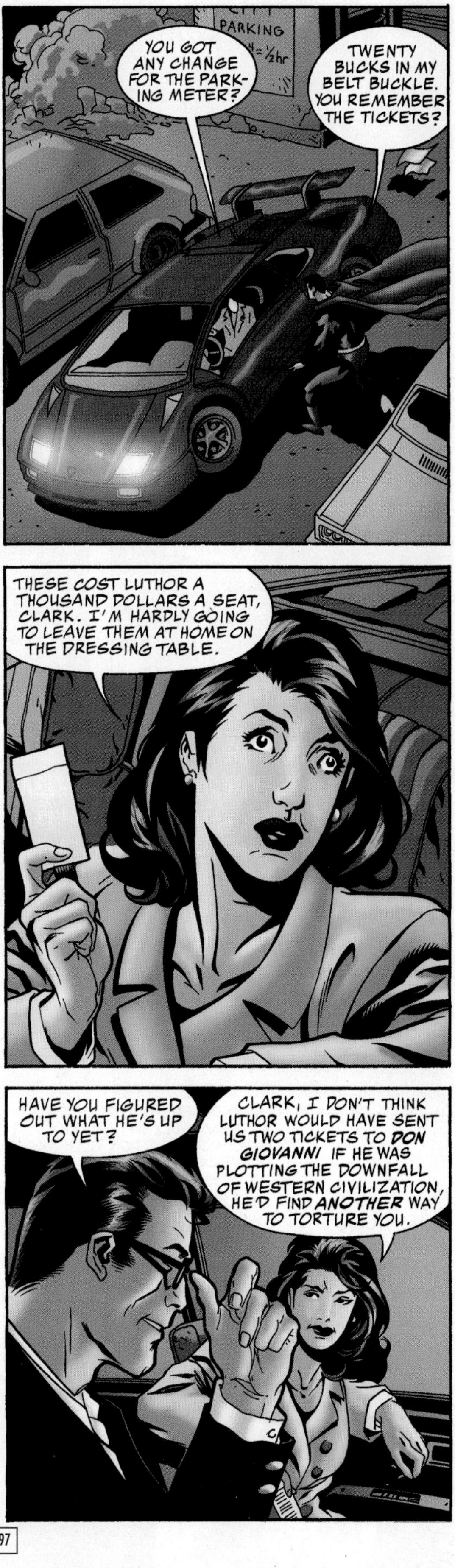
CITY PARKING
YOU GOT ANY CHANGE FOR THE PARK-ING METER?
TWENTY BUCKS IN MY BELT BUCKLE. YOU REMEMBER THE TICKETS?
THESE COST LUTHOR A THOUSAND DOLLARS A SEAT, CLARK. I'M HARDLY GOING TO LEAVE THEM AT HOME ON THE DRESSING TABLE.
HAVE YOU FIGURED OUT WHAT HE'S UP TO YET?
CLARK, I DON'T THINK LUTHOR WOULD HAVE SENT US TWO TICKETS TO *DON GIOVANNI* IF HE WAS PLOTTING THE DOWNFALL OF WESTERN CIVILIZATION, HE'D FIND ***ANOTHER*** WAY TO TORTURE YOU.

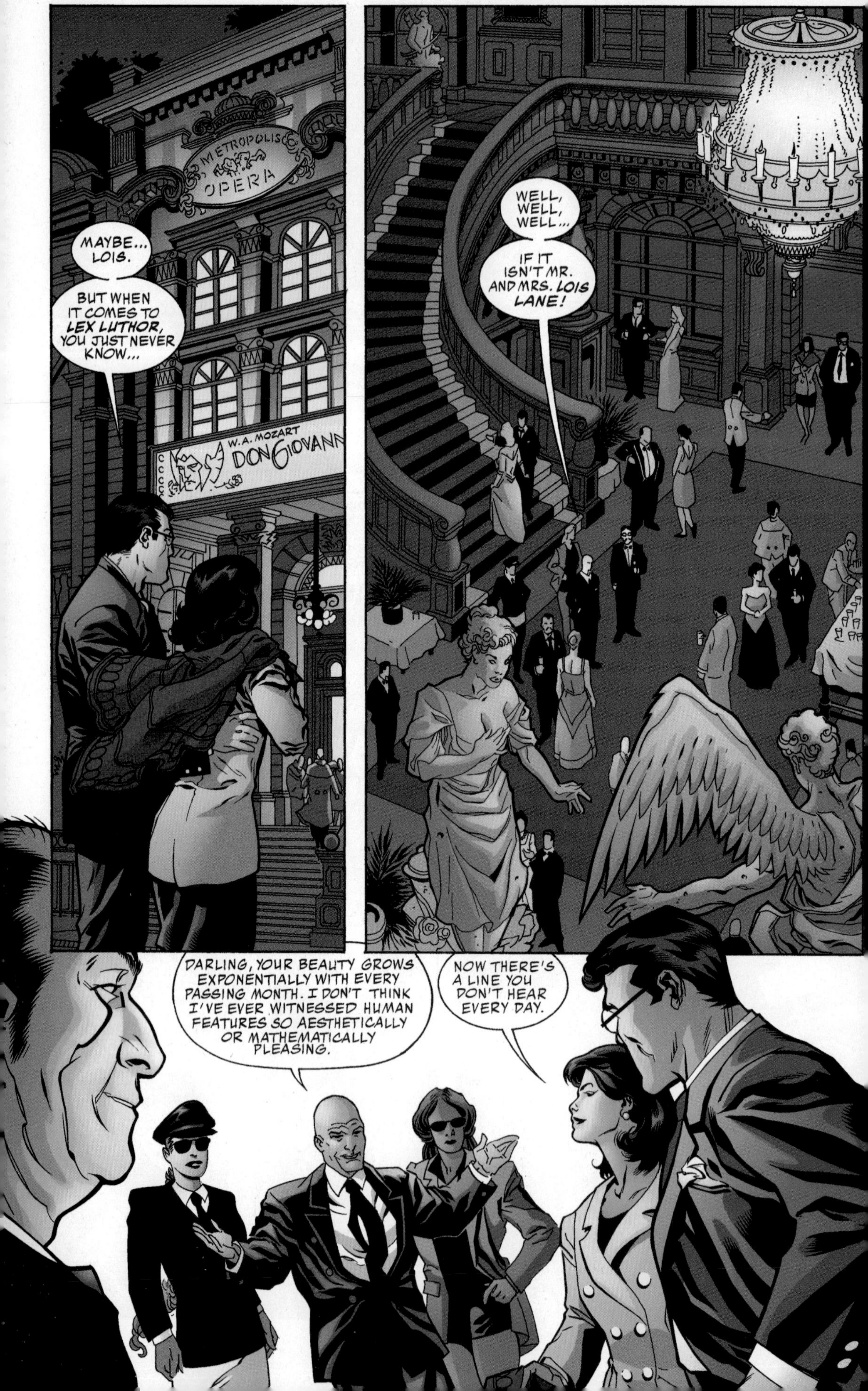
METROPOLIS OPERA
MAYBE... LOIS.
BUT WHEN IT COMES TO LEX LUTHOR, YOU JUST NEVER KNOW...
W. A. MOZART DON GIOVANNI
WELL, WELL, WELL...
IF IT ISN'T MR. AND MRS. LOIS LANE!
DARLING, YOUR BEAUTY GROWS EXPONENTIALLY WITH EVERY PASSING MONTH. I DON'T THINK I'VE EVER WITNESSED HUMAN FEATURES SO AESTHETICALLY OR MATHEMATICALLY PLEASING.
NOW THERE'S A LINE YOU DON'T HEAR EVERY DAY.

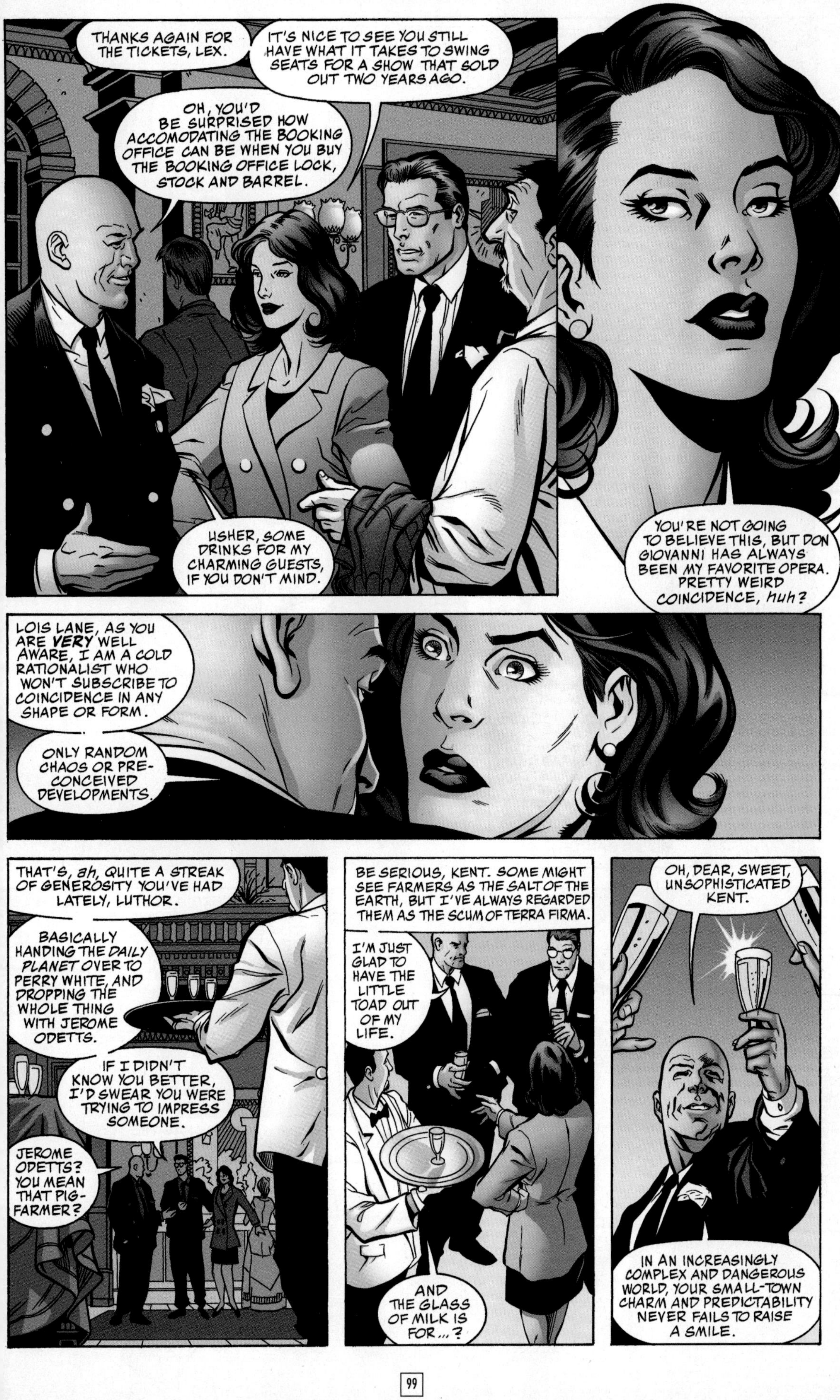
THANKS AGAIN FOR THE TICKETS, LEX.
IT'S NICE TO SEE YOU STILL HAVE WHAT IT TAKES TO SWING SEATS FOR A SHOW THAT SOLD OUT TWO YEARS AGO.
OH, YOU'D BE SURPRISED HOW ACCOMODATING THE BOOKING OFFICE CAN BE WHEN YOU BUY THE BOOKING OFFICE LOCK, STOCK AND BARREL.
USHER, SOME DRINKS FOR MY CHARMING GUESTS, IF YOU DON'T MIND.
YOU'RE NOT GOING TO BELIEVE THIS, BUT DON GIOVANNI HAS ALWAYS BEEN MY FAVORITE OPERA. PRETTY WEIRD COINCIDENCE, *huh?*
LOIS LANE, AS YOU ARE ***VERY*** WELL AWARE, I AM A COLD RATIONALIST WHO WON'T SUBSCRIBE TO COINCIDENCE IN ANY SHAPE OR FORM.
ONLY RANDOM CHAOS OR PRE-CONCEIVED DEVELOPMENTS.
THAT'S, *ah,* QUITE A STREAK OF GENEROSITY YOU'VE HAD LATELY, LUTHOR.
BASICALLY HANDING THE *DAILY PLANET* OVER TO PERRY WHITE, AND DROPPING THE WHOLE THING WITH JEROME ODETTS.
IF I DIDN'T KNOW YOU BETTER, I'D SWEAR YOU WERE TRYING TO IMPRESS SOMEONE.
JEROME ODETTS? YOU MEAN THAT PIG-FARMER?
BE SERIOUS, KENT. SOME MIGHT SEE FARMERS AS THE SALT OF THE EARTH, BUT I'VE ALWAYS REGARDED THEM AS THE SCUM OF TERRA FIRMA.
I'M JUST GLAD TO HAVE THE LITTLE TOAD OUT OF MY LIFE.
AND THE GLASS OF MILK IS FOR...?
OH, DEAR, SWEET, UNSOPHISTICATED KENT.
IN AN INCREASINGLY COMPLEX AND DANGEROUS WORLD, YOUR SMALL-TOWN CHARM AND PREDICTABILITY NEVER FAILS TO RAISE A SMILE.

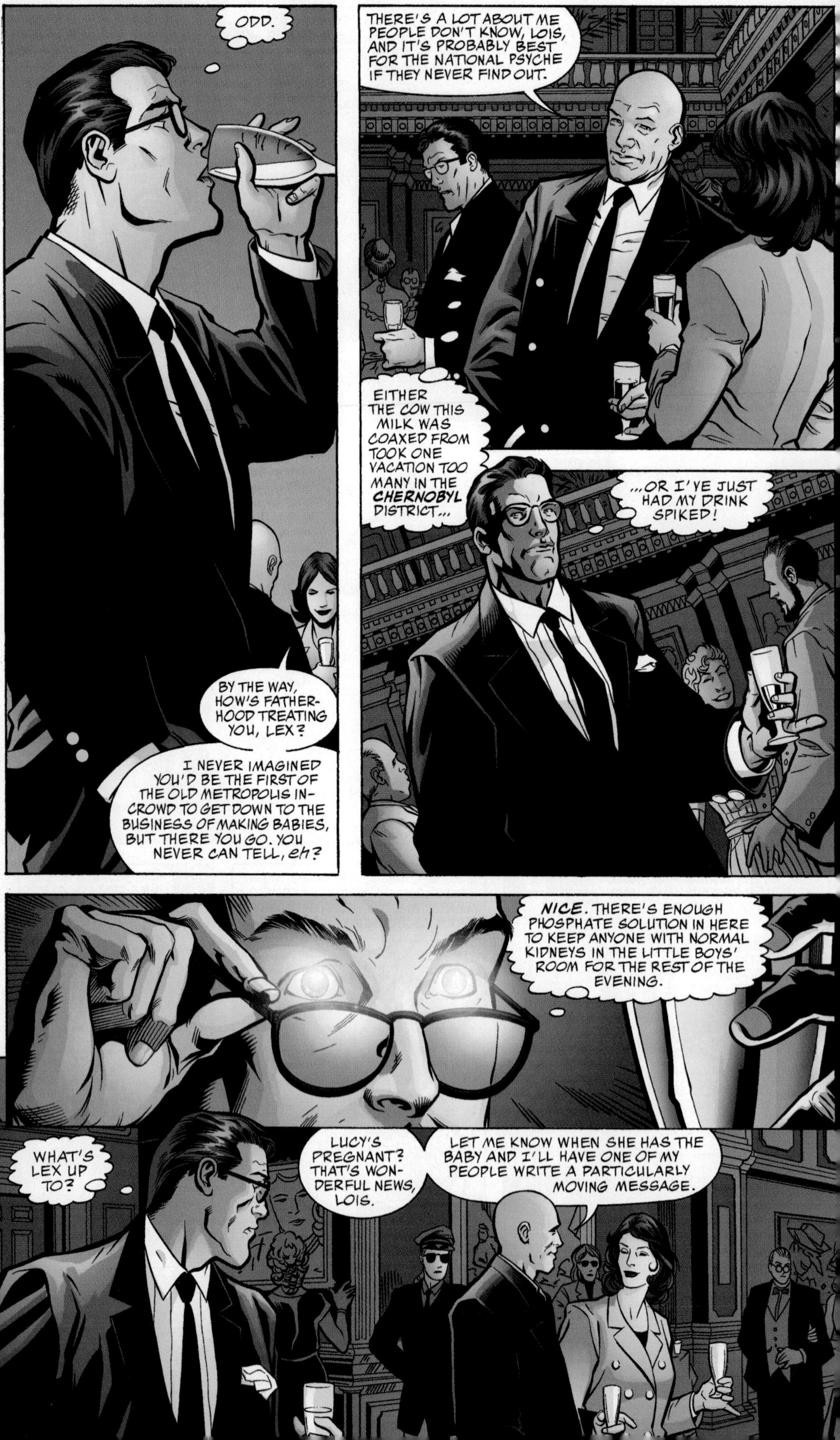

ODD.
BY THE WAY, HOW'S FATHER-HOOD TREATING YOU, LEX?
I NEVER IMAGINED YOU'D BE THE FIRST OF THE OLD METROPOLIS IN-CROWD TO GET DOWN TO THE BUSINESS OF MAKING BABIES, BUT THERE YOU GO. YOU NEVER CAN TELL, *eh*?
THERE'S A LOT ABOUT ME PEOPLE DON'T KNOW, LOIS, AND IT'S PROBABLY BEST FOR THE NATIONAL PSYCHE IF THEY NEVER FIND OUT.
EITHER THE COW THIS MILK WAS COAXED FROM TOOK ONE VACATION TOO MANY IN THE **CHERNOBYL** DISTRICT...
...OR I'VE JUST HAD MY DRINK SPIKED!
NICE. THERE'S ENOUGH PHOSPHATE SOLUTION IN HERE TO KEEP ANYONE WITH NORMAL KIDNEYS IN THE LITTLE BOYS' ROOM FOR THE REST OF THE EVENING.
WHAT'S LEX UP TO?
LUCY'S PREGNANT? THAT'S WON-DERFUL NEWS, LOIS.
LET ME KNOW WHEN SHE HAS THE BABY AND I'LL HAVE ONE OF MY PEOPLE WRITE A PARTICULARLY MOVING MESSAGE.

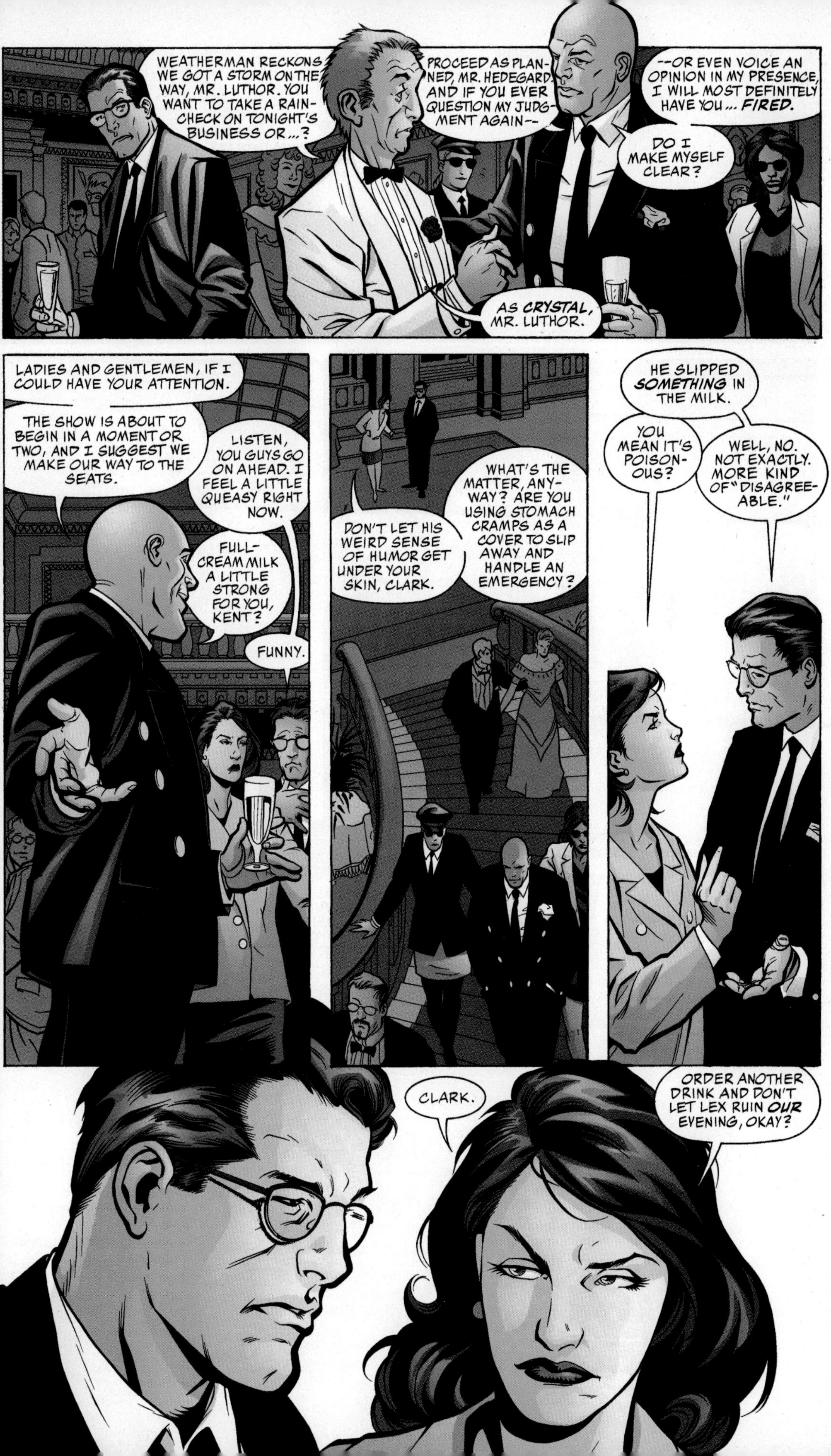
WEATHERMAN RECKONS WE GOT A STORM ON THE WAY, MR. LUTHOR. YOU WANT TO TAKE A RAIN-CHECK ON TONIGHT'S BUSINESS OR...?
PROCEED AS PLANNED, MR. HEDEGARD. AND IF YOU EVER QUESTION MY JUDGMENT AGAIN--
--OR EVEN VOICE AN OPINION IN MY PRESENCE, I WILL MOST DEFINITELY HAVE YOU... **FIRED.**
DO I MAKE MYSELF CLEAR?
AS **CRYSTAL,** MR. LUTHOR.
LADIES AND GENTLEMEN, IF I COULD HAVE YOUR ATTENTION.
THE SHOW IS ABOUT TO BEGIN IN A MOMENT OR TWO, AND I SUGGEST WE MAKE OUR WAY TO THE SEATS.
LISTEN, YOU GUYS GO ON AHEAD. I FEEL A LITTLE QUEASY RIGHT NOW.
FULL-CREAM MILK A LITTLE STRONG FOR YOU, KENT?
FUNNY.
DON'T LET HIS WEIRD SENSE OF HUMOR GET UNDER YOUR SKIN, CLARK.
WHAT'S THE MATTER, ANYWAY? ARE YOU USING STOMACH CRAMPS AS A COVER TO SLIP AWAY AND HANDLE AN EMERGENCY?
HE SLIPPED **SOMETHING** IN THE MILK.
YOU MEAN IT'S POISONOUS?
WELL, NO. NOT EXACTLY. MORE KIND OF "DISAGREEABLE."
CLARK.
ORDER ANOTHER DRINK AND DON'T LET LEX RUIN **OUR** EVENING, OKAY?

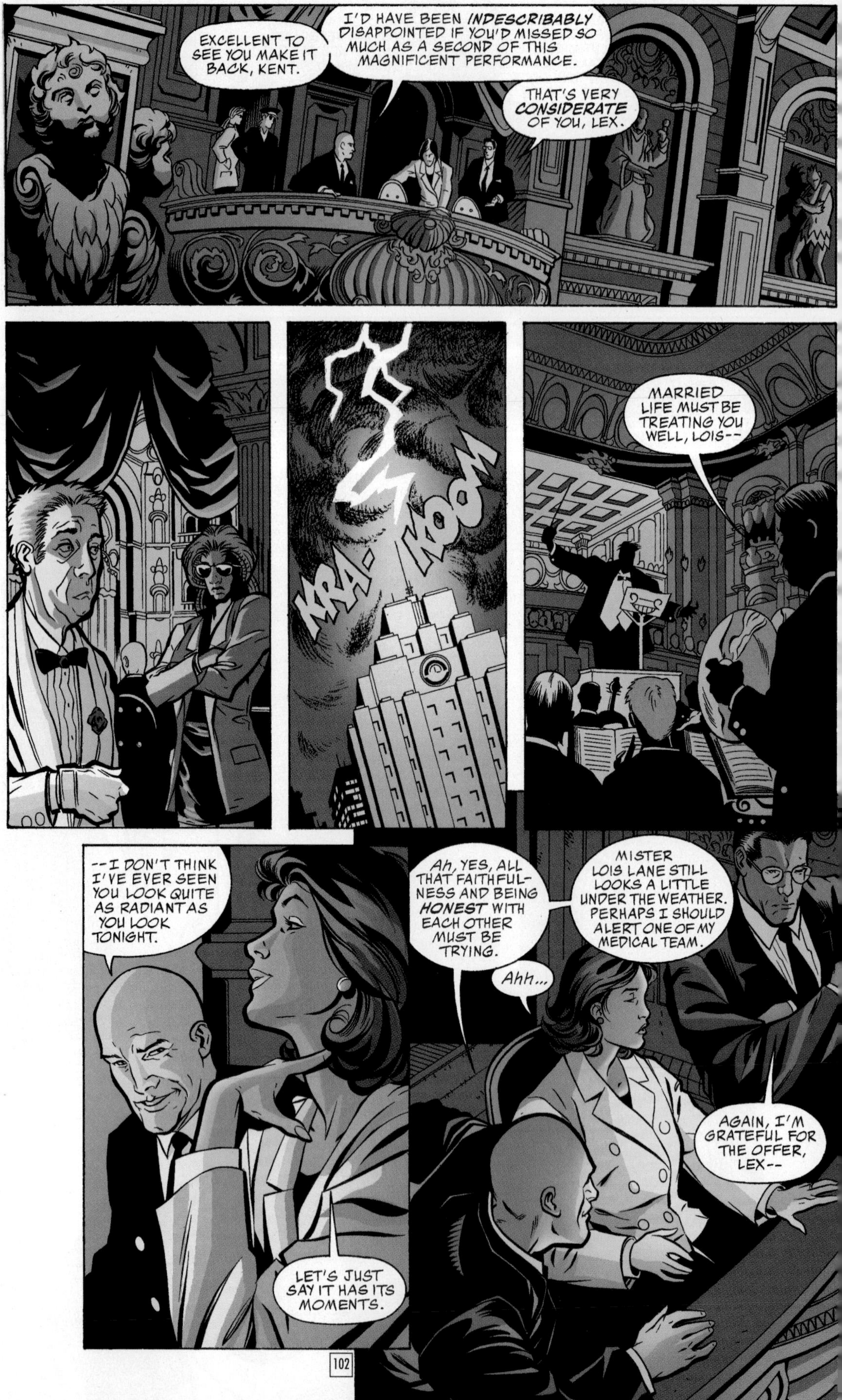
EXCELLENT TO SEE YOU MAKE IT BACK, KENT.
I'D HAVE BEEN *INDESCRIBABLY* DISAPPOINTED IF YOU'D MISSED SO MUCH AS A SECOND OF THIS MAGNIFICENT PERFORMANCE.
THAT'S VERY *CONSIDERATE* OF YOU, LEX.
KRA-KOOM
MARRIED LIFE MUST BE TREATING YOU WELL, LOIS--
--I DON'T THINK I'VE EVER SEEN YOU LOOK QUITE AS RADIANT AS YOU LOOK TONIGHT.
LET'S JUST SAY IT HAS ITS MOMENTS.
Ah, YES, ALL THAT FAITHFULNESS AND BEING *HONEST* WITH EACH OTHER MUST BE TRYING.
MISTER LOIS LANE STILL LOOKS A LITTLE UNDER THE WEATHER. PERHAPS I SHOULD ALERT ONE OF MY MEDICAL TEAM.
Ahh...
AGAIN, I'M GRATEFUL FOR THE OFFER, LEX--

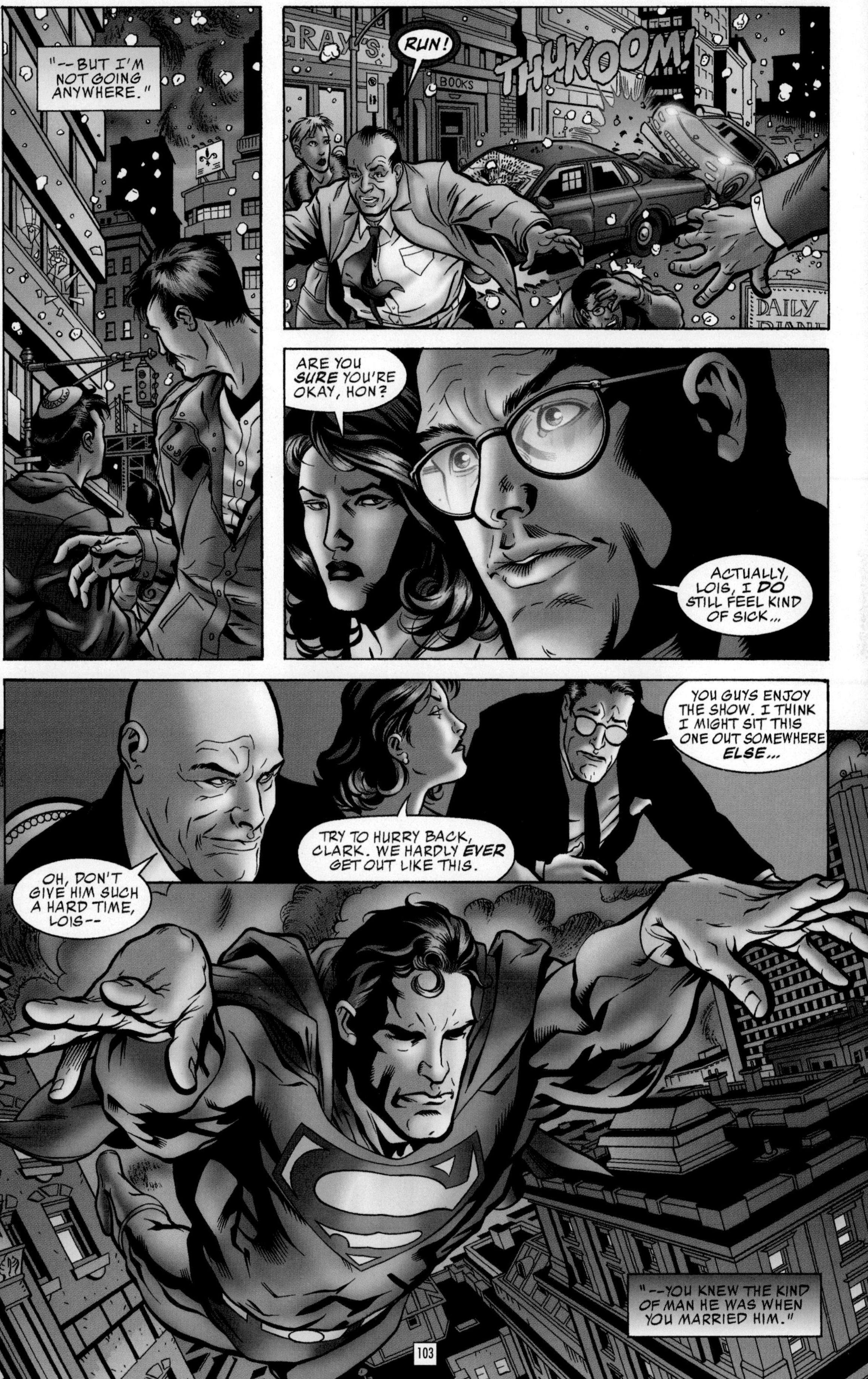

"--BUT I'M NOT GOING ANYWHERE."
GRAY'S
BOOKS
RUN!
THUKOOM!
DAILY
ARE YOU SURE YOU'RE OKAY, HON?
ACTUALLY, LOIS, I DO STILL FEEL KIND OF SICK...
YOU GUYS ENJOY THE SHOW. I THINK I MIGHT SIT THIS ONE OUT SOMEWHERE ELSE...
TRY TO HURRY BACK, CLARK. WE HARDLY EVER GET OUT LIKE THIS.
OH, DON'T GIVE HIM SUCH A HARD TIME, LOIS--
"--YOU KNEW THE KIND OF MAN HE WAS WHEN YOU MARRIED HIM."

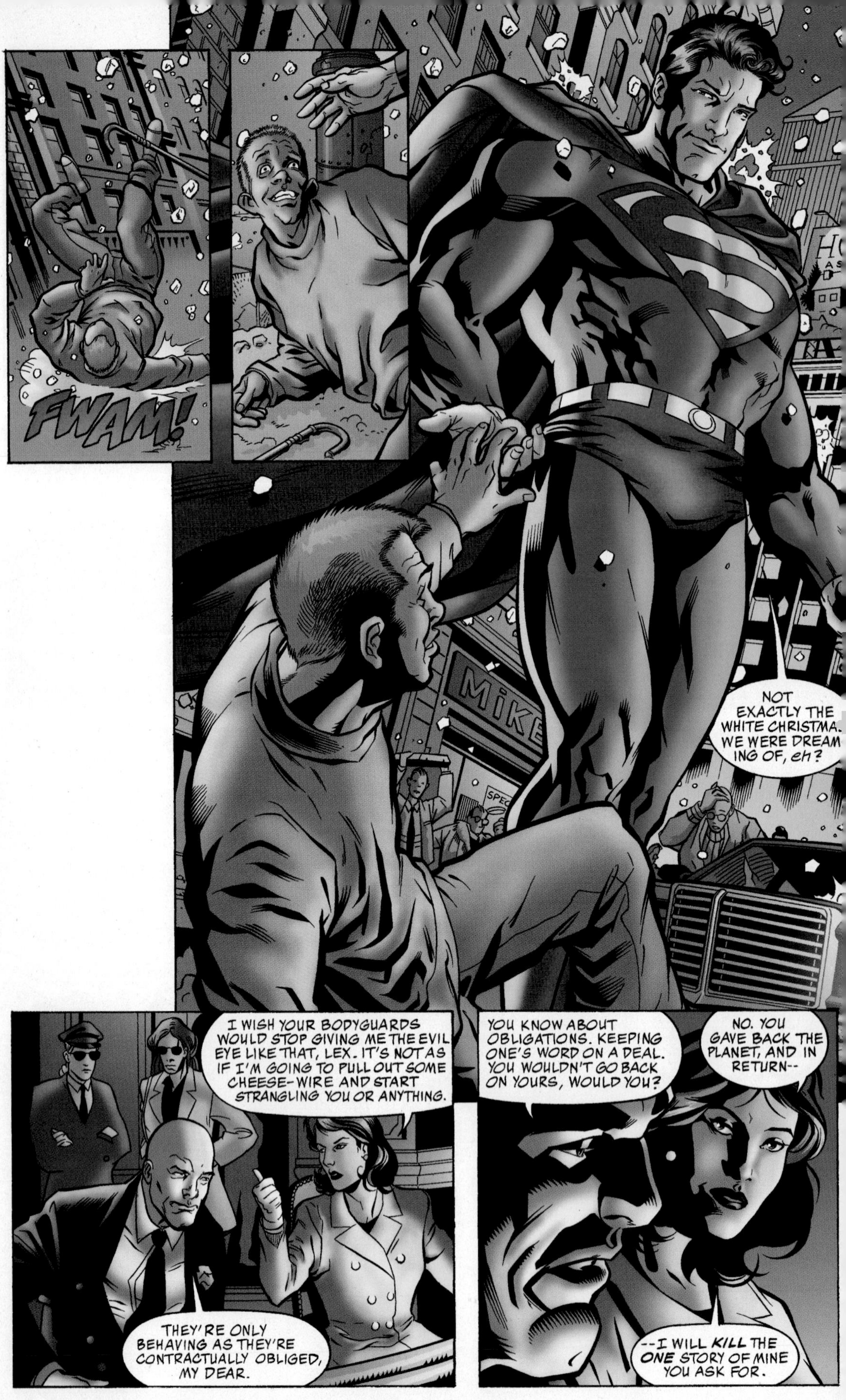
FWAM!
NOT EXACTLY THE WHITE CHRISTMA WE WERE DREAM ING OF, eh?
I WISH YOUR BODYGUARDS WOULD STOP GIVING ME THE EVIL EYE LIKE THAT, LEX. IT'S NOT AS IF I'M GOING TO PULL OUT SOME CHEESE-WIRE AND START STRANGLING YOU OR ANYTHING.
THEY'RE ONLY BEHAVING AS THEY'RE CONTRACTUALLY OBLIGED, MY DEAR.
YOU KNOW ABOUT OBLIGATIONS. KEEPING ONE'S WORD ON A DEAL. YOU WOULDN'T GO BACK ON YOURS, WOULD YOU?
NO. YOU GAVE BACK THE PLANET, AND IN RETURN--
--I WILL KILL THE ONE STORY OF MINE YOU ASK FOR.

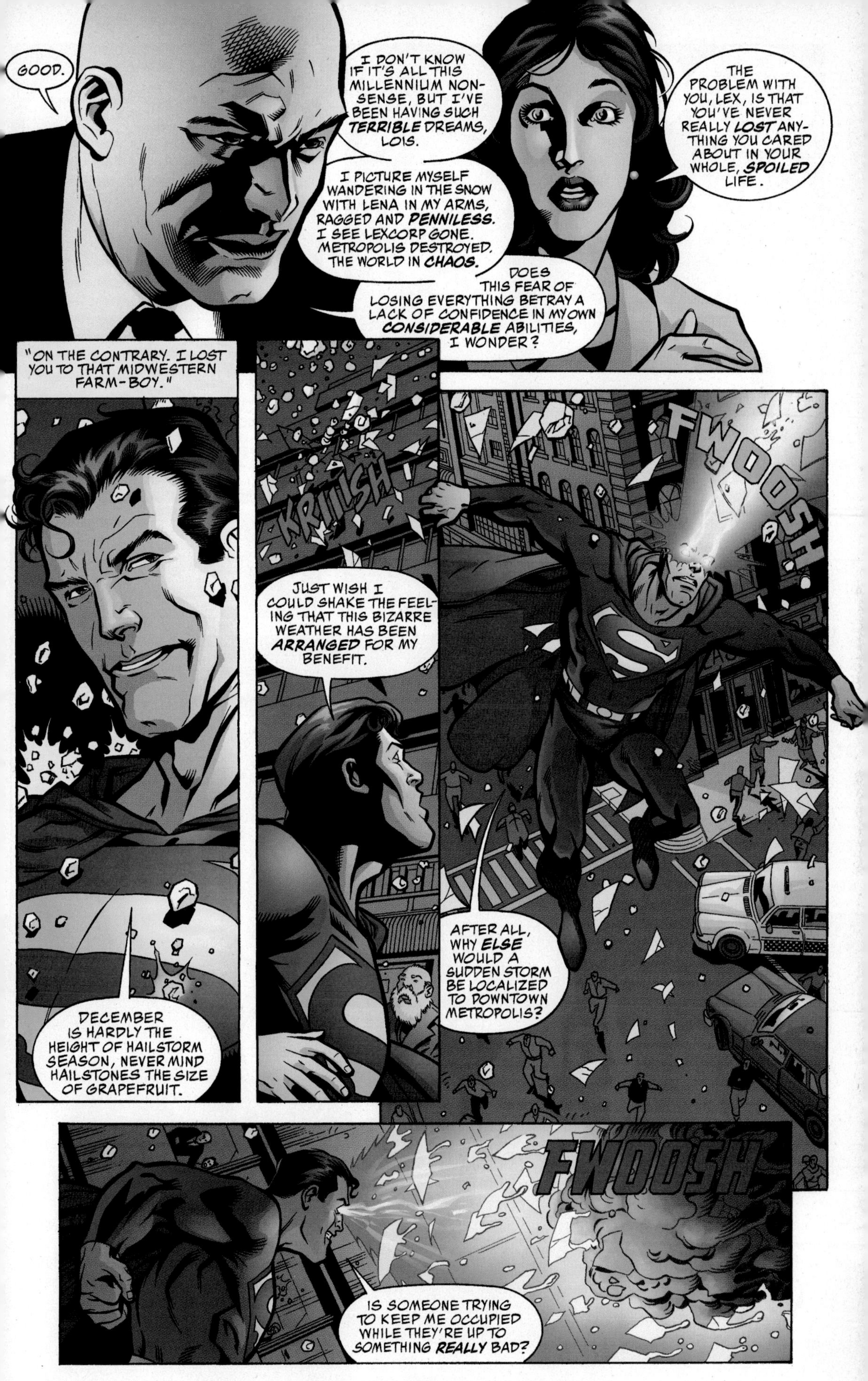
GOOD.
I DON'T KNOW IF IT'S ALL THIS MILLENNIUM NON-SENSE, BUT I'VE BEEN HAVING SUCH TERRIBLE DREAMS, LOIS.
I PICTURE MYSELF WANDERING IN THE SNOW WITH LENA IN MY ARMS, RAGGED AND PENNILESS. I SEE LEXCORP GONE. METROPOLIS DESTROYED. THE WORLD IN CHAOS.
DOES THIS FEAR OF LOSING EVERYTHING BETRAY A LACK OF CONFIDENCE IN MY OWN CONSIDERABLE ABILITIES, I WONDER?
THE PROBLEM WITH YOU, LEX, IS THAT YOU'VE NEVER REALLY LOST ANY-THING YOU CARED ABOUT IN YOUR WHOLE, SPOILED LIFE.
"ON THE CONTRARY. I LOST YOU TO THAT MIDWESTERN FARM-BOY."
DECEMBER IS HARDLY THE HEIGHT OF HAILSTORM SEASON, NEVER MIND HAILSTONES THE SIZE OF GRAPEFRUIT.
KRUUSH
JUST WISH I COULD SHAKE THE FEEL-ING THAT THIS BIZARRE WEATHER HAS BEEN ARRANGED FOR MY BENEFIT.
FWOOSH
AFTER ALL, WHY ELSE WOULD A SUDDEN STORM BE LOCALIZED TO DOWNTOWN METROPOLIS?
FWOOSH
IS SOMEONE TRYING TO KEEP ME OCCUPIED WHILE THEY'RE UP TO SOMETHING REALLY BAD?

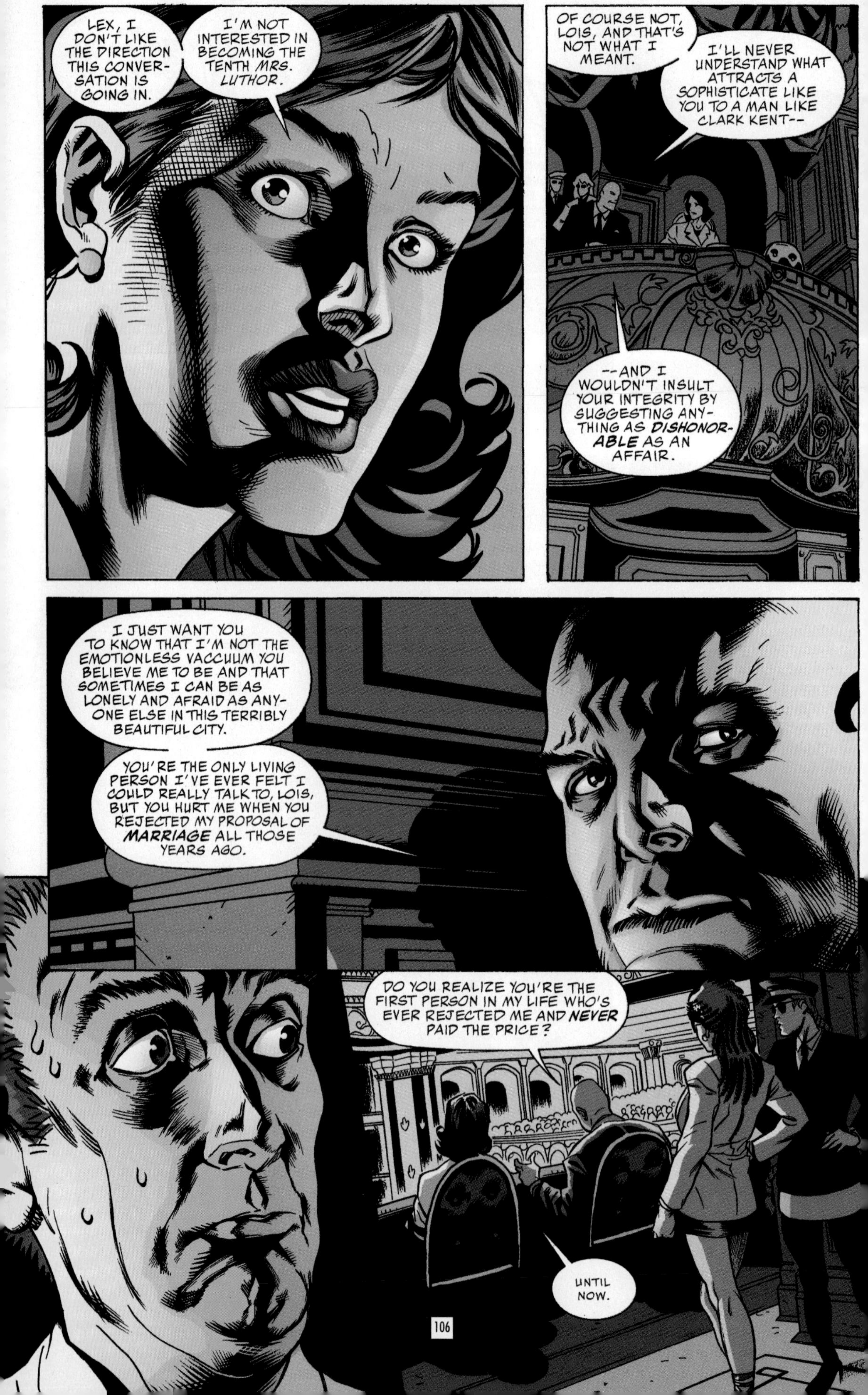
LEX, I DON'T LIKE THE DIRECTION THIS CONVERSATION IS GOING IN.
I'M NOT INTERESTED IN BECOMING THE TENTH *MRS. LUTHOR*.
OF COURSE NOT, LOIS, AND THAT'S NOT WHAT I MEANT.
I'LL NEVER UNDERSTAND WHAT ATTRACTS A SOPHISTICATE LIKE YOU TO A MAN LIKE CLARK KENT--
--AND I WOULDN'T INSULT YOUR INTEGRITY BY SUGGESTING ANYTHING AS ***DISHONORABLE*** AS AN AFFAIR.
I JUST WANT YOU TO KNOW THAT I'M NOT THE EMOTIONLESS VACCUUM YOU BELIEVE ME TO BE AND THAT SOMETIMES I CAN BE AS LONELY AND AFRAID AS ANYONE ELSE IN THIS TERRIBLY BEAUTIFUL CITY.
YOU'RE THE ONLY LIVING PERSON I'VE EVER FELT I COULD REALLY TALK TO, LOIS, BUT YOU HURT ME WHEN YOU REJECTED MY PROPOSAL OF ***MARRIAGE*** ALL THOSE YEARS AGO.
DO YOU REALIZE YOU'RE THE FIRST PERSON IN MY LIFE WHO'S EVER REJECTED ME AND ***NEVER*** PAID THE PRICE?
UNTIL NOW.

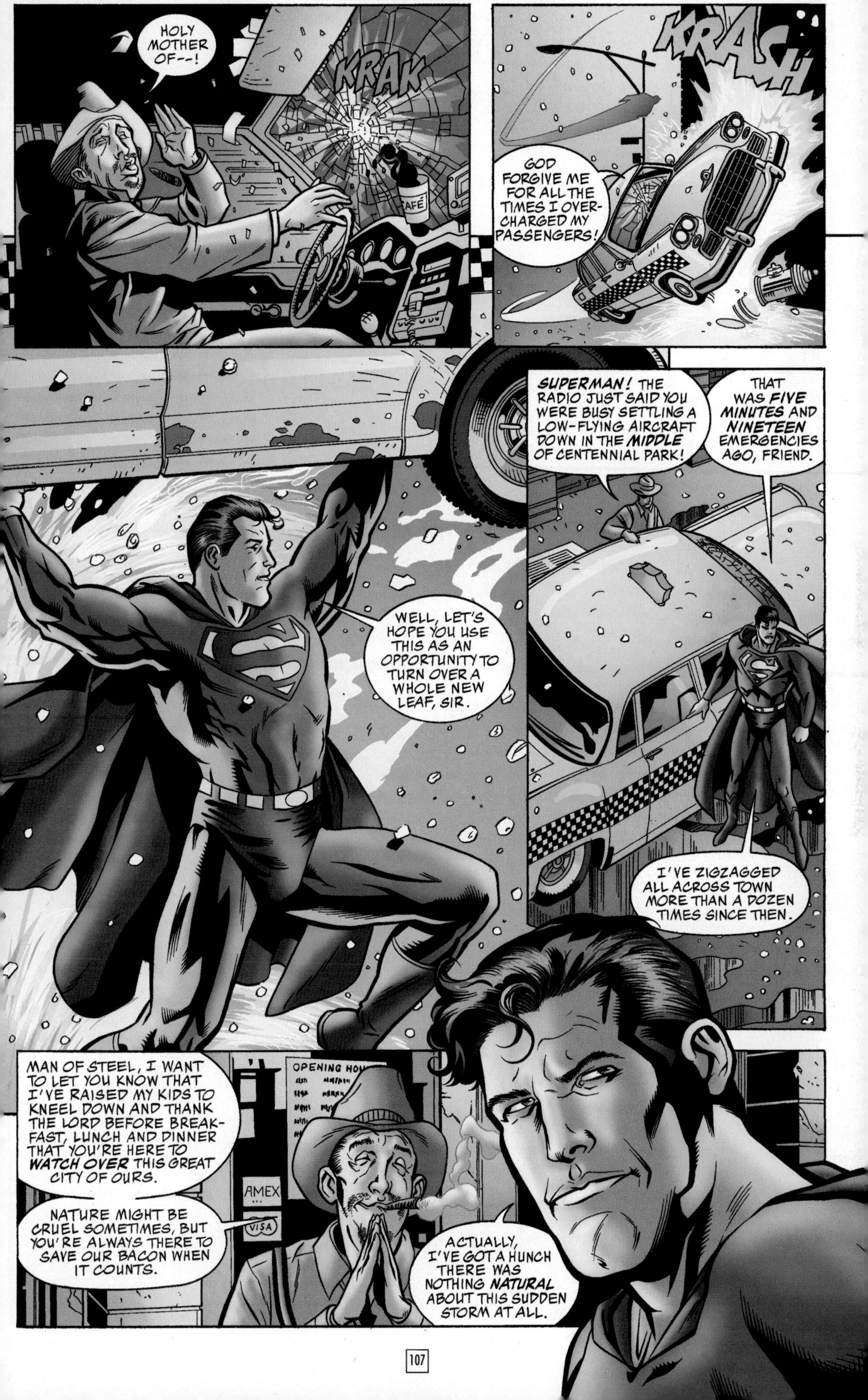

HOLY MOTHER OF--!
KRAK
KRASH
GOD FORGIVE ME FOR ALL THE TIMES I OVER-CHARGED MY PASSENGERS!
CAFÉ
WELL, LET'S HOPE YOU USE THIS AS AN OPPORTUNITY TO TURN OVER A WHOLE NEW LEAF, SIR.
SUPERMAN! THE RADIO JUST SAID YOU WERE BUSY SETTLING A LOW-FLYING AIRCRAFT DOWN IN THE MIDDLE OF CENTENNIAL PARK!
THAT WAS FIVE MINUTES AND NINETEEN EMERGENCIES AGO, FRIEND.
I'VE ZIGZAGGED ALL ACROSS TOWN MORE THAN A DOZEN TIMES SINCE THEN.
MAN OF STEEL, I WANT TO LET YOU KNOW THAT I'VE RAISED MY KIDS TO KNEEL DOWN AND THANK THE LORD BEFORE BREAK-FAST, LUNCH AND DINNER THAT YOU'RE HERE TO WATCH OVER THIS GREAT CITY OF OURS.
NATURE MIGHT BE CRUEL SOMETIMES, BUT YOU'RE ALWAYS THERE TO SAVE OUR BACON WHEN IT COUNTS.
OPENING HOU
AMEX
VISA
ACTUALLY, I'VE GOT A HUNCH THERE WAS NOTHING NATURAL ABOUT THIS SUDDEN STORM AT ALL.

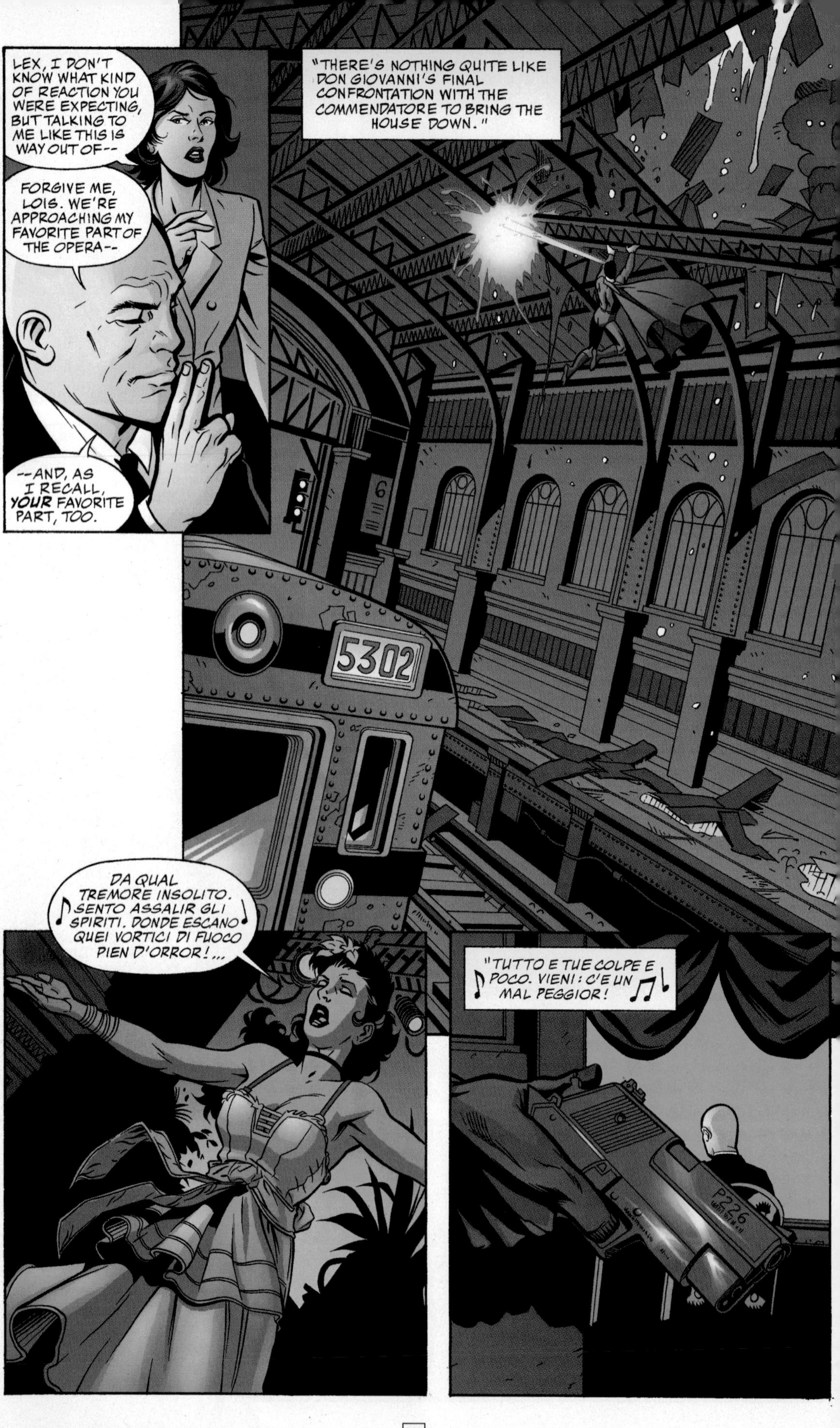

LEX, I DON'T KNOW WHAT KIND OF REACTION YOU WERE EXPECTING, BUT TALKING TO ME LIKE THIS IS WAY OUT OF--
FORGIVE ME, LOIS. WE'RE APPROACHING MY FAVORITE PART OF THE OPERA--
--AND, AS I RECALL, ***YOUR*** FAVORITE PART, TOO.
"THERE'S NOTHING QUITE LIKE DON GIOVANNI'S FINAL CONFRONTATION WITH THE COMMENDATORE TO BRING THE HOUSE DOWN."
5302
DA QUAL TREMORE INSOLITO. SENTO ASSALIR GLI SPIRITI. DONDE ESCANO QUEI VORTICI DI FUOCO PIEN D'ORROR!...
"TUTTO E TUE COLPE E POCO. VIENI: C'E UN MAL PEGGIOR!
P226

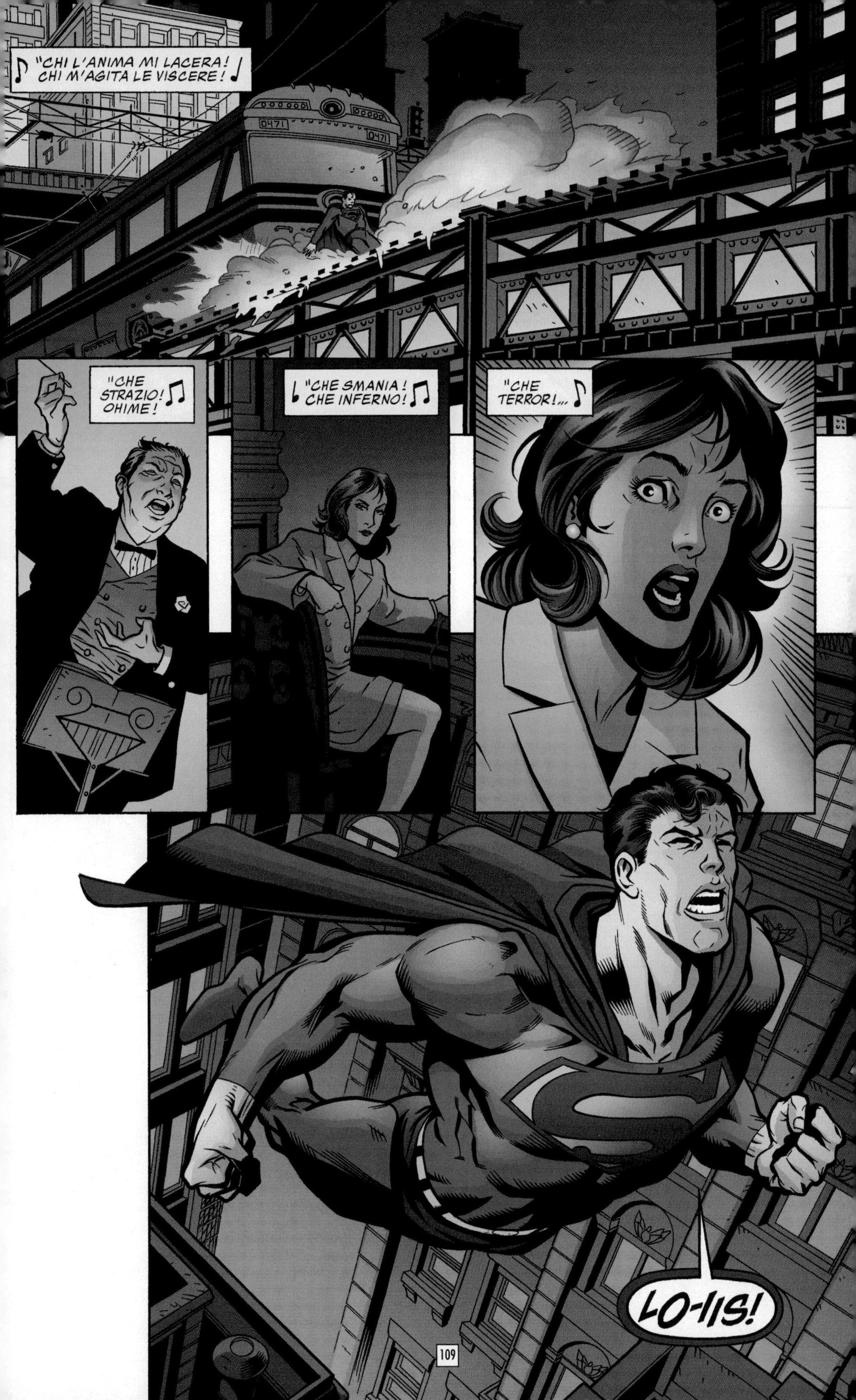
"CHI L'ANIMA MI LACERA! CHI M'AGITA LE VISCERE!
"CHE STRAZIO! OHIME!
"CHE SMANIA! CHE INFERNO!
"CHE TERROR!...
LO-IIS!

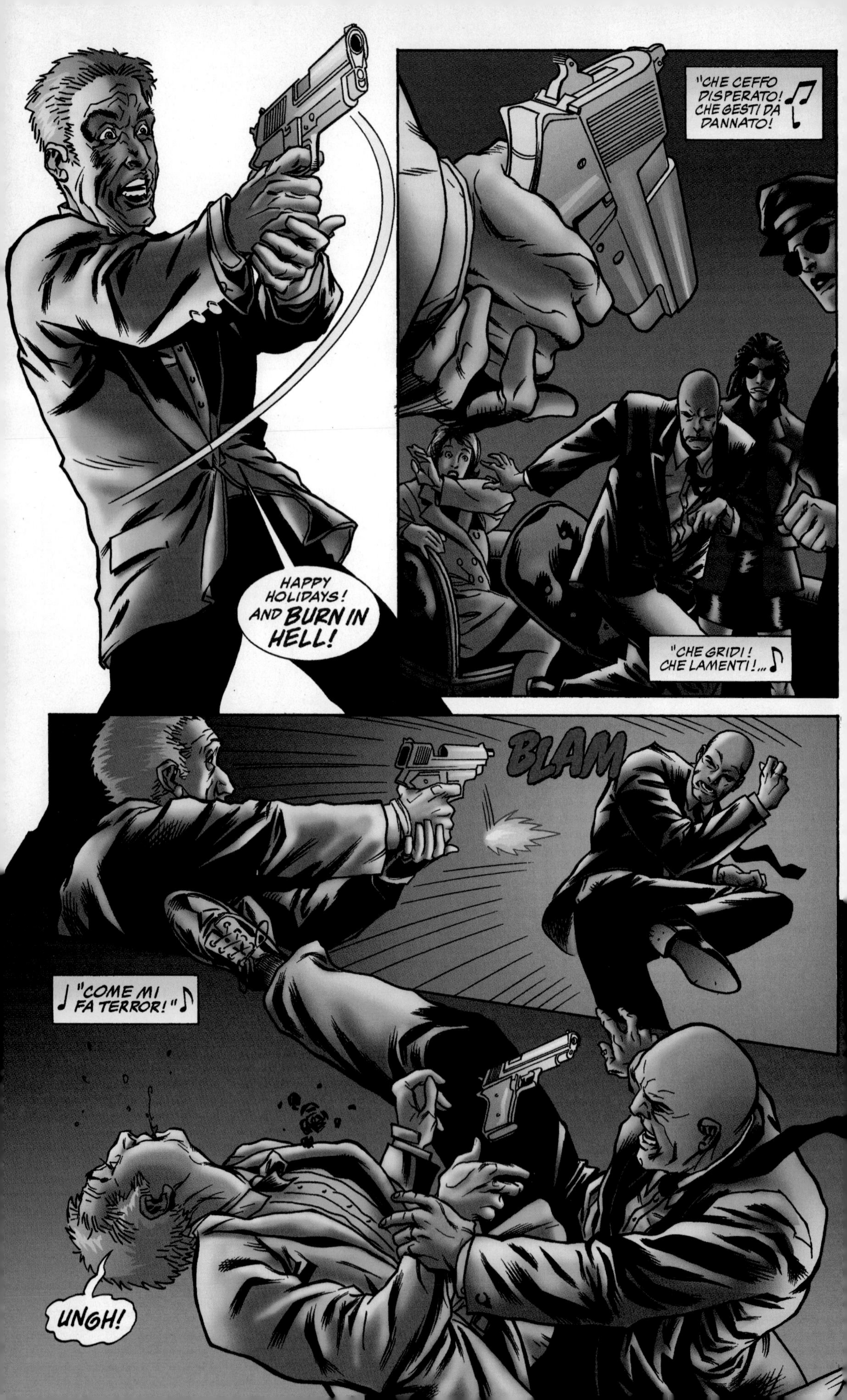
HAPPY HOLIDAYS! AND BURN IN HELL!
"CHE CEFFO DISPERATO! CHE GESTI DA DANNATO!
"CHE GRIDI! CHE LAMENTI!...
BLAM
"COME MI FA TERROR!"
UNGH!

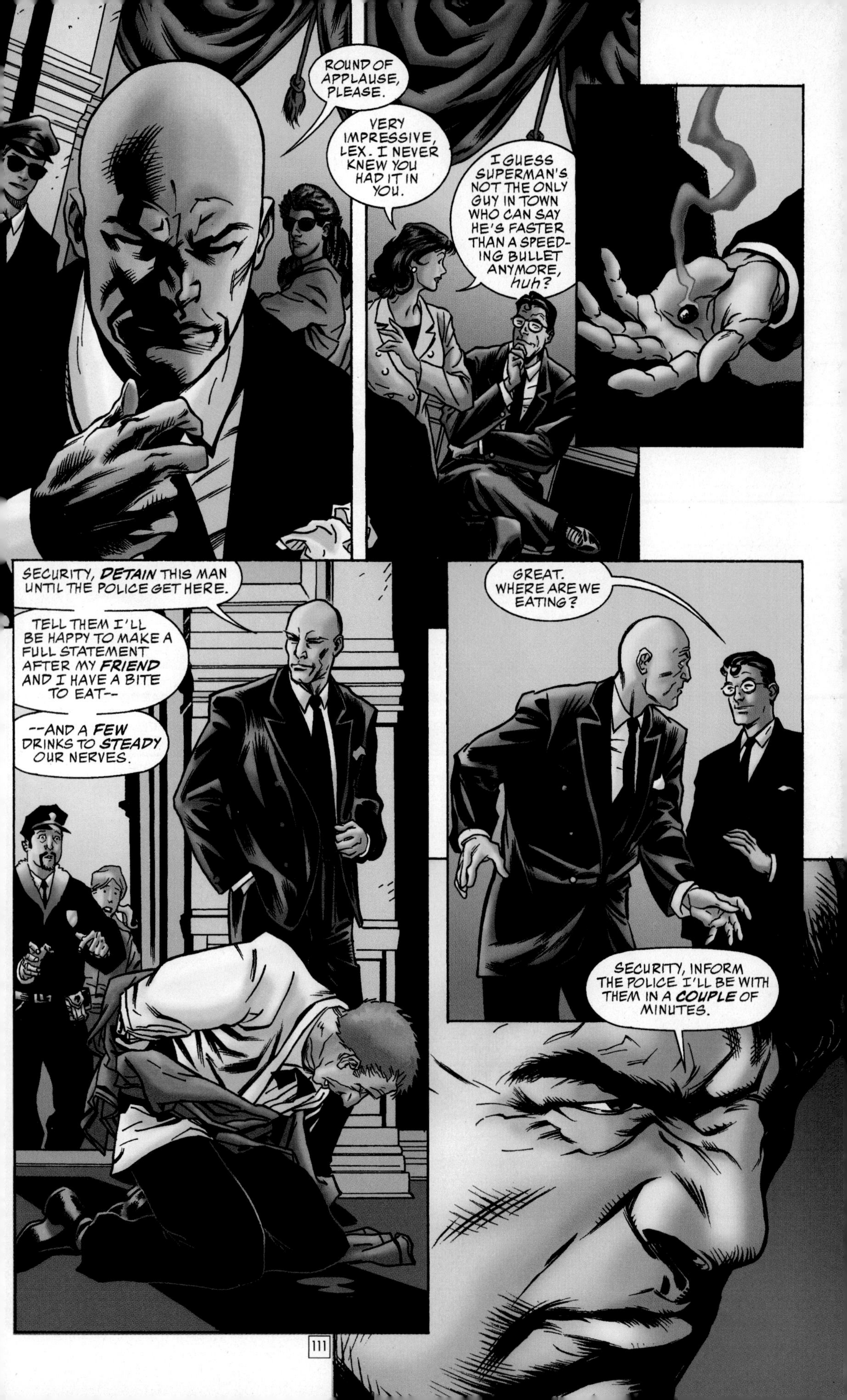
ROUND OF APPLAUSE, PLEASE.
VERY IMPRESSIVE, LEX. I NEVER KNEW YOU HAD IT IN YOU.
I GUESS SUPERMAN'S NOT THE ONLY GUY IN TOWN WHO CAN SAY HE'S FASTER THAN A SPEEDING BULLET ANYMORE, *huh?*
SECURITY, ***DETAIN*** THIS MAN UNTIL THE POLICE GET HERE.
TELL THEM I'LL BE HAPPY TO MAKE A FULL STATEMENT AFTER MY ***FRIEND*** AND I HAVE A BITE TO EAT--
--AND A ***FEW*** DRINKS TO ***STEADY*** OUR NERVES.
GREAT. WHERE ARE WE EATING?
SECURITY, INFORM THE POLICE I'LL BE WITH THEM IN A ***COUPLE*** OF MINUTES.

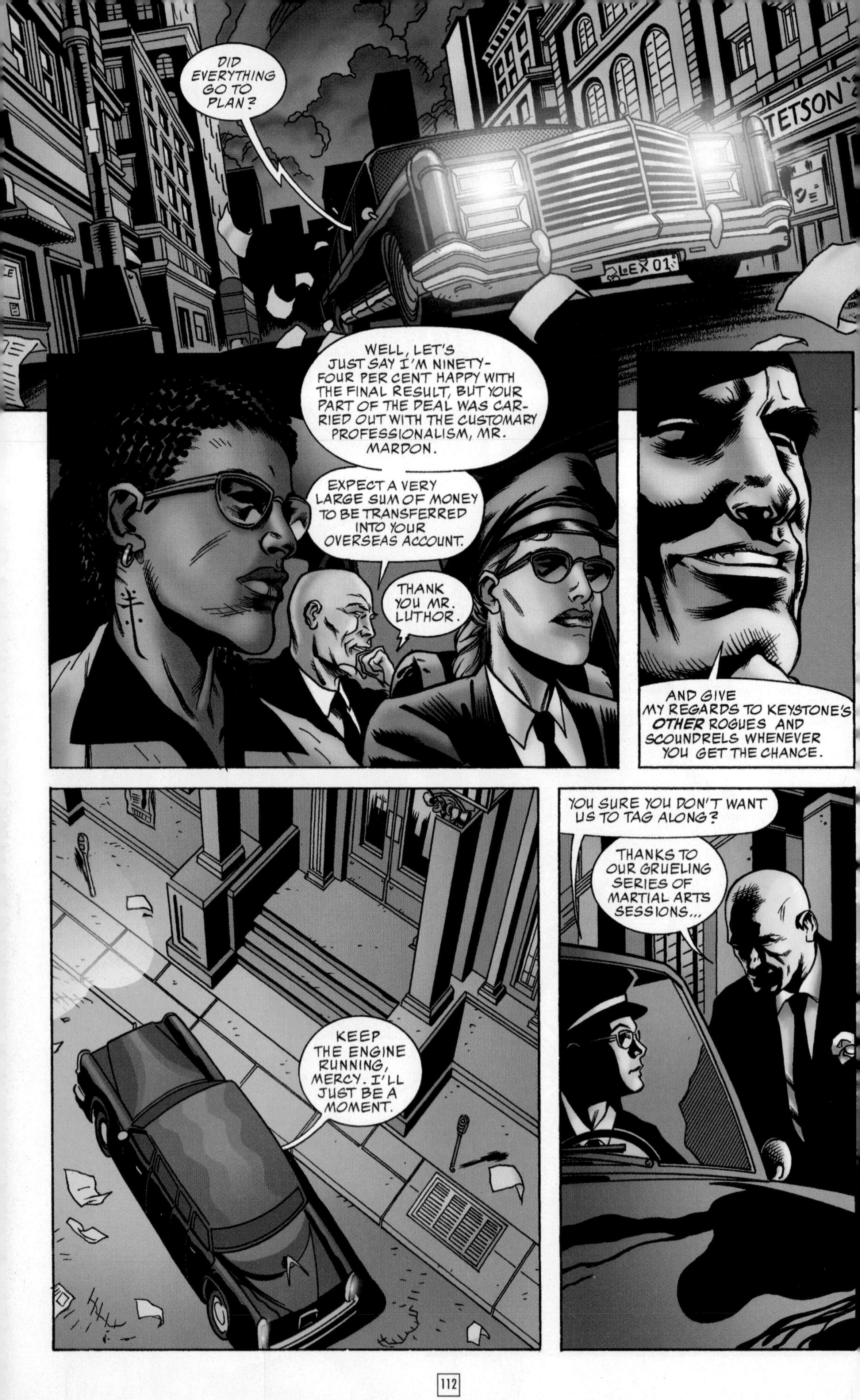
DID EVERYTHING GO TO PLAN?
TETSON
LEX 01
WELL, LET'S JUST SAY I'M NINETY-FOUR PER CENT HAPPY WITH THE FINAL RESULT, BUT YOUR PART OF THE DEAL WAS CARRIED OUT WITH THE CUSTOMARY PROFESSIONALISM, MR. MARDON.
EXPECT A VERY LARGE SUM OF MONEY TO BE TRANSFERRED INTO YOUR OVERSEAS ACCOUNT.
THANK YOU MR. LUTHOR.
AND GIVE MY REGARDS TO KEYSTONE'S OTHER ROGUES AND SCOUNDRELS WHENEVER YOU GET THE CHANCE.
KEEP THE ENGINE RUNNING, MERCY. I'LL JUST BE A MOMENT.
YOU SURE YOU DON'T WANT US TO TAG ALONG?
THANKS TO OUR GRUELING SERIES OF MARTIAL ARTS SESSIONS...

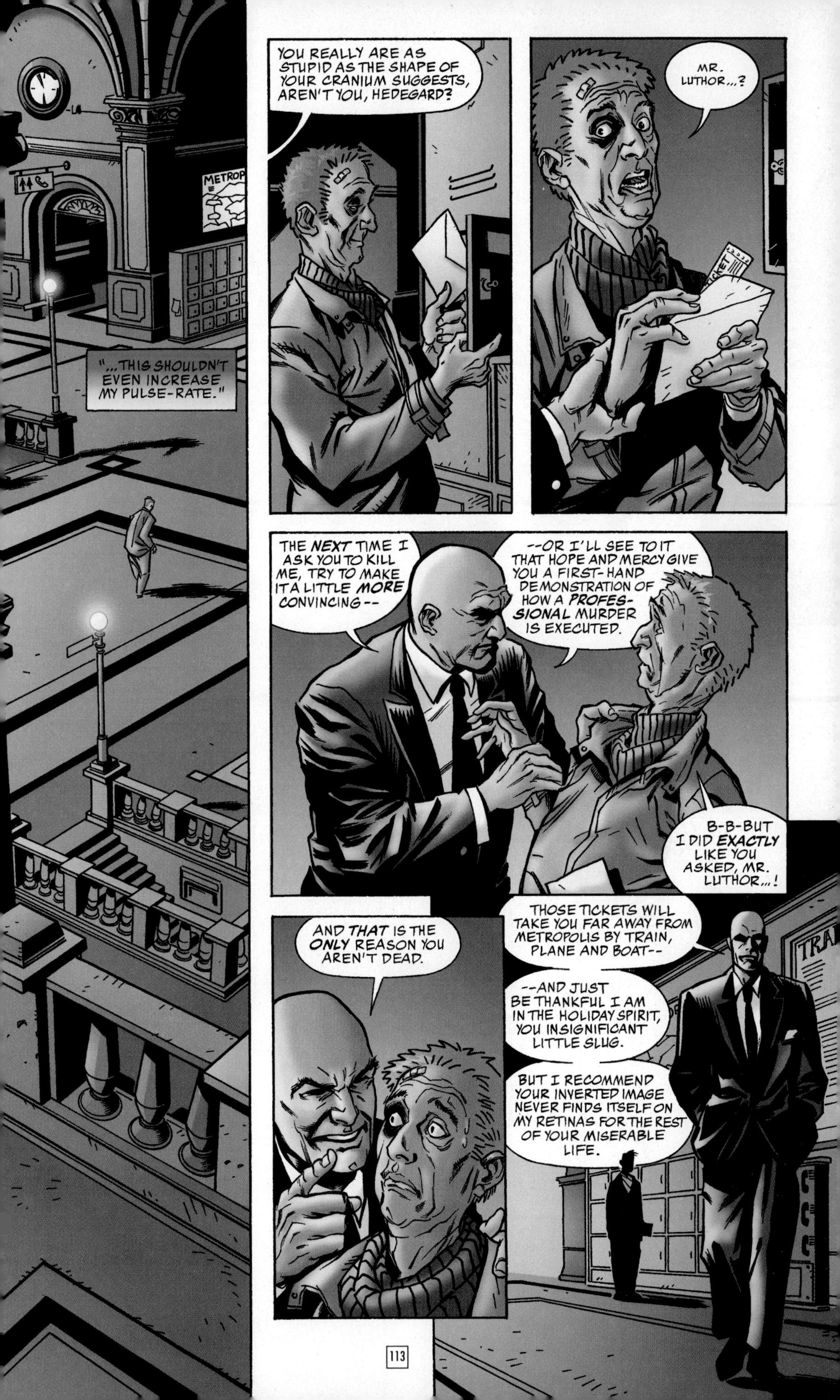
"...THIS SHOULDN'T EVEN INCREASE MY PULSE-RATE."
METROP
YOU REALLY ARE AS STUPID AS THE SHAPE OF YOUR CRANIUM SUGGESTS, AREN'T YOU, HEDEGARD?
MR. LUTHOR...?
TICKET
THE NEXT TIME I ASK YOU TO KILL ME, TRY TO MAKE IT A LITTLE MORE CONVINCING--
--OR I'LL SEE TO IT THAT HOPE AND MERCY GIVE YOU A FIRST-HAND DEMONSTRATION OF HOW A PROFESSIONAL MURDER IS EXECUTED.
B-B-BUT I DID EXACTLY LIKE YOU ASKED, MR. LUTHOR...!
AND THAT IS THE ONLY REASON YOU AREN'T DEAD.
THOSE TICKETS WILL TAKE YOU FAR AWAY FROM METROPOLIS BY TRAIN, PLANE AND BOAT--
--AND JUST BE THANKFUL I AM IN THE HOLIDAY SPIRIT, YOU INSIGNIFICANT LITTLE SLUG.
BUT I RECOMMEND YOUR INVERTED IMAGE NEVER FINDS ITSELF ON MY RETINAS FOR THE REST OF YOUR MISERABLE LIFE.

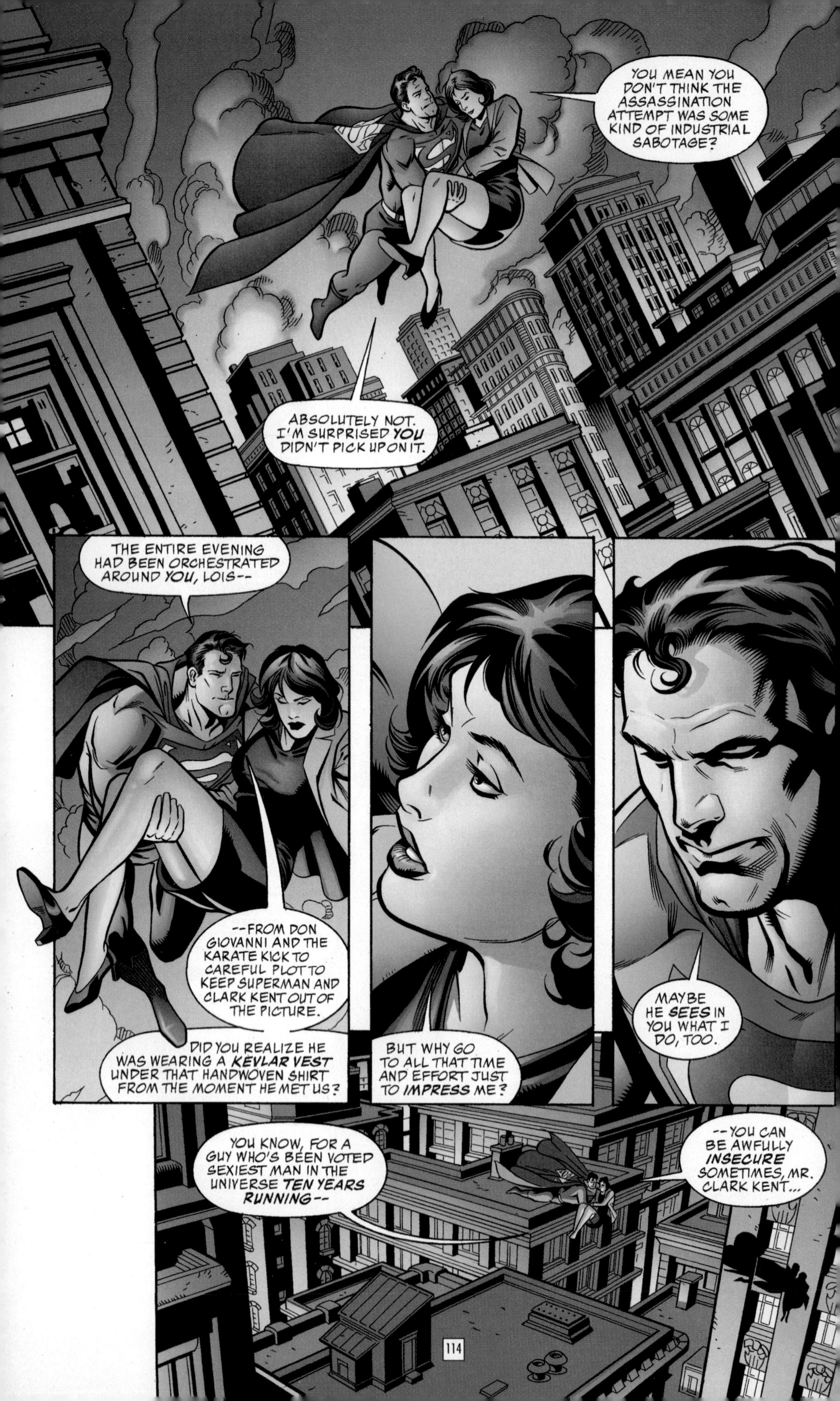
YOU MEAN YOU DON'T THINK THE ASSASSINATION ATTEMPT WAS SOME KIND OF INDUSTRIAL SABOTAGE?
ABSOLUTELY NOT. I'M SURPRISED YOU DIDN'T PICK UP ON IT.
THE ENTIRE EVENING HAD BEEN ORCHESTRATED AROUND YOU, LOIS--
--FROM DON GIOVANNI AND THE KARATE KICK TO CAREFUL PLOT TO KEEP SUPERMAN AND CLARK KENT OUT OF THE PICTURE.
DID YOU REALIZE HE WAS WEARING A KEVLAR VEST UNDER THAT HANDWOVEN SHIRT FROM THE MOMENT HE MET US?
BUT WHY GO TO ALL THAT TIME AND EFFORT JUST TO IMPRESS ME?
MAYBE HE SEES IN YOU WHAT I DO, TOO.
YOU KNOW, FOR A GUY WHO'S BEEN VOTED SEXIEST MAN IN THE UNIVERSE TEN YEARS RUNNING--
--YOU CAN BE AWFULLY INSECURE SOMETIMES, MR. CLARK KENT...

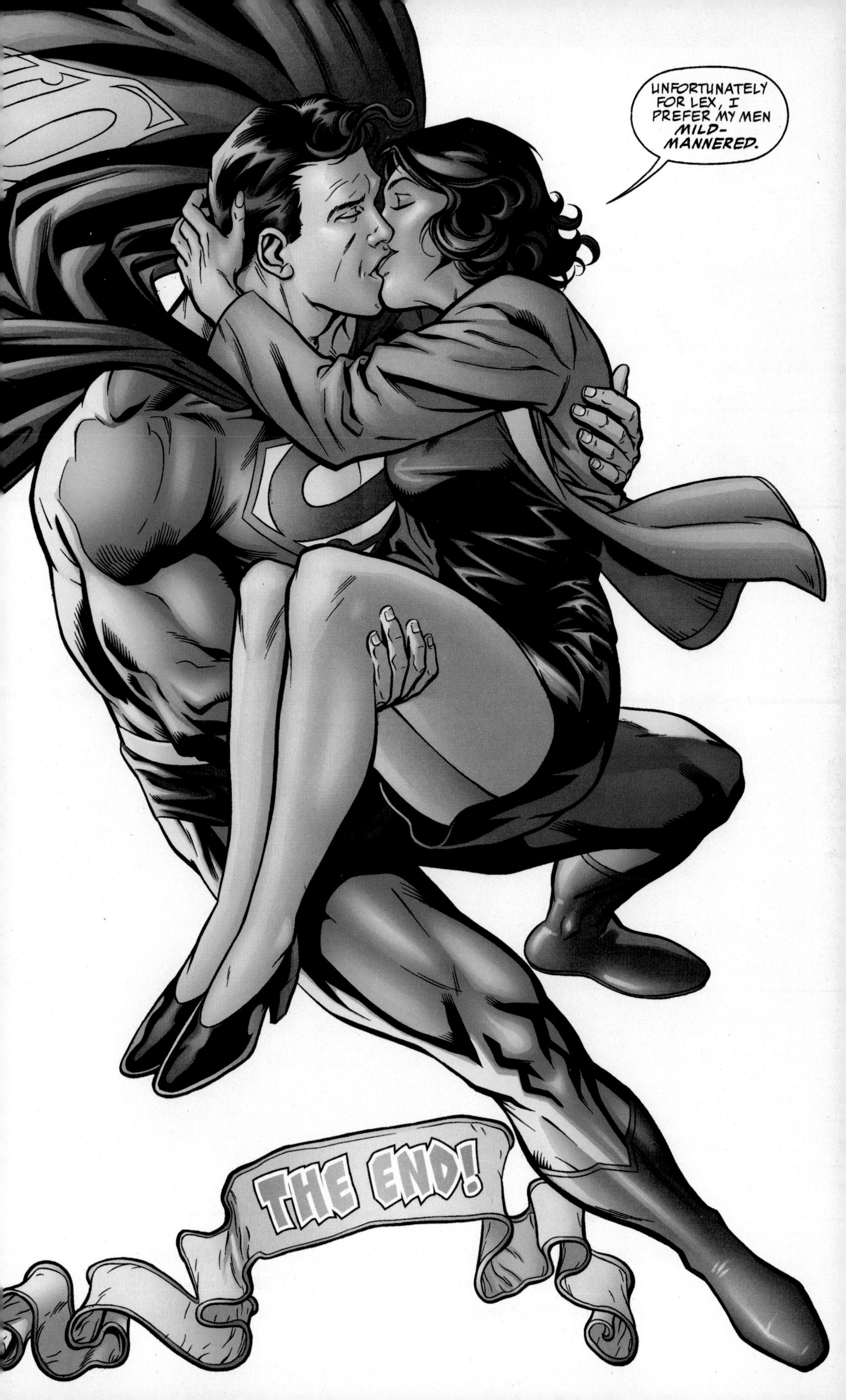
UNFORTUNATELY FOR LEX, I PREFER MY MEN MILD-MANNERED.
THE END!

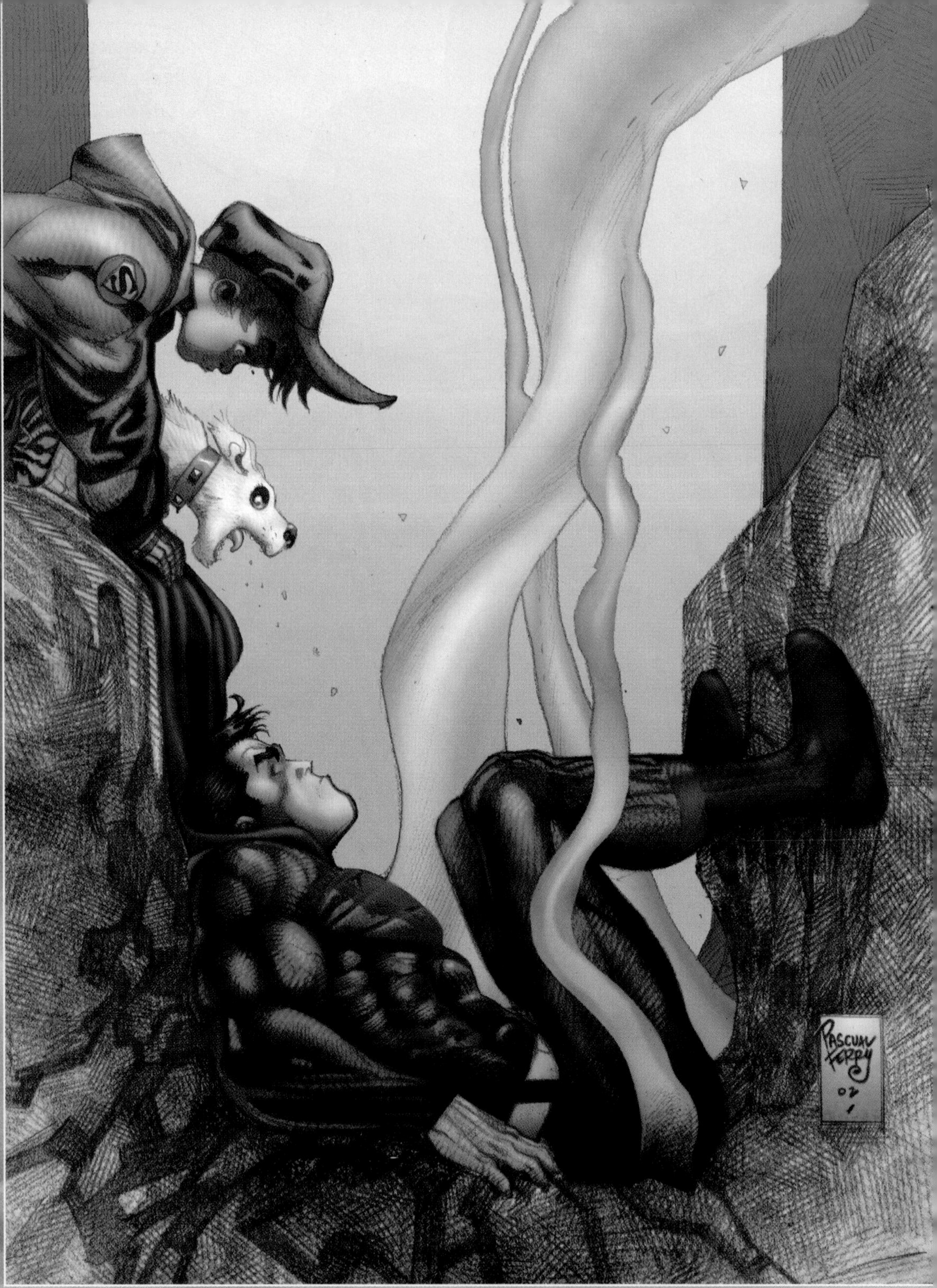
PASCUAL FERRY 02

"The Second Landing"

GEOFF JOHNS writer **BRENT ANDERSON** penciller **RAY SNYDER** inker
TANYA & RICHARD HORIE colorists **COMICRAFT** letterer
PASCUAL FERRY WITH TANYA & RICHARD HORIE cover artists

From the pages of the SUPERMAN comic...
What's more American than baseball and Superman?

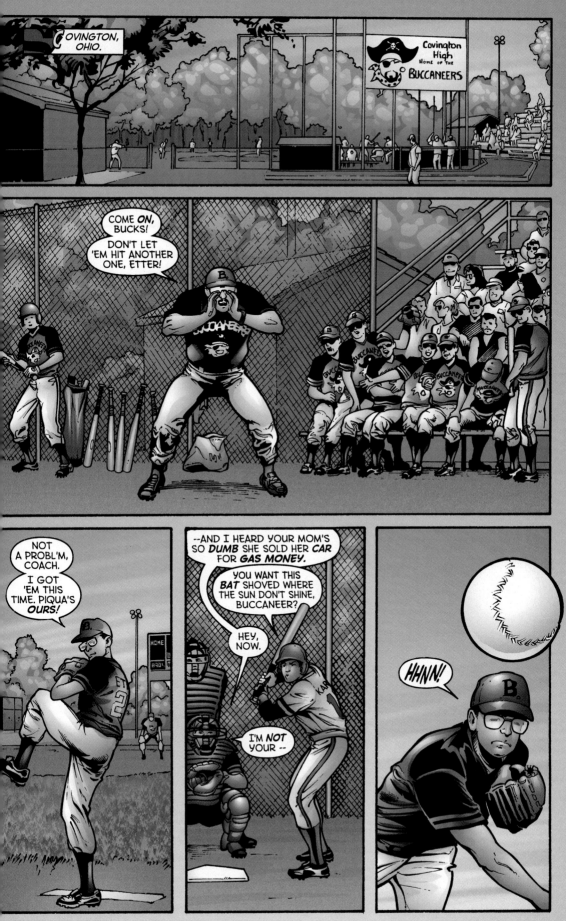

COVINGTON, OHIO.

Covington High
HOME OF THE
BUCCANEERS

COME ON, BUCKS!

DON'T LET 'EM HIT ANOTHER ONE, ETTER!

NOT A PROBL'M, COACH.

I GOT 'EM THIS TIME. PIQUA'S OURS!

--AND I HEARD YOUR MOM'S SO DUMB SHE SOLD HER CAR FOR GAS MONEY.

YOU WANT THIS BAT SHOVED WHERE THE SUN DON'T SHINE, BUCCANEER?

HEY, NOW.

I'M NOT YOUR --

HHNN!

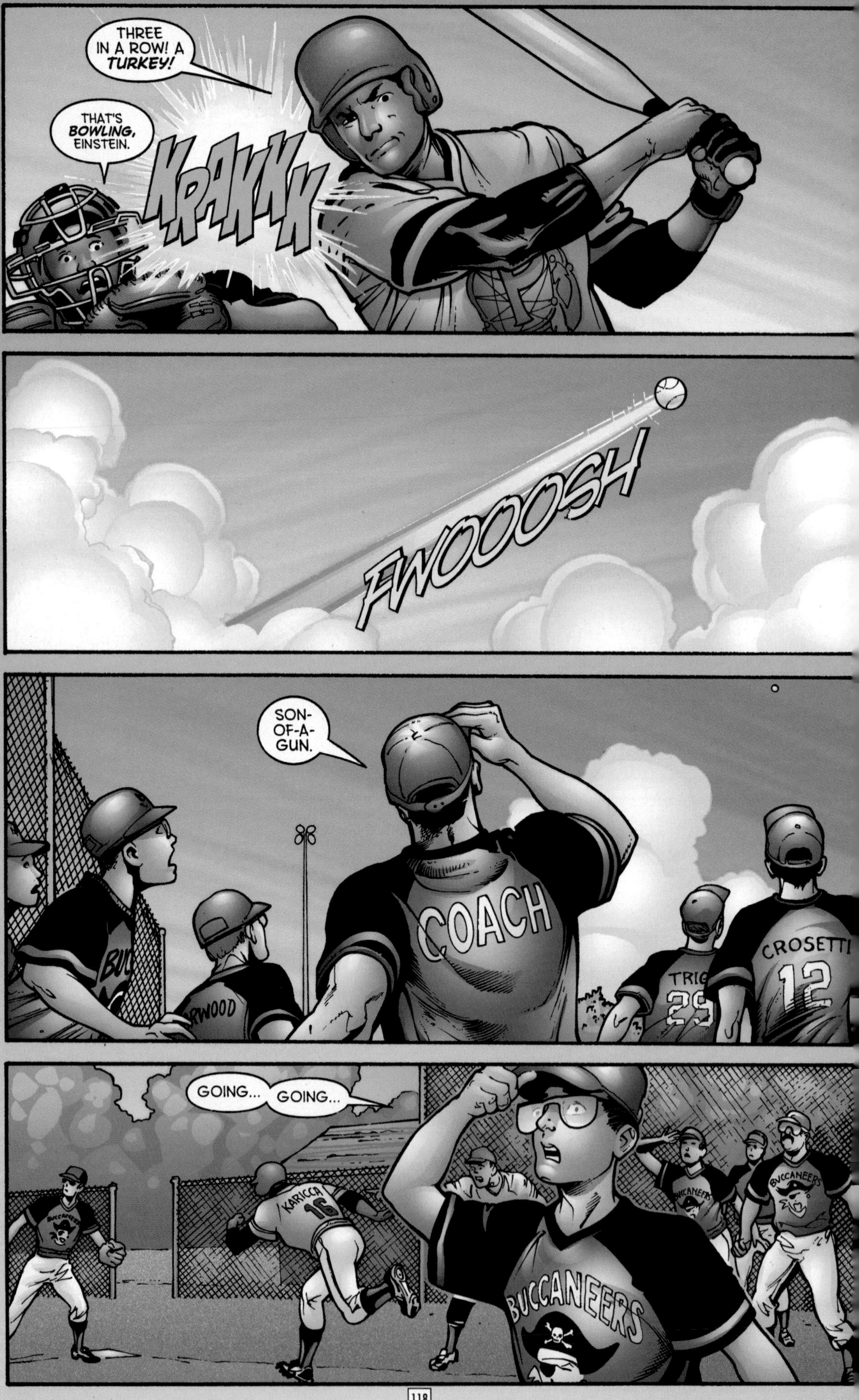
THREE IN A ROW! A *TURKEY!*
THAT'S *BOWLING,* EINSTEIN.
KRAKKK
FWOOOSH
SON-OF-A-GUN.
COACH
RWOOD
TRIG 29
CROSETTI 12
GOING...
GOING...
KARICCA 16
BUCCANEERS

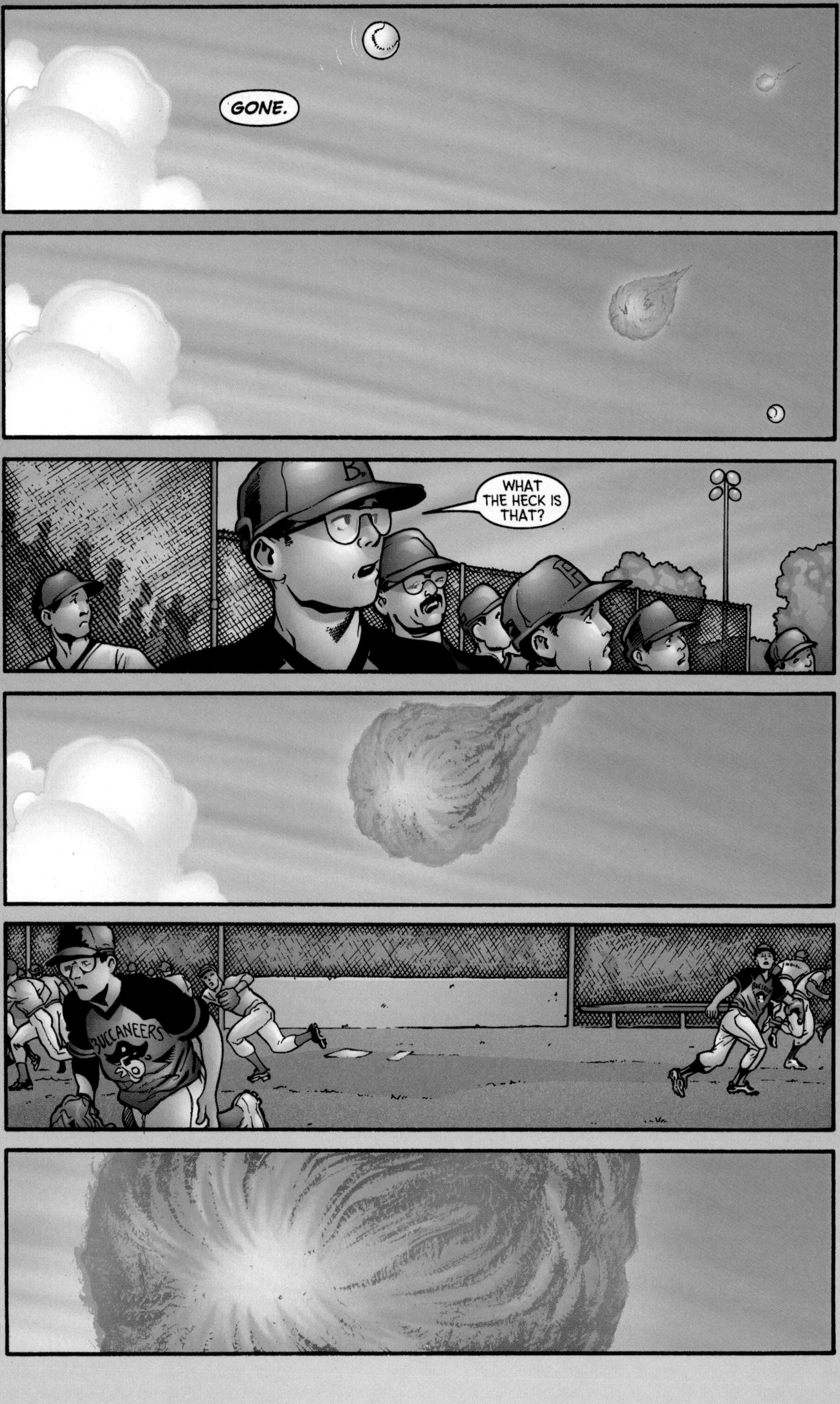
GONE.
WHAT THE HECK IS THAT?
BUCCANEERS

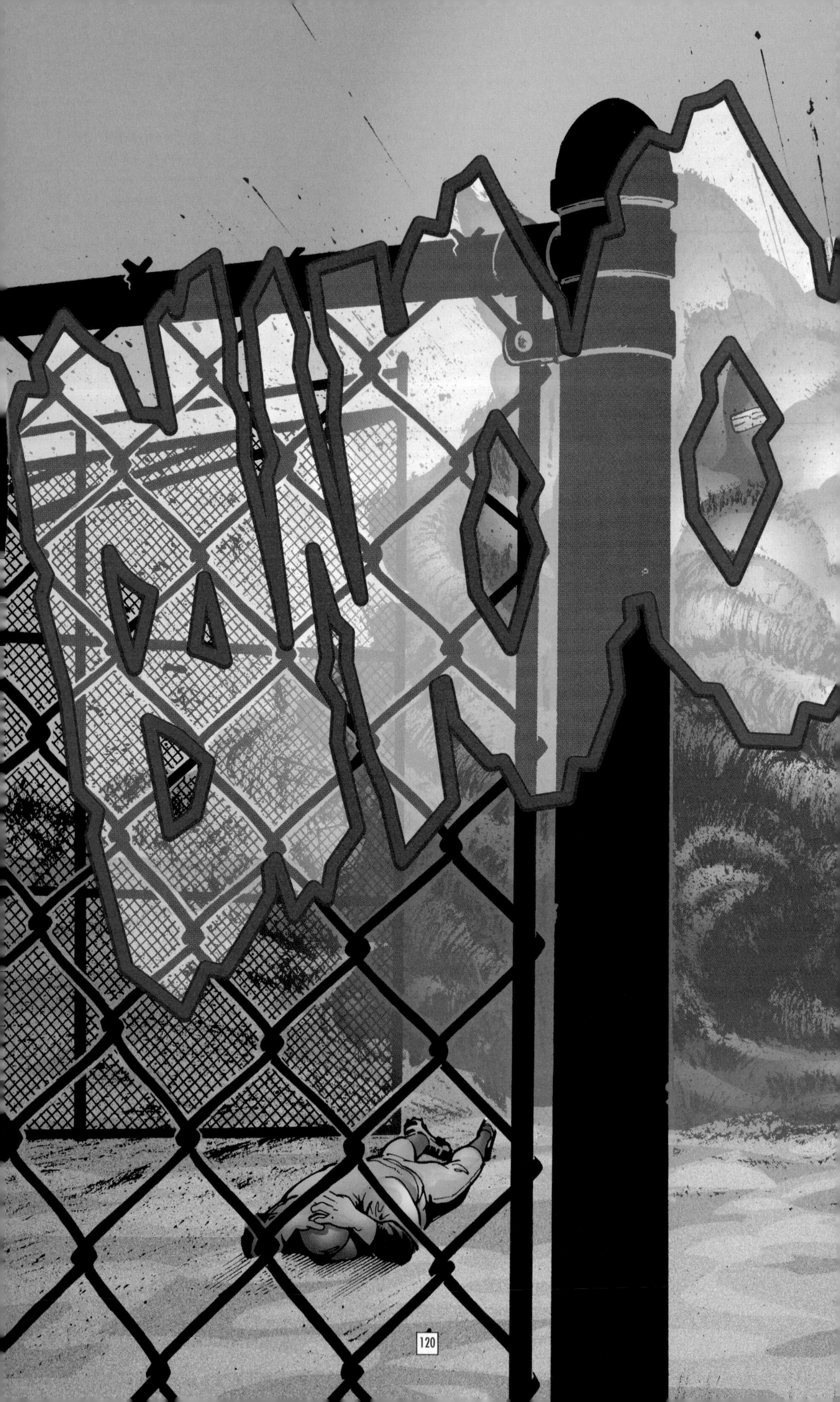

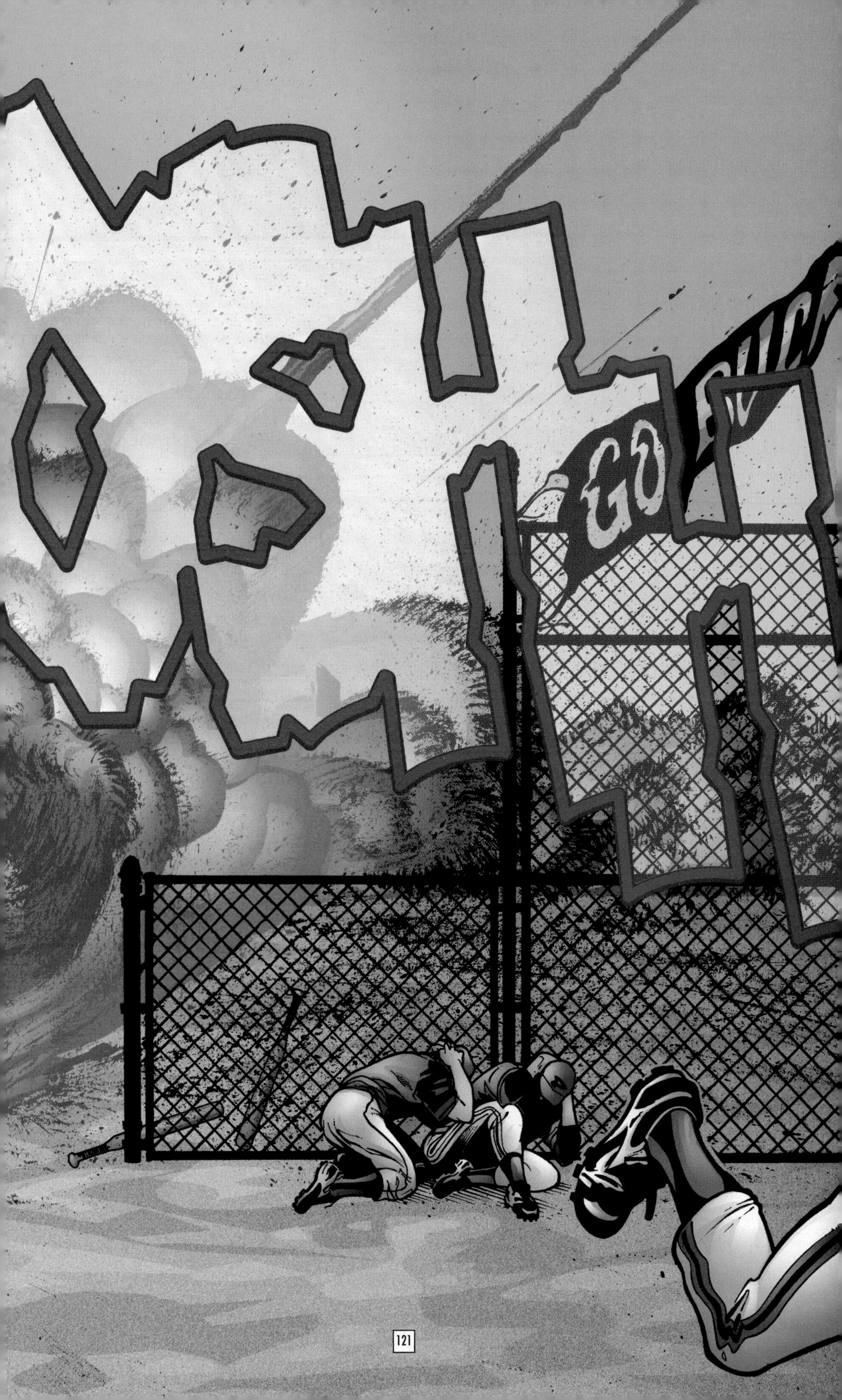
GO

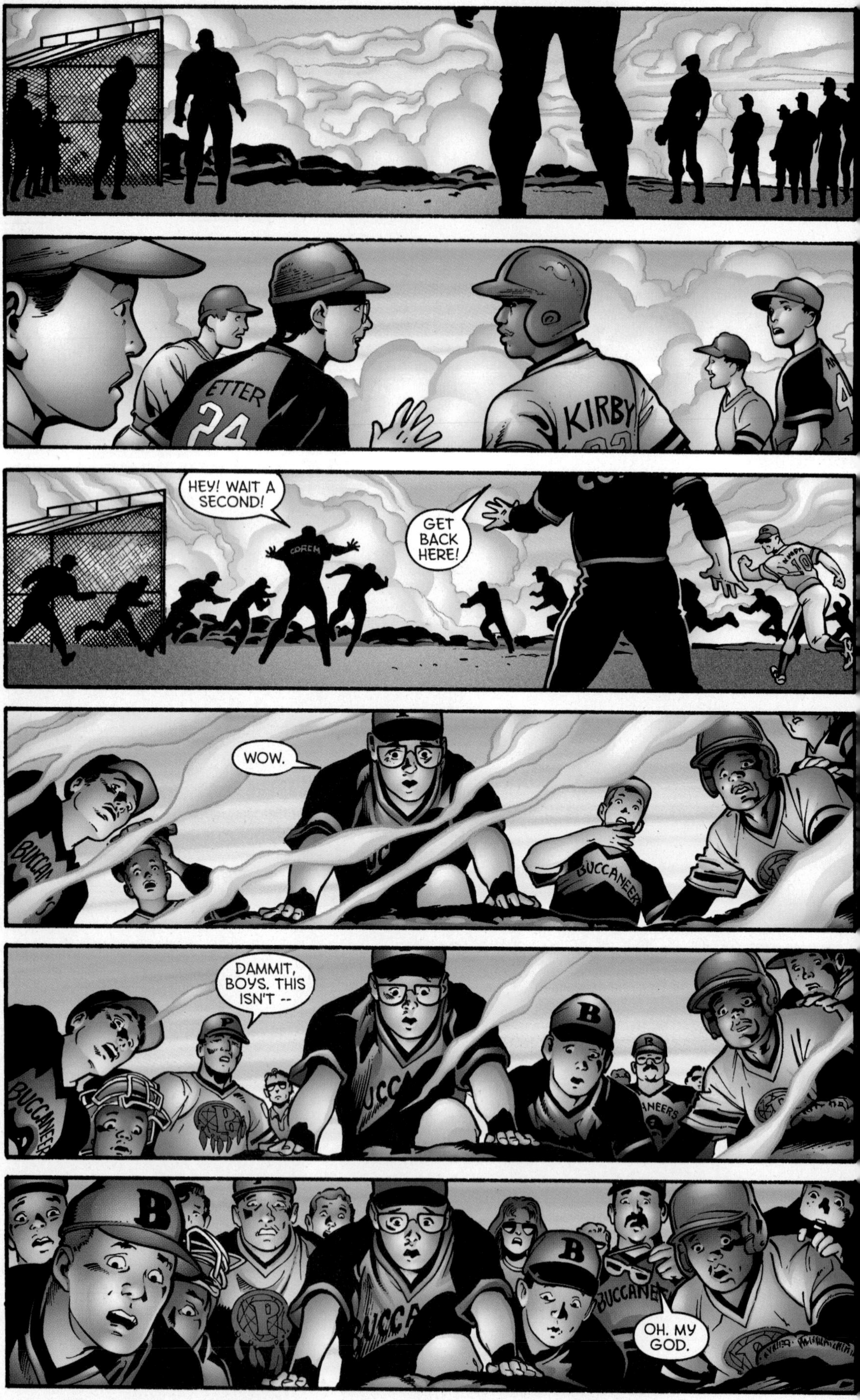
ETTER
24
KIRBY
HEY! WAIT A SECOND!
COACH
GET BACK HERE!
WOW.
BUCCANEER
DAMMIT, BOYS. THIS ISN'T --
BUCCANEER
OH. MY GOD.

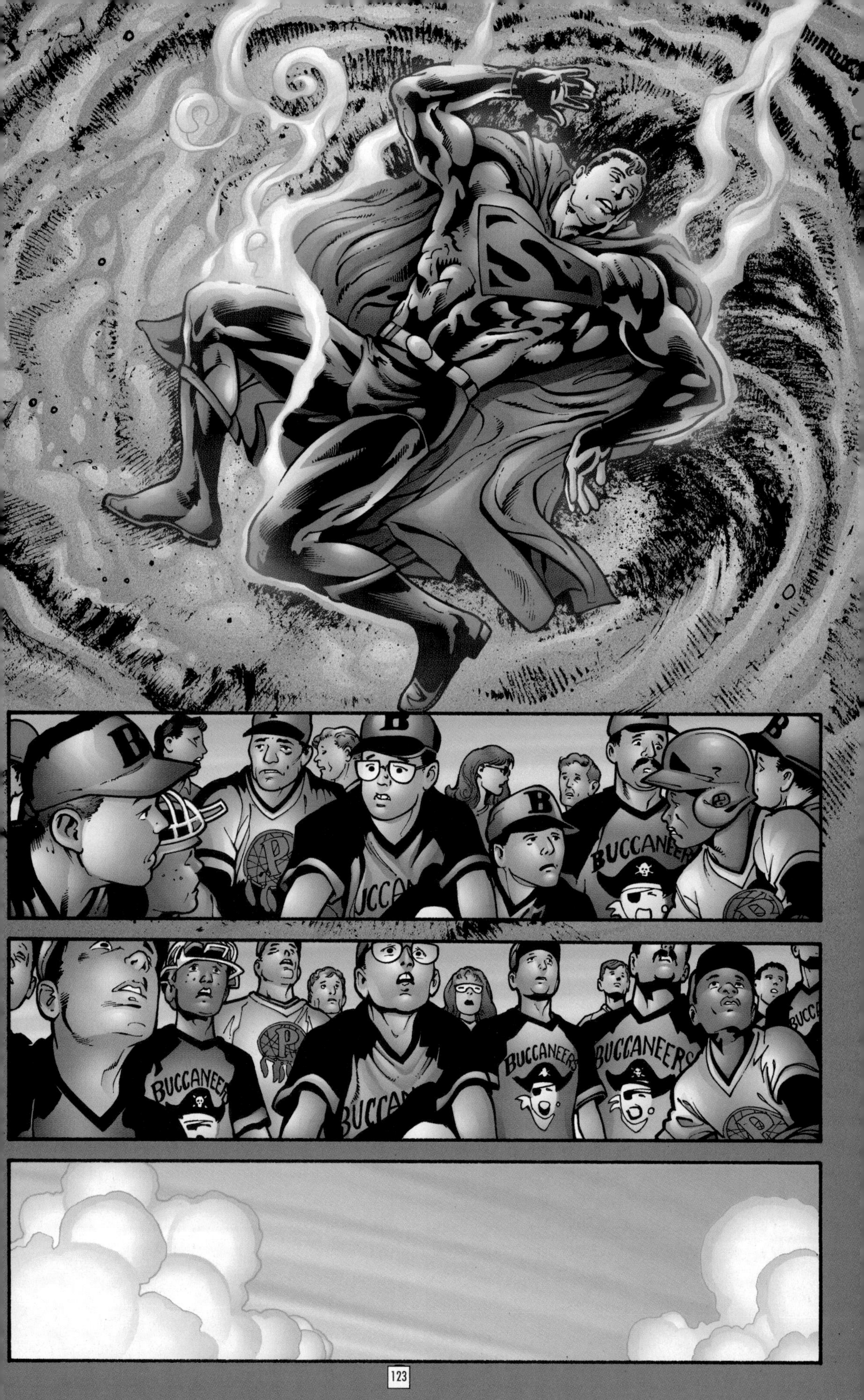
BUCCANEERS
BUCCANEERS
BUCCANEERS

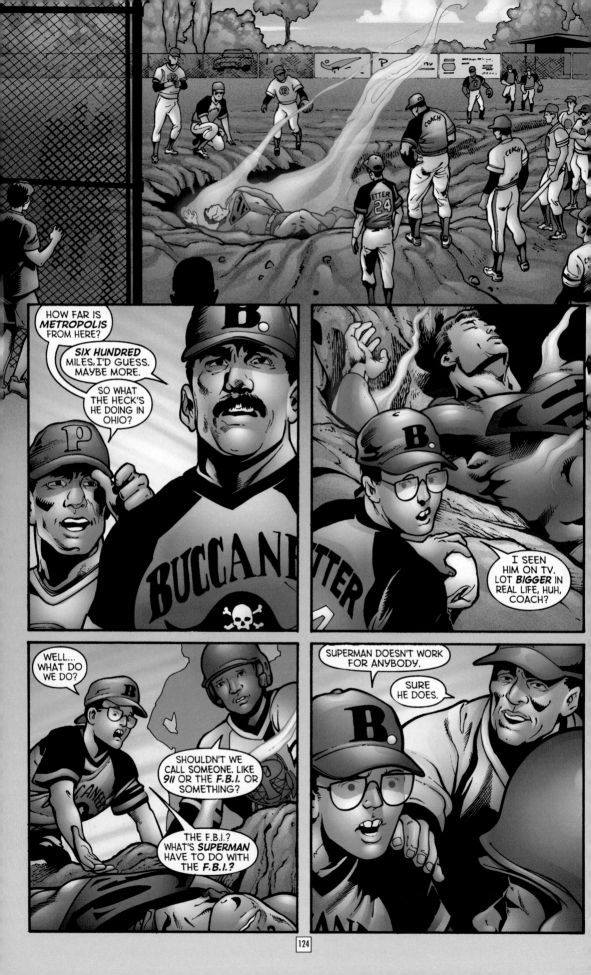

HOW FAR IS *METROPOLIS* FROM HERE?

SIX HUNDRED MILES, I'D GUESS. MAYBE MORE.

SO WHAT THE HECK'S HE DOING IN OHIO?

I SEEN HIM ON TV. LOT *BIGGER* IN REAL LIFE, HUH, COACH?

WELL... WHAT DO WE DO?

SHOULDN'T WE CALL SOMEONE. LIKE *911* OR THE *F.B.I.* OR SOMETHING?

THE F.B.I.? WHAT'S *SUPERMAN* HAVE TO DO WITH THE *F.B.I.*?

SUPERMAN DOESN'T WORK FOR ANYBODY.

SURE HE DOES.

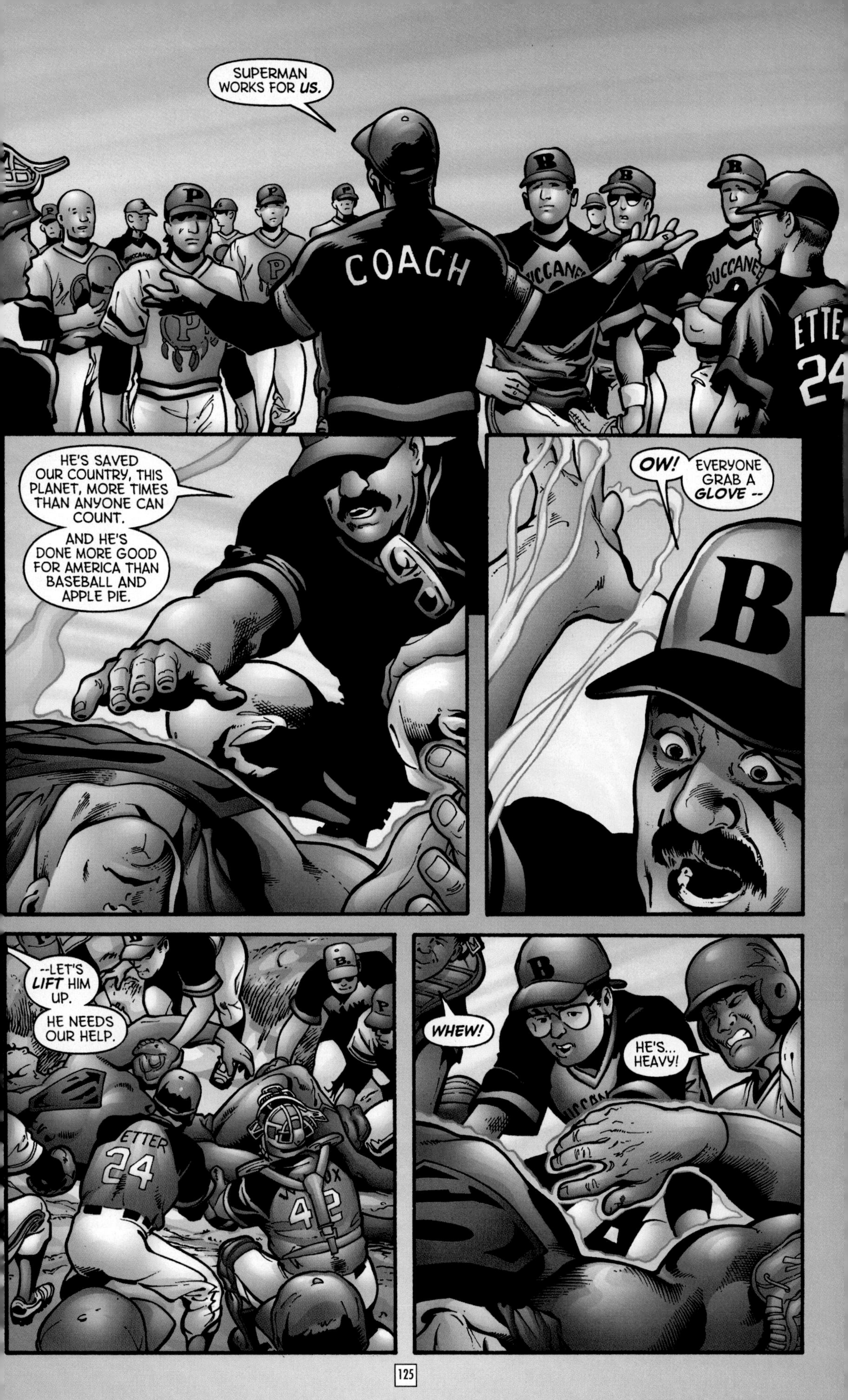

SUPERMAN WORKS FOR *US.*
COACH
HE'S SAVED OUR COUNTRY, THIS PLANET, MORE TIMES THAN ANYONE CAN COUNT.
AND HE'S DONE MORE GOOD FOR AMERICA THAN BASEBALL AND APPLE PIE.
OW!
EVERYONE GRAB A *GLOVE* --
--LET'S *LIFT* HIM UP.
HE NEEDS OUR HELP.
ETTER 24
WHEW!
HE'S... HEAVY!

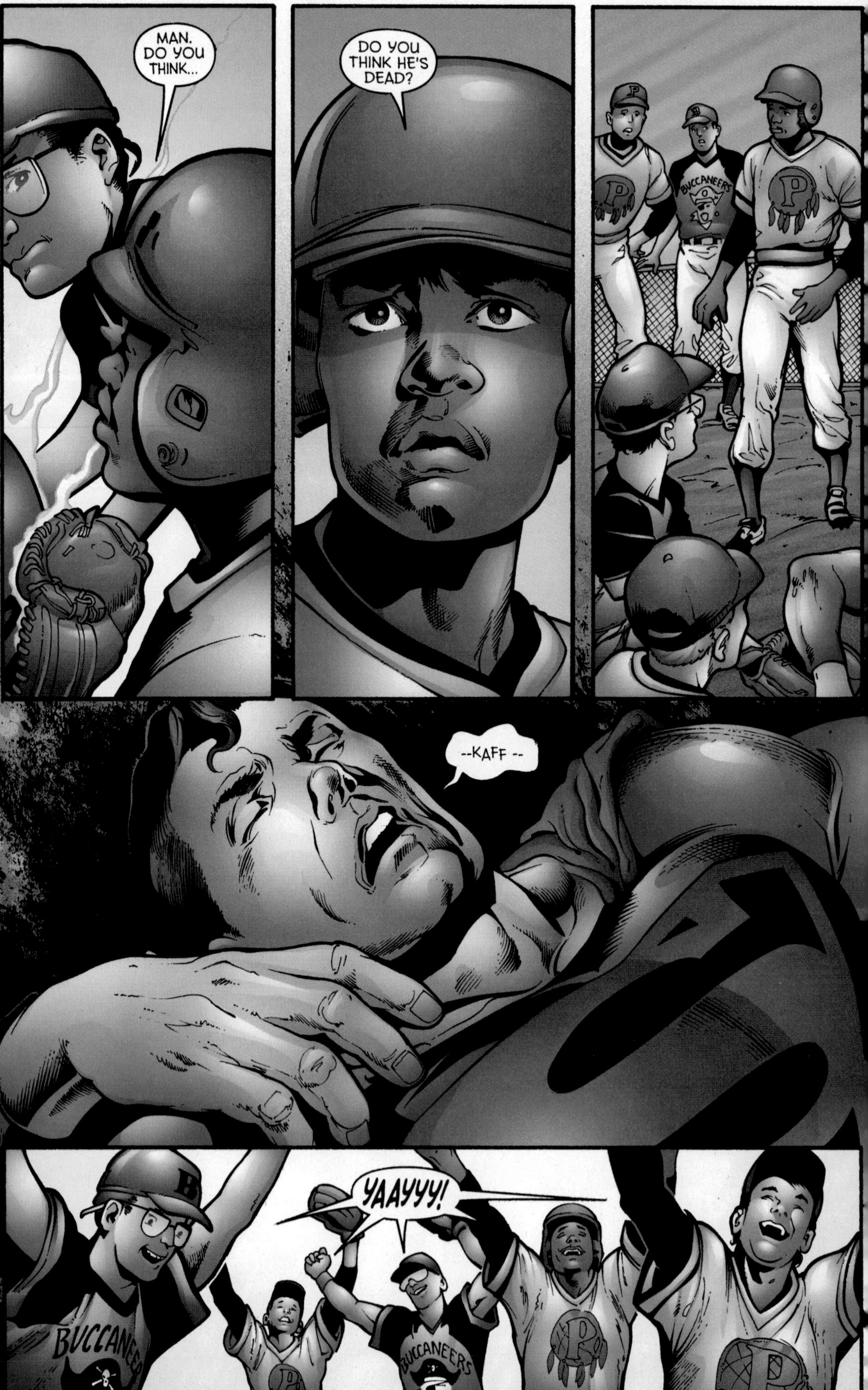
MAN. DO YOU THINK...
DO YOU THINK HE'S DEAD?
--KAFF --
YAAYYY!

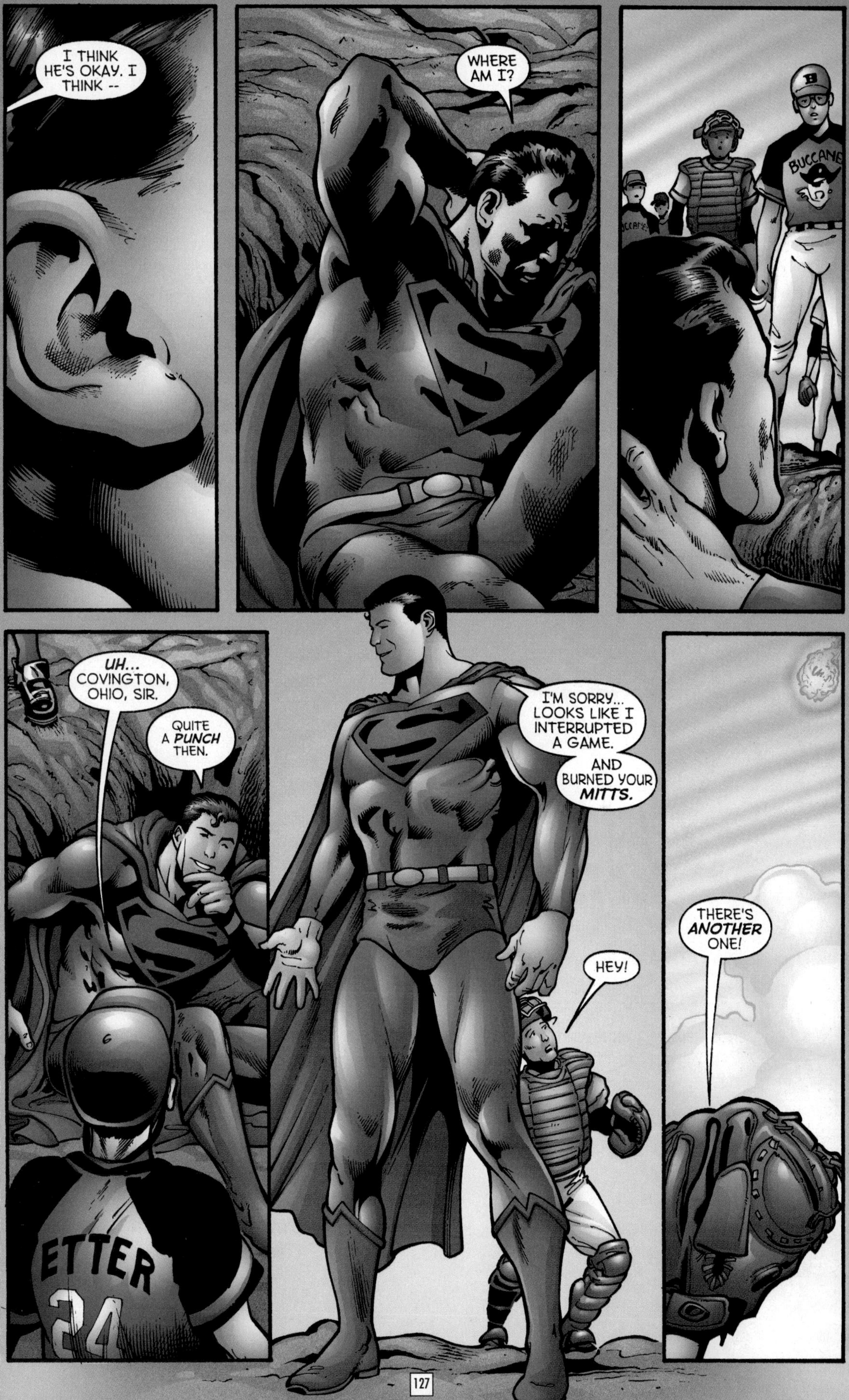
I THINK HE'S OKAY. I THINK --
WHERE AM I?
UH... COVINGTON, OHIO, SIR.
QUITE A *PUNCH* THEN.
I'M SORRY... LOOKS LIKE I INTERRUPTED A GAME.
AND BURNED YOUR ***MITTS.***
HEY!
THERE'S ***ANOTHER*** ONE!

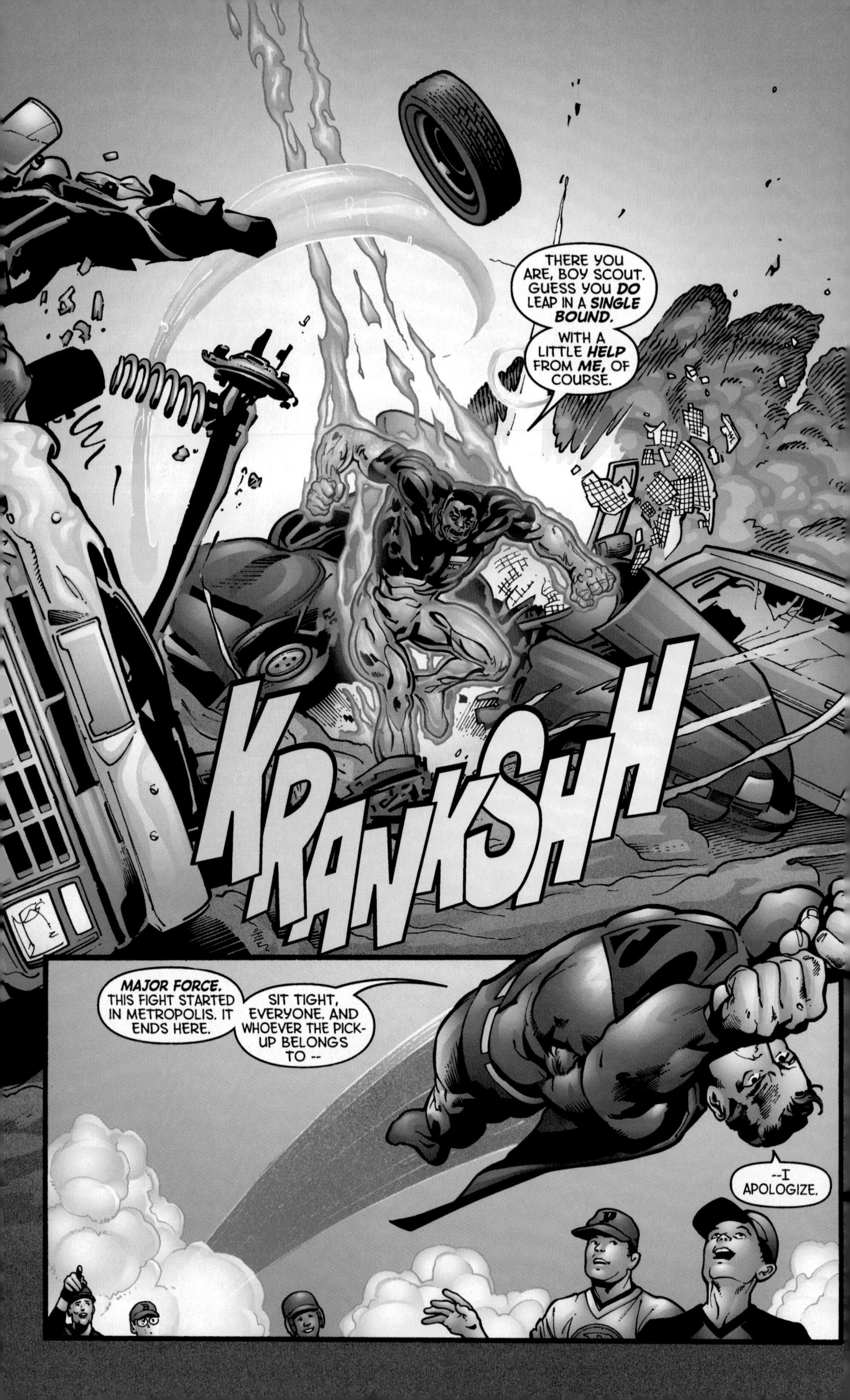
THERE YOU ARE, BOY SCOUT. GUESS YOU **DO** LEAP IN A **SINGLE BOUND.**
WITH A LITTLE **HELP** FROM **ME,** OF COURSE.
KRANKSHH
MAJOR FORCE. THIS FIGHT STARTED IN METROPOLIS. IT ENDS HERE.
SIT TIGHT, EVERYONE. AND WHOEVER THE PICK-UP BELONGS TO --
--I APOLOGIZE.

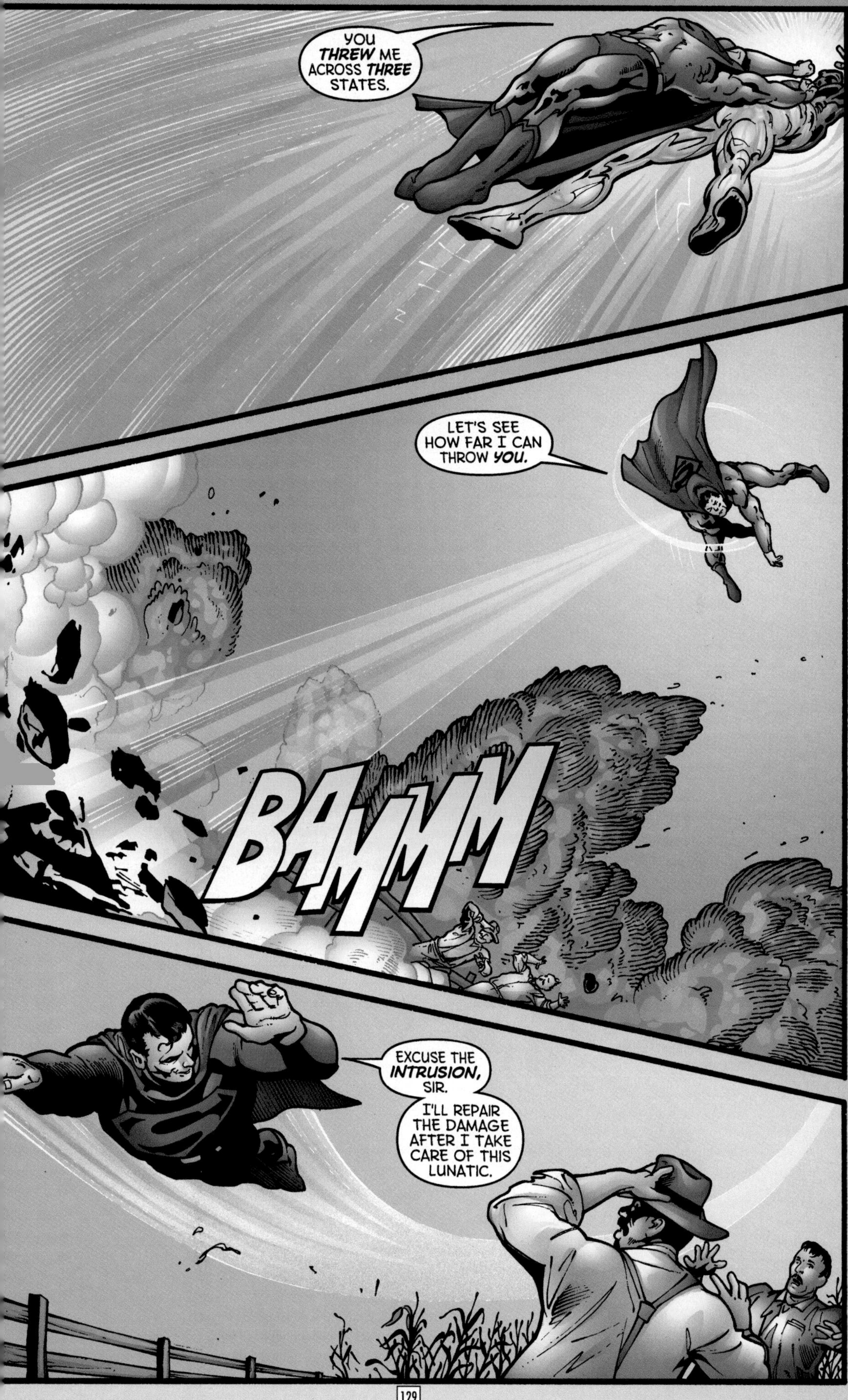
YOU *THREW* ME ACROSS *THREE* STATES.
LET'S SEE HOW FAR I CAN THROW *YOU.*
BAMMM
EXCUSE THE *INTRUSION,* SIR.
I'LL REPAIR THE DAMAGE AFTER I TAKE CARE OF THIS LUNATIC.

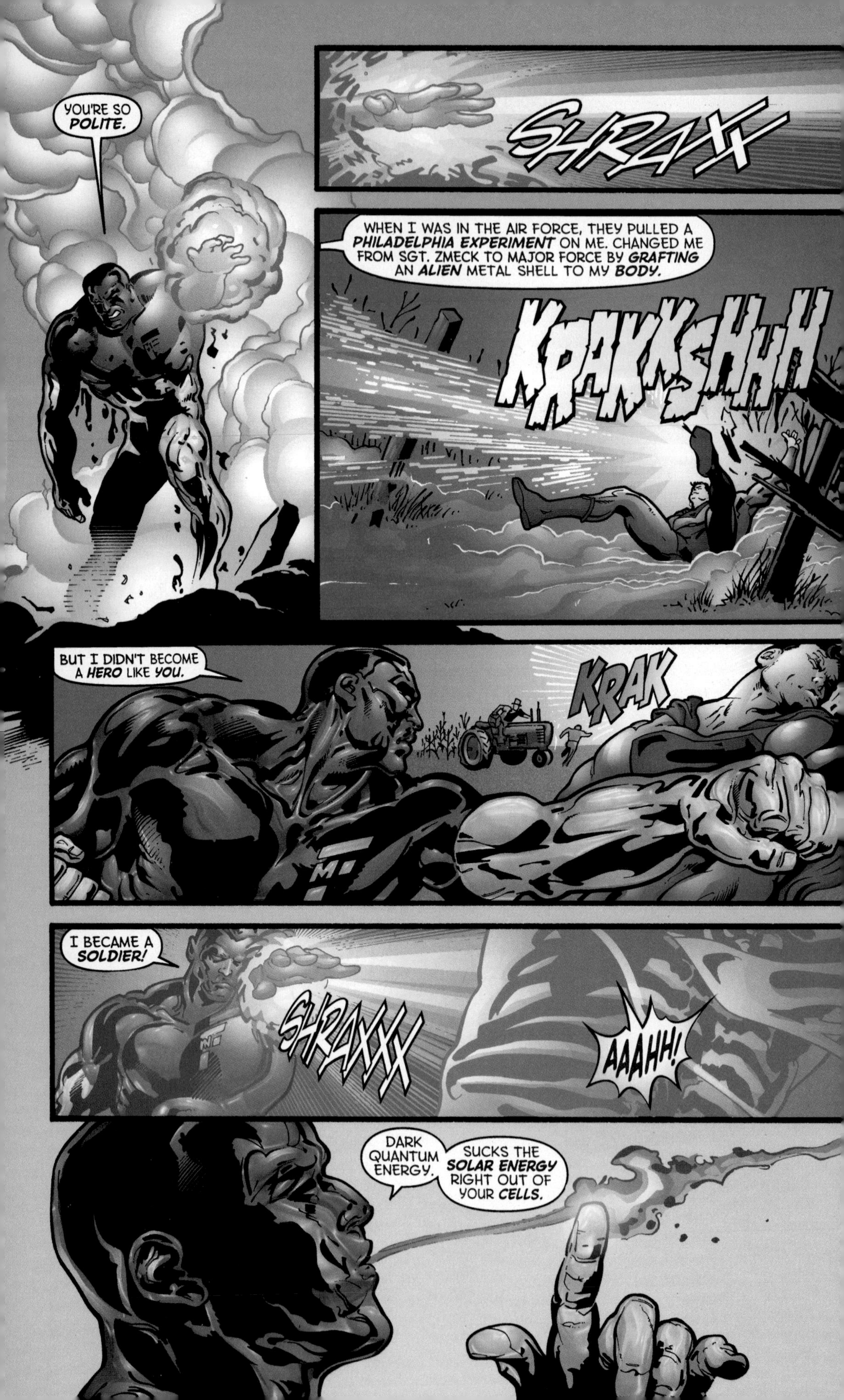
YOU'RE SO POLITE.
SHRAXX
WHEN I WAS IN THE AIR FORCE, THEY PULLED A PHILADELPHIA EXPERIMENT ON ME. CHANGED ME FROM SGT. ZMECK TO MAJOR FORCE BY GRAFTING AN ALIEN METAL SHELL TO MY BODY.
KRAKKSHHH
BUT I DIDN'T BECOME A HERO LIKE YOU.
KRAK
I BECAME A SOLDIER!
SHRAXXX
AAAHH!
DARK QUANTUM ENERGY.
SUCKS THE SOLAR ENERGY RIGHT OUT OF YOUR CELLS.

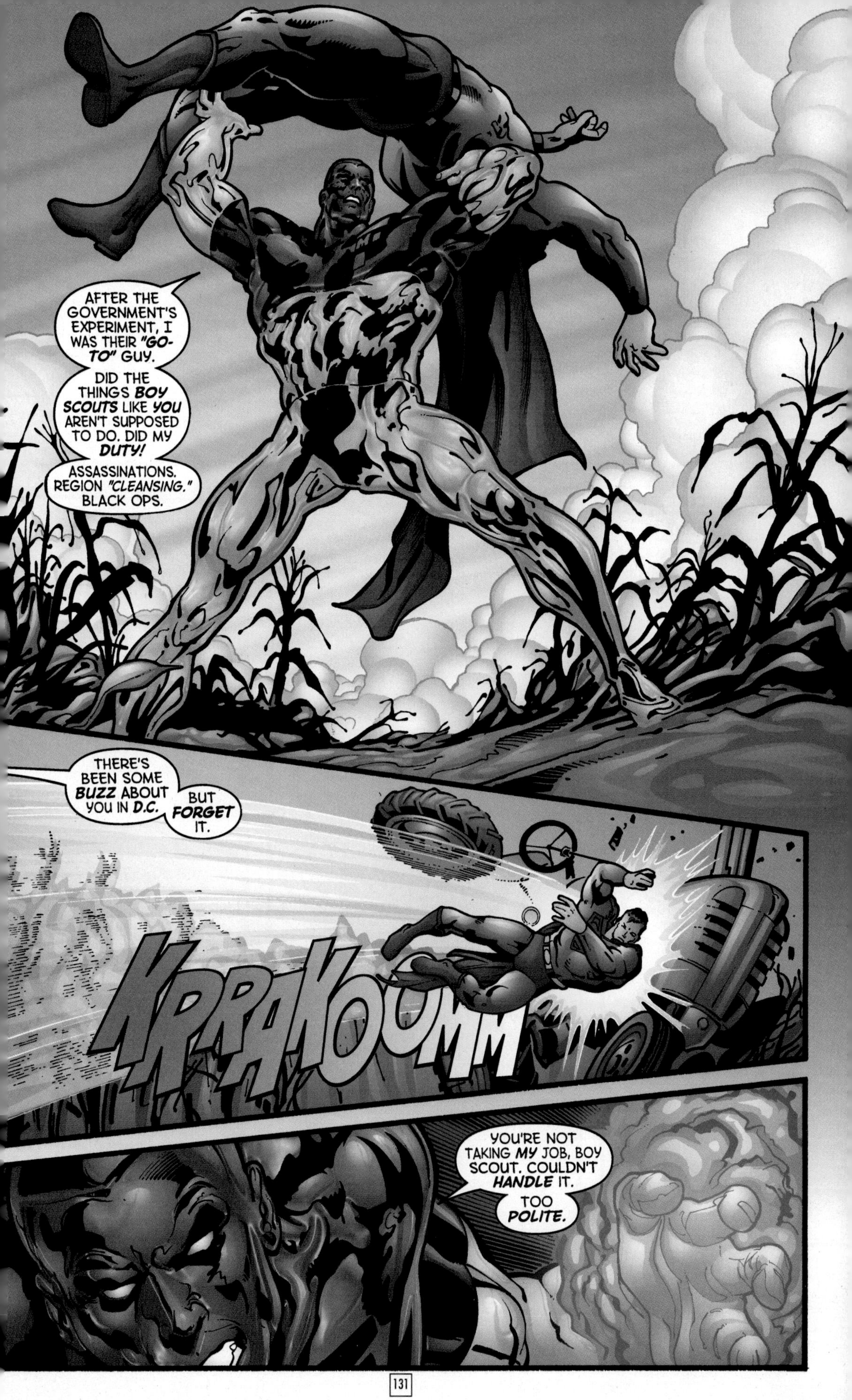
AFTER THE GOVERNMENT'S EXPERIMENT, I WAS THEIR "GO-TO" GUY.
DID THE THINGS BOY SCOUTS LIKE YOU AREN'T SUPPOSED TO DO. DID MY DUTY!
ASSASSINATIONS. REGION "CLEANSING." BLACK OPS.
THERE'S BEEN SOME BUZZ ABOUT YOU IN D.C.
BUT FORGET IT.
KRRAKOOMM
YOU'RE NOT TAKING MY JOB, BOY SCOUT. COULDN'T HANDLE IT.
TOO POLITE.

KAAKRAKK

THAT'S A COMMON **MISCONCEPTION.**

COMMON MISCONCEPTION? WHAT ARE YOU TALKING ABOUT?

THE *BOY SCOUT* THING, MAJOR.

AND BEING *POLITE.*

KRRAKKANG

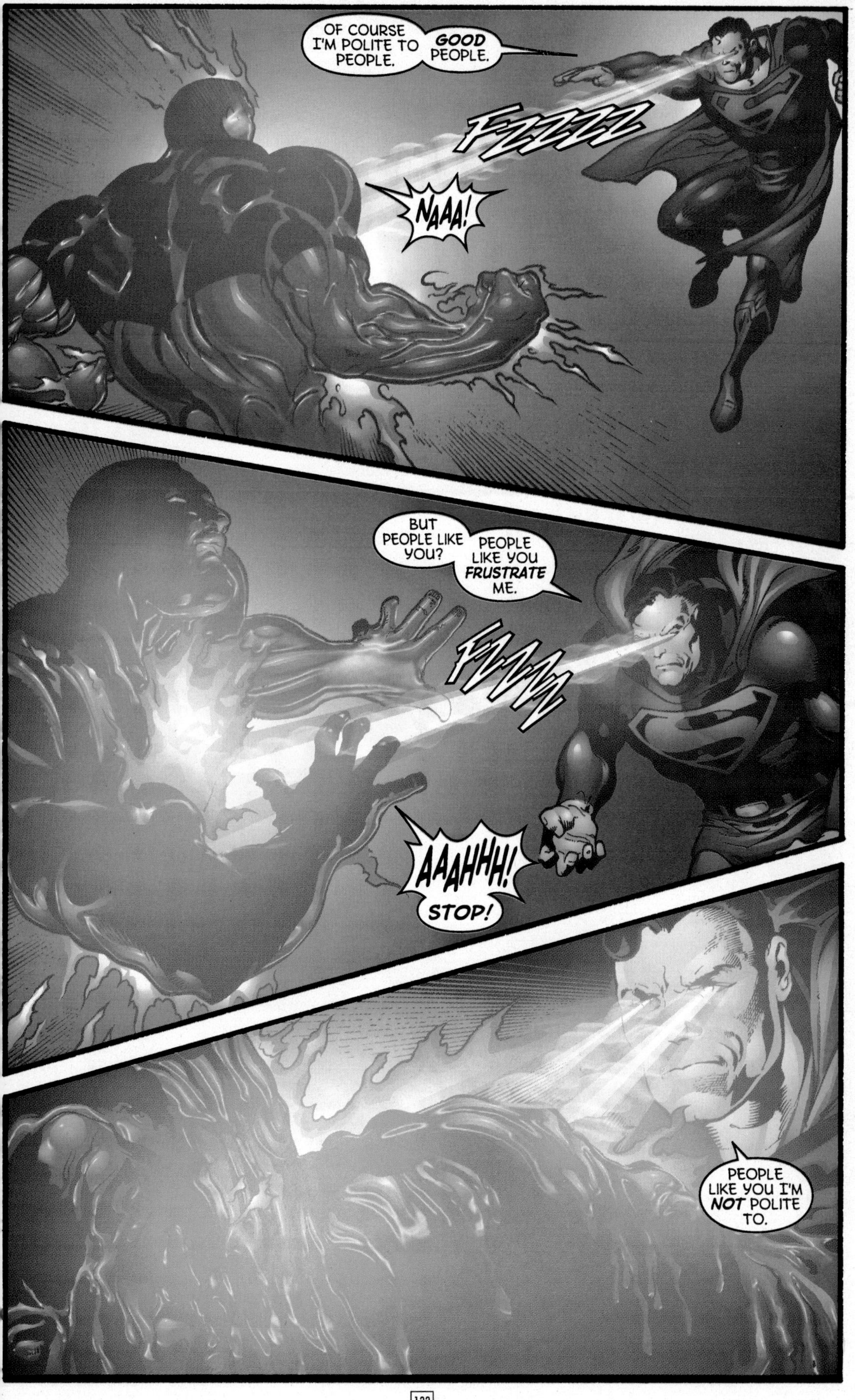
OF COURSE I'M POLITE TO PEOPLE.
GOOD PEOPLE.
FZZZZ
NAAA!
BUT PEOPLE LIKE YOU?
PEOPLE LIKE YOU FRUSTRATE ME.
FZZZZ
AAAHHH! STOP!
PEOPLE LIKE YOU I'M NOT POLITE TO.

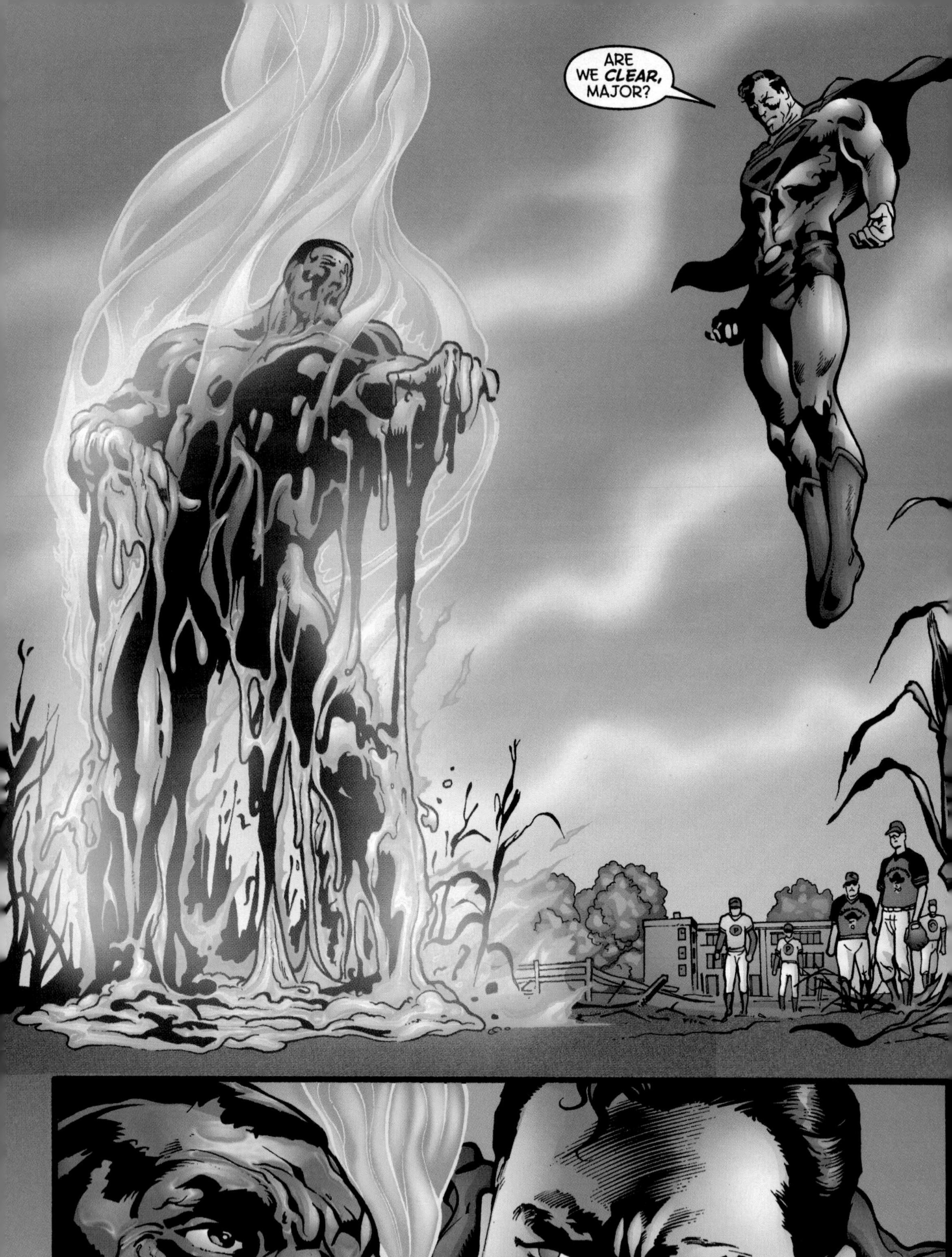
ARE WE CLEAR, MAJOR?

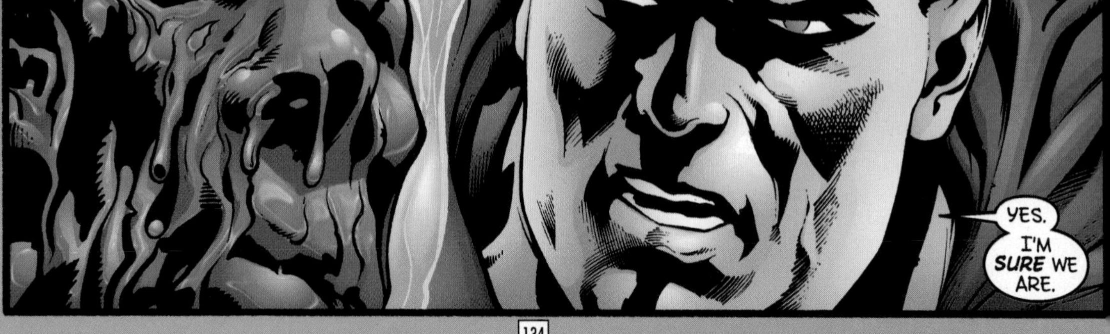
YES. I'M SURE WE ARE.

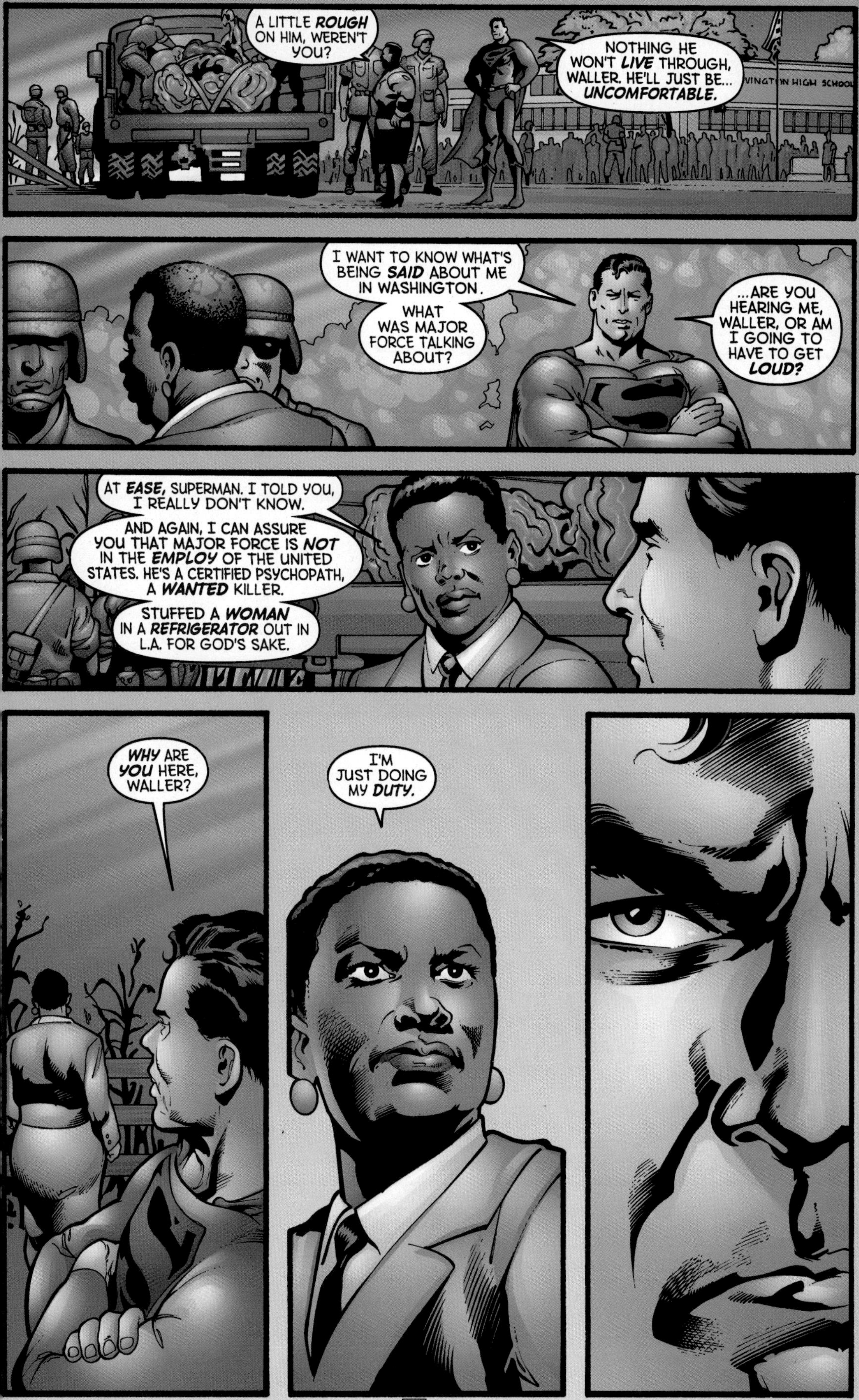
A LITTLE ROUGH ON HIM, WEREN'T YOU?
NOTHING HE WON'T LIVE THROUGH, WALLER. HE'LL JUST BE... UNCOMFORTABLE.
VINGTON HIGH SCHOOL
I WANT TO KNOW WHAT'S BEING SAID ABOUT ME IN WASHINGTON.
WHAT WAS MAJOR FORCE TALKING ABOUT?
...ARE YOU HEARING ME, WALLER, OR AM I GOING TO HAVE TO GET LOUD?
AT EASE, SUPERMAN. I TOLD YOU, I REALLY DON'T KNOW.
AND AGAIN, I CAN ASSURE YOU THAT MAJOR FORCE IS NOT IN THE EMPLOY OF THE UNITED STATES. HE'S A CERTIFIED PSYCHOPATH, A WANTED KILLER.
STUFFED A WOMAN IN A REFRIGERATOR OUT IN L.A. FOR GOD'S SAKE.
WHY ARE YOU HERE, WALLER?
I'M JUST DOING MY DUTY.

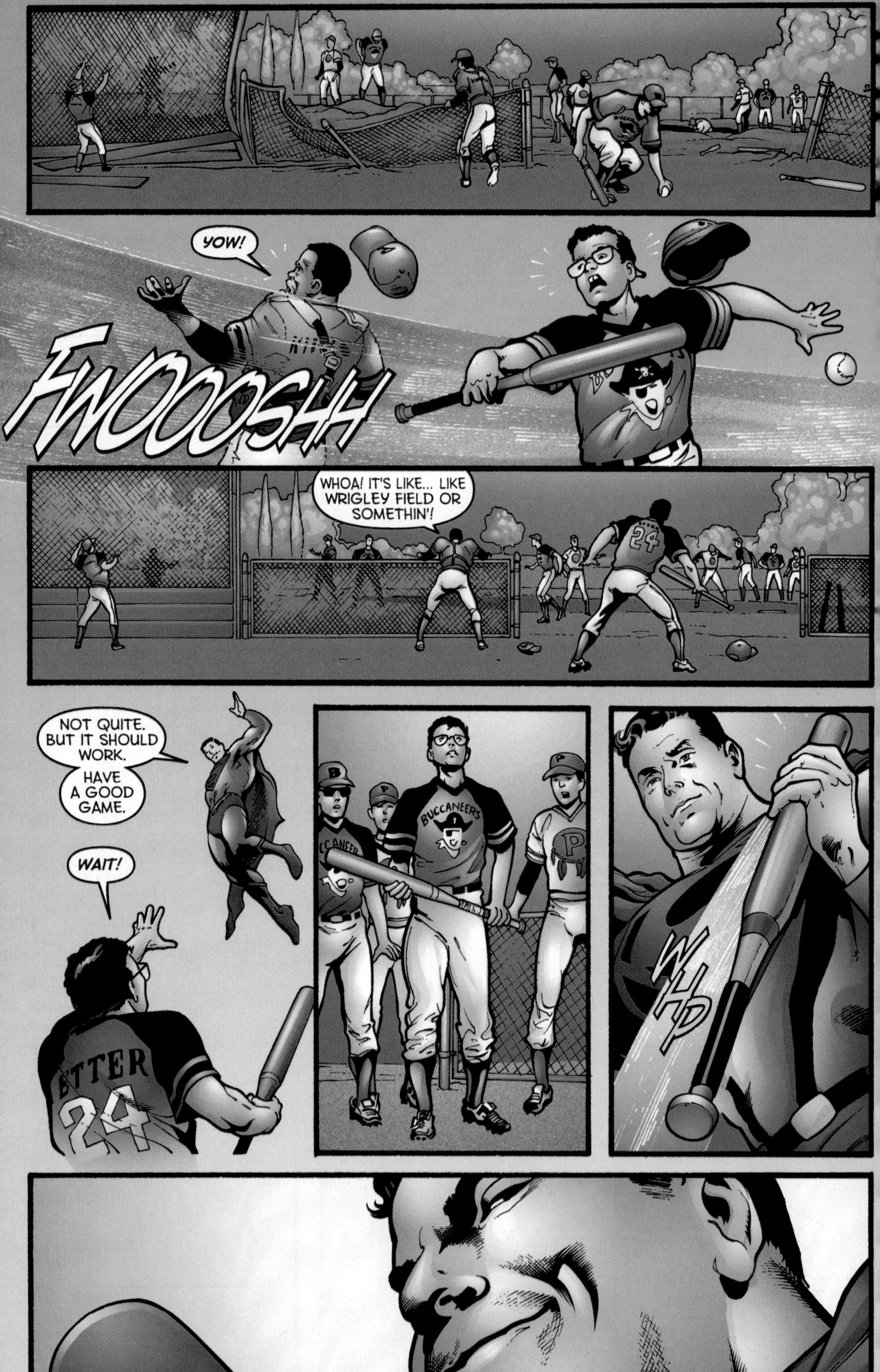
YOW!
FWOOOSHH
WHOA! IT'S LIKE... LIKE WRIGLEY FIELD OR SOMETHIN'!
NOT QUITE. BUT IT SHOULD WORK.
HAVE A GOOD GAME.
WAIT!
ETTER
24
BUCCANEERS
WHP

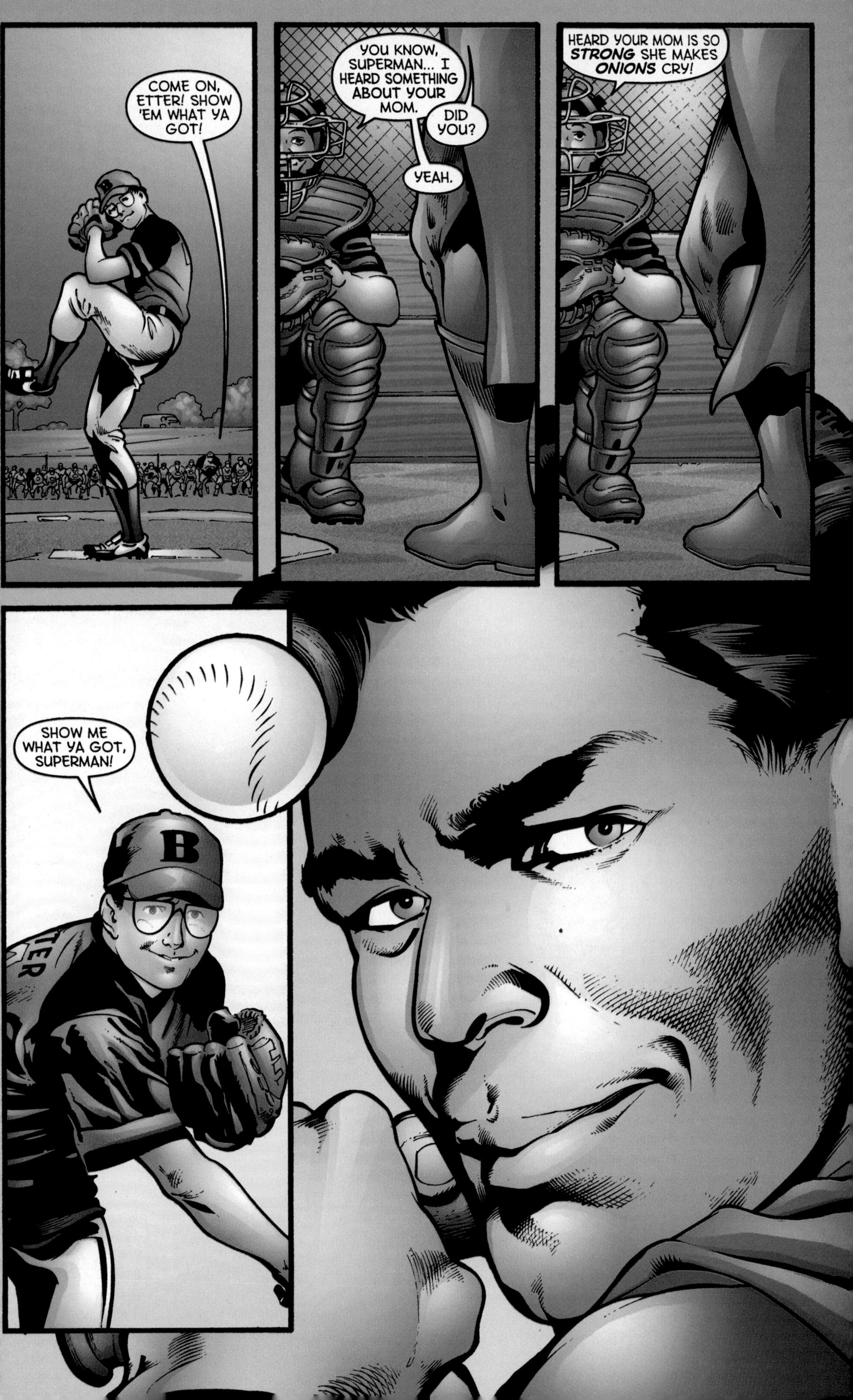
COME ON, ETTER! SHOW 'EM WHAT YA GOT!
YOU KNOW, SUPERMAN... I HEARD SOMETHING ABOUT YOUR MOM.
DID YOU?
YEAH.
HEARD YOUR MOM IS SO **STRONG** SHE MAKES **ONIONS** CRY!
SHOW ME WHAT YA GOT, SUPERMAN!

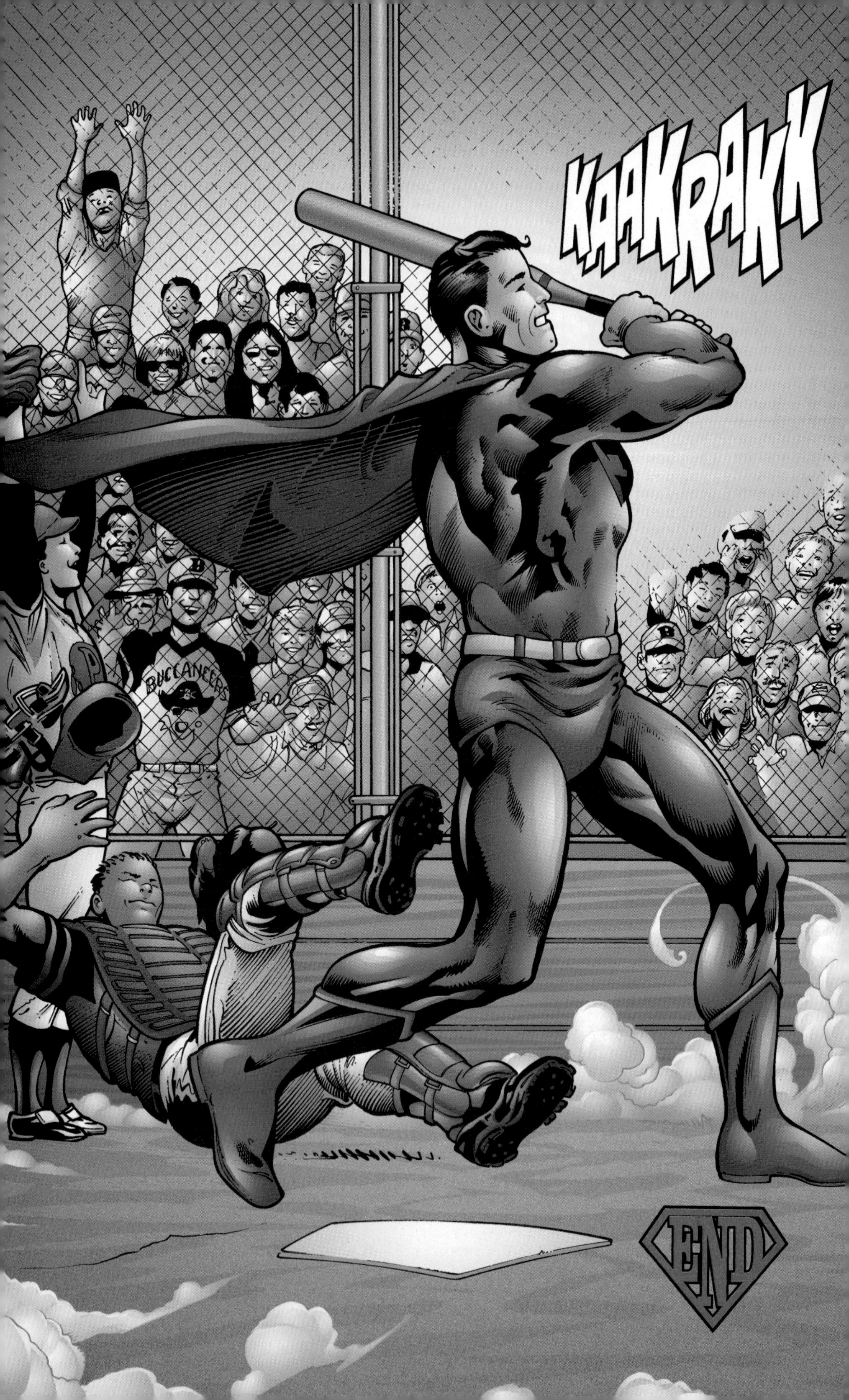
KAAKRAKK
BUCCANEERS
END

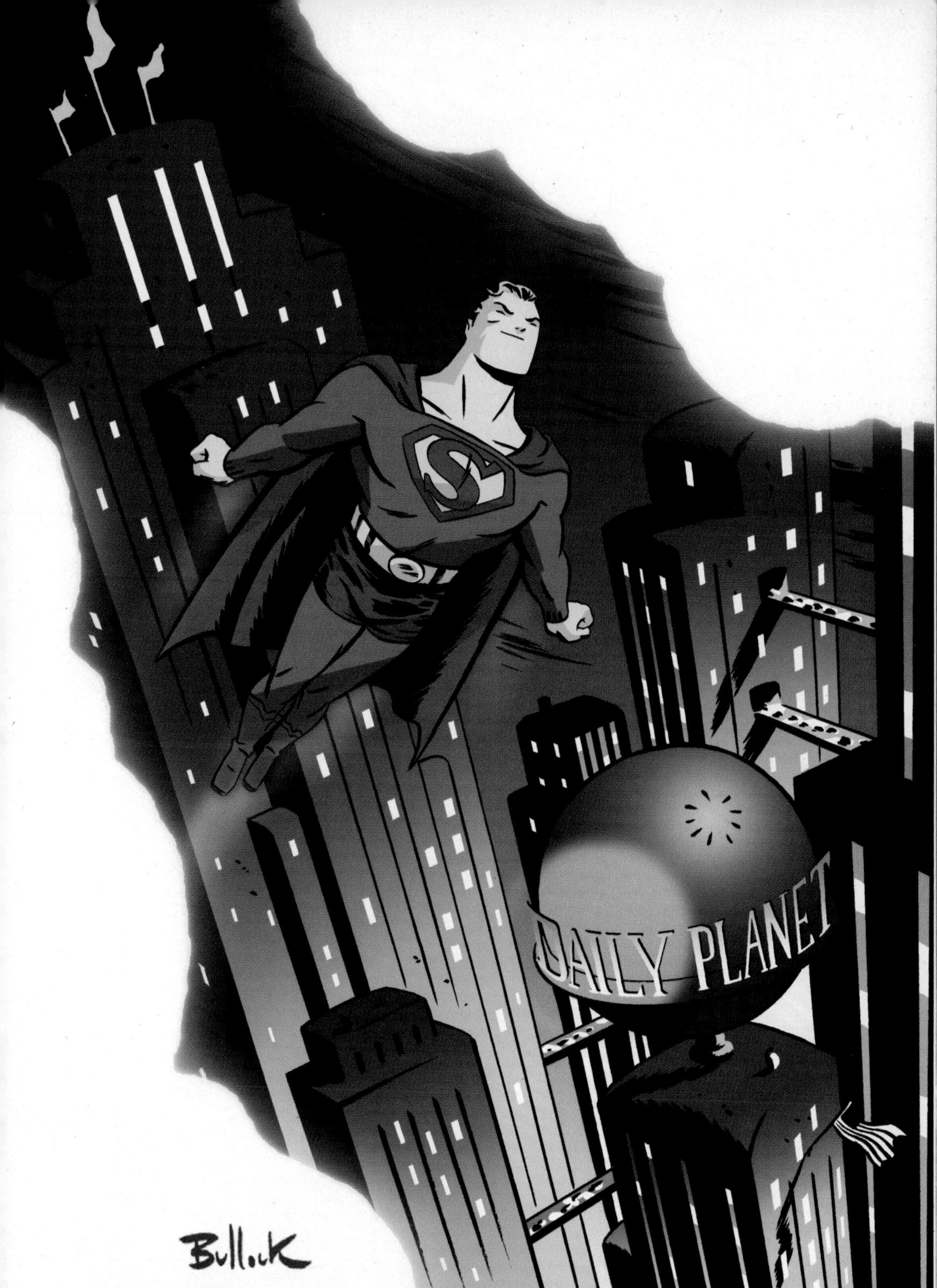
DAILY PLANET
Bullock

"Walking Midnight"

JOE KELLY writer

PASCUAL FERRY, KANO, DAVE BULLOCK, DUNCAN ROULEAU, RENATO GUEDES pencillers

MARLO ALQUIZA, KEITH CHAMPAGNE, JORGE CORREA, JAIME MENDOZA, CAM SMITH inkers

GUY MAJOR colorist **COMICRAFT** letterer **DAVE BULLOCK** cover artist

From the pages of one of DC's longest-running comics, and the debut title for Superman, comes this ACTION COMICS story showing how the Man of Steel spends New Year's Eve...

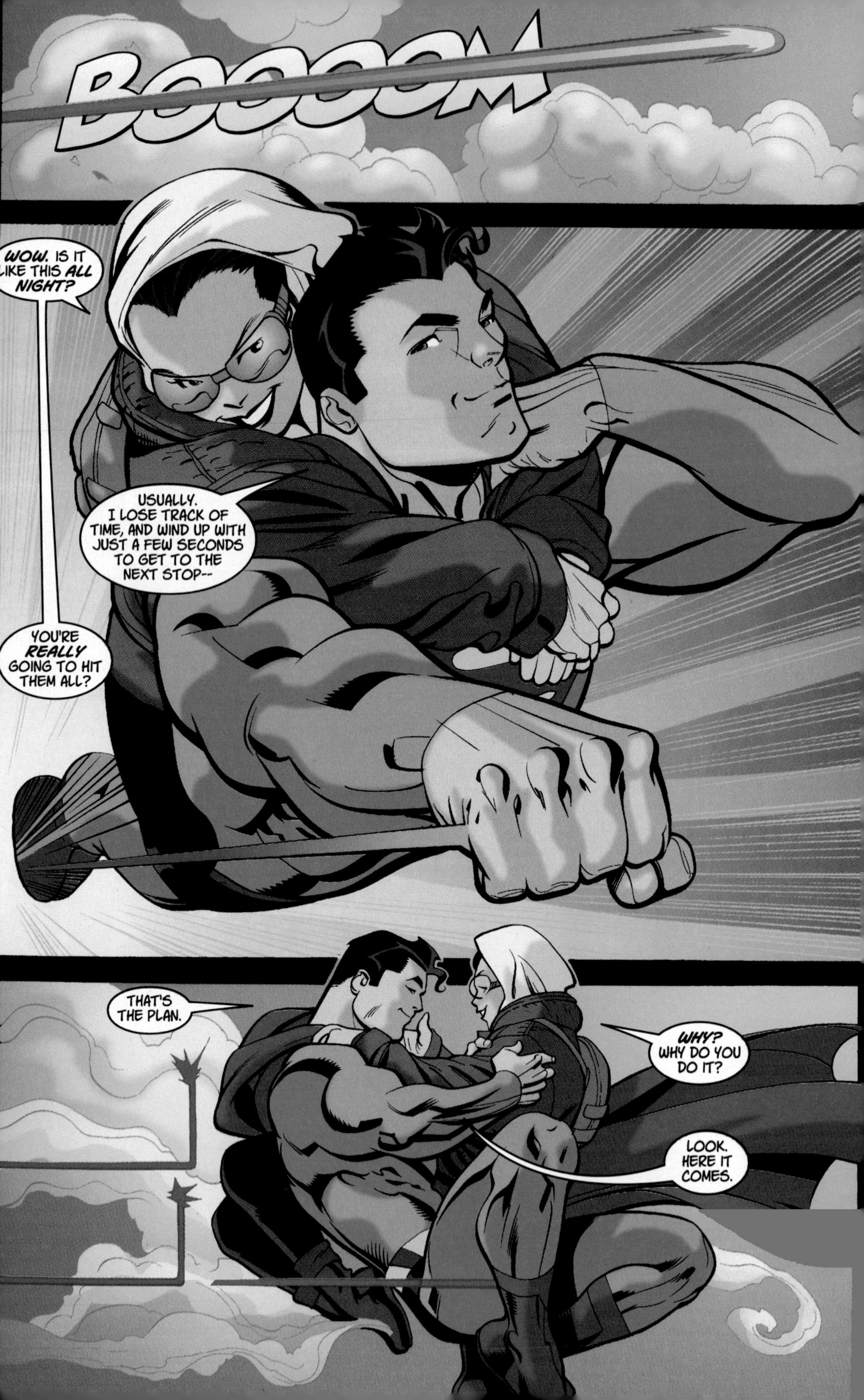
BOOOOOM
WOW. IS IT LIKE THIS ALL NIGHT?
USUALLY. I LOSE TRACK OF TIME, AND WIND UP WITH JUST A FEW SECONDS TO GET TO THE NEXT STOP--
YOU'RE REALLY GOING TO HIT THEM ALL?
THAT'S THE PLAN.
WHY? WHY DO YOU DO IT?
LOOK. HERE IT COMES.

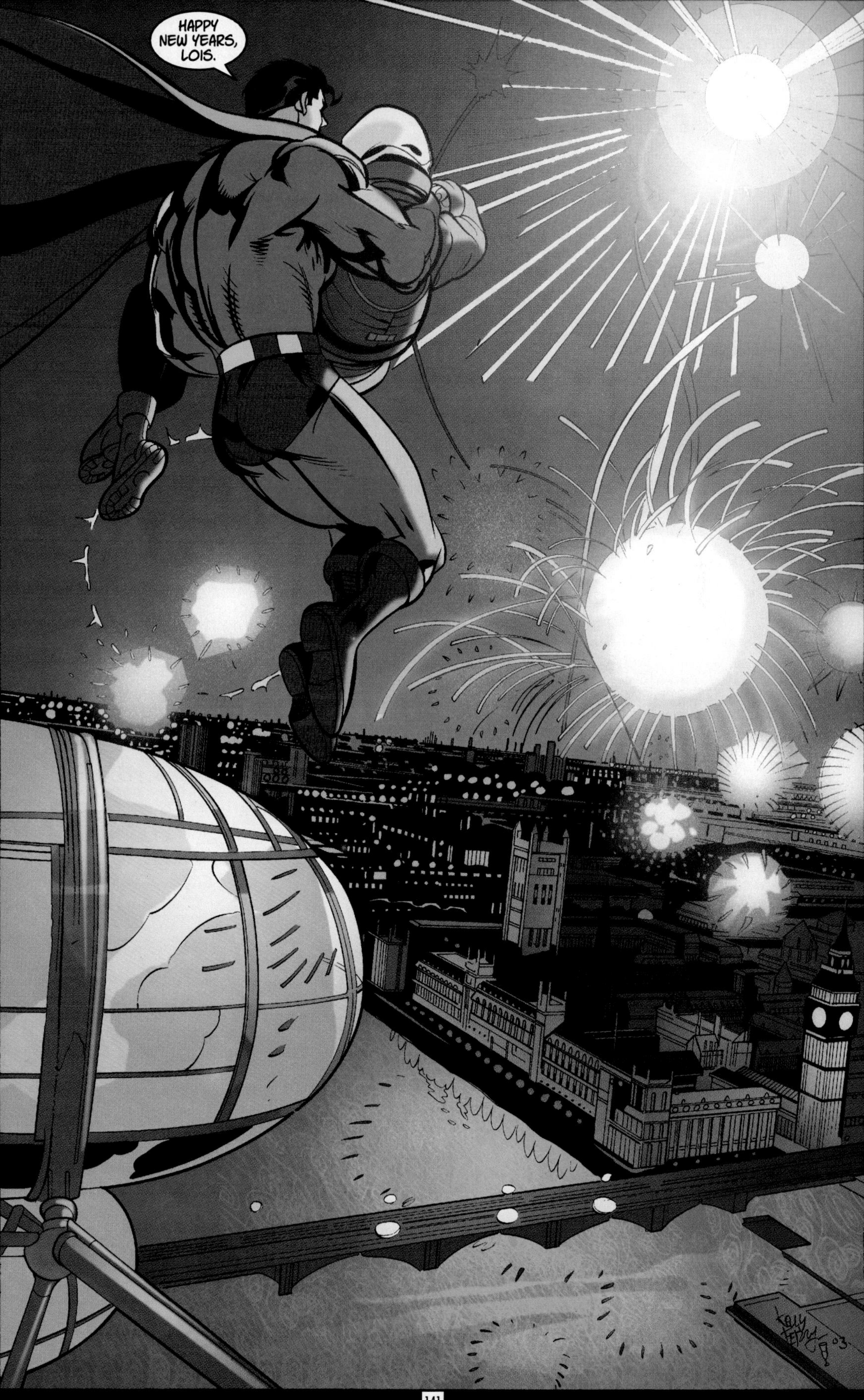
HAPPY NEW YEARS, LOIS.

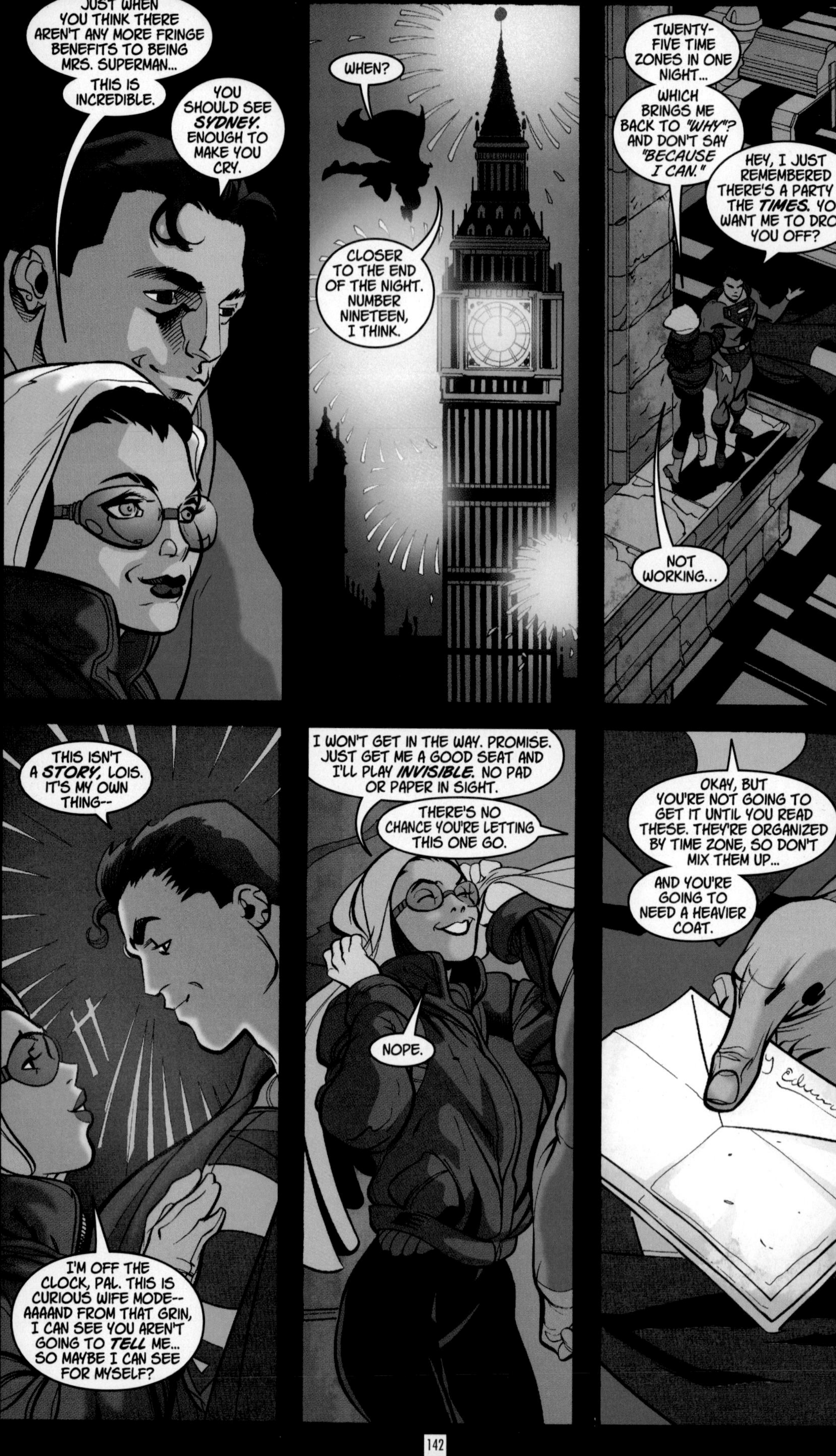
JUST WHEN YOU THINK THERE AREN'T ANY MORE FRINGE BENEFITS TO BEING MRS. SUPERMAN...
THIS IS INCREDIBLE.
YOU SHOULD SEE SYDNEY. ENOUGH TO MAKE YOU CRY.
WHEN?
CLOSER TO THE END OF THE NIGHT. NUMBER NINETEEN, I THINK.
TWENTY-FIVE TIME ZONES IN ONE NIGHT...
WHICH BRINGS ME BACK TO "WHY"? AND DON'T SAY "BECAUSE I CAN."
HEY, I JUST REMEMBERED THERE'S A PARTY AT THE TIMES. YOU WANT ME TO DROP YOU OFF?
NOT WORKING...
THIS ISN'T A STORY, LOIS. IT'S MY OWN THING--
I'M OFF THE CLOCK, PAL. THIS IS CURIOUS WIFE MODE-- AAAAND FROM THAT GRIN, I CAN SEE YOU AREN'T GOING TO TELL ME... SO MAYBE I CAN SEE FOR MYSELF?
I WON'T GET IN THE WAY. PROMISE. JUST GET ME A GOOD SEAT AND I'LL PLAY INVISIBLE. NO PAD OR PAPER IN SIGHT.
THERE'S NO CHANCE YOU'RE LETTING THIS ONE GO.
NOPE.
OKAY, BUT YOU'RE NOT GOING TO GET IT UNTIL YOU READ THESE. THEY'RE ORGANIZED BY TIME ZONE, SO DON'T MIX THEM UP...
AND YOU'RE GOING TO NEED A HEAVIER COAT.

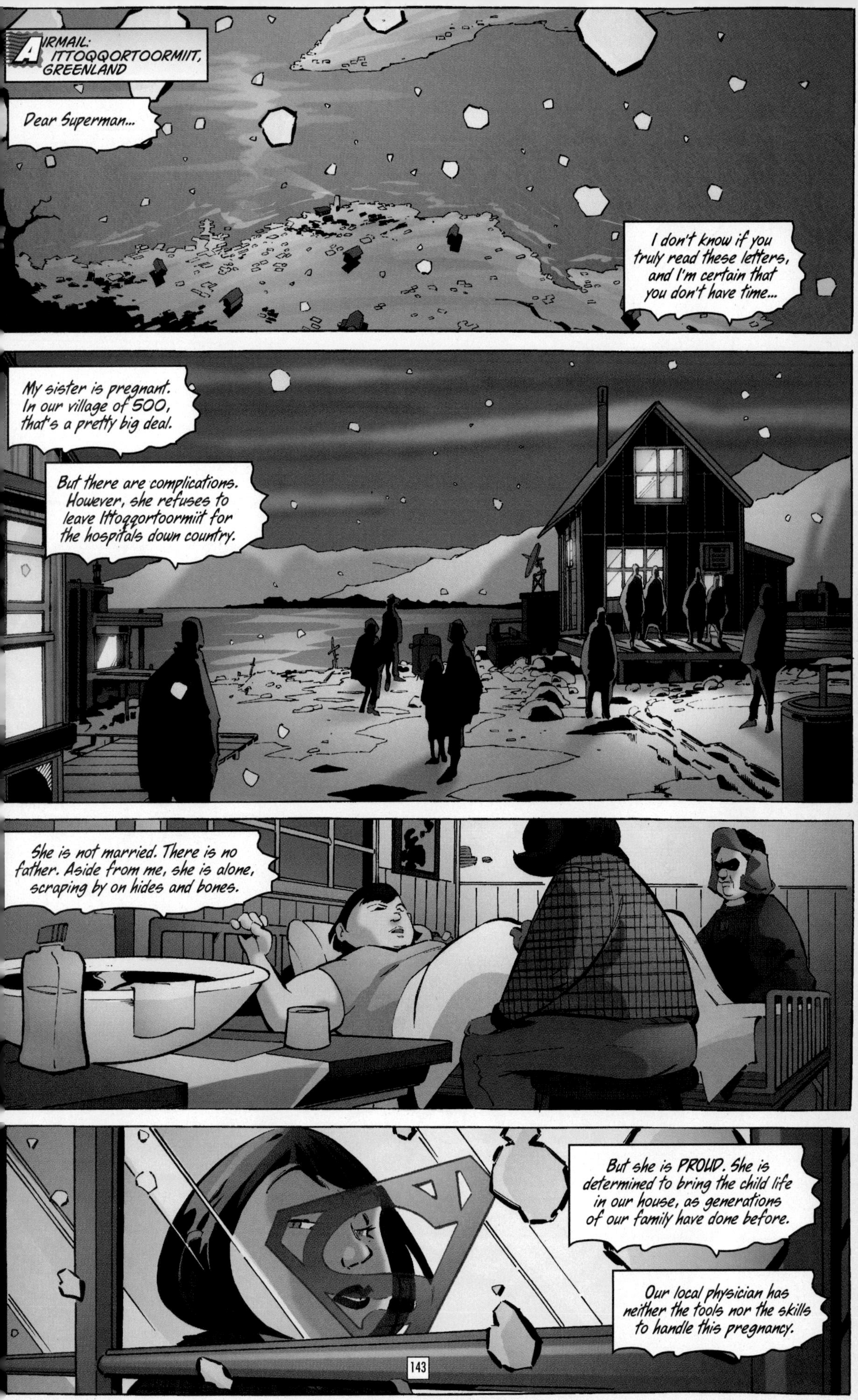
AIRMAIL: ITTOQQORTOORMIIT, GREENLAND
Dear Superman...
I don't know if you truly read these letters, and I'm certain that you don't have time...
My sister is pregnant. In our village of 500, that's a pretty big deal.
But there are complications. However, she refuses to leave Ittoqqortoormiit for the hospitals down country.
She is not married. There is no father. Aside from me, she is alone, scraping by on hides and bones.
But she is PROUD. She is determined to bring the child life in our house, as generations of our family have done before.
Our local physician has neither the tools nor the skills to handle this pregnancy.

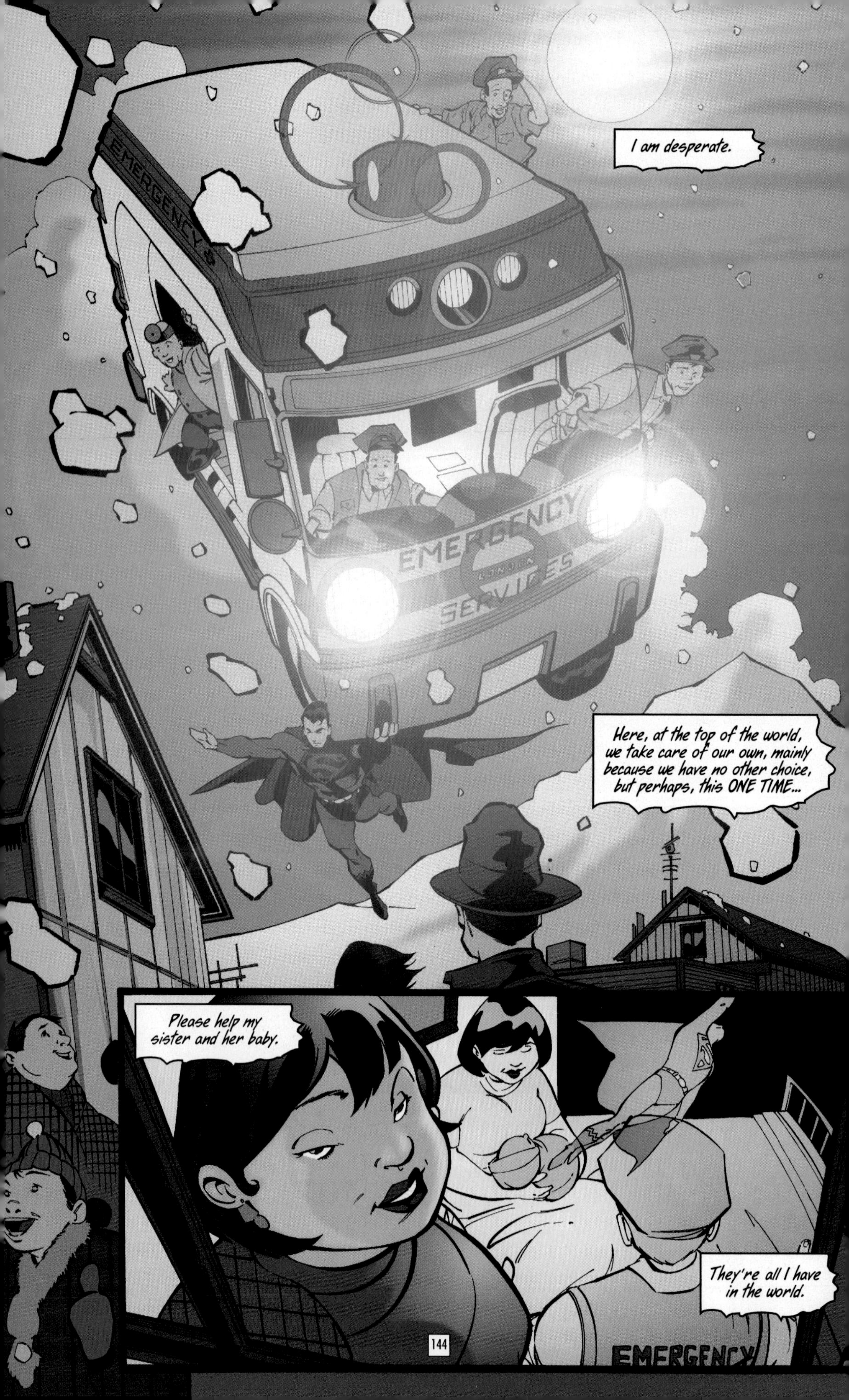
I am desperate.
EMERGENCY
EMERGENCY
LONDON
SERVICES
Here, at the top of the world, we take care of our own, mainly because we have no other choice, but perhaps, this ONE TIME...
Please help my sister and her baby.
They're all I have in the world.
EMERGENCY

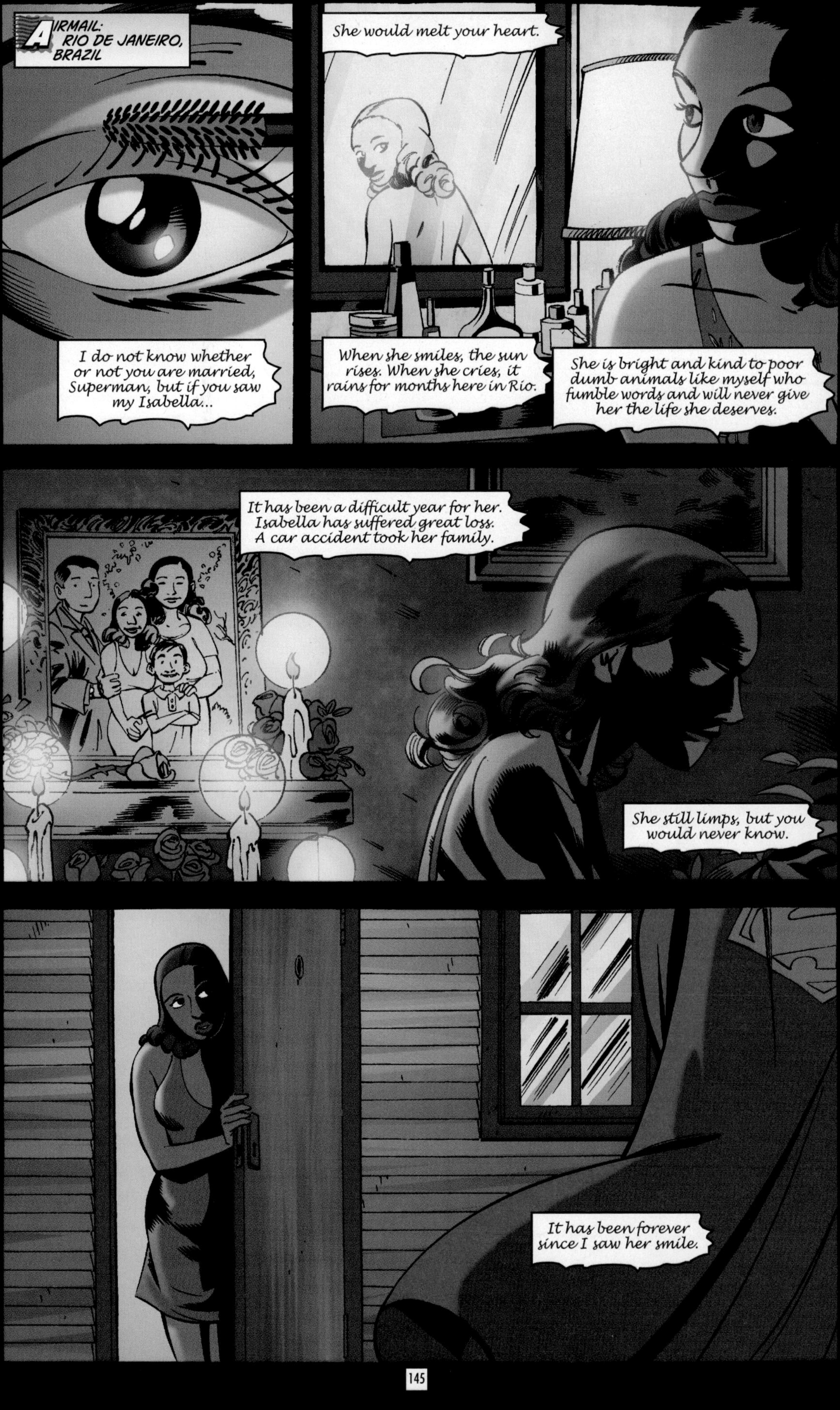
AIRMAIL: RIO DE JANEIRO, BRAZIL
I do not know whether or not you are married, Superman, but if you saw my Isabella...
She would melt your heart.
When she smiles, the sun rises. When she cries, it rains for months here in Rio.
She is bright and kind to poor dumb animals like myself who fumble words and will never give her the life she deserves.
It has been a difficult year for her. Isabella has suffered great loss. A car accident took her family.
She still limps, but you would never know.
It has been forever since I saw her smile.

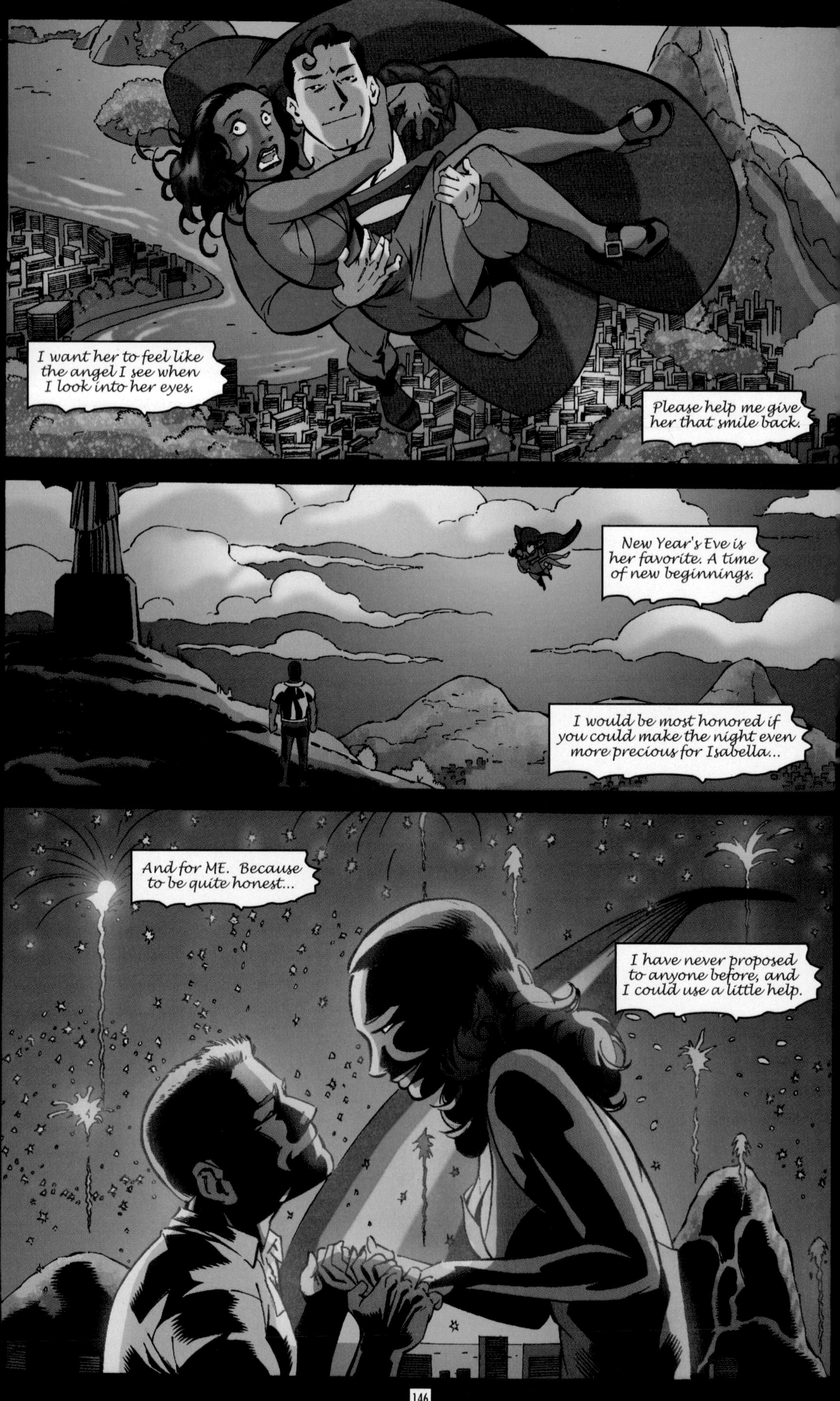
I want her to feel like the angel I see when I look into her eyes.
Please help me give her that smile back.
New Year's Eve is her favorite. A time of new beginnings.
I would be most honored if you could make the night even more precious for Isabella...
And for ME. Because to be quite honest...
I have never proposed to anyone before, and I could use a little help.

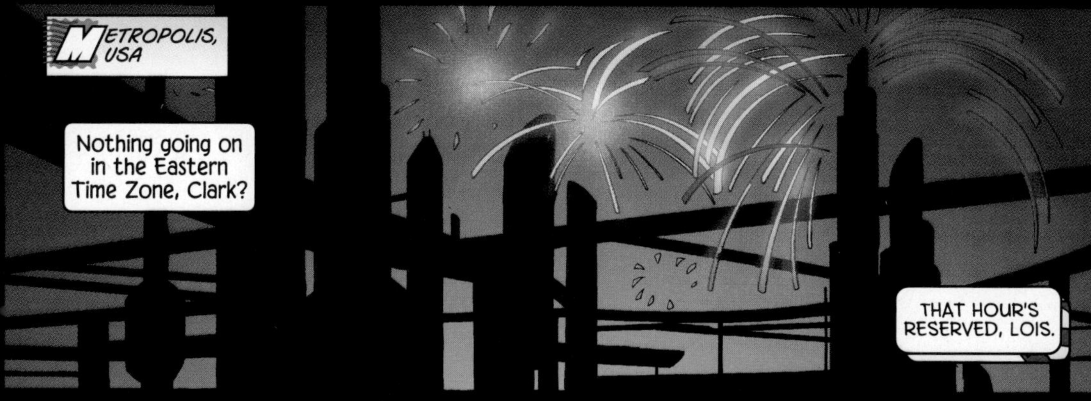
METROPOLIS, USA
Nothing going on in the Eastern Time Zone, Clark?
THAT HOUR'S RESERVED, LOIS.

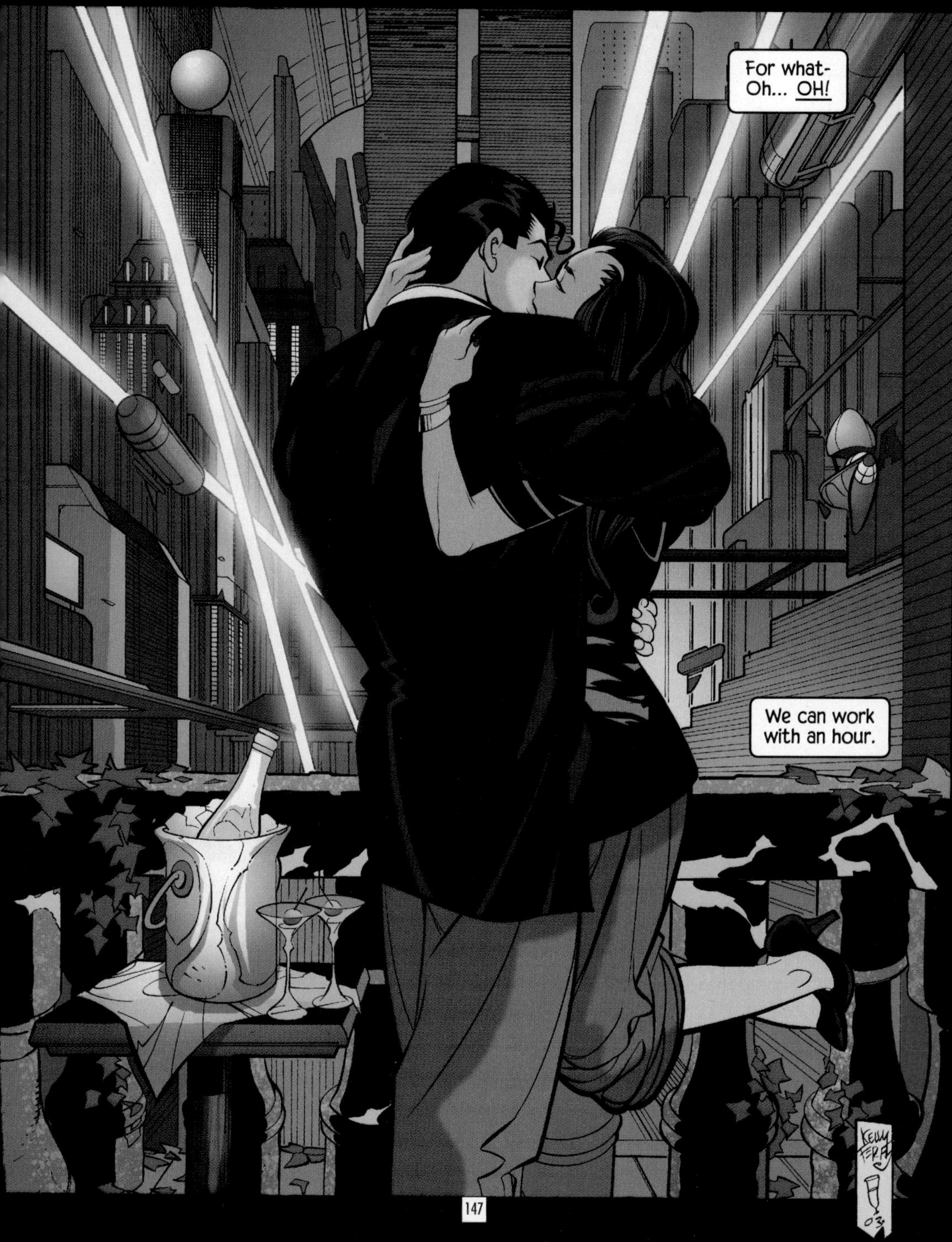
For what- Oh... OH!
We can work with an hour.

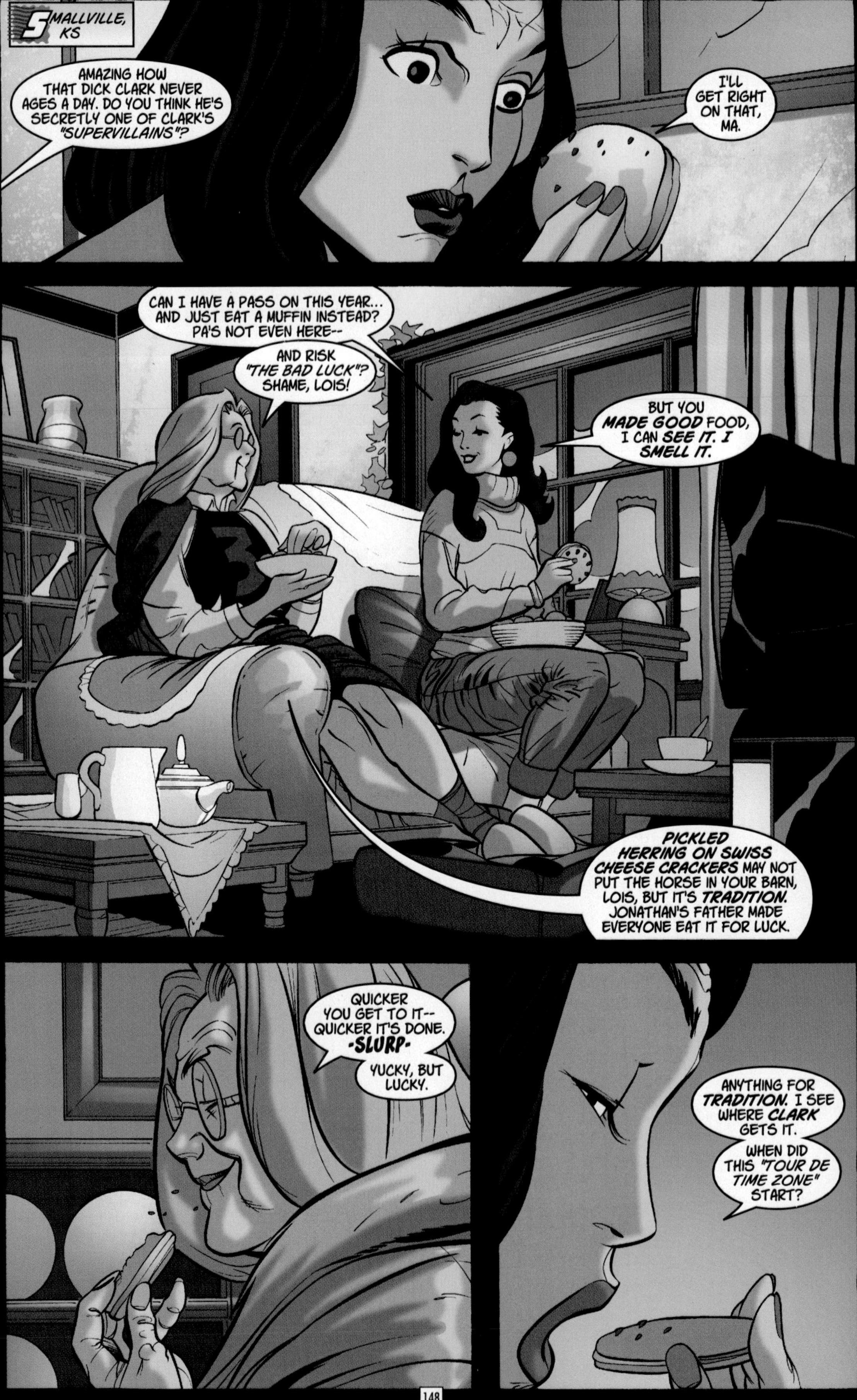
SMALLVILLE, KS
AMAZING HOW THAT DICK CLARK NEVER AGES A DAY. DO YOU THINK HE'S SECRETLY ONE OF CLARK'S "SUPERVILLAINS"?
I'LL GET RIGHT ON THAT, MA.
CAN I HAVE A PASS ON THIS YEAR... AND JUST EAT A MUFFIN INSTEAD? PA'S NOT EVEN HERE--
AND RISK "THE BAD LUCK"? SHAME, LOIS!
BUT YOU MADE GOOD FOOD, I CAN SEE IT. I SMELL IT.
PICKLED HERRING ON SWISS CHEESE CRACKERS MAY NOT PUT THE HORSE IN YOUR BARN, LOIS, BUT IT'S TRADITION. JONATHAN'S FATHER MADE EVERYONE EAT IT FOR LUCK.
QUICKER YOU GET TO IT-- QUICKER IT'S DONE.
-SLURP-
YUCKY, BUT LUCKY.
ANYTHING FOR TRADITION. I SEE WHERE CLARK GETS IT.
WHEN DID THIS "TOUR DE TIME ZONE" START?

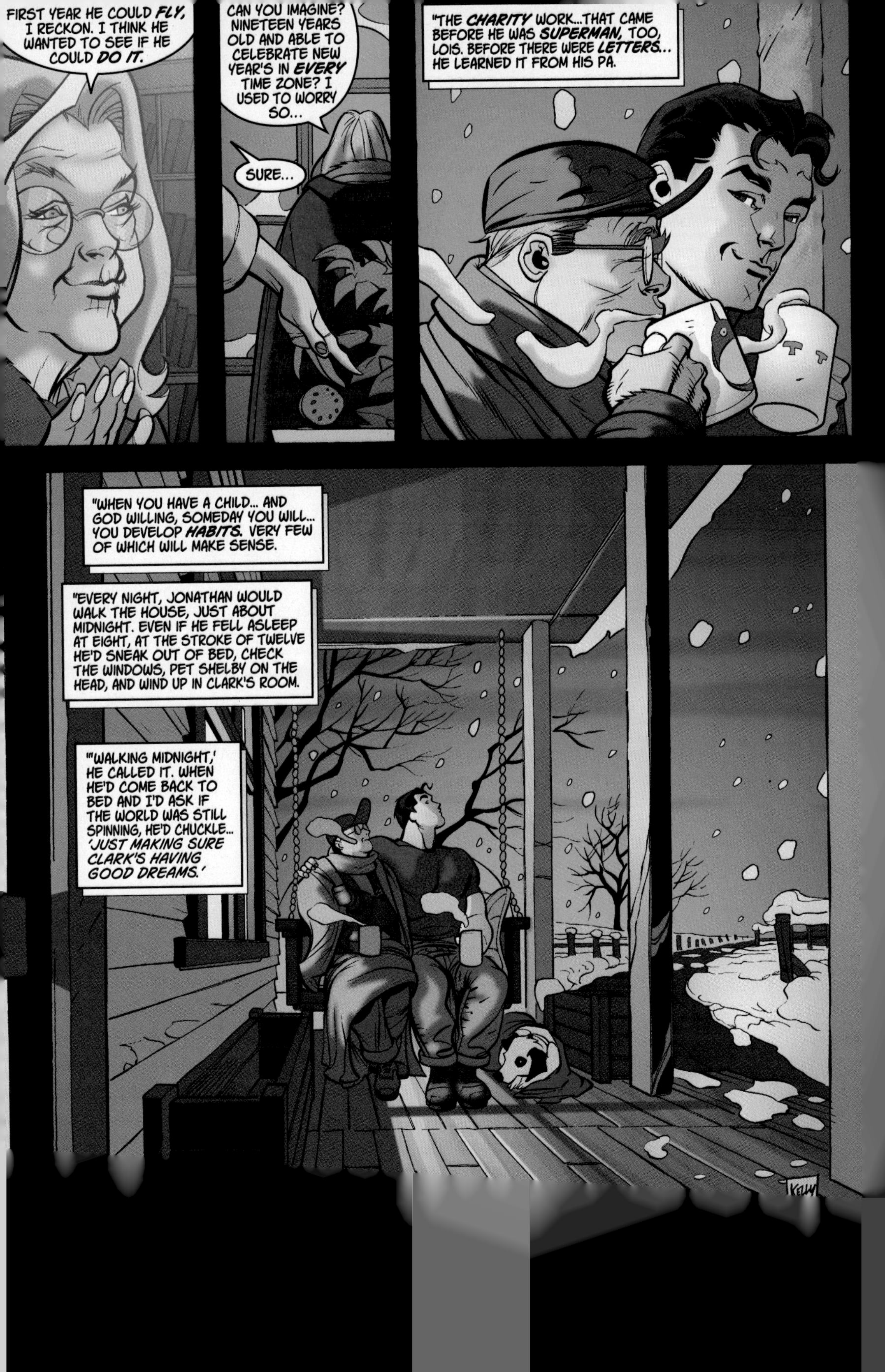
FIRST YEAR HE COULD FLY, I RECKON. I THINK HE WANTED TO SEE IF HE COULD DO IT.
CAN YOU IMAGINE? NINETEEN YEARS OLD AND ABLE TO CELEBRATE NEW YEAR'S IN EVERY TIME ZONE? I USED TO WORRY SO...
SURE...
"THE CHARITY WORK...THAT CAME BEFORE HE WAS SUPERMAN, TOO, LOIS. BEFORE THERE WERE LETTERS... HE LEARNED IT FROM HIS PA.
"WHEN YOU HAVE A CHILD... AND GOD WILLING, SOMEDAY YOU WILL... YOU DEVELOP HABITS. VERY FEW OF WHICH WILL MAKE SENSE.
"EVERY NIGHT, JONATHAN WOULD WALK THE HOUSE, JUST ABOUT MIDNIGHT. EVEN IF HE FELL ASLEEP AT EIGHT, AT THE STROKE OF TWELVE HE'D SNEAK OUT OF BED, CHECK THE WINDOWS, PET SHELBY ON THE HEAD, AND WIND UP IN CLARK'S ROOM.
"'WALKING MIDNIGHT,' HE CALLED IT. WHEN HE'D COME BACK TO BED AND I'D ASK IF THE WORLD WAS STILL SPINNING, HE'D CHUCKLE... 'JUST MAKING SURE CLARK'S HAVING GOOD DREAMS.'

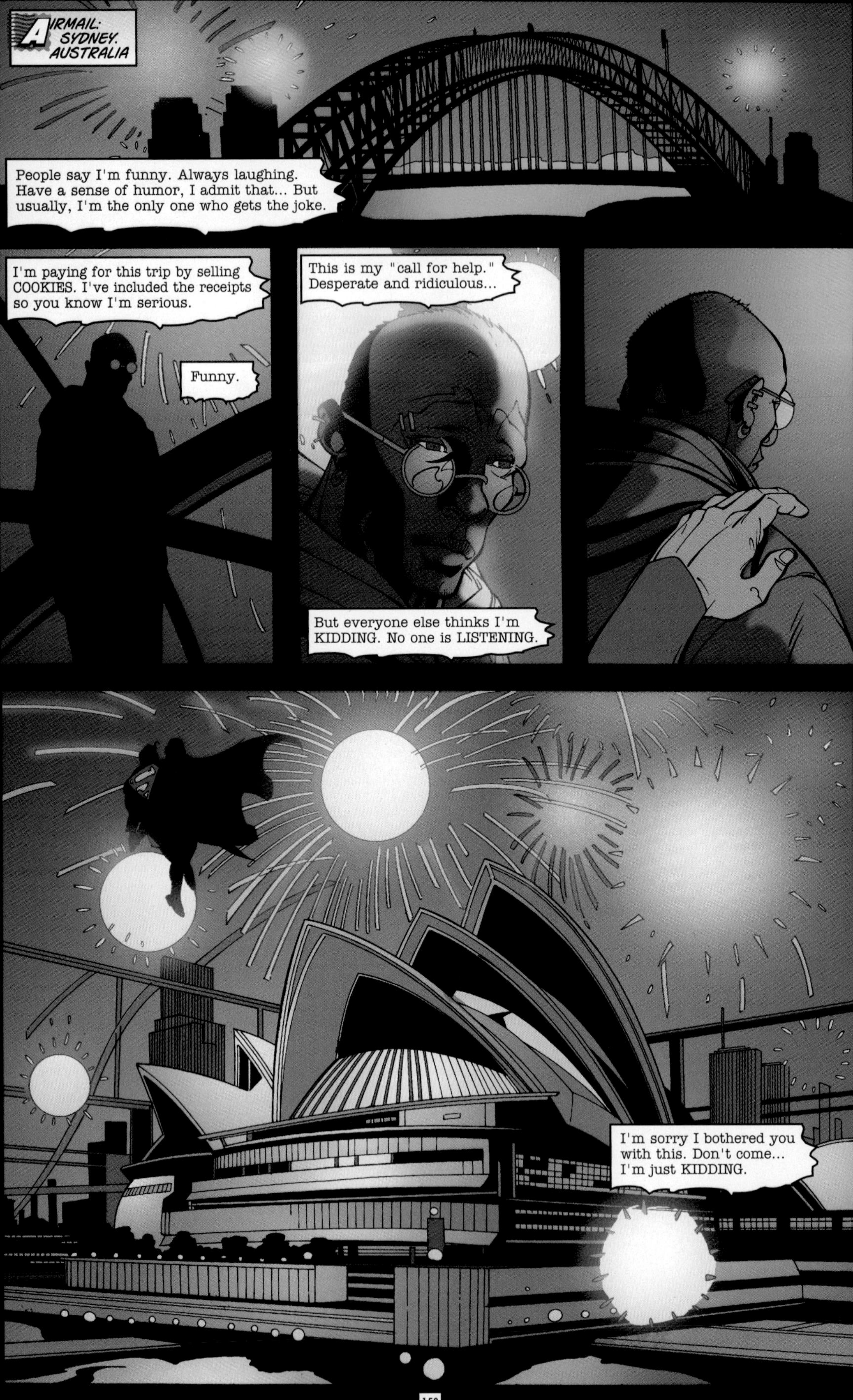
AIRMAIL: SYDNEY. AUSTRALIA
People say I'm funny. Always laughing. Have a sense of humor, I admit that... But usually, I'm the only one who gets the joke.
I'm paying for this trip by selling COOKIES. I've included the receipts so you know I'm serious.
Funny.
This is my "call for help." Desperate and ridiculous...
But everyone else thinks I'm KIDDING. No one is LISTENING.
I'm sorry I bothered you with this. Don't come... I'm just KIDDING.

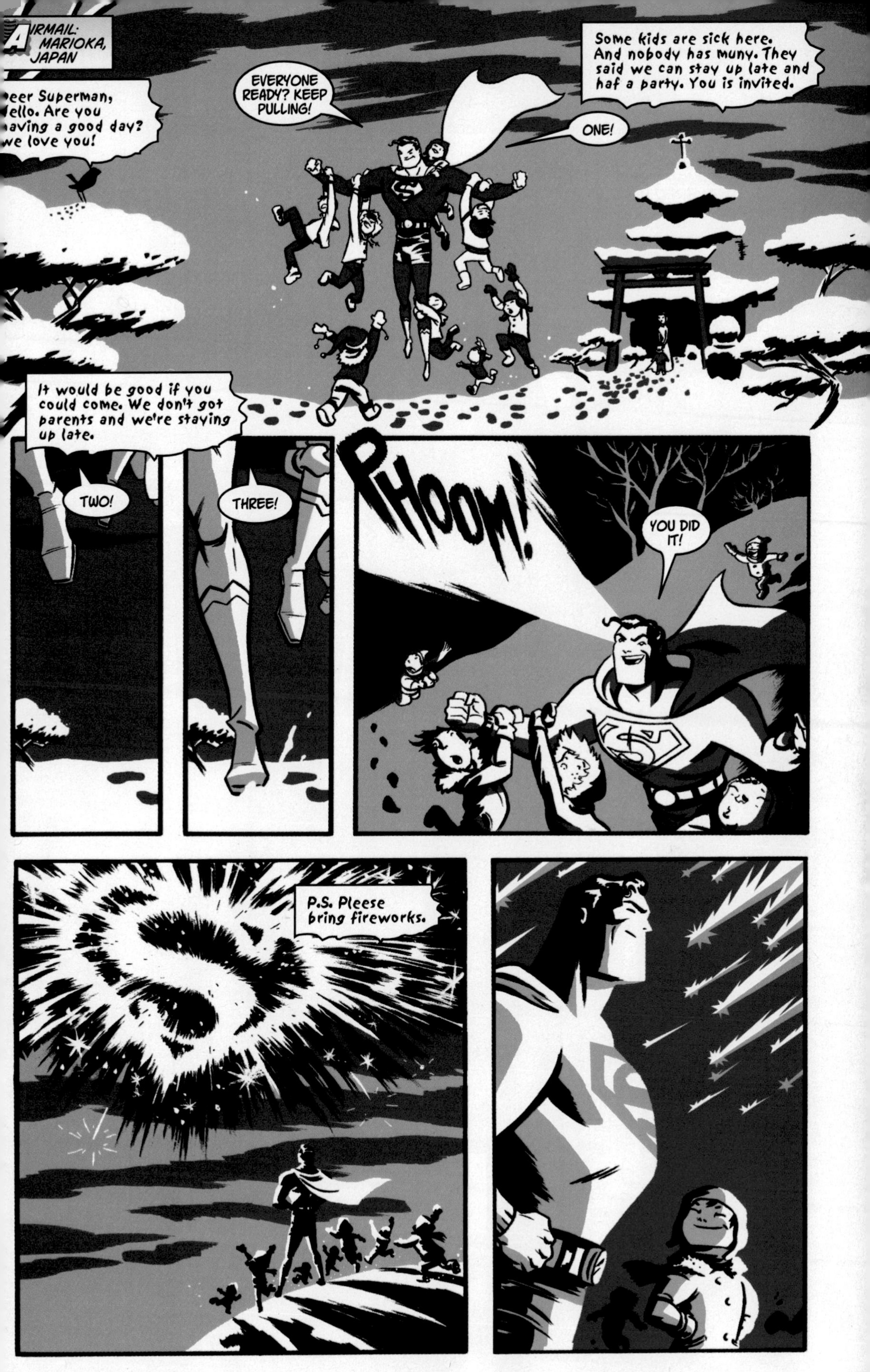
AIRMAIL: MARIOKA, JAPAN
eer Superman, ello. Are you aving a good day? we love you!
EVERYONE READY? KEEP PULLING!
Some kids are sick here. And nobody has muny. They said we can stay up late and haf a party. You is invited.
ONE!
It would be good if you could come. We don't got parents and we're staying up late.
TWO!
THREE!
PHOOM!
YOU DID IT!
P.S. Pleese bring fireworks.

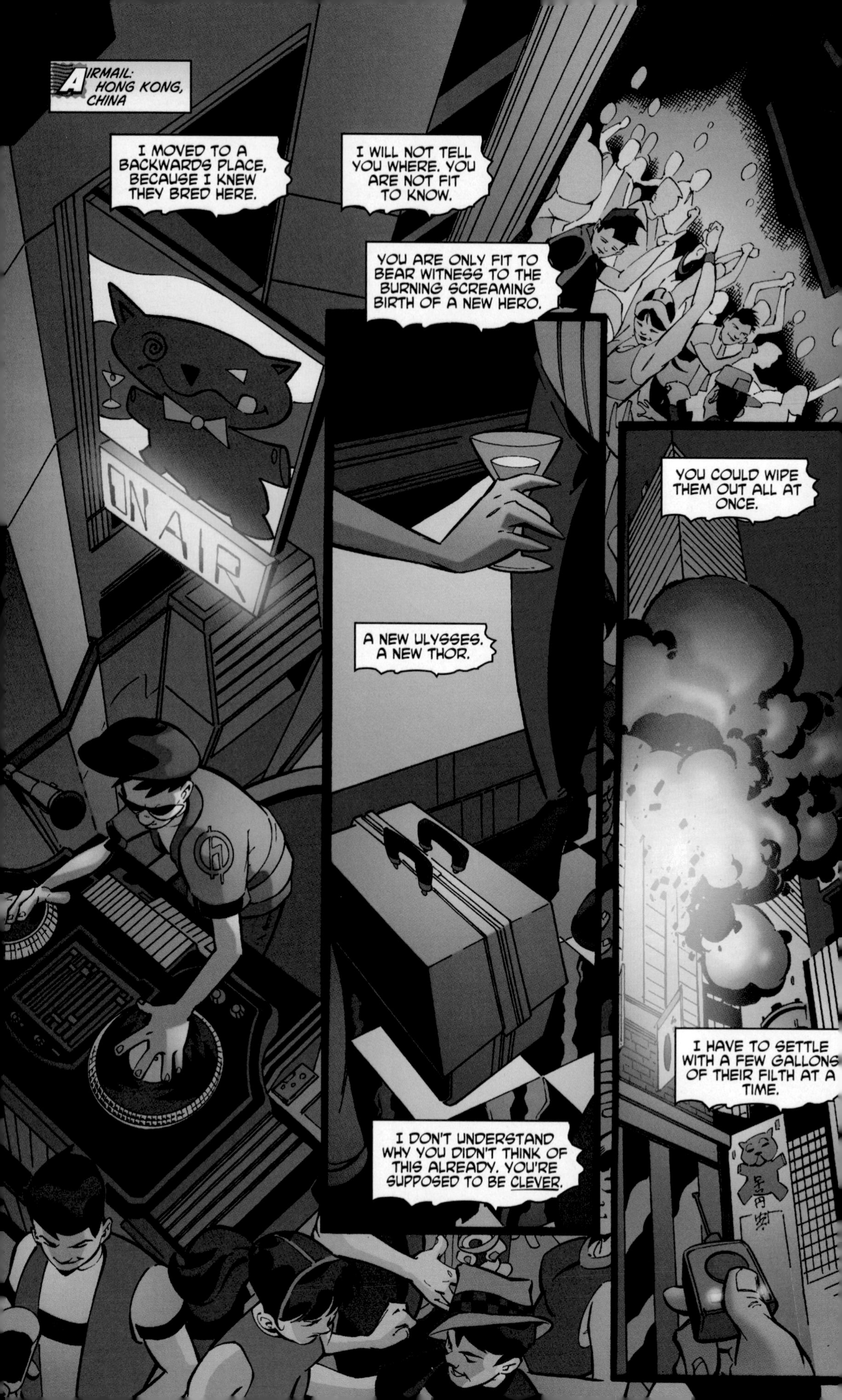
AIRMAIL: HONG KONG, CHINA
I MOVED TO A BACKWARDS PLACE, BECAUSE I KNEW THEY BRED HERE.
I WILL NOT TELL YOU WHERE. YOU ARE NOT FIT TO KNOW.
YOU ARE ONLY FIT TO BEAR WITNESS TO THE BURNING SCREAMING BIRTH OF A NEW HERO.
ON AIR
A NEW ULYSSES. A NEW THOR.
I DON'T UNDERSTAND WHY YOU DIDN'T THINK OF THIS ALREADY. YOU'RE SUPPOSED TO BE CLEVER.
YOU COULD WIPE THEM OUT ALL AT ONCE.
I HAVE TO SETTLE WITH A FEW GALLONS OF THEIR FILTH AT A TIME.

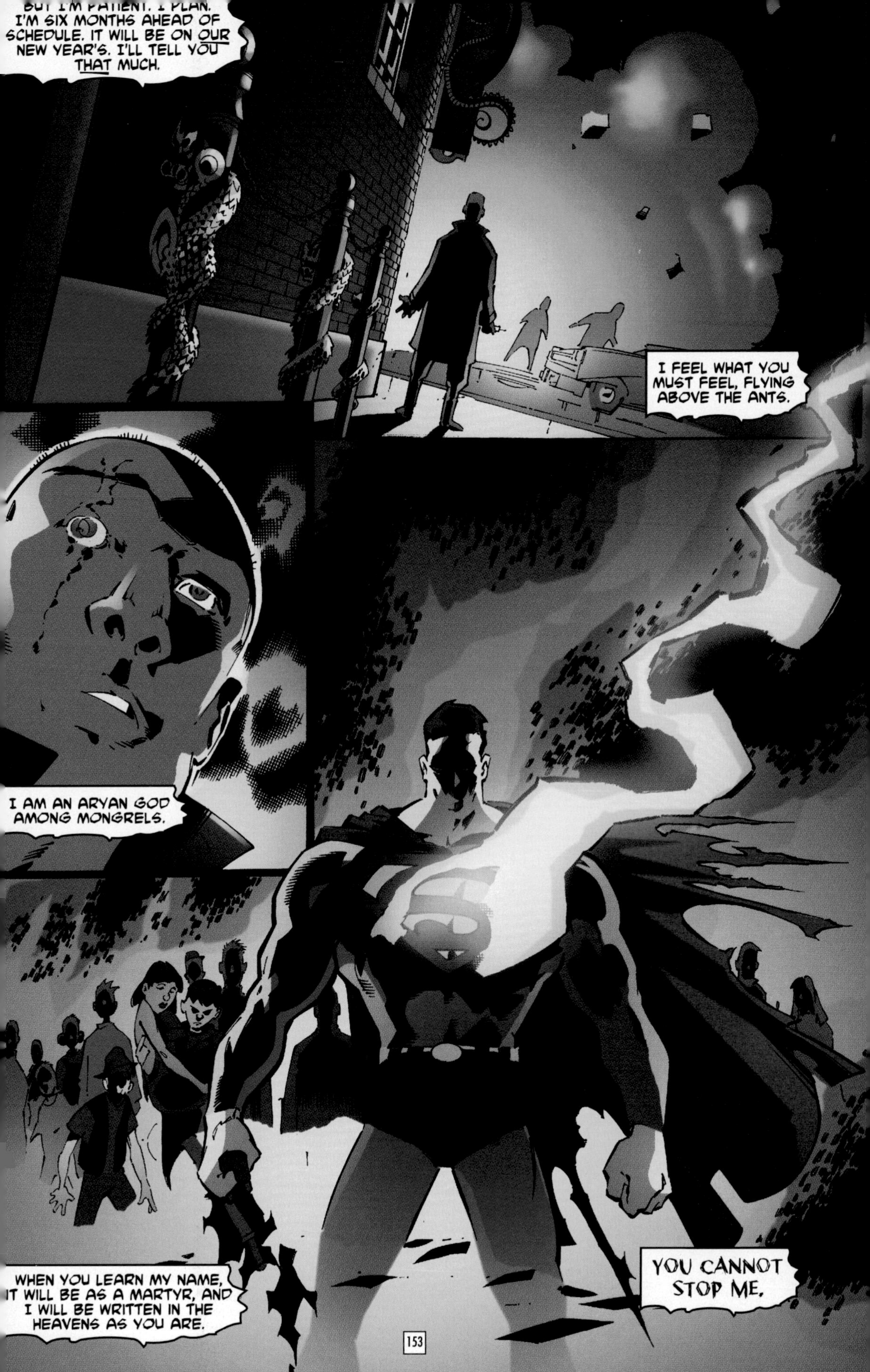
BUT I'M PATIENT. I PLAN. I'M SIX MONTHS AHEAD OF SCHEDULE. IT WILL BE ON OUR NEW YEAR'S. I'LL TELL YOU THAT MUCH.
I FEEL WHAT YOU MUST FEEL, FLYING ABOVE THE ANTS.
I AM AN ARYAN GOD AMONG MONGRELS.
WHEN YOU LEARN MY NAME, IT WILL BE AS A MARTYR, AND I WILL BE WRITTEN IN THE HEAVENS AS YOU ARE.
YOU CANNOT STOP ME.

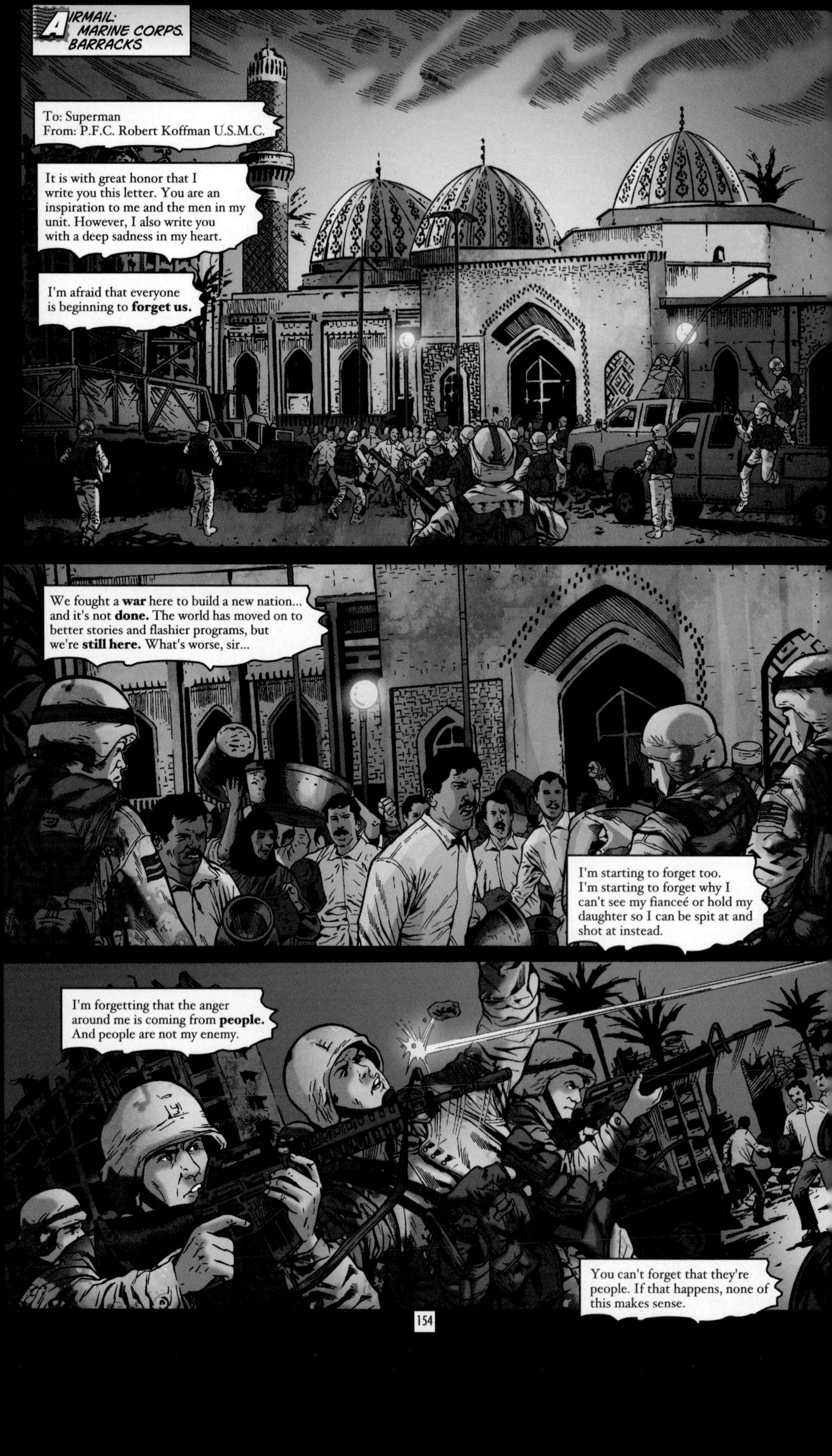
AIRMAIL: MARINE CORPS. BARRACKS
To: Superman
From: P.F.C. Robert Koffman U.S.M.C.
It is with great honor that I write you this letter. You are an inspiration to me and the men in my unit. However, I also write you with a deep sadness in my heart.
I'm afraid that everyone is beginning to **forget us.**
We fought a **war** here to build a new nation... and it's not **done.** The world has moved on to better stories and flashier programs, but we're **still here.** What's worse, sir...
I'm starting to forget too. I'm starting to forget why I can't see my fianceé or hold my daughter so I can be spit at and shot at instead.
I'm forgetting that the anger around me is coming from **people.** And people are not my enemy.
You can't forget that they're people. If that happens, none of this makes sense.

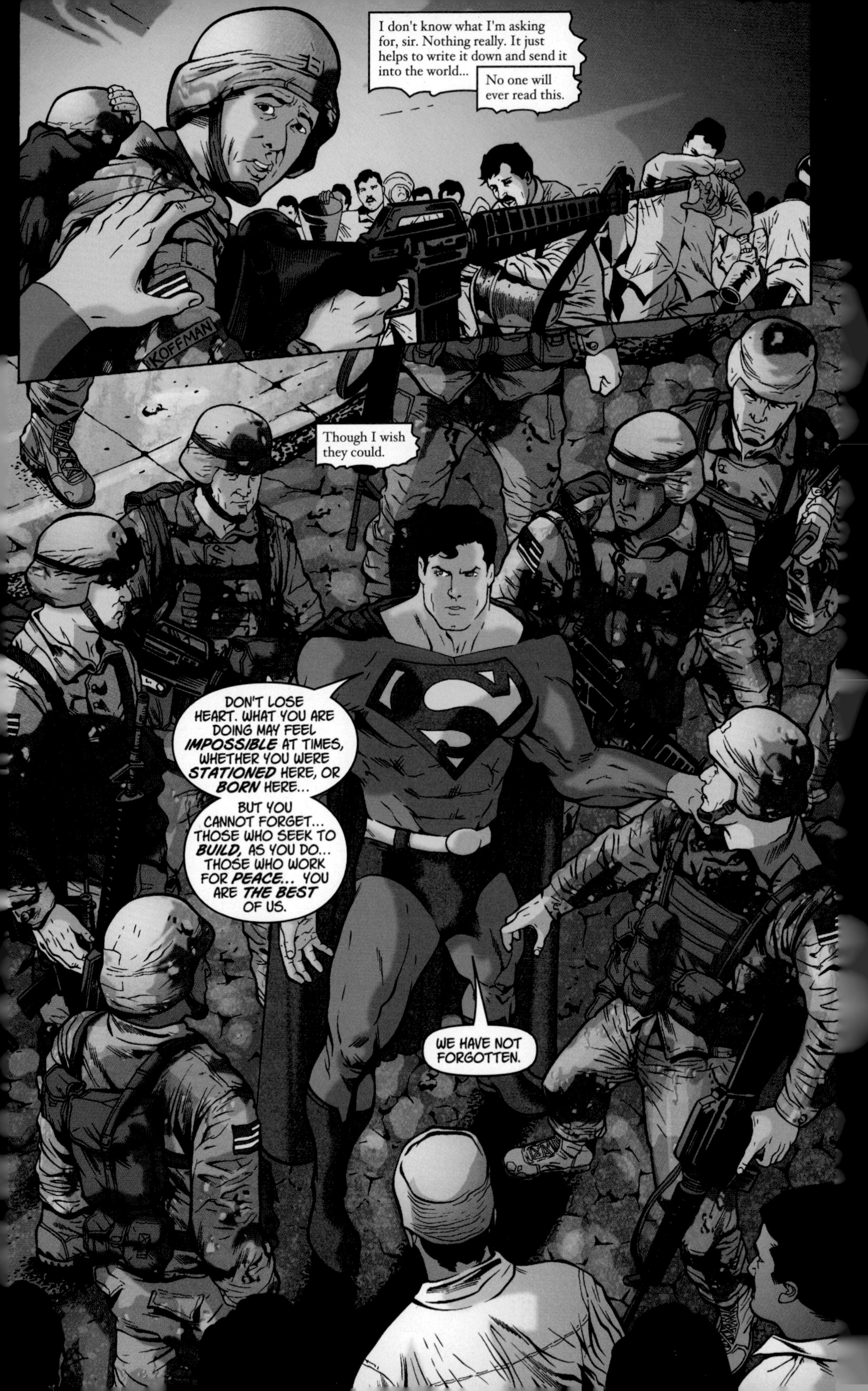
I don't know what I'm asking for, sir. Nothing really. It just helps to write it down and send it into the world...
No one will ever read this.
KOFFMAN
Though I wish they could.
DON'T LOSE HEART. WHAT YOU ARE DOING MAY FEEL IMPOSSIBLE AT TIMES, WHETHER YOU WERE STATIONED HERE, OR BORN HERE...
BUT YOU CANNOT FORGET... THOSE WHO SEEK TO BUILD, AS YOU DO... THOSE WHO WORK FOR PEACE... YOU ARE THE BEST OF US.
WE HAVE NOT FORGOTTEN.

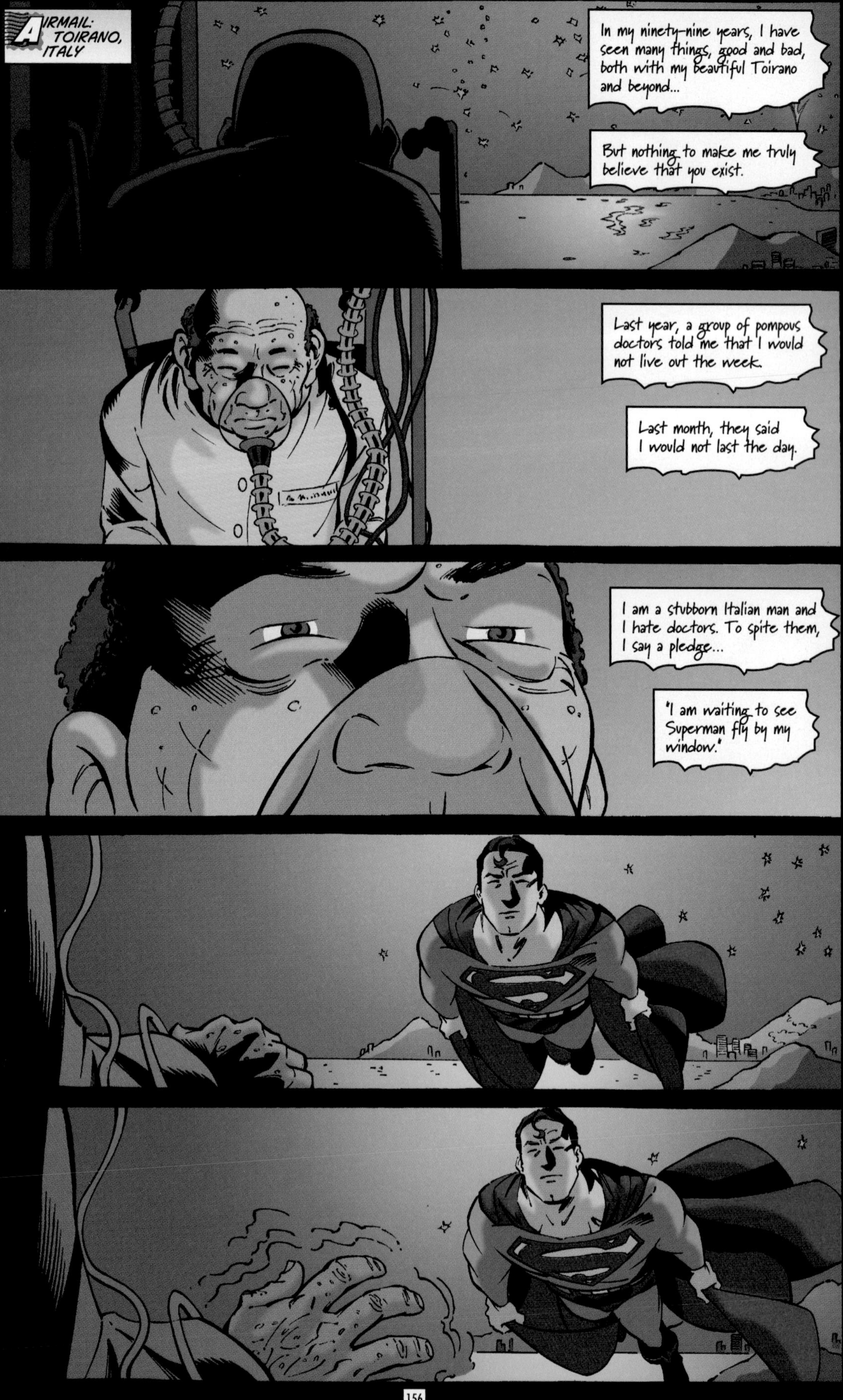
AIRMAIL: TOIRANO, ITALY
In my ninety-nine years, I have seen many things, good and bad, both with my beautiful Toirano and beyond...
But nothing to make me truly believe that you exist.
Last year, a group of pompous doctors told me that I would not live out the week.
Last month, they said I would not last the day.
I am a stubborn Italian man and I hate doctors. To spite them, I say a pledge...
"I am waiting to see Superman fly by my window."

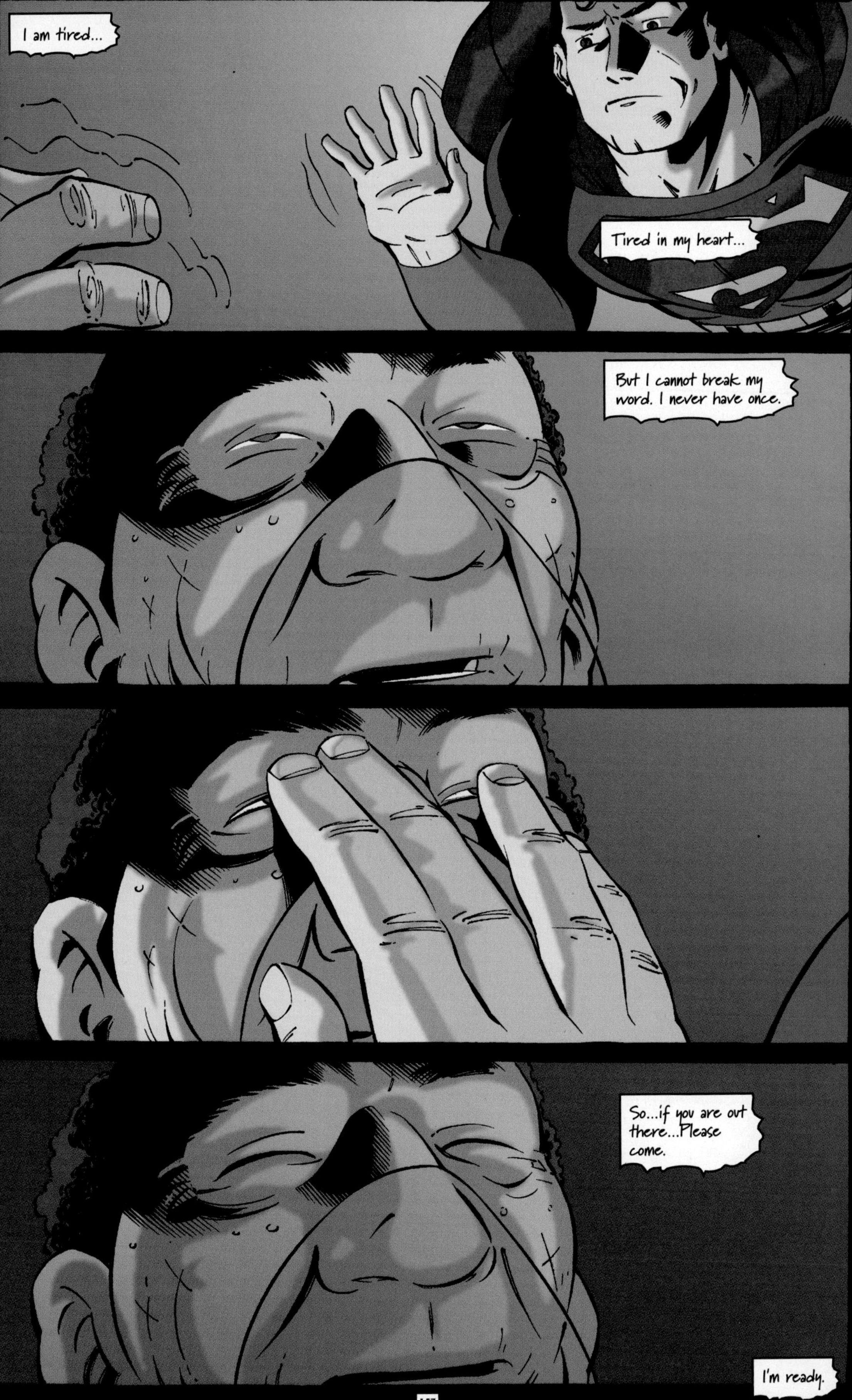
I am tired...
Tired in my heart...
But I cannot break my word. I never have once.
So...if you are out there...Please come.
I'm ready.

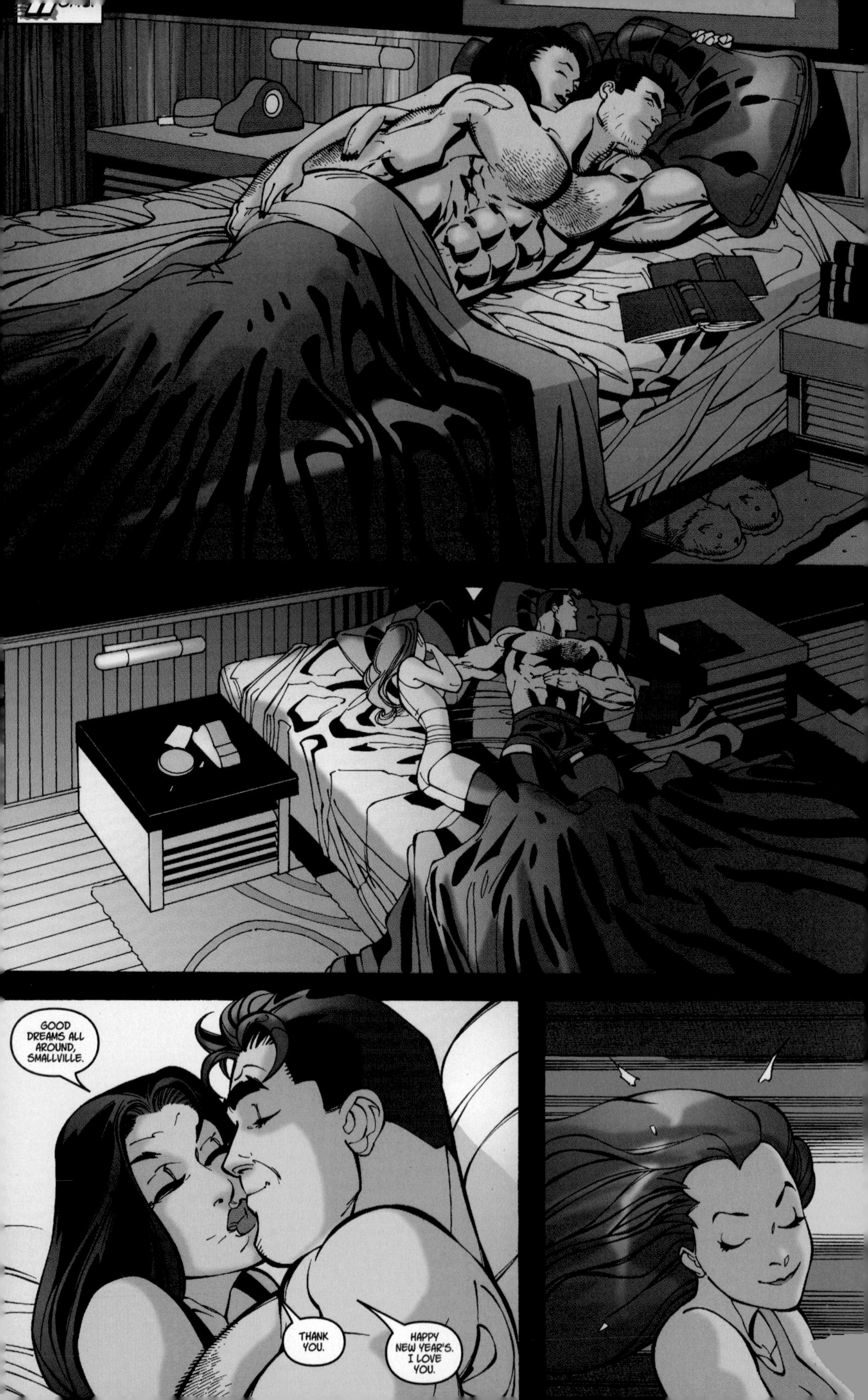
GOOD DREAMS ALL AROUND, SMALLVILLE.
THANK YOU.
HAPPY NEW YEAR'S. I LOVE YOU.

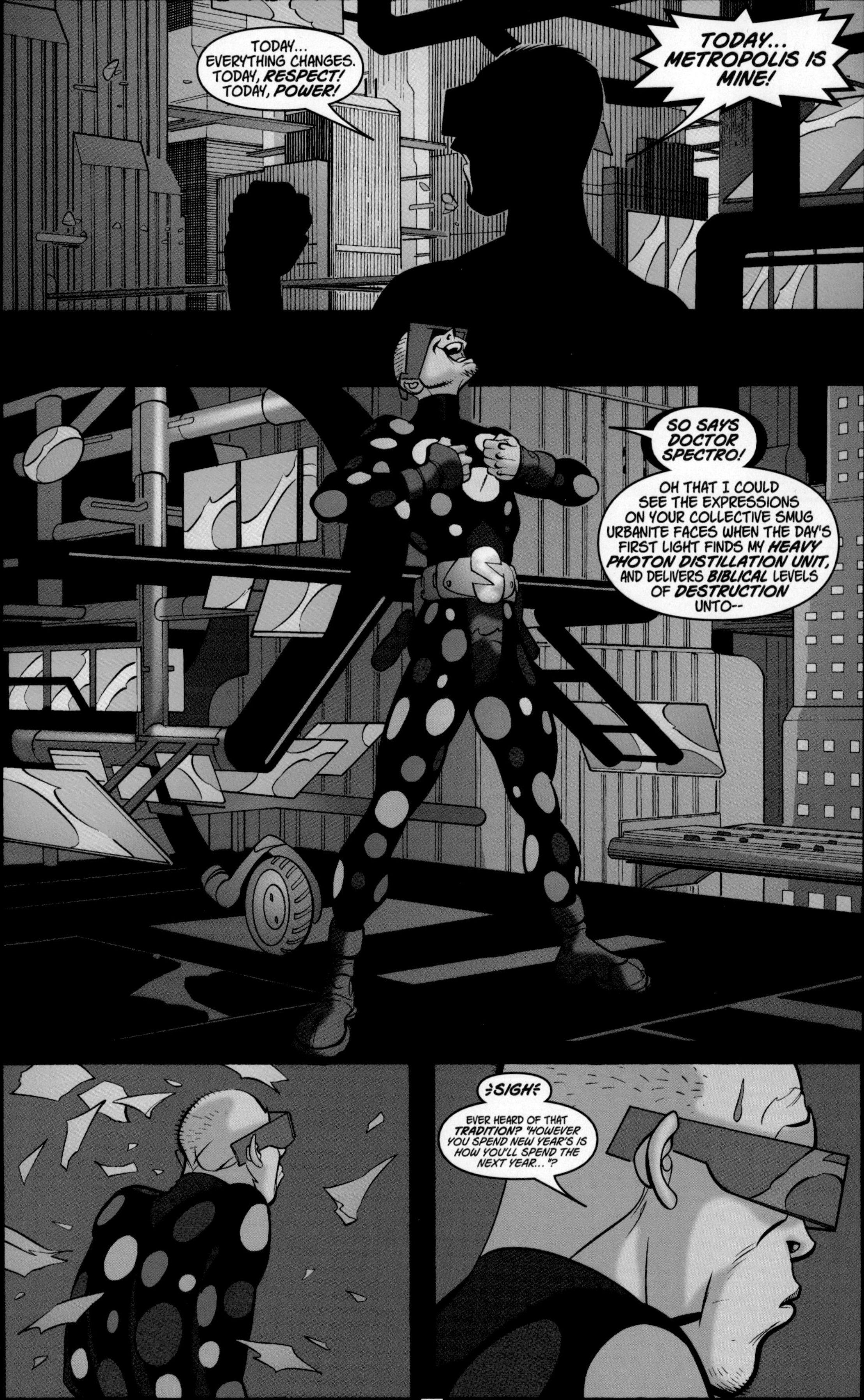
TODAY... EVERYTHING CHANGES. TODAY, RESPECT! TODAY, POWER!
TODAY... METROPOLIS IS MINE!
SO SAYS DOCTOR SPECTRO!
OH THAT I COULD SEE THE EXPRESSIONS ON YOUR COLLECTIVE SMUG URBANITE FACES WHEN THE DAY'S FIRST LIGHT FINDS MY HEAVY PHOTON DISTILLATION UNIT, AND DELIVERS BIBLICAL LEVELS OF DESTRUCTION UNTO--
SIGH
EVER HEARD OF THAT TRADITION? "HOWEVER YOU SPEND NEW YEAR'S IS HOW YOU'LL SPEND THE NEXT YEAR..."?

LAST NIGHT, I TURNED MY BACK ON THE ONE SHOT I HAD AT *LOVE* TO FINISH BUILDING *THAT*--

THAT PIECE OF POST-MODERN *GARBAGE ART.* I'LL NEVER SEE THAT WOMAN AGAIN.

I'M SORRY TO HEAR THAT, DOCTOR. I AM.

I DO NOT *REGRET* MY STAB AT *GREATNESS,* SUPERMAN. *I CANNOT...* BUT IT OCCURS TO ME THAT I WILL *DIE* WONDERING WHAT *COULD* HAVE BEEN, IF I HAD JUST *STAYED HOME* AND STARTED THE NEW YEAR IN HER ARMS.

WHAT DID YOU DO LAST NIGHT?

...

EVERYTHING.

"*EVERYTHING.*" OF COURSE YOU DID... WOULD YOU--

COULD YOU TELL ME WHAT IT'S LIKE? TO BE YOU?

YOU WANT TO KNOW THE *TRUTH...?*

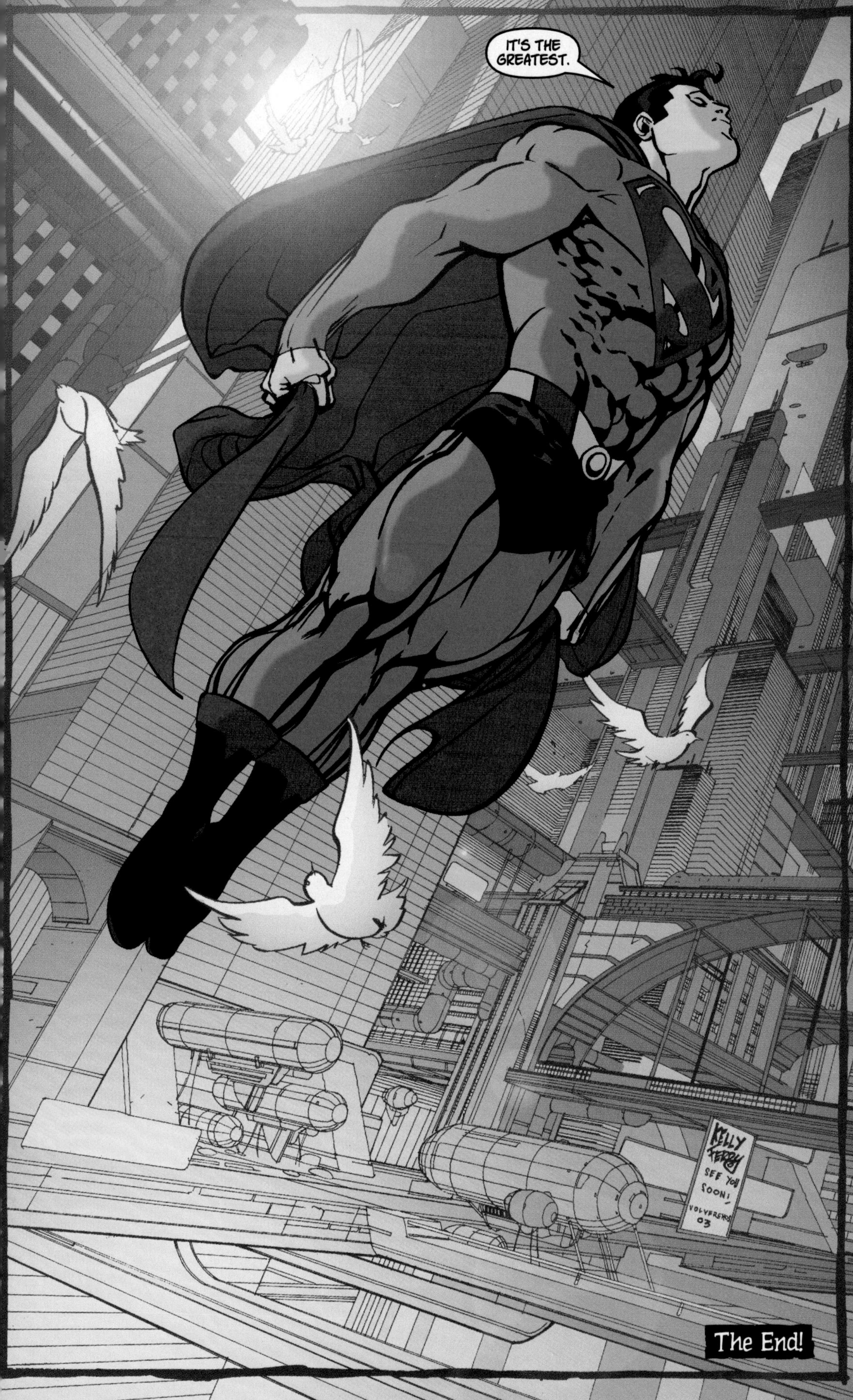
IT'S THE GREATEST.
KELLY FERRY
SEE YOU SOON!
The End!

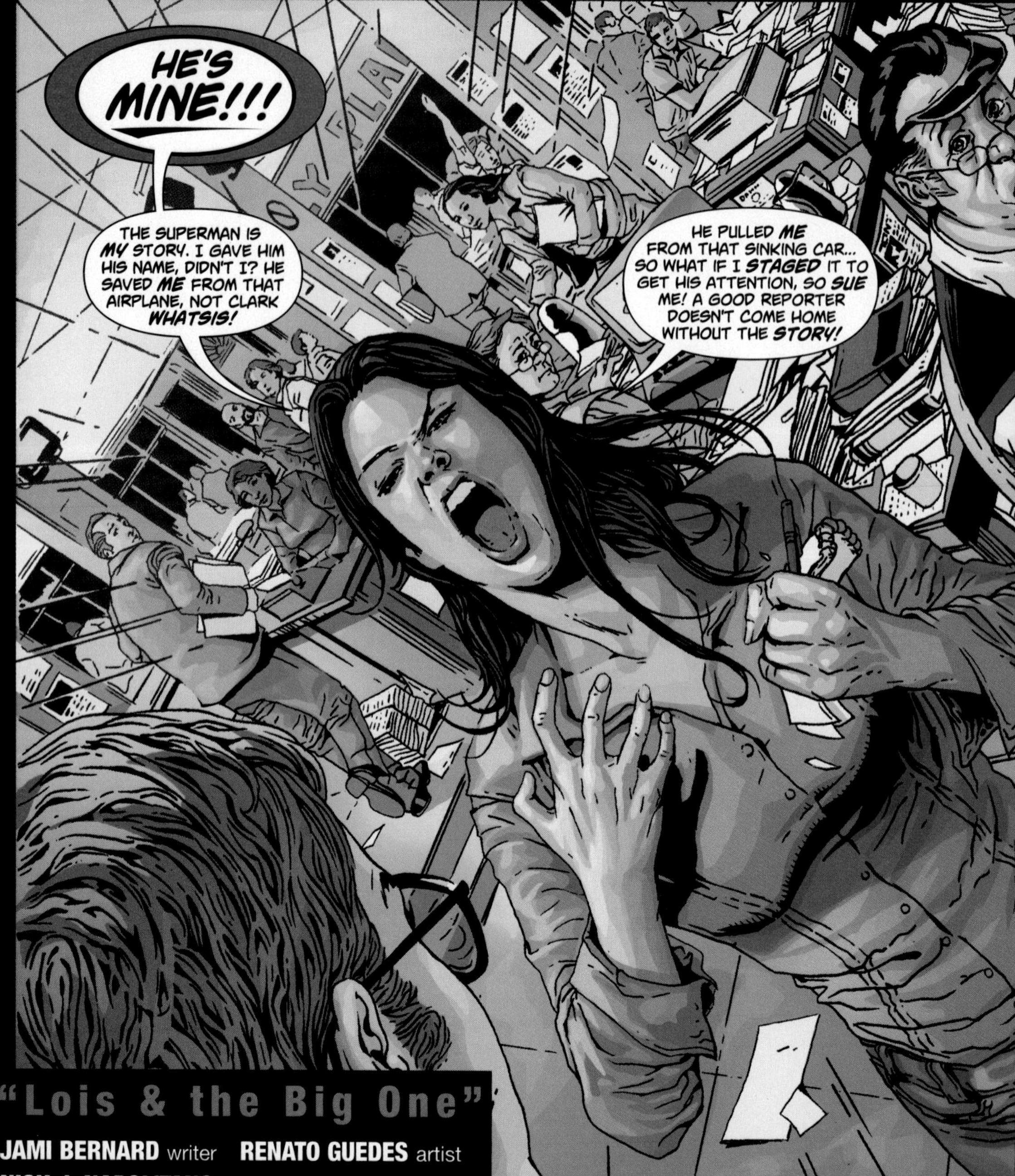
HE'S MINE!!!
THE SUPERMAN IS MY STORY. I GAVE HIM HIS NAME, DIDN'T I? HE SAVED ME FROM THAT AIRPLANE, NOT CLARK WHATSIS!
HE PULLED ME FROM THAT SINKING CAR... SO WHAT IF I STAGED IT TO GET HIS ATTENTION, SO SUE ME! A GOOD REPORTER DOESN'T COME HOME WITHOUT THE STORY!

"Lois & the Big One"

JAMI BERNARD writer **RENATO GUEDES** artist
NICK J. NAPOLITANO letterer

From SUPERMAN SECRET FILES comes this short story about Lois Lane's desire for the scoop on Superman...

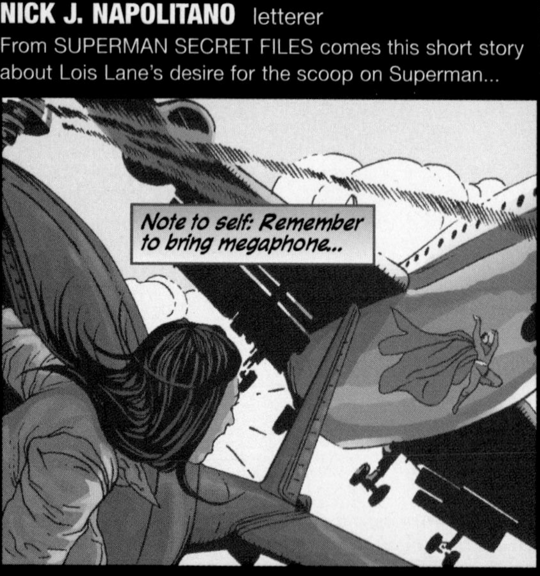
Note to self: Remember to bring megaphone...

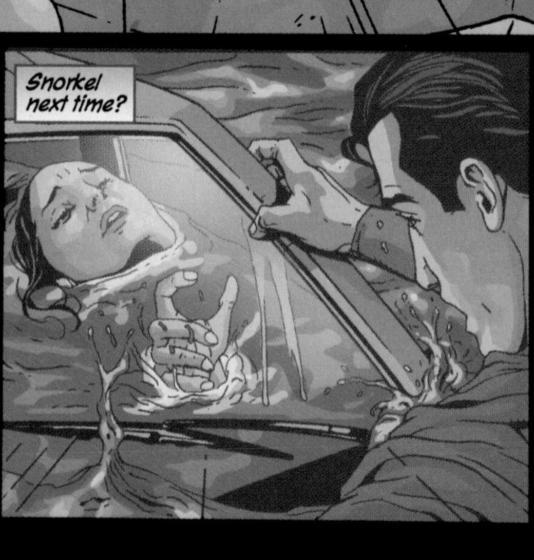
Snorkel next time?

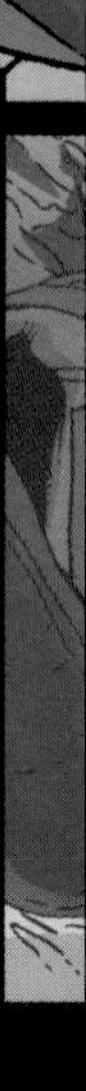

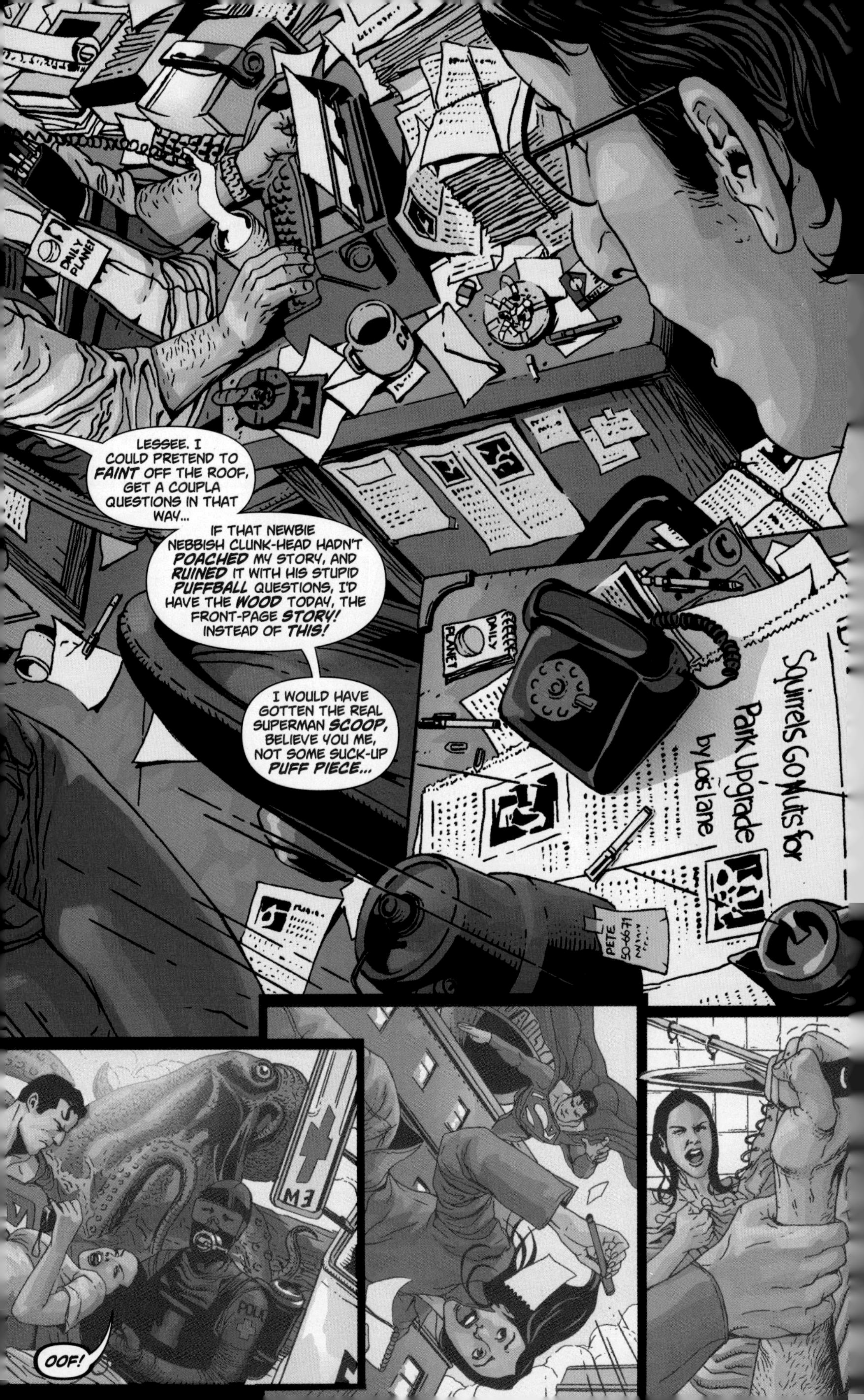
DAILY PLANET
LESSEE. I COULD PRETEND TO FAINT OFF THE ROOF, GET A COUPLA QUESTIONS IN THAT WAY...
IF THAT NEWBIE NEBBISH CLUNK-HEAD HADN'T POACHED MY STORY, AND RUINED IT WITH HIS STUPID PUFFBALL QUESTIONS, I'D HAVE THE WOOD TODAY, THE FRONT-PAGE STORY! INSTEAD OF THIS!
I WOULD HAVE GOTTEN THE REAL SUPERMAN SCOOP, BELIEVE YOU ME, NOT SOME SUCK-UP PUFF PIECE...
DAILY PLANET
Squirrels Go Nuts for Park Upgrade
by Lois Lane
PETE
OOF!

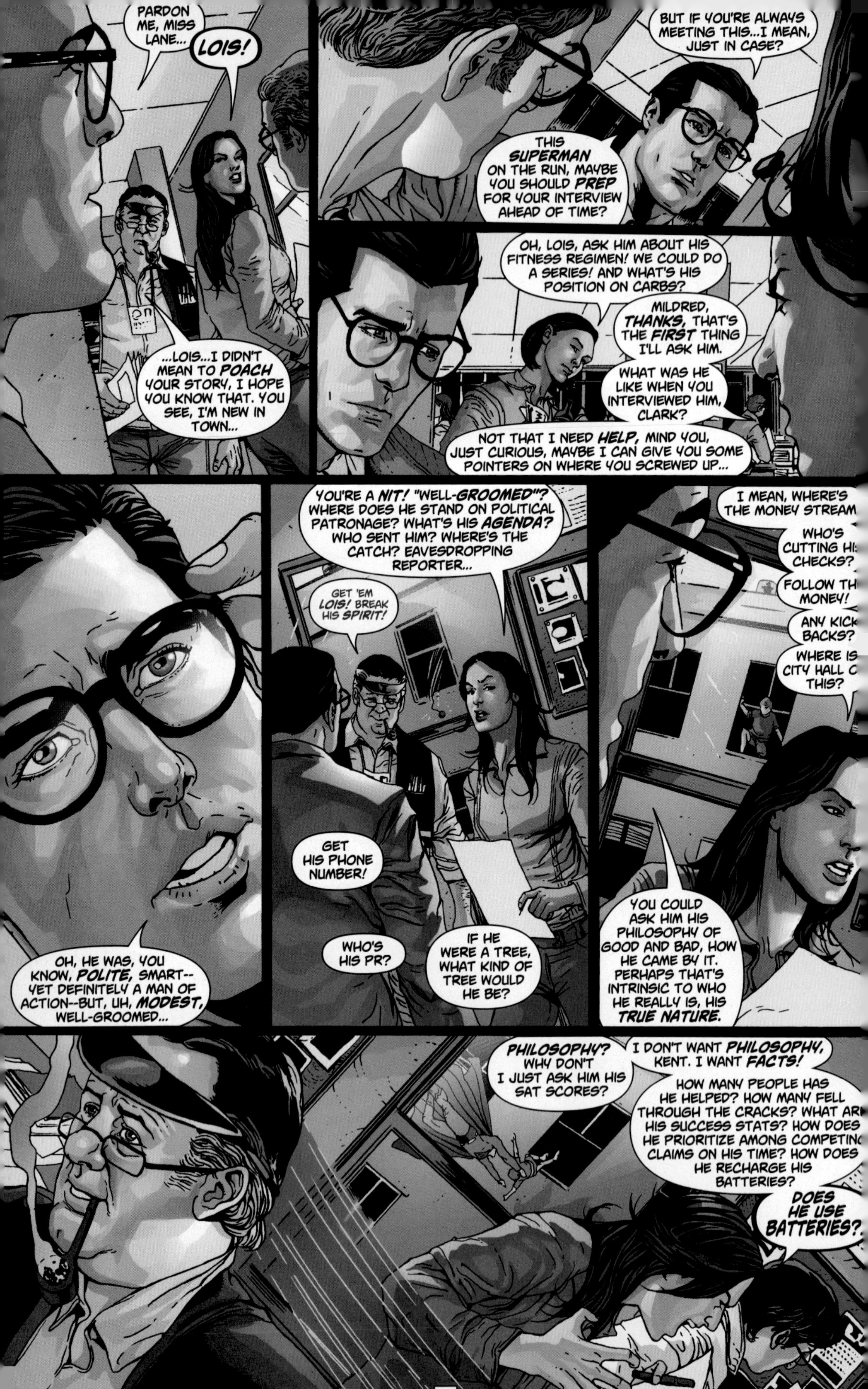
PARDON ME, MISS LANE...
LOIS!
...LOIS...I DIDN'T MEAN TO POACH YOUR STORY, I HOPE YOU KNOW THAT. YOU SEE, I'M NEW IN TOWN...
BUT IF YOU'RE ALWAYS MEETING THIS...I MEAN, JUST IN CASE?
THIS SUPERMAN ON THE RUN, MAYBE YOU SHOULD PREP FOR YOUR INTERVIEW AHEAD OF TIME?
OH, LOIS, ASK HIM ABOUT HIS FITNESS REGIMEN! WE COULD DO A SERIES! AND WHAT'S HIS POSITION ON CARBS?
MILDRED, THANKS, THAT'S THE FIRST THING I'LL ASK HIM.
WHAT WAS HE LIKE WHEN YOU INTERVIEWED HIM, CLARK?
NOT THAT I NEED HELP, MIND YOU, JUST CURIOUS, MAYBE I CAN GIVE YOU SOME POINTERS ON WHERE YOU SCREWED UP...
OH, HE WAS, YOU KNOW, POLITE, SMART-- YET DEFINITELY A MAN OF ACTION--BUT, UH, MODEST, WELL-GROOMED...
YOU'RE A NIT! "WELL-GROOMED"? WHERE DOES HE STAND ON POLITICAL PATRONAGE? WHAT'S HIS AGENDA? WHO SENT HIM? WHERE'S THE CATCH? EAVESDROPPING REPORTER...
GET 'EM LOIS! BREAK HIS SPIRIT!
GET HIS PHONE NUMBER!
WHO'S HIS PR?
IF HE WERE A TREE, WHAT KIND OF TREE WOULD HE BE?
I MEAN, WHERE'S THE MONEY STREAM
WHO'S CUTTING HI
CHECKS?
FOLLOW TH
MONEY!
ANY KICK
BACKS?
WHERE IS
CITY HALL C
THIS?
YOU COULD ASK HIM HIS PHILOSOPHY OF GOOD AND BAD, HOW HE CAME BY IT. PERHAPS THAT'S INTRINSIC TO WHO HE REALLY IS, HIS TRUE NATURE.
PHILOSOPHY? WHY DON'T I JUST ASK HIM HIS SAT SCORES?
I DON'T WANT PHILOSOPHY, KENT. I WANT FACTS!
HOW MANY PEOPLE HAS HE HELPED? HOW MANY FELL THROUGH THE CRACKS? WHAT AR
HIS SUCCESS STATS? HOW DOES HE PRIORITIZE AMONG COMPETIN
CLAIMS ON HIS TIME? HOW DOES HE RECHARGE HIS BATTERIES?
DOES HE USE BATTERIES?

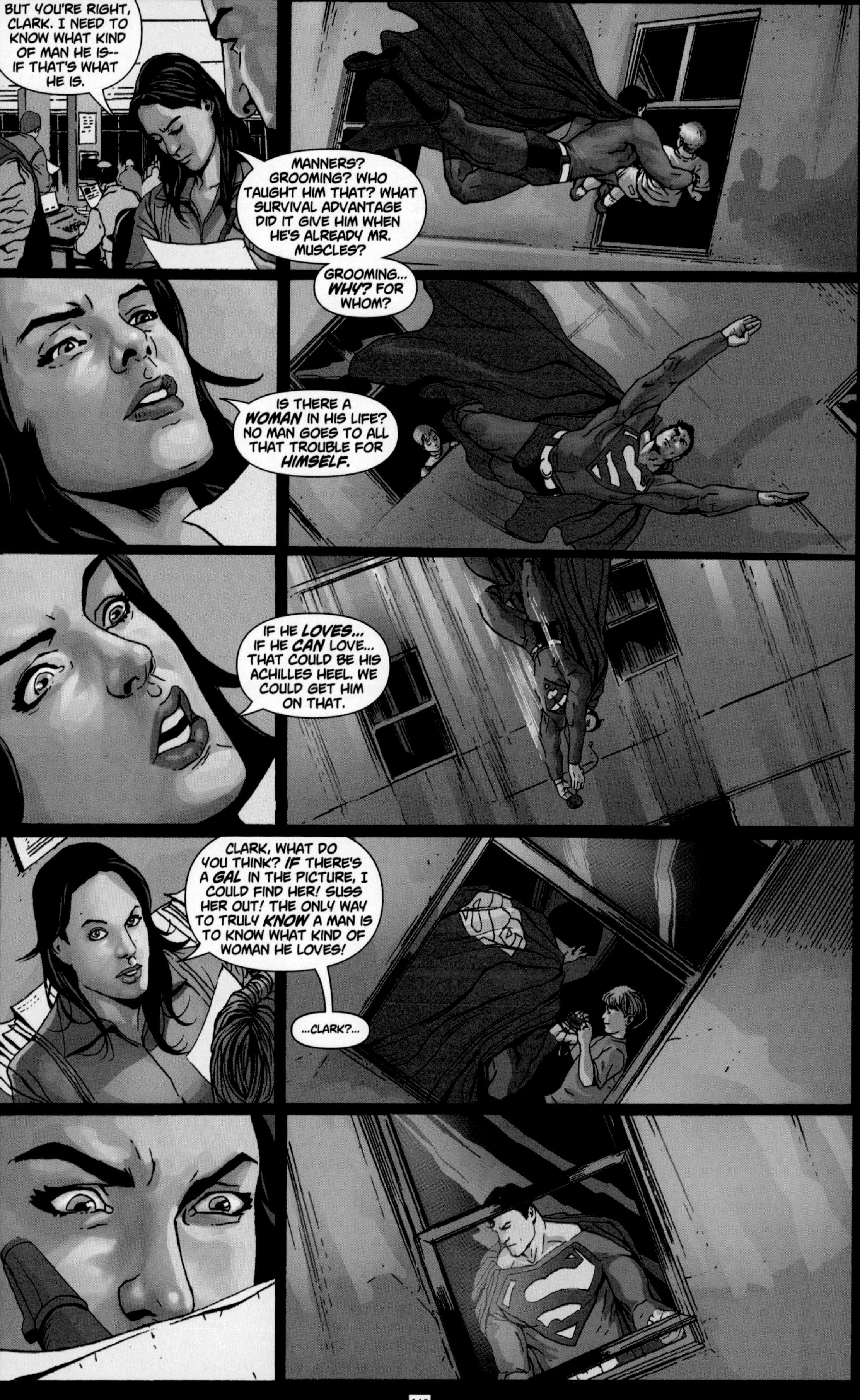
BUT YOU'RE RIGHT, CLARK. I NEED TO KNOW WHAT KIND OF MAN HE IS-- IF THAT'S WHAT HE IS.
MANNERS? GROOMING? WHO TAUGHT HIM THAT? WHAT SURVIVAL ADVANTAGE DID IT GIVE HIM WHEN HE'S ALREADY MR. MUSCLES?
GROOMING... WHY? FOR WHOM?
IS THERE A WOMAN IN HIS LIFE? NO MAN GOES TO ALL THAT TROUBLE FOR HIMSELF.
IF HE LOVES... IF HE CAN LOVE... THAT COULD BE HIS ACHILLES HEEL. WE COULD GET HIM ON THAT.
CLARK, WHAT DO YOU THINK? IF THERE'S A GAL IN THE PICTURE, I COULD FIND HER! SUSS HER OUT! THE ONLY WAY TO TRULY KNOW A MAN IS TO KNOW WHAT KIND OF WOMAN HE LOVES!
...CLARK?...

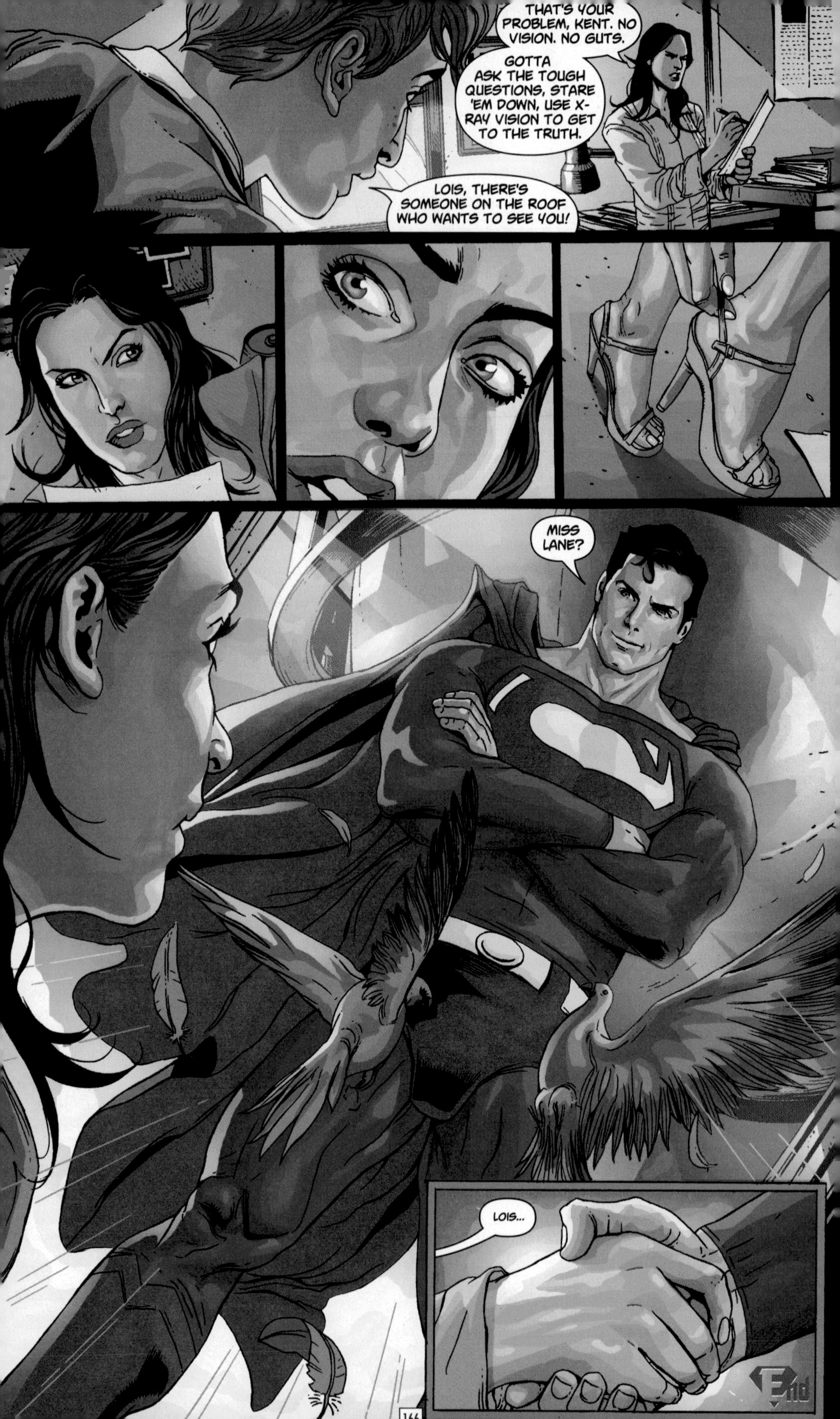
THAT'S YOUR PROBLEM, KENT. NO VISION. NO GUTS.
GOTTA ASK THE TOUGH QUESTIONS, STARE 'EM DOWN, USE X-RAY VISION TO GET TO THE TRUTH.
LOIS, THERE'S SOMEONE ON THE ROOF WHO WANTS TO SEE YOU!
MISS LANE?
LOIS...
End

The Gunfighter: Man or Myth?

The

Gun fighter

Man or Myth?

Joseph G. Rosa

University of Oklahoma Press : Norman and London

By Joseph G. Rosa

They Called Him Wild Bill: The Life and Adventures of James Butler
  Hickok (Norman, 1964)
The Gunfighter: Man or Myth (Norman, 1969)
The West of Wild Bill Hickok (Norman, 1982)
Rowdy Joe Lowe: Gambler with a Gun (Norman, 1989)

For Bruce and Michael Snell,
  who will, I know, grow up to appreciate
  the American West as much as their English friend does

Library of Congress Catalog Card Number: 68-31378

ISBN: 0–8061–1561–0

8 9 10 11 12 13 14 15 16 17 18 19 20

Introduction

THE WESTERN GUNFIGHTER was the New World's counterpart of the knights in armor and the Robin Hoods of the Old. His sword was a Colt .45, and his armor the ability to outdraw and outshoot any rival. For generations he has represented to the nation's youth the heroic image of the lone crusader who fights evil in order that good may prevail—a paragon of virtue, beyond reproach.

It is this concept of the gunfighter that is generally uppermost in our minds—surely in our imaginations. Few people who profess to be knowledgeable about the American West can in all honesty say that their opinions or conclusions have not in some way been influenced by childhood reading and trips to the movies. We all treasure fond memories of a hero or heroes whose exploits served as a guide to our youthful behavior, even though we may now recognize the mythical nature of these early heroes, as well as of the villains whose evil plans they thwarted. When we seek the truth about the gunfighter as a man, myth must be distinguished from reality, and he must be viewed as but one of the many personalities that thronged the West—not as the principal character.

There are many obstacles to such a course. Even the origin of the word "gunfighter" is obscure. "Bat" Masterson used it in his *Human Life* articles as early as 1907 but preferred the term "mankiller." A noted Western historian believes that it gained popularity with the early movies and adds, "I think the early Westerners themselves spoke of the *gunman* rather than gunfighter."[1] Eugene Manlove Rhodes once wrote that the Old West considered a "gun-

[1] Ramon F. Adams to the author, December 2, 1965.

man" comparable to a "swordsman" of earlier centuries but that, with the arrival of the Chicago gangsters, the word came to suggest something evil, of "helpless victims 'taken for a ride' or 'put on the spot'; of time fuse bombs and steel vests, armored cars and machine guns; the safe and shameless!"[2]

Although *A Dictionary of Americanisms* lists no use of "gunfighter" before 1894, the term was used at least twenty years earlier. In 1874 several newspapers carried a story of a gentleman calling himself "Cemetery Sam" who appeared in Eureka, California, where he politely (but loudly) informed the local residents that he was "from Pioche" and was a "gunfighter."[3] Occasionally we find the word "shootist" applied to a gun-toting individual, but mostly this term was applied to prominent marksmen. It was left to Clay Allison, the famed killer, to say, "I am a shootist," and mean "gunfighter."[4]

Today, however, the outlaw killer is commonly a "gunman" and the peace officer a "gunfighter," though I use the latter term to cover both good and bad.

In the terminology of the time this book covers, a pocket pistol was "carried," and a holstered weapon was "worn." A pistol was not "drawn" but "pulled," and to all but a tenderfoot, revolvers were "guns." Revolvers were, of course, the principal fighting weapons, but derringers and knives played their parts. The most deadly weapon of them all was the sawed-off shotgun. Very few men dared stand up to an adversary armed with one.

The gunfighter might never have emerged but for the conditions in the country he operated in—the American wild West. Although Australia, South Africa, and other newly populated countries experienced similar periods of lawlessness and violence, it was the American West that bred the men whose exploits, both real and imagined, created the myth of the hero without fear, fault, or flaw —the hero whose virility and virtue have been immortalized in

[2] Eugene Manlove Rhodes, in Eugene Cunningham, *Triggernometry*, xi.

[3] Topeka *Daily Commonwealth*, July 19, 1874.

[4] St. Louis *Republican*, July 25, 1878.

hundreds of moving pictures, thousands of novels, and millions of anecdotes.

When I planned this book, it was my intention to avoid too many references to individuals, but as my research progressed, I realized that the personalities *were* the legend. In my opinion only two of the gunfighters who became famous—Hickok and Masterson—lived lives resembling the legends that have sprung up about them. Hickok did perform some of the feats associated with his legend; Masterson achieved a genuine frontier reputation and was greatly respected. Their legendary rivals are just that—legendary. The present-day reputation of Wyatt Earp is a case in point. His legend was created by Stuart Lake and spread by television.

This book is a very informal study, but I have endeavored, so far as possible, to base my findings on the records of the time or upon the word of experts who had access to material not available to me. Every effort has been made to verify all statements presented as fact; any errors of interpretation are mine alone.

JOSEPH G. ROSA

Ruislip, Middlesex, England

Acknowledgments

I SHOULD LIKE TO EXPRESS my thanks to the following persons for their patience and unselfish efforts to provide me with advice or information: Henry Newcombe, who originally encouraged me to write the book and has given advice during its writing; Joseph W. Snell, who read the manuscript and made many useful suggestions, especially in regard to the cow-town chapters; C. Leland Sonnichsen, who read my original draft and loaned material from his Western collection; and Waldo E. Koop, whose researches have turned up items of interest long overlooked by less diligent researchers. Thanks are also due to Savoie Lottinville, Arthur Carmody, Ramon F. Adams, Paul D. Riley, Donald F. Danker, Lucile Stevens, Don Russell, Earle R. Forrest, E. B. Mann, Edward Knowles, William Peacock, Jr., and many others who will, I hope, approve the result of their efforts.

I am also indebted to the following organizations for making available material which would otherwise have been unobtainable: the Kansas State Historical Society, the Denver Public Library, the Wyoming State Archives and History Department, the Nebraska State Historical Society, the Texas State Archives, and the El Paso Public Library. My thanks, too, to Mrs. Eileen Mulford, who assisted with the typing of the manuscript.

J. G. R.

Contents

ix

Illustrations

Part 1. The Myth and the Man

1.

The Gunfighter Legend

IT IS NOON. The sun blazes down on a sun-baked, dusty street. Except for an occasional cow pony standing with lowered head at a hitching rail, its tail switching idly at the ever-present flies, no living thing is to be seen. Suddenly the street is no longer deserted. Two men have walked out from the shade of buildings some fifty yards apart. Almost casually they step to the center of the street and stand facing each other. They begin to move forward slowly but steadily, spurs jingling softly, boot heels raising small clouds of dust.

One of the men carries himself arrogantly erect, his lips drawn back in a sneer, aware that hidden along the street are people watching him with hate—a hatred born of fear. His expression is contemptuous as his hand hovers near the butt of an ornate six-shooter that flashes brightly in the harsh rays of the sun with each movement of his body. His eyes are snakelike, unblinking, cold, and cruel. For he is a killer, determined that the man now approaching him shall die—as all others have died who have dared to challenge him or his ruthless ambition. But he is also fearful because he knows that the man he is facing represents everything that he is not.

The other man is tall, and his well-proportioned body moves with a panther-like grace as he paces down the street. Looking neither to the right nor to the left, he walks with deadly purpose toward his antagonist. His features are grim, his mouth a taut slash marring a normally handsome face. His blue-gray eyes, usually relaxed and smiling, are now implacable as they watch the man ahead. At

each step his hands brush against the polished butts of twin Colt .45's nested in holsters hanging low from crossed cartridge belts. The lower ends of the holsters are lashed to his thighs with rawhide thongs to give him just that extra speed on the draw which might mean the difference between life and death. Staring mortality in the face, he dare not show fear as he stalks toward the man whose depravity has led to this duel to the death. On him depend the future of the town and the welfare of the people who at this moment are crouching in the shadows, fearfully awaiting the next few seconds.

Hands flash down, and the thunderous roar of heavy Colts fills the air. When the acrid blue smoke clears, our hero stands alone, guns in hand, his enemy dead in the dust. Once more good has triumphed over evil. From the shadows of the buildings people slowly emerge to shake his hand and thank him for saving them. This is the hero of countless Western movies and novels—the big, sometimes cruel, magnificent demigod we call the "gunfighter."

There is no Western legend as enduring as that of the overrated gunfighter. He is the embodiment of every hero of all time, and yet no one can say for sure what really inspired his legend. It is not enough to say that he was a product of the time. What is there about this figure that has such mass appeal? Principally it is his character that attracts such a wide audience. Modern society's organizations devoted to law and order attempt to apprehend and punish the wrongdoer when crimes against persons or property are committed, but this is normally a long-drawn-out process, and the results are not always satisfactory. In real life individuals are not allowed to take the law into their own hands, but in fiction the legendary gunfighter can act as judge, jury, and executioner. In him people see themselves reacting to similar situations.

In a Western movie or book all manner of injustices are put right by the gunfighter hero, a two-gun Galahad whose pistols are always at the service of those in trouble. Tales of his heroic exploits and of feats impossible for man and weapon have stimulated a world-wide interest in the American West. Since it is essential that

4

the gunfighter's pistol prowess be beyond reproach, he is gifted with phenomenal reflexes which enable him to draw and fire a revolver with incredible speed and accuracy. There is no room for any weakness in his legend.

The instrument of a gunfighter's appeal is his pistol. Without it he is meaningless, for the gun signifies his strength and purpose. In his hands it is the tool of justice or destruction, each shot finding its mark, for "Judge Colt and his jury of six" is unerring in its verdict of death to wrongdoers. No other make of revolver has enjoyed the fame of the Colt, both as a military arm and as a Western civilizer. Of the many different guns used in the West, the gunfighter's particular favorite was the 1873 Army model, the Peacemaker—without doubt the most famous firearm ever made. A six-shot single-action (that is, cocked by hand for each shot) revolver, it became the instrument of both lawmaker and lawbreaker during the last twenty-five years of the nineteenth century and is today an integral part of the gunfighter legend. Weighing just over three pounds fully loaded, well balanced and hard-hitting, it was an ideal fighting man's weapon.

Belief in the superhuman skill of gunfighters and their weapons is not restricted to modern times. In the heyday of the Old West particular attention was paid to a man's ability with a six-shooter. In 1879 a Cheyenne newspaper described the accomplishments of "Wild Bill" Hickok with his cap-and-ball Colt revolvers. The "Prince of Pistoleers" had been dead but three years; nevertheless, his legendary marksmanship was firmly fixed in the public mind:

> His ivory handled revolvers . . . were made expressly for him and were finished in a manner unequalled by any ever before manufactured in this or any other country. It is said that a bullet from them never missed its mark. Remarkable stories are told of the dead shootist's skill with these guns. He could keep two fruit cans rolling, one in front and one behind him, with bullets fired from these firearms. This is only a sample story of the hundreds which are related of his incredible dexterity with these revolvers.[1]

[1] Cheyenne *Daily Leader*, July 1, 1879.

The Western town of books and movies usually has only one street, flanked by dust-covered, sun-drenched, false-fronted buildings—the marshal's office, a saloon, a bank, and sometimes a general store. Almost always the saloon, where good in the form of the gunfighter has its first meeting with evil, is the center of the stage. Here the villain—a rustler, outlaw, or other undesirable whose hold on the town threatens its existence—holds court. Nobody seems to be employed except the bartender, who is forever polishing glasses or pushing bottles to the loafers who are awaiting the inevitable tragedy that will take place during the last five minutes of the story.

On the rare occasions when there is any insight into the characters of the protagonists, it is quickly apparent that they are both something more and something less than human. This situation in the movie Western creates stereotyped characters that eventually begin to pall on the most ardent of fans. In many television and movie Westerns the hero appears to have little or no interest in the opposite sex. Most of the time he leans against a post outside the marshal's office or perches on the hitching rail alongside the saloon, watching all that goes on. The villain plots the acquisition of a ranch, a bank robbery, or some other nefarious scheme which will force the men into open conflict.

The gunfighter legend has been fostered by continuous repetition in books and short stories, but the movie, more than any other medium, is responsible for the legend's world-wide appeal. In 1903, when Edwin S. Porter produced *The Great Train Robbery* (filmed in the wilds of New Jersey), audiences loved it and demanded more. Even while Porter's primitive cameras were filming what was to give a significant boost to the myth, trains were still being robbed, men were being killed in gunfights, and the frontier tradition was very much alive. Thirty years before, William F. Cody, better known as "Buffalo Bill," had enthralled audiences with his gory dramas of Western life. Small wonder that those who had watched Cody act out on the stage the role they fondly imagined he

performed in real life should react favorably toward the new motion pictures.

It is unlikely that Buffalo Bill realized what he was starting in the 1870's, when he featured Wild Bill Hickok, already a part of the legend, in his Wild West stage show. Although Hickok's name drew crowds, he was not a success as a performer and soon left to return to the West. But this brief appearance, in which he performed exaggerated versions of some of his real-life adventures, firmly established a heroic image in the public mind. Cody later toured the world with his show and did more to foster the wild West legends than any other individual. Those years of public acclaim made it fitting that the West should be the scene and subject of the first motion-picture drama.

The early Western movie featured another legendary hero— a "King of the Cowboys." G. M. Anderson, better known as "Broncho Billy," a bit player in *The Great Train Robbery*, was the first "king" and appeared in a number of pictures that embodied most of the now-familiar Western situations. Emphasizing action and featuring stars who could ride well, the early Westerns rapidly gained popularity. It became a tradition for villains to wear black hats, in contrast to the heroes' white ones, and each character was portrayed a little larger than life. There never has been or ever will be a hero quite like the Western hero.

In 1914 an erstwhile Broadway actor of considerable fame, then forty-three years old, decided to go into the moviemaking business. He was William Surrey Hart, probably the most famous Western actor of them all. During the twelve years that he appeared in Westerns, a number of subtle changes crept into the films. In place of the endless fights and chases, he substituted comparatively good plots and a sense of realism. Despite modern-day techniques, few Western pictures better than his have been made. It was Hart who first attempted to depict the "good" bad man of the Old West as a human being. One of his favorite roles was that of the reformed killer whose ultimate death or heroics assured the triumph of good

7

over evil. Hart tried to depict the harsh struggles of the frontier West. If he overplayed the two-gun civilizer somewhat, it seems evident that he did so to emphasize the moral theme of his pictures. But his realism and insistence on detail were his undoing. After World War I most people wanted to forget problems and were eager for light entertainment. Hollywood, quick to respond, adopted a more lighthearted approach to the West.

Close on Hart's heels came Tom Mix, the ultimate in Western movie heroes. His exploits on and off the screen served to furnish material for his own personal legend. Many people came to associate his flashy suits and gaudy regalia with the actual dress of the cowboy. Mix made a star of his horse, Tony, and rode him to a fame undreamed of by any of the old-time cowboys he claimed to emulate. The fact that Mix had never been or done half the things his publicity claimed for him meant nothing to moviegoers. They wanted escapism, and the moviemakers catered to this desire in every possible way.

Buck Jones, a former cavalryman and cowboy, replaced Mix as the top-drawing Western star. With his horse, Silver, he vied with Mix and Tony for "king" status for almost ten years. Jones made his career in sound Westerns and became one of the most beloved of the Western stars. Both Mix and he met tragic ends—Mix in an automobile crash in 1940 and Jones in the terrible night-club fire at Cocoanut Grove, in Boston, Massachusetts, in 1942. There were many other cowboy stars during the days of the last silent and the first sound pictures that furthered the image of the cowboy-gunfighter hero, including such stars as former Army chaplain Fred Thomson, Tom Tyler, and one-time world champion trick rider Ken Maynard.

The old-time Westerns, lacking authenticity, romanticized an already semifictional theme and added to the legend of the gunfighter. These heroes of gun smoke and gallop, who had shot their way through thousands of blanks into the hearts of millions the world over, were replaced by the heroes of the most ridiculous Westerns of all—the musical Westerns. The novelty caught on and

lasted until the early 1950's, when audiences finally tired of the effeminate clothing and impossible situations.

William Boyd established himself in the role of Clarence E. Mulford's most famous character, Hopalong Cassidy, in the middle 1930's, but it was television, after World War II, that gave him the opportunity to ride again on film with a whole new generation. The Hopalong Cassidy films became staple afternoon and Saturday-morning television fare. Television also extended the fame of another hero, the Lone Ranger. The masked rider and his faithful Indian companion, Tonto, rode the justice trail through the media of radio, comic strip, and finally TV, advocating and supporting purity and mercy. The Lone Ranger (who used silver bullets) shot only to wound, never to kill.

Movie audiences are fickle, and the absurdities of the musical Western and the unbelievable goodness of the Lone Ranger finally gave way to a more authentic treatment of the Old West and to more believable situations. This changing attitude was in reality a return to a trend that was briefly apparent during the 1920's and revived briefly in the 1940's. For a hundred run-of-the-mill "oaters" that played to packed audiences, there were a few major productions that became near-classics. John Ford's *The Iron Horse* and James Cruze's *The Covered Wagon*, perhaps the most important of the earlier attempts to establish the Western movie as a work of art, were not just stories of gunfights between cowboys and Indians. Later *The Ox-Bow Incident* and *Red River*, both mature Westerns, were aimed at depicting the West as a harsh land, the people roughened and toughened by their efforts to settle it. The present-day Westerns, with little attempt at authenticity, have made changes in format that are evident even in the most juvenile of pictures. The do-gooder heroes have had their day, and in their wake what can only be called Western morality plays have emerged to depict a more subtle relationship between the hero and the villain; both realize that one answers only to his own conscience and the other to the conscience of society.

The heroine of the Western has changed little. Traditionally she

9

is a rancher's daughter, a schoolteacher, or a store owner whose main attribute is an almost impervious respectability. In the mature movie she may be a saloon girl or a prostitute—but she is "morally pure," and her heart is at least gold-plated. She secretly loves the hero but never lets on, convinced that he would never love a girl like her, a situation suggesting again that he is someone forever apart. Recently, hints of more realistic male-female relationships have been creeping into Westerns. On occasion the stereotyped cry, "Don't go; you'll be killed!" is supplemented by down-to-earth advice. The man about to fight it out is likely to find himself confronted by a woman demanding that he face reality. The sexless superhuman is giving way to a more lifelike character.[2]

Despite subtle changes and a tendency to portray some depth of character in the Western movie and story hero, there is one facet of the myth that may never change, for it is the very essence of the myth—the gunfight. A remarkable transformation takes place in the hero during the moments just before the fight. Gone is his lazy, almost apathetic approach to life. As the adrenaline begins to flow, he becomes alert, cautious, and almost lion-like, stalking down the street to meet his destiny. This is what he was created for, and this is what he must do. For the moment he has no other purpose in life, and he knows it. When the shooting is over and the smoke has cleared, the hero reverts to his nonchalant manner, ready for new drama. Sometimes, his job done, he rides out of town, a silent, lonely man without friends, his goals a distant town, another gunfight, and still more long rides—a man eternally condemned to loneliness.

This characterization is remote from the make-up of the real-life gunfighter, who is thought, by those who indulge in character analysis, to have been bolstering a weak ego with a display of physical strength. His desperate desire to be top dog was manifest in the gunfight. Living on the edge of self-destruction for so long, he wore on his face a fixed expression of pain and misery. Because of his way of life the gunfighter was the most pitied, and sometimes

[2] "The American Morality Play," *Time*, March 30, 1959.

the most despised, Old West character. This man, who held the power of life and death in his hands and used guns to solve his problems, was a mixture of fears. Condemned by his reputation to continue a life of danger, the gunfighter was in reality a composite of many characteristics, the overriding one being that he was a killer. Environment made him; circumstance guided him.

He was not a difficult man to spot. Treading the thin line between life and death made him a more than cautious individual. He avoided dark alleyways and the direct glare of street lamps. Indoors he kept a wall at his back. He was a drifter; where he came from few people cared, and where he was going only the devil knew. He was the product of a violent era that encompassed the struggle for Texas, the California gold rush, and the Kansas-Missouri border wars. It might be said that he was conceived when Samuel Colt patented his first revolver in England in 1835.

But the gunfighter came into his own during the period of the great cattle drives from Texas after the Civil War. Up the cattle trails into Kansas—ending at Abilene, Newton, Ellsworth, Dodge City, and other railhead cowtowns—came prosperity and violence. The Texas cowboy was easy game for the gamblers, pimps, and prostitutes who frequented the towns, and his only recourse was his gun. Marshals, hired for their skill with guns and not for their policing abilities, were expected to maintain a reasonable state of order. The cowtown marshal rarely mixed with the town's citizens during a cattle-drive season, being far too busy controlling the transient cowboys and others who were trying to take over the town. The average person knew little about the gunfighting marshals until long after they were gone, when their heroic or villainous exploits became the subjects of stories and novels. Tales of their deeds aroused controversies among people who had little or no knowledge about frontier life. Attitudes toward the gunfighters ranged from hatred to hero-worship, with the latter feeling generally predominating, even though most people know that folk heroes are products of the imagination coupled with nostalgia and national pride.

The gunfighter of fact and fiction is now a firmly established character in American folklore, even though his contribution to the conquering of the West is still hotly debated. The dust from the last cattle drive has long since settled; the mountain trails and sun-baked streets the gunfighter traveled are no more. But his ghost still rides, and the marks he made on the land are cut deep into the American heritage.

2.

The Wild West

THE WILD WEST, the scene of the gunfighter's exploits, is as much a part of America's folklore as are its innumerable characters, whose adventures have thrilled a world-wide audience for more than a century. Of particular interest to Europeans is the period from 1850 to 1900, the period of the conflict between immigrants and Indians, the westward extension of the railroads, the rise of the cattle industry, and the near extermination of the buffalo, all important aspects of the Western panorama.

To the American, the story of the West is the story of his country's youth—a brief yet long-to-be-remembered stage in the growth to maturity—a time when the frontier was an indefinable place without distinct boundaries, a place apart. The frontier promised freedom and a chance to plan anew. No map could pinpoint it, for it was a concept, not a geographical entity, and the closest the pioneers could come to describing its location was somewhere to the west, beyond civilization.

The wild West, roughly the land west of the Mississippi River, comprised millions of square miles of almost every type of terrain imaginable: prairies, deserts, quicksands, mountains, and rivers—some of the roughest country on earth. Its geography dictated the destiny of the men who came to it. Its natural barriers forced them to plan geographically. Thus the flat plains of Texas and the grassy prairies and high plains of Oklahoma and Kansas made cattle raising and cattle driving feasible.

Today's Americans are not particularly impressed by the vastness of the United States (encompassing almost three million

square miles), but a century ago the time taken to travel from one region to another could be soul-destroying, especially when the nearest friendly person might be a hundred miles or more away. At that time a trip west could take six months or more to complete. The West was a harsh, rugged, and often desolate land, to be conquered only by those strong enough and brave enough to face it and tame it.

There was never a shortage of would-be settlers. Like the ripples from a stone cast into a pool, the waves of settlers spread outward from the townships on the Atlantic coast, up and over the Appalachians (more than fifteen hundred miles of mountain ranges extending south from Maine to Alabama), through the Northwest Territory, across the Mississippi, onto the Great Plains, and through the Rocky Mountains and the Sierras, the final great mountain barriers to the Pacific. The land between the two oceans provided a stage and a backdrop for the drama of the greatest migratory movement of modern times.

The Louisiana Purchase of 1803 almost doubled the size of the United States, and the vast wilderness beyond the Mississippi beckoned man to explore a country of a size that could only be guessed. There were plains that seemed endless, mountains eternally snow-capped, and wildlife beyond belief. Europeans had ventured into this vast territory before the United States took possession of it, but it was not until 1804–1806 that the first official exploration, led by Lewis and Clark, trekked across uncharted wilderness to the Pacific and found that the far West could be reached and settled.

The thousands who made the long, hazardous trip to the Oregon country in the 1840's were followed by tens of thousands in the great overland rush in 1848–49 to the newly discovered gold fields in California. Hard-working people eager for an opportunity to start afresh and gold seekers avid for wealth made the Far West a scene of frenzied activity. The names Oregon and California were on everyone's lips. Mention of the Oregon Trail still conjures up a

vision of hundreds of white-topped covered wagons drawn by slow-moving oxen steadily plodding their way to a promised land.

It is something of a paradox that occupation of the land bordering the Pacific Ocean preceded the settlement of the plains that had to be crossed to reach it. The vast area west of the Missouri and Mississippi rivers (now comprising Oklahoma, Nebraska, Kansas, North and South Dakota, and that region of Colorado east of the Rocky Mountains), an area of about half a million square miles, was often called the "Great American Desert." The entire region was considered by most early travelers to be arid and worthless, habitable only by the Indian tribes and the millions of buffaloes that roamed its prairies. Even after the Civil War there were still those who regarded the region as a desert, a natural barrier preventing any great extension of the population westward.[1] But still men pushed west.

Before the new lands could be reached and settled, the threatening presence of the Indians was a constant reminder that the land was not free for the taking. It had to be fought for. Many pioneers considered the Indians less than human—wild creatures to be killed or driven away to make room for the newcomers. As the settlers advanced, the Indians were forced to retreat or be eliminated. The buffaloes, upon which the Plains Indians were utterly dependent, were hunted for meat and hides and sometimes just for sport, until the great herds were decimated. Early views that the Indians should be allowed to occupy the southern part of the desert region were rejected.[2] Despite efforts by leaders on both sides, the increasing land hunger of the whites hastened the tragic decline of the red men. Treaties made with the Indians were quickly broken as more settlers pushed west in the wake of the pathfinders. The Indians had always waged intertribal wars, but the threat and then the reality of the white invasion served to make some of them forget their age-old differences and band together to

[1] Walter Prescott Webb, *The Great Plains*, 157.
[2] Robert E. Riegal and Robert G. Athearn, *America Moves West*, 194–95.

fight against a civilization that had little place for them and their ways. From the early Indian wars of colonial times until the last battle, at Wounded Knee in 1890, it was the Indians who were destined to be the ultimate losers. But their determined resistance, which contributed to the hazards of the western movement, left behind a saga of courage and determination that will never be forgotten.

Despite Indians, weather, rough country, and all the other hardships of pioneering, the settlers persisted in the movement west, driven by post–Civil War economic pressures or simply by the need for change. The railroads, facilitating the exodus of pioneers and businessmen from the East, also carried less desirable passengers. Criminals, too, became aware of the wealth the West had to offer. On October 6, 1866, the Reno gang, led by John Reno, committed the first of many post–Civil War train robberies. All over the West outlaw activity became a problem.

Law and order were slow to follow the surge of settlement, and local crime problems had to be solved by individual communities. People were forced to make their own laws and dispense justice on the spot. A man on the run had many things in his favor. Provided he got a head start from the scene of the crime, the chance of capture and punishment was remote. He could change his name and disappear into the wilderness of Texas, the deserts of Nevada, or the mountains of Colorado. If he was familiar with the desert or mountains, he would know where to hide, where to find water, and how to cover his tracks. The only way to track him down would be to employ someone also familiar with the country—if such a man was available. It is likely that the frontier tradition of not prying into a stranger's private affairs may be traced to those days—hunted men had to be very careful and closely guarded their true identities.

Communication was extremely limited in the early days. Months might pass before information about a wanted man reached his pursuers. By then, of course, he could be well beyond reach. In the absence of organized law enforcement outlaws had little to fear. If

a man's cattle were stolen, his crops destroyed, or he and his family attacked, it was up to him to track down the culprits. What lawmen there were might be many miles away, and by the time they could be summoned, it would be too late. Neighbors who could help him might not be available. The westerner often had to face such dangerous situations on his own.

The telegraph system, installed in the West in the early 1860's, does not seem to have been fully utilized in the pursuit of outlaws until the 1870's, by which time law-enforcement bodies were rapidly expanding their scope and abilities, aided, after 1876, by the rapid communication provided by the telephone. With these means of communication they began to turn the tide against lawless elements that still terrorized parts of the West. But the outlaws were far from beaten. In the 1890's the infamous "Wild Bunch," led by George Leroy Parker, alias Butch Cassidy, had their own methods of beating the telegraph or telephone. Their plans for robberies of banks, trains, or mines included series of relay stations where fresh horses were available. In an emergency they "borrowed" mounts from ranches along their escape route.

Cassidy and his gang made their headquarters in some of the most inaccessible country in the West. One of their hiding places was in a barren, desolate part of northern Wyoming. In prehistoric times the waters of a lake had eaten into the towering mountain walls that surrounded the lake, which in time dried up, leaving a huge basin hemmed in by sheer cliffs of red sandstone. During the summer months there was plenty of grass and water in the basin, and in the winter snowdrifts cut it off from the rest of the world. A narrow gorge, which the gang called the Hole in the Wall, was the only entrance or exit.

The remote areas of Utah, Colorado, and other regions had similar places of refuge. But the world of outlawry began to shrink as bands of ranchers, farmers, and peace officers invaded these retreats to fight pitched battles that decided the fate of good men and bad. In the early 1900's train robbery became a dangerous occupation, banks began to take stricter precautions, and the might

17

of the Pinkerton private police organization was employed to fight criminals. In 1902 the Oregon National Guard was called out to help track down Harry Tracy, one of the most ruthless of the Wild Bunch riders, who had escaped from jail. He evaded the guardsmen, but after remaining free for fifty-nine days, he was eventually traced to a ranch near Creston, Washington. In the gunfight that followed, Tracy was wounded in the leg. Unable to stop the bleeding, and aware that escape was impossible, Tracy placed the muzzle of his rifle in his mouth and pulled the trigger.[3]

The people's attitude toward the lawless element was mixed. Some secretly considered the outlaws romantic figures, while others believed that they were the victims of social conditions. Such attitudes may well explain the tolerance that Missourians first felt toward the James brothers, who turned to crime after the Civil War, believing that they were being persecuted by vindictive Yankees. However, when the economy of the state began to suffer because of their robberies and outrages, which seriously affected the running of the railroads, the people turned against them and other outlaws.

In the Western tradition horse stealing was a more serious crime than shooting a man. Such standards seem ludicrous today, but in frontier days horses were essential to the well-being of individuals and communities. In 1869 a Kansas newspaper editor remarked that hardly "a day passes without one or more cases of horse-stealing coming to our ears. At the penitentiary one-fourth of the convicts are in durance for offenses connected with the horse, and there are many more outside than there are in."[4]

His concern was shared by other Kansans. Between 1869 and 1875 horse stealing was the favorite occupation of a gang of outlaws headquartered in the southern part of the state and in Indian Territory to the south. The thievery aroused much concern, for when a settler lost his horse, he lost his living. Appeals to the law proved

[3] James D. Horan, *The Wild Bunch*, 154–55; Stacy Osgood, "Harry Tracy—Meanest Man, Alive or Dead," The Westerners' *Brand Book* (Chicago), Vol. XVI, No. 6 (August, 1959), 41–43, 46–48.

[4] Leavenworth *Daily Commercial*, October 5, 1869.

fruitless; few sheriffs dared venture south of Marion County, and many of them stopped before they got that far. So well organized were the outlaws that the settlers deemed it necessary to form the Anti-Horse Thief Association. There were two rules the association members followed when they set out after thieves. If a stolen horse was found in a man's possession, he was questioned thoroughly about how he got it and what he intended to do with it, and a verdict was rendered on the spot. The second rule was even more direct. If the association members came across known thieves in hiding or overtook them on the trail, no quarter was given. On one occasion, when the association members brought back some stolen horses, they volunteered no details about how they had retrieved them. One member of the posse merely said, "We just left the men."[5]

One of the earliest attempts by the citizenry to gain control over the violent gangs that rampaged through the West took place in California following the 1849 gold rush. Swarming into the gold camps, thousands of men crowded each other at the diggings and the small townsites. In the absence of formal law, to protect their interests the men formed committees, or courts, to handle civil cases. Disputes about mining claims and other matters were resolved by these committees with the active support of the miners. When criminals began flocking to the diggings, the miners formed vigilance committees, each of which elected a jury. At first claim jumping, sluice-box robbing, and other crimes were punished by whipping or banishment and, for repeated crimes, even by death. The proceedings were unencumbered by such technicalities as appeals, and punishment was generally carried out soon after the verdict. A man might be hanged within minutes or hours after sentence was passed.[6]

San Francisco, a thriving metropolis by the middle of 1849, was also a dangerous one. At night it was almost impossible to walk the streets, lined with saloons, gambling houses, and brothels, without

[5] J. A. McClellan, "Joseph McClellan," Kansas State Historical Society (hereinafter cited as KSHS) *Collections*, Vol. XVII (1926–28), 863–64.

[6] Wayne Gard, *Frontier Justice*, 151.

being molested by pickpockets and thugs. Among its population were hardened criminals, lured to California by gold. A particularly notorious band of ruffians was known as the "Hounds." Some members of the gang were veterans of the Mexican War, and others hailed from the streets of New York City.

On Sundays the Hounds paraded the streets carrying flags and accompanied by a fife-and-drum band. At night they terrorized foreign-born San Franciscans, particularly Mexicans, Peruvians, and Chileans. In response to public criticism the Hounds changed their name to the Society of Regulators, but continued their raids. Finally, in July, 1850, the outraged citizens banded together and rounded up nineteen of the gang, including the leader, and proceeded to try them. The court followed traditional legal processes, employed prosecution and defense counsel, and allowed the defense to call witnesses. Nine of the accused were convicted, and since there was no prison in which to confine them, they were banished from the city.[7]

By 1851 the power of the California vigilantes was the cause of much concern in other parts of the country. Membership in the committee had reached seven hundred, and few people knew the identities of the members, although it was claimed that they included "our finest merchants, bankers, &c., in whom the public have confidence."[8] In the East these self-appointed enforcers of their own laws were viewed with disfavor, principally because few easterners could comprehend the difficulties involved in establishing law and order in the mining camps. Reports of what was going on reached England, where one case in particular aroused interest. This case concerned James Stuart, an Englishman, who at the age of sixteen had been banished to Australia for forgery. In 1850 he went to California, where he gained notoriety as a horse thief, robber, and burglar. Later he murdered a mining-camp merchant. A man named Thomas Burdue was arrested for the crime at Marysville, California, and was tried and convicted but was released when

[7] *Ibid.*, 152–53.

[8] London (England) *Morning Chronicle*, September 3, 1851.

it was learned that the vigilantes had arrested the guilty man, Stuart. In defiance of a request by the United States Supreme Court to deliver Stuart to legally constituted authorities, the San Francisco vigilantes met in secret session to try him.

The press deplored this action by a "self-organised body, unknown to the law, which assumed the functions of a judicial tribunal to punish offences against life and property, alleged to have become alarmingly frequent through the remissness of the legally constituted authorities in executing the laws of the land."[9] The vigilance committee was compared with the Committee of Public Safety of the French Revolution.

When it was decided that Stuart should hang, he was taken to the place of execution, handcuffed, and surrounded by a large body of men. When the rope was placed around his neck, those present removed their hats, and he was hanged "in general silence." In summing up, the paper commented:

> If the state of society in California demands the existence of a "Committee of Vigilance," the action of that body should be in cooperation with the officers of justice. Acting in defiance of the law, it perpetrates abuses more dangerous than those which it seeks to remedy. The defenders of this association point to its rapid increase in numbers as an evidence of its popularity. No wonder that people aspire to enrol themselves on its lists. It is the supreme power in the State. Its control is unlimited. Life, liberty, property, and reputation are at its mercy. In the language of the local judiciary, it "over-rides the laws and sets the constitution at defiance." Its organisation is extending itself by branches throughout the whole of California.[10]

Californians were not the only westerners to organize vigilance committees. All over the West citizens were forced to defend themselves against the thieves and murderers that abounded. During the years when North and South were locked in combat, the West was waging its own battles in places like Montana, where the gold fields near Bannack and Virginia City provided steady work for vigilantes.

In 1862, when gold was discovered at Grasshopper Creek, a

[9] *Ibid.*   [10] *Ibid.*

21

tributary of Beaverhead River in Washington Territory, thousands swarmed into the region (which later became Idaho Territory and included part of present-day Montana). Among its earliest settlements was the town of Bannack. Bannack was soon invaded by thieves and murderers, and efforts were made to bring law to the area. On May 24, 1863, Henry Plummer was elected sheriff. But because of the crimes committed by road agents in the next eight months and the apparent inability of Plummer to combat them, the citizens decided to form a vigilance committee. Then the citizens were shocked to discover that Henry Plummer, in whom they had placed their trust, was the leader of the outlaws. Swiftly the angry vigilantes went into action. Three members of the gang, including Plummer, were hanged.[11]

If Plummer's exploits gained notoriety, those of Joseph A. (Jack) Slade were destined to become a part of frontier legend. Born about 1824 at Carlyle, Illinois, Jack Slade was a veteran of the Mexican War. Normally a quiet and well-behaved individual, Slade was a terror when he was drunk. In 1858 or 1859 he was hired as a line superintendent for the Central Overland California and Pike's Peak Express Company. Slade was responsible for that part of the route known as the Sweetwater Division, which began at the Upper California Crossing of the South Platte River and extended to Rocky Ridge.

It was Slade's feud with Jules Bene, a French Canadian, which began and ended in violence, that publicized Slade's name all over the West. Slade had been superintendent for about a year when the two men had their first encounter at Julesburg, Colorado. Julesburg was situated on the bank of the South Platte River, opposite the mouth of Lodge Pole Creek, at the fork of the roads to Denver and the Oregon Trail and was a station on the Pony Express route. The section was known as "Jules' Stretch." Benjamin Ficklin, the general superintendent of the Overland Company, ordered Slade to investigate charges that Jules was mixed up in horse stealing and that he harbored outlaws. Slade set to work to recover the com-

[11] Thomas J. Dimsdale, *The Vigilantes of Montana*, 147–49.

pany's stolen stock and keep the line open. But Jules refused to submit to his authority. According to one account, the trouble came to a head when Slade re-engaged a man Jules had dismissed. In reprisal Jules went after Slade with a gun. Some men saw him coming and shouted a warning to Slade, but before he could pull his pistol, Jules shot him three times. Still on his feet, Slade was then shot twice more as Jules emptied both barrels of a shotgun into him. Thinking Slade was dead, Jules told the onlookers to bury him. Instead, infuriated by his act, the men attacked Jules and swiftly arranged a necktie party. Just as Bene was being swung from a pole erected between two wagons, Ben Ficklin arrived and ordered him cut down. Learning that Slade was still alive, Ficklin gave Jules a chance to live, provided he left the country. Jules eagerly accepted and left.

In spite of his wounds Jack Slade recovered and returned to his position as line superintendent. But he did not forget Jules Bene. Hearing that Bene had returned to the region, he ordered his men to find and hold him. They captured Jules at Slade's Cold Springs ranch and tied him to a corral post. Slade arrived and between drinks slowly shot Bene to pieces. Finally tiring of it all, Slade shoved the muzzle of his revolver into Bene's mouth and blew his brains out. He then cut off the dead man's ears. Some versions of the story claim that Slade used one ear as a watch fob and the other to pay for drinks.

Many years later, Jules Bene's widow gave a different version of the Julesburg fight. She claimed that Slade was the aggressor and that, to save his life, Jules had used his shotgun before Slade could draw his pistol. According to her story, Jules then paid part of the expenses to send Slade to Denver for treatment of his wounds and left the region, believing that the incident would be forgotten. Some time later he returned to collect some cattle he had left behind and stopped off—unarmed, his wife claimed—at Slade's ranch, where Slade killed him. When Bene's widow learned of his death, she fled to St. Joseph, Missouri, and did not come forward to tell her version of the story until the early 1930's.

Slade's career after Jules Bene's death was not a peaceful one, although his reputation continued to inspire awe among tenderfeet. Mark Twain, who met him in 1861, found him "so friendly and so gentle-spoken that I warmed to him in spite of his awful history."[12] Slade was discharged by the Overland Company after he shot up the post canteen at Fort Halleck. His drunken brawls and rowdyism had finally proved to be too much. His wife, Virginia, persuaded him to move to Virginia City, Montana, to operate a ranch. An important factor in his decision to leave Colorado was a warrant that had been issued for his arrest following a grand-jury indictment for assault with intent to kill.

In Montana Slade pursued his old ways. He terrorized the citizens of Virginia City with his rows and disregard for property. In his sober moments Jack Slade was a worthy citizen, but the citizens of Virginia City, already plagued by outlaws, had neither the time nor the patience to fathom the depths of his character. Finally, they gave him just one more chance to redeem himself. Slade ignored their ultimatum, and on March 10, 1864, he was arrested by the vigilantes and sentenced to be hanged.

Some people felt that his arrest and sentence was a mistake. One man who heard the decision was so overcome that he walked off weeping like a child. When Slade learned of the vigilantes' verdict, he broke down and cried repeatedly, "My God! my God! must I die? Oh, my dear wife!" Someone hastily left to get her. But the vigilantes wasted no time. Slade was taken out and placed upon a box, and a rope was put around his neck. Ignoring his desperate pleas to wait until his wife arrived, someone shouted the command, "Men, do your duty!" The box was pulled away, and the rope jerked tight, killing the man some had feared "more than the Almighty."

Slade's wife arrived soon after the hanging. Seeing his body laid out at the Virginia Hotel, she threw herself across it and between sobs screamed curses at the men who had hanged him. She abused his cronies for not shooting him before the rope could do its work,

---

[12] Clemens, Samuel L., *Roughing It*, 75.

to save him from the dishonor of hanging. When she had calmed down somewhat, she had his body placed in a tin coffin, filled with alcohol to act as a preservative. She planned to take his body to his birthplace, Carlyle, Illinois, for burial, but upon reaching Salt Lake City, she had his body buried there, in the Mormon cemetery, on July 20, 1864. Back in Colorado a marshal wrote on the unserved warrant: "Slade is dead, defunct."[13]

Vigilantes often acted hastily and, as we have seen, overreached themselves in their desire to mete out justice. Little more than lynch mobs unwilling to wait for the due process of law, they broke into jails, hauled prisoners away, and hanged them. Justice could be harsh on the frontier.

In the cattle country rustlers and horse thieves captured by ranchers and cowboys were also summarily hanged, often without benefit of "trial" by committee. Maintaining vigilance committees could be extremely difficult. Most of the members were storekeepers, businessmen, and working people who could not stand by ready to ride at a moment's notice and who might be miles from the scene of the action when needed.

Keeping the peace on the frontier involved other problems than outlaws. Among cattlemen economic pressures and disputes over grass and water rights frequently led to bloodshed. The arrival of settlers, or "nesters," in cattle country often provoked range wars, as did the conflicting interests between cattlemen and sheepmen. When the Tewksbury family brought sheep to Pleasant Valley, Arizona, in the late 1880's, the war that broke out between the Tewksburys and the Grahams (who had already been feuding for some time) resulted in the annihilation of all the male members of the Graham family, and all but one of the Tewksbury men.[14]

13 Bene's wife was never sure whether his name was Bene or Reni. Boulder County *Miner and Farmer*, February 1, 1940; J. Sterling Morton, *Illustrated History of Nebraska*, 180–81; James A. Long, "Julesburg—Wickedest City on the Plains," *Frontier Times*, Vol. XXXVIII, No. 2 (February–March, 1964), 24; Dean Ducomb, "A Silent Drum Beside the Okaw," The Westerners' *Brand Book* (New York) Vol. IV, No. 1 (1957), 1–8; Forbes Parkhill, *The Law Goes West*, 55–57; Dimsdale, *The Vigilantes of Montana*, 194–205.

14 Earle R. Forrest, *Arizona's Dark and Bloody Ground*, 276.

Wars among ranchers competing for land or cattle supremacy were important aspects of Western history. Some of the men who came to the plains and the brush country of Texas after the Civil War began amassing fortunes and founding dynasties by rounding up wild cattle. The cattle barons gathered enormous herds, built huge ranches, and grazed their cattle on public lands. Self-sufficient and independent, developing his own culture and way of life, the cattleman had his own brand of law and a Western code that allowed him to enforce that law the way he saw fit. The westerner responded to the demands of the moment, while the easterner abided by convention, and neither completely understood the other.[15] Of course, there were some men, notably John Chisum, who built cattle empires without relying on the gun, and such men were highly respected. Among the less highly esteemed cattlemen was Isom Prentice ("Print") Olive, a believer in the might of the gun. Born in Mississippi in 1840, Olive was taken to Texas as a small boy. After serving in the Confederate Army during the Civil War, Olive went into the cattle business and grew rich. In the middle 1870's Olive and his family decided to leave Texas for the Platte River country in Nebraska. There he laid claim to a vast region of land, from which he was determined to exclude settlers. When the families of Luther Mitchell and Ami Ketchum moved to Clear Creek, in Custer County, the Olives decided to drive them out. When they tried to do so in November, 1878, Print's younger brother, Robert, who was a hotheaded youth with a record of violence and was wanted by the Texas Rangers, was mortally wounded. The homesteaders fled, and efforts were made to protect them until the authorities could arrange a court hearing.

Print Olive had other ideas. With the help of corrupt officials he succeeded in obtaining custody of Mitchell and Ketchum and lynched both of them, after shooting Mitchell in the back, as, he claimed, Mitchell had shot his brother. When the bodies were found, they were badly burned, and there are conflicting stories about this aspect of the affair. There was a public outcry, and

[15] Webb, *The Great Plains*, 207.

Olive and one of his men, Fred Fisher, went on trial. Feeling was so high both for and against the pair that the governor of the state telegraphed the President for troops to keep the peace and guard the court. The arrival of the troops dispelled any thoughts of rescue harbored by the large crowd of cowboys in town for the trial.

Olive and Fisher were found guilty and sentenced to life imprisonment. But they did not remain in prison very long. Two years later the Nebraska Supreme Court ruled that the trial had been improper, since it had not been held in Custer County, where the Ketchum and Mitchell killings occurred. Both men were released pending a retrial in that county. The new trial was never held, but the days of the all-powerful cattle barons were over in Nebraska. Aware of the feeling against him and his kind, Olive moved his family and diminished herds across the line into Kansas in October, 1882. He made a new home in Dodge City and engaged in various interests until his career came to an abrupt end at Trail City, Colorado, in 1886. Joe Sparrow, who owed Olive ten dollars and resented the way he had demanded repayment, drew a gun and shot Olive in the chest as he entered Olive's saloon. Killed instantly, the saloon owner never felt the succeeding shots as Sparrow emptied his six gun into him. Olive, the man who had lived by the gun, died unarmed.[16]

There was also violence when barbed wire was introduced to the West. Cattlemen in Kansas and Indian Territory used the wire to control their stock in crowded regions, but cattlemen on the larger ranges bitterly opposed fences, and many men were killed before cattlemen realized that barbed wire had come to stay. It signified permanent settlement and spelled the end not only of the open range but also of the old-style cattle baron.[17]

In the meantime, the problems that had taxed the resources— and the abilities—of the vigilance committees were being solved by sheriffs and regular police forces. Cities, counties, states, and territories gradually managed to establish law in the West, sometimes

[16] Harry E. Chrisman, *The Ladder of Rivers: The Story of I. P. (Print) Olive,* 24–25, 250–58; Richard Crabb, *Empire on the Platte,* 228–349.

[17] Gard, *Frontier Justice,* 119.

only after many serious setbacks. The six-shooter became the instrument of the lawman as well as that of the lawless. Its part in taming the country cannot be overemphasized. Whereas the long rifle had been the weapon of the early days of the nation, the six-shooter was the weapon of the West. It was the horseman's weapon and the plainsman's. Armed with a six-shooter and a carbine, a man could do battle against almost any comer.[18] In close combat the six-shooter was unexcelled in fire power and reliability. In the hands of an expert gunfighter it was a highly persuasive instrument of law and order.

It would be incorrect to assume that the West was tamed by the gunfighter alone. Certainly the man with the gun played a big part, but the common, ordinary, hard-working people, the small ranchers and farmers and their wives, who lived quiet lives and raised families, contributed much toward the establishment of law-abiding communities.

Many men became peace officers in the early days because it gave them social standing and the promise of an easier living than herding cattle or plowing the prairies. A few were dedicated to the law and brought a sense of purpose and dedication to their jobs, but these men were rare. For most of the regularly employed peace officers the job was routine, unrewarded, and thankless. Although they had probably as much courage and ability as the men who achieved fame, most of them died in obscurity. It should be emphasized that for every man who sought notoriety there were many who avoided it. Trouble had a habit of developing at almost any time, and they saw little reason to attract it.

This, then, was the wild West, the setting for the drama of lawmen and lawless, whose final act saw the transformation of a wild, untamed wilderness into a continent-wide nation. It was also the setting that produced the most enduring of Western myths—the gunfighter.

[18] Webb, *The Great Plains*, 179.

3.

Frontier Origins

IT MIGHT BE ARGUED that the gunfighter of Western history
evolved from the men with the long rifles who proved their worth
in the Revolutionary War and the early wars against the Indians.
"Gun" in "gunfighter" means "pistol," and since the primary concern of this book is the fighter who used the true revolver, or, as
Samuel Colt described it, the "revolving pistol," it is in the era of
the revolver's invention—the 1830's—that the origin of the gunfighter is to be found.

The American frontier bred heroes and legends. Many people
of the new country were eager to escape the restrictions of their
former environment and wanted an identity of their own. In the
process of achieving it, they produced a unique character, the
frontiersman. The frontiersman lived off the land, abided by his
own rules, and owed allegiance to no one. Having severed his ties
with the old civilization, he was also free of its responsibilities.
Considered antisocial because of his "uncivilized" way of life, he
was recognized as someone apart. From this small group of men,
constantly pushing farther west to escape the net of civilization,
came the trail blazers, forever crossing the next hill in search of
new horizons. The typical frontiersman of the 1820's lived in that
part of the country west of the Appalachians encompassing Tennes-
see, the Great Lakes region, and the central Mississippi Valley.
Regardless of where he lived, he was generally called a Kentuckian.[1] By the early 1830's, the westward movement of the

---

[1] Joseph Leach, *The Typical Texan*, 13.

frontiersmen was well under way, and the penetration into Texas had begun.

The migration to Texas led to considerable friction with the Mexican government. The routes of the migrants were comparatively simple; they crossed the Sabine River from various points or journeyed by ship across the Gulf of Mexico and landed on the southern coast. Most of them merely wanted land and the chance to live on it peacefully, but Texas was still under Mexican rule, and the politicians among the new settlers became concerned with establishing the independence of the territory or bringing it within the jurisdiction and under the protection of the United States. The Mexicans, naturally, bitterly resented these efforts, and conflict was inevitable. The Revolution of 1835 led to support for the "Texians" from all parts of the United States. The fall of the Alamo on March 6, 1836, when all the members of a courageous band of Texans were massacred by a far larger Mexican force, inspired others to fight on. Led by Sam Houston, the Texans had their revenge at the Battle of San Jacinto some weeks later, and Texas was acknowledged by the captured General Santa Anna to be independent.

While these events were taking place, the legend of the Texas gunfighter was in the making. Stories of the heroic efforts of Davy Crockett, James Bowie, and William B. Travis at the Alamo infused a spirit into those who followed that would manifest itself in the "typical" Texan,—a figure who even earlier, in 1835, had inspired the comment, "The Texians are mostly muscular, powerful men and great marksmen; and whether at a distance with the rifle, or in close combat they will be terrible."[2] The influx of thousands into Texas during this and the following decade further aggravated the situation with Mexico, and trouble between the two countries continued until the Mexican War of 1846 to 1848 forced Mexico to accept the independence of Texas.

The frontier character typified by the rifle-carrying buckskin-clad Boones and Crocketts, was soon to be joined by another

[2] *Ibid.*, quoting the New York *Star*, 25.

personage—the Texas Ranger. From him sprang both the flesh-and-blood and the legendary gunfighter. From the time of their origin as an irregular force in 1823 the Texas Rangers were very much in the public eye. Their most glorious period was from 1840 to 1900, when they successfully combated outlaws and Indians and Mexicans still unwilling to accept Texas' sovereignty.

Their experiences with Mexicans and Indians taught the Texans a hard lesson—to survive they had to fight. The Mexican, with his musket and lance, had proved a worthy opponent, but the bow-wielding or rifle-carrying Plains Indian, who could use either weapon with alarming rapidity and accuracy on foot or on horse-back, was far more dangerous, for he never accepted defeat and was generally merciless to captives. Far from daunted by this fearsome enemy, one Ranger claimed that "a Texas Ranger can ride like a Mexican, trail like an Indian, shoot like a Tennessean, and fight like a very devil."[3] Moreover, the Texans had a weapon that could not be matched by their adversaries—the revolver.

When the Texas government negotiated with Samuel Colt for percussion rifles and revolvers in 1839, the Texas navy received the new five-shot revolvers that would revolutionize warfare on the frontier. It was not long before the Rangers also became aware of the value of the Colt. Their first issue of Colt revolvers was supplied by the navy. Despite the worn condition of some of the weapons, which had been used by the navy for more than four years, the Rangers welcomed them. They were five-shot, .36-caliber Paterson-model revolvers with nine-inch barrels, and were known as No. 5 pistols.[4]

Armed with his five-shot pistol and a rifle, the Ranger was theo-retically six times more effective than a musket-carrying Mexican soldier or a bow-wielding Indian, though the Rangers never under-estimated their foes. Riding in companies of ten, fifteen, or more, the mounted Rangers were practically invincible. As early as 1835

---

[3] Webb, *The Great Plains*, 166.

[4] William B. Edwards, *The Story of Colt's Revolver*, 99; James E. Serven, *Colt Firearms*, 10.

a newspaper had predicted, "Who knows what embryo heroes this Texian war may not bring forth?"[5] What heroes indeed! The descendants of these heroes would drive cattle to Kansas, and make or break gunfighting reputations as they did so.

The fighting qualities of the Texas Rangers under their leader, Colonel John C. (Jack) Hays, during the early 1840's and the Mexican War, were proved over and over again. They had no uniform and dressed in all manner of assorted coats, pants, and hats, with their long matted hair and full beards, they could have been taken for a gang of cutthroats.[6]

Many and varied are the accounts of how in 1844 Colonel Hays and fifteen Rangers engaged a force of about eighty Comanches and, armed with their five-shot Colts, defeated them in a determined charge. One of the two Rangers wounded in the rout, Samuel Walker, wrote to Colonel Colt and praised his pistols, adding, "The Texans who have learned their value by practical experience, their confidence in them is so unbounded, so much so that they are willing to engage four times their number."[7]

Samuel Walker influenced the design of Colt's later revolvers. Early in 1846 he was appointed a lieutenant colonel in the Texas Rangers and later a captain in the newly formed Regiment of Mounted Rifles, organized specifically for duty in the Mexican War. It was largely through his influence that Colt, whose Paterson, New Jersey, gun-manufacturing venture had failed, was able to get back into the gunmaking business and produce the first of the famed six-shooters.[8]

The early-day exploits of the Texas Rangers were many and heroic, but it was not until the Civil War that the Texans were pitted against well-armed adversaries on equal terms. As fighting men, the Mexicans were inferior to the Texans—not in courage, perhaps, but certainly in incentive. Moreover, their arms were no match for the superior weapons of the Rangers. Just what might

[5] Boston *Times*, quoted by the New York *Herald*, June 15, 1836.

[6] Walter Prescott Webb, *The Texas Rangers*, 118; Leach, *The Typical Texan*, 48.

[7] Edwards, *The Story of Colt's Revolver*, 99.

[8] *Ibid.*

have happened had the enemies met on equal terms is open to speculation, but in the circumstances the Rangers established themselves as a superior fighting force.[9]

The Texas Ranger's success with his weapon anticipated the role the Colt revolver was to play all over the West. It had been proved that any man armed with such a weapon would be equal in fire power to any opponent, and the significance of the revolver was quickly recognized. The Rangers had taken the first step toward the establishment of a pistol-packing tradition, and the miners in California took the next.

There was a great demand for pistols among the thousands who joined the California gold rush. The multibarrel pepperbox and other types of weapons gave way to the more reliable and improved models of the Colt. The gold seekers had to be largely self-reliant; the vigilance committees helped keep the lawbreakers under control, but few men cared to be without personal protection. The first Colt revolvers to reach the diggings directly from the factory were 1849 .31-caliber pocket pistols with three- or four-inch barrels, as well as some .44-caliber Dragoon Army revolvers. These weapons appear to have arrived in January, 1850. Later the new .36-caliber Navy pistols arrived, to be greeted with much enthusiasm. The light weight and excellent balance of this pistol was well appreciated, and the Californians quickly adopted it as their weapon.[10] It was featured in many duels among the gold seekers. The acceptance of the revolver in California presaged the eventual demand in other parts of the West. From there the scene shifted to the Middle West, where an even greater need arose for weapons in Kansas Territory.

The question of slavery was uppermost in the minds of the people who settled in Kansas. They had to decide whether Kansas would be a free or a slave state. Hundreds of Missourians who supported slavery crossed the border to claim land, believing that if Kansas became a free state the slaveowners in western Missouri would lose many slaves, who would flee to Kansas. Many of these

[9] Leach, *The Typical Texan*, 52.
[10] Edwards, *The Story of Colt's Revolver*, 259, 261.

Missourians had no intention of settling in Kansas; they wished only to hold it long enough to vote for slavery.

In opposition to the "Border Ruffians," as the Missourians were called, hundreds of "Free Soil" party members streamed into the territory to establish homes.[11] Several societies were formed by pro- and antislavery advocates to assist people wishing to settle in Kansas. Prominent among them was the Massachusetts Emigrant Aid Society (later reorganized as the New England Emigrant Aid Company). From Missouri came members of proslavery organizations, including such secret societies as Blue Lodges, Social Bands, and Friendly Societies, to bolster the position of earlier settlers from Missouri who did plan to stay permanently. In July, 1854, the first organized bands of New England immigrants arrived at the site of Lawrence, Kansas, and river steamers from St. Louis brought many more settlers, most of them from the Middle States. Soon there were several free settlements in Kansas, as well as proslavery towns, among them Atchison and Lecompton.[12] Many people arriving from the North found that the best homesteads near the Missouri border had already been claimed. Undaunted, they pushed deeper into Kansas. Leavenworth drew many settlers, as did Topeka, later to become the state capital. The Free Staters thus became firmly entrenched, and the struggle for Kansas began in earnest.

When Andrew H. Reeder, the first governor of the territory, called an election to choose a territorial delegate to Congress, a band of Missouri Border Ruffians took over the polling places on election day to elect their candidate, John W. Whitfield, a former Indian agent, as the proslavery delegate to Congress. To prevent fraud in a new election held on March 30, 1855, the governor divided the territory into election districts and appointed enumerators to take a census that revealed some eighty-five hundred qualified voters in Kansas. On election day, however, the Border

[11] James P. Callahan, "Kansas in the American Novel and Short Story," KSHS *Collections*, Vol. XVII (1926–28), 139–88; William Cullen Bryant and Sydney Howard Gay, *A Popular History of the United States*, IV, 406–408.

[12] William Frank Zornow, *Kansas: A History of the Jayhawk State*, 67–68.

Ruffians again arrived, took over the polls, and assured a victory for the proslavery factions.[13]

Both the Border Ruffians and the Free Staters displayed the characteristics that were to become associated with the men who wielded the six-shooter after the Civil War. The Border Ruffians were for the most part cold-blooded murderers. They invaded the territory with abundant arms and ammunition, and were well stocked with whisky by Missouri plantation owners and their friends, in return for the Ruffians' proslavery votes and their intimidation of the Free Staters. Living up to their part of the bargain, they destroyed homes, crops, or other possessions and murdered men trying to defend their families.[14]

A Kansas pioneer left behind this exaggerated but revealing description of a typical Border Ruffian:

> He was rather undersized than oversized, dirty rather than dark; he wore long, straight, greasy hair, had a small head, grey eyes, small hands and feet; his favorite animal was a good horse. He never smiled, but grinned; never laughed, but chuckled.
>
> Tobacco to him was a natural luxury, to which he took as easily as a duck to water. His native drink was corn whiskey as much so as New England rum was to a Yankee. Profanity was born in him; an oath was ready to pop out every time he opened his mouth. He prefaced every sentence with an oath and ended in the same way. He never sat on his horse, he just hung there; his feet ornamented with spurs, a pair of navy revolvers and a large knife attached to his belt; a skillful rider, an excellent shot and I might say when in the minority, like the savage Indian, the most sneaking, cringing coward of the plains. But when in the majority, the most braggardly, overbearing, insolent, tyrannical and brutal of creatures. And the border country was full of just such fellows as I have described, and they were a menace to Kansas, particularly along her eastern border for more than four years.... These were the kind of men that Quantrill invaded Lawrence with in August, 1863.[15]

13 *Ibid.,* 70.

14 Callahan, "Kansas in the American Novel and Short Story," KSHS *Collections,* Vol. XVII (1926–28), 145–46.

15 William W. Denison, "Early Days in Osage County," KSHS *Collections,* Vol. XVII (1926–28), 379.

Allied against the Ruffians were the "Jayhawkers," Free Staters who thought little of stealing from proslavery Missourians (or Kansans) in retribution for alleged depredations. "The term 'Jayhawker,'" wrote John McReynolds, "was applied by the pro-slavery men to mean 'thief' and after it became of general use, they ceased using any other term than 'Jayhawkers' to all the Free State people of the territory."[16] During the Civil War, Colonel C. R. Jennison's Seventh Kansas Cavalry was known as the Jayhawker Regiment, and most Union soldiers spoke of "jayhawking" from the enemy, much as soldiers in later wars spoke of "liberating" property.[17]

Among the leaders of the Jayhawkers were men whose names have become permanently linked with the state's struggle for freedom. There was James H. Lane, the "Grim Chieftain of Kansas," a former soldier in the Mexican War, whose deeds during the Kansas struggle and the Civil War have been the basis of much controversy. And there was the fiery John Brown, whose soul marched on through impassioned political and patriotic disturbances for generations after his death. The sporadic Kansas-Missouri border skirmishes continued until they became part of a larger, more intense war. The worst of the prewar fighting came during the years 1855 to 1858. It is not known how many revolvers were used during the prewar struggle, nor can it ever be accurately estimated, for people coming into Kansas brought with them all manner of weapons.

When the Civil War erupted, Ruffians and Jayhawkers along the Kansas-Missouri border joined the guerrilla bands that were to commit some of the most brutal acts of violence of the war. The most notorious guerrilla band on either side was that of William Clarke Quantrill, a northerner who had come to Kansas in 1857, when he was not quite twenty. He taught school for a time before throwing in his lot with the Southern states. His depredations against the Kansans culminated in a raid on Lawrence, Kansas, on

---

[16] Fort Scott *Weekly Monitor*, May 13, 1868.
[17] Joseph W. Snell to the author, January 20, 1966.

August 21, 1863, in which 150 citizens were killed. The raid was staged in reprisal for alleged atrocities by Kansas guerrillas. The bitterness went back to September, 1861, when James Lane led a band of men across the Missouri border in pursuit of General Sterling Price, who had attacked Lexington, Missouri, earlier in the month with a large force.

Setting out after Price, Lane adopted a tactic that was to be copied by Quantrill and other guerrillas: tracing Price's route, he punished all those he believed had welcomed the rebel troops as they marched toward Lexington. Everyone along the route was treated as an enemy, and the expedition degenerated into a looting spree. Horses, cows, clothing, furniture, and anything else that could be moved were gathered up, homes were robbed, and people were murdered. At Osceola, Missouri, on September 22, nine people were "court-martialed" and shot, and all but three of the town's buildings were destroyed. It was this act that prompted Quantrill's retaliatory raid on Lawrence, Kansas, without doubt the most shocking guerrilla atrocity of the war.[18]

Union and Southern guerrilla bands, largely composed of hotheads and other irresponsible individuals, though there were some honorable men among their number, became famous for their hit-and-run raids during the war. In the South John Singleton Mosby's Rangers earned a reputation that made them the foremost "Grey Ghosts of the Confederacy." In the North Jennison's Jayhawkers also earned considerable renown. The most famous of the Union guerrillas from Kansas were the "Red Legs," formed in 1862 to guard against Confederate guerrilla incursions into Kansas. Their name came from the red-dyed sheepskin boot tops which they "jayhawked" from a cobbler's shop during a raid on Independence, Missouri. Historians differ in their views of the character of this organization. Some maintain that it was an outlaw band, while others argue that its members were predominantly patriotic men drawn by the exigencies of the time into the savage ruthlessness of war. The roster of the Red Legs reads like a who's who of the West

18 E. R. Archambeau, Jr., to the author, March 30, 1964.

and includes the names of such personalities as William F. Cody and James Butler Hickok, and was led by Theodore Bartles, who was rated an even better shot than Hickok.[19]

A typical guerrilla of the Civil War was heavily armed, sometimes carrying four or more six-shot revolvers, which gave him impressive fire power. There are conflicting reports about the models of pistols carried by the guerrillas. The Navy revolver was a popular weapon, as was the heavier .44 Army. In his old age Bill Stewart, a former member of Quantrill's guerrillas, recalled: "We always kept right at revolver practice. All of us had two, some more, all of them .44 caliber cap and ball dragoon revolvers—captured of course."[20] Of far more interest to those who could obtain one, however, was the new Colt 1860 Army revolver. This, like the Dragoon, was a .44-caliber weapon, but two pounds lighter. Another popular weapon was the .44-caliber Remington New Model Army.

In 1906 the claim was made that "each of Mosby's men [had been] armed with two Colt's .45 calibre muzzle-loading revolvers. Long practice had made a good shot of every man in the command and each was sure with his revolver just as every cowboy is sure with his six-shooter. The Colonel admonished his men never to fire a shot until the eyes of the enemy were visible. It was no uncommon thing for a Mosby man to gallop by a tree at full tilt and drop three bullets into the trunk in succession."[21] However, Colt never produced a .45-caliber cap-and-ball revolver. Their weapons were probably Dragoons or the 1860 model. Even so, the marksmanship credited to Mosby's men at full gallop would have to be seen to be believed.

Bill Stewart's claim that Quantrill's men were armed with cap-

---

[19] William E. Connelley to Frank J. Wilstach, October 27, 1926, Wilstach Collection, New York Public Library; Lela Barnes (ed.), "An Editor Looks at Early-Day Kansas—The Letters of Charles Monroe Chase," KSHS *Quarterly*, Vol. XXVI, No. 2 (Summer, 1960), 113–51, 121 n.

[20] Columbia *Daily Tribune*, undated clipping (December, 1945), supplied by Edward Knowles, Topeka, Kansas.

[21] Robert A. Kane, "The D.A. vs. S.A. Controversy" (letter to the editor), *Outdoor Life*, Vol XVII, No. 6 (June, 1906), 589–92.

tured weapons is historically valid. The Colt Company sold 129,730 .44-caliber revolvers to the North during the Civil War, most of which were the New Model Army and the remainder Dragoons. Later the Northern forces were supplied with 17,010 1851- and 1861-model Navy revolvers. And, of course, there were other Northern contractors for various types of revolvers.[22] In the South weapons and ammunition were always in short supply. Thus a captured Yankee Colt or Remington was much prized by a Confederate soldier.

The Union blockade of Southern ports caused severe problems to the Confederacy. English and other European manufacturers were urged to supply arms in exchange for gold or cotton as long as they were available, and so began the adventurous period of blockade running. But the Confederacy was not entirely dependent on outside help. A number of Southern manufacturers were producing arms. Among the most prominent were David and George Dance, of Columbia, Texas; Leech and Rigdon, of Greensboro, Georgia; Spiller and Burr, of Atlanta, Georgia; and Griswold and Greer, of Griswoldville, Georgia. Most of the weapons produced by these manufacturers were copies of the standard Colt, Remington, and Whitney arms. In fact, the only revolver patented in the Confederacy during the war (on August 12, 1861) was the .36-caliber pistol made by Thomas W. Cofer. Cofer's revolver resembled the Whitney pistol, except that it was fitted with a sheathed trigger.[23]

The conflicts in Texas and California, the dangers of frontier life, the border wars, the guerrilla activities of the Civil War, and, above all, Colt's sophisticated handguns, which made it easy to settle problems with bullets—all these experiences and influences produced a breed of men accustomed to violence and indifferent to human life. With the end of the Civil War, the era of the gunfighter had arrived.

---

[22] Col. Berkeley R. Lewis, *Notes on Cavalry Weapons of the American Civil War (1861–1865)*, 30.

[23] Richard D. Steuart, "The Story of the Confederate Colt," *Army Ordnance*, Vol. XV, No. 86 (September–October, 1934), 90–91.

4.

The Bad Man

THE IMPACT THE GUNFIGHTING ELEMENT had on Western society in the years immediately after the Civil War was caused largely by conditions in the West. The men who came back from the war were well trained in the basic skills required of gunmen: they could handle weapons, and they knew how to kill. Some of the men who returned from war never had cause to take up arms again, while others, adept in the use of the six-shooter and immune to feelings of guilt about killing a man, lived and died with guns in their hands. Not all gunmen could be classified as bad men. The true bad man, or outlaw killer, was entirely different from the law-abiding man with a reputation as a good shot, or from the man who was known as a tough customer in a fight, or dangerous only when provoked, or "a bad man to fool with."

The real and legendary exploits of bad men have provided inspiration for much of the Western myth. The following description of a typical bad man from Bodie is, though written with tongue in cheek, an indication of how well the myth had been established by 1880:

> One of the peculiarities of the Bad Man from Bodie is his profanity. A Bad Man from Bodie who never used an oath is as impossible as perpetual motion or an honest election in Nevada. This trait is especially noticeable whenever he kills a man or endeavours to kill one. Whenever you hear of a man from Bodie who did not swear when he "pulled his gun" you may depend upon it that he is base metal, a tenderfoot, a man from Pioche, or Cheyenne, or Leadville. The oath of the Bad Man from Bodie is like the cheerful warning of the rattle

snake, and like that warning blow follows close upon its heels. This brings us to another peculiarity of the Bad Man from Bodie, namely, his excessive prudence. Ill-natured critics have designated this morbid caution of the Bad Man from Bodie to cowardice, but every true bad man knows this to be wholly false, and will resent the imputation as a personal insult. Whenever a Bad Man from Bodie dons his war paint and strikes the bloody trail of carnage he is prepared for every contingency. His little gun nestles cosily in his right hand coat pocket, the latter generally being lined with velvety buckskin to prevent the hammer from catching and frustrating his purpose of converting his enemies into fully fledged angels. Meeting an eligible candidate for a place in his graveyard he emits his stereotyped oath and "blazes away." This mode of procedure is termed in the elegant vocabulary of the Bodie classics "getting the drop on his Injun"—the vulgar bad man of other inferior localities term it "getting the bulge on the bloke," a highly reprehensible and slangy way of expressing the idea. Sometimes the bad man from Bodie entertains his victim with a short oration before butchering him. . . . I have seen him leap upon a billiard table and shout his defiance in the following stirring manner: "Here I am again, a mile wide and all wool. I weigh a ton and when I walk the earth shakes. Give me room and I'll whip an army. I'm a blizzard from Bitter Creek. I can dive deeper and come up drier than any man in forty counties. I'm a sand storm mixed with a whirlwind. . . . I was born in a powder house and raised in a gun factory. I'm bad from the bottom up and clear grit plumb through. . . . I'm chief of Murdertown, and I'm dry. Whose treat is it? Don't all speak at once, or I'll turn loose and scatter death and destruction full bent for the next election."[1]

The image of the "good" bad man as a young Robin Hood became well established soon after the close of the Civil War. The old-time novelist often treated the bad man with considerable sympathy and, aware that no one is all good or all bad, found sufficient reason to excuse his faults. Evidence about the actual nature of the Western bad man disproves many of the "kind to animals, women, and children" characteristics attributed to him by the eulogizers. A more realistic approach places greater stress on

[1] Sacramento *Daily Bee*, October 12, 1880.

the qualities of greed and arrogance that made the average bad man a taker rather than a giver. One authority with considerable perceptiveness has expressed the opinion that the whole business of American frontier outlawry could stand re-examination and stresses the need to distinguish between the man who killed out of meanness or for revenge and the man who became an outlaw because he believed there was no other way for him to ensure that no one took unfair advantage of him.[2]

The real bad man, the outlaw killer, was selfish, willing to steal and kill to get what he wanted. He had no scruples to speak of and believed that his needs and wants came first. Although he may not have been entirely responsible for his behavior, having been born in an era of violence, yet he rarely tried to improve his relationship with society.

Many of the bad men came from among the unemployed thousands of easterners who drifted west only to find that there, too, jobs were scarce. Some of these thousands found employment in the revived cattle industry; others entered government service or enlisted in the frontier army. Some turned to crime, leading a nomadic life. They became self-reliant and hardened by the rigors of the continuous fight for survival. To them, other men's lives were cheap, and it is not surprising that they held the view that "Mexicans don't count" or that "the only good Indian is a dead one."[3]

Thousands of men drifted westward after the Civil War, dreaming of riches that proved elusive. Disillusioned, many of them wandered on. But some, going to any length to achieve wealth with a minimum of effort, gambled, fought, and robbed to get what they wanted. Some killed. After the first killing each subsequent killing became easier. So it went, until eventually justice caught up with them, or, more often than not, they died in violence among people who cared little for them or for their sudden end.

Harry Tracy, a member of the Wild Bunch, and one of those

[2] C. L. Sonnichsen, *Outlaw: Bill Mitchell, Alias Baldy Russell, His Life and Times*, 14–15.

[3] George Hendricks, *The Bad Man of the West*, 5.

men who regarded killing, robbing, and violence as a way of life, was a cold-blooded fighting machine. His philosophy was simple— if you want something, take it with a gun. "I kill only those who get in my way," he said. His companion in crime, Harvey Logan, better known as "Kid Curry," would ride a thousand miles to kill a man. Perhaps the most remarkable man to ride with the Wild Bunch was their chief, Butch Cassidy. Oddly enough, this man, who led the most desperate gang of robbers and killers in the West, never killed a man during a robbery. Sentenced in 1894 to five years in the Wyoming State Penitentiary for horse stealing, he was pardoned a year later when he promised the governor of Wyoming that he would never again terrorize that state.

The battle of wits waged between the Wild Bunch and the Pinkerton Detective Agency makes exciting reading. The Pinkerton organization made robbing trains and banks extremely hazardous. Eventually remnants of the gang transferred their activities to South America, where they proved such a formidable threat that various governments requested assistance from the United States government to combat them. Cassidy and Harry Longbaugh, "The Sundance Kid," last members of the original gang, died in Bolivia in 1911, after robbing a mule train carrying silver. After a day-long fight with some Bolivian cavalry that had trapped them in a small village, the Kid was fatally wounded, and Butch, rather than be taken alive, shot himself.[4]

The South produced many bad men during the bitter period of defeat and Reconstruction. It was in this atmosphere that two of the most notorious Texas bad men, William P. Longley and John Wesley Hardin, started down the outlaw trail killing what they classified as belligerent Negroes, a practice that became all too common in the postwar years. Fleeing the wrath of both blacks and whites, Hardin and Longley asserted that the Negroes were the aggressors, though a cursory examination of their careers suggests that neither man had much respect for anyone—black or white.[5]

[4] Horan, *The Wild Bunch*, 19, 25, 188–90.

[5] Cunningham, *Triggernometry*, 15; John Wesley Hardin, *The Life of John Wesley Hardin*, 121–24.

Jesse James, considered to be America's most infamous outlaw, was in his early teens when some Kansas militiamen came looking for his elder brother, Frank, during the spring of 1863. Frank was a known rebel and was suspected of being a member of Quantrill's guerrillas. Jesse's stepfather was taken to a tree, a rope was tied around his neck and thrown over a branch, and he was "lifted" a few times to force information from him. The militiamen also badly mistreated Jesse's mother. Next they turned their attention to young Jesse and whipped him, but he refused to talk. The humiliation of this incident left a deep impression on Jesse. At the first opportunity, he joined Quantrill—probably in late 1863 or early 1864, since there is no evidence that he took part in the Lawrence massacre in the summer of 1863.

Shortly after the close of the war Jesse was severely wounded during an exchange of shots between some Southern guerrillas and Union soldiers near Lexington, Missouri. It is probably because his wound was thought to be fatal that his name does not appear on the list of guerrillas who were offered pardons if they surrendered. (According to Jesse's son, no pardon was granted.) It has been asserted that Jesse was so persecuted for sixteen years by his vengeful enemies that he had no recourse but to turn to crime. But the fact that Jesse committed no known robberies until some years after the war suggests that the alleged persecution is only another part of the James myth. One expert on the James story has reached the conclusion that James suffered from paranoia.[6]

The attempts of some bad men to get even with society for imagined or genuine grievances reveal their basic sense of inferiority and their lack of maturity. Unable to solve their personal problems, they turned to violence to ease their frustrations and achieve recognition. Such a man was Sam Bass. When Bass was about seventeen, he ran away from his home in Indiana and traveled to Texas. There, discontented with his life as a common laborer, teamster, and itinerant cowboy, he went to the quarter-horse race tracks in Denton County, Texas, and made a reputation with his

[6] Interview with Edward Knowles, Topeka, Kansas, October 8, 1966.

famous "Denton Mare." Then he fell in with an unscrupulous individual named Joel Collins, who soon transformed the good-humored but weak youngster into a petty gambler, horse thief, and train robber. In Nebraska the pair and their confederates robbed a Union Pacific train of sixty thousand dollars in gold. Bass then formed his own gang and led a series of stagecoach and train robberies in Texas in 1878. Pursued by the Texas Rangers and betrayed by a member of the gang, Bass was severely wounded in a gun battle at Round Rock on July 19, 1878, and died two days later, on his twenty-seventh birthday.[7]

Another of the famed bad men was William H. Bonney, alias Billy the Kid. According to legend, he was a native of New York City, where he was born on November 23, 1859, but there is no actual record of where or when he was born, though it is generally accepted that his real name was Henry McCarty. Robert N. Mullin found a record of Patrick Henry McCarthy born in New York on September 17, 1859, the son of Catherine and Patrick McCarthy. It is also possible that Billy was the son of a William and Katherine McCarty Bonney of New York. Another possible birthplace was Indiana, where a Joseph McCarty of Cass County was listed in the 1880 census as the father of two sons, Joseph and Henry. Mullin concludes, "Regardless of which of these or other beliefs one accepts, it seems safe to surmise that in choosing the name Bonney, Henry McCarty was probably reverting to a parental family name."[8]

According to another historian, whose version of Billy's origins is the generally accepted one, Billy's father was a Michael McCarty, who died during the Civil War. In the years following the war, this McCarty's widow, Catherine, and her sons, Joseph and Henry, lived in Indianapolis, Indiana. There she became friendly with a William Antrim. In the summer of 1870 the family accompanied him to Wichita, Kansas, where Mrs. McCarty went into the real-estate business and ran a laundry.

[7] Gard, *Frontier Justice*, 228–29; Cunningham, *Triggernometry*, 274–97.

[8] Robert N. Mullin, "The Boyhood of Billy the Kid," *Southwestern Studies*, Vol. V, No. 1 (1967), 7.

Wichita was at that time a frontier village on the Chisholm Trail, though not yet a railroad town. The McCarty boys undoubtedly experienced many exciting moments as the Texas herds thundered past town, amid clouds of dust, on their way to Abilene. The colorful drovers and the soldiers, scouts, Indians, and buffalo hunters that passed through Wichita also provided thrills for the McCarty youngsters. In 1871 Catherine McCarty's health began to fail. It is probable that she was a victim of tuberculosis. In August the family sold out and, accompanied by William Antrim, went to New Mexico, where the climate would be better for her condition.

Antrim and Mrs. McCarty were married at Santa Fe on March 1, 1873, and Antrim decided to become a miner and took the family to Silver City. Catherine kept a boarding house there until she died on September 16, 1874. Her death left the two boys largely on their own. Henry worked at odd chores, went to school in Silver City, and led the life of a schoolboy until a childish prank involving the theft of some laundry belonging to two Chinese involved him with the law. He and George ("Sombrero Jack") Shaffer were arrested, but escaped. The local press noted that McCarty was probably the tool of Shaffer and only hid the clothes while the other boy did the stealing, but Henry left town and made his way to Arizona.

Completely alone for the first time in his life, the boy wandered around New Mexico and Arizona for two years, working at almost anything he could find. For a time a cowboy and possibly a sheepherder, he was known as "Kid" or "Kid Antrim," by the time his first killing of record took place in Arizona Territory at or near Camp Grant, on August 17, 1877. Apparently a blacksmith named Frank P. Cahill had called Billy a pimp, and Billy had retorted by calling Cahill a son of a bitch. In the ensuing fight the boy realized that he was no match for the man, drew his gun, and shot him. Cahill died the next day. Locked up in the post guardhouse to await trial, Billy escaped and from then on was involved in one fracas after another.

The life story of Billy the Kid has been written and rewritten so

many times that it is hard to know where fact ends and fiction begins. It is known that he took part in the Lincoln County, New Mexico, cattle war and that by 1880 he was one of the most wanted outlaws in the West. His career was brought to a sudden end by his former friend, Sheriff Pat Garrett, on the night of July 14, 1881, at Fort Sumner (in New Mexico Territory). Garrett and his deputy, John W. Poe, had reached the fort late in the evening, and Garrett went in to see a Pete Maxwell who he believed knew where the Kid was hiding. As Garrett sat talking in Maxwell's darkened bedroom, Billy walked in. Garrett, recognizing Billy in the darkness, shot him. Billy the Kid was dead, but in his story, heavily encrusted with fancied adventures, he lives on, a demigod of the wild West myth.[9]

The admiration of people who led prosaic lives soon made folk heroes of Jesse James, Billy the Kid, and others. William Martin, better known as "Hurricane Bill," was a well-known bad man of Kansas. As early as 1870 he was involved in rustling sixty head of cattle southeast of Abilene. A posse hastily formed in Marion overtook the rustlers, recovered the cattle, and drove off Martin and his gang.[10] By 1874 Hurricane Bill had begun to gain a reputation as a bad man—and at least one young admirer. A Wichita newspaper commented:

> "Hurricane Bill," or Wm. A. Martin, as he signs himself, favors the *"Eagle"* with a communication dated this week, Eagle Block, in which he sets forth some of his grievances. According to his own view of the surroundings, he had hardly disposed of one case by giving bonds "for good behavior and kindness toward a policeman who shot him down four years ago" until his valuable but wounded person is required for having traded ponies with his red brethren and having treated their lady squaws to a little redeye. All that William desires in the premises is a massing of all the charges and accusations, as he has to answer for many who get the profits.

[9] *Ibid.*; Kent Ladd Steckmesser, *The Western Hero in History and Legend*, 58–70; Waldo E. Koop, "Billy the Kid—The Trail of a Kansas Legend," *The Trail Guide*, Vol. IX, No. 3 (September, 1964).

[10] Junction City *Union*, February 26, 1870; Floyd B. Streeter, *Prairie Trails and Cow Towns*, 65.

We also have a letter in our possession containing a photograph of Sumner Beach of Ellsworth, to Hurricane Bill asking for a job of adventuring. Evidently Beach's case is one of abuse and misplaced confidence, while the hard row of his friend Hurricane Bill is not yet hoed out. If one only knew one half that was going on around him it would turn the hair white. We advise young Beach to stay with his aunt and Wm. A. Martin to join the army against the Indians or turn cowboy.[11]

Driven from Wichita by the police, Hurricane Bill appears to have made his headquarters in Texas. In 1876 he and two others were arrested at Fort Griffin for "playing cards in a saloon," but the case was dismissed. At the time gambling went on day and night. Apparently the arrest was an early example of "rousting" by the police.[12]

Martin's young Ellsworth, Kansas, admirer, Sumner J. Beach, was an interesting character. In 1874 he was seventeen years old and was evidently a blacksmith. Some months before his letter to Hurricane Bill, he wrote several illuminating letters to Daniel B. Wesson, of the gunmaking firm of Smith & Wesson. Signing himself "Cimmarron," Beach said that he liked and used a Smith & Wesson revolver, although it was not as easy to repair as the Colt. He added: "I have been shooting your make and find it a perfect revolver. I can kill a man at 100 yards with my revolver every time." In a subsequent letter he told Wesson that he was the correspondent for the *American Sportsman* in "this country," and letters signed Sumner Beach, date-lined Ellsworth, did appear in the magazine during 1873–74. Beach also informed Wesson that all "the notorious desperadoes have your rev. The notorious Hurricane Bill has a pair of your revolvers. He kills annually from 25 to 30 Indians." Beach then offered to capture Wesson a wild horse in exchange for a .44-caliber Russian model revolver. Wesson sent him the revolver but never received his horse.[13]

[11] Wichita *Weekly Eagle*, July 30, 1874.

[12] Carl Coke Rister, *Fort Griffin on the Texas Frontier*, 139.

[13] 1875 Census for the State of Kansas (Ellsworth County, Ellsworth Township),

One enduring aspect of the legendary good bad man is his Robin Hood qualities, which make it easy to excuse or justify his activities. The real bad man, however, remained outside the law, found it easier to take than to give, kept the element of surprise in his favor, and had few scruples. The feuds and range wars that gripped parts of Texas, Wyoming, and Arizona during the 1840's and again in the late 1890's provided the necessary conditions for the evolution of the professional killer. During these bloody clashes the hired killer was in great demand. He was well paid for his services, which ranged from defending a rancher's property to murder, all of which duties required competence with a six-shooter.

The murder of a man named Joseph G. Goodbread, in Shelbyville, Texas, in 1840 by Charles W. Jackson led to repercussions throughout the territory. Alfred George, a prospective candidate for sheriff of Shelby County, had given Goodbread a Negro slave in exchange for land certificates purported to be exchangeable for more than forty thousand acres of land. The certificates turned out to be bogus, as were thousands of others issued by fraudulent land commissioners. When a traveling board of inquiry invalidated the fake certificates, George demanded compensation from Goodbread. Thinking that Goodbread, by publicly airing the story, might hinder his political career, George enlisted Jackson's aid by telling him that, spiteful over a previous row, Goodbread had threatened to shoot Jackson. Surprised and angered, Jackson agreed to kill the unarmed Goodbread, and so fired the shot that sparked the first big Texas feud, the one between the "Regulators" and the "Moderators."[14]

Pursued by Goodbread's friends, Jackson posted bond to appear at the next district-court term. When he learned that he was to be indicted for murder, he quickly applied for a change of venue to nearby Harrison County. The change of venue was granted and George, now sheriff, was ordered to keep Jackson in the Shelbyville

copy of entry supplied by Waldo E. Koop; John E. Parsons, *Smith and Wesson Revolvers*, 82.

[14] Gard, *Frontier Justice*, 22–24; C. L. Sonnichsen, *I'll Die Before I'll Run*, 15.

jail without bail. Pleading disrepair of the jailhouse, the sheriff promised to keep Jackson under guard, but as soon as the judge had gone, he freed Jackson.

Shortly after this Jackson organized "The Shelby Guards," actually to protect him, though their avowed purpose was to stamp out the alarming increase in rustling. After the gang had made several attacks on Goodbread's friends and damaged their property, anti-Jackson feeling began to grow in the county. When Jackson came to trial for killing Goodbread, the presence of 150 armed Regulators around the courthouse so alarmed Judge John M. Hansford that he failed to appear for the second day. He had fled to Marshall, not wishing to expose "my person in the courthouse any longer where I see myself surrounded by bravos and hired assassins, and no longer left free to preside as an impartial judge at this special term of court." The jury quickly acquitted Jackson, and he was released. Not long afterward Judge Hansford was shot and killed under mysterious circumstances.[15]

Jackson next took upon himself and his gang the duty of capturing Texans wanted in Louisiana for stealing Negro slaves. One of the seven men they captured was the probate judge of Harrison County, who received a seven-year sentence.[16] Friends of Goodbread's and men who had suffered at the hands of Jackson's Regulators organized the Moderators, killed Jackson from ambush, and lynched or shot a number of other men. The feud continued for four years, until August, 1844, when the Texas President Sam Houston went to San Augustine and, backed by four companies of militia, ordered the fighting stopped. The Moderators surrendered, the Regulators dispersed, and the leaders of both factions signed an agreement to end hostilities. Except for a few sporadic outbursts, the fighting was over.[17]

This localized war between private armies set the pattern for similar feuds. Feuding in Texas intensified during the seventies,

---

[15] Gard, *Frontier Justice*, 25–26.
[16] *Ibid.*, 26.
[17] *Ibid.*, 39; Sonnichsen, *I'll Die Before I'll Run*, 15–16.

slackened off in the eighties (thanks mainly to the Texas Rangers), revived in the nineties, and then died away. Whatever the cause, a feud bred hatred and often was climaxed by bloodletting and violent death.[18]

The gunman was at the top of his form in the era of the range wars, when men died violently in quarrels over sheep, cattle, fences, grass, and water or combinations of any of these issues. Economic or social pressure brought out the worst and best in men. In the middle of any trouble was the killer employed by men who were often as cold-bloodedly ruthless as they and who were prepared to go to any lengths to keep or increase what they had. Taking full advantage of the situation created by the Civil War, some ranchers had amassed great herds of cattle and, in attitude akin to the feudal barons of Europe, treated their employees as though they were serfs. The influx of small ranchers, farmers, and others eager to settle on what had been open range created friction and tensions that quickly led to violence. The promise of free land provided under the Homestead Act of 1862 and later laws brought thousands west only to find most of the best land controlled by cattlemen bitterly resentful of any intrusion. For more than twenty years after the Civil War cattlemen used the open ranges to graze their cattle, and they saw no reason to change things.

Although Texas had most of the cattle business in the years after the war, during the last twenty years of the century Montana and Wyoming began claiming their share of the market. In 1866 Nelson Story, an Ohioan, had driven cattle from Texas to Montana, in a trek that has become an epic in Western trail-driving history and legend. Having fought the innumerable dangers of the country and hostile Indians, Story reached his goal in December. He built a corral near Livingston, on the Yellowstone, and started a new era in cattle raising.

Ten years were to pass, however, before any great steps were taken to further this new branch of the cattle industry. Story's back trail to Texas was practically sealed off by the Indian wars that

[18] Sonnichsen, *I'll Die Before I'll Run*, 3, 9.

culminated in the subjugation of the hostile tribes and the ultimate tragedy at Wounded Knee in 1890. Indian wars, the massacre of Custer's men at the Little Big Horn in 1876, and other outbreaks did not deter the cattlemen of Montana and Wyoming. Slowly the industry grew, the herds replenished with cattle, mostly of short-horn stock, driven eastward from Oregon. In the early eighties, when the Texas–Kansas cattle drives became less profitable, many Texans moved their stock and holdings to Montana and Wyoming. During this period British and other European interests also began to invest in Western cattle.

Folk drawn to cattle-raising country expecting to put down roots and share in the prosperity found fences around most of the best land and water. Infuriated when the newcomers tore down the fences, the cowmen accused them of stealing cattle. In return the settlers charged the cattlemen with poisoning water holes and branding calves that belonged to the settlers. Tension mounted through the eighties and had reached a point just short of open warfare when disaster hit.

On January 28, 1887, the worst blizzard in many years struck the Northwest. There had been storms in the region for several months, but none to compare with this one. Thousands upon thousands of cattle perished in the snowdrifts. Many that survived the forty-below-zero temperatures died from starvation. Cowboys and ranchers died in desperate efforts to save the stock. When the snows began melting in March, the ranchers assessed their losses. Many of them found that they were ruined. Before they had time to plan future moves, homesteaders took advantage of the lull in hostilities and moved onto the range land, along with cowboys who had lost their jobs, reformed outlaws, and rustlers driven from distant areas.

The cattle boom was over, but there were still men with money to promote large herds, although they sensed that the range land would soon be taken over by small landholders and fenced in. For three years tension mounted between cattlemen and settlers. By 1890 the rift between the factions was very wide and there were

many acts of violence. Gunmen from Texas and the declining cow-towns of Kansas were employed as "detectives" or "range inspectors" to spy on, harass, and intimidate homesteaders and in other ways protect the cattlemen's interests.

For some months there were sporadic lynchings and other violent outbursts. One incident in particular aroused considerable feeling—the hanging of Ella Watson ("Cattle Kate") and James Averill for rustling. In October, 1891, as part of the continual effort to intimidate the homesteaders, the powerful Wyoming Stock Growers' Association, through the State Board of Livestock Commissioners, instructed livestock brokers to confiscate stock bearing the brands appearing on a list they provided. They were told to ignore the bills of sale offered as proof of ownership of such cattle; furthermore, they were empowered to retain the money realized from the sale of the cattle. Only members of the Stock Growers' Association could legally sell stock under these stipulations. The homesteaders and small ranchers interpreted this move to mean that they were all prejudged guilty of rustling. In a defiant move to market their stock, they formed the Northern Wyoming Farmers and Stock Growers Association and rounded up their cattle.

To put an end to this defiance, on April 5, 1892, a special train left Cheyenne for Casper carrying more than fifty heavily armed men, led by Major Frank Wolcott and Frank Canton, a well-known peace officer familiar with the country. In the subsequent "Johnson County War," as it came to be called, many men on both sides of the controversy were killed. The war also illustrated the tragic result of allowing killers a free hand.

Nathan D. Champion, a cowboy turned homesteader, had been accused by Wolcott's gunmen of being a rustler, and he and his friend Nick Rae were on their wanted list. The gunmen attacked them at the K C Ranch, leased to Rae by John Nolan. Champion had a claim about two miles away, but was in the K C Ranch cabin at the time. Rae was wounded as he stepped out the door. Champion dragged him inside, where he died. In a grim seige that lasted almost twenty-four hours, Champion bravely held his own and even

53

managed to record what was happening. Finally, when they set fire to the place, he was forced to run. Twenty-eight bullets cut him down.[19]

The cult of the West tends to overlook the bad man's violent side, his selfishness, and his cruelty, romanticizing his character and his life. The bad man was as much a part of the society as was the farmer or cowboy, but his deeds hindered the settlement of the West; moreover, to oppose him, people had to rely on still more violence—personified by the man whose gun would be used in defense of society. Six-shooter justice was to be inflicted in earnest on the bad man, who, though he might disregard laws and courts, could not ignore the fact that this kind of judgment was final.

[19] Gard, *Frontier Justice*, 121–45; Dee Brown and Martin F. Schmitt, *Trail Driving Days*, 179–231.

5.

The Lawman

IN 1834 A MAN IN IOWA TERRITORY killed a companion, apparently without provocation. It was decided to try him, though the participants in the trial were not empowered by any law to do so. The defendant was found guilty, and the date for his execution was set. In an effort to obtain a pardon, friends sent a petition to the governor of Missouri (Iowa had been part of the original Missouri Territory), but the governor replied that he had no authority to act and suggested that they write President Andrew Jackson. President Jackson replied that since the laws of the United States had not yet been extended to Iowa he was powerless to act and suggested that the pardoning power rested with those who had passed the sentence. The murderer was hanged.[1]

Citizens' courts, squatters' courts, and vigilance committees played an important part in establishing law and order in the West. They were the common people's efforts to fill a desperate need. Law-abiding people had to make laws and establish courts and, in short, *become* the law. It existed only in them. But they needed a police force, or forces, that would be able to cope with criminals and prevent crime. A realization of the need for police inspired Texans, cognizant of the futility of waiting for law to come to them, to organize the Texas Rangers. The Rangers maintained order and fought the enemies of Texas until they were superseded by the Northern Army of Occupation during Reconstruction. Texas' Reconstruction governor, Edmund J. Davis, formed a state

[1] Paul E. Wilson, "Law on the Frontier," *The Trail Guide*, Vol. V, No. 3 (September, 1960), 8–9.

police in 1870, but it was largely ineffective because it was resented by Texans and because it largely failed to keep order. It may, indeed, have served to increase rather than reduce crime.[2]

Governor Davis' brief and disastrous term in office was accompanied by an upsurge in outlawry. The situation, serious enough during the 1860's, became far worse in the 1870's. Texas outlaws were well organized and did as they pleased. They and the gunmen hired by the feudal cattle barons were formidable obstacles to the establishment of a settled society in Texas.

In 1874, however, a new governor, Richard Coke, took action and organized the Texas Rangers once again. The newly constituted force enlisted men who prided themselves on their ability to uphold the old Ranger tradition. One section of the new organization, headed by Major John B. Jones, was known as the "Frontier Battalion." It was responsible for keeping order in the Indian country and settling disputes among white men. The other section, the "Special Force of Rangers," was placed under the command of Captain L. H. McNelly, a young Civil War veteran. McNelly had served in the state police, but had not been tainted by that experience and was highly regarded. The duty of the Special Force was to be confined to controlling cattle rustlers and border bandits. Both forces had their hands full. Without the Rangers Texas would have been in very poor straits. Under appallingly difficult and dangerous conditions they eventually brought to justice the outlaws and desperadoes who infested the state.[3]

One of the Rangers' more colorful feats was the capture of John Wesley Hardin in 1877. Already wanted for murder, Hardin shot and killed a deputy sheriff named Charles Webb in Comanche on May 26, 1874 (Hardin's twenty-first birthday). According to Hardin's account, Webb, who had just been introduced to him, immediately shot him in the side. Wes then shot Webb through the left cheek. Webb fell against a wall and then fell to the ground

[2] Gard, *Frontier Justice*, 224.

[3] Sonnichsen, *I'll Die Before I'll Run*, 119; Gard, *Frontier Justice*, 224; Webb, *The Texas Rangers*, 233.

dead. Hardin's friends, Jim Taylor and Bud Dixon kept firing at Webb's body. Wes surrendered to sheriff John Karnes but escaped when a mob formed to lynch him. After three years of hiding and running, constantly pursued by the Rangers, he went to Alabama and then to Florida.

When a chance meeting with a young man impersonating Hardin interested Ranger Lieutenant John B. Armstrong in the Hardin case, he applied for permission to work on the capture of the desperado. He was aided by a young detective, John Duncan, who rented a farm near the home of one of Hardin's relatives (perhaps Hardin's father). Armstrong began sifting through the conflicting reports about the killer's whereabouts. Duncan learned that his neighbor had a wagon or team belonging to Wes and offered to purchase it. The unsuspecting relative wrote to Hardin, living under an alias in Alabama, for permission to sell it. Duncan somehow intercepted the letter and told Armstrong the name of the person to whom it was addressed. Certain that the letter was intended for Hardin, Armstrong left for Alabama with Duncan, after requesting the Texas authorities to send him two warrants for Hardin's arrest, one in Hardin's real name and one in the name on the letter. One warrant was to be mailed to Alabama by mail, and the other was to be sent by express.

In Alabama Armstrong learned that Hardin was leading a gang of train robbers, and the railway company was only too willing to assist the Rangers. However, it appeared that Hardin was now in Pensacola, Florida. Without waiting for the warrants to arrive, Armstrong and Duncan took the next train to Florida.

At a small depot outside Pensacola, accompanied by the town's law officers, they waited for a train on which they believed Hardin was traveling. Sure enough, when the train clanked and steamed its way into the station, Hardin was seen sitting by a window with his arm on the sill, facing forward. Four of his men were traveling with him. Armstrong decided to enter the car from the front and asked the local policemen to come in from the rear. Duncan was to try to grab Hardin's arm through the window. It was a dangerous plan,

but they did not have time to work out a safer one. Armstrong climbed aboard prepared for action. Unfortunately, Duncan and the Pensacola policemen did not go into action as planned, and he found himself facing five outlaws.

Ranger Armstrong carried a stick in his left hand and his six-shooter in his right. Hardin saw Armstrong's 7½-inch-barrel Peacemaker, called out, "Texas, by God!" and reached for his own gun. Hardin's pistol caught in his suspenders as he tried to pull it clear, and he "almost pulled his breeches over his head." One of the outlaws fired a shot through the Ranger's hat and was repaid with a bullet through the heart. The man jumped through a train window, staggered a few paces, and dropped dead. Armstrong struggled desperately to take Hardin alive, and as the desperado tried to get his revolver free, struck him on the side of the head with the barrel of his Colt, hitting him so hard that Hardin was knocked out for two hours. Armstrong then disarmed the three remaining members of the gang and placed them under arrest. In Hardin's later version of this fight and arrest he implies that he battled a large posse of officers before finally being overpowered.[4]

Tales of the Texas Rangers' exploits were told and retold all over the West, and many state and federal law-enforcement bodies, as well as private organizations, began imitating their methods. One private organization that became well known was General David J. Cook's Rocky Mountain Detective Association. A former deputy marshal, county sheriff, and chief of police, Cook devoted most of his life to law enforcement and compiled a set of basic rules which became almost a standard guide among Western peace officers. It might be headed "Self-Preservation":

I. Never hit a prisoner over the head with your pistol, because you may afterwards want to use your weapon and find it disabled. Criminals often conceal weapons and sometimes draw one when they are supposed to have been disarmed.

II. Never attempt to make an arrest without being sure of your

[4] Gard, *Frontier Justice*, 227–28; Webb, *The Texas Rangers*, 297–99; Hardin, *Life*, 93–94, 117–18.

authority. Either have a warrant or satisfy yourself thoroughly that the man whom you seek to arrest has committed an offense.

III. When you attempt to make an arrest, be on your guard. Give your man no opportunity to draw a pistol. If the man is supposed to be a desperado, have your pistol in your hand or be ready to draw when you make yourself known. If he makes no resistance, there will be no harm done by your precaution. My motto has always been, "It is better to kill two men than to allow one to kill you."

IV. After your prisoner is arrested and disarmed, treat him as a prisoner should be treated—as kindly as his conduct will permit. You will find that if you do not protect your prisoners when they are in your possession, those whom you afterwards attempt to arrest will resist you more fiercely, and if they think they will be badly dealt with after arrest, will be inclined to sell their lives as dearly as possible.

V. Never trust much to the honor of prisoners. Give them no liberties which might endanger your own safety or afford them an opportunity to escape. Nine out of ten of them have no honor.[5]

Perhaps the most famous of the private police forces was the Pinkerton Detective Agency. Allan Pinkerton, its founder, was born in Scotland on August 25, 1819, the son of a Glasgow police sergeant. As a young man he emigrated to Canada and then moved to the United States, where he went to work as a cooper in Chicago. One day, while cutting poles for barrel hoops on a small island near the small town of Dundee, Michigan, he noticed that the place was used as a campsite. He spoke to the local sheriff about it, and the result was the arrest of a gang of counterfeiters. Soon Pinkerton's skill in detection gained attention, and finally he organized his own detective agency, which achieved world-wide fame during and after the Civil War. In the hectic post–Civil War days the agency was active in pursuit of Western bad men, most notably the James gang and Butch Cassidy's Wild Bunch.[6]

Also enlisted in the early-day war against crime were the United

---

[5] Gen. David J. Cook, *Hands Up; or, Twenty Years of Detective Life in the Mountains and on the Plains*, 9–10.

[6] Sigmund A. Lavine, *Allan Pinkerton: America's First Private Eye*, 3–4, 49–64, 143ff.

States marshals, officers so surrounded by the aura of heroics that even today mention of their title fires the imagination. Under the Judiciary Act of 1789 marshals were appointed by the President, subject to confirmation by the Senate. The act also specified their duties and gave them authority to command all necessary assistance —which meant appointing deputies. Until 1896 deputies were paid under a fee system, after which they were paid salaries. Many of the duties once assigned to United States marshals are carried out today by the Federal Bureau of Investigation. In the early days a United States marshal was rarely a peace officer. His appointment was often a political one, though his responsibility covered a wide range of duties. Among other things he was responsible for prisoners during trial and for delivery of convicted prisoners to prison or to a place of execution.

The actual tracking down of criminals was generally the job of the marshal's deputies. And it was they who performed most of the legendary deeds of daring attributed to United States marshals. The crimes that came under the jurisdiction of the United States marshal included desertion from the Army, mail robbery, and offenses committed on government property or on Indian reservations. Early-day newspaper reports and other documentation indicate that the services of a deputy United States marshal were also welcomed in apprehending thieves and murderers.[7]

The real and imagined exploits of the deputy marshals continue to be popular subjects to build myths on. One female admirer recalls the thrilling experience she had in 1905 when, as a little girl in Wellington, Kansas, she saw a deputy marshal on his way down to Indian Territory (now Oklahoma) to quiet some unruly Indians. Advised never to forget what she saw, she never did: "He was a tall, gray-haired man, the far-away gaze of a plainsman in his eyes, gun at belt, and he walked as I have not seen a man walk for years,

[7] Thad Page (chief archivist, General Records Division, National Archives) to the author, January 28, 1958; Zoe A. Tilghman, *Spotlight: Bat Masterson and Wyatt Earp as U.S. Deputy Marshals*, 1–2; Topeka *Daily Commonwealth*, August 22, 1871 (in connection with Newton's General Massacre). See also Chapter 7 below.

light and fearless and free. I don't think men will ever walk that way again."[8]

In spite of the state police organizations, the private agencies, and the federal officers, law enforcement was so sketchy and intermittent that almost every man was used to owning firearms for his own and his family's protection. In the 1850's a writer noted that "there are probably in Texas about as many revolvers as male adults,"[9] a situation that was not to change for many years. Members of the average Western community accepted guns as part of their basic equipment, though little sympathy was felt for those who used guns in criminal activities, and few cared when gunmen were killed. Ambushing or sniping was not condoned, and killing someone while committing a robbery was unpardonable. Shoot-outs were accepted, though most people felt that those who lost their lives in gunfights "needed shooting anyway." Even in early days shoot-outs frequently led to official enquiries. However casual these investigations may have been, they satisfied the letter of whatever law then existed. Sometimes the miscreant was told to get out of town and never come back or was warned that future misbehavior might result in far more serious consequences. However, as more people moved west, the increase in population meant that the rules had to change. In time laws regulating the possession and use of firearms were enacted, and police forces were strengthened to enforce the laws. The police force of a typical Kansas cowtown consisted of a city marshal (the chief of police) and as many policemen as necessary. There were seldom more than five, some of whom were hired during the cattle-driving season and dismissed when it ended. On occasion, special police would be employed to supervise certain establishments known for rowdyism or violence. The "lone man" cowtown marshal popularized in legend never really existed. His police force might not always be at full strength, but a marshal was never alone. The duties of the town's police force varied in

[8] Mrs. Lucile Stevens to the author, September 10, 1964.

[9] Frederick Law Olmsted, *A Journey Through Texas; or, a Saddle-Trip on the Southwestern Frontier*, 75.

detail from place to place, but followed an over-all pattern. The police had power to enter any saloon, billiard hall, or other place of amusement and arrest drunks or others who refused to "be restored to order and quiet." Following an arrest, the officer then had to report his action to a magistrate within twenty-four hours.[10] Other duties might be to remove traffic obstructions from the streets, shoot stray dogs, stop runaways, and inspect chimneys, flues, and sidewalks.

Two pressing problems confronted all town councils: a shortage of trained policemen and a shortage of money to pay good men. These problems were especially severe in cattle-driving seasons. Many kinds of men, hired for their reputations as good shots or for their courage under fire, served as cowtown marshals. It was not uncommon for a town council to hire a man from among those they had difficulty controlling. This practice involved a calculated risk, for such a man might resort to intimidation and violence to keep order and thus provoke rather than prevent trouble.[11]

Violence associated with the cattle trade was difficult to stop. Stringent measures against carrying firearms, tied in with various state laws, were rarely enforced. One unenforceable Kansas law prohibited former Confederate soldiers from carrying "a pistol, bowie-knife, dirk or other deadly weapon" on penalty of a maximum fine of one hundred dollars and a jail sentence of one to three months.[12] For various reasons, most of them relating to economics, most town councils preferred fining troublemaking cowboys to jailing them. In June, 1873, the county commissioners of Ford County, Kansas, passed a motion aimed at the suppression of firearms in Dodge City: ". . . any person or persons found carrying concealed weapons in the city of Dodge or violating the laws of the State shall be dealt with according to law."[13] Two years earlier, in

[10] Robert R. Dykstra, "The Cattle Town Experience" (Doctoral dissertation, University of Iowa, 1964), 149.

[11] *Ibid.*, 154.

[12] *Kansas Statutes*, 1868, 378. This law remained in force for the whole of the cowtown era.

[13] Dykstra, "The Cattle Town Experience," 145.

1871, the Wichita council had ordered the city marshal to erect two signboards warning visitors that weapons were strictly forbidden. The following year the toll collectors at the privately owned Chisholm Trail bridge were sworn in as special police and empowered to relieve all visitors of their arms in exchange for a metal token. By 1873, however, the signboards were back advising visitors to "leave your revolvers at police headquarters, and get a check."[14]

These were by no means the first efforts to control firearms in Kansas. In March, 1869, the editor of a Lawrence, Kansas, paper, had commented on the alarming increase in firearms and some shootings that had resulted and added: "Let every man, not an officer, carrying fire arms, be summarily taken before some magistrate and fined to the full extent of the law."[15] An Abilene editor added a touch of moralizing to the argument and declared:

> *Fire Arms.*—The Chief of Police [James B. Hickok] has posted up printed notices, informing all persons that the ordinance against carrying fire arms or other weapons in Abilene, will be enforced. That's right. There's no bravery in carrying revolvers in a civilized community. Such a practice is well enough and perhaps necessary when among Indians or other barbarians, but among white people it ought to be discontinued.[16]

Many difficulties hampered efforts to keep firearms at a minimum, and guns presented many problems. "Unreconstructed Rebels" and equally belligerent "Yankee" police officers were bound to clash. The southerners always outnumbered the cowtown police, and some refused to give up their arms, even if it meant that they had to conceal them on their persons. Consequently the police wore their revolvers openly, as a symbol of authority and as a warning to troublemakers that, if need be, they would use them in their efforts to maintain or establish order. It is not, therefore, particularly surprising that the cowtown police killed more people than did the bad men they were keeping in check. The number of

[14] *Ibid.*
[15] Lawrence *Daily Tribune*, March 3, 1869.
[16] Abilene *Chronicle*, June 8, 1871.

homicides in the five principal cowtowns was far less than folklore and fictionalized accounts would lead one to believe. Some of the frontier "gunfighters" who became legendary spent considerable time in these towns, but few of them were involved in shooting escapades. In the years 1870 to 1885 forty-five men died by violence in Abilene, Ellsworth, Wichita, Dodge City, and Caldwell, most of them cowboys and gamblers shot by town marshals.[17]

From these killings evolved one of the most durable elements of the Western legend—the "war" between the Texas cowboys and the Kansas marshals.

[17] Dykstra, "The Cattle Town Experience," 167; see table, "Circumstances of Homicides," 168.

6.

Cowboys and Cowtowns

Today's concept of the cowboy as an expert horseman and crack shot leading a romantic, exciting life is not confined to the United States. The cowboy has been admired in most parts of the world since Buffalo Bill Cody helped create a heroic image for him in both hemispheres. When Cody featured the exploits of cowboys and Indians in his wild West show, his portrayal of the cowboy set the pattern, which was further followed and elaborated in such works as Owen Wister's *The Virginian*.

The flesh-and-blood cowboy of the Old West was a worker employed in herding, rounding up, branding, and driving cattle to market. Over the years his image has become blurred with that of the gunfighter, a distortion of fact that can largely be laid at the door of the House of Beadle and Adams. In 1887 *Beadle's Dime Novels* depicted Buck Taylor as "King of the Cowboys," a title Taylor used in Cody's wild West shows. Identified with the already legendary frontier heroes, he was the original "cowboy hero" of folklore. Beadle's cowboy fought Indians, rescued maidens from a fate worse than death, and generally assumed the role of knight in dusty leather. In every situation he displayed brilliant horsemanship and superb marksmanship. It was this characterization of the heavily armed horseman clad in a gaudy stage costume that was to become the stock Western movie hero in the 1920's.[1] It was an almost totally misleading characterization, all the more ironic because the cowboy's true story is as interesting as the legend.

[1] Henry Nash Smith, *Virgin Land: The American West as Symbol and Myth*, 123–24.

It is not known precisely when or how the cattle herder of the American West came to be called "cowboy." The first use of the word has been traced to the time of the American Revolution, when Americans referred to Tory marauders active near New York as "cowboys." Anglo-Americans in the cattle country generally referred to a herder as a "drover," until the word "cowboy" took its place. (Cowboys who "drove" herds up the trails to Kansas continued to be called "drovers" until the final days of trail driving.) Apparently the term "cowboy" was in early usage synonymous with "rustler," which originally meant one who gathered up, or "rustled," unowned wild cattle, and only later was applied to one who stole cattle from their legal owners.

In regions of the Southwest and the West under Spanish influence the Spanish *vaquero* ("cowherd") continued in use long after "cowboy" had come into general use. The American cowboy also owed much of his equipment, nomenclature, and clothing styles to the Mexican herdsmen, who had adapted Spanish equipment and methods to the new environment.[2]

Cattle were introduced into the New World by Columbus in 1493, when his expedition landed on the island of Hispaniola. In the years after Cortes began his conquest of New Spain (Mexico), cattle were brought to the mainland. Many of the cattle escaped from the missions and forts for which they were imported and roamed wild. The gradual intermingling of Spanish and, later, Anglo-American stock produced a lean, narrow-faced, longhorned creature ideally suited to the land in which it thrived, an animal that men would fight and die to own and would become the economic backbone of Texas—the Texas longhorn.[3]

By 1830 there were said to be 100,000 cattle in Texas, including both branded stock and wild cattle. Though movement of cattle from Texas was slow and difficult, and markets were few and widely

[2] Bryant and Gay, *A Popular History of the United States*, IV, 22; Arnold R. Rojas, "The Vaquero," *The American West*, Vol. I, No. 2 (Spring, 1964), 48.

[3] Donald R. Ornduff, "Aristocrats in the Cattle Country," *The Trail Guide*, Vol. IX, No. 2 (June, 1964), 2.

separated, by 1837–38 herds of three hundred to one thousand head of wild, unbranded cattle of the Nueces and Rio Grande regions had been rounded up and driven to the interior. In 1842 Texas cattle were driven as far as New Orleans, and by 1848 to markets in the East, but not until the California gold rush brought demands for beef from the West Coast did it become profitable to drive cattle to far-off markets. In 1849–50 the demand for beef began to increase steadily. Chicago received its first shipment of Texas steers in 1856, and soon other herds were being driven north.

In 1859, to avoid conflicts with Kansans and Missourians who were determined to keep Texas cattle out because of their fear of Texas fever,[4] cattlemen drove their herds north through Colorado over a trail laid out by Oliver Loving, but suitable transportation to markets in the East was not yet available. When the Civil War broke out, trail drives to the North stopped, and at first there was little market in the South for beef. Later in the war, when beef was desperately needed in the Confederacy, most of the thousands of head of Texas cattle were running wild and unobtainable.[5]

When the war ended, the cattle allowed to wander by the exigencies of war had multiplied and moved into the Texas brush country. Few ranchers had the resources to go after cattle in the brush, and those who did found it no easy task to round up cattle

[4] In 1868 John Gamgee, the English author of *The Cattle Plague* (London, 1866), visited the United States. He diagnosed Texas fever for the U.S. Commissioners of Agriculture, and some of his reports on the "splenic or periodic fever of cattle" were published in *Reports on the Diseases of Cattle in the United States Made to the Commissioner of Agriculture, with Accompanying Documents* (Washington, 1869). A revised edition appeared in 1871. Charles F. Gross, bookkeeper for Joseph G. Mc-Coy in 1871, stated that deaths of local cattle from fever almost led to a range war. Finally the cattlemen and traders raised "a big fund of money, sent to England & got Prof. Gamgee, the most noted scientist in England, to come over [to] investigate & report. After his report showed that the Texas cattle were responsible for the deaths of the native stock (he never said just how), the dealers arranged to pay & did pay most for the dead native cattle, and a partial peace was obtained." (Charles F. Gross to J. B. Edwards, April 13, 1922, Manuscripts Division, KSHS.)

[5] Wayne Gard, *The Chisholm Trail*, 23, 36–37; Everett Dick, "The Long Drive," KSHS *Collections*, Vol. XVII (1926–28), 29; Charles F. Gross to J. B. Edwards, April 13, 1922, Manuscripts Division, KSHS; Webb, *The Great Plains*, 211.

that, after years of freedom, were wild and unwilling to be herded. Texas longhorns were ferocious animals, and even after they had been rounded up, getting them to market presented many problems.[6] Early drives to Baxter Springs, on the southern border of Kansas, met with much opposition from armed mobs of Kansans who believed that all Texas cattle were infected with Texas fever. Many members of these mobs were veterans of the Missouri-Kansas border wars. Though some of them had been proslavery Missourians, the Texans with fine impartiality called all of them Jayhawkers. Despite opposition the drives continued, and Texas cattlemen prospered.[7]

Of all the routes taken by the cattlemen driving their herds to the railroads, the most famous was the Chisholm Trail, named after Jesse Chisholm, a half-blood trader. The Chisholm Trail formed part of a long route which ran from the Rio Grande River, through Indian Territory, to Abilene, Kansas. A pamphlet published by the Kansas Pacific Railroad in 1874 called the route the "Texas Cattle Trail" as far north as Wichita.[8] From there to the Kansas Pacific railhead at Abilene it was sometimes called "McCoy's Extension" or the "Abilene Trail." Over the years the pounding hoofs beat the earth of the routes into hard-packed trails two to four hundred yards wide.

Despite their massive horns that had a spread of six to seven feet or more, the longhorns were remarkably agile and capable of great speed. Held in check at night by the soothing voices of the night guards and generally obedient to the directions of mounted men in daylight, the unpredictable creatures could be "spooked" by a man on foot, by the wind, or by any unusual phenomenon. A flash of lightning or a clap of thunder could set them off in a mad stampede. Faced with death and destruction as he raced to stop and pacify the terrified beasts, the cowboy earned his thirty or forty dollars a month and his reputation as a horseman.

[6] Gard, *The Chisholm Trail*, 151–57.

[7] Dick, "The Long Drive," KSHS *Collections*, Vol. XVII (1926–28), 37.

[8] Gard, *The Chisholm Trail*, 72–73; *Guide Map of the Great Texas Cattle Trail, 1874*.

An almost self-sufficient nomad, a drover enjoyed few luxuries and rarely dressed in the splendor associated with the fictional counterpart. When he was paid off at the end of a drive, he replaced his clothing and had a bath and a haircut. On the trail the cowboy endured considerable hardship. As one old-time cowboy described it:

> The old open range days was a great life. It was hard, that is the work was hard and dangerous and you had to stand all kinds of weather, but in the winter we were genally at the home ranch or in a snug line cabin somewhere on the range. But it was healthy. You could have stood it. Many an Easterner went to the rough life of a cowboy to save his last lung and did save it. I didn't go for that purpose. I went because I wanted to be a cowboy.
>
> The first time I went was in 1902 to southwestern Colorado. I was just 19, and father was dubious about letting me go to the "wild and wooly." Finally, mother came to my aid (as she always did) when she said to father: "Well, he is older than you were when you ran away and joined the Union Army." That kind of settled it because he had no comeback for that, and I went. It was a great life, and we all loved it. I disliked the rainy season more than snow and cold weather when we were out with the wagon. Of course we slept on the ground. We each had his own bed made of a heavy canvas wagon sheet about 14 feet long and seven feet wide. We would make up a bed of blankets and soughans (comforts) on one half and then pull the rest of the canvas sheet up over that. Of course . . . if it rained that night, well, you just got good and wet. The canvas tarp kept you pretty dry on top, but the water had a habit of running along the ground and under you and soaking up through everything. Like everything else you got used to that in time. When it snowed it was much more comfortable because the snow formed a protective covering over you, and it was kind of warm. . . . It was sure a great life and I never knew a cowboy of the old open range that didn't love it.[9]

The cowboy's life evolved around the cow, but he owed that life to the horse. Although he usually had a string of horses at his disposal, he generally had a preference for one particular animal, and

[9] Earl R. Forrest to the author, February 16, 1967.

death was considered the only fitting punishment for the man who tried to steal it.

Also indispensable to the cowboy was his pistol. Though he was capable of some alarming antics with this weapon, he used it primarily to defend himself against hostile Indians, rustlers, and rattlesnakes, or to shoot a crazed steer or an injured horse. Rarely did he use it on a companion. More often than not, his pistol grew rusty from disuse and was only "aired" when used to hurrah a town. The cowboy delighted in appearing rougher than he really was, and his reputation for rowdyism made him greatly feared in some quarters. He enjoyed such stories as the probably apocryphal one about the Indian chief who asked General Phil Sheridan for a cannon. "What! Do you want to kill my soldiers with it?" asked the general. "No," replied the chief. "Want to kill cowboy; kill soldier with a club."[10]

Though in actual fact the cowboy seldom cared to pit his skill against the semiprofessional gun wielders who policed the Kansas cowtowns, legend has him willing to fight at the drop of a hat to save a comrade in danger, and portrays him as generous, brave, and scrupulously honest. According to one of his contemporaries, the typical cowboy was imbued with "a strange, paradoxical code of personal honor, vindication of which he will obtrude his life as though it were but a toy."[11]

A considerably less romantic view of the cowboy goes to the other extreme and depicts him as a ruffian or ne'er-do-well. One newspaper described the typical trail hand as "unlearned and illiterate, with few wants and meager ambition," and further observed:

> His diet is principally Navy plug and whisky, and the occupation of his heart is gambling. His dress consists of a flannel shirt with a handkerchief encircling his neck, butternut pants, and a pair of long boots in which are always to be found the legs of his pants. His head is

[10] Robert M. Wright, *Dodge City: The Cowboy Capital*, 279–80.

[11] "Over Sunday in New Sharon," *Scribner's.* Vol. XIX (March, 1880), 771, quoted in Smith, *Virgin Land*, 122.

covered with a sombrero, which is a Mexican hat with a low crown and a brim of mammoth dimensions. He generally wears a revolver on each side, which he will use with as little hesitation on a man as on a wild animal. Such a character is dangerous and desperate, and each one generally has killed his man. There are good and even honorable men among them, but run-away boys and men who find it too hot for them even in Texas join the cattle drovers and constitute a large proportion of them. They drink, swear, and fight; and life with them is a round of boisterous gaiety and indulgence in sensual pleasure.[12]

This view was shared by many of the early cowtown residents. One Abilene citizen recalled that a cowboy with too much tangle-foot aboard was likely to use his Navy six-shooters at the slightest provocation: "Drunk or sober they would shoot a plug hat if the fancy took them."[13]

Any fair assessment of the cowboy would recognize that, while he was not the most highly civilized of individuals, he operated in times and under circumstances that were not conducive to peace-able conduct. The Texas cowboy hated the idea of being beholden to anyone, and particularly to a northerner. The fact that the Texas cattle trade depended on Northern buyers and Yankee money was a thorn in his side. After months on the trail, coaxing and bullying longhorns to keep moving, hoarse from dust, sodden with rain, "poisoned" by what passed for food, he longed for the sights and the enjoyments of the cowtowns, and it was a bitter shock to find them policed by Yankee marshals bent on frustrating his need to let off steam.

Abilene, the first of the important Kansas cowtowns, was the creation of Joseph G. McCoy, one of the brothers of the firm of William K. McCoy and Brothers, which was engaged in shipping cattle to various markets. In 1867, beset by Kansas quarantine laws that barred Texas cattle from most parts of the state for most of the year, McCoy looked for a shipping point in an area with good grazing land. He eventually found it—Abilene—on the Kan-

---

12 Topeka *Daily Commonwealth*, August 15, 1871.
13 J. B. Edwards, *Early Days in Abilene*, 3.

sas prairie. McCoy described it as "a place of about a dozen log huts with dirt-covered roofs, the one exception being a place shingle-covered. . . . The business of the burg was conducted in two small rooms, mere log huts, and of course the inevitable saloon, also a log hut, was to be found."[14]

On June 18, 1867, McCoy, convinced that Abilene would be ideal for his purpose, purchased 250 acres of land at the northeastern edge of the village. Within three months he had built a shipping yard large enough to hold one thousand head of cattle. A barn, a livery stable, an office, the later-celebrated three-story Drovers Cottage hotel, and a bank were also constructed. The shipping pens could load forty railroad cars in two hours, and McCoy induced the Kansas Pacific Railroad to build a one-hundred-car switch at Abilene and transfer pens and feed yards at Leavenworth. On September 5, 1867, the first cattle were dispatched from Abilene to Chicago, and the town was in business.[15]

All the Kansas cowtowns were similar in appearance. The town's main street and business section ran east to west, parallel to the railroad. The streets, ankle-deep in dust in dry weather, became quagmires of mud in rainy periods. In Abilene the Drovers Cottage on "A" Street served as the principal meeting place for the cattlemen and buyers. The dance halls and brothels were on the north side, the "wrong side of the tracks."[16] Abilene, Newton, Ellsworth, Wichita, Dodge City, Caldwell, and several other places enjoyed brief periods of prosperity as cowtowns. Although Dodge City was to achieve the greatest fame, owing to its famous residents and its longer period as a cattle shipping point, it was in Abilene that the Texas cowboy was discovered and brought to national prominence.[17]

[14] Joseph G. McCoy, *Historic Sketches of the Cattle Trade of the West and Southwest*, 44.

[15] Gard, *The Chisholm Trail*, 65–66, 69.

[16] George L. Cushman, "Abilene, First of the Kansas Cow Towns," KSHS *Quarterly*, Vol. IX, No. 3 (August, 1940), 243–44.

[17] Joe B. Frantz and Julian E. Choate, *The American Cowboy: The Myth and the Reality*, 32.

The arrival in Abilene or any other cowtown of a herd of cattle meant different things to different people. Some looked upon the cattle trade as a necessary evil because it brought them a profitable living. Others greatly feared and despised the Texans, who, aware of the feeling they caused in town, made it a point to put on a show upon arrival or departure, heralding the event with a fusillade of revolver shots that shattered the peace and smoked up the air. At first the Kansans simply watched such performances in awe, but they soon learned to hurry to safety when they heard the signal crack of a pistol shot fired by one of the boys as they raced by on their way to or from the cow camps across Mud Creek.[18]

If some of the permanent inhabitants resented the arrival of the drovers, the saloonkeepers and gamblers welcomed them. During the cattle season, from May to September, their main business was the entertainment of drovers. The Texans wanted excitement, and people flocked to the cowtowns to supply it. In April, 1871, the population of Abilene was no more than five hundred, but by June 1 it held about seven thousand people:

. . . . eating wherever they could and sleeping everywhere, some in houses, some in tents, but the greater number under blankets spread upon the prairie. As to drink, there was probably more whiskey drank than water, and of quality that would make rabbits fight a bull dog. On the first of June, 1871, the fiery furnace of the Abilene Texas cattle trade was in full blast; it was red hot, everything sizzled. On the southwest corner of First and Cedar Streets was Jake Karatofsky's General Merchandise Store. Whiskey included in the "General" department. From this corner to the southeast corner of Mulberry and First was a solid wall of saloons, gambling houses and other dents [*sic*] of perdition. From the northeast corner of First and Cedar around to the Gulf House (now National Hotel) was also a solid row of gambling dens and saloons. These dens were run 24 hours of the day and 30 and 31 days of the month and fresh relays of victims always ready to take the places of those who had lost their last penny at the wheel of fortune, or rather misfortune, and they who were lying dead

18 Theophilus Little, "Early Days of Abilene and Dickinson County," in Adolph Roenigk, *Pioneer History of Kansas*, 36.

drunk on the floor or sidewalk. Brass bands, string bands, piano, vocal music were installed inside and at the doors of these places to attract the passer-by and retain the sucker already in the toils, and too, the "Soiled Dove" was there; bedizzened in her gaudy dress, cheap jewelry and high colored cosmetics, and then the Devil himself was there night and day. Talk about "Hell down below." Why, Abilene was a setthing [*sic*], roaring, flaming Hell.

Thousands and tens of thousands were staked and lost and won at these gaming tables. One Texas cattle man lost $30,000 at one sitting. I have seen a hatful of gold lying loose in a pile on these tables. Some body steal it? you ask. He would have been bored full of bullets in the twinkling of an eye.[19]

Violence growing out of drinking, gambling, and prostitution beset every cowtown. The Texans brought with them a prosperity that could not be ignored, but storekeepers, hardware dealers, and others who had goods or services to sell did not relish the stories circulated about the disturbances, fearing that such reports would keep settlers and investors away and would eventually be bad for business and growth. The newspapers often denounced the visitors' unseemly behavior. The season of 1872 was forecast by a concerned Wichita editor: "During the coming season Wichita desires law and order, with their consequent peace and security, and not bloodshed and a name that will cause a thrill of horror whenever mentioned and which will effectually deter the most desirable class of people from coming among us. Right speedily will the latter follow if the former are not maintained."[20] Other writers in towns along the cattle trail voiced similar opinions.[21]

The Kansas Code empowered mayors to call upon men between the ages of eighteen and fifty to help enforce the law. However, the mayors rarely did so because it created resentment among the cowboys who were likely to take their trade elsewhere.[22] Aware that the Texans had them over a barrel, city fathers contented themselves with passing local ordinances against wearing arms, gamb-

[19] *Ibid.*, 35–36.
[20] Wichita *Eagle*, June 7, 1872.
[21] Dykstra, "The Cattle Town Experience," 137–38.

ling, and prostitution and making violators liable to token fines. Money from the routine fines was channeled into the town treasury, and there was no interruption of activities.[23]

If today the leniency toward the Texans and those who entertained them seems hypocritical, it must be remembered that, after all, it was easier and cheaper to fine a cowboy for carrying a gun in town than it was to jail him. City officials by and large preached tolerance. According to one authority:

> In such cases citizens invariably inclined toward a degree of forgiveness, especially if the perpetrator could invoke youth, intoxication, or some other extenuating circumstance. Of particular appeal was word that a young killer came from a good family, so that, with typical Victorian sentimentalism, it could be said of him that he fell temporarily upon evil ways. . . . "We have no personal ill-will against the accused," mused an Abilene editor of a young Texan just acquitted of murder. "If he now reforms his life will give us pleasure to note the fact, as it will certainly rejoice the hearts of his father and good mother, who are said to be highly respectable people."[24]

The saloon was a favorite meeting place of the cowboys and cattlemen, for there they could combine business and pleasure. The saloon's entertainments were somewhat limited, but the proprietors endeavored to appeal to all types of clientele. The better saloons served fine imported liqueurs, wines, and cigars. Beer of varying grades was also provided. A favorite import was Guinness from Ireland.

Saloons also prided themselves on their ability to provide good music for their customers. Chalkey M. Beeson—"Chalk" to his friends—of Dodge City, was described as an accomplished musician who "delights frequent appreciative audiences with his fine musical skill," and it was a "rare treat to drop in at the Saratoga upon Mr. Beeson, and listen to his last and best musical combination." In addition to drink and music a good saloon also provided billiard tables.

[22] *Ibid.,* 140.   [23] *Ibid.,* 148.
[24] *Ibid.,* 151–62; Abilene *Chronicle,* June 8, 1871.

Some establishments catered to those who wanted quieter surroundings. Dodge City's Alamo, which opened in June, 1877, had no music but offered a parlor for those who wanted to talk or think at leisure over cigars and refreshments.[25]

Some saloons provided other things besides quiet and quality liquor to appeal to men just off the trail. The more lavish the saloon's decor the better most of them liked it. One of these saloons, Abilene's Alamo, was described thus:

> It was housed in a long room with a forty-foot frontage on Cedar Street, facing the west. There was an entrance at either end. At the west entrance were three double glass doors. Inside and along the front of the south side was the bar with its array of carefully polished brass fixtures and rails. From the back bar across a large mirror, which reflected the brightly sealed bottles of liquor. At various places over the walls were huge paintings in cheaply done imitations of the nude masterpieces of the Venetian Renaissance painters. Covering the entire floor space were gaming tables, at which practically any game of chance could be indulged. The Alamo boasted an orchestra, which played forenoons, afternoons, and nights.[26]

A considerably less elaborate establishment was the Gold Room in Newton. An 1871 description dwelt at length on its half-dozen gaming tables, mammoth bar, music, and shows. It was regarded as the "pivot" of the town, and nearly every adult male inhabitant spent a few minutes or more each day at the tables or bar. On Main Street, midway between the railroad depot and the post office, the Gold Room was a large frame building about sixty feet long and thirty feet wide. It had been very roughly put together and the Gothic A-shaped roof was freely ribbed with timbers slanting downward and outward. Daylight shone through cracks in the roof, and spider webs hung from the corners and rafters. According to the Topeka *Daily Commonwealth,* "the place throughout has a new,

[25] Dodge City *Times,* June 2, September 29, 1877.

[26] Cushman, "Abilene, First of the Kansas Cow Towns," KSHS *Quarterly,* Vol. IX, No. 3 (August, 1940), 244.

fresh, rough look that well accords with the general appearance of the town."

On entering the main door, the customer saw a twenty-foot bar on the left, behind which was a row of barrels containing all kinds of liquors and wines. Above them was "the mantle or show part of the bar, lined with clusters of decanters daintily arranged and polished until their shimmer is like that of diamonds." Close to the wall opposite the bar were the gaming tables. The tables were square and covered with green baize, with little semicircles cut out of one of the sides for the dealer, to bring his board closer and give him better control of his layout.

Around the room were scattered small, round tables for the use of private gamblers. At the rear of the hall was a raised platform for entertainers. There was also a stage for a piano and musicians. In the rear of the building there was a friendly calaboose for drunken clients. Rooms used by the waitresses and other employees, situated alongside the icehouse, were especially attractive when the outdoor temperature was one hundred degrees and above.[27] The saloons of the end-of-track railroad towns and mining towns had provided the models for the cowtown establishments. Few of them resembled the palatial establishments that were to be built on Hollywood sets. Most were about eighty by twenty-four feet. The bar occupied most of the saloon and was usually about twenty feet long and eight feet wide.[28] Bat-wing doors, the swinging doors of Western-movie saloons, were not in general use during the sixties and seventies. Saloons usually had standard doors with or without glass panels. Most bars were equipped with a footrail and cuspidors. Sawdust was strewn upon the floor, and over the rooms hung the characteristic saloon odor—a combination of stale beer, sweat, and tobacco smoke—an odor that by and large produced a congenial atmosphere.

An 1880 prohibition amendment to the Kansas State Constitution drastically altered the drinking habits of Kansans and led to

---

[27] Topeka *Daily Commonwealth*, September 17, 1871.
[28] Yankton *Press and Dakotaian*, December 5, 1876.

the famous "Dodge City War" of 1883, in which gambler Luke Short, a member of the semipolitical faction made up of saloon-keepers and gamblers and known as the "Gang," became involved in a dispute with a "reform" group composed of other saloon owners. Other members of the Gang included James H. ("Dog") Kelley, Bat Masterson, and W. H. Harris. The reform group was led by Alonzo B. Webster, Lawrence E. Deger, and Mike Sutton.

Some members of the Gang had been accused of engaging in criminal pursuits—rigged games, confidence tricks, holdups, and land frauds. These accusations, combined with Dodge City's reputation as a "wicked city," made it difficult to persuade settlers to come to the region. The election of Alonzo B. Webster as mayor of Dodge City in 1881 put an end to most of the criminal activities and imposed on the town's entertainment industry a quasi-moral set of restrictions.

On the night of April 28, 1883, Luke Short and W. H. Harris, who had bought the Long Branch Saloon, defied a new ordinance, and the city police raided the saloon and arrested their girl "singer" for soliciting. Luke claimed discrimination because the Long Branch was the only saloon raided, and later in the evening he exchanged shots with L. C. Hartman, a special policeman, but no one was hurt. Luke was arrested but was later released by a committee headed by the reform mayor and told to stay out of town "permanently." Short headed for Topeka, where he aired his complaint to the governor and the press.[29]

When news got around that Luke Short had appealed to his gun-fighting friends to support him in his fight with the Dodge City officials, the citizens of the town asked the governor to send troops for their protection. The governor refused to do so, and Luke's friends, among them Wyatt Earp and Bat Masterson, began to drift into town. It is also possible that Doc Holliday came from Denver, although his presence has not been generally recorded.[30]

[29] Dykstra, "The Cattle Town Experience," 326; Joseph W. Snell, "The Wild and Woolly West of the Popular Writer" (paper given before the Western History Association at El Paso, Texas, October 14, 1966).

[30] Interview with John Gilchriese, El Paso, Texas, October 15, 1966.

By the end of May the group was firmly entrenched. No gunplay erupted, but Luke was reinstated as a citizen of Dodge in June. To celebrate his return, Luke, his partner, Harris, and some friends were photographed in a group. Today the picture is labeled "The Dodge City Peace Commission"—but there was no contemporary reference to that name.

Gambling brought into the saloons large amounts of money, and in time rooms and even whole establishments were given over to betting games. The gambling ordinances were generally mild or unenforced, and all kinds of people were drawn to the games. Most of the gunfighters gambled, but few were professionals. Fly-by-night gamblers soon earned themselves the much-reviled title "tin-horn" and a swift death with a Boot Hill burial. The professional gamblers, "the red pepper of the compound," were a breed apart. The 1871 season in Newton was presided over by such fascinating characters as John Gallagher, known variously as "Corn-Hole Johnny," "Three-card Johny," and "Chuck-luck Johnny." Although he was only twenty-six years old, he was a veteran gambler. Other professionals were Dick Clark, the most impassive and stony-faced of them all; his partner, New York gambler Jim Moon; and the monte dealers, "Pony" Reid and Texan "Trick" Brown. Such men kept the continual rounds of monte, faro, chuck-a-luck, three-card monte, and mustang raking in the profits.[31]

Brothels and dance halls were also big business in the cowtowns. Each new season brought trainloads of get-rich-quick gamblers, pimps, and prostitutes from the East. Many of the girls were as hard as their male companions. One buffalo hunter never forgot a visit he paid one night to a saloon in Dodge City. As he started through the door, he saw a man put his gun to the ear of another man standing at the bar and practically blow his head off. A girl sitting cross-legged on a billiard table jumped down and rubbed her hands in the blood running across the floor. Then leaping to her feet, she cried out, "Cock-a-doodle-doo! clapped her hands, and spattered blood all over her dress. Considerably shaken by the "wicked

[31] Topeka *Daily Commonwealth*, September 17, 1871.

bitch," the buffalo hunter turned right around and went back to his camp.[32]

There was nothing particularly unusual about the women employed in cowtowns to entertain the men. In general they differed but little from the whores of mining camps and seaports. Occasionally their escapades provided newspapers with ribald anecdotes:

> A desperate fight occurred at the boarding house of Mrs. W., on "Tin Pot Alley," last Tuesday evening, between two of the most fascinating doves of the roost. When we heard the noise and looked out the front window, which commanded a view of the situation, it was a magnificent sight to see. Tufts of hair, calico, snuff and gravel flew like fir [*sic*] in a cat fight, and before we could distinguish how the battle waned a chunk of dislocated leg grazed our ear and a cheer from the small boys announced that a battle was lost and won. The crowd separated as the vanquished virgin was carried to her parlors by two "soups." A disjointed nose, two or three internal bruises, a chawed ear and a missing eye were the only scars we could see.[33]

Sometimes such a girl became infatuated with one of her customers. The unfortunate outcome of one such affair was reported in a Kansas City paper. A girl from St. Louis who had made her way to Newton fell in love with a railroad man, who rejected her. In desperation she tried to obtain poison, and when that failed, she acquired a pistol and slipped away to her room:

> A deafening report, a fall of a heavy body, a piercing shriek, soon brought a crowd to the bedside, across which the unfortunate girl lay, her clothes blacked and smoking with the fire which the fatal powder had ignited. The pistol had been held firmly against the pit of the stomach and the ball had passed through the body to the skin of the back.
>
> A bed was at once made on the floor and the dying girl was placed upon it. At the latter's request, the unwilling and unfortunate cause of the tragedy was sent for. He came and her eyes never left him from the

---

[32] Walter S. Campbell (Stanley Vestal), *Dodge City: Queen of the Cow Towns*, 23.
[33] Ford County *Globe*, January 21, 1879.

moment he entered until the film of death shut out all sight of the outer world.[34]

The business of prostitution flourished. Many of the girls had rooms or cabins well away from the saloons. Some of them solicited business while serving drinks in the many dance halls, which were usually housed in long, narrow one- or two-story frame buildings. The dance area was on the first floor at the front. In one corner was a raised platform for the "orchestra" (usually a sole violinist or pianist), and in the rear were small rooms for the use of the girls and their customers. The various city ordinances kept prostitutes and gamblers happily in business but under control. Their contributions to the city treasuries and the slush funds of politicians and police departments were quite impressive and most welcome.[35]

The proprietors of the brothels, gambling dens, and saloons were a hard bunch—they had to be to stay in business. "Rowdy Joe" Lowe, owner of a saloon in Wichita, in company with his equally colorful wife, "Rowdy Kate," was one of the many who kept reporters supplied with material for their papers. Rowdy Joe administered his own brand of law, occasionally administering a pistol whipping to someone who got out of hand. He moved to Newton in 1871. There he was involved in a gunfight with a man named Sweet over Kate, a fight that resulted in Sweet's death. In 1873, back in Wichita again, he fought a duel with another saloonkeeper, E. T. ("Red") Beard. Beard, a veteran of many fights, did not survive this one. At the hearing the evidence was so confused that no one could say for sure that Joe actually killed Red.[36]

The toughness of saloonkeepers was often reflected in the attitude adopted toward their establishments by newspapermen, one of whom recalled: "There is a row of saloons on the Kansas Pacific

[34] Kansas City *Times*, September 6, 1871.

[35] Nyle H. Miller and Joseph W. Snell, *Why the West Was Wild*, 15.

[36] *Ibid.*, 255–56; State of Kansas *vs.* Joseph Lowe, Sedgewick County District Court Records, 1873, Manuscripts Division, KSHS.

Railway called Hays City; having visited the place, we should call it the Sodom of the Plains." With tongue in cheek he continued:

> Its saloons, as we have observed, are among its chief attractions. On entering one, you are astonished at the warlike appearance of the place, as it looks more like an arsenal than a bar room. The adroitness with which the skilled barkeepers there handle their weapons is a marvel. When a noisy crowd enters, the keeper of the arsenal retreats gracefully behind his fortifications, and "smiles blandly upon his baffled pursuers." He is surrounded with a halo of knives and pistols, and strikes an attitude of defiance among the spigots. Immediately upon the least sign of hostile demonstrations, he displays his skill as a marksman upon some unfortunate victim, and taking a piece of chalk in his hand, turns lithely to the French plate mirror at his back, and writes in large letters, "to be continued." This exhibition of trained dexterity wins for him the reputation of a "thoroughbred," and one not to be trifled with. Such scenes made up the daily routine of life there, in the days of Wild Bill, sometimes called William Severe, and they are frequently repeated in commemoration of the ancient chivalry of the city.[37]

Saloonkeepers and the police seemed to appreciate the difficulties of their respective professions, and, as is the usual procedure in all times in all places, arrangements were worked out. Policemen also had arrangements with bawdyhouse owners, madams, pimps, and whores. Policemen were regular visitors to the brothels, and their presence often led to arguments and violence.

One evening, as Frank Hunt, a former policeman in Caldwell, was sitting near a window in the Red Light dance hall after an argument with another man over a girl, an unknown person took a shot at him through the window and killed him. On another occasion, George Brown, city marshal of Caldwell, entered the same establishment with constable Willis Metcalf, looking for a man reported to be armed. As they started up the stairs to the second floor, they were set upon by four armed men. In the struggle Brown was shot through the head. The bullet splattered his brains "on the wall and

---

[37] Junction City *Union*, July 8, 1871.

floor of the building, while the gore dripped through the floor to the rooms below." The murderers escaped.[38]

These were the Kansas cowtowns, hard, tough, catering to the needs and urges of trail-weary, drive-hardened cowboys. In this atmosphere it is small wonder that gunplay and violence were common occurrences—or that cowboys gained reputations as gunfighters and peace officers became legendary.

[38] Caldwell *Commercial*, October 14, 1880, June 29, 1881.

7.

Policing the Cowtowns

IN THE SUMMER OF 1869 a special correspondent for a Leavenworth paper visited Abilene, Kansas. Ignoring the lawless element, he spoke favorably of the town's businessmen, but added that "Abilene . . . might be called a Texan town, so much of the Texan being apparent on the surface. In the busy season thousands of Texan steers are the principal inhabitants, but at present the Texan drovers take a prominent position."[1] One of the Texans he spoke of recalled: "We found the town was full of all sorts of desperate characters, and I remember one day one of these bad men rode his horse into a saloon, pulled his gun on the bartenders, and all quit business. When he came out several others began to shoot up the town."[2] Such shooting scrapes were carefully avoided by residents. One of them recalled, "When you heard one or two shots, you waited breathlessly for a third. A third shot meant a death on Texas Street."[3]

On September 3, 1869, some responsible citizens of Abilene appeared before Cyrus Kilgore, probate judge of Dickinson County, with a petition "praying for incorporation" of Abilene. Judge Kilgore duly granted the request and until an election could be held appointed as trustees K. B. Shane, Theodore C. Henry, Thomas Sherran, T. F. Hersey, and Joseph G. McCoy. This group selected Henry to act as mayor, and he remained in this capacity until 1871.[4]

[1] Leavenworth *Times and Conservative*, June 25, 1869.

[2] J. Marvin Hunter (ed.), *The Trail Drivers of Texas*, 503.

[3] Stuart Henry, *Conquering Our Great American Plains*, 82.

[4] Cushman, "Abilene, First of the Kansas Cow Towns," KSHS *Quarterly*, Vol. IX, No. 3 (August, 1940), 249; Dykstra, "The Cattle Town Experience," 142.

When the 1870 cattle season arrived, the trustees tried to curb the activities of the town's thirty-two saloons and to prohibit brothels within city limits. An ordinance against the carrying of firearms was passed, but proved almost unenforceable. The Texans riddled the ordinance posters with bullets as they galloped into or out of town and showed similar disrespect for the city's first jail by tearing it down. It was rebuilt under extreme difficulty and guarded day and night. The jail's first prisoner, a Negro cook, was "rescued" by a band of drovers, who chased off the guards. Not content with this achievement, they forced businesses to close and shot up the town. Some of the more daring citizens organized a posse and pursued them as they left. Several were captured and imprisoned, but this did not deter the Texans, who continued to terrorize the inhabitants.[5]

The position of marshal, created on May 2, 1870, by a city ordinance, was not successfully filled until June 4, when the council appointed a man they had originally turned down. Although his "personal appearance belied his reputation, and his credentials were acceptable, the idea of inaugurating the reign of good government through the agency of such a person seemed inconsistent and objectionable."[6] This man was Thomas J. Smith, better known as "Bear River Tom" Smith, in recognition of his exploits as a trouble shooter for the Union Pacific Railroad during the riots at Bear Town, or Bear River, Wyoming, in November, 1868.

In Abilene, Marshal Smith achieved everything that his predecessors had failed to do. He stopped cowboys from carrying firearms in the streets and exercised a brand of law enforcement completely alien to the Texans—he used fists instead of pistols to make an arrest. Baffled by this approach, everyone in town allowed himself to be completely ruled by Smith. His personality was such that few dared tangle with him, and although he rarely used them,

[5] Cushman, "Abilene, First of the Kansas Cow Towns," KSHS *Quarterly*, Vol. IX, No. 3 (August, 1940), 250.

[6] Miller and Snell, *Why the West Was Wild*, 576; Theodore C. Henry, "Two City Marshals, Thomas James Smith of Abilene," KSHS *Collections*, Vol. IX (1905–1906), 528.

the two silver-plated Colts in his belt reminded would-be trouble-makers that he could shoot. His very lack of a reputation as a gunfighter may have been partly responsible for the way he held his own in Abilene. Apart from his performance at Bear River he was very much a man of mystery. Used as they were to settling all quarrels with weapons, the Texans failed to appreciate his methods, although they obeyed his orders. The citizens of Abilene, however, looked upon Smith as an ideal policeman and as a gesture of their faith on August 9 increased his salary from $150 to $225 a month, retroactive to July 4. He was also appointed deputy and under-sheriff of the county. Under the guardian care of Smith and his deputy, James H. McDonald, Abilene began to show some respect for law and order.[7]

On November 2, at the request of County Sheriff Joseph Cramer, Smith and McDonald left Abilene to arrest Andrew McConnell, charged with the murder of John Shea, near Chapman Creek. McConnell, backed by his neighbor, Moses Miles, had pleaded self-defense, but it had been learned that both men had lied. When Smith arrived at McConnell's dugout and told him that he was under arrest, McConnell shot him in the chest. Smith fired back, grappled with McConnell, and found the strength to overpower him. At that moment Moses Miles came up behind the struggling pair and struck Smith on the head with his gun. Not content with knocking Smith down, Miles grabbed an ax and all but decapitated the marshal. Deputy McDonald took no part in the fray and fled to Abilene to obtain assistance. According to one resident, he bolstered his courage in a saloon, where, "leaning against the bar, with a drink of whiskey in his hand, he blubbered out his yarn. There being nobody to dispute him, his story had to go. But I can still recall the looks that passed between men who had been raised from birth to eat six-shooters. It was so rank that no one could say a word."[8]

[7] Miller and Snell, *Why the West Was Wild*, 576.

[8] Abilene *Chronicle*, November 3, 1870; Charles F. Gross to J. B. Edwards, August 23, 1922, Manuscripts Division, KSHS.

Miles and McConnell were captured three days after the killing. In March, 1871, they were sentenced to hard labor in the state penitentiary, Miles for sixteen years, McConnell for twelve. The comparatively lenient sentences aroused much anger in Abilene and prompted the comment: "Twelve and sixteen years in the penitentiary seem long periods, but the condemned ought to be thankful that they got off with even such sentences. Never during their natural lives can they atone for their great crime."[9]

After Tom Smith's murder, gunsmith Patrick Hand was appointed to serve as the town policeman until a strong man could be found to succeed the marshal. According to the council minutes James H. McDonald was a member of the police force, perhaps as acting marshal, for as long as the Henry administration remained in office. On April 1, 1871, it was recorded: "On motion J. H. McDonald was allowed one hundred and fifty Dollars ($150) for services as policeman."[10]

On April 3, 1871, the date of the first election held in Abilene, Joseph G. McCoy became mayor. Among the many problems the new mayor had to face was the one of devising effective measures to control Abilene's brothels and gambling dens. Above all, he had to find a suitable man for marshal. Charles Gross, who kept McCoy's books and worked as a room clerk at the Drovers Cottage, recommended a man he had known back in his home state of Illinois, James B. Hickok. McCoy met Hickok, was impressed by him, and recommended him for the job. On April 15, 1871, the council unanimously confirmed McCoy's choice, and Hickok became marshal at a salary of $150 per month plus 25 per cent of all fines imposed in court.[11]

Wild Bill Hickok was marshal of Abilene for eight months, a period that brought him criticism as well as praise. Unlike Smith, he used pistols to maintain law and order and relied to some extent

[9] Abilene *Chronicle*, March 23, 1871.

[10] Minute Book of the City Council of Abilene, Kansas, 1871, KSHS, 49.

[11] *Ibid.*, 55; Charles F. Gross to J. B. Edwards, April 13, 1922, Manuscripts Division, KSHS.

upon his already well-established reputation as a gunfighter to keep the peace. Hickok displayed all the traits that have become associated with the gunfighter of legend, but by and large his actions were dictated by necessity. Distrustful of his deputies (one of whom was the unreliable McDonald) and his many lady friends, and because his reputation with a gun was such that he was in perpetual fear of assassination by glory hunters, he carefully avoided bright lights and dark alleyways. The few times that he patrolled the streets (a task he usually left to others) he kept to the center, ever watchful against sudden attack. In saloons or other public places he always kept his back to a wall, even when addressing a crowd. Although he did not strictly enforce the no-guns rule in Abilene, few of those carrying arms cared to challenge him, and when, in September, 1871, on the council's orders he closed the saloons and gambling establishments, he met little opposition.[12]

Wild Bill's policing of Abilene was beset by several difficulties. A strong individualist, he resented interference with his methods, but he was not above interfering with those of the city council, where, in fact, most of his problems originated. On one occasion he picked up a councilman and carried him over his shoulder to a council meeting.[13] At another time Mayor McCoy, in a dispute with two councilmen over the amount saloons were to be taxed, embarrassed Hickok by saying that any loss of revenue resulting from the low tax he favored would be made up by the marshal, who would collect fines from all incoming gamblers and prostitutes, and "no one would be the wiser for it." The local paper quickly took McCoy to task for the scheme but expressed no opinion about Hickok's connection with it.[14]

The ups and downs of the council's policy toward the Texas cattle trade clearly reflected the tension that existed between the procattle members and those representing the growing farm popu-

[12] Joseph G. Rosa, *They Called Him Wild Bill: The Life and Adventures of James Butler Hickok*, 118–42; Minute Book, Abilene, Kansas, 1871, KSHS, 88, 94.

[13] Minute Book, Abilene, Kansas, 1871, KSHS, 64; Abilene *Chronicle*, May 18, 1871.

[14] Abilene *Chronicle*, May 18, 1871.

lation. Among the miscellaneous ordinances passed by the council on June 24 was one banning the carrying of dirks or bowie knives and the discharging of firearms within city limits.[15] In enforcing this latter ordinance, Hickok became involved in one of his most controversial gunfights.

On October 5, Hickok and Phil Coe, a former partner of Ben Thompson and a member of the gambling element in Abilene, came to a showdown outside the Alamo. Reports of the battle are conflicting, but it appears that Coe, surrounded or supported by about fifty armed Texans, got into an argument with the marshal, who was trying to curb their rowdyism. In a sudden exchange of shots Coe was hit twice in the stomach. Two of his bullets cut through Hickok's coat. Hickok's friend, Mike Williams, ran into the line of fire and was killed. Shocked and outraged by his friend's death, Hickok swept through the town and cleared out all the saloons, brothels, and gambling dens. The local newspaper supported the marshal's action and his handling of the situation.[16]

The reaction from the Texans, already resentful of the encroachment by farmers on the land through which they drove their herds to Abilene, was predictably violent. In Texas, Hickok was much reviled, and reports of Coe's death referred to him as "Wild Bill, the terror of the West," a "notorious gambler and desperado." One report late in October recorded that " 'Wild Bill,' the marshal of Abilene, shot and instantly killed two of his policemen on the night of the 4th instant. This is the same man that killed Phil Coe, of this city, a few weeks ago. The gallows and penitentiary are the places to tame such blood thirsty wretches as 'Wild Bill.' "[17]

15 Minute Book, Abilene, Kansas, 1871, KSHS, 69–73.

16 Abilene *Chronicle*, October 12, 1871. Many writers have questioned the story that Hickok paid the funeral expenses, contending that it was invented by the New York press. Custer included the story in *My Life on the Plains*. On October 16, 1871, the Topeka (Kansas) *State Record* stated: "Mike Williams, the policeman who was accidentally shot at Abilene by Wild Bill was buried at Kansas City last Sunday afternoon. Wild Bill paid the funeral expenses."

17 Austin *Democratic Statesman*, October 12, 26, 1871; Austin *Weekly State Journal*, October 26, 1871.

By far the most distorted account of the incident came from Oxford, Kansas, a report that was evidently the basis for many of the Texas legends asserting that Hickok shot Coe in the back, when in fact they were face to face. The Oxford paper's story reads:

WILD BILL KILLS TWO MEN

We this week present to our readers the particulars of the shooting affray in Abilene briefly mentioned last week. It is stated that on the night of the fifth instant, a large party of men were drinking together in the Alamo saloon, Wild Bill and other city officials among the number, and that Philip H. Wilson [*sic*], one of the murdered men and the marshal seemed to be on the most friendly terms, and took a drink together just before the firing. A young man named Harding [apparently no relation to John Wesley Hardin], one of the party, was getting rather drunk, and for fear of accidents, Coe took his revolver from him, holding it in his hand. A short time after this, a pistol shot was heard, and Wild Bill went to the door and asked who fired it, when Coe said he had fired at a dog. Bill asked him what he was doing with the pistol in his hand, but before Coe could answer, a friend to one side called to him and while his head was turned, Bill drew a pistol and fired. Coe instantly fired three shots at the Marshal from the pistol he had in his hand, but the latter dodged behind a door and escaped. Coe then fell into the arms of his friends. With a revolver in each hand, Bill then started to run down the stairs from the saloon which is in the second storey, and meeting Mike Williams at the bottom, fired a shot from each revolver, both balls passing through his body. It is said that the above are the facts in the case, and that there was no other provocation for the shooting. Coe is said to have been a kind and generous hearted man well thought of by all who knew him. He had many friends among the Texans and cattle dealers about Abilene. It is darkly hinted that avengers are on the trail and we will probably soon hear of another tragedy in Abilene.[18]

According to other contemporary accounts a showdown between Hickok and Coe had been expected for some time, and there was talk that they had quarreled over a prostitute. One old-timer who knew Coe in Abilene recalled him as "a red mouthed, bawling

[18] Oxford *Times*, October 21, 1871.

'thug'—'plug' Ugly—a very dangerous beast.''[19] Late in November a "darkly hinted" attempt to kill Wild Bill was made as he traveled by train to Topeka from Abilene, but he successfully circumvented the parties without bloodshed.

The recent discovery of a watch presented to Hickok for his services suggests that there were many in Abilene who supported his actions and respected him for his policing abilities. The back of the watch is inscribed "J. B. Hickok from His Friends, October 26, 1871." In the center of the inscription is engraved a six-pointed star with the legend "Marshal Abilene Kansas.''[20]

By this time Abilene's days as a cowtown were numbered. The farmers of Dickinson County joined forces to ban the cattle trade, and animosity toward the unsavory aspects of the Texas cattle business was building. At the end of the 1871 season the council decided to cut down on the police force and ordered Hickok to dismiss Deputy Tom Carson and J. W. ("Brocky Jack") Norton, a special deputy hired to cover the brothel district under the provisions of an ordinance passed in June of that year. It is possible that Hickok refused to carry out these orders, because at a special meeting of the council held on December 12 a motion was made that Hickok be discharged. On December 13 he was dismissed "for the reason that the City is no longer in need of his services." There was also the cryptic comment, "Also that all of his Deputies be stopped from doing duty." Evidently the council had decided that Abilene

[19] Little, "Early Days of Abilene and Dickinson County," in Roenigk, *Pioneer History of Kansas*, 37.

[20] Abilene *Chronicle*, November 30, 1871. It is claimed that the watch was taken from Hickok's body by Charles Utter in 1876 and carried by him until 1906, when it was sold to an Abilene bartender. The present owner is Lou R. Mahnic, of La Salle, Illinois. I examined the watch in October, 1967, and found it to be a key-winder with a one-quarter-carat ruby in the stem. The coin-silver case was made by the Western Watch Company, Chicago, Illinois. The serial number of the case is 6429, and the movement number is 15926. A search of the Chicago directories from 1845 to the present revealed a listing only for the Western Watch Case Company, which first appeared in 1887 and was last listed in 1956. (Larry A. Viskochil, reference librarian, Chicago Historical Society, to the author, March 22, 1968.)

no longer needed such an expensive law enforcer; his successor, James A. Gauthie, was hired for fifty dollars a month.[21]

The argument raged in Abilene over the enormously lucrative Texas cattle trade. Of the estimated 600,000 to 700,000 Texas longhorns that arrived in south-central Kansas during the summer of 1871, Abilene dispatched fifty thousand head by rail to the East, and three times that many were driven from Abilene to other states. But the great cattle days were over for Abilene. On February 22, 1872, the Farmers' Protective Association announced in the columns of the Abilene *Chronicle* that it "most respectfully" requested that the Texans seek some other point for shipping their cattle as they would "no longer submit to the evils of the trade."

In the meantime, Newton, in Harvey County, Kansas, had begun playing its role as a cowtown. Like other towns, Newton had sprung up along the rails to share in the cattle boom. McCoy, his Abilene enterprise at an end, moved to Newton, where he supervised the building of shipping pens for the Santa Fe Railroad.[22]

Newton had been founded in March, 1871, by two pioneers who had arrived in a bull-team wagon and built a shack east of Sand Creek, some thirty miles north of Wichita. The settlers had heard rumors that the Santa Fe Railroad would be routed past that point. They called the place Newton, and by July 17, when the railroad reached the spot, a hotel, a blacksmith shop, and a saloon had already been built. By August the town had ten dance halls, and more were under construction. Soon twenty-seven saloons, eight gambling halls, and a flourishing brothel district known as "Hide Park" were catering to all comers, as were hotels, restaurants, grocery stores, and other essential establishments for the twelve to fifteen hundred residents. The town was completely lawless. Saloons and gambling dens that never closed offered shows, music, and free lunches.[23]

[21] Minute Book, Abilene, Kansas, 1871, KSHS, 105.

[22] "Statistics of Agriculture," *Tenth Census Report of the United States, 1882*, III, 975; Gard, *The Chisholm Trail*, 157–58.

[23] Gard, *The Chisholm Trail*, 151, 157–58.

On August 11, 1871, Newton's citizens were scheduled to vote on a proposal to issue twenty thousand dollars in county bonds to aid in the building of the Wichita and Southwestern Railroad. A former night policeman for the Santa Fe Railroad, Mike McCluskie, or McCluskey (sometimes known as Art Delaney), was commissioned a "special policeman" for election day. An Ohioan, McCluskie had been in trouble most of that summer. Captain A. R. French, of the Kansas City Railroad, had charged him with attempted garroting, but the case had been dismissed.[24] Another policeman hired for the election was a Texas gambler named William Wilson, also known as Billy Bailey, who had been the victor in three previous gunfights. Wilson exchanged harsh words with McCluskie on election day and later in the evening got into a row with him over which one of them should set up drinks in the Red Front, a notorious saloon. Blows were struck, and they left the saloon to shoot it out in the street. Wilson died the next morning from a gunshot in the chest. Strong feeling against McCluskie was aroused among the Texans in town, and he was advised to leave.[25]

On the night of August 19 McCluskie returned to Newton and celebrated Saturday night in the usual manner at Perry Tuttle's saloon. The Texans in town were ready for him and plotted to kill him. The Texans chose for their leader Hugh Anderson, the son of a wealthy cattleman and himself something of a hard case. Anderson had joined John Wesley Hardin in the pursuit and slaying of Juan Bideno, the Mexican who had killed William C. Cohron some weeks before. Gathering his friends together, Anderson led them into Tuttle's saloon. What happened next was to go down in Western history as "Newton's General Massacre."[26]

About 2:00 A.M. on Sunday, August 20, the Texans went into

[24] Colin W. Rickards, "Vengeance: Kansas 1870's Style," The English Westerners' *Brand Book*, Vol. IV, No. 1 (October, 1961), 2; Emporia *News*, August 25, 1871; Zornow, *Kansas*, 153.

[25] Gard, *The Chisholm Trail*, 159; Topeka *Daily Commonwealth*, August 17, 1871; Abilene *Chronicle*, August 20, 1871.

[26] Streeter, *Prairie Trails and Cow Towns*, 87; Abilene *Chronicle*, July 13, August 17, 1871.

action. A great many shots were fired, and John Martin, a Texan popular among both Texans and Newtonians, was killed when he tried to intercede. McCluskie received three wounds, any one of which would have proved fatal, and died several hours later. Others in the crowd were hit by flying lead, some of them innocent bystanders, three of whom died. It is a part of Newton legend that a youngster named Riley, a consumptive befriended by McCluskie, killed several Texans in revenge for his idol's death.[27] The battle caused widespread concern and prompted one editor to comment: "How all this will end is a problem that must yet be solved. It seems to be a great mistake that a town can only be incorporated and get organization in the three first months of the year, as something seems to be quite necessary in Newton—a good efficient police force and a set of officers that mean business and will take some measures to make it safe for people to walk the streets. It is worse than 'Tim Finnegan's wake.' "[28]

Deputy United States Marshal Harry Nevill served a warrant on Anderson, also wounded in the massacre, but no direct action was taken against him. His father came from Texas and arranged for his transportation, by way of Kansas City, back to Texas. The young Texan recovered from his wounds, but on July 4, 1873, near Medicine Lodge, Kansas, he fought a duel to the death with Mike McCluskie's brother Arthur. The two shot each other full of holes, ending the gory encounter with knives after crawling the few yards that separated them.[29]

In the days following the massacre serious thought was at last given to the establishment of a permanent police force in Newton. On August 25, 1871, an election was held for this purpose. The officials thus elected hired Thomas Carson and Carlos B. King. Carson was much disliked by the Texans, who threatened to kill

[27] Theodore F. Price, "Newton: A Tale of the South-West" (poem, *ca.* 1872), Snyder Collection, University of Missouri, Kansas City.

[28] Topeka *Daily Commonwealth*, August 22, 1871.

[29] Rickards, "Vengeance: Kansas 1870's Style," The English Westerners' *Brand Book*, Vol. IV, No. 1 (October, 1961); Topeka *Daily Commonwealth*, August 24, 1871.

him. During his service under Hickok in Abilene he had angered the Texans and had also had a dispute with fellow policeman James H. McDonald. Nor had he got along very well with Hickok. The Texans regarded Carson as a bully and accused him of threatening someone with a shotgun.[30]

Carlos King's tenure in Newton was short. On September 23 he saw Thomas Edwards wearing a pistol in a dance hall and told him to take it off. Edwards refused, and not until Tom Carson appeared with a leveled revolver would he give it up. Shortly after Carson had left on his rounds of the town, Edwards crept up to King, pushed a derringer against his chest, shot him, and fled. King died a few minutes later; Edwards escaped.[31]

Soon after this incident Tom Carson left Newton and returned to the Abilene police force, but he was soon discharged from the force for shooting a bartender through the hip without provocation. Brocky Jack Norton was fired at the same time. The pair later had a row, and in January, 1872, Carson was arrested for shooting Brocky Jack. On February 18, Carson and three others escaped from the Abilene city jail and disappeared.[32]

James H. McDonald, who had been dismissed from the Abilene police force on September 2, became a Newton policeman at the end of the year, but his career was short-lived; accused of stealing four hundred dollars, he left town when a warrant was issued for his arrest. There were rumors that Hickok had been offered the job as marshal of Newton at two hundred dollars a month, but he never accepted the position. Perhaps he believed that McDonald was still in residence.[33]

[30] Charles F. Gross to J. B. Edwards, April 20, 1922, Manuscripts Division, KSHS; Topeka *Daily Commonwealth*, August 27, September 28, 1871; Minute Book, Abilene, Kansas, 1871, KSHS, 73.

[31] Topeka *Daily Commonwealth*, September 26, 1871.

[32] Minute Book, Abilene, Kansas, 1871, Manuscripts Division, KSHS, 105; Junction City *Union*, November 25, 1871; Abilene *Chronicle*, February 1, 22, 1872.

[33] Waldo Koop to the author, November 28, 1961 (Mr. Koop also confirmed that McDonald was considered to be town marshal as late as October 11); Topeka *Daily Commonwealth*, December 6, 1871.

William L. Brooks, a former stagecoach driver, was marshal of Newton during the 1872 cattle season, its last season as an important cattle town. Brooks was appointed in April, some two months after the town was incorporated as a city. On June 9 Brooks was involved in a shooting scrape with several Texans in a dance hall. Though wounded, Brooks chased two of the men out of town. One story implied that he had been hit in the collarbone by a shot fired by one Joe Miller. In his official complaint, Brooks merely stated that one John Doe and Richard Roe "did unlawfully make an assault with a loaded pistol, and did then and there, shoot at and towards the said W. L. Brooks with intent then and there to kill the said W. L. Brooks." "Doe" was later identified as James Hunt, a man who had once fought Red Beard. Hunt was bound over to the next term of the district court, but the outcome of the trial is not known. Brooks remained in Newton as marshal through the summer and may have served on the Ellsworth police force in August, before moving on to Dodge City.[34]

Ellsworth had been steadily moving into the cattle business since its founding in January, 1867, and by July, 1871, an estimated thirty-five thousand head of cattle had been shipped from there.[35] The town had been established on the north bank of the Smoky Hill River. A disastrous flood in July of its first year destroyed all the buildings, and a new township was laid out some two miles northwest of the original site. Until wooden buildings were erected, business was conducted in tents, and, as the new town grew, virtually every other building became a saloon, a brothel, or a gambling den. The town was the headquarters for all southwest freight traffic of the Union Pacific Railroad, Eastern Division.[36]

In August, 1867, the county of Ellsworth held its first election. The Junction City *Union* had reported that "on the 10th of August, next, they hold a special election in Ellsworth county, for county

[34] Miller and Snell, *Why the West Was Wild*, 52; Wichita *Eagle*, June 14, 1872, November 13, 1873; Topeka *Daily Commonwealth*, June 15, 1872.

[35] Topeka *Daily Commonwealth*, July 16, 1871.

[36] George Jelinek, *Ellsworth, Kansas, 1867–1947*, 9; Miller and Snell, *Why the West Was Wild*, 630.

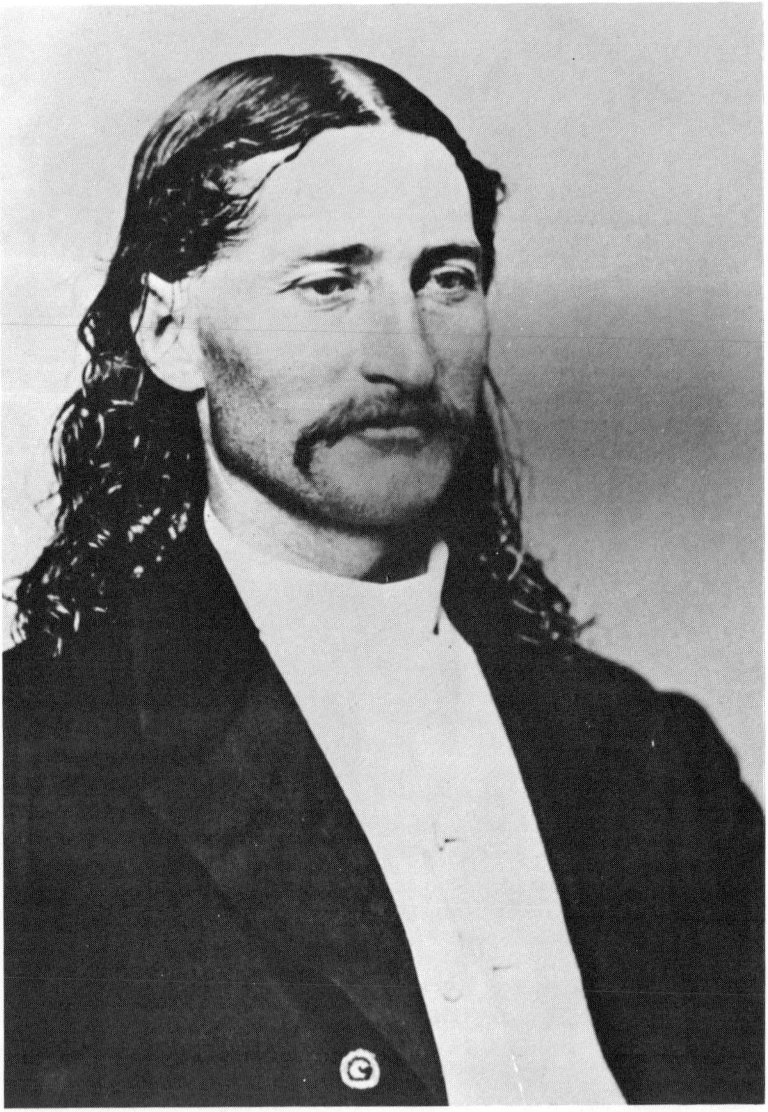

James Butler ("Wild Bill") Hickok, the "Prince of Pistoleers." From the original glass plate made by E. E. Henry at Leavenworth, Kansas, in 1867.

COURTESY MARY E. EVERHARD

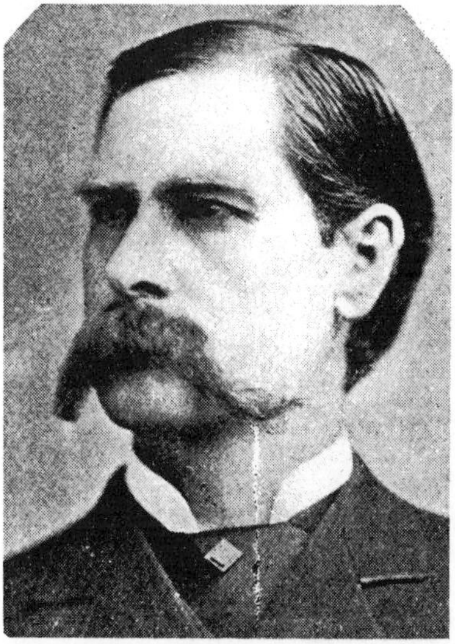

COURTESY KANSAS STATE HISTORICAL SOCIETY

Wyatt Earp. From a photograph in *Human Life*, February, 1907.

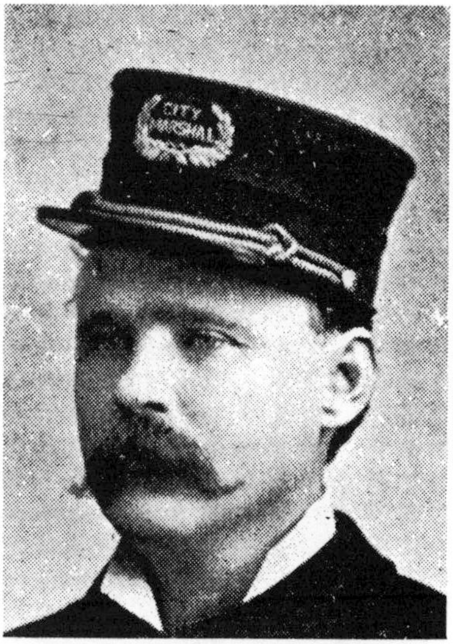

COURTESY KANSAS STATE HISTORICAL SOCIETY

Ben Thompson, city marshal of Austin, Texas. From a photograph in *Human Life*, January, 1907.

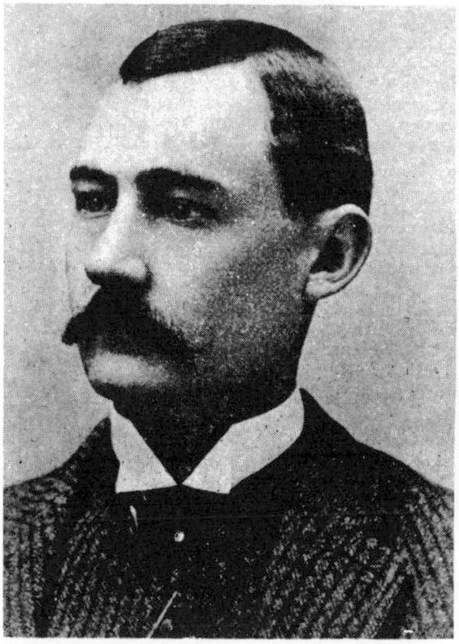

COURTESY KANSAS STATE HISTORICAL SOCIETY

Luke Short. From a photograph in *Human Life*, April, 1907.

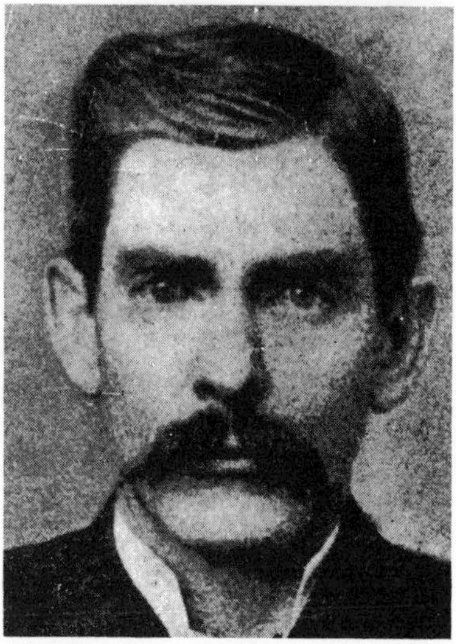

COURTESY KANSAS STATE HISTORICAL SOCIETY

John H. ("Doc") Holliday. From a photograph in *Human Life*, May, 1907.

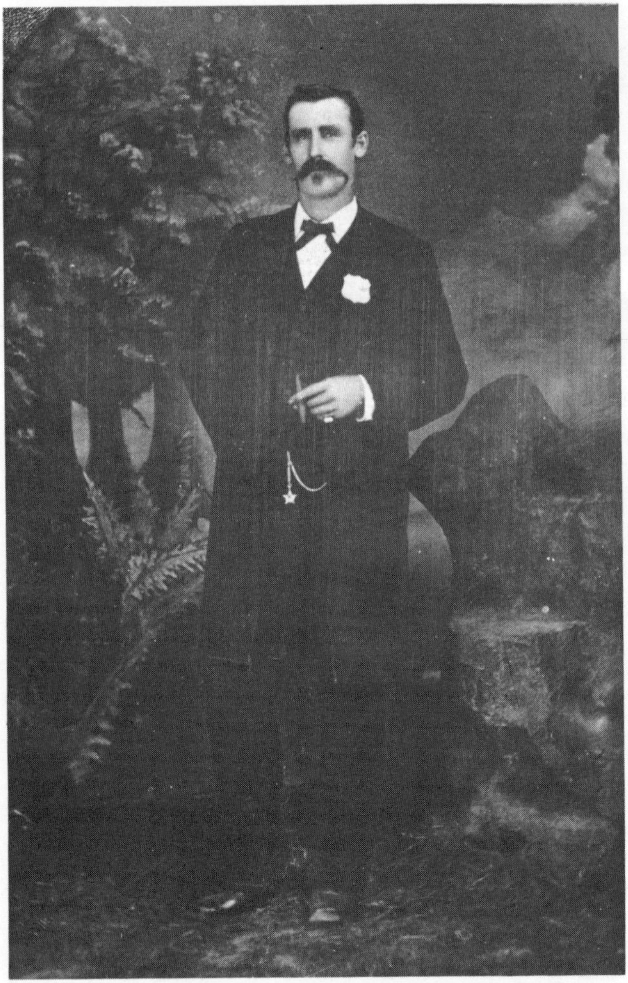

Dallas Stoudenmire, marshal of El Paso, Texas, in 1881.

COURTESY ROSE COLLECTION,
UNIVERSITY OF OKLAHOMA LIBRARY

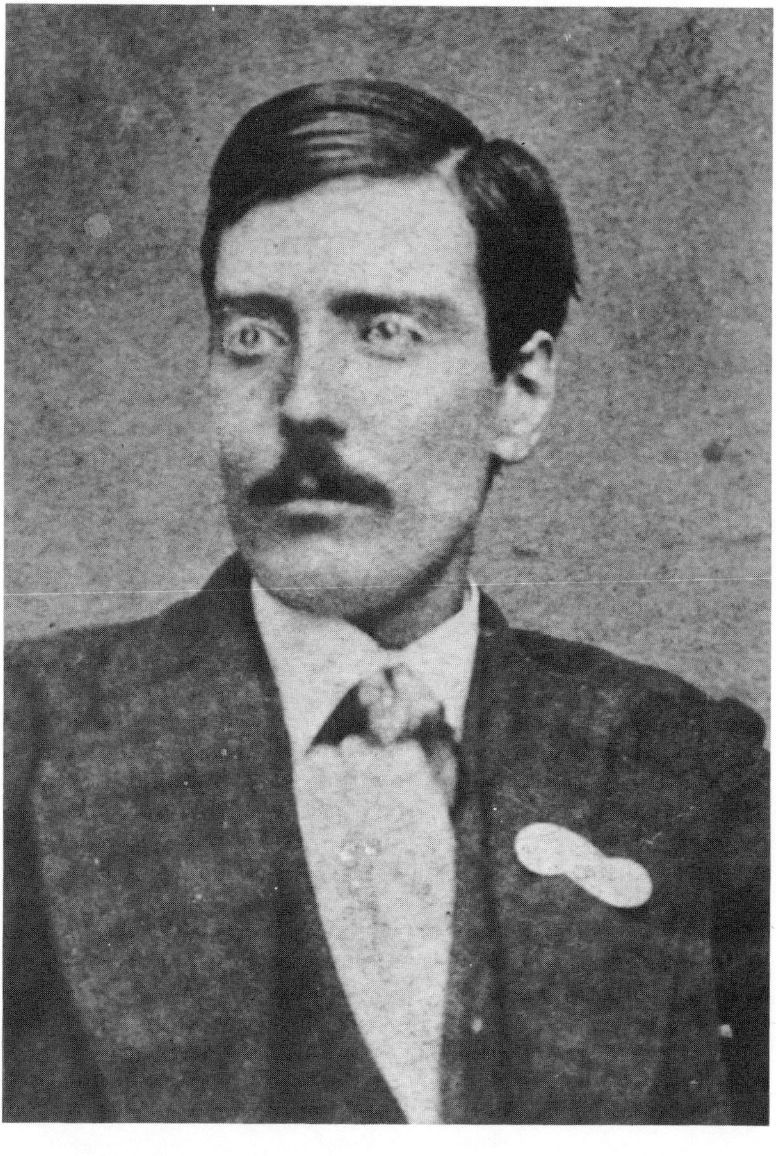

Edward J. Masterson, when he was marshal of Dodge City, Kansas.

COURTESY KANSAS STATE HISTORICAL SOCIETY

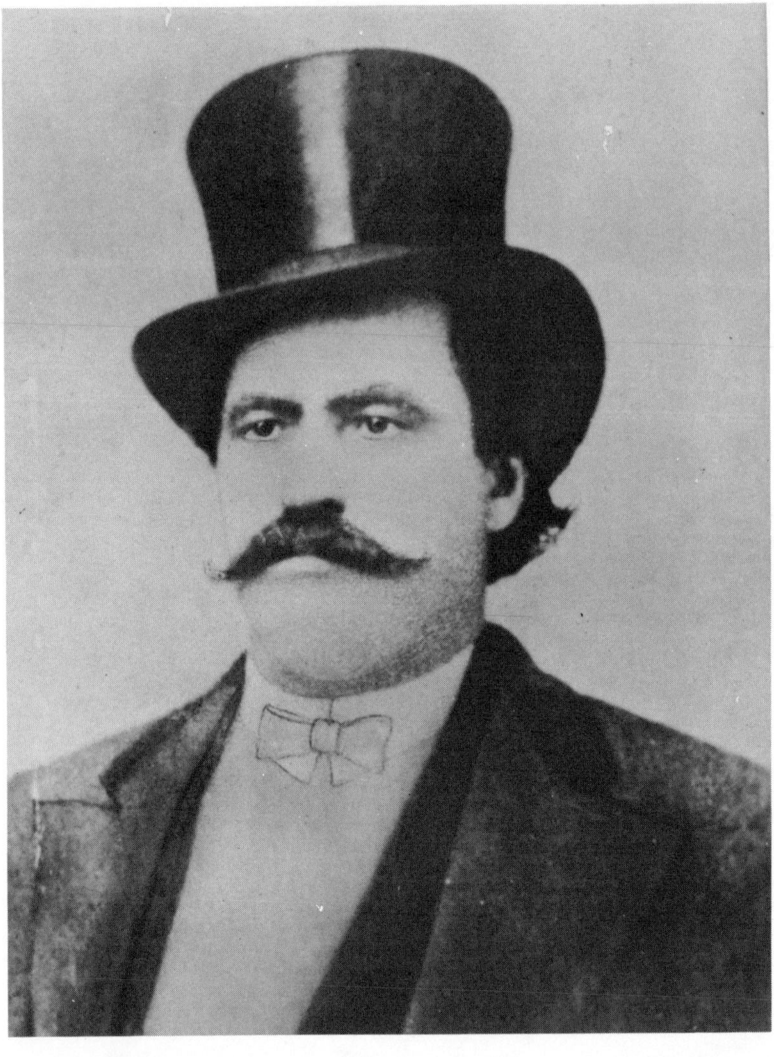

Joseph ("Rowdy Joe") Lowe, Wichita, Kansas, saloonkeeper and gunfighter.

COURTESY KANSAS STATE HISTORICAL SOCIETY

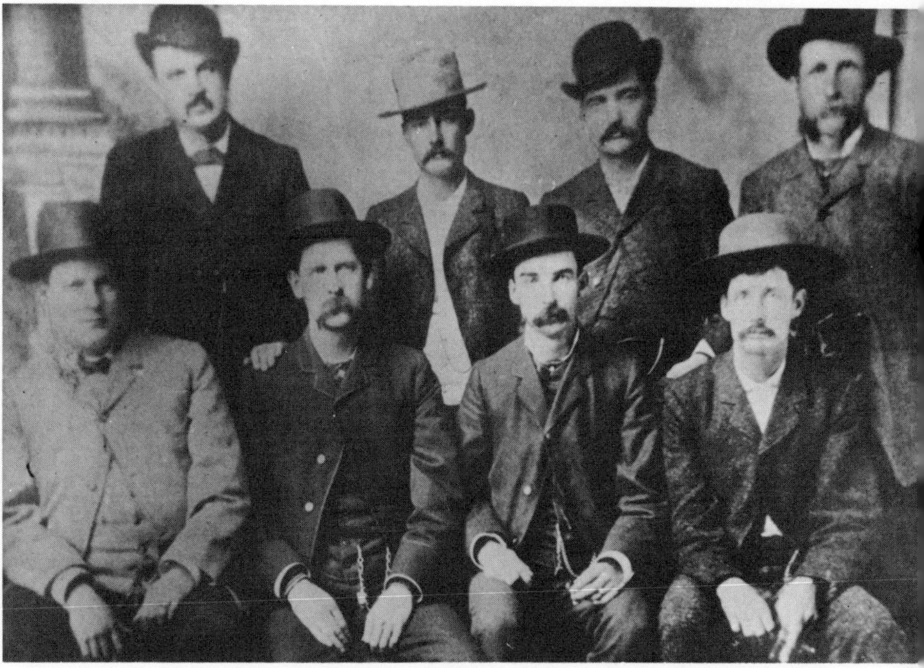

The "Dodge City Peace Commission," 1883. Back row, left to right: W. H. Harris, Luke Short, William Barclay ("Bat") Masterson, and W. F. Petillon. Front row, left to right: Charles Bassett, Wyatt Earp, M. F. McClain, and Neal Brown.

COURTESY KANSAS STATE HISTORICAL SOCIETY

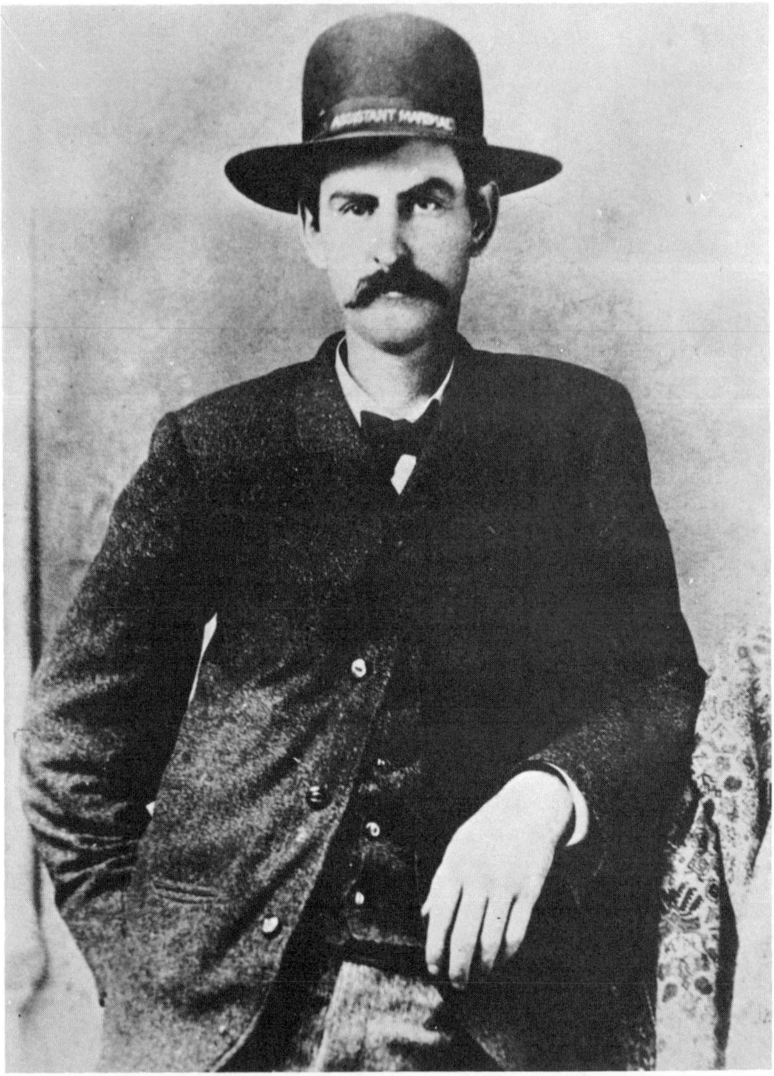
ASSISTANT MARSHAL

David ("Mysterious Dave") Mather, assistant marshal of Dodge City, Kansas.

COURTESY KANSAS STATE HISTORICAL SOCIETY

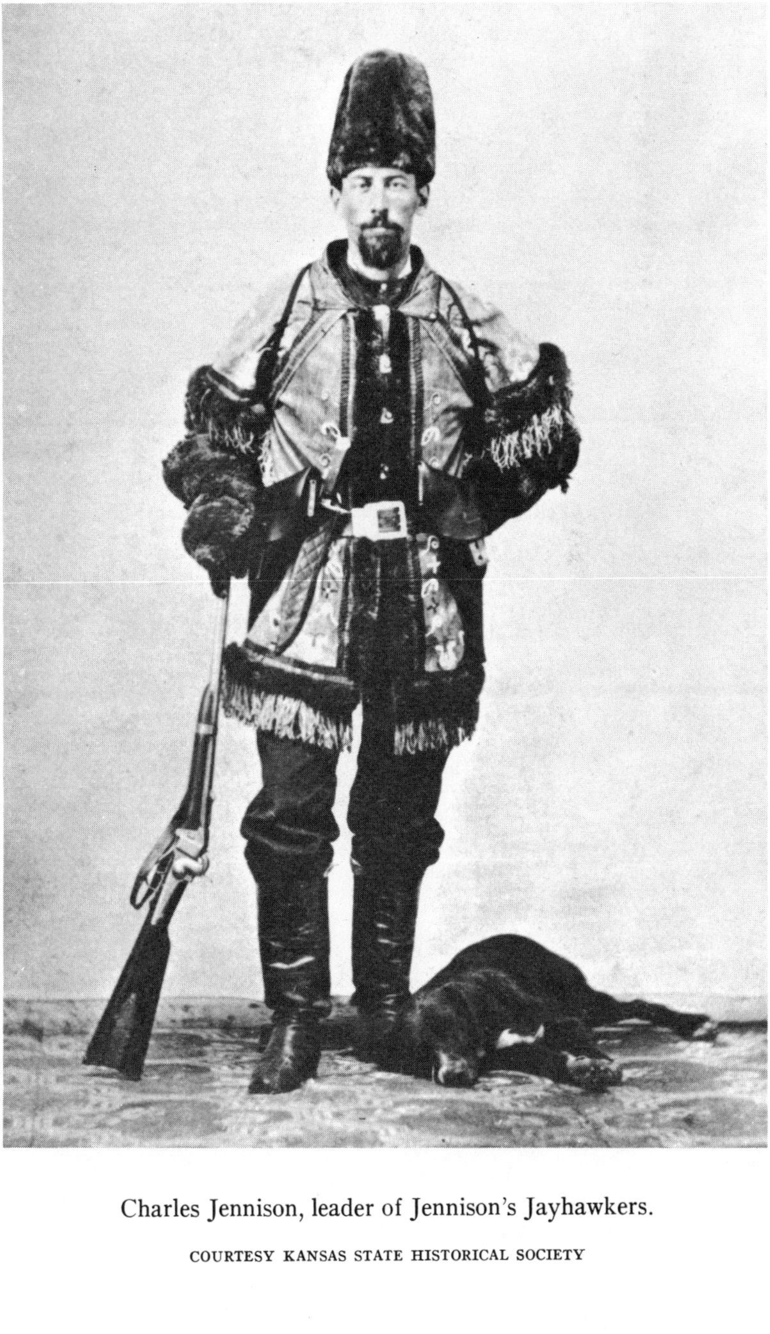

Charles Jennison, leader of Jennison's Jayhawkers.

COURTESY KANSAS STATE HISTORICAL SOCIETY

A group of Kansas Free Staters photographed in July, 1859, after rescuing John Doy (seated) from jail. This heavily armed band was typical of the time.

COURTESY KANSAS STATE HISTORICAL SOCIETY

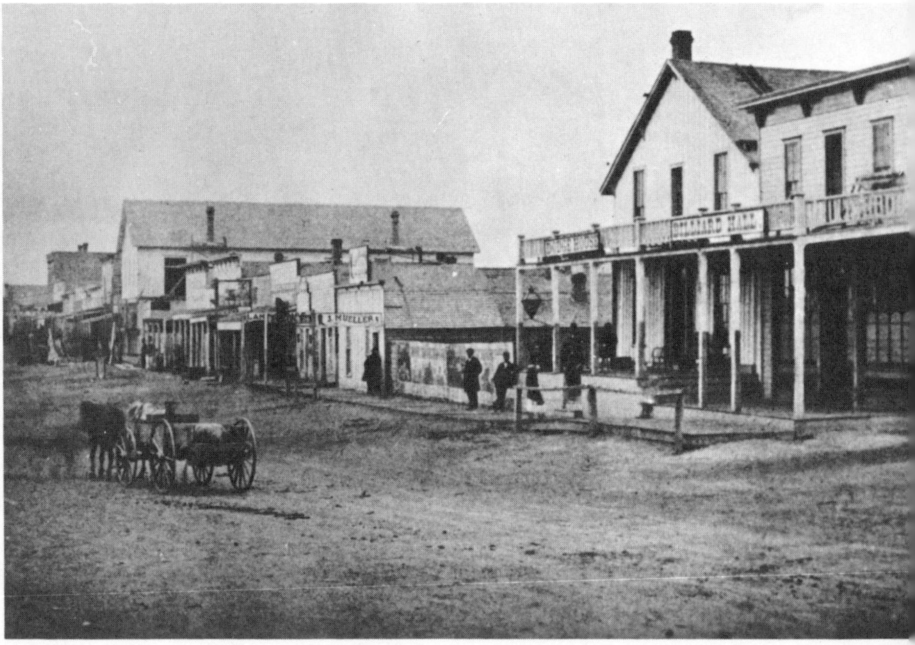

Front Street, Dodge City, Kansas, in 1878.

COURTESY KANSAS STATE HISTORICAL SOCIETY

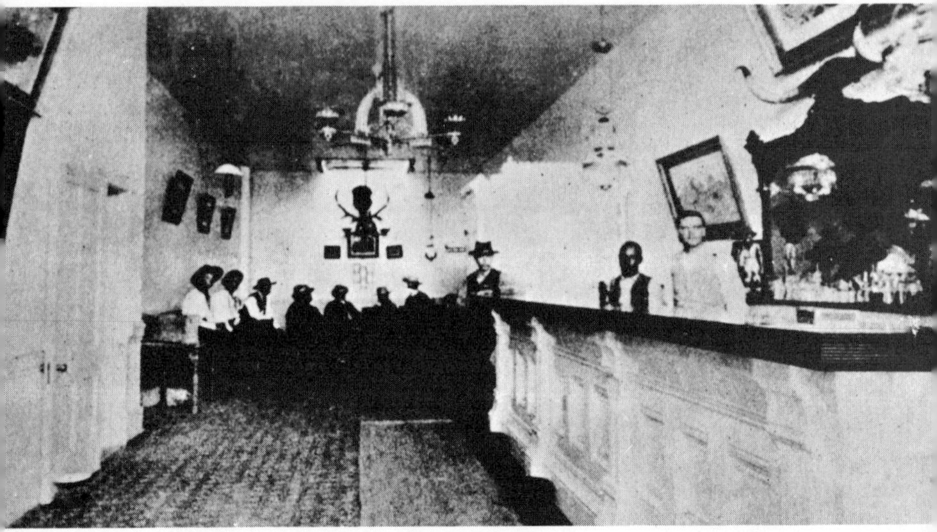

The Long Branch Saloon, Dodge City, Kansas.

COURTESY KANSAS STATE HISTORICAL SOCIETY

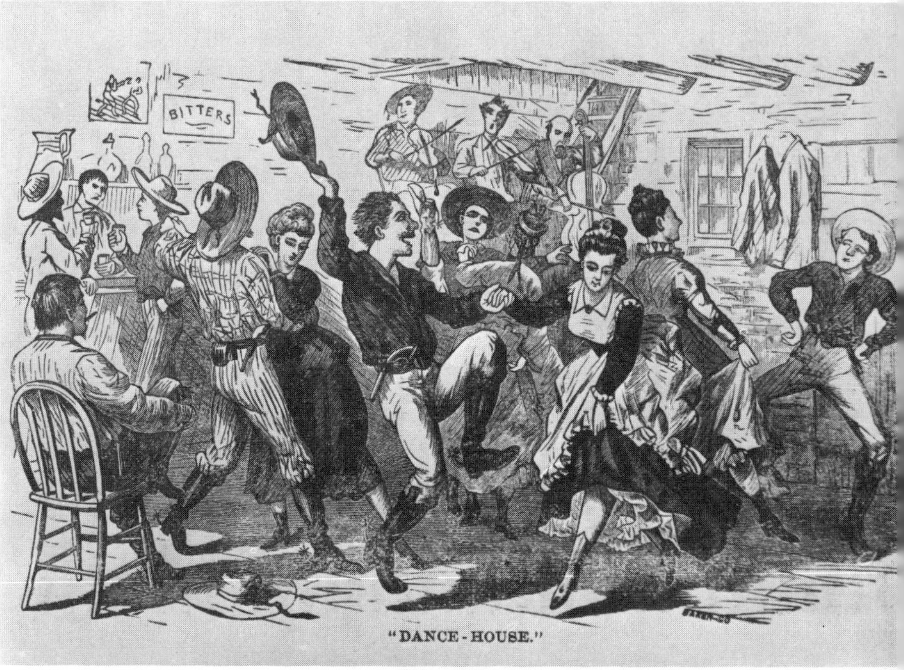
BITTERS
"DANCE-HOUSE."

A typical cowtown dance hall of the 1860's and 1870's.

COURTESY KANSAS STATE HISTORICAL SOCIETY

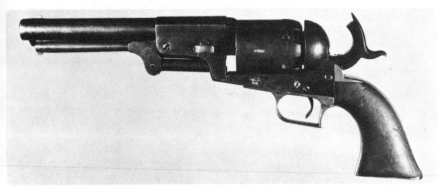

Colt .44 1848 Dragoon (second model), said to be the one taken from John Brown at Harper's Ferry in 1859.

COURTESY KANSAS STATE HISTORICAL SOCIETY

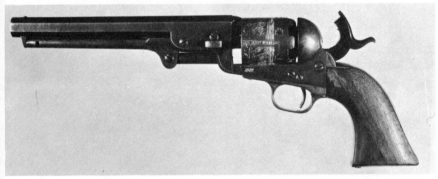

John Brown's Colt .35 Navy revolver, 1851 model.

COURTESY KANSAS STATE HISTORICAL SOCIETY

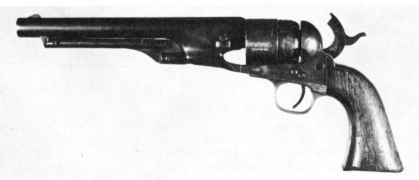

Colt .44 Army revolver, 1860 model.

COURTESY KANSAS STATE HISTORICAL SOCIETY

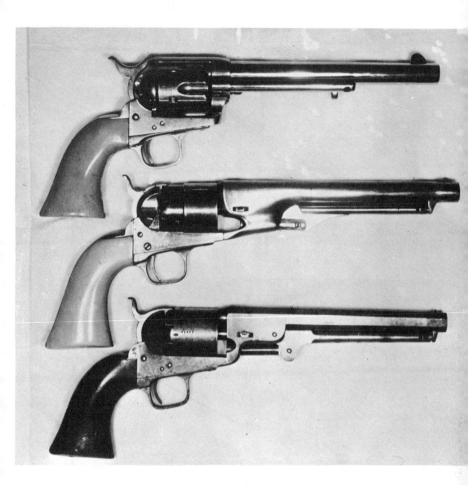

Three famous Colts. Top: Colt .45 single-action Army revolver, 1873 model, the Peacemaker. Center: Colt .44 New Model Army revolver, 1860 model. Bottom: .36 Colt Navy revolver, 1851 model (made in London). Author's collection.

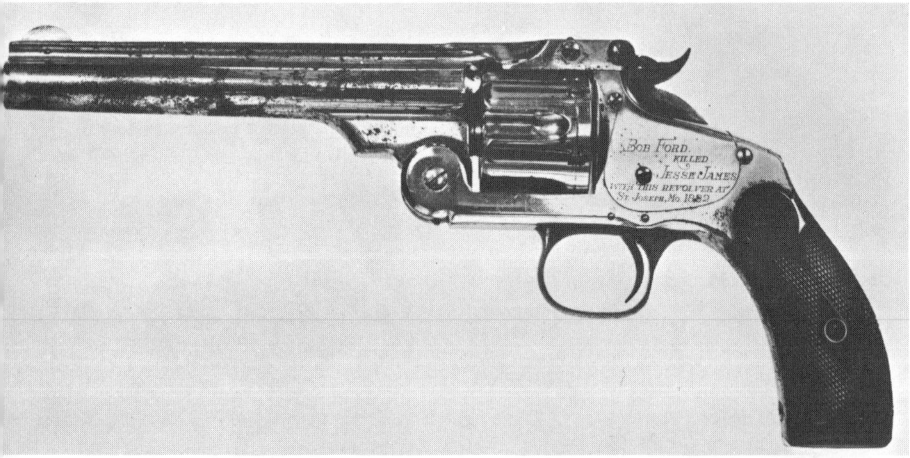
BOB FORD.
KILLED
JESSE JAMES
WITH THIS REVOLVER AT
ST. JOSEPH, MO. 1882

The Smith & Wesson .44 New Model No. 3 (American), said to have been used by Bob Ford to kill Jesse James.

COURTESY SMITH & WESSON

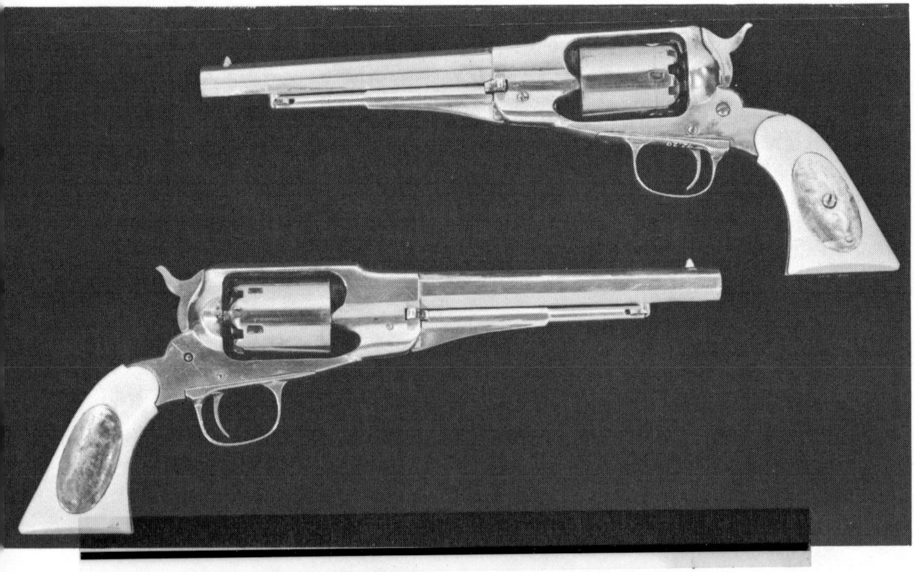

Pair of Remington .44 New Model Army revolvers, 1863 model. The weapons are silver-plated with gold-plated cylinders and ivory butts.

COURTESY KANSAS STATE HISTORICAL SOCIETY

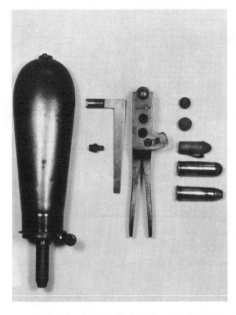

Left: Dixon powder flask for Colt percussion arms. Center: percussion nipple, nipple wrench, .36-caliber Colt bullet mold. Right, top to bottom: .36-caliber round ball, .44-caliber round ball, Eley foil cartridge, .45 long Colt cartridge, and .44-40 cartridge. Author's collection.

Top: Civil War holster, belt, and ca pouch. Center: Typical belt and ope top holster of the 1860's and 1870's. Bo tom: Early cartridge belt and open-to holster of the 1880's and later. Author collection.

TOP AND MIDDLE BELTS
COURTESY OF WILLIAM AYTON

and town officers. Kingsbury wants to be sheriff. . . . and Wild Bill wants to be marshal of Ellsworth City."[37] Captain E. W. Kingsbury was elected sheriff and set up headquarters in the city. Chauncey B. Whitney was elected township constable. Between the two of them they kept the rowdy element fairly quiet during the summer and fall. In the fall Whitney checked business licenses and made improvements to the building that was to be used as the city jail.[38] During the summer Hickok had spent much of his time in and around the city, scouting for the government and carrying out his duties as deputy United States marshal. On November 5 he was among the five contenders for the post of sheriff, as were Kingsbury and Whitney. Wild Bill polled the largest number of votes within the city of Ellsworth (155) but received little support in the rest of the county, and Kingsbury was re-elected.

At one point in the election campaign Hickok had accused M. R. Lane, another candidate for sheriff, of making a defamatory remark about him. Lane denied the accusation, and, in the confrontation, the crowd of onlookers fully expected to witness a gunfight. Neither man would back down, and some of the witnesses thought that if a fight developed Hickok would undoubtedly get his gun into action first but that the armed men who would leap to Lane's aid would, no doubt, kill Hickok. Against these odds Hickok stood little or no chance, and his friends and other interested persons intervened to prevent what could have been a gory battle.[39]

Whitney continued in his capacity as constable and was re-elected in the township election of April, 1868. In August he joined Colonel George A. Forsyth's scouts and took part in the Battle of Beecher's Island. On December 31 he returned as constable and undersheriff. Sheriff Kingsbury's bonds were found insufficient on February 11, 1869, and since he had left the state, the county commissioners declared the position vacant.[40] Whitney, considered to be an ideal

[37] Junction City *Union*, July 27, 1867.

[38] Miller and Snell, *Why the West Was Wild*, 630.

[39] *Ibid.*; Cyrus Edwards to J. B. Edwards, April 8, 1926, Manuscripts Division, KSHS.

[40] Miller and Snell, *Why the West Was Wild*, 630–31.

successor to Kingsbury, was not appointed. Instead, E. A. Kesler was named sheriff on March 1, 1869, and Whitney was not a candidate at the November election because he was once more in Army uniform because of an Indian scare.[41]

Although the settlement at Ellsworth was incorporated as a village in 1868, it was 1871 before it became a city.[42] By the middle of 1869 several herds of Texas cattle had arrived in the town via the route from Fort Cobb, Indian Territory. The drovers found that before their arrival Ellsworth's citizens had decided to purge the town of lawlessness, perhaps hoping thereby to set a good example to the Texans. On May 12 they had dragged a man named Fitzpatrick from jail, where he was awaiting trial for murder, and lynched him. The same evening someone took a shot at Judge Westover, apparently in retaliation for the lynching.[43] Such acts did not put an end to the town's prospects as a cattle-shipping center. The herds came trickling in, and in their wake came the undesirables who invariably presented themselves in the cattle towns.

In August, 1869, "Apache Bill" Semans, who had been a scout for the Nineteenth Kansas Cavalry during Custer's Washita River campaign, was serving on the city's police force. Apache Bill had had several brushes with the law. He had been jailed in Topeka for stealing government mules. Hickok had arranged his release, and eventually he had arrived in Ellsworth. During a disturbance in a dance hall, Apache Bill, acting in his capacity as a policeman, tried to stop a Texan who was shooting off a pistol and was shot through the lungs. He died shortly afterward.[44]

The summer of 1871 saw an expansion of the cattle trade, and by the following year shipments of cattle had increased so greatly that it was apparent that Ellsworth had become a principal cowtown. McCoy's Drovers Cottage in Abilene was dismantled and

---

[41] *Ibid.*, 632.

[42] Streeter, *Prairie Trails and Cow Towns*, 93.

[43] Robert Dykstra, "Ellsworth, 1869–1875: The Rise and Fall of a Kansas Cowtown," KSHS *Quarterly*, Vol. XXVII, No. 2 (Summer, 1961), 167.

[44] KSHS *Collections*, Vol. XVII (1926–28), 106, 362, 364; Leavenworth *Times and Conservative*, August 4, 1869.

moved to Ellsworth to compete with the Grand Central and other establishments. The influx of business also attracted to Ellsworth the pimps and prostitutes driven out of Abilene by Hickok the previous season. The record is incomplete, but it seems evident that Chauncey B. Whitney was elected sheriff of Ellsworth in November and also held the position of city marshal from July 27, 1871, to April 3, 1872, when he resigned this position to devote more time to his duties as sheriff. His successor as marshal, John L. Councell, was fired on July 24, as was Assistant Marshal Brocky Jack Norton. Norton had recovered from his wound in Abilene and had moved to Ellsworth with the cattle trade. The council replaced the men with Edward O. Hogue as "Chief of Police," the only man to have that title during Ellsworth's period as a cowtown. At each meeting of the council Hogue's appointment was reaffirmed until, on August 26, he was appointed city marshal.[45]

On July 27, 1872, occurred the first shooting of the Ellsworth cattle season. Seated at a table in the Ellsworth Billiard Saloon, Print Olive, the Texas cattle king, whose other scrapes were related in Chapter 2, was shot by James Kenedy, son of Miflin Kenedy, a well-known cowman from Corpus Christi, Texas. In a row over cards Olive had accused Kenedy of unfair dealing, and Kenedy, unarmed at the time, had threatened revenge. He bided his time until he found Olive unarmed in the saloon. When Kenedy pulled his pistol, Olive begged him not to shoot and threw up his hands, but took a ball in the groin and was also wounded in the thigh and hand. As Kenedy prepared for a fourth shot, "Nigger Jim" Kelly, Olive's trail boss, who had been sitting outside on the veranda, fired through the window. Kenedy was hit in the thigh and knocked off balance. The crowd quickly disarmed Kenedy, and two doctors attended Olive. Their prompt action undoubtedly saved his life, but he carried an unusual scar as a reminder—part of his gold watch chain had been driven into his groin and could not be removed. Kenedy escaped with the help of friends. He is believed to have been the same James Kenedy who later killed Dora Hand in Dodge

[45] Miller and Snell, *Why the West Was Wild*, 218.

City by accident when he tried to assassinate Mayor James "Dog" Kelley, with whom he had had a row. Unaware that the mayor was at Fort Dodge being treated for an illness, Kenedy fired through the mayor's bedroom wall and killed the woman who had been given the use of the room.[46]

On October 8, 1872, Hogue was replaced as marshal by Norton. Demoted to policeman, Hogue continued to do a good job. During 1873 he was active in making arrests and on June 11 arrested Ben Thompson's brother, Billy, for being disorderly and for possessing a revolver, which he had carelessly fired in the street. Thompson was fined five dollars and ten dollars in court costs. The Thompson brothers had been in town only a few days. Ben had planned to open a saloon as he had in Abilene, but he decided that gambling might prove more lucrative.[47]

The steady influx of cattle for shipment filled the area that summer, and by July an estimated 177,000 head awaited their turn at the pens. Ellsworth was not slow to do business with the army of drovers that descended upon the town. Their number seemed to grow daily, and the citizens feared that the police force might not be able to control them.

In the summer of 1873 the cattle business was slow, and there were few cattle buyers, a situation that presaged the financial panic that followed in the autumn. The inactive drovers in town waiting for their herds to be shipped from the railhead were restless and eager for entertainment. The ninety-degree heat shortened the tempers of both cowmen and police. The get-tough policy inaugurated by the police caused much bad feeling among the Texans. One officer in particular upset the cattlemen. He was John ("Happy Jack") Morco, an illiterate, surly fellow who claimed to be from California, where, he said, he had slain twelve men. In June, 1873, Morco was arrested in Ellsworth for vagrancy. A week later he was hired as a policeman. He soon made himself disliked among the

[46] Ellsworth *Reporter*, August 1, 1872; Chrisman, *The River of Ladders*, 119–22; Campbell, *Dodge City*, 162.

[47] Police Court Docket, Records of the City of Ellsworth, Kansas.

Texans, who deplored his zeal in making arrests. On June 30 he arrested Billy Thompson, charging that Thompson had assaulted him with a pistol. Billy paid his second fine of the month—ten dollars and fifteen dollars in court costs. There was soon a state of undeclared war between the police and the Texas drovers and wealthy cattlemen.[48]

The gamblers had no love for Morco either. On August 15, Ben Thompson financed John Sterling in a high-stake monte game, being assured that he would get a split of the winnings, but at the end of the game, in which Sterling won more than a thousand dollars, he carefully avoided Ben. Thompson finally cornered Sterling in Nick Lentz's Saloon and asked for his share, whereupon Sterling struck Ben in the face. Before the situation could get worse, the pair were separated by John Morco, who pulled a gun and persuaded Ben to leave. Thompson then made his way to Brennan's Saloon. Some minutes later Morco and Sterling, heavily armed, stood in the doorway of Brennan's and invited Ben to come out to the street. Realizing that they wanted a fight, Thompson quickly ducked out the back door and ran to Jack New's Saloon, where he had left his pistol and a Winchester rifle. He was joined there by his brother, Billy, who was armed with Ben's prized English double-barreled, center-fire shotgun.[49] The brothers stepped into the street, where Billy, who was drunk, carelessly discharged one of the shotgun barrels, narrowly missing the feet of two passing Texans. The Thompsons then turned and walked to the railroad, where they could continue the fight without injuring bystanders.[50]

From this vantage point Ben called, "Bring out your men if you want to fight." Sheriff Whitney came over and persuaded the pair

[48] Gard, *The Chisholm Trail*, 200–202; Streeter, *Prairie Trails and Cowtowns*, 101; Dykstra, "The Cattle Town Experience," 157.

[49] The weapon, made about 1870 by George Gibbs, of Corn Street, Bristol, was a gift to Ben Thompson from Cad Pierce and was worth about $150. Left by Ben with Chalk Beeson in 1877 as security for a loan of $75, it has remained in Dodge. When I examined it in October, 1966, it was in good condition, although, many years before, some cowboys had taken it on a hunting trip, got snow in the muzzles, and blew the ends out, making it necessary to cut off six inches of barrel.

[50] Gard, *The Chisholm Trail*, 202.

to return with him to Brennan's. At the doorway, hearing a warning shout, Ben turned to see Morco coming toward him, gun in hand, and took a shot at him. The ball hit the door jamb of a store as Morco swiftly ducked inside. At the sound of the shot both Billy and Whitney dashed out to the street. Then Billy suddenly turned on Whitney and pointed the shotgun at him. The sheriff hastily backed away. "Don't shoot," he begged. But Billy pulled the trigger. Whitney screamed as he was hit by the charge of buckshot and collapsed in the street. As the fallen man called for his wife, Billy turned and fled into the saloon. Shortly afterward he ran out, leaped onto a horse, and rode to the Grand Central Hotel. There Ben gave him a pistol and some advice: "For God's sake leave town, you have shot Whitney, our best friend!" Billy's reported response was that he did not give a damn and that he would have shot "if it had been Jesus Christ." He then rode out of town, leaving Ben to keep the citizens at bay.

For over an hour Ben Thompson, surrounded by a crowd of sympathetic Texans, refused to give up his arms despite a plea by Mayor James Miller. The policemen had made themselves scarce, "loading their muskets." The mayor, impatient at the delay, fired them all. Many considered this to be an unwise move, since even a bad police force was better than none. Ben at last agreed to surrender his weapons to Deputy Sheriff Hogue if Morco would also give up his guns. This was agreed to.

Whitney, in critical condition, had been carried to his home, where an examination showed that a full charge of buckshot had entered his shoulder, ripped through his lungs, and lodged in his spine. For three days he lingered in great agony and died on August 18.[51]

A witness to the killing, William Purdy, stated that after Billy Thompson shot him Whitney said, "He did not intend to do it, it was an accident, send for my family." There was no indication at any time that the Thompsons and Whitney were not on the best of terms.[52] Ben Thompson's comments on the shooting indicate

[51] Ellsworth *Reporter*, August 21, 1873.

that he considered his brother was so drunk that he did not know what he was doing.[53] In September, 1877, Billy Thompson was arrested in Texas and brought to Ellsworth for trial. He was acquitted on the grounds that the shooting was an accident. There were those who thought that the jury was bribed to acquit him.[54] Many years later, when cowtown legends were accepted as fact, it was claimed that when the mayor dismissed the police force Wyatt Earp stepped out of the crowd and offered to bring in Thompson, but no record placing Wyatt Earp anywhere near Ellsworth on that day has been found.[55]

A council meeting hastily called after Mayor Miller dismissed the police force produced a stormy session. Once again economics decided the issue: Some councilmen were for banning the cattle trade, but those who made their living and profits from the Texans won the day. The police force was reorganized. Ed Hogue was again appointed marshal, and John DeLong, John Morco, and Ed Crawford were hired as policemen. Then, on August 20, John Morco tried to make the three leading lights in the Texans' camp, Cad Pierce, John Good, and Neil Kane, leave town, claiming he had eviction orders issued by the marshal. The three Texans protested to Hogue, who denied any knowledge of the orders. Ed Crawford, in an attempt to intimidate Pierce, drew his pistol and, in the ensuing argument, shot him. The enraged Texans threatened to kill Crawford, but Ed shrugged off the threats. However, he promptly left town on August 27, when the city council fired the whole police force again. In November Crawford came back, much to the surprise of the townsfolk, and the inevitable happened. He was murdered in a brothel, presumably by Texans.[56]

[52] Testimony of William Purdy, State of Kansas *vs.* William Thompson, Records of the Ellsworth County District Court, 1877.

[53] Testimony of Ben Thompson, State of Kansas *vs.* William Thompson, Records of the Ellsworth County District Court, 1877.

[54] Streeter, *Prairie Trails and Cowtowns*, 124–26.

[55] *Ibid.*, 108–10; Stuart N. Lake, *Wyatt Earp, Frontier Marshal*, 87–94; Frank Waters, *The Earp Brothers of Tombstone*, 47.

[56] Miller and Snell, *Why the West Was Wild*, 507; Ellsworth *Reporter*, August 28, November 13, 1873.

Shortly after being fired, Morco had gone to Salina to avoid the aggravated Texans but for some reason returned to stalk around the streets of Ellsworth attached to a brace of ivory-handled six-shooters. The new marshal, J. Charles Brown, ordered him to disarm, but he refused, and Brown shot him through the heart.[57]

Ellsworth by that time was sharing her place in the sun with Wichita. The Wichita and Southwestern Railroad had reached Wichita on May 11, 1872, and the town was then ready for the cattle business.[58] Wichita had been incorporated in July, 1870, and elevated to city status in April, 1871. During its first three years several marshals were engaged, but for various reasons none of them lasted long. On April 13, 1871, the city council hired Mike Meagher as marshal. He held the position for five years with only one break, from 1874 to 1875.[59] Like other cowtowns Wichita was lawless in its first years, when shootings were almost daily hazards. One fight especially worthy of note was the one between Deputy United States Marshal Jack Bridges and the proprietor of the Harris House, John E. (Jack) Ledford.

Old-timers were divided in their opinions of John Ledford. Some of them regarded him as a substantial citizen, while others considered him a desperado. He was born in North Carolina about 1843, and was believed to have ridden with Quantrill during the Civil War. It is known that he and Marshal Bridges had served together as scouts for the United States Army in conflicts with the Indians. Ledford and the Army parted company following a drunken spree at Fort Dodge in April, 1869. Soon afterward he was arrested and lodged in the Shawnee County jail, charged with larceny or misappropriation of government property. He was not convicted of the charge and was released. There are conflicting stories about his associations with known rustlers and outlaws, some of whom were involved in the theft of 144 government mules on April 5, 1870, at Bluff Creek, Indian Territory.

[57] Salina County *Journal*, September 4, 1873; Ellsworth *Reporter*, September 11, 1873.

[58] Gard, *The Chisholm Trail*, 183–84.

[59] Miller and Snell, *Why the West Was Wild*, 481.

In November, 1870, Ledford ran unsuccessfully for sheriff of Wichita. There was evidently some irregularity in the election, for although Ledford received 240 votes, the declared winner, a man named Walker was appointed to the office of sheriff by the governor. On December 22, Ledford married Alice Harris and with her ran the Wichita Hotel, renaming it Harris House. In 1871 he was charged by a woman named Pauline Hall with interfering with her lawful business. It was not disclosed what the business was, and the charge was dismissed.

The events leading to Ledford's battle with Bridges are not known, but it seems obvious that the mule-stealing incident in 1870 had something to do with it. Second Lieutenant C. E. Hargous of the Fifth Infantry, the officer who had been in charge of the mule train, was also second-in-command of a detachment of troops from the Fifth Infantry and the Seventh Cavalry which left Fort Harker on February 26, provisioned for a twelve-day trek and "liberally supplied with ammunition." Led by Jack Bridges and a scout, Lee Stuart, the twenty-four soldiers arrived in Wichita on February 28 and surrounded Ledford's hotel.

The charge against Ledford was one of resisting a United States officer, but it is hardly likely that the Army would have sent out a force of heavily armed men for such a minor offense. In the gun-fight that followed, Ledford was severely wounded but had the satisfaction of seeing Bridges and two companions turn and flee after emptying their pistols at him. Bridges was also badly wounded but recovered. Ledford did not. A warrant was issued charging Bridges and Stuart with the premeditated murder of Ledford, but it is not known whether the warrant was ever served. Conflicting versions of the shooting were published, including a statement by Bridges that Ledford had fired first. There was also a rumor that Ledford had once given Bridges a sound thrashing and that Bridges had threatened to shoot Ledford on sight.[60]

[60] Waldo Koop to the author, January 28, 1967. Mr. Koop made available to me his copies of the Fort Harker records and newspaper accounts contained in his Ledford file.

When Wichita began sharing in the cattle trade, she also gained a share of the violence. Tough characters, among them William ("Hurricane Bill") Martin, the leader of the desperadoes known as the "Texas Gang," who frequently shot up the town, made life difficult for the citizens. On July 6, 1874, Hurricane Bill and fourteen companions threatened Samuel Botts, a policeman, when Botts tried to arrest a Texan. The Texas Gang galloped up and down the street shooting guns and terrorizing the citizens, who rang the police alarm. At least fifty armed men answered the call and faced the Texas Gang in the street. City Marshal William Smith hurried to the scene and tried to persuade both groups to disperse. As tension mounted, S. M. Tucker, a lawyer, took a hand. Armed with a shotgun, he pushed his way through the crowd saying that while he felt he had been called out for no purpose now that he was there he would arrest anyone the marshal cared to name.

Smith pointed to the Texans and said, "All right, arrest Hurricane Bill." Without hesitation Tucker cocked one barrel of his shotgun and called on Martin to surrender. Martin took a long look down the barrels of the shotgun and gave up his revolvers. "You can have me," he said. Perplexed and demoralized, the other Texans followed suit and submitted to arrest. They were fined a total of six hundred dollars. For weeks afterward people found pistols in weed patches on Horse Thief Corner, where Texans had dropped them.[61] The records show that Wyatt Earp served as a policeman in Wichita during 1875 and 1876,[62] but by this time Wichita's day as a cowtown was past. The cattle trade had moved on to the town that would witness the end of the great cattle boom—Dodge City.

Dodge City was founded in July, 1872. Originally known as Buffalo City, it was located five miles from Fort Dodge. The name was changed to Dodge City either because of its close proximity to the fort or because Colonel Richard I. Dodge, commander of the

[61] Gard, *The Chisholm Trail*, 214–15; Streeter, *Prairie Trails and Cowtowns*, 151–53.
[62] Miller and Snell, *Why the West Was Wild*, 145–46.

Army post,[63] was a member of the town company.[64] Until the early days of the cattle trade, the town served as the headquarters for buffalo hunters and for the buffalo-hide trade. From its founding violence stalked its streets. In December, 1872, Billy Brooks, the erstwhile marshal of Newton, got into a gunfight with a man named Brown, a former yardmaster for the Santa Fe Railroad at Newton. Both men fired three shots; Brown's first bullet injured Brooks, whose third shot killed Brown and wounded another man.[65]

In the winter of 1872–73, in order to legalize the sale of liquor in Dodge City (the Kansas Code forbade its sale in unorganized regions) the citizens petitioned for organization of Ford County, including in their census return the names of a number of transients as bona fide residents. The request was granted on April 5, 1873. The Santa Fe Railroad, fearing high local taxes on its property, went to court to claim that the census was fraudulent. Refusing the railroad's claim, the legislature legalized the organization of Ford County on March 7, 1874, and Dodge City was incorporated the following year.[66]

In November, 1872, Billy Brooks was elected Dodge City's first marshal, though his office was unofficial since the town was not yet incorporated. Often called "Bully" Brooks, he swaggered around the town with a pair of Colt Navy revolvers very much in evidence.[67] H. H. Raymond, then a young man starting out on a career as a buffalo hunter, recalled his first sight of the marshal, in a saloon early one morning in November, 1872: "The man with his back to me as I entered wore a blouse and protruding below it were the barrels of two large revolvers. I learned later this was Bill Brooks. Quite an unusual sight for a tenderfoot!"[68] On March 4,

[63] Dodge was the author of several important works, including *The Hunting Grounds of the Great West* (London, 1877) and *Our Wild Indians* (London, 1882).

[64] Wright, *Dodge City*, 9.

[65] Wichita *Eagle*, January 2, 1873.

[66] Dykstra, "The Cattle Town Experience," 144.

[67] Miller and Snell, *Why the West Was Wild*, 51–57; Joseph W. Snell to the author, May 19, 1965.

[68] Joseph W. Snell (ed.), "Diary of a Dodge City Buffalo Hunter, 1872–73," KSHS *Quarterly*, Vol. XXXI, No. 4 (Winter, 1965), 346.

1874, Raymond noted in his diary that "Bill Brooks got shot at with needle gun and the ball passing through two barrels of watter [*sic*] lodging in outside iron hoop. Jerdon [*sic*] shot at him." Apparently Kirk Jordan, a buffalo hunter, had accused Brooks of killing a friend of his and had lain in wait for Brooks. Hidden in a doorway, he lined up Brooks in his sights. When someone walked across the line of fire, Jordan raised his gun to let the man pass, but Brooks saw a flash of light on the gun and jumped behind two barrels of water. When he tried to get his gun out, it stuck in the holster. When Jordan fired, the heavy ball smashed through both barrels and smacked into the barrel hoop on the far side next to Brooks. Before Jordan could reload, Billy sprang to his feet and fled to a hiding place under a bed in a livery stable. The next day Raymond noted that he "saw Brooks and Jerden [*sic*] compromise today." Some friends had arranged the meeting, and when Jordan rode up unarmed to a hitching rack, he remarked, "Boys, you've got me into it!" At that moment Brooks emerged from a nearby building, wearing a white starched shirt but no gun. He approached Jordan with a smile on his face and offered him his hand. Jordan shook hands but did not smile and remarked, "What we've got to say we don't need to say to this crowd. Let's go inside!"[69]

Brooks did not stay around Dodge for long. One among the many rumors about him said that he was involved in the assassination of Matt Sullivan, a Dodge City saloonkeeper. In 1877 he was reported killed near Butte, Montana, by Morgan Earp, but this information was not corroborated. Another version of the end of Billy Brooks was reported in a story of the arrest and lynching of a number of horse thieves in July, 1874, among whom was a "W. L. Brooks."[70]

Dodge City's first official marshal was Lawrence E. Deger, appointed in the spring of 1876.[71] On December 4, 1877, he was

[69] *Ibid.*, 362; Wright, *Dodge City*, 167–68.

[70] Sumner County *Press*, July 30, 1874; Lake, *Wyatt Earp, Frontier Marshal*, 186; interview with John Gilchriese, El Paso, Texas, October 15, 1966.

[71] Miller and Snell, *Why the West Was Wild*, 129.

replaced as marshal by Edward J. Masterson, the older brother of Bat Masterson, then sheriff of Ford County.[72] Ed was a good officer and displayed great courage in his dealings with the lawless. On April 9, 1878, during his evening round, he came across some drunken cowboys carrying arms. He promptly disarmed one of them, Jack Wagner, and handed the pistol to a friend of Wagner's. Masterson then offered the men some advice on obeying the law. As he started to turn away, Wagner pulled a hide-out pistol, pushed the barrel into the marshal's stomach, and fired. The flash of flame from the powder set Ed's clothing on fire; nonetheless he immediately shot Wagner and Wagner's friend, Alf Walker, who tried to intervene. Legend has it that Bat Masterson, hearing the first shot, rushed to the scene and while still on the run fired the shots that wounded Wagner and Walker. However, modern historians are convinced that Bat was not involved.[73]

Ed Masterson was helped to his room, where he died within half an hour, a brave man to the end. He was buried the next day. The only member of his family present was his brother, Bat. Wagner died the day after the shooting. Walker, wounded in the left lung and with his right arm broken, was taken to Kansas City by his father.[74]

Dodge City's reign as "Queen of the Cowtowns" ended in 1885, at a time when the West was beginning to feel the effects of civilization. Settlers were arriving in ever-increasing numbers. Wheat farmers were putting to the plow the prairies once used for longhorn grazing grounds and were blocking the Chisholm Trail with fences. Many people who had come up the Chisholm Trail had stayed to settle in Kansas and become permanent citizens. Local administrations became more efficient in keeping the peace and

[72] *Ibid.*, 134.

[73] Chris Penn, "Edward J. Masterson: Marshal of Dodge City," The English Westerners' *Brand Book*, Vol. VII, No. 4 (July, 1965), 6–12; Vol. VIII, No. 1 (October, 1965), 1–9.

[74] Miller and Snell, *Why the West Was Wild*, 299–306; Penn, "Edward J. Masterson: Marshal of Dodge City," The English Westerners' *Brand Book*, Vol. VII, No. 4 (July, 1965), 6–12; Vol. VIII, No. 1 (October, 1965), 1–9.

maintaining order. As the economy became independent of the cattle trade, penalties for carrying and using weapons grew stricter.

In 1885 the Kansas cattle boom was ended by passage of a state law banning the trail-cattle industry. Soon the boom days were only memories—of two-gun marshals who shot it out with the lawless on the dusty streets or in the smoky saloons of the cowtowns. The days of the men who ruled with revolvers were at an end.

8.

The Man-Killers

TODAY THE BEHAVIOR of the early-day "shootist," bad man, or man-killer is greatly misunderstood, as is his significance. Certainly the adulation heaped upon the better-known gunfighters is not justified. In their own time the gunfighters were accepted as a part of Western life, and they were respected for their capabilities and certainly for their potential violence. Only later did they become the objects of hero-worship.

Debunkers of the gunfighter myth have suggested that the old-time man-killers were rarely brave, for a brave man never used his gun until he had to.[1] Yet many a brave police officer has died because he followed the rules of society and let the criminal make the first move. The old-time gunmen had few rules; they were guided by instinct and experience, without which they could not have survived for long. Hesitancy could mean death or crippling wounds. Certainly some of them were caught off guard and paid for their carelessness with their lives. They carried a gun for one main reason—self-preservation.

In 1910 Edgar Beecher Bronson classified the types of killers in the Old West:

> On the plains thirty years ago there were two types of man-killers; and these were subdivided into classes. The first types numbered all who took life in contravention of the law. This type was divided into three classes: A, Outlaws to whom blood-letting had become a mania; B, Outlaws who killed in defense of their spoils or their liberty; C, Otherwise good men who had slain in the heat of private quarrel, and

[1] Ramon F. Adams, *Six-Guns and Saddle Leather*, 2.

111

either "gone on the scout" or "jumped the country" rather than submit to arrest.

The second type included all who slew in support of law and order.[2]

By and large, Bronson was on the right track, although his characterizations could and did often overlap. It is certain that the gunfighter as a paragon of virtue simply could not exist—ever. Somewhat more realistic is the good bad man so much admired by some Western writers early in this century and depicted in the movies of William S. Hart.

The following facetious description of a "typical killer" indicates something of the attitude the gunfighters' contemporaries had toward them:

The gentleman who has "killed his man" is by no means a *rara avis* in Kansas City. He is met daily on Main street, and is the busiest of the busy throng. He may be seen on 'change, and in the congregations of the most aristocratic churches. He resides on "Quality hill," or perhaps on the East Side. . . . This ubiquitous individual may be seen almost anywhere. He may be found behind the bar in a Main street saloon; he may be seen by an admiring audience doing the pedestal clog at a variety theater; his special forte may be driving a cab, or he may be behind the rosewood counters of a bank.

If he has been here any great number of years, his "man" was

PROBABLY A PIONEER,

and died in the interest of "law and order"—at least so the legend runs. And no one dares dispute the verity of the legend, for behold the man who executed a violator of the law without waiting for the silly formalities of a judge and jury, mayhap now sits in a cushioned pew at an aristocratic church, and prays with a regularity, grace and precision only equaled by his unerring arm with a revolver, the great Western civilizer.

The gentleman who has killed his man is therefore a ubiquitous individual in this city, and may be met at every corner. He is usually quiet

2 Edgar Beecher Bronson, *The Red-blooded Heroes of the Frontier*, 70. Bronson supposedly was a nephew of Henry Ward Beecher and a cousin of the Lieutenant Frederick H. Beecher killed in the fight at Beecher Island on the Arickaree in 1868 (*Gun Digest* [1958], 63).

in demeanor, sober and thoughtful in aspect, somber in dress, and the last man on earth one would suspect of having notches on the butt end of his pistol. He may take a drink occasionally, but seldom gets drunk. He plays a game of pool at times, but never quarrels over the game. He perhaps goes down to West Kansas and tackles the tiger, but when there are loud words over the cloth of green he is not the man who utters them. He is quiet—fatally quiet. Your gentleman who has dropped his man is a blue eyed or gray eyed man in nine cases out of ten, and his hair and beard are brown, unless grizzled or whitened with the frosts of the many winters which have come and gone since the glories of the old Santa Fe trail began to wane.

Your gentleman who has dropped his man is, therefore, no uncommon individual, but when you see a man who has entered upon

HIS THIRD DOZEN,

it is about time to be civil, for he may begin to fear that material is about to run out, and may have an uncontrollable desire to hurry up and finish that third dozen.[3]

This editor, while poking fun at the number of killings attributed to individuals (which increased with each telling), nonetheless had respect for the potential danger of the man who shot to kill. It is interesting to note that apparently even as early as 1881 it was believed that man-killers notched their pistols.

Boot Hill, the cemetery of the gunfighter, is part of the Old West legend. Traditionally no town worth its salt was without one. The first graveyard so named was evidently the one at Hays City, Kansas. In 1871 a visitor noted the wickedness that abounded in Hays City and declared: "Were the dead that sleep on the lonely hill behind the city, to get up from their graves, they might be able to give reminiscences of the place that would cause the hairs of the head to stand on end, and the blood to curdle in its natural channels."[4] Boom towns, mining camps, and cowtowns in all parts of the West had Boot Hills, but the most famous of them all was the one at Dodge City. In Dodge City's first year of existence twenty-five men were reportedly killed in brawls and buried on Boot Hill.

[3] Kansas City *Journal*, November 15, 1881.
[4] Junction City *Union*, July 8, 1871.

A dead man was generally laid out in a back room of a saloon until he could be taken out to the burial ground, where the body was disposed of with a minimum of ceremony. Boot Hill was essentially a paupers' graveyard and also contained the bodies of many poor who had died peacefully. Coffins were expensive and rare; many a dead man was interred wrapped in a blanket from his bedroll, if he had one.[5] In 1877 a writer moralized thus:

> Most places are satisfied with one abode for the dead. In the grave there is no distinction. The rich are known from the poor only by their tombstones, so the sods upon the grave fail to reflect the characters buried beneath them; and yet Dodge boasts two burying spots, one for the tainted, whose very souls were steeped by immorality, and who have generally died with their boots on. "Boot-Hill" is the somewhat singular title applied to the burial place of the class just mentioned. The other is not designated by any particular title, but is supposed to contain the bodies of those who died with a clean sheet on their bed—the soul in this case is a secondary consideration.[6]

Few of the old-time gunfighters lived long enough to write their memoirs. One who did, Bat Masterson, left behind several recollections, all aimed at readers of the time and designed to suit the requirements of the publishers. Masterson was a legend in his own time.[7] In 1882 a Kansas newspaper claimed that Bat was a member of the "killer class," probably basing its opinion on some highly inaccurate reporting that had appeared in the New York *Sun* the previous November. The *Sun* reported that Bat had killed twenty-six men—seven of whom had died within a few minutes of being shot—in revenge for the murder of his brother, Ed. In Kansas the story inspired numerous comments. One editor reflected that a

[5] Campbell, *Dodge City*, 15–16.

[6] Dodge City *Times*, September 1, 1877.

[7] He was born on November 26, 1853, in the parish of St. George, County Rouville, Quebec Province, Canada, and the records show that his only Christian name was Bartholomew. (Chris Penn to the author, August 10, 1967.) Bat wished to be known as William Barclay Masterson, and his will dated August 3, 1907, bears this signature. See also Snell (ed.), "Diary of a Dodge City Buffalo Hunter, 1872–73," KSHS *Quarterly*, Vol. XXXI, No. 4 (Winter, 1965), 349n.

total of twenty-six men was "too much for a small man only twenty-seven years of age, and we call for a recount."[8] In fact there is doubt about the actual number of men Masterson killed in gunfights; his only known victim was a Sergeant Melvin A. King, of the Fourth Cavalry.[9] It is evident that Masterson gained his frontier reputation not only with the gun but also with the pen.

In 1907, having abandoned the West for a career in journalism, Bat wrote a series of articles on the West for *Human Life*. Historians find the factual content debatable, but no one can deny that Masterson knew his subject. His comments on some of the old-time gunfighters are very illuminating. His readers' knowledge of the West was already confused by legend, and he attempted to define the early man-killers in a way they would understand:

> I have been asked . . . to write something about the noted killers of men I am supposed to have personally known in the early days on the western frontier and who of their number I regarded as the most courageous and the most expert with the pistol.
>
> In making this request, I may reasonably assume the editor did not consider that he was imposing on me very much of a task, and had it embodied nothing more than the question of proficiency with the pistol, such would have been the case; but in asking me to offer an opinion on the question of physical courage as sometimes exemplified by them under nerve-trying conditions, he has placed a responsibility on my shoulders that I hardly care to assume. I have known so many courageous men in that vast territory lying west and south-west of the Missouri River—men who would when called upon face death with utter indifference as to consequences, that it would be manifestly unjust for me even to attempt to draw a comparison.
>
> Courage to step out and fight to the death with a pistol is but one of three qualities a man must possess in order to last very long in this hazardous business. A man may possess the greatest amount of courage possible and still be a pathetic failure as a "gun fighter," as men are often called in the West who have gained reputations as "man-killers."

[8] Ford County *Globe*, November 22, 1881, July 25, 1882; Atchison *Champion*, November 17, 1881.

[9] Miller and Snell, *Why the West Was Wild*, 322.

Courage is of little use to a man who essays to arbitrate a difference with the pistol if he is inexperienced in the use of the weapon he is going to use. Then again he may possess both courage and experience and still fail if he lacks deliberation.

Any man who does not possess courage, proficiency in the use of fire-arms, and deliberation had better make up his mind at the beginning to settle his personal differences in some other manner than by an appeal to the pistol. I have known men in the West whose courage could not be questioned and whose expertness with the pistol was simply marvelous, who fell easy victims before men who added deliberation to the other two qualities.[10]

In making his comparisons, Masterson referred at some length to the careers of Ben Thompson, Wyatt Earp, Luke Short, Doc Holliday, and Bill Tilghman. They had all been friends or associates of his in earlier days. Each man, in Masterson's opinion, shared with Wild Bill Hickok and Rowdy Joe Lowe the quality of courage that showed itself in nerves of steel. Any one of them, he says, "would not have hesitated a moment to put up his life as the stake to be played for." Thompson, he recalled, "possessed a much higher order of intelligence than the average 'gun fighter' or mankiller of his time." Doc Holliday, he noted:

... had a mean disposition and an ungovernable temper, and under the influence of liquor was a most dangerous man. . . . Physically [he was] . . . a weakling who could not have whipped a healthy fifteen-year-old boy in a go-as-you-please fist fight, and no one knew this better than himself, and the knowledge of this fact was perhaps why he was so ready to resort to a weapon of some kind whenever he got himself into difficulty. He was hot-headed and impetuous and very much given to both drinking and quarrelling, and among men who did not fear him, was very much disliked.[11]

Such comments from a man who was described as a member of the "killer class" suggests that their common bond was the ability

10 W. B. (Bat) Masterson, "Famous Gun Fighters of the Western Frontier," *Human Life*, Vol. IV (January, 1907), 9.

11 Masterson, "Famous Gun Fighters of the Western Frontier," *Human Life*, Vol. IV (May, 1907), 5.

to kill. Man-killing was not always premeditated. Harsh words, sudden anger, or a heated quarrel often led men to draw their pistols and fire. It happened so quickly that the sudden end was an anti-climax. Such a row could involve a whole crowd in a general fusillade in which onlookers might also be shot down.

Some men killed because of a sadistic streak, the feeling of power the act gave them, or the elation of seeing a victim writhing and kicking in the dust as he died slowly and agonizingly. These men clearly came under Bronson's heading of the type for whom bloodletting had become a mania—pathological killers who were perhaps the most dangerous gunmen of them all. The least insult or imagined slight could trigger an explosion of killing. Such a man was Bass Outlaw. A one-time Texas Ranger who had been fired for drunkenness, Outlaw nursed a grudge against several former comrades and in a drunken rage killed a young Ranger friend who tried to stop him from shooting off his pistol in the back yard of a brothel in El Paso. In a swift exchange of shots with John Selman, the town constable (and the killer of John Wesley Hardin), Bass wounded Selman in the leg, but the policeman shot him just above the heart and killed him.[12]

Among the gunfighters death was never far away; many of them had lived with death as a companion and were conditioned to it. Those who had fought in the Civil War were especially haunted by the specter of imminent death. For most men the ending of hostilities had meant that they could stop killing and return to normal lives. But veterans of frontier conflicts, spies, sharpshooters, and guerrillas were conditioned to view killing as a means to an end. The unwary sentry whose throat had been cut, the unarmed men shot down for the information they could reveal, meant little to such men. Self-reliant and independent men who had learned to abide with death found the restrictions of civilized society intolerable. The idea of a life without danger in a world where they were not masters of their own destiny appalled them. To them there was only one alternative—an occupation suited to their par-

[12] Cunningham, *Triggernometry*, 236–48.

117

ticular talents. A Kansas newspaper editor noted the effect that the Civil War had had on the men who later became scouts and guides for the United States Army against the Indians:

> What a pity that young men so brave and daring should lack the discretion to sheath their daggers forever when the war terminated! But such is the demoralizing effect of war upon those who engage in it and certainly upon all who love the vocation.
>
> We learn from a gentleman who has frequently met these wild and reckless young men, that they live in a constant state of excitement, one continual round of gambling drinking and swearing, interspersed at brief intervals with pistol practice upon each other.
>
> At a word any of the gang draws his pistol and blazes away as freely as if all mankind were Arkansas Rebels, and had a bounty offered for their scalpes [*sic*].
>
> How long these Athletes will be able to stand such a mode of life; eating, drinking, sleeping (if they can be said to sleep) and playing cards with their pistols at half cock, remains to be seen. For ourself, we are willing to risk them in an Indian campaign for which their cruelty and utter recklessness of life particularly fit them.[13]

Pointed but undiscerning comments of this nature reveal a lack of understanding of the feelings, reactions, and motives of the men who got into gunfights. A man who could draw his gun and shoot another man without hesitation had a cold-blooded attitude toward life that most people were spared. The man-killers of the West thus had an advantage over men basically reluctant to kill. When his life was threatened, the gunfighter could and would shoot to kill. Although he might appear calm and cool-headed under fire, his inner feelings were probably in turmoil. This man, facing death and wrestling with thoughts and emotions, was a far cry from the gunfighter of fiction. For him each fight, which could easily be his last, was a fight for life—his own.

Opinions held by commentators on the subject of man-killing as practiced by noted gunfighters of the early West are varied and con-

[13] Manhattan *Independent*, October 26, 1867.

tradictory. In most instances it is difficult to learn whether the views of the writers of the time are honest ones or embellished comments. One interview that led to much controversy was the one Wild Bill Hickok granted to Colonel George Ward Nichols, who had been aide-de-camp to General Sherman on the march through Georgia. Nichols met Hickok in Springfield, Missouri, in the fall of 1865, just after Wild Bill had been acquitted of the murder of Davis (or David) Tutt in a duel on Market Square. Nichols asked Hickok what he thought about killing men and reported Hickok's reply in an article in *Harper's Monthly*: " 'As ter killing men, I never thought much about it. The most of the men I have killed it was one or t'other of us, and at such times you don't stop to think; and what's the use after it's all over?' "[14]

Though Nichols quoted Hickok as speaking in a crude dialect, Henry M. Stanley, who interviewed Wild Bill a few months after the article was published, remarked that he was not as "coarse and illiterate as *Harper's Monthly* portrays him." Stanley then described his conversation with Hickok on the subject of man-killing:

"I say, Bill, or Mr. Hickok, how many white men have you killed to your certain knowledge?" After a little deliberation, he replied, "I would be willing to take my oath on the Bible tomorrow that I have killed a hundred, a long ways off."

"What made you kill all those men; did you kill them without cause or provocation?"

"No, by Heaven! I never killed one man without good cause."[15]

Some years later a lady asked Hickok about his reputation as a killer, and he is supposed to have replied:

"I suppose I am called a red-handed murderer, which I deny. That I have killed men I admit, but never unless in absolute self-defense, or in the performance of an official duty. I never, in all my life, took any mean advantage of any enemy. Yet understand," he added, with a

[14] Col. George Ward Nichols, "Wild Bill," *Harper's New Monthly Magazine*, Vol. XXXIV, No. 150 (February, 1867), 280.

[15] St. Louis *Weekly Missouri Democrat*, April 16, 1867.

dangerous gleam in his eyes, "I never allowed a man to get the drop on me. But perhaps I may yet die with my boots on."[16]

Later writers quoted what they claimed were other comments by Hickok on his reasons for killing men, but only one recorded a pertinent remark about his method. Charles Gross claimed that Bill said, "Charlie, I hope you never have to shoot any man, but if you do shoot him in the guts near the navel; you may not make a fatal shot, but he will get a shock that will paralize his brain and arm so much that the fight is all over."[17]

Hickok's comments upon the stopping power of a bullet are valid. But stopping power is not necessarily the same as killing potential. Sometimes fatal wounds at first appear to be only slight ones. On the other hand, a man severely wounded by a "man stopper" could be out of action for some time and yet live.[18] The man-stopping potential of various weapons had much to do with a gunfighter's choice of weapons. Often a man owed his life to the instantaneous effect his gun had upon his enemy. In most communities a man shot in a gunfight usually received prompt medical treatment, but the location of his wound generally determined his chances of survival. A stomach wound nearly always proved fatal, whereas an arm or leg wound or a body wound that did not injure a vital organ or smash a bone would respond to treatment—provided, of course, blood poisoning did not set in. Death was not uncommon from this cause, and to fend it off, if no other antiseptic was available, whisky was poured into the wound. Sometimes gunpowder was sprinkled on it and set afire, cauterizing the wound but producing an effect on the patient that is best left to the imagination.

Heavy-caliber lead balls wrought havoc on the tissues of the body, and shots fired at close range sometimes set clothing on fire. Traveling at a relatively slow speed (seven hundred to one thousand feet per second) a .44 or .45 ball was sufficiently powerful to stop a

[16] Annie D. Tallent, *The Black Hills, or Last Hunting Grounds of the Dakotas,* 100.
[17] Charles F. Gross to J. B. Edwards, June 15, 1925, Manuscripts Division, KSHS.
[18] Jeff Cooper, *Fighting Handguns,* 116.

man in his tracks. Only by experimenting with different grades of powder, bullet weights, and types of weapons could a gunfighter find the pistol and ammunition that suited him best. A man who killed buffaloes for a living chose a hard-hitting rifle with a large-caliber ball, or a gun especially made for the purpose, and the gunfighter adopted the same logic in man-killing: he picked a weapon for a variety of reasons—accuracy, balance, dependability, and, above all, stopping potential in action. For close action the revolver was unsurpassed. Hickok favored the accurate, hard-hitting .36 Colt Navy revolver. Others preferred the deadlier, at close range, .44 or .45. Backed by forty grains of black powder, the .44 ball of the Dragoon Colt, the 1860 Army, or the Frontier had tremendous stopping power.

Through experience westerners learned exactly what they wanted of a gun. On notepaper imprinted "Opera House Saloon" and date-lined "Dodge City, Kansas, July 24, 1885," Bat Masterson wrote to the Colt Company, in Hartford, Connecticut:

GENTS

Please send Me one of your nickle plated short 45. calibre revolvers. it is for my own use and for that reason I would like to have a little Extra pains taken with it. I am willing to pay Extra for Extra work. Make it very Easy on the trigger and have the front Sight a little higher and thicker than the ordinary pistol of this Kind. put on a gutta percha handle and send it as soon as possible, have the barrel about the same length that the ejecting rod is

Truly Yours
W B MASTERSON[19]

In a postscript Bat ordered a duplicate .45 for a friend. Over a period of years he proved to be a good customer of Colt's, ordering eight single-action revolvers. His first purchase was in October, 1879, when he purchased a 7½-inch Peacemaker. This pistol was silver-plated and had a Mexican eagle carved on the pearl handle. On the backstrap was inscribed "W. B. Masterson." Of the other

[19] This letter is now in the Connecticut State Library Collections, Hartford, Connecticut.

seven pistols Masterson owned, two had 5½-inch barrels, and five had 4¾-inch barrels (the same length as the ejector rod). So far only one of these pistols has come to light. The others are eagerly sought—to prevent faking, the Colt Company will not divulge the serial numbers.[20]

In his later years Bat was not above pulling the leg of gullible collectors who wanted one of his revolvers. To get rid of one determined collector, Bat bought a cheap old .45 Colt, cut twenty-two notches in the handle, and presented it to the collector. Open-mouthed, the collector asked Bat whether he had actually killed that many men with it. "I didn't tell him yes, and I didn't tell him no," Masterson later recalled, "and I didn't exactly lie to him. I simply said I hadn't counted either Mexicans or Indians, and he went away tickled to death."[21]

Masterson's concern about the sights and the barrel lengths of the pistols he ordered from Colt was typical of the individualism of the gunfighter, who would go to great lengths to modify his gun to his personal taste. The action had to be smooth and fast. A new standard Colt or Remington revolver (of either the percussion or the cartridge type) needed expert attention. The trigger pull was too heavy, and the factory mainspring required firm pressure on the hammer spur to cock the pistol. To overcome these difficulties, the gun was stripped, and special care was paid to the half-cock and full-cock notches, or "bents," on the hammer. A hard file or whetstone was used on the edges to reduce them sufficiently to give an easy let-off when pressure was applied to the trigger. Then, after final polishing, they were rehardened to prevent excessive wear.

The revolver's mainspring also received special attention. Success or failure in a gunfight often depended on the ease with which a hammer could be cocked. In place of the strong factory mainspring, a specially tempered version was fitted. The hammer could then be cocked with less effort but would still come down on the

[20] Larry R. Wilson, *Bat Masterson (Colt's Firearms Lawman Series)*, 18; John E. Parsons, *The Peacemaker and Its Rivals*, 91.

[21] Lake, *Wyatt Earp, Frontier Marshal*, 42.

primer or cap with enough force to explode it. Eventually this combination of filing, polishing, and tempering made the action of the pistol smooth and reliable.

The standard Colt, Remington, and other large-caliber revolvers of the time were usually six-shot weapons, but they were rarely loaded with more than five bullets—a safety precaution. On the early Colt revolvers small pins were set in the rear of the cylinder between the nipples. A corresponding hole or slot to fit the pins was cut in the lower lip of the hammer face. When the hammer was lowered, it held the cylinder rigid and its striking face away from the cap, but constant use or mishandling soon wore out the pins. For complete safety a pistol was carried with the hammer resting on an empty chamber. An 1859 patent for a cylinder with twelve locking notches enabled the cylinder-locking bolt to be used as a safety catch when the hammer rested between chambers. The idea was not generally adopted, although the Springfield Armory did convert several Colt revolvers to this mechanism.[22]

The arrival of the Colt Peacemaker in 1873 brought with it another form of safety device, a third notch on the hammer. A slight pressure on the hammer spur would draw it back just enough to keep the firing pin away from the cartridge. Balanced on the sear of the trigger, it was prone to fracture. A hard jolt or other shock could easily dislodge it, and, occasionally, the trigger sear was snapped off. To avoid such accidents, cautious gunmen took various precautions. Some filed off the safety notch, while others continued to employ the old reliable method of carrying only five bullets in the cylinder.

The gunfighter was reputed to be able to fan a six gun so fast that the five or six shots sounded like one shot. Tests made in 1933 by marksmen proved that this feat was possible. To perform it, the pistol was gripped in one hand with the trigger held back, tied to the guard, or removed, as the other hand brushed rapidly back and forth against the hammer spur so that it cocked and fired the pistol with each movement. But, contrary to legend, fanning was not a

[22] U.S. Patent No. 26,641, December 27, 1859.

common practice in the Old West, partly because the mechanism of the gun suffered from such ill-treatment.

Some six-shooter experts "slipped" the hammer by allowing the thumb to slide off the spur at full cock. This method was not very accurate, but in a barroom brawl two or three shots fired in this manner could have a very demoralizing effect on a crowd.

Getting a six-shooter into action at speed in the heat of battle was not a common accomplishment, even among the expert gunfighters. Few incidents of "quick drawing" are recorded, and even these are questionable. A man usually had his pistol out and ready if he expected to get into a gunfight. As in any battle condition, the element of surprise counted a lot with the gunfighting elite. Evenly matched opponents generally killed each other, but few gunfights took place between experts. Usually it was the inexperienced braggart or troublemaker trying to take on the professional who died in the fight.

The famous gunfighters earned their reputations the hard way. They rarely looked for trouble, but somehow it found them, usually with fatal results for the challengers. Few of the top-notch man-killers resorted to violence unless forced into it, and they did so then only for self-preservation. This fact is often overlooked by those who dwell on the agonies of the losers in such encounters. Certainly there was nothing pleasant about a Phil Coe or a Charlie Harrison groaning in pain with bullets in the stomach or groin, but it must be said that when they took on the gunfighters they knew what they were getting into.[23]

[23] Steckmesser, *The Western Hero*, 139.

9.

The Gunfight

THE GUNFIGHT IS THE CLIMAX of most Western stories. The fictional gunfighter's appeal stems from his actions when the chips are down. In reality a shoot-out was a sobering, often one-sided spectacle. The face-to-face duel at high noon rarely occurred in real life; gunfights had no set pattern. Nor is it safe to over-generalize about the quarrels that sparked the gunfights. Too often the cause of a fight was never determined, or never reported. It appears that women, gambling, or revenge were at the root of most killings.[1] One of Dodge City's most famous gunfights, the shoot-out between Levi Richardson and Frank Loving, occurred over a woman.

Richardson, a buffalo hunter turned freighter, had a reputation for bravery and as a pistol and rifle shot had few equals in Dodge. Although he was a hard-working individual, and was well liked, he had a quick temper. During his stay in Dodge he fell in love with a young woman who preferred a young gambler named Frank Loving—"Cock-eyed Frank"—who was a cool individual, the opposite of quick-tempered Richardson, and consequently more dangerous. In their first quarrel over the young lady the two men came to blows. Then, on the night of April 5, 1879, they had a showdown in the Long Branch Saloon.

Levi Richardson was on the point of leaving the saloon when Loving came in, passed Levi with hardly a glance, and seated himself at a card table. Richardson hesitated and then turned and took a seat at the same table. Loving immediately got up and made some

[1] Dykstra, "The Cattle Town Experience," 169.

remark to Richardson. The two men exchanged insults. Then Richardson pulled his pistol, and Loving reached for his. The men were so close that "their pistols almost touched each other." Richardson fired first, just as Loving drew his revolver, but the shot was wide. Then Cock-eyed Frank's first shot missed its target, and he ran behind a large stove a few feet from the table. Levi chased him, firing three shots, all misses. Loving then stood his ground and coolly shot Richardson in the left breast. As Richardson staggered back, Frank fired two more shots, one of which found its mark. Though mortally wounded, Levi got off one more shot before Deputy Sheriff William Duffey, who had been in the saloon throughout the fight, wrested his pistol from him, and Charles Bassett, the town marshal, ran into the saloon and disarmed Loving. In the scuffle Levi and Duffey fell to the floor. Levi struggled to his feet, staggered toward the billiard table, and fell for the last time.

The room was full of gun smoke and confusion. Miraculously, none of the onlookers were hit. Marshal Bassett examined Loving's .44 Remington and found that all the chambers had been fired; Richardson's pistol contained five empty shells. A coroner's jury found that "the said Levi Richardson came to his death by a bullet wound from a pistol fired by Frank Loving in self-defense." Loving was released. Richardson was buried the following afternoon. The editor of the Ford County *Globe* hinted that the police should have enforced the city ordinance against the carrying of firearms, adding: "Gamblers as a class, are desperate men. They consider it necessary in their business that they keep up their fighting reputation, and never take a bluff. On no account should they be allowed to carry deadly weapons."

Those who witnessed the fight were surprised by its outcome: Richardson, the victor in several other gunfights and a crack target shot, had been killed by a man with no reputation. Wyatt Earp, according to his biographer, claimed that Richardson lost because he fanned his pistol and tried to rush the fight while Loving took his time, aimed deliberately, and hit his man. Cock-eyed Frank's

career as a gambler-gunfighter ended several years later, Earp recalled, in Trinidad, Colorado, when he was killed by James Allan.[2]

Two gunfights that attracted considerable attention took place in El Paso, Texas, on the night of April 14, 1885. The county sheriff, the city marshal, and their deputies were out of town, attending a murder trial in nearby Presidio County. This left law enforcement in the hands of Charles M. ("Buck") Linn, a former Ranger and now city jailer, who was described by a contemporary as well-mannered when sober but "crazy" when drunk. That night he was drunk. Sam Gillespie, a local citizen, had said that Linn should be indicted by the grand jury for pistol-whipping one of Gillespie's friends, who had cursed Linn when he locked him up for drunkenness. Linn heard about Gillespie's comment and was so infuriated that he sent word to Gillespie that he was going to kill him. Gillespie armed himself, and when he saw Linn walking down the street, drew his gun and stood in full view in a doorway. Linn got the idea and went back to the Gem Saloon, where he met an old friend, William P. Raynor, "the best-dressed bad man in Texas." Raynor had been a collector of customs at Clinton, Texas, and had also served for a time on the El Paso police force, but was then employed as a gambler at the Gem. Although Raynor was considered an entertaining companion by his friends, others considered him an officious person who was continually interfering in matters that were none of his affair. He was quite proud of his reputation as a gunfighter and had recently been involved in two cases of assault. He and Linn spent several hours wandering from saloon to saloon, drinking heavily at every stop.

After becoming involved in a mild argument in the Gem with a young faro dealer named Bob Cahill, Linn and Raynor separated. George Look, who had been watching Linn and Raynor, warned J. J. Taylor, owner of the Gem, that trouble could be expected, since both men were having their drinks "charged up on the ice," which kept them going after their money had run out. But when

[2] Ford County *Globe*, April 8, 1879; Campbell, *Dodge City*, 188–94; Lake, *Wyatt Earp, Frontier Marshal*, 223–24.

Raynor showed no signs of hostility, Look and Taylor went into the theater that opened off the bar. The theater was filled with soldiers who had just arrived in town. Suddenly Raynor appeared in the entrance, drew his pistol and shouted, "Where is that son of a bitch who came to town tonight?" The soldiers immediately panicked and ducked beneath their seats or ran toward the exits. Only then did Raynor notice that Taylor and Look were seated in the audience. He holstered his gun, removed his hat, and bowed. "Excuse me, gentlemen—excuse me," he apologized, and then turned and walked out. The man Raynor was looking for wisely kept out of sight.

Back in the bar, according to Wyatt Earp's biographer, Raynor met Earp, who was in town to visit his friend Lou Rickabaugh, and tried to provoke him into a fight. When Earp pointed out that he was unarmed and had no intention of fighting a man who was obviously glory hunting, Raynor turned his attention to a man at the bar who was wearing a white cowboy hat. He taunted him for a few minutes but, on finding that he too was unarmed, moved on to the billiard room and sat where he could see over a partition that separated it from the bar. The man in the white hat, "Cowboy" Bob Rennick, although not well known in El Paso, had a reputation as a hard character. After Raynor left the bar, Rennick brooded for a time over Raynor's insults and then walked over to the faro table and asked the dealer for a pistol, saying, "I have been imposed on enough and won't stand for it." The dealer replied, "Have no trouble—go on out," but Rennick reached into the drawer and grabbed the dealer's gun.

At that moment Raynor burst into the room, firing wildly. Rennick quickly knelt on the floor and, holding the gun in both hands, fired at his adversary, hitting him in the shoulder and the stomach. Dazed, Raynor emptied his gun into a billiard table before he turned and staggered out to a streetcar and collapsed across one of the seats, mumbling that his mother should be told he died "game." Rennick followed him but made no further attempt to shoot. George Look persuaded Rennick to leave. "Go on out back and get out of

the way," he told him. Rennick took his advice and crossed the border to await developments.

When Linn learned that his friend had been mortally wounded, he started back to the saloon, looking for Cahill, the faro dealer, whom he evidently believed had done the shooting. Someone warned Cahill that Buck was coming after him, and he quickly armed himself. According to Wyatt Earp, Cahill, never in a gunfight until that night, eagerly took Earp's advice: "He'll come shooting," Wyatt said. "Have your gun cocked, but don't pull until you're certain what you're shooting at. Aim for his belly, low. The gun'll throw up a bit, but if you hold it tight and wait until he's close enough, you can't miss. Keep cool and take your time."

Linn came through the door with his gun in his hand. Cahill tried to make him drop it, but he refused, and the shooting commenced. Cahill hit Linn twice. One bullet went through his heart, killing him instantly, almost on the spot where his friend, Raynor had earlier been shot. Cahill then left town and joined Rennick across the border.[3]

Raynor was carried to his home. Although his condition was serious, he was convinced that he would recover and attend to Rennick himself. One man declared that he was "damned glad" that Raynor might die, commenting that he "ought to have been killed years ago," and then carefully adding, "If Bill gets well, what I said don't go."[4] Shortly afterward, however, Raynor died. Cahill and Rennick returned to El Paso, and both were acquitted of charges arising from what became known as "The Gem Saloon Shoot-Out."

Following the Short-Webster feud—the "Dodge City War of 1883" described earlier—the Santa Fe Railroad demanded an improvement in the moral climate in Dodge, a city it considered a

---

[3] Lake, *Wyatt Earp, Frontier Marshal*, 361–65; "Recollections of George Look" (manuscript), (copy supplied by C. L. Sonnichsen), El Paso Public Library, El Paso, Texas; *The Lone Star* (El Paso), April 15, 1885; El Paso *Times*, April 15, 16, 19, 1885.

[4] "Recollections of Frank E. Hunter," Manuscript Collection, El Paso Public Library, El Paso, Texas.

company town, threatening to deprive Dodge of its division terminus and its status as a major cattle town. In response the city administration closed all places of business and entertainment on Sundays, music was abolished from dance halls, and gambling was confined to back rooms.[5]

In July, 1884, a feud developed in Dodge between Assistant Marshal Thomas C. Nixon and former Assistant Marshal David ("Mysterious Dave") Mather. Nixon had achieved considerable fame in the early 1870's as a buffalo hunter operating out of Dodge. It was claimed that on one occasion he had killed 120 buffaloes without moving his rifle's rest sticks (he also ruined his Sharps in the process).[6] After he retired from buffalo hunting, he undertook several ventures connected with that business and also became a partner in the Bond and Nixon Saloon. He served two periods as an assistant city marshal, in 1881–82, and again in 1884. He had many friends in the city.[7]

David Mather, according to one old-timer, was said to be "a very wicked man, a killer of killers," who, if he "promised a man he would kill him, . . . was sure to do it."[8] At various times he associated with horse thieves and was suspected of being a train robber. There is reliable evidence that he was for a brief period a police officer in Las Vegas, New Mexico, in 1879–80. On January 25, 1880, he shot and killed a drunken railroad man named Joe Costello, who had threatened him with a pistol.[9]

In April, 1880, Mather appeared in Dodge in company with Charlie Basset and other friends in search of "greener fields and pastures new." Later he returned to New Mexico, where he was believed to have assisted in a jail break. He next appeared in Fort Worth, Texas, where he was accused of robbing the proprietress of a "house" in Dallas. Armed with a butcher knife and a pistol, the woman gave chase and followed him to Fort Worth, only to be

[5] Dykstra, "The Cattle Town Experience," 327–28.

[6] Lake, *Wyatt Earp, Frontier Marshal*, 52.

[7] Topeka *Commonwealth*, August 3, 1884.

[8] Wright, *Dodge City*, 215–16.

[9] Las Vegas *Gazette*, November 4, 1879; Las Vegas *Daily Optic*, January 26, 1880.

arrested before she could reach Mather, who had been taken from a train just as it was leaving the depot and jailed. The woman was released after paying a fine of $8.25, but Dave, possibly for his own safety, was taken in custody to Dallas and then released.[10]

In June, 1883, Mather was back in Dodge City as an assistant marshal, an appointment which did not meet with general approval. After several changes in the police force during the early part of the year, he was ousted at the municipal elections held in April, 1884. Tom Nixon was made assistant to Marshal William (Bill) Tilghman, but no other policemen were appointed.[11]

Late in the autumn of 1883 Mather had entered into a partnership to operate the Mather and Black Opera House and Dancehall. Owing to legal restrictions and what the partners considered to be police interference, their dance hall did not materialize. In reprisal against Nixon, Mather and his partner sold their beer at considerably less than the going rate of two glasses for twenty-five cents. The other saloonkeepers, including Bond and Nixon, then put pressure on the wholesalers to cut off supplies of beer to Mather's establishment.[12] Dave apparently became convinced that Nixon was behind the suppression of his business and sought him out. Nixon, aware that Mather was looking for him, made the first move. On the evening of July 18, 1884, he took a shot at Dave. The following day the citizens, already aware that trouble was brewing, were not surprised when they opened their papers and read:

ANOTHER SHOOTING

About 9 o'clock last night the city was thrown into considerable excitement by the report that Deputy Marshal Thos. Nixon had shot ex-Marshal Dave Mather. Investigation showed that Nixon had fired one shot from his six-shooter at Mather from the foot of the Opera House stairs, Mather at the time standing at the head of the stairs. The bullet went wild, and struck the woodwork of the porch. Mather's face was considerably powder burned, and the little finger of his left

10 Fort Worth *Democrat-Advance*, January 27, 1882.
11 Miller and Snell, *Why the West Was Wild*, 459.
12 Dykstra, "The Cattle Town Experience," 330.

hand was injured by a splinter. The shooting was the result of an old feud, and as both men tell different stories about the shooting, and there were no witnesses, it is impossible to state who provoked the quarrel. Sheriff Sughrue promptly disarmed Nixon and he was taken to jail. Mather claimed to have been unarmed, while Nixon claims Dave reached for his gun before he attempted to draw his own. Mather says he will make no complaint, but from all appearances the end is not yet.

Nixon gave bonds before Judge Cook in the sum of $800 for his appearance at the next term of court. The charge is assault with intent to kill.[13]

It was later reported that Nixon was under the impression that his shot had killed Mather, and he expressed "no regrets." On July 21 Nixon appeared before Judge Cook and was released because Mather refused to make a statement.[14] On the evening of the same day, while Nixon was on duty, standing at the corner of Front Street and First Avenue, Mysterious Dave came up behind him, called his name, and fired four shots as Nixon started to turn. Two shots hit Nixon in the right side, and one went through the left. One of the first persons to reach Nixon was his friend Bat Masterson, who later said that the wounded man was "lying on his right side and back, and had his feet to the northeast, his head southwest, his left hand down by his left leg, and his right hand up. That was a minute after the last shot was fired. He had his revolver on him. He was lying on it. It was partially drawn out. He had no other weapons that I saw."[15]

Mather was released on a six-thousand-dollar bond put up by Mike Sutton and others, who evidently believed that he should be compensated for having "spread confusion among the saloonists and the reigning city fathers" and also because he had rid the town "of a character it could do without." Dave's trial was fixed for the December term and took place at Kinsley. Regardless of the motives which led to the killing, Mather had murdered Nixon; yet

13 Dodge City *Democrat*, July 19, 1884.

14 Dodge City *Times*, July 24, 1884.

15 Dodge City *Globe Stock Journal*, August 5, 1884.

the general opinion was that Nixon had been the original aggressor. When the jury acquitted Dave after thirty minutes of deliberation on December 30, the announcement of the verdict was "interrupted by demonstrations of approval by the audience."[16]

Mather had had his revenge. By not making sure he had killed Mather, Nixon had left himself open for retaliation by a man noted for his vengeful nature. Mysterious Dave was involved in another killing in Dodge City and later served elsewhere as a lawman. His eventual disappearance was as mysterious as his name.

Political ambitions, personal feuds, and possible involvement in stagecoach robberies brought Wyatt, Morgan, and Virgil Earp and their friend Doc Holliday to a gunfight that has since become a "classic" in American folklore: the controversial "Gunfight at the O K Corral" on October 26, 1881, in Tombstone, Arizona. The stories of the events which led to the fight are as confused and conflicting as the testimony of those who witnessed or participated in the shoot-out. In a fight which lasted about thirty seconds, three men died and two were badly wounded. Nearly ninety years have passed since it took place, during which time there have been many private and official re-evaluations of the events and the participants. It is still considered the prime example of the gunfight.

After brief periods of service as a Wichita policeman and as an assistant marshal in Dodge City, Wyatt Earp accompanied his brothers, Virgil, Morgan, and James, and their wives to Tombstone, Arizona Territory. They arrived there on December 1, 1879.[17] Wyatt found employment as a shotgun messenger with Wells, Fargo and Company. Later he became a deputy sheriff of Pima County.

On March 15, 1881, a Kinnear and Company stagecoach was attacked while reportedly carrying eight thousand dollars in gold. As the coach left Drews' Station, a passenger and the driver, Bud Philpot, who had temporarily changed places with the shotgun

---

[16] *Kansas Cow Boy*, August 23, 1884; Dodge City *Times*, January 8, 1885; Dykstra, "The Cattle Town Experience," 330–31.

[17] Waters, *The Earp Brothers of Tombstone*, 98.

messenger, Bob Paul, were shot and killed by some unmounted masked men who attempted to stop the coach. The horses bolted at the gunfire. Bob Paul clambered down to the wagon tongue, retrieved the reins, and brought the horses under control. After Paul saved the coach from destruction, he drove it safely to Benson.

When news of the killing reached Tombstone that night, two posses were formed, one by Sheriff John Behan and his deputy, Billy Breakenridge, and the other by the Earps, Bat Masterson, and "Buckskin" Frank Leslie. A local tough named Luther King, found hiding at Len Radfield's ranch on the San Pedro, admitted to holding the horses while Bill Leonard, Harry Head, and Jim Crane tried to rob the coach. King was taken to Tombstone by Behan's posse. While everyone's attention was diverted for a moment, King stepped outside the jail, reached a waiting horse, and made his escape. When the Earp party returned and were told of King's escape, and also of a rumor that Doc Holliday had been implicated in the attempted robbery, they were furious. Holliday's connection with the holdup was never proved, though one authority is convinced that he had a hand it it.[18]

Wyatt tried to bribe Ike Clanton, a penny-ante rustler and outlaw, and a known friend of the wanted men, to betray them. Wyatt wanted credit for their capture although Clanton would receive the reward money. All three men were killed before Earp could get anywhere near them. Leonard and Head died in a gun battle with the Haslett brothers in Eureka, New Mexico, in June, 1881, and Crane perished at the hands of Mexican regulars in August of the same year.[19] Stories about Wyatt's offer got out, and Ike Clanton began shouting all over town that Earp was telling lies about him. He claimed he had refused the offer and assumed that this would save him from being branded a Judas. Around him Ike gathered a crowd of partisans, including Billy Clanton, Frank and Tom McLaury (spelled McLowery or McLowry in most contemporary accounts), and Billy Claiborne.

18 Interview with John Gilchriese, El Paso, Texas, October 15, 1966.
19 Patricia Jahns, *The Frontier World of Doc Holliday*, 129, 132.

Several times the antagonists came perilously close to a gun battle. Anticipating the eventual outcome, Virgil Earp, who was a deputy United States marshal as well as city marshal, appointed his brothers and Doc Holliday as deputies. Late on the evening of October 25, Ike Clanton had a run-in with Holliday at a lunch counter. Doc called Ike a "son of a bitch of a cow-boy," told him to get a gun and go to work, and accused him of threatening the Earps, which Ike denied. Again Doc demanded that he fight. At the counter Morgan Earp, seated with his feet up and his hand inside his coat as if holding a pistol, watched the dispute. Ike got to his feet and went outside, followed by taunts and invitations to get himself "heeled." Some ten feet or more away on the sidewalk he saw Virgil Earp, who was soon joined by Wyatt and by Morgan, who had emerged from the lunchroom to join in the taunts. Clanton merely asked Morgan not to shoot him in the back and walked off.

Later in the evening, undaunted, Ike played poker with Virgil, Tom McLaury, Sheriff Behan, and an unknown man. Early the next morning he approached Virgil and told him that if he was one of the bunch who had threatened his life he could have his fight. At half-past one that afternoon he was stopped on the street by Virgil and Morgan. As they argued, Virgil suddenly drew his six-shooter and struck Ike on the head. Virgil and Morgan then dragged the dazed man to the courthouse, where Judge Wallace fined him twenty-five dollars for carrying concealed weapons. During the hearing Ike and Morgan had another row. As they left the courtroom, Tom McLaury appeared, and this time Wyatt Earp took a hand. When tempers flared, Wyatt drew his revolver, laid it alongside McLaury's head, and left him lying in the gutter.

The Earps had been warned earlier that morning that Clanton had threatened to kill them and Holliday, and they were not taking chances. When someone informed them that Ike and Billy Clanton, the two McLaurys, and Claiborne were all down at the O K Corral (actually in the vacant lot behind the corral, facing Fremont Street), Wyatt and Morgan set off toward Fremont Street prepared for a showdown. On the way they were joined by Holliday.

Sheriff Behan was having a shave when he heard that the Earps and the Clantons were about to fight it out. He hurried to Fourth and Allen Streets, where a crowd was gathering. Outside the Hafford Saloon he met Virgil, who told him there were men in town looking for a fight but did not name them. Behan advised him to disarm them. Virgil refused, saying that he would rather give them a chance to fight. Behan then reminded him it was his duty to disarm them rather than encourage a fight. When Virgil made no reply, Behan said that he was going to disarm the "boys."

As he moved off down Fourth Street, he noticed that Morgan and Doc Holliday had arrived and that Virgil was now carrying a shotgun. At the corner of Fremont Street he met Frank McLaury holding a horse. Behan told him that he would have to disarm him and that he intended to disarm anyone in town who was carrying guns. Frank said that he did not want any trouble but refused to give up his arms. The pair then walked toward Fly's Photographic Gallery. Standing outside the gallery were Ike and Billy Clanton, Tom McLaury, and Billy Claiborne. Ike said he did not have any weapons. Behan searched him and found this to be true. Tom McLaury then opened his coat to show that he too was unarmed. Billy Clanton said that he was ready to leave town, and Claiborne claimed that he was not a member of the party and was merely endeavoring to persuade them all to leave.

Sheriff Behan tried to persuade them all to go with him to his office, but before they made any definite move, he looked down the street and saw the Earps approaching. Leaving the Clanton group, he hurried to tell Virgil he had the party in charge. The Earps ignored him and continued on down the street. Wyatt, who had been holding his pistol under his coat, now put it in his overcoat pocket. The overcoat was brand-new and had been fitted with a special canvas-lined, wax-rubbed pocket designed for carrying a pistol and getting it into action at speed.[20]

Later Behan was to testify that when the Earps reached the Mc-

[20] John P. Clum (with annotations by John Gilchriese), *It All Happened in Tombstone*, 1; interview with John Gilchriese, El Paso, Texas, October 15, 1966.

Laurys one of them—he thought it was Wyatt—said, "You sons of bitches, you have been looking for a fight, and now you can have it." Wyatt testified that as his group came up to the Clantons Billy Clanton and the two McLaurys had their hands by their sides and Frank McLaury's and Billy Clanton's six-shooters were in plain sight. Virgil ordered them to throw up their hands, saying that he had come to disarm them. Immediately Billy Clanton and Frank McLaury dropped their hands to their pistols. Virgil called out, "Hold, I don't mean that; I have come to disarm you."

Billy Clanton cried out, "Don't shoot me, I don't want to fight." Tom McLaury quickly threw open his coat to show that he was not armed saying either, "I have nothing," or "I am not armed" (according to Behan, who later reported the conversations under oath). Behan claimed that Holliday fired the first shot from a nickel-plated pistol. Almost instantaneously two more shots were fired. No two accounts of the fight seem to agree, but it is apparent that Wyatt Earp and Billy Clanton got off the first shots. Wyatt Earp gave his account of the fight to a Tombstone paper:

> Billy Clanton and Tom McLowry commenced to draw their pistols; at the same time Tom McLowry threw his hand to his right hip, throwing his coat open like that (showing), and jumped behind a horse. I had my pistol in my overcoat pocket, where I put it when Behan told us he had disarmed the other parties. When I saw Billy Clanton and Frank McLowry draw their pistols, I drew my pistol. Billy Clanton leveled his pistol on me, but I did not aim at him. I knew that Frank McLowry had the reputation of being a good shot and a dangerous man and I aimed at Frank McLowry. The first two shots which were fired were fired by Billy Clanton and myself, he shooting at me and I at Frank McLowry. I do not know which shot was fired first. We fired almost together. The fight then became general.
>
> After about four shots were fired, Ike Clanton ran up and grabbed my left arm. I could see no weapon in his hand, and I thought at the time he had none, and so I said to him, "The fight has now commenced; go to fighting, or get away." At the same time I pushed him off with my left hand. He started and ran down the side of the building and disappeared between the lodging house and photograph gallery; my first

137

shot struck Frank McLowry in the belly; he staggered off on the sidewalk, but first fired one shot at me; when we told them to throw up their hands Claiborne held up his left hand and then broke and ran, and I never seen him afterwards until late in the afternoon; I never drew my pistol or made a motion to shoot until after Billy Clanton and Frank McLowry drew their pistols; if Tom McLowry was unarmed I did not know it; believe he was armed and fired two shots at our party before Holliday, who had the shotgun, fired at and killed him, if he was unarmed there was nothing in the circumstances, or in what had been communicated to me, or in his acts or threats that would have led me even to suspect his being unarmed; I never fired at Ike Clanton, even after the shooting commenced, because I thought he was unarmed; I believed then and believe now, from the facts I have stated and from the threats I have related, and other threats communicated to me by different persons, as having been made by Tom McLowry, Frank McLowry and Ike Clanton, that these men last named had formed a conspiracy to murder my brothers, Morgan and Virgil, Doc Holliday and myself; I believe I would have been legally and morally justifiable in shooting any of them on sight, but I did not do so, nor attempt to do so; I sought no advantage when I went, as Deputy Marshal, to help disarm them and arrest them; I went as a part of my duty and under the directions of my brothers, the marshals; I did not intend to fight unless it became necessary in self-defense or in the rightful performance of official duty; when Billy Clanton and Frank McLowry drew their pistols; I knew it was a fight for life and I drew and fired in defense of my own life and the lives of my brothers and Doc Holliday.[21]

Ike Clanton, the instigator of the trouble, and Billy Claiborne escaped unhurt. Billy Clanton was not as lucky. Only nineteen years old, he put up a game fight, and even while he lay dying outside Fly's gallery, he was still trying to use his pistol. When it was taken away from him, he was heard to murmur, "Give me some more cartridges."

Virgil had handed Holliday the shotgun which Doc used to kill Tom McLaury. The coroner found that McLaury's body con-

---

[21] Tombstone *Daily Nugget*, November 17, 1881.

tained twelve wounds on the "right side of his body near together, underneath the arms, between the third and fifth ribs; my opinion was that they were buckshot wounds; laid the palm of my hand on them; it would cover the whole of them, about four inches in space." Frank McLaury was dead from a wound in the stomach, one inch left of the navel. Billy Clanton had two wounds, one two inches from the left nipple into the lungs and the other six inches right of the navel.

Virgil was badly wounded in the leg, and Morgan suffered a chipped vertebra. All the Earps survived the fight. A bullet had cut through Holliday's pistol holster and torn a strip of skin from his back. The next day he and Wyatt Earp were arrested on warrants made out by John Behan and Ike Clanton. Several friends of the Earps put up a twenty-thousand-dollar bond, guaranteeing that on October 30 Wyatt and Holliday would appear before Justice of the Peace Wells Spicer. Neither Virgil (who was dismissed as city marshal) nor Morgan was ever called as a witness. Both were considered too seriously wounded to attend.

There was no trial. The preliminary hearing lasted for nearly a month, and at its conclusion Justice Spicer carefully considered all the evidence and dismissed the charge that the Earps shot down an unarmed Tom McLaury, pointing out that McLaury had had access to a rifle in a saddle scabbard on his horse. The exoneration was not well received. On November 28 Virgil Earp was crippled for life when someone (probably acting in revenge) emptied a load of buckshot into his left side and arm as he left the Oriental Saloon. On March 17, 1882, Morgan Earp was shot through the back as he played pool in Bob Hatch's Saloon. His killers were identified as Pete Spence, Frank Stilwell, and several half-bloods. It was known that Spence had no liking for the Earps, who had brought about his arrest in September, 1881, while he was a deputy sheriff, for robbing the Bisbee stage. The Earps realized that things were getting too hot in Arizona, and Wyatt arranged for Virgil to accompany Morgan's body to their parents' home in Colton, California. Wyatt went as far as Tucson with Virgil and the body.

At Tucson Frank Stilwell tried to kill Wyatt in front of the Union Pacific depot, but Earp shot him down. From then on the Earps were finished in Arizona. Opinions differ about the fight at the O K Corral, but it seems certain that pride and personal ambition were the basic causes.[22]

Earlier in 1881, before the Earp-Clanton shoot-out, Luke Short, the fiery little gambler, was a faro dealer at the Oriental Saloon in Tombstone. On February 21, 1881, Luke, the undertaker's friend— "he shot 'em where it didn't show"—came up against the gunfighter Charlie Storms. Storms had been among the hordes of gold seekers in Deadwood, Dakota Territory, and had enjoyed something of a reputation there, although he never became involved in disputes with the top-notch gunfighters, such as Wild Bill Hickok. If it is true that, when Hickok was murdered Storms took one of Wild Bill's pistols, the acquisition did not bring him luck.[23]

In Tombstone Short and Storms had apparently fallen out on the evening of February 20. As Storms grew drunker and more belligerent, everyone knew that the incident would end in shooting. Bat Masterson wrote that he witnessed the events which led up to the killing and tried to stop the quarrel between his friends:

> Charlie Storms and I were very close friends,—as much so as Short and I were—and for that reason I did not care to see him get into what I knew would be a very serious difficulty. Storms did not know Short and . . . had sized him up as an insignificant-looking fellow, whom he could slap in the face without expecting a return. Both men were about

[22] Clum, *It All Happened in Tombstone*, 1; Frank Mason, "What Really Happened at the O.K. Corral?" *True West*, Vol. VIII, No. 1 (September–October, 1960), 35, 44; Gary L. Roberts, "O.K. Corral: The Fight That Never Dies!" *Frontier Times*, Vol. XXIX, No. 6 (October–November, 1965), 6–9, 40–42, 44–45; Robert L. Thomas, "Gunfight at Iron Springs," *True West*, Vol. XII, No. 3 (January–February, 1965), 38–39; Jahns, *The Frontier World of Doc Holliday*, 106–72; Lake, *Wyatt Earp, Frontier Marshal*, 231–358; Waters, *The Earp Brothers of Tombstone*, 98–207.

[23] Frank J. Wilstach, *Wild Bill Hickok: The Prince of Pistoleers*, 11. I did extensive research into this incident but could not get beyond Wilstach's story; see Joseph G. Rosa, "Are These the Hickok Guns?" *Guns Quarterly*, Vol. I, No. 1 (Spring, 1960).

to pull their pistols when I jumped between them and grabbed Storms, at the same time requesting Luke not to shoot—a request I knew he would respect if it was possible without endangering his own life too much. I had no trouble in getting Storms out of the house, as he knew me to be his friend. When Storms and I reached the street I advised him to go to his room and take a sleep, for I then learned for the first time that he had been up all night, and had been quarreling with other persons.

He asked me to accompany him to his room, which I did, and after seeing him safely in his apartments, where I supposed he could go to bed, I returned to where Short was. I was just explaining to Luke that Storms was a very decent sort of man when, lo and behold! there he stood before us. Without saying a word, he took hold of Luke's arm and pulled him off the sidewalk, where he had been standing, at the same time pulling his pistol, a Colt's cut-off, 45 calibre, single action; but . . . he was too slow, although he succeeded in getting his pistol out. Luke stuck the muzzle of his own pistol against Storms' heart and pulled the trigger. The bullet tore the heart asunder, and as he was falling, Luke shot him again. Storms was dead when he hit the ground. Luke was given a preliminary hearing before a magistrate and exonerated.[24]

Another witness to the shooting, George Parsons, heard the first two shots but thought little of it. At the third his interest was aroused. In his journal he wrote:

I seized hat and ran out into the street just in time to see Storms die—shot through the heart. Both gamblers. L.S. running game at Oriental. Trouble brewing during night and morning and S was probably aggressor though drunk. He was game to the last & after been shot through the heart by a desperate effort steadying revolver with both hands fired four shots in all I believe. Doc Goodfellow bro't bullet into my room and showed it to me. .45 caliber and slightly flattened. Also showed a bloody handkerchief, part of which was carried into wound by pistol. Short very unconcerned after shooting—probably a case of kill or be killed. Forgot to say that the Faro games went right on as

[24] Masterson, "Famous Gun Fighters of the Western Frontier," *Human Life*, Vol. IV (April, 1907), 10.

though nothing had happened after body was carried into Storms' room at the San Jose house.[25]

A less well publicized shoot-out involving Luke Short took place in 1887. This time his adversary was long-haired Jim Courtright, marshal of Fort Worth, Texas. After his Dodge City troubles Luke had transferred his business interests to Fort Worth, where he came up against the protection racket. He refused to be intimidated by several visits Courtright made to his White Elephant Saloon. Trouble between the two came to a head on the evening of February 8, 1887. Informed that Courtright wanted him in the street, Short casually walked out and faced the marshal with his thumbs hooked into the armholes of his vest and started to argue. As though he were smoothing wrinkles in his vest, Short lowered his hands, and Courtright ordered him not to pull a gun. "I'm not trying to pull a gun!" cried Luke in a pained tone. "I haven't got a gun there, see!" He pulled at his coat to prove his point, but Courtright, no fool, went for his gun. Short drew his and fired wildly. By a strange quirk of fate his shot hit and smashed the marshal's thumb as Courtright drew and cocked his gun. In desperation Courtright tried to shift the weapon to his left hand, but Short steadied himself and put three bullets into him. Courtright was dead, killed as the result of one of the strangest flukes in frontier history.[26]

Newspaper stories of gunfights of any consequence were often colored by the editors' personal comments and also by moralizing, if the incident could be made to fit a pet theme of the moment. Although dislike of one or more participants might be displayed, rarely did the press hide the truth for fear of reprisal. Some of the stories provide insight into the attitudes of the time. One fight that inspired considerable comment was the one in Cheyenne between Charlie Harrison and Jim Levy, who failed to kill each other at first go, although both had achieved reputations in various parts of the West for courage and for dexterity with guns. Years after the event Bat Masterson wrote:

[25] Quoted in Jahns, *The Frontier World of Doc Holliday*, 121.
[26] Cunningham, *Triggernometry*, 215–16.

Charlie Harrison was one of the best-known sporting men west of the Missouri River. His home was in St. Louis but he traveled extensively throughout the West and was well-known through the Rocky Mountain region. He was of an impetuous temperament, quick of action, of unquestioned courage and the most expert man I ever saw with a pistol. He could shoot faster and straighter when shooting at a target than any man I ever knew; then add to that the fact that no man possessed more courage than he did, the natural conclusion would be that he would be a most formidable foe to encounter in a pistol duel.[27]

The other man was Jim Levy. Although he was not as well known to Masterson as Harrison was, Levy has been included among the outstanding gunfighters of Deadwood. According to one old-timer, he was "the top-notcher of them all, except Wild Bill."[28] On Friday, March 9, 1877, Levy and Harrison met in Cheyenne, Wyoming. Soon after six in the evening they entered Shingle and Locke's Saloon and sat down at a table. Both had been drinking. Gradually their conversation turned into an argument over a game in which Levy had been "cinched." Eventually Levy, irked by Harrison's remarks, drew his pistol, but Harrison told him to wait until he could get his hands on a gun, when he would gladly accommodate him. Levy agreed to this, and both men went up the street to the Senate Saloon. Harrison went into the saloon and picked up a revolver. Then he walked up the street to Frenchy's Saloon. Levy was waiting for him across the street from the saloon.

Harrison raised his pistol and fired, but missed. Levy immediately returned the fire. About six shots were exchanged, one hitting Harrison in the left breast. He fell down, raised himself, and fired once more at Levy and missed again. Levy ran across the street, shot Harrison in the right hip, and left. This wound was a bad one. The ball had taken a circular course across the lower abdomen and lodged close to the surface in the left hip, lower down than the point of entrance. Harrison was given immediate medical care but

[27] Masterson, "Famous Gun Fighters of the Western Frontier," *Human Life*, Vol. IV (January, 1907), 9.

[28] Wilstach, *Wild Bill Hickok*, 268.

refused to allow the doctor to take out the ball. He was at first reported to be recovering, but two weeks later it was announced that he had died, leaving his wife and daughter destitute.

Angered by Levy's action in shooting Harrison again as he lay wounded, the press editorialized: "The pleas of self-defense might well be set up in Levy's behalf had he not done this, but we believe he should be made to suffer the severist penalty of the law for thus carrying into effect an evident intention to kill his man." However, it was later reported that "Levy, the pistoliferous gambler, has secured bail and is at large."[29]

Whatever the inner turmoil that he suffered during a gun battle, without coolness, deliberation, and excellent reflexes no gunfighter could hope to survive for long. Charlie Harrison paid the penalty for not having—in addition to superior marksmanship and undoubted nerve—the qualities of deliberation and self-control. Anxious and hurried, he underestimated his man, and Levy took advantage of him.

Stories of gunfights and gunfighters improve with age. The Dave (or Davis) Tutt duel with Wild Bill Hickok in Springfield, Missouri, on July 21, 1865, perhaps inspired the "showdown at noon" movie sequences, and exaggerated accounts of several fights have become the basis for stock situations, such as the killing of an enemy by trickery or firearm gymnastics.

Using a trick as old as duels between men, Hickok is said to have killed Bill Mulrey (or Mulvey), a drunken desperado, in August, 1869, at Hays, Kansas. Mulrey had pulled two pistols on Hickok. Wild Bill said, supposedly to someone behind Mulrey, "Don't shoot him, boys." Thrown off guard, Mulrey looked behind him, and Hickok then drew his own gun and killed Mulrey.

A now-legendary example of firearm gymnastics was for the hero to dispose of a would-be assassin by catching sight of him in a barroom mirror and shooting him from under the arm or over the shoulder without turning around. This is what is said to have hap-

---

[29] Cheyenne *Weekly Leader*, March 15, 22, 29, 1877.

pened in a fight between Hickok and Samuel Strawhim in Hays, Kansas, later in 1869.

Sam Strawhim was well known in Hays as a bad man. In July, 1869, angered by a vigilance committee's order to leave town, he and Joe Weiss tried to beat up Alonzo B. Webster, then a clerk in the post office. Webster shot Weiss, but Strawhim escaped and went to Ellsworth. Later he returned to Hays, and on September 27 he and some cronies caused a riot in John Bittles' Saloon. Sheriff Hickok was summoned to restore order. In the melee that followed, Strawhim was killed. A coroner's jury exonerated the sheriff, and the story of the mirror trick was woven into the threads of the truth to improve the story. What actually happened was recorded by a witness:

PARTICULARS OF THE KILLING OF STRANHAN
AT HAYS CITY.

Hays City, September 30, 1869.

EDS. COMMERCIAL:—Allow me, an eye witness, to relate to you the details of the shooting affair last Sunday night, during which a certain Sam Stranhan [Strawhim] was killed.

It seems that there was on the part of this Stranhan and some of his associates bad feeling against certain citizens of this town, and members of the Vigilance committee. To satisfy their hatred they mobbed together and went on Sunday night, about half-past 11 o'clock to the saloon of Mr. John Bitter [Bittles], with the intent to break up the establishment. The crowd, numbering about fourteen to eighteen persons, called for beer in a frantic manner. The glasses had to be filled up continually. Meanwhile the men were passing in and out of the saloon, and as it afterwards appeared carried the glasses to an adjoining vacant lot. Mr. Bitter remarked that the number of glasses was diminishing, and saw that Stranhan carried out some of them. The noise was fearful, all the men crying at the top of their voices, beer! beer! and using the most obscene language. This went on for a short time, when they began throwing the beer at each other. During all the noise one could hear threats as: "I shall kill someone to-night just for luck," or "some one will have to go up to-night," etc.

Mr. Bitter finally called the policeman, Mr. Wm. Hickock [*sic*],

145

known as "Wild Bill," asking him to go out and fetch the missing glasses back. Wild Bill shortly returned with both hands full of glasses, when Stranhan remarked that he would shoot anyone that should try to interfere with his fun. Wild Bill set the glasses on the counter, Stranhan took hold of one and took it up in a threatening manner. He had no time to execute his design for a shot fired by Mr. Hickock killed him. He dropped down dead. The inquest was held next morning at 9 o'clock. The verdict of the jury was that deceased was shot by Mr. Hickock, and that the homicide was justifiable, the same being in self-defense.

Too much credit cannot be given to Wild Bill for his endeavor to rid this town of such dangerous characters as this Stranhan was.[30]

In 1876 a friend of Hickok's recalled that when Wild Bill carried the glasses back into the saloon the conversation went as follows: "Boys," Wild Bill remarked, "you hadn't ought to treat a poor old man [Bittles] in this way." Strawhim said he would throw them out again. "Do," retorted Bill, "and they will carry you out."[31] Then Hickok displayed the true gunfighter's reaction to danger—he shot first and considered the outcome later.

When men were determined to kill, they did so in the quickest way they knew. An example of such determination was recalled by Luther North, writing of a visit he made in 1867 to Julesburg, Colorado. Julesburg was a town of about two thousand inhabitants. Nearly all the men went about armed, and there were killings almost daily. One evening, as North sat outside the hotel talking with half a dozen fellow loungers, a man appeared on the street carrying a heavy Colt revolver in his hand. One of the men in the crowd remarked, "That is Slim Jim, he runs the dance hall up on the corner, and Swede Charley got one of his girls from him and he is going over to kill him." "Charley is a bad man," someone else added. "Jim better let him alone."

Crossing the street, Slim Jim entered Swede Charley's restaurant, closing the door behind him. Two shots were heard. Several minutes

---

30 Leavenworth *Daily Commercial*, October 3, 1869.
31 Wichita *Eagle*, September 14, 1876.

later Jim came out, crossed the street, stooped down, pulled up his trouser leg, examined his ankle, and pushed the trouser leg down again. He then straightened up and walked a full block to his dance hall. Several of his girls watched as he got to within twenty feet of where they were standing, stumbled, dropped his gun, and fell face forward, dead. Swede Charley had shot Slim through the heart, but Swede was never arrested for the killing since it was obviously done in self-defense.[32]

The behavior of Dallas Stoudenmire when he was marshal of El Paso, Texas, also exemplified that of the man who shot first and asked questions later. During his brief period as El Paso's guardian of the law, Stoudenmire established a reputation that was to survive long after his lifetime.

The El Paso of the 1880's was a growing but still lawless border town. Just across the Rio Grande was Paso del Norte,[33] its Mexican counterpart. On January 28, 1881, occurred an incident that would eventually draw Stoudenmire into a gun battle. It seems that some Americans were jailed in Paso del Norte for robbing a Mexican peddler. Several El Paso girls smuggled guns across the border to aid the men's escape. The local Mexican garrison rounded up all but three of the escapees. The three managed to reach an irrigation ditch at the border but were killed by a *vaquero* with a Winchester as they struggled through the muddy water. In El Paso there was a great outcry, and the unidentified *vaquero* was a wanted man.[34]

Leading the revenge seekers were three brothers, James, Frank, and Dr. George ("Doc") Felix Manning. The Mannings had interests in saloons and owned a ranch some ten miles above El Paso. John Hale, their foreman, who also owned a small spread, was ordered to watch the Mexicans who crossed the border in search of lost or stolen cattle.

After the initial furor over this incident died down, the people

---

[32] Luther North, *Man of the Plains*, 58–59.

[33] On September 16, 1882, the name was changed from Paso del Norte to Ciudad Juárez.

[34] "Recollections of George Look," El Paso Public Library.

of El Paso began to concern themselves about the political situation. The city officials, unwilling to clean out the practitioners of vice because of the revenue they provided, had difficulty in acquiring a police force capable of keeping the peace. The appointment of a young Kentuckian, George Campbell, on December 1, 1880, had led to dissension over his salary. Well aware that he had the city council at a disadvantage, Campbell conspired with the local saloonkeepers to supplement his income. Upon learning about the deals being made by their policeman, the councilmen sent for the Texas Rangers, and had a warrant issued for Campbell's arrest. When the Rangers, led by Sergeant James Gillett, arrived in El Paso, Campbell hid out at John Hale's ranch until, after some negotiation, the council withdrew the warrant and allowed Campbell to resign.[35]

In his place Ed Copeland, owner of the Occidental Saloon, was appointed marshal at a salary of fifty dollars a month. However, he could not put up the required bond, and was replaced by his deputy, Bill Johnson, the town drunk. Then, on April 11, 1881, a new man was appointed marshal—Dallas Stoudenmire—at a salary of one hundred dollars a month.[36]

Stoudenmire, a former Confederate soldier, deputy sheriff, and Ranger, was six feet two inches tall. He had hazel eyes and auburn hair, a broad, pale face, and a granite jaw.[37] He was said to be utterly fearless and capable of killing without compunction. The townspeople felt that at last they had a strong man in charge. Disdaining holsters, Dallas stuffed his two short-barreled, silver-plated, pearl-handled .45 Colts into leather-lined hip pockets. Even when he was wearing a frock coat, he seemed to have no difficulty getting the revolvers into action.

Rustling activities in the area were gradually increasing and were of concern to the Texas Rangers. Soon after Stoudenmire's appoint-

[35] Capt. George Baylor to Gen. W. H. King, 1881–82 correspondence, University of Texas Archives, Austin, Texas. See also the Minute Books of the El Paso City Council.

[36] Minute Book B, El Paso, Texas, 1881, 94.

[37] Roll of Company A Frontier Men, Texas Rangers, 1874 (copy supplied by James M. Day), Texas State Archives, Austin, Texas.

ment thirty head of cattle were stolen from the mayor of Paso del Norte and driven across the border. Captain Baylor of the Rangers was asked to investigate rumors that the cattle had been traced to Hale's ranch and that the Manning-Hale faction was leading the rustlers. On April 14 Ranger Ed Fitch set out for the ranch, accompanied by ten Mexicans who could identify the cattle. On the way to the ranch two of the Mexicans, Juarique and Sanchez, decided to do some investigating on their own, and were ambushed and murdered by two former Rangers.[38]

When the news of the murders reached Mexico, a force of about seventy-five armed Mexicans crossed the border, and their leader sought out Spanish-speaking Gus Krempkau, a one-time Ranger and now a constable in El Paso. With his help the bodies were recovered and brought into El Paso. An inquest was held in Judge Buckler's office on April 15, with Krempkau as interpreter. By lunchtime tension was mounting between the Americans and the Mexicans, and it was decided to terminate the inquest. The Mexicans took the bodies across the border, and Stoudenmire, who had taken no part in the activities, sauntered over to the Globe Restaurant, owned by his brother-in-law, "Doc" Cummings, for lunch.

About this time Gus Krempkau left Judge Buckler's office and went into Keating's Saloon next door, where he had left his rifle during the inquest. When he came out with the gun, he saw George Campbell, drunk, in the middle of the street, shouting that Stoudenmire should have arrested the Mexicans, who had ridden into town armed. A number of Rangers nearby ignored the drunken shouts. Krempkau walked over to his mule and pushed the rifle into the saddle scabbard. Around his waist was a fine gun belt of which he was very proud, but he was not a gunfighter; he only used a gun when his life was threatened. Campbell watched his movements, and it was obvious he was looking for trouble.

[38] There is reason to suppose that one of these Mexicans was the *vaquero* who had shot the three Americans. The former Rangers were Frank Stevenson and Chris Peveler. This information was brought to light by Leon C. Metz, of El Paso, Texas, who has conducted an exhaustive study of the career of Dallas Stoudenmire.

"Any American that would befriend the Mexicans ought to be hanged!" Campbell shouted. Krempkau looked embarrassed and then angry. Reddening, he turned. "George," he said quietly, "I hope that you don't mean me."

Campbell snapped his fingers angrily. "If the shoe fits you, wear it." He turned to his own mule. John Hale was sitting in a window near the door of Keating's Saloon. He had been watching the exchange through an alcoholic haze. Suddenly he jumped to his feet and ran to Krempkau. He drew his pistol, pushed the barrel under the constable's arm, and shouted, "Turn loose, Campbell, I have got him covered." Then he pulled the trigger. The bullet tore its way through both Krempkau's lungs. Sobered by his hasty action, Hale panicked and jumped behind a pillar at a corner of Keating's Saloon. Hearing the shot, Stoudenmire came running, pulled both pistols, and opened fire on Hale. The first shot brought down a Mexican bystander, but the next one buried itself in Hale's brain as he peered around the pillar, killing him instantly.

Campbell pulled his pistol and covered the crowd. "Gentlemen," he yelled, "this is not my fight!" Gus Krempkau, sagging against the saloon door numbed by pain and bleeding to death, did not hear him. As he slid to the ground, he drew his pistol. Slowly cocking and firing, in a deliberate manner, he emptied the gun at Campbell. One shot smashed Campbell's wrist, forcing him to switch his pistol to his left hand, and another hit him in the foot. The rest of the shots went wild. Stoudenmire also shot at Campbell, and it was his shots that finally brought Campbell down. If Stoudenmire had heard Campbell's disclaimer, he ignored it. As Dallas ran to the dying man, Campbell turned on his back and gasped out, "You big son of a bitch, you murdered me." Doc Cummings now appeared, still wearing his bartender's apron and waving a shotgun. He joined Dallas in the middle of the street, and both men cried out, "Where are you, Rangers? Close in, Rangers!" But the Rangers, though they were standing by with guns drawn, did not intervene.[39]

[39] "Recollections of George Look," El Paso Public Library.

Pat Shea, a friend of the dying man, darted forward and picked up Campbell's gun, a weapon he particularly prized. "George," he yelled, "do you want your gun?" Stoudenmire promptly shoved the muzzles of his pistols into Shea's face, who dropped the weapon, threw up his hands, and backed away. The pistol was retrieved by an eyewitness, George Look, and handed to the bartender at Keating's. Before he died, Campbell asked Look to give the gun to Shea.[40]

The Rangers had not interfered because they felt that Stoudenmire was in command of the situation. Ranger Captain Baylor thought that Campbell's death, although regrettable, was unavoidable in the circumstances and that, in defending another policeman, Stoudenmire had acted in the interests of law and order. In his report he also noted that it was possible that one of Krempkau's stray bullets might have cut down the Mexican bystander, although most witnesses agreed that it was Stoudenmire who killed him.[41]

A temporary calm returned to the city. Stoudenmire clamped down on the saloons, and the rough element kept fairly quiet. But everyone was sure that there would be more trouble. On April 17 Bill Johnson tried to kill Stoudenmire and Cummings with a shotgun as they made the night rounds of the city. Both men returned Johnson's fire, and he fell to the ground with eight bullet wounds. The darkness was lit by flashes of gunfire as other men also started shooting. Instead of running for cover, Stoudenmire became angry. He ran toward his unknown assailants and emptied his pistols at them, but they escaped into the night. Apart from a bullet nick in a heel he was unhurt. A vigilance committee was quickly organized. Cummings blamed the Mannings for the attack, but nothing was done to verify his allegation.

After Johnson's killing the town again became peaceable. Stoudenmire was presented with a gold-headed cane in recognition of his services, and for a time he was a highly respected citizen.

---

[40] *Ibid.*

[41] Capt. George Baylor to Gen. W. H. King, 1881–82 correspondence, University of Texas Archives, Austin, Texas.

Then he took to drink, perhaps because the place was too quiet and he was bored, or perhaps for a different reason. No one knows.

When Dallas took time off to go to Columbus, Texas, to marry Isabella Sherrington,[42] James B. Gillett, a deputy marshal, was left in charge, with Cummings to help him. On February 14 Gillett was sick and remained in bed. For weeks Cummings had been brooding about the feud between Stoudenmire and the Mannings, and now he decided to do something about it. He made the rounds of the saloons, getting drunker at each bar, until he finally arrived at the Manning Brothers' Coliseum. He was met by Jim Manning, who tried to dissuade him from entering, but Cummings began insulting him, getting angrier by the minute. J. C. Kling, the bartender, was also drawn into the argument. There was an exchange of shots—witnesses were uncertain who fired first—and Cummings was killed. Later investigation showed that one of the chambers of Manning's pistol had been fired, and many believed that Kling had fired the second shot, but this charge was never proved.[43]

When Dallas returned to El Paso, Jim Gillett met him at the depot and broke the news of Cummings' death to him. Furious, Stoudenmire let it be known that if the Mannings wanted trouble they could have it. Some of the townspeople, hoping to avert more bloodshed, persuaded Dallas and the Mannings to sign an agreement not to fight. The effect of this frustration upon Stoudenmire was to make him drink more and more heavily. In March, 1882, he was temporarily replaced by Deputy Gillett until he sobered up. It was later learned that he had accepted an appointment as a deputy United States marshal in New Mexico. Dallas did not leave town, but the position of city marshal was declared vacant, and W. W. Mills was nominated for the post. However, Stoudenmire was re-elected.[44]

[42] The Colorado County records, at Columbus, Texas, contain an entry stating that a marriage license was issued February 20, 1882 (details confirmed by C. L. Sonnichsen).

[43] James B. Gillett, "The Killing of Dallas Stoudenmire," *Frontier Times*, Vol. I, No. 10 (July, 1924), 24.

From that time on, Dallas Stoudenmire went downhill fast. The situation became so serious that the council threatened to cut his salary. Dallas took the hint and resigned after a stormy session in the council chamber. Gillett took his place. Stoudenmire became a familiar sight in the saloons, and there were rumors of an impending showdown between him and the Mannings. On September 18, 1882, it came. Early that morning, after an all-night drinking session, Stoudenmire met Gillett on the street, and Gillett tactfully suggested that Dallas go home to bed. Dallas did go home, but was up again at 3:00 P.M. and on the streets. It was then that he learned that the Mannings had been told to expect trouble from him. Protesting that the story was untrue, he set out to clear up the matter, accompanied by a friend, Walt Jones, a former policeman.

When Dallas and Jones entered the Coliseum, they found Jim Manning standing by the bar and Doc Felix Manning playing billiards. Dallas approached Jim and said that he wanted to straighten things out. Jim left to get Frank, and Doc Manning dropped his cue and walked over. He accused Dallas of not keeping his part of the bargain, and they began arguing heatedly. When they went for their guns, Walt Jones tried to intervene, but Stoudenmire pushed him aside, a movement that cost him vital moments. Doc got his gun, a double-action .44, into action and shot Dallas. The ball lodged in a large pocketbook and a packet of letters in Dallas' right breast pocket. Again Doc Manning fired, and this time the bullet smashed into Stoudenmire's left breast, high up near the shoulder. By this time Dallas had his gun out and working. He shot Manning through the right arm above the elbow, knocking the pistol from Doc's hand. Immediately the little doctor flung himself at his huge adversary, throwing his arms around him to keep Stoudenmire from shooting him.

Locked together, the pair crashed and staggered around the saloon, through the doorway, and into the street. At this point Jim Manning, armed with a .45, rushed out. His first shot splintered a barber's pole, and his second hit Stoudenmire in the brain, killing

[44] Minute Book C, El Paso, Texas, 1882, Part 1, 46, 62.

153

him instantly. Dragging himself free, Doc Manning took one of Stoudenmire's pistols and began to batter the dead man about the head.

The two brothers were arrested for the killing. Jim Manning stood trial, but was acquitted. The official interpretation of the circumstances—that Jim Manning had attacked Stoudenmire to protect his unarmed brother, who had been trying to stop Stoudenmire from using his guns—made possible no other verdict.[45]

Not all the gunfights described above were hot-blooded, spur-of-the-moment actions. Some were culminations of earlier incidents destined to end in violence. Many things contributed to the final showdown, when a shoot-out settled the matter. There was little romance—it was a harsh game of life and death.

[45] Gillett, "The Killing of Dallas Stoudenmire," *Frontier Times*, Vol. I, No. 10, (July, 1924), 24

10.

The Man

THE GUNFIGHTER WAS NO SUPERMAN; although he had certain talents and abilities that set him apart from other men, he shared their failings and weaknesses. Rarely the lone wolf, he was often a good mixer because that was the best way to keep track of his friends—and enemies. Most of the gunfighters associated with women, and many of them married, one of the few indications they gave of desiring to form permanent attachments or conform to the codes of society.

Bat Masterson, in his youthful years, enjoyed the company of prostitutes, and at one time is supposed to have vied with Sergeant Melvin A. King, of the United States Cavalry, for the affections of Molly Brennan, a saloon girl in Sweetwater, Texas. One of the several versions of her death claims that she was killed in a pitched battle between troopers and some buffalo hunters. But the most popular story is that, upon finding Bat with Molly one evening, Sergeant King started shooting and the girl was fatally wounded when she threw herself in front of Bat. According to this story, Bat, although injured, managed to get his gun working and killed the sergeant. The Jacksboro, Texas, newspaper referred to the girl as Molly Braman and to King's killer as "a citizen." A story that Ben Thompson intervened when Bat's life was threatened by King's friends does not stand up to examination.[1]

Strangely enough, Bat Masterson never earned notoriety as a

---

[1] Jacksboro (Texas) *Frontier Echo*, February 11, 1876; Richard O'Connor, *Bat Masterson*, 53–55; Lake, *Wyatt Earp, Frontier Marshal*, 133; Floyd Benjamin Streeter, *Ben Thompson: Man with a Gun*, 125.

lady killer, perhaps because in most instances he was more discreet about his amorous affairs than some of his contemporaries.[2] In 1880, following his term as sheriff of Ford County, Kansas, and a visit to Colorado, Bat returned to Dodge City. The official Tenth United States Census taken in Dodge City on June 22, 1880, listed him as a resident and described him as a laborer of twenty-five living with a nineteen-year-old girl named Annie Ladue. Later Masterson was involved in the divorce action of a Mrs. Lou Spencer. On November 21, 1891, five days before his thirty-seventh birthday, he married Emma Walters. Three years his junior and a former saloon girl, Emma apparently understood and tolerated Bat's erratic way of life, for they remained together until he died on October 25, 1921—a month before their thirtieth wedding anniversary.[3]

Wyatt Earp's biographer states that at the age of twenty Wyatt married a girl of sixteen but that she died shortly afterward in a typhus epidemic. Another writer gives the date of the marriage as January 10, 1870, and the girl's name as Willa [or Urilla] Sutherland.[4] Wyatt's second wife (no records of this marriage have been found) was a girl called Mattie. When Wyatt deserted her in Tombstone, she turned to prostitution. Six years later, in July, 1888, she drank a bottle of laudanum and died.[5] Wyatt had left Mattie to take up with a saloon girl named Sadie. When he left Tombstone, she also disappeared, to reappear later under her real name, Josephine Sarah Marcus. Whether or not she ever married Wyatt, researchers have established that she was a shrew and gave Wyatt hell in his later years.[6]

Ben Thompson, of Texas and Kansas gunfighting fame, was born in Knottingley, Yorkshire, England, on November 11, 1842.

[2] Miller and Snell, *Why the West Was Wild*, 317–21; O'Connor, *Bat Masterson*, 31–40.

[3] Miller and Snell, *Why the West Was Wild*, 409; O'Connor, *Bat Masterson*, 152.

[4] Lake, *Wyatt Earp, Frontier Marshal*, 29; Waters, *The Earp Brothers of Tombstone*, 38.

[5] Waters, *The Earp Brothers of Tombstone*, 225.

[6] Interview with John Gilchriese, El Paso, Texas, October 15, 1966.

In 1849 his family emigrated to Texas. In 1863, after recovering in San Antonio from wounds received while serving with the Second Texas Cavalry, Ben went home to Austin and met Catherine Moore, the daughter of Martin Moore, a former Austin merchant. They were married soon afterward.

The early years of the marriage were marred by a series of catastrophic events. Ben had trouble with his brother-in-law, Jim Moore. One day Ben came home to find that Jim had hit Catherine and knocked her down. Ben took after Jim with a pistol and wounded him. Thompson had been in scrapes with the Army before, and this time the military pressed charges. Ben was given a four-year sentence in the state penitentiary. Two years later, at the end of the period of postwar military rule, the civilian government reviewed his case and released him.

Leaving his family in Texas, Ben went to Kansas, where he was a principal in a number of incidents. In the summer of 1871, after he had established a profitable saloon and gambling business in Abilene, Ben arranged to bring his wife and son from Texas. On the evening of the day they arrived in Kansas City, he took them for a ride. On the excursion their buggy hit a pothole and turned over, throwing all of them into the road. Ben broke a leg already weakened by a war injury. His wife's arm was fractured, and his son's foot crushed. Ben's and the boy's injuries healed, but Catherine's arm had to be amputated. Early in October, 1871, Ben decided to take them back to Austin.

For Ben Thompson, settled family life was impossible. He was constantly traveling about the country setting up businesses in various cowtowns or becoming embroiled in trouble stirred up by his homicidal brother, Billy, and other people, and he found little time to be at home. Although his family was well provided for during his lifetime, when he died, his accumulated debts deprived them of most of the money he had invested in property.[7]

Even John Wesley Hardin, probably the most ferocious of all the Texas gunfighters, made a stab at matrimony, when he married

[7] Streeter, *Ben Thompson*, 47, 79, 202–203.

157

Jane Bowen in 1872. Although they had three children, a boy and two girls, it is doubtful that their married life consisted of much more than fleeting moments together. Wes Hardin was always on the run. Eventually he was captured by the Texas Rangers and sentenced to twenty-five years in the state penitentiary. Hardin kept in constant touch with his wife, and she figured greatly in his plans for the future. But she died on November 6, 1892, a little over fifteen months before he was paroled on February 17, 1894.

Hardin's years in prison had enabled him to gain an education of sorts. He had studied law and planned to hang up his shingle after his release. But the woman he had planned his new life for was dead. For a time after he was paroled he and his children lived with Fred Duderstadt, an old friend of trail-driving days. Then they moved to Gonzales, Texas, where Hardin, headstrong and ill-tempered, fell afoul of local politicians. He moved on, first to Riddleville and then, in December, 1894, to Junction, where he opened a law office. A young girl, Callie Lewis, whom he met in the nearby town of London, became infatuated with him and his reputation. Seizing a chance for happiness, Wes married her on January 8, 1895. But the marriage was short-lived. Callie soon grew tired of the relationship and left him, refusing to see him again. Hardin began to drink, got into fights, and was finally murdered.[8]

Just how many women Wild Bill Hickok had during his hectic twenty years on the frontier is unknown. The scraps of information that are available suggest that the relationships were marked by jealousy. Hickok is supposed to have killed David C. McCanles at Rock Creek, Nebraska, on July 12, 1861, in a dispute over money, but there is evidence to suggest that their differences actually arose over McCanles' mistress, Sarah Shull. It is likely that David (or Davis) Tutt died in Springfield, Missouri, on July 21, 1865, in a gunfight with Hickok over the favors of a woman, perhaps Susannah Moore (a mystery girl from the Ozarks, whose presence is felt but not positively identified in the wealth of Hickok material). Hickok had several mistresses in Abilene, and according to local legend, it

8 Hardin, *Life*, xiii–xiv, 64, 135–47.

was a prostitute named Jessie Hazell who sparked off the gunfight with Phil Coe.

A few women crossed Hickok's path without causing bloodshed. Indian Annie, of Ellsworth, was rumored to have borne him a child in 1867, but what evidence is available indicates that Hickok was not the child's father. Calamity Jane, Emma Williams, Mattie Silks, Annie Anderson (a former waitress in Abilene), are among those said to have shared Bill's bed. When Hickok finally married, at the age of thirty-eight, it was to a woman whose charms had failed to appeal to him the first time he encountered her. Agnes Lake Thatcher, five years older than Bill and the widow of a circus owner, William Lake Thatcher, had led the sort of exciting life that appealed to a man of Hickok's temperament. They first met in Abilene, in July, 1871, and again in Rochester, New York, when Bill was appearing in Buffalo Bill's stage show "Scouts of the Plains." Still later they renewed their acquaintance in Cheyenne, Wyoming, where they decided to be married.

The Reverend W. F. Warren, who officiated at the simple ceremony held on March 5, 1876, appears to have had his doubts about the marriage. He wrote in the remarks column of the Methodist church register, "I don't think the[y] meant it." Two weeks later Hickok was off to the Black Hills with a band of gold prospectors, convinced that he would make a strike that would permit him to retire. But in August he was dead. It is evident from letters written by Agnes to Wild Bill's mother that she was very fond of her "James" and honestly believed that they would be happy together when he returned from the Black Hills. Two of Bill's letters to his wife have survived (though their present whereabouts is unknown), and both contain expressions of his love for her. On September 27, 1877, Agnes married a George Carson in Cheyenne; however, he soon disappeared from her life, and it was as Mrs. Wild Bill Hickok that she preferred to be remembered until her death in 1907.[9]

[9] Marriage Record of the Methodist Church, Cheyenne, Wyoming Territory, 1876, Wyoming State Archives, Cheyenne, Wyoming; Laramie County Records, Book C, September 27, 1877, Carnegie Public Library, Cheyenne, Wyoming. New Jersey

Anyone inquiring into the habits and personalities of the old-time gunfighters quickly becomes convinced that very few of them were suited to marriage. They were not the sort to settle down to the routine or responsibilities of married life. The gunfighter who followed the outlaw trail saw his family but rarely, and the hasty visit, usually one jump ahead of a posse, was marred by fear as he listened for the knock at the door that might announce the arrival of the law. As his notoriety grew and a price was placed on his head, there was the added fear that an informer would turn him in for the reward. Some fugitives changed their names, moved to new locations where they were not known, and managed to live in peace. Others, like the James brothers, would not or could not reform and spent their lives on the run. Even for those who succeeded in building new lives, there was always the risk that sometime, somehow, their past would be discovered.

One outlaw spent thirty-three years on the run. During that time he married and made several efforts to settle down and raise a family. This man was William Mitchell, who was involved in the Mitchell-Truitt feud in Texas in the early 1870's. In a gunfight between the two families in 1874 two of the Truitts were killed by Bill Mitchell and Mit Graves, a boy who worked for the Mitchells. Bill fled after the fight, and his father was arrested and hanged for his part in the affair. Years later Bill, determined on revenge, rode hundreds of miles to kill James Truitt, the only surviving Truitt who had participated in the fight.

From 1874 to 1907 Bill Mitchell, alias Baldy Russell (and other names), was on the run, a wanted man but not a notorious killer. On the occasions when he was arrested, he was usually freed on bail. But in 1912 he was sentenced to life imprisonment. He either escaped or was allowed to escape, and no effort seems to have been made to bring him in again. He died in 1928, a free but still-wanted man. Throughout their precarious life, his wife had remained by

Mirror (Jersey City), August 31, 1907. I have read the letters from Agnes Lake to Mrs. Polly Hickok, now in the possession of the family, in Troy Grove, Illinois.

his side, a loyal and patient woman. It is regrettable that her story has never been told. It would doubtless have provided insight into the emotions and frustrations of a woman married to a gunfighter.[10]

Some men on the run took their women with them, and some of the women also earned fame as outlaws. While Butch Cassidy and the Wild Bunch were at the height of their fame, Laura Bullion (a fitting name for a robber) rode with them. Laura was a part-Indian girl with black, flashing eyes, high cheekbones, and thick, coarse black hair. She was no raving beauty, but she was adored by Ben Kilpatrick, the "Tall Texan." She acted as cook and housekeeper for the gang, and when another hand was needed, she readily rode out on raids. She could ride and shoot with the best of them, and the gang knew that she had little use for anyone who might double-cross her or the gang.

Finally Laura and Kilpatrick were captured and imprisoned. When she was released, Laura promised to wait for Ben, and she kept her word. In 1911, however, when his sentence expired, he had to face a murder charge (of which he was later acquitted), and Laura and Kilpatrick parted. Ben disappeared into Texas, where he and a man named Ole Beck held up a train near Sanderson and were killed by a Wells, Fargo messenger. It was March 13, 1912, and train robbers were supposed to be a thing of the past. Perhaps Kilpatrick realized this but could not resist the temptation to stage just one more "raise." When Laura heard of his death, she wrote to his mother, "He swore he would never be taken alive again."[11]

Descriptions of a legendary gunfighter's personal character follow a pattern. Almost without exception they were generous to a fault, chivalrous, and fond of children. It is possible that certain individuals among the actual gunfighters possessed these qualities. But it is important to remember that these qualities were high on the list of desirable characteristics of the Victorian era and that the legend makers would naturally endow their heroes with them. Thus

[10] Sonnichsen, *Outlaw: Bill Mitchell.*
[11] Horan, *The Wild Bunch*, 104–105, 184–87.

it is easy to understand why such scoundrels as Billy the Kid were included in the good-bad category by misguided admirers.

Believers in and perpetrators of the Western myth also contend that the gunfighters shared certain physical characteristics. Great attention has been paid to the color of their eyes and hair and to fancied similarities in physical appearance. One modern writer has devoted a whole book to the subject,[12] claiming also to list all the facets that went into making a typical bad man. Nevertheless, there was only one personality trait they all shared: the disposition to kill when provoked. In physical attributes they were as individual as any random group of men. In the few available photographs of members of the gunfighting fraternity, their expressions reveal varying degrees of intelligence. The legendary "sadness" to be seen in their eyes was probably eyestrain caused by the length of time they had to sit unblinking for an early-day portrait.

The so-called "Western Code" never really existed. Men bent on killing did so in the most efficient and expeditious way they knew. Jesse James was shot in the back by Bob Ford as he stood on a chair adjusting a picture. Ben Thompson was led into a trap in a theater and shot down with his friend King Fisher. Billy the Kid died as he entered a darkened room. Wild Bill Hickok was shot from behind while he was playing poker. In each case the victim had no chance to defend himself.

It has been pointed out that the gunfighters—especially those who allied themselves with some aspect of law enforcement—were accepted by the society on whose fringes they lived. Another factor in a gunfighter's acceptance was whether or not he was regularly employed. If he was out of a job, he was likely to be arrested for "vagrancy," a catchall charge that served to discourage potential troublemakers from staying in town. Even Hickok was not immune to such charges. On June 17, 1875, Wild Bill was charged with vagrancy in Cheyenne, Wyoming Territory, and a warrant for his arrest was issued the same day. A $200 bail bond was ordered and was returned and filed on June 18 and approved on June 22. By

[12] Hendricks, *The Bad Man of the West.*

August 4 the charge had cost the county $5.25 in expenses. In November, however, when the case was to be tried, Bill had disappeared, and a continuance was ordered. On June 12, 1876, Hickok had still not been apprehended, although he was known to be in town or nearby preparing for his trip to the Black Hills. The case was again continued to the next term. When Hickok was murdered, a clerk wrote across the docket entry, "Deft dead. Dismissed."[13]

Contemporary reports of his death hinted that the town marshal was afraid to bring in Wild Bill, a suggestion the marshal angrily denied. No one seemed to know why Hickok had been charged in the first place. As one historian commented, "Bill was always classed as a law and order man."[14] The explanation appears to be that Hickok was believed to be potentially dangerous, and the vagrancy charge was the easiest means of safeguarding the town against trouble.

No discussion of the gunfighter as a man would be complete without mentioning the men in official positions who used their offices to act on the wrong side of the law. Their activities have provided the basis for innumerable plots in Western books, movies, and television shows, in which the crooked banker or sheriff has become a familiar figure. One of the most notorious of such men was Henry Newton Brown, marshal of Caldwell, Kansas. Believed to have been a former associate of Billy the Kid, Brown had served briefly as assistant marshal of Caldwell early in 1882, and on December 21 of that year was appointed marshal. His effective policing of the town was appreciated by the citizens, who presented him with a fine, handsomely engraved Winchester rifle. As far as the townspeople were concerned, Marshal Brown and his assistant, Ben Wheeler, were ideal peace officers.

In May, 1884, the bank at Medicine Lodge was held up and the president and the cashier were killed. The robbers were pursued by

[13] Laramie County Clerk of Court Criminal Appearance Docket, Book II, 230, June 17, 1875–June 12, 1876, copy supplied by the Wyoming State Archives, Cheyenne, Wyoming.

[14] Russell Thorp to the author, October 14, 1960.

163

a hastily organized citizens' posse, who captured the gang after trapping them in a canyon. The gang's leaders were none other than Brown and Wheeler.

Retribution was swift. That evening an armed mob invaded the jail where the gang was being held and overpowered the sheriff and his posse. Shots were fired, and during the confusion the prisoners tried to escape. Wheeler, badly wounded, and two others were quickly captured. Brown managed to run several blocks before he was killed by a charge of buckshot and several rifle bullets. The remaining outlaws were taken to an elm tree east of town and hanged.[15]

The more deeply a historian delves into the activities of the heroes and villains of the Old West the clearer becomes the image of the men behind the legend. All of them were flawed. Some had strengths of character which tended to overshadow their faults and weaknesses; others had few visible virtues and little to commend them. The qualities they shared—pride, arrogance, and indifference to human life—and the destructive emotions that drove them— fear, anger, resentment, and jealousy—place them well and truly among men and not immortals.

[15] Miller and Snell, *Why the West Was Wild*, 67–84.

Part 2. The Pistoleer

11.

Six-Shooter Rivals

IN 1835 SAMUEL COLT PATENTED a percussion "revolving breech pistol" in England, and a year later the weapon was patented in the United States. The principle was not original, but Colt's version was the most practical developed to that time. During the next twenty-five years his revolver underwent numerous modifications and was the model for many imitations. All the imitations contributed to the rapidly expanding firearms industry, but it was the Colt revolver more than any other weapon that made possible the evolution of the gunfighter.

Between 1836 and 1841 Colt's Paterson was produced in a variety of calibers, from .28 to .36, at his Patent Arms Manufacturing Company, in Paterson, New Jersey. Equipped with the folding triggers so popular in Europe, these earliest pistols were five-shot weapons. The largest size, the .36, first sold as a "belt" pistol and later as a modified "holster" pistol, could be obtained with any barrel length from 4 to 12 inches, but the 7½-inch and 9-inch versions proved to be the most popular. The acceptance of the Paterson by the Texas Navy and the Texas Rangers influenced others to use the new revolvers. However, when Colt's business failed, production was halted. It was the outstanding performance of its successor—the Walker Colt—in the Mexican War that made Colt's name famous throughout the world. When the Texas government first approached Colt to make the arms, he was unable to find a specimen of his earlier Paterson pistol to use as a model. "I advertised in the newspapers for a specimen of my own arm," he recalled,

"as I had given my samples and models all away to friends; but I did not find one at the time; and in getting up the new ones I made improvements on the old."[1]

According to one expert, the Walker pistol, firing a 219-grain lead bullet backed by 50 grains of black powder, had a muzzle velocity of at least fifteen hundred feet per second—a velocity not exceeded until the introduction of the .44 Smith & Wesson "Magnum type." Although there were no facilities at that time to gauge its capabilities accurately, Captain Walker noted that the pistol was as effective as a rifle at one hundred yards and superior to a musket at two hundred yards.[2]

The Walker weighed four pounds nine ounces, and with its nine-inch barrel it looked more like a cannon than a revolver. Gone was the folding trigger of the Paterson. The new pistol had a more conventional gunlock, a trigger protected by a guard, and only five moving parts. Its mechanism was almost identical to that of the later Peacemaker.

Partly because of its fantastic performance the Walker Colt was a short-lived weapon. The powder charge was so powerful that on occasion the gun would blow itself apart. But with it Colt achieved his goal: he re-established himself in the gunmaking business. Colt had no factory in which to produce the pistol, and he negotiated with Eli Whitney, Jr., to produce at cost the one thousand pistols ordered by the government for use in the Mexican War. The weapons were manufactured at Whitney's factory near New Haven, Connecticut. Eventually eleven hundred Walkers were turned out.

Colt, none too happy about the way the Whitney workmen, unfamiliar with gunmaking, were producing his pistols, was in no position to complain, for Whitney had been the only manufacturer able to undertake the work. As soon as the success of the Walker Colt was assured, Sam Colt was able to open his own factory, and by October, 1847, his now-famous Hartford factory was in opera-

---

[1] Evidence of Samuel Colt Before the Select Committee on Small Arms, London, 1854, The Guildhall Library, London, England.

[2] Jeff Cooper, *Guns of the Old West*, 11.

tion. The next year another large pistol, the 1848 Dragoon, was brought out. This pistol continued to be produced, with slight modifications, until 1873. Weighing a few ounces less than the Walker, the Dragoon had a slightly smaller cylinder which reduced the powder charge to 40 grains, although the ball weight remained at 219 grains, or 48 round balls to the pound.

Colt's quest for a lighter and more easily handled weapon led to the appearance in 1850 of a pistol that more than any other of its time encouraged the use of revolvers by military personnel and civilians. This was the Navy revolver, originally designed as a "New Improved Ranger Size Pistol" in honor of Colt's friend Colonel Jack Hays. The Ranger appellation was dropped in favor of the Navy designation, possibly because a number of the new pistols were tested and adopted by the United States Navy, or perhaps because the cylinder was engraved with a rolled-on scene depicting a battle between the Texas navy and some Mexican ships on May 16, 1843. A two-pound ten-ounce, .36-caliber, six-shot weapon with a 7½-inch octagonal barrel, the Navy had lightness, balance, and hard-hitting accuracy that soon made it very popular.

In 1851 Samuel Colt was among the American exhibitors at the Great Exhibition held in London's Hyde Park in the Crystal Palace, where England played host to the world's inventors and craftsmen. English restrictions on the importing of foreign arms had prevented him from shipping his arms in quantity to Great Britain, but when the law was changed in time for the exhibition, Colt crammed his stand with specimens of his arms. Although he received only honorable mention for his revolvers, interest in them was marked, and the British government made some purchases for the Twelfth Lancer Regiment.

After some negotiation Colt set up a factory in London and opened his books for orders on January 1, 1853. Until December, 1856, the factory produced the Navy pistol and the 1849 pocket model. Approximately thirty-eight to forty thousand Navy pistols and about ten thousand pocket models were manufactured, with steel supplied by Thomas Firth and Sons, the Sheffield manufac-

turers, who exported large quantities of metal to Colt's Hartford factory as well.[3]

The London factory attracted many public figures, including Prince Albert and Charles Dickens. Dickens commented at length on the cleanliness of the factory and the excellent working conditions provided for the staff and workmen.

The British government purchased approximately twenty-four thousand Navy pistols, as well as a number of Dragoon pistols, for use in the Crimean War. By 1856, however, the opposition and strong competition of English gunmakers forced Colt to move his machinery and equipment to Hartford. But the mass-production methods he introduced in England remained to influence European manufacturing methods.[4]

In the years before the Civil War Colt devoted himself to designing a revolver that would combine the power of the Dragoon with the lightness and balance of the Navy. The resulting weapon, the New Model Army revolver of 1860, used the basic Navy frame stepped down a little at the front to take a rebated cylinder bored to house the .44 ball of the Dragoon and forty grains of black powder. The round barrel was eight inches long, and the handle was a quarter of an inch longer than the handle of the Navy, to absorb the increased recoil. Over 200,000 of these revolvers were produced. They became the most popular Civil War pistols and were much in demand for years after the war.

Colt did not long monopolize the pistol-making industry. His basic patents ran out, and other companies began competing for small-arms sales. In England Robert Adams and William Tranter were producing superior pistols, expertly made and finished, though lacking the attributes that kept Colt's weapons in the forefront— ruggedness and reliability. English gunmakers adopted the top

[3] Order Book of Thomas Firth and Sons, 1851–1854. For more information on Colt's London enterprise, see Edwards, *The Story of Colt's Revolver.* Joseph G. Rosa, "Sam Colt Opted for British Steel," *The Gun Report,* Vol. XIV, No. 2 (July, 1968) 8–14.

[4] Howard L. Blackmore, "Address: Colonel Colt London," *Gun Digest* (1958), 79–84, 309–12.

strap as a standard fitting, as did the Remington Arms Company, producer of Fordyce Beals's solid-frame, single-action revolver, patented September 14, 1858. There were several modifications in its design, culminating in the most popular of the Remington cap-and-ball arms, the .44 New Model Army of 1863. This gun and the .36 single- or double-action Navy version were extremely popular among Union and Confederate troops and were widely used in the West.[5]

Another rival of the Colt during the war years was the .44 double- or single-action Starr revolver. A few .36-caliber Starrs were made, but the .44 was by far the more popular of the two weapons. Some twenty-five thousand revolvers of the single-action type were purchased by the Union. More rigidly constructed than the Colt 1860 Army, with a top strap similar to that used on the Remington, the Starr had the advantage of being easily disassembled without the use of a screwdriver; a knurled screw at the rear of the recoil shield was removed, and the barrel tipped forward to allow a quick removal of the cylinder. The Starr failed to be generally accepted in the West, and in the late 1860's the company was dissolved. However, Starr revolvers, converted to five-shot cartridge weapons in Belgium, were used in the Franco-Prussian War of 1870.[6]

The resurgence of the Western movement at the end of the Civil War brought with it a need for modernized arms and ammunition. For years experiments had been carried out in an effort to produce a cartridge that would replace the cap-and-ball system. At the London exhibition in 1851 Casimir Lefaucheux had displayed single-shot and five-barrel pin-fire cartridge pistols that had been praised but not widely used.[7] In 1852 Robert Adams had developed a metal cartridge for use in his percussion revolver, and between 1862 and 1865 Deane-Harding, William Tranter, and John Adams produced true cartridge revolvers in England. Notwithstanding the new developments, British Army officers stuck to the percussion revolver

[5] William B. Edwards, *Civil War Guns,* 192–95.

[6] *Ibid.,* 196–203.

[7] *Illustrated London News,* July 5, 1851.

as a service weapon as late as the Ashanti War in 1872, and many officers stationed outside the United Kingdom continued to rely on percussion weapons long after the metal cartridge had come into use.[8]

Early in the 1850's Samuel Colt had rejected as impractical an idea for metal-cartridge weapons put to him by an employee, Rollin White. White went ahead with his experiments, and on April 3, 1855, was granted a patent for a revolver whose chambers were bored end to end. The newly formed partnership between Horace Smith and Daniel B. Wesson, who had joined forces to produce a metal-cartridge weapon, was granted the exclusive rights to produce bored-through cylinder arms on payment of royalties to White, in an arrangement that remained effective until April 3, 1869.[9]

For years the company produced only small-caliber weapons which did not compete with the larger military sizes manufactured by Colt and Remington. Samuel Clemens commented upon their apparent ineffectiveness when he described the weapon he carried on his 1861 stagecoach trip to the West:

> I was armed to the teeth with a pitiful little Smith and Wesson's seven-shooter, which carried a ball like a homeopathic pill, and it took the whole seven to make a dose for an adult. But I thought it was grand. It appeared to me to be a dangerous weapon. It only had one fault—you could not hit anything with it. One of our "conductors" [shotgun guard] practiced a while on a cow with it, and as long as she stood still and behaved herself she was safe; but as soon as she went to moving about and he got to shooting at other things, she came to grief.[10]

Clemens' pistol was probably the earliest of the Smith & Wesson revolvers, a .22-caliber, seven-shot revolver available from early 1857. This weapon underwent several modifications. In June, 1861, just about the time Clemens was preparing for his trip west, Smith & Wesson produced the No. 2 revolver. It resembled the modified

[8] John Darwent to the author, 1965 correspondence.
[9] Parsons, *Smith and Wesson Revolvers*, 3–4, 41–54.
[10] Samuel Langhorne Clemens, *Roughing It*, 31–32.

versions of the No. 1, but was a six-shot weapon in .32 caliber. Available in four-, five-, and six-inch barrel lengths, it was very popular during the Civil War, especially the six-inch-barrel model, which was most favored by officers and their men.[11] However, the caliber was too small, and the company planned a successor to the No. 2 in the military .44 caliber as early as 1862, but it was not until 1869 that such a revolver became practicable.[12]

The prototype of the No. 3 revolver was completed in May, 1870, and was submitted to the United States Board of Ordnance for tests. The board concluded that the weapon was "decidedly superior to any other revolver submitted," and placed an order for one thousand revolvers. Thus, on December 28, 1870, the Smith & Wesson No. 3 became the first cartridge revolver to be adopted by the United States government.[13] Although it was generally known as the American Model, that designation was not officially applied to the gun by the company until 1874, the last year it was manufactured.

Unlike its contemporaries, which were loaded and unloaded through a gate device on the right-hand side of the recoil shield, the Smith & Wesson American had a break-open action that allowed the barrel to drop down, ejecting all the cartridge cases as the cylinder and barrel cleared the frame. This action proved excellent for cavalry use, because the whole operation could be performed with one hand. There was, however, one disadvantage: if only a couple of shots had been fired and the user decided to reload it, all six cartridges were ejected at once. The Colt, despite the fact that both hands were required to load it (difficult to accomplish while riding a galloping horse) did not present this problem.

The Smith & Wesson American was originally issued as a six-shot weapon with an eight-inch barrel, but when requests came in for different barrel lengths, the company altered the gun to order. An officer in the Seventh Cavalry declared that his "8 inch shoots

[11] Parsons, *Smith and Wesson Revolvers*, 29.
[12] *Ibid.*, 66–67.
[13] *Ibid.*, 71.

splendidly and carries well. On the saddle the barrel is a little long, for the belt holster when a person is mounted punches against the horse's back and saddle."[14]

John B. Omohundro, better known as "Texas Jack," was an admirer of Smith & Wesson arms. While serving as a scout at Fort McPherson, Nebraska, he was issued an American and had engraved on it "Texas Jack Cottonwood Spring 1872." He later purchased other revolvers from the company.[15]

Sometime in the early 1870's Buffalo Bill Cody ordered a No. 3 equipped with a shoulder stock, and had "Buffalo Bill" engraved on it. In 1879 he ordered a nickel-plated American with a gold cylinder and a pearl stock and five hundred .44 cartridges loaded with five grains of powder. Smith & Wesson instructed the Union Metallic Cartridge Company to "put cut paper wad on powder. These are for a special order from W. F. Cody ('Buffalo Bill') who is to use them for stage target shooting." Later he ordered another five hundred cartridges, this time to be loaded with fifteen grains because "the 500 loaded some time since with 5 grains do not shoot strong enough." Buffalo Bill was now using blanks on stage. A year before he had wounded a fourteen-year-old boy in the gallery with a careless shot from his Winchester (loaded with ball and a small charge) as he rode off the stage of a Baltimore theater. The boy fortunately recovered, but Cody, shaken by the accident, decided that the risk of using live ammunition was too great.[16]

In 1871 the Russian government placed an order for twenty thousand Smith & Wesson pistols and specified certain changes in the cartridge design which distinguished them from the standard American model.[17] A visit to the United States by Grand Duke Alexis included a tour of the Smith & Wesson factory on December 7, 1871, where he was presented with a finely engraved No. 3 with

---

[14] *Ibid.*, 77.

[15] *Ibid.*, 134–36; Herschel C. Logan, *Buckskin and Satin*, viii.

[16] Parsons, *Smith and Wesson Revolvers*, 147; Baltimore *American*, September 10–12, 14, 1878.

[17] See Chapter 14 below.

a pearl butt bearing on one side the arms of the United States and on the other those of Russia. On a buffalo hunt the Duke was persuaded to try out his new pistol but failed to bring down a buffalo.[18]

The initial success of Smith & Wesson with the monopoly on bored-through cylinders had not been shared by the company's rivals, and those who tried to pirate the design found themselves involved in legal disputes. In 1867, however, Smith & Wesson licensed Remington to convert certain revolver frames on hand at the factory. Remington produced 4,541 rim-fire revolvers in .46 caliber before the Rollin White patent expired. These revolvers had to be fitted with five-shot cylinders because of difficulties in the placement of six chambers in the existing frames. The converted pistols made during this period did not have ejectors. When the White patent expired, Remington modified the standard percussion revolvers to take the six-shot cartridge cylinder and ejector.[19]

The Colt Company decided to perfect a method of converting its arms which did not infringe on the White patent. Adverse comment at the Paris International Exhibition about the marked differences between the Colt and the Smith & Wesson arms on view did not please the Colt Company, and the following comments in one of England's most influential magazines may have prompted the company to find a quick solution to the problem: "It may perhaps not be impossible to contrive a pistol adapted to self-igniting cartridges, the chambers of which are not bored from end to end, such an arrangement is necessarily a roundabout way of achieving what Messrs. Smith and Wesson, by virtue of their patent, accomplish more simply."[20]

In September, 1868, F. Alexander Theur, of the Colt Company, patented a system whereby cartridges could be front-loaded into a converted Colt cylinder and ejected by means of an attachment

[18] Parsons, *Smith and Wesson Revolvers*, 105; Don Russell, *The Lives and Legends of Buffalo Bill*, 177–78; Logan, *Buckskin and Satin*, 55–56.

[19] Parsons, *Smith and Wesson Revolvers*, 62–63; Parsons, *The Peacemaker and Its Rivals*, 12.

[20] *Illustrated London News*, August 31, 1867.

worked by the hammer. The "Theur Conversion" was complicated and unsatisfactory and found little favor.

Meantime, the Colt Hartford factory was busy making plans. An application to renew the expiring patent of Rollin White had been refused, and the way was clear for Colt, Remington, and other companies to compete with Smith & Wesson. Colt used this period to convert existing pistols as a preliminary to the introduction of a new revolver. Old percussion pistols were converted to rim- and center-fire ammunition, and new transition models were produced using the remaining stock of percussion barrels, frames, and other parts. During 1871 and 1872 several new models were also manufactured under the Richards-Mason patents, all of which were basically percussion weapons with open frames. Then, in 1872, William Mason patented an entirely new Colt revolver.

The new pistol retained the old cap-and-ball mechanism, detachable trigger guard, and handle strap, but it had a solid frame and a screw-in barrel. The cartridges were loaded and ejected from a side gate cut in the recoil shield, with an ejector housed alongside the barrel. This was the New Model Army revolver of 1873— the Peacemaker.

Produced in a wide variety of calibers, from .45 to .476, the Peacemaker became the most popular revolver ever made, and, except for a fourteen-year period from 1941 to 1955 has been in continuous production. In 1878, in response to many demands, the Frontier Six-Shooter, a .44-40 version chambered for the same cartridge as the 1873-model Winchester rifle, was brought out. Whether in .45 or .44-40, the Colt single-action revolver became the most highly favored fighting man's weapon in the West.

The United States government became interested in the new Colt in December, 1872. After several good reports on its performance trials were ordered for the Peacemaker, the Colt 1872 Richards model, and the Smith & Wesson No. 3 American model. All three pistols were chambered for standard service ammunition in .44 caliber. Each weapon fired eight hundred rounds. The two Colts functioned perfectly throughout the test. The American

tended to clog and was difficult to dismantle for cleaning. The Colts, with fewer parts, withstood ill-treatment better than the American, whose only superiority lay in speed of loading and ejecting. Both Colts were found to be more accurate than the American model and had greater penetration. The open-frame Richards model was more accurate and had greater penetration than the new Colt in .44 caliber, although the latter functioned better. The Peacemaker's top strap and improved base pin (fitted into a bushing independent of the actual cylinder) reduced the tendency to clog, and it was easier to dismantle for cleaning.

Several other trials were arranged between the new Colt, now in .45 caliber, and various Smith & Wesson arms, and the Colt proved superior to all the other arms tested. Under a contract dated July 23, 1873, the United States government ordered eight thousand of the new Army revolvers for cavalry use.[21]

In 1875 the Remington Company produced its first cartridge revolver, which was given a government trial against the Colt, and the improved Smith & Wesson revolver, patented by Major George W. Schofield, an officer in the Tenth Cavalry Regiment. The tests, conducted under the supervision of the United States Board of Ordnance, took place at the Springfield Arsenal, beginning on February 23, 1876.[22]

The first trial tested rapidity of loading and ejection. Eighteen shots were fired from each revolver, the chambers being empty before and after firing. The Schofield took only fifty-nine seconds against the Colt's one minute fifty-four seconds and the Remington's comparable time (including one misfire). During the next few days all three revolvers were subjected to very stiff tests for rust and fouling resistance and endurance. At the conclusion of the tests it was decided that the Colt was the weapon "best adapted to meet all the requirements of the military service." Nevertheless, 8,005 Schofields were ordered by the government because the Board of Ordnance believed that they "would be in demand by a

[21] Parsons, *The Peacemaker and Its Rivals*, 20–21.
[22] *Ibid.*, 36.

177

large class of commissioned officers in time of war." Peacemakers remained official side arms of the cavalry until 1892.[23]

Although the Remington model was not adopted for military use, some ten thousand were sold to the Egyptian government, and they were widely used in the West. To compete with the Colt, the Remington was produced in calibers of .45, .44-40, and the standard .44. A modified version of the .44-40 appeared in 1890, but only about two thousand guns of that model were manufactured. It was the last of a long line of Remington handguns.[24]

The Colt, Remington, and Smith & Wesson arms had no monopoly in the West, but comparatively few other guns were sold in that region. When it first appeared in the East, the standard Peacemaker cost seventeen dollars. In the West, where demand exceeded supply and the new weapon did not appear in quantity in gun dealers' stocks until 1876, prices were much higher. Undoubtedly the revolver best suited to the rough conditions of military and frontier use, the Peacemaker became the gun of the West—and "Colt" became a synonym for "pistol."

[23] *Ibid.*, 36–42; Parsons, *Smith and Wesson Revolvers*, 94–95.
[24] Parsons, *The Peacemaker and Its Rivals*, 42; *Gun Digest* (1958), 269.

12.

The Dead Shot

GOOD PISTOLEERS "never missed"—they always "got their man."
A cursory examination of the facts surrounding this claim reveals that few men during any period of revolver history could be classified as "dead shots," and those whose prowess amazed the most reliable witnesses often admitted that the "experts" could and did sometimes miss their targets.

There was great rivalry among top-notch gunfighters in the use of a pistol. Though few of them cared to exchange shots with each other in a serious gunfight, they readily took part in pistol matches and constantly practiced to improve their marksmanship. Bat Masterson contended that skill in the use of a pistol was invariably inborn but added that "there were plenty who learned to shoot simply because they had to. Everybody who was not a reasonably good shot went back to where he came from and quickly."[1]

The better target shot was not necessarily the victor in a gunfight. A gunfighter who displayed little skill at target practice often won a gunfight because of his state of mind—to which Masterson added another important requirement—deliberation. In a fight to the death a good shot might hesitate for a moment, during which his opponent, whose killer instinct was stronger or whose reaction was quicker, shot him dead. Many great pistol men went down before an opponent with less skill simply because their presence of mind did not equal their skill.

Bill Hickok, the legendary "Prince of Pistoleers," took part in

[1] Bat Masterson, "The Tenderfoot's Turn (an abridgment of a booklet written for the Savage Arms Company), *Guns Quarterly*, Vol. II (Summer, 1960), 10–13, 66–67.

shooting matches against anyone who cared to take him on. Most times he won (and his ability improved with the telling), but he did on occasion meet his match. Whenever he visited Theodore Bartles, a one-time leader of the Red Legs who kept the Six-Mile House on the Leavenworth Road in Wyandotte County, Kansas, the neighbors had a chance to see two famous shots in action. Bartles usually won but readily admitted that he would not like to go up against Wild Bill in a fight.

It was generally believed that in a fight to the finish Hickok was in a class by himself, gifted as he was with the cold-blooded nerve essential to the man who could shoot while being shot at. Luther North, who met Hickok in the early 1870's, often wrote about Hickok's pistol prowess. Luther's brother, Major Frank North, of the famous Pawnee Battalion of Indian scouts, was rated as one of the finest target shots with a revolver in the frontier Army. At one time Major North, Hickok, and John Talbot used to meet about twice a week at Talbot's Roadhouse, between Cheyenne and Fort Russell, to compete in target shooting. North invariably won, closely followed by Talbot. "I never saw Wild Bill shoot with his left hand either, although he was always called a two-gun man," commented Luther. Describing one contest, Luther reported that Wild Bill "was very deliberate and took careful aim closing his left eye. If he could shoot from the hip he never did it there." Luther later said that "Wild Bill was a man of Iron Nerve and could shoot straight enough to hit a man in the right place when the man had a gun in his hand and just between you and me not many of the so called Bad Men could do that."[2]

Legend has made all the shootists appear much better shots than they were. But there can be no doubt that some of them were great pistol men. The predominant weapon during the 1860's and 1870's, the cap-and-ball revolver, was slow-loading but rugged and reliable—ideal for the plainsman miles from civilization. The Colt

[2] North, *Man of the Plains*, 150–51, 310; Luther North to Richard Tanner, December 31, 1930, MS1345 Tanner, Manuscripts Division, Nebraska State Historical Society, Lincoln, Nebraska.

and Remington revolvers produced between the 1850's and 1890's may have lacked certain refinements (they had, for instance, open sights), but they were far from crude. They served their purpose, and the accuracy of some of them compares favorably with weapons in use today. In his gunfighting days Bat Masterson considered Colts such good pistols that he ordered eight of them. But in retrospect, after he had become acquainted with newer types of guns, he had some rather uncomplimentary things to say about the old-time six-shooters. Writing for a rival gunmaker, the Savage Arms Company, he indirectly criticized the Colt:

> With the clumsy monstrosities which they were able to obtain, from the heavy "monkey-wrench" cap-and-ball revolver to the more modern but just as cumbersome six-shooter, men all learned to "throw lead" quick and straight without taking sight. To do this, even if he had the natural gift of the born dead shot, required a man to practice hard and long; for although he might have the necessary sense of direction well developed, the hand and the wrist had to be trained to fit the pistol, since the pistol did not fit the hand. . . .
>
> To accustom his hands to the big, cumbersome pistols of those days, the man who coveted a reputation started in early and practiced with them just as a card sharp practices with his cards, as a shell-game man drills his fingers to manipulate the three walnut shells and the elusive pea; or a juggler must practice to acquire proficiency. When he could draw, cock and fire all in one smooth lightning-quick movement, he could then detach his mind from that movement and concentrate on accuracy.
>
> That required even more practice, for no time should be wasted in taking aim, and unless the hand grasped the handle just right and held the pistol in exactly the proper relation to the wrist, on the sensitive ball-and-socket joint of which the aim in pistol shooting always depends, he missed. . . .
>
> It was necessary for our aspiring six-shooter man to accustom himself not only to the exact manner of grasping the handle of his gun so that it pointed where the wrist pointed, but he also had to learn all over to point straight with his wrist twisted sharply downward and out of its natural pointing position. . . .

In short, the crude six-shooter, with its walking-stick handle and its trigger so placed that the trigger-finger had to reach down for it at an angle of 45 degrees, had a tendency to shoot too high and to the left.[3]

Bat was stretching the truth somewhat in these remarks, especially in his reference to a "lightning-quick movement." No doubt because he was promoting the Savage Automatic Pistol, he exaggerated the "clumsiness" of the six-shooters. Sam Colt designed his pistols on the principle that each one should act as an extension of the arm, the barrel resembling a pointing finger.

In Hickok's lifetime various writers credited him with fantastic feats with weapons. Colonel George Ward Nichols has described how Wild Bill put six balls into a letter *O* in a signboard some fifty or sixty yards from where they were standing. In itself this feat should not be difficult for a good shot, but Nichols added that Hickok accomplished it "without sighting the pistol with his eye." Wyatt Earp's biographer wrote that Earp saw Hickok perform a similar feat in Kansas City, only this time the distance was one hundred yards. But Earp witnessed no such feat—he never met Wild Bill.[4]

The legend builders were humorous at times, some deliberately so to be entertaining, and others inadvertently so in the belief that they were repeating fact. Samuel Clemens repeated a highly amusing anecdote he heard about Jack Slade during Clemens' trip west in 1861:

> Slade was a matchless marksman with a navy revolver. The legends say that one morning at Rocky Ridge, when he was feeling comfortable, he saw a man approaching who had offended him some days before—observe the fine memory he had for matters like that—and, "Gentlemen," said Slade, drawing, "it is a good twenty-yard shot—

[3] Masterson, "The Tenderfoot's Turn," *Guns Quarterly*, Vol. II (Summer, 1960), 10–13, 66–67.

[4] Interview with John Gilchriese, El Paso, Texas, October 15, 1966. Mr. Gilchriese assured me that Lake had used one of the many Hickok legends merely to get Wyatt into the act. Nothing in his material suggests that they ever met, although Wyatt claimed to own a coin he said that Hickok had sent him for some unknown reason. The coin has now disappeared.

I'll clip the third button on his coat!" Which he did. The bystanders all admired it. And they all attended the funeral too.[5]

In his classic account of the outlaw days of early Montana, Thomas J. Dimsdale cited numerous instances of six-shooter prowess among both the good and the bad men of the territory. Of Henry Plummer, the road agent, Dimsdale wrote:

> The headquarters of the marauders was Rattlesnake Ranch. . . . Two rods in front of this building was a sign post, at which they used to practice with their revolvers. They were capital shots. Plummer was the quickest hand with his revolver of any man in the mountains. He could draw the pistol and discharge the five loads in three seconds. The post was riddled with holes, and was looked upon as quite a curiosity until it was cut down in the summer of 1863.[6]

The speed and accuracy of the old-timers was enlarged upon by the nineteenth-century purveyors of sensationalism. Unless a pistol was drawn and fired with fantastic speed and accuracy, the story seemed to be lacking in effect. Occasionally doubt about the writers' veracity was expressed. Of Wild Bill's mastery of the six-shooter, one Missouri editor remarked, when reviewing the Nichols article about Hickok in *Harper's*: "No superior skill with the pistol . . . could any man of the million Federal soldiers of the war, boast of. . . . But Nichols 'cuts it very fat' when he describes Bill's feats of arms."[7]

The only possible way to verify the truth of some of the claims made for frontier marksmen is to test weapons like the ones they used. With cap-and-ball revolvers it is possible to put six shots into a two-foot circle at one hundred yards, hit tin cans thrown into the air, or drive a can along the ground with bullets carefully shot from behind it. But such tests do not prove that all the old-timers could shoot that well. One old man swore that one time Hickok, walking his horse down a street in Hays, Kansas, drew two re-

---

[5] Clemens, *Roughing It*, 73.

[6] Dimsdale, *The Vigilantes of Montana*, 25.

[7] Springfield *Weekly Patriot*, January 31, 1867.

volvers, spun them forward so that as they came level his thumbs caught the hammers, and cocked and fired the guns at a tin can he kept jumping for a whole block. It can only be assumed that Wild Bill's horse was exceptionally well trained or insensitive to the noise and smoke.[8]

Although military evaluations of handguns indicate quite clearly that Colt's revolver was a much-respected weapon, some of the feats attributed to the Colt's users were beyond the skills of any marksman. In 1924, in an effort to see just how accurate the old cap-and-ball revolvers were, two experts selected a .36 Navy Colt and a .44 Remington, both in almost new condition, and put them to a test. Using round balls cast from the molds supplied with the revolvers, they had no difficulty putting them inside circles five inches in diameter at fifty yards. When using conical bullets, however, they found that the circles had to be seven inches in diameter. Before each test great care was taken to load the weapons correctly, and grease-soaked felt wads were placed under the balls, which were themselves smeared with grease when rammed into the chambers to reduce the leading in the rifling.[9] Even then, fouling from the black powder affected the weapons' accuracy. Consequently, it may be assumed that only if owners of cap-and-ball weapons were careful to keep them extremely clean, well oiled, and properly loaded could they expect to achieve reasonable accuracy with them.

Despite the range and accuracy of the old-time revolvers, their sights left much to be desired. On the Colt Navy the front sight was normally a brass pin or post, though occasionally there was a blade sight of the type used on the Dragoon and 1860 Army models. The Colt rear sight, a notch cut into the lip of the hammer, could only be of use when the weapon was at full cock. If the hammer or its pivot screw was worn, accuracy was reduced. Users of the Reming-

8 Jeff Cooper, "How Good Was Hickok?" *Guns and Ammo*, Vol. II, No. 3 (March, 1960), 22–27; Hays *Daily News*, March 27, 1955.

9 Roy C. McHenry, "In Re: Wild Bill Hickok," *The American Rifleman*, Vol. LXIII, No. 25 (June 1, 1926), 865.

ton, Starr, and other solid-frame revolvers did not have this problem, because the rear sights on those guns were milled into the top strap.

Even though careful attention was paid to the sights and to the loading and oiling of the weapons, a further problem remained. Black powder creates a great deal of smoke. Writers who credited trick shots with the ability to hit repeatedly hats, tin cans, or other targets tossed into the air rarely considered the effect of the smoke. When attempting some of the shots (with varying degrees of success), I have found that the target is soon obscured unless there is a strong breeze to blow away the smoke.

Among the most important tests ever made of various military revolvers were those conducted by the United States Army from 1872 to 1876. In those tests the Peacemaker had a mean absolute deviation at 50 yards of 3.11 inches, compared with the Smith & Wesson's 4.39. At 25 yards the penetration of the Colt was 4.1 inches, compared with the Smith & Wesson's 3.33. In 1898 it was officially stated that the mean absolute deviation of the Peacemaker at 50 yards was 5.3 inches; at 100 yards, 8.3 inches; at 150 yards, 12.3 inches; at 200 yards, 15.9 inches; at 250 yards, 24.9 inches; and at 300 yards, 28.7 inches.

It is interesting to note that on recommendations of the War Department the Peacemaker was sighted in for 25 yards in the early 1870's but that in the 1890's it was sighted in for 50 yards. The revolver was considered to be a close-range weapon, particularly among mounted troops. The speed of a cavalry charge quickly brought men into contact with the enemy and allowed maximum use of the revolver. As with the earlier cap-and-ball experiments, however, it was established that the Peacemaker was also capable of great range. The United States Army tests reveal some interesting facts. To compensate for trajectory and drift, the correct point of aim at 150 yards was found to be 4 feet above the target and at 200 yards 8 feet above the target.[10]

[10] *Description and Rules for the Management of the Springfield Rifle, Carbine, and Army Revolvers,* 67–68; Parsons, *The Peacemaker and Its Rivals,* 20.

These test results serve to disprove many of the claims of the legend builders. Once the absolute limits of any weapon are established, no marksman can exceed those limits, regardless of his ability. Bat Masterson emphasized this point when he quoted Pat Garrett on the possibility of hitting a 1½-inch bull's-eye twice out of five shots at fifteen paces. "I would call that very good shooting myself," said Garrett, "if I took careful aim and did my best."[11]

Al Jennings, an Oklahoma bad man, was credited to be among the all-time champions with a six-shooter. One of his reported tricks was to hit a can thrown into the air, or move it over the ground, with well-placed shots. Men who knew Jennings personally denied such stories. One man remarked, "I happen to know that Mr. Jennings can't hit a gallon can at twenty yards with aimed fire once out of ten times. I've seen him try." General Roy Hoffman, a Rough Rider and veteran of World War I, commented, "I knew Al Jennings personally, and his marksmanship was notoriously poor. He was one of the kind of fellows who could have qualified as the traditional bad shot who couldn't hit the side of a barn."[12]

It is regrettable that few reports of the prowess of old-time pistol shots can be substantiated. There were very fine marksmen among them, and some of their feats were witnessed by credible people. Walter Winans, whose feats are reliably recorded, was perhaps the finest shot of all time. When in 1897 he won ten out of twelve revolver matches at Bisley, England's famed target range, his skill was considered little short of marvelous—he had achieved almost unbelievable possibles with such weapons as a Smith & Wesson .44-caliber Russian, a Colt .44-40 Frontier Six-Shooter, a Bisley-model Colt, and later a .45 Smith & Wesson revolver, in which he used U.M.C. smokeless ammunition and which he equipped with his own patented foresight. His views on the subject of target shooting and target shooters might well have been echoed by any one of a half-dozen top-notch gunfighters. He wrote:

[11] Masterson, "The Tenderfoot's Turn," *Guns Quarterly*, Vol. II (Summer, 1960), 12.

[12] Wilbur Cooper (Jack Roban, ed.), "Hickok-Hoakum Case Goes to Jury," *The American Rifleman*, Vol. LXXIII, No. 26 (June 15, 1926), 900–902.

In my opinion revolver shooting is essentially a matter of firing rapidly at short ranges. Deliberate shooting at stationary targets, especially at long ranges, is all wrong. To begin with, the revolver is not accurate enough for such work. When a revolver is used, either in war or in self defence, the shooting is generally done at a few yards' distance, and at a rapidly moving object. Further, it often happens that a succession of shots has to be fired in a few seconds.

Commenting on the fact that target shooting in the 1890's was regarded in some circles as training for combat, Winans went on:

> The man who can make a possible at 20 or even 50 yards, but who takes from one to two minutes for each shot would be killed before he could loose off a round. It therefore seems to me that the deliberate shooting at the revolver clubs and at Bisley is worse than useless, because it teaches the man to shoot the wrong way. The disappearing target, which is in sight for three seconds for each shot, is too slow, for it is practically a stationary target.[13]

Today, seventy years later, Winans' comments are still recognized for their common sense, and military practice now follows this theory. Even in his own day Winans' ideas had some supporters. W. W. Greener, the renowned gunmaker and firearms expert, commented on the revolver of 1898: "The modern revolver is designed for quick work at close quarters. The qualities of paramount importance are therefore, rapidity of fire, accuracy and penetration at short range, handiness and quick re-loading. A weapon which is for use in a melee, need not have much range; of greater moment is the simplicity of the mechanism, which should make no demand upon the shooter's attention."[14]

Perhaps Greener had in mind the then new double-action arms of Colt, Smith & Wesson, and Webley, but his reference to "simplicity of the mechanism" suggests the old single-action Peacemaker. What the Colt may have lacked in workmanship and finish,

---

[13] Capt. Leo Milligan, "Pistol Aces of a Past Era," *Guns Review*, Vol. III, No. 3 (March, 1963), 18–19.

[14] *Ibid.*

compared with other precision-made arms, it made up for in simplicity of design, ruggedness, and reliability.

Winans' records have yet to be bettered by anyone using similar weapons. A later "pistoleer," Edward McGivern, whose experiments and feats were also impressive, established beyond all doubt the absolute limits of the revolver. He proved, for instance, that the stories centering around the capabilities of the old single-action revolver were not entirely legend. In January, 1934, he drew and fired five shots into a man-sized target at ten feet in 1.6 seconds, drew and fired one shot into a man-size target at ten feet in .25 second, and by drawing and fanning the hammer put five shots into a target in 1.2 seconds. In the last stunt all five shots were close enough that they could be covered by the palm of the hand. During most of his long career McGivern used double-action pistols. He practiced a great deal to achieve near-perfection, but unlike the old-timers, he never used his gun on another man.

13.

The Cult of the Six-Shooter

THE MEN WHO PROVIDED THE INSPIRATION for the gunfighter myth are long dead, but their weapon has survived. Something akin to hero-worship—gun worship—has grown up around the six-shooter.

An important element of the six-shooter legend was the gunfighter's dexterity in performing all manner of tricks, draws, spins, and rolls. Perhaps the most famous trick of all was the Curly Bill, or road agent's, spin. There are many conflicting accounts of its origin and its use. It may have originated with the production of the Walker Colt, whose trigger guard made possible numerous stunts. At any rate, by the 1880's the spin was an established part of Western folklore.

The gun spin figured in stories of the death of Fred White, the first marshal of Tombstone. One evening in October, 1880, a group of cowboys were shooting and whooping it up in town. White deputized Virgil Earp to help him arrest them. As the two lawmen moved in, the group dispersed. White and Earp cornered one man in the darkness, and White demanded his pistol. One version of the tale claims that the man held out his pistol barrel first, and the marshal pulled the cocked gun, causing it to fire and shoot him in the stomach. A more popular version is that the man held out the weapon butt first and that as White reached for it the man promptly spun the butt into his own hand and cocked the pistol. Whether he then deliberately fired, or, as he testified, Earp seized him from behind, causing the hair-triggered pistol to fire, is not known.

The man who held the gun was William ("Curly Bill") Brocius.

An examination of his weapon after the incident showed five shots still in the cylinder, evidence that he had not been one of the men shooting up the town. Brocius was taken to Tucson for trial and acquitted of the murder charge.[1] The story of the spin soon circulated through the West. In 1884 a correspondent for the New Mexico *Globe-Democrat* made a visit to a gun store in El Paso and wrote about some of the interesting people he met and heard about:

> While your correspondent was inspecting the glittering array of pistols of all kinds which filled half a dozen show-cases, a young fellow about 23 entered. He was dressed in approved frontier style, sombrero it would take three days to walk round the rim of, white handkerchief tied loosely round the neck, blue shirt, pants stuck in his boots, and large Mexican spurs upon his heels, jingling as he walked. He wished to buy a "gun." In the expressiveness and laconic tongue of the frontier a "gun" is a revolver, a rifle is called by the name of the maker, and the weapon of the sportsman, uncurtailed of its fair proportions, is known as a shot-gun.
>
> Selecting from a case a handsomely mounted 45-caliber revolver the clerk said: "How would you like this? It is the newest thing out—double-action forty-five."
>
> "Ain't worth a row of beans. No man 'cept a tenderfoot wants that kind of thing. Give me an old reliable all the time. Ye see a man that's used to the old style is apt to get fooled—not pull her off in time—and then he'll be laid out colder'n a wedge."
>
> He was handed out a single-action of the same model, which after carefully examining, he proceeded to cock and fire, twirling the pistol around his forefinger and cocking and pressing the trigger the moment the butt came into the palm of his hand. After some little "kick" about the price the weapon was paid for and the customer left the store.
>
> "There are few men," observed the clerk as his customer left, "that can do that trick. I have been ten years on the southwest frontier, among the worst classes, and don't know more than half a dozen. 'Bill the kid' could do it, so can Pat Garret [*sic*], former-sheriff of Lincoln county; so can Dan Tucker, deputy sheriff of Deming. Curly Bill

---

[1] Lake, *Wyatt Earp, Frontier Marshal*, 244; Waters, *The Earp Brothers of Tombstone*, 116; Jahns, *The Frontier World of Doc Holliday*, 113–14.

could do it best of the lot, and that's how he killed Sheriff White at Tombstone."

A TREACHEROUS TRICK.

"How was that?" queried the correspondent.

"Well, you see Curly Bill was trying to paint the town red, and White heard of it, and going up to him covered him with his six-shooter and told him he had got to give up his gun. Bill handed the gun out butt first, but kept his finger inside the guard, and as the sheriff reached for it he gave it that twist you've seen, turned her loose, and the sheriff passed in his checks."[2]

John Wesley Hardin claimed to have tricked Hickok with a gun spin during the summer of 1871. Hardin's description of the incident leaves much to be desired, and exactly what the trick was is open to conjecture. Most authorities agree that if he did, indeed, perform such a trick it was the Curly Bill spin. Hardin wrote that, when asked by Hickok to hand over his pistols: "I said all right and pulled them out of the scabbard, but while he was reaching for them, I reversed them and whirled them over on him with the muzzles in his face, springing back at the same time. I told him to put his pistols up, which he did."[3] How Hickok could have been holding his own pistols and at the same time reaching for Hardin's was not explained. It is also interesting to note that until the publication of Hardin's book no one had heard that he once forced the redoubtable Wild Bill to back down.

Although the tricks that can be performed with a six-shooter are numerous and showy, it was far more important to the gunfighter to be able to get a gun out and working quickly and accurately. Fancy rolls and spins meant nothing when death was a heartbeat away.

As emphasized earlier, the single-action revolver was without doubt the most popular weapon in the West. The young pistoleer in El Paso was not alone in his derisive comments about the double-action revolver. The gun-store clerk was eager to air his own views on the subject to the newspaper reporter, who asked:

[2] Wichita *Daily Eagle*, October 11, 1884.　　　　[3] Hardin, *Life*, 45.

"Do you sell many of the bull-dog pistols?"

"Yes. They are chiefly bought by railroad laborers, tramps, and boys. Men who are used to the country either buy a caliber-41 or carry a 44 or 45 in a shoulder scabbard."

"What is that?'

"Well, it's a pistol scabbard with a strap passing over the right shoulder, and supports the pistol under your coat on the left side. It enables you to draw while a man is thinking that you are only looking for your handkerchief. The bull-dog is a poor pistol, shoots wild and can't be depended upon for over fifteen feet. The great trouble with all these pistols are that they are hard on the trigger. The boys get over this by having the catch filed down. The pistol of the cowboy is as fine on the trigger as were the hair-triggers of the old dueling days."[4]

The controversy over the single-action versus the double-action revolvers became a matter of contention between two experts following an article in the April, 1906, issue of *Outdoor Life*. The merits of both pistols were discussed by Robert A. Kane in a letter to the editor:

Mr. Wertman claims that one can get greater rapidity of fire with equal accuracy from the D.A. than with the S.A. Now, are we to understand that Mr. Wertman uses his D.A. in the manner its inventor intended it should be used, or does he use it as a S.A.? If the former, any marksman who has had sufficient experience to be classified as such can challenge his statement and prove the opposite. If he adopts the more popular method of using his D.A. revolver as a S.A., cocking it with the hammer for each shot, then Mr. Wertman proves our contention that the S.A. is the more accurate weapon in practical use. Now, as Mr. Wertman has referred to some of the methods of manipulating a S.A. six-shooter common among the frontiersmen of the Old West, and seems to doubt the sources of his information, it may not be amiss to describe some of their stunts, and in so doing I shall confine my statements to descriptions of performances which I have witnessed. . . . [Here followed a lengthy description of Hickok's ability with a single-action revolver.]

Stewart Edward White in his book "The Mountains," in a chapter

[4] Wichita *Daily Eagle*, October 11, 1884.

on cowboys, writes as follows: "The average cowboy is only a fair target shot, but he is chain lightning at getting his gun off in a hurry. . . . the cowboy is prejudiced against the double action gun, for some reason or another. He manipulates his single action fast enough, however." . . .

The D.A. .45 was NEVER adopted by the government, and the .38 D.A. not until 1892 or 1893, or nearly two years after the engagement at Wounded Knee. . . . Both the tenderfoot and his D.A. revolver were misfits on the frontier.[5]

Despite the low repute of the double-action pistol, there were some people who preferred it, although few of them belonged to the gunfighting fraternity. To supply their needs, during the 1870's Smith & Wesson produced double-actions in competition with Colt's.[6]

A gunfighter armed with two revolvers and the ability to use both at one time or to shoot with either hand with equal skill is an accepted personality of the legendary West. The true purpose of the pair of guns carried by the real gunfighter has been forgotten or ignored, and the result has been to make of the gunfighter an oftentimes ridiculous figure—a grandstander who wore two guns for show or to impress the crowd—or worse, a coward. The gunfighters carried two guns because of a tradition that grew out of the era of the flintlock, a slow-loading and unreliable weapon that made it necessary to carry a brace of pistols in order to have something in reserve.

To overcome the failings of single-shot pistols, a wide variety of double-barreled and multishot weapons appeared in the late 1700's. Some of these weapons were quite ingenious. There were pistols with clusters of barrels welded together on a central axis, and others with a number of barrels drilled from one large piece of metal and rotated by hand. Elisha Haydon Collier's flintlock "revolver," developed from earlier weapons, employed a cylinder similar to that of a modern revolver, but it was too cumbersome to

[5] Kane, "The D.A. vs. S.A. Controversy," *Outdoor Life*, Vol. XVII, No. 6 (June, 1906), 589–92.

[6] Parsons, *Smith and Wesson Revolvers*, 164–66.

be carried or used effectively by most people. After the invention by Alexander Forsyth in 1807 of an ignition system using fulminate of mercury, the development of the percussion cap soon followed to revolutionize the arms industry.

In turn the percussion cap, a far more positive system than the flintlock, inspired many more inventions. But the problem of fire power remained. Development of weapons along the lines of Collier's principle seemed to be the next logical step, but instead gunsmiths returned to the multibarrel pistols. These weapons, with various modifications, remained in use until the 1860's, despite the introduction of the true revolver. Owing to a slight similarity in appearance, multibarrel weapons were often called "pepperboxes." Samuel L. Clemens (Mark Twain) described one carried by a fellow traveler named Benis on his 1861 Western trip:

> He wore in his belt an old original "Allen" revolver, such as irreverent people called a "pepperbox." Simply drawing the trigger back, the hammer would begin to rise and the barrel speed the ball. To aim along the turning barrel and hit the thing aimed at was a feat which was probably never done with an "Allen" in the world. But George's was a reliable weapon, nonetheless, because, as one of the stage drivers afterward said, "if she didn't get what she went after, she would fetch something else." And so she did. She went after a deuce of spades nailed against a tree, once, and fetched a mule standing about thirty yards to the left of it. Benis did not want the mule; but the owner came out with a double-barreled shotgun and persuaded him to buy it anyhow. It was a cheerful weapon—the "Allen." Sometimes all its six barrels would go off at once, and then there was no safe place in all the region roundabout but behind it.[7]

Colt's improved partitioning of chambers and the cylinder that replaced the revolving barrel lessened considerably the danger of multiple discharge. It was not unknown for a Colt to misfire, but Sam Colt always argued that if his weapons were loaded properly such accidents could not occur.

Like most of its predecessors, the Colt was frequently sold in

[7] Clemens, *Roughing It*, 32.

pairs. The first one thousand .44-caliber Walker Colt Dragoons delivered to the United States Mounted Rifles in 1847 were issued in pairs, as was customary for mounted soldiers, and Sam Walker arranged for double saddle holsters in which to carry them.[8] Regular Army troops were later provided with carbines and sabers, and then only one revolver was issued to each man. The military mind still believed that the carbine and saber were superior to the revolver.

Among civilians the time taken to load or reload a cap-and-ball revolver often meant the difference between survival and death. The practical solution was to carry two revolvers, or at least a spare loaded cylinder, a practice that originated with Pony Express riders. In the early days each rider was armed with a carbine and two Navy revolvers. Later it was decided that the extra pistol and the carbine were unnecessary weight, and they were dispensed with, leaving the riders with one revolver and occasionally a spare loaded cylinder.[9]

In the percussion pistol there was a tendency for spent caps to drop back into the mechanism through the hammer channel, rendering the weapon inoperative until it had been stripped and cleaned out. Even a broken mainspring was less serious than the effects of a spent cap, because the user could always use a rock or other hard object to hit the hammer spur and set off the cap. Accuracy was much reduced by this method, but at least the weapon was still usable. Colt recognized the dangers of spent caps and milled a groove in the recoil shield so that as the cylinder turned the caps dropped away. But this provision was by no means foolproof. In the solid-frame Remington arms the hammer face struck the cap through a corresponding hole through the frame, and spent caps rarely gave trouble. But after a short time in action the cylinder pin sometimes became so fouled that the cylinder was likely to freeze, and only by removing the base pin (sometimes a difficult operation)

[8] Col. Berkeley R. Lewis, "Colt Walker-Dragoon Holsters," *Gun Digest* (1958), 43–45.

[9] Serven, *Colt Firearms*, 101.

could it be cleaned. With such hazards as these, as well as the reloading problem, to contend with, the old-timers found a second gun to be a necessity.

True fixed ammunition was unavailable for general use until 1870, and it was not always possible to obtain the prepared paper or foil cartridges. Thus the early westerners had to rely on loose powder and caps and therefore had to carry extra weapons. Some of the members of the Civil War guerrilla bands carried as many as four revolvers. "Bloody Bill" Anderson is said to have carried eight revolvers spread around his belt, as well as a hatchet and additional Dragoons in saddle holsters. This claim may well be fiction, but photographs of some of the old-time guerrillas reveal that they were, indeed, walking arsenals.

The practice of carrying two guns during the early days did not necessarily mean that both weapons were used at once. The fictional gunfighter pulls both guns and fires them simultaneously. The real-life gunfighter may have done so on rare occasions, especially during a saloon brawl, but the basic purpose for the second gun was to have something in reserve. Usually one gun was emptied before the second one was brought into action.

Few gunfighters were ambidextrous. Hickok's exploits with two pistols indicate that he may have been so, but his left-hand shots were not as good as his right-hand shots. One man recalled watching Hickok put six quick shots into a target twenty paces away with his right hand and then follow this feat with another six shots into the target with the left hand. The witness said that of the first six shots two were in the center spot and the others within an inch of it. Of the left-hand shots all six were in the target but none in the center spot. Hickok's only comment on the matter was that he had never shot a man with his left hand.[10]

Metallic ammunition became commonplace in the 1870's, but it was of poor quality and subject to misfire, and men continued to carry more than one pistol in the event of an emergency. Even in the 1880's, after ammunition had become more reliable, few gun-

[10] Charles F. Gross to J. B. Edwards, June 15, 1925, Manuscripts Division, KSHS.

fighters failed to carry some type of reserve or hide-out gun. Many carried derringers, the deadly short-barreled .41- or .36-caliber, single-shot pistols invented by Henry Deringer. John Wilkes Booth used a derringer in the assassination of Abraham Lincoln and forever branded the derringer as an assassin's weapon. Gamblers, prostitutes, and petty criminals carried derringers. There were many versions of the gun, the most popular being the cartridge-model Colt, the Williamson, and especially the two-shot Remington. The most interesting version was the Williamson, a .41 or .36 weapon designed to fire fixed rim-fire ammunition or powder and ball.

By the 1890's the two-gun men had nearly disappeared, but their tradition is a long time dying. Dime novels and wild West shows kept it alive, as did the movies of William S. Hart, whose two-gun good bad men maintained a rate of fire that would have done credit to a Gatling gun.

A desire to preserve the gunfighter legend, a refusal to let the old days die, served to give the legend another twist—the fast draw. All over the United States and in many parts of the world this feat has captured the imagination of gun lovers and Old West fans. In a little less than a hundred years the gunfighter legend has turned full circle. *Beadle's Dime Novels*, Buffalo Bill's wild West shows, and modern Western novels, movies, and television shows all contributed to the myth. Admirers of the fast draw, caring not that the supposed originator wore a tarnished halo, elevate his modern counterpart to a kind of sainthood. Feats of speed and marksmanship attributed to the legendary gunfighter are duplicated and bettered by modern-day marksmen. For many people the fast draw is an inseparable part of the cult of the six-shooter.

In place of the early-day leather holsters, built for the dual purpose of carrying and protecting a pistol, modern fast-draw holsters are steel-lined, cut away to a minimum, and specially molded to fit the gun. Some are even designed to allow the cylinder to turn so that the gun can be cocked in the holster by the heel of the hand. The time taken to draw and fire one shot has improved consider-

ably since Ed McGivern set his record of .25 second in 1934—
and thereby helped create general interest in the fast draw.

The fast draw, which really caught on in 1954, seems to have
been the creation of Dee Woolem, who practiced fast draw between
acts at his job of "robbing" an excursion train at a tourist exhibition
in Orange County, California. He built an electric timer to time his
speed, and others copied him. Within five years the fast draw had
aroused nation-wide interest.[11] By the middle 1960's the fast draw
had practitioners around the world. Today competitions are held
to determine the "fastest gun alive" among the synthetic gunfighters, and the competition is very keen. There are rules and strict
supervision to ensure that no one uses anything but blanks or wax
bullets. Whether one condones or condemns the fast draw, it does
illustrate the fantastic appeal of the legendary gunfighter and
his weapons.

The old-time gunfighters and the modern-day fast-draw addicts
have one thing in common—similar weapons. There the similarity
ends. The gunfight was a fact; the fast draw, a fantasy.

The fast draw has become the subject of controversy among
target shooters and others devoted to various forms of sport shooting. Many dedicated sportsmen regard it as childish and irresponsible and damaging to the sport of shooting. This view is reinforced
by the antics of the lunatic fringe, who really believe that their
speed identifies them with the early-day westerners. Disparagers of
the cult take the more realistic view expressed by a much-respected
authority in the gun world, who summed it up as follows:

> I have never happened to meet a Fast Draw addict who claimed he
> could excel the old timers in guts, but when a good one tells you that he
> can excel the old timers in speed, he's 100 per cent right! I know a
> hundred men who can draw, fire, and hit a target in less time than
> Hickok or any old timer could ever have done. I know this can't be
> proved, simply because no old timer ever was timed. But it must cer-
> tainly be accepted—because no old timer ever had the gun or the

[11] Dee Woolem, "Fast Draw—From Six to Sixty," *Guns Quarterly*, Vol. I (Spring,
1960), 18–21, 56–58.

holster essential to such speeds. Hickok, with his sash-held guns, would have been blown apart before he could get those guns clear, given a face to face test against today's speedsters. I don't say the modern boys would have killed him—that's a very different kettle of fish. Almost everyone, in a kill situation, is reluctant to shoot. I would expect most of today's fast gunmen to draw, see that they had the opponent hopelessly beaten, and stop, expecting him to accept defeat. Whereupon Hickok (or Hardin, or Earp, or Breakenridge, et al) would proceed to kill him! Because I don't believe those men *had* much, if any, such reluctance!

But I know several modern gunmen who could and would kill any one of the old timers, given their own modern equipment against that of the old timers. Only a few days ago, I saw Bill Jordan (Captain, Border Patrol, and a noted exhibition shooter and fast draw artist), hold a coin on the back of his right hand at less than shoulder height, drop his hand from under the coin, draw (with the same hand), and intercept the coin with the barrel of the gun at hip level. The coin dropped not more than 14 inches; you can figure the speed of the draw. This was done in a motel room; but I have seen Jordan do this with a loaded gun, let the coin drop past his gun and then hit it with a bullet before it touched the floor. No old time gunman ever approached this speed; and I say Jordan not only could but would have killed them, because Jordan has killed a few men himself, in the course of some 35 years of law enforcement.

Actually, there never were any face to face, Hollywood-type, draw-and-shoot duels between known old timers. And if there had been, between men of anything like equal skill, the man who *started* to draw first would always win. Why? Simply because it takes even a man with quick reactions 20 to 25 hundredths of a second to respond to any "signal." And hundreds of today's gunmen can draw, fire, and hit in half a second or less. . . . If Gunman A waited for Gunman B to "go for his gun," Gunman B's starting movement would be Gunman A's starting signal. It will take him 20 hundredths of a second, at the very least, to see that signal and react to it by starting for his own gun. If both men can draw, fire, and hit in half a second, Gunman B will beat Gunman A by 20 hundredths of a second, right? . . . You *can* set up a fair draw-and-shoot duel, only by letting both men get set, then giving both a starting signal. This way, and this way only, can they match

their reaction time-gun dexterity speed. And I never heard of this being done, in the Old West. Nobody then was splitting seconds into fractions; and nobody then ever thought of such a thing as "reaction time." (A good fast draw man will have you stand facing him with your open hands a foot apart, tell you to clap your hands when you see him start to move—and then draw and put his gun between your hands before you can clap them—merely proving that his draw speed excels your reaction time.) ...

I agree with you that the methods of handgun combat of today and those of Hickok's era are a world apart. We know the old timers tried for some degree of speed in getting their guns into action, even dreaming up trick ways of carrying the guns to permit quicker shots—such things as bottomless holsters, guns worn with no holsters at all but with metal studs fitting into metal sockets on the belt to permit swiveling the gun to firing position, etc. Hickok's own carry must have been aimed toward quickness, among other things. But nobody ever, in those days, came up with any holster or any method of carrying that approached the speed potential of modern, steel-stiffened holsters; and, as you say (and in spite of all the fictional poppycock about giving the other guy the first move), the old timers took a pretty practical approach to the problems of getting a gun into action. . . .[12]

The Captain Jordan mentioned above has written a book on the subject of guns and shooting from a policeman's point of view and has explained at length the difficulties in deciding when and when not to draw a gun, in action or in preparation for action. Perhaps his most pertinent remark was, "Speed's fine but accuracy's final."[13]

[12] E. B. Mann to the author, June 6, July 13, 1966.
[13] William H. Jordan, *No Second Place Winner*, 57.

200

14.

Bullets and Holsters

WHEN THE OLD-TIME GUNFIGHTER went into action, he made sure that he was armed with the most efficient weapon and the best ammunition he could obtain. The kind of ammunition he used was important. Until metallic cartridges were devised, only loose powder and ball or the prepared paper or tinfoil cartridge was available. Various types of cartridges had been in use as early as the wheel lock. In the middle of the sixteenth century paper cartridges containing powder and ball were common to the military, and elaborate cartridge boxes were in use among civilian shooting enthusiasts. By the time of the Napoleonic Wars prepared ammunition was in general use.[1]

In using the early cartridges it was necessary to bite off one end before pouring the powder into the barrel. In the heat of battle precious powder was spilled, and alternative methods of loading and preparation were eagerly sought. In 1846 Houiller of France patented a rim-fire system similar to that employed in modern .22 ammunition. A year before, in 1845, a fellow countryman of Houiller's, Louis Flobert, had invented the BB cap—a small-caliber ball inserted into an oversize percussion cap—and in 1849 Flobert produced a metallic cartridge of modern form charged with black powder. The rim of the case was covered with fulminate of mercury and was exploded by a ridged striker on the hammer. A number of the Flobert-designed small-caliber arms have been called "saloon pistols," a name that led some people to believe that they were used in saloons for friendly shooting matches. In fact, they were de-

[1] Howard L. Blackmore, *British Military Firearms*, 22, 30, 143.

signed for use in a *pistolet de salon*, or "shooting gallery." Later Lefaucheux simplified earlier systems and produced the pin-fire cartridge. This cartridge had a metal base, a paper or metal tube containing a powder charge, and a conical bullet. At the base of the charge was a percussion pellet attached to a small pin which protruded from the side of the case, an arrangement to detonate the charge when the pin was struck by the hammer.[2]

Many rim- and center-fire cartridge designs of the early 1850's were years ahead of their time. Charles Lancaster, the London gunsmith, patented a center-fire cartridge in 1852, but it was the inventor of a firearm, Robert Adams, who first produced a percussion-revolver cartridge that did not require ramming. Patented in 1851, it consisted of a bullet formed with a projecting tang which passed through a wad into a metal tube, where it was riveted in place. The tube was filled with powder, and the end sealed with a thin disk of paper. Placed over this end was a small cap, or lid, which was removed before loading. Because of this last feature the cartridge was known to the British as the "Adams dustbin cartridge."[3]

In England in 1854 Samuel Colt and William Thomas Eley patented a cartridge consisting of a conical bullet cast with a groove that facilitated the attachment of a case or chamber made of tin foil. A piece of tape was attached to the cartridge, which was then wrapped in paper, with one end of the tape on the outside. Before the cartridge was loaded, the tape was torn off, taking the paper with it. Part of the case was ripped away, exposing the powder to the flash of the cap when it was rammed into the chamber. A similar cartridge without the tape was also produced, supplied in "envelopes" of five or six. When loaded straight into the chamber, this cartridge, too, was burst by the force of the rammer.[4]

Meantime, in the United States, where Flobert-type pistols were

[2] Edwards, *Civil War Guns*, 164; Hank Wieand Bowman, *Famous Guns from the Winchester Collection*, 45–46; Cooper, *Guns of the Old West*, 17.

[3] R. Bedford, "The Adams Dustbin Cartridge," *Guns Review*, Vol. II, No. 2 (April, 1962), 18–20.

[4] Serven, *Colt Firearms*, 149.

manufactured by Horace Smith, there was increasing interest in metallic cartridges. Smith & Wesson set about devising a reliable one. Flobert's 1849 cartridge provided a suitable model, and in 1856 the Smith & Wesson version was patented. It had one advantage over preceding designs—a lubricated bullet. In 1857, when the company began producing revolvers under Rollin White's patent for bored-through chambers, an improved version was made.[5]

In the years just before the Civil War other firms were busily engaged in perfecting metallic cartridges, among them Maynard and Burnside. During the war breech-loading carbines and rifles were widely used, including the Spencer, the Henry, the Sharps, and the Hankins. The most common ammunition was the prepared paper or foil cartridges designed for percussion arms; nevertheless, the trend was clearly toward metallic ammunition.

Though the plainsmen of the 1850's and 1860's naturally preferred prepared ammunition, it was not always available on the frontier. So each man carried a bullet mold, a powder flask, and a supply of percussion caps, and usually spare nipples and springs as well. Black powder was the subject of many campfire chats and arguments. For many years American-made powder was considered inferior to English powder. One of the problems facing American powder manufacturers was difficulty in obtaining saltpeter, most of which was imported and of inferior quality. About 1863 manufacturers began converting Chilean nitrate of soda, and by 1864 the Union had fourteen powder mills producing varying grades of powder. Even after the war, however, the quality of the powder was not high. One old-time buffalo hunter recorded that two of the leading brands of American powder burned hot and dry, caked up the barrels of his rifles, and made cleaning difficult. When he came across some much more expensive powder of English manufacture, he found that it burned decidedly moister and developed greater energy, and he used it exclusively thereafter.[6]

[5] Bowman, *Famous Guns from the Winchester Collection*, 50.
[6] Col. Berkeley R. Lewis, *Notes on Ammunition of the American Civil War, 1861–1865*, 1–3; Frank H. Mayer and Charles B. Roth, *The Buffalo Harvest*, 41.

A serious drawback to all percussion caps of the era was the fulminate of mercury, which soon corroded the nipples. When checking his weapons, the experienced pistol man also regularly inspected the nipples. To guard against misfire, at each loading he pushed a pin or spike through the flash hole to remove any dirt or unburned powder. Explaining this precaution to Charles F. Gross in 1871, Wild Bill Hickok said, "I ain't ready to go yet, and I am not taking any chances when *I draw and Pull I must be sure*." Hickok also made a practice of periodically firing and reloading his pistols to avoid overnight dampness, which affected the salt-laden black powder of the day.[7]

In the early 1870's, when Colt, Smith & Wesson, and Remington were vying for weapons supremacy, they also worked to improve the ammunition used in their revolvers. Smith & Wesson's first large-caliber revolver, the .44 American, was designed for a 218-grain lead bullet and 25 grains of black powder. This bullet had good stopping power, but it was in no way comparable to the .45 Colt cartridge.[8]

The original .45 Colt cartridge case could hold 40 grains of black powder, and the bullet varied in weight from 233 to 265 grains. With this load behind it, a 250-grain bullet could travel 910 feet per second—delivering a jolt to stop any enemy in his tracks. This speed was less than the estimated 1,500 feet per second of the .44 Walker bullet backed by 50 grains of black powder; however, the Peacemaker could take this load with safety, whereas the Walker was overloaded.

The old-timers well understood that bullet weights and powder charges affected the efficiency of their weapons, and there is little doubt that most of them were as particular about the ammunition they used as they were about the guns they wore. United States Army tests revealed that the Peacemaker bullet would penetrate a 3¾-inch white-pine board at fifty yards, and a 3½-inch board at one hundred yards. Even at three hundred yards its penetration was

[7] Charles F. Gross to J. B. Edwards, June 15, 1925, Manuscripts Division, KSHS.
[8] Parsons, *Smith and Wesson Revolvers*, 104.

$2\frac{1}{4}$ inches (in the opinion of the Army experts, a penetration of 1 inch corresponded to a very dangerous wound).[9] The gunfighter armed with a Peacemaker was a formidable opponent, indeed.

The gunfighter had to have some convenient and accessible means of carrying his weapons and ammunition. The now-familiar body belt and holster were not common when Colt patented his first revolver in 1835. In those days the holster was normally attached to the saddle. The use of a body belt and holster did not become common until the 1850's, when the ordinary flap saddle holster, of the type supplied with the 1847 Walker and the 1848 Dragoon, was modified for belt wear. The holster completely enclosed the gun and protected it from sand, dirt, and moisture.[10]

The few surviving Colt percussion-revolver holsters are mostly "left-handed," and designed to be worn on the right side to allow the butt of the pistol to point forward—the long-barreled pistol was easier and safer to handle this way. It was a simple matter to draw the pistol with the right hand by inverting the palm, slipping the index finger through the guard, and placing the thumb over the hammer spur. The action of throwing it forward in a twisting motion as it came out cocked it and lined it up on the target. Photographs taken just before and during the Civil War show many pistols worn in this fashion. Artists depicted cowboys of the trail-driving era wearing pistols in belts or holsters with the butts forward. In some instances the pistol was carried with the butt in the small of the back.

A famous portrait of Hickok, an exponent of the reverse, or twist, draw, shows him carrying a pair of Colts thrust in a belt, butts forward. An earlier photograph, taken in 1865 and reproduced as a woodcut in *Harper's*, shows him wearing a reverse-draw holster at his right hip. For the most part, however, he carried his pistols in a belt, a waistband, or a silk sash.[11]

[9] Cooper, *Guns of the Old West*, 11, 22; *Description and Rules for the Management of the Springfield Rifle, Carbine, and Army Revolvers*, 67–69.

[10] Edwards, *The Story of Colt's Revolver*, 266; Lewis, "Colt Walker-Dragoon Holsters," *Gun Digest* (1958), 43–45.

[11] The photographer was Charles W. Scholten, who seems to have made a number

The two-inch-wide military belt worn by Frank James at the time of his surrender was a converted Army belt to which he had added cartridge loops. The 1851 Army sword-belt buckle he wore caused some comment, but Frank informed Governor Crittenden, to whom he had surrendered, that he had taken it from the body of a Union officer he had killed at Centralia, Missouri. His pistol was an 1875-model .44-40 Remington. Governor Crittenden's family also received the .45 Schofield Smith & Wesson revolver, belt, and holster that Jesse James had thrown on a bed moments before he was killed by Bob Ford on April 3, 1882. The presentation of these items to the Crittendens was a gesture of gratitude for their kindness to the James family after Jesse was slain. Jesse's belt was a plain one, two inches wide, with cartridge loops and an oblong metal buckle.[12]

In the frontier days when a man without a revolver was only half-dressed, the way one wore a revolver was a personal matter. Charlie Forbes, a member of Henry Plummer's gang considered by some to exceed Plummer in quickness and dexterity with guns, believed in making the best use of his equipment. He had "the scabbard sewn to the belt, and wore the buckle always exactly in front, so that his hand might grasp the butt, with the forefinger on the trigger and the thumb on the cock, with perfect certainty, whenever it was needed, which was pretty often."[13] The description does not indicate whether Forbes wore a cross-draw or a reverse-draw holster.

At the end of the Civil War, when cartridges for rifles and for some models of revolvers became available, revolvers were still carried in belts, pockets, and occasionally in holsters (some of

---

of portraits of Wild Bill in Springfield in 1865, though there are no known copies of them. The drawing which illustrated the *Harper's* story was said by the editor of the Springfield *Weekly Patriot* (January 31, 1867) to be a Scholten photograph.

[12] Miles Standish, "Guns That Won the West," *The Trail Guide*, Vol. IV, No. 2 (June, 1959), 7, 10; see also Harold L. Peterson, *The Book of the Gun*, 222–23, for a colored photograph of these weapons.

[13] Dimsdale, *The Vigilantes of Montana*, 79.

military origin, sometimes with the flap cut off to allow a speedy draw), and the ammunition had to be carried in pouches or pockets, where it was often not readily accessible. Some more practical arrangement for carrying ammunition was needed by civilians and military personnel alike. Soon the Army was provided with a cartridge belt, and harness makers and saddlers quickly copied it for civilian use. By the middle 1870's the cartridge belt was a common sight in the West.

Some of the early holsters were sewed to the belt or fitted tightly to it by means of a loop; others were fitted with a backing, or "skirt," that allowed them to be slipped over the belt and positioned as the wearer desired. Some men fixed pegging or thongs to the bottoms of the holsters and tied them to their legs. Tying the holster in this fashion kept it out of the way when the wearer was working and prevented it from riding up when the gun was drawn. Eventually the practice became part of the gunfighter myth, when it was interpreted to have been a means of gaining speed on the draw.

Holsters were worn in other places than at the waist or in the armpit. Some men had strange preferences for the placement of such items. Hardin was said to have worn two holsters sewn to a vest. The pistol butts pointed inward across his chest. To draw, he had to cross his arms.[14]

In the old days belt holsters were almost invariably worn high on the hip, where they were handy and comfortable. The wearer did not give primary importance to speed of draw. If he expected trouble, he placed his gun where he knew he could get to it, and he usually drew before he entered a dangerous situation.

By the end of the nineteenth century holsters were undergoing changes in design. The old flap holster that had given way to the open-top variety, which covered everything but the handle of the pistol, was in turn replaced by a series of modified holsters. One was the buscadero holster, designed by Sam Myres, of El Paso, Texas, who followed suggestions made by Captain John R. Hughes, of the

[14] Cunningham, *Triggernometry*, 426, 431.

Texas Rangers. This holster was attached to or hung from the belt by means of slits cut at an angle on the back. From this practical and unadorned holster came the now-familiar Hollywood gun belts with steel-lined holsters and other refinements, the likes of which the old-time gunfighters never saw.[15]

[15] Haldeen Braddy, "The Birth of the Buscadero," *Guns*, Vol. VIII, Nos. 1–85 (January, 1962), 38–39, 60.

15.

The Legend Lives On

THE GUNFIGHTER OF LEGEND is now too firmly established in American folklore for any factual treatment to be able to strip him entirely of his glory. Through the media of fiction, television, and movies he continues to ride from one adventure to another, and will doubtless continue to do so for a long, long time. To his many admirers the idealized Western hero seems to embody many things Americans believe in—freedom, democracy, and one's right to defend his home and family. Moreover, the wild West legend is an expression of the New World's need for recognition by the Old.

Despite America's accelerating trend toward urbanization and her technologically based economy, there still exists a fascination with her frontier past which tends to affect many Americans' attitudes toward their society. Perhaps the past is not yet remote enough to permit an impartial examination of the West and its characters. Despite sporadic efforts to present realistically the settlement of the West and to overcome the cowboy-and-Indian oversimplification, there still exists in many people a sympathy and vicarious identification with the man with a gun.

Some of the most effective perpetuators of the gunfighter legend and the Western myth have been the novelists. Owen Wister's *The Virginian* gave us one character. Zane Grey, Ernest Haycox, Clarence E. Mulford, and Max Brand gave us many others, as they stirred the hearts and the imaginations of millions the world over with stories of heroes of the Old West. They and hundreds of other writers have written millions of words about this subject that will no doubt continue to enthrall audiences in years to come.

Occasionally, in attempts to circumvent the legend and explain what the West was "really like," more or less realistic films have been produced. *The Gunfighter*, a film produced in the 1940's, depicted the loneliness of the man behind the gun in something approaching a believable fashion. It was a story, told without glamor, of a young killer, flushed with pride in his new-won reputation, who was quickly made to learn that, no matter where he went, somewhere, somehow, someone would shoot him down.

In the movie *Shane*, based on a best-selling Western novel, a further attempt was made to portray the gunfighter as a human being. This film also captured the sense of loneliness that was the lot of most real-life gunfighters. Yet Shane himself was an embodiment of the legend—courageous, compassionate, loyal, willing to sacrifice himself for the good of society.

To date the finest Western of them all is undoubtedly *High Noon*. Filmed in the early 1950's, at the time of Senator Joseph R. McCarthy's investigation of "Communists in high places," the movie has been interpreted both as a classic Western and as a means to strike back at the witch hunters who were assaulting Hollywood. The dual purpose, if there was one, may have partly accounted for the film's excellence. At any rate, it achieved a maturity no other Western has matched. The climactic scene, the marshal's lone confrontation with the outlaw, would never have happened in the real West, but this is the only important concession in the film to the gunfighter legend.

In Western movies of the 1950's action was played down in favor of "psychological" treatment of the characters which, though it may have damaged the heroic-gunfighter image, failed to provide a realistic substitute. The erstwhile gunfighting marshal was reduced to a father confessor who tried to reason with a killer and explain why he was bad. The 1960's have brought further changes in the format. Gunfights are back, but there seems to be a struggle to give the action a vestige of meaningfulness in the face of opposition from the diehards who want only action for action's sake.

The Western, no longer a purely American institution, is now

produced in many areas of the world. In Japan it is big business, and in Spain, Italy, and Germany Westerns are turned out by the score. One of the successful Italian-Spanish Westerns, *A Fistful of Dollars*, made in Spain and set in Mexico, is a violent film, outstanding only for its savagery. The sadism of the "hero" certainly damages the legendary image of the gunfighter but counters with a character of unrelieved evil equally remote from reality. The most charitable interpretation of the film is that it is a brutal parody of the gunfighter legend. The film has inspired several imitations, and it seems evident that, in Europe at least, the more death the better the box-office receipts.

Today the Western, as story, movie, and television series, is at the crossroads. Gone are the old-time stars who inspired the adulation of millions. Youngsters of today tend to worship different idols. But the Western picture as entertainment or as an art form, in a world beset by violence, uncertainty, and fear, will probably continue to provide an escape for millions of Western fans for years to come. Whether it will be a new format in which realism and symbolism are effectively blended or only a vehicle for the fast draw and sadism, only time will tell. The Western gunfighter is a part of the American myth, and I suspect that the lonely two-gun Galahad will continue to ride into the sunset of another day and into still another adventure for a very long time. What was an epitaph for the "Two-Gun Man" can also be a salute to the legendary gunfighter:

> One day, rode forth this man of wrath,
>   Upon the distant plain,
> And ne'er did he retrace his path,
>   Nor was he seen again;
> The cow town fell into decay;
>   No spurred heels pressed its walks;
> But, through its grass-grown ways, they say,
>   The Two-Gun Man still stalks.[1]

[1] "The Two-Gun Man" (final verse), a poem originally published in the Denver *Republican* and reproduced in Wright, *Dodge City*, 178–79.

Bibliography

I. Books and Pamphlets

Adams, Ramon F. *Burs Under the Saddle*. Norman, 1964.
————. *Six-Guns and Saddle Leather*. Norman, 1954.
Ashbaugh, Don. *Nevada's Turbulent Yesterday*. Los Angeles, 1963.
Beidler, X. X. *Beidler: Vigilante*. Norman, 1965.
Billington, Ray Allen. *Westward Expansion: A History of the American Frontier*. New York, 1949.
Blackmore, Howard L. *British Military Firearms*. London, 1961.
Botkin, B. A. *A Treasury of Western Folklore*. New York, 1955.
Bowman, Hank Wieand. *Famous Guns from the Winchester Collection*. Greenwich, Conn., 1958.
Bronson, Edgar Beecher. *The Red-blooded Heroes of the Frontier*. New York, 1910.
Brown, Dee, and Martin F. Schmitt. *Trail Driving Days*. New York, 1952.
Bryant, William Cullen, and Sydney Howard Gay. *A Popular History of the United States*. 4 vols. New York, 1884.
Campbell, Walter S. *Dodge City: Queen of the Cowtowns*. London, 1955.
Chrisman, Harry E. *The Ladder of Rivers: The Story of I. P. (Print) Olive*. Denver, 1962.
Clemens, Samuel Langhorne. *Roughing It*. New York, 1962.
Clum, John P. (with annotations by John Gilchriese). *It All Happened in Tombstone*. Flagstaff, 1965.
Connelley, William Elsey. *Quantrill and the Border Wars*. Topeka, 1910.
————. *Wild Bill and His Era*. New York, 1933.
Cook, Gen. David J. *Hands Up; or, Twenty Years of Detective Life in the Mountains and on the Plains*. Norman, 1958.

Cooper, Jeff. *Fighting Handguns.* Los Angeles, 1958.

———. *Guns of the Old West.* Los Angeles, 1958.

Crabb, Richard. *Empire on the Platte.* Cleveland, 1967.

Cunningham, Eugene. *Triggernometry.* Caldwell, Idaho, 1941.

Custer, George Armstrong. *My Life on the Plains.* New York, 1874.

Description and Rules for the Management of the Springfield Rifle, Carbine, and Army Revolvers. Washington, 1898.

Dimsdale, Thomas J. *The Vigilantes of Montana.* Norman, 1953.

Edwards, J. B. *Early Days in Abilene.* Abilene, 1940.

Edwards, William B. *Civil War Guns.* Harrisburg, 1962.

———. *The Story of Colt's Revolver.* Harrisburg, 1953.

Forrest, Earle R. *Arizona's Dark and Bloody Ground. London,* 1953.

Frantz, Joe B., and Julian E. Choate. *The American Cowboy: The Myth and the Reality.* Norman, 1955.

Gard, Wayne. *The Chisholm Trail.* Norman, 1954.

———. *Frontier Justice.* Norman, 1949.

George, John Nigel. *English Pistols and Revolvers.* London, 1961.

Hardin, John Wesley. *The Life of John Wesley Hardin.* Norman, 1961.

Hawgood, John A. *The American West.* London, 1967.

Hendricks, George. *The Bad Man of the West.* San Antonio, 1950.

Henry, Stuart. *Conquering Our Great American Plains.* New York, 1930.

Holloway, Carroll C. *Texas Gun Lore.* San Antonio, 1951.

Horan, James D. *The Wild Bunch.* London, 1960.

———, and Paul Sann. *Pictorial History of the Wild West.* New York, 1954.

Hunter, J. Marvin, ed. *The Trail Drivers of Texas.* Nashville, 1925.

Jahns, Patricia. *The Frontier World of Doc Holliday.* New York, 1957.

Jelenik, George. *Ellsworth, Kansas, 1867–1947.* Salina, 1947.

Jordan, William H. *No Second Place Winner.* Shreveport, 1965.

Lake, Stuart N. *Wyatt Earp, Frontier Marshal.* Boston, 1931.

Lavine, Sigmund A. *Allan Pinkerton: America's First Private Eye.* London, 1965.

Leach, Joseph. *The Typical Texan.* Dallas, 1951.

Lewis, Col. Berkeley R. *Notes on Ammunition of the American Civil War, 1861–1865,* Washington, 1959.

———. *Notes on Cavalry Weapons of the American Civil War, 1861–1865,* Washington, 1961.

Logan, Herschel C. *Buckskin and Satin.* Harrisburg, 1954.

McCoy, Joseph G. *Historic Sketches of the Cattle Trade of the West and Southwest*. Kansas City, Mo., 1874.

Mayer, Frank H., and Charles B. Roth. *The Buffalo Harvest*. Denver, 1958.

Miller, Nyle H., and Joseph W. Snell. *Why the West Was Wild*. Topeka, 1963.

Morton, J. Sterling. *Illustrated History of Nebraska*. Lincoln, Neb., 1907.

North, Luther. *Man of the Plains*. Lincoln, Neb., 1961.

O'Connor, Richard. *Bat Masterson*. London, 1960.

Olmsted, Frederick Law. *A Journey Through Texas; or, a Saddle-Trip on the Southwestern Frontier*. New York, 1857.

Parkhill, Forbes. *The Law Goes West*. Denver, 1956.

Parsons, John E. *The Peacemaker and Its Rivals*. New York, 1950.

———. *Smith and Wesson Revolvers*. New York, 1957.

Peterson, Harold L. *The Book of the Gun*. London, 1962.

Richmond, Robert W., and Robert W. Mardock. *A Nation Moving West*. Lincoln, Neb., 1966.

Riegel, Robert E., and Robert G. Athearn. *America Moves West*. New York, 1964.

Rister, Carl Coke. *Fort Griffin on the Texas Frontier*. Norman, 1956.

Roenigk, Adolph. *Pioneer History of Kansas*. Lincoln, Kan., 1933.

Root, Frank A., and William Elsey Connelley. *The Overland Stage to California*. Topeka, 1901.

Rosa, Joseph G. *They Called Him Wild Bill: The Life and Adventures of James Butler Hickok*. Norman, 1964.

Russell, Don. *The Lives and Legends of Buffalo Bill*. Norman, 1960.

Sandoz, Mari. *The Cattlemen*. New York, 1958.

Serven, James E. *Colt Firearms*. Santa Ana, Calif., 1954.

Smith, Henry Nash. *Virgin Land: The American West as Symbol and Myth*. Cambridge, Mass., 1950.

Smith, W. H. B. *Book of Pistols and Revolvers*. Harrisburg, 1965.

Sonnichsen, C. L. *I'll Die Before I'll Run*. New York, 1962.

———. *Outlaw: Bill Mitchell, Alias Baldy Russell, His Life and Times*. Denver, 1965.

Steckmesser, Kent Ladd. *The Western Hero in History and Legend*. Norman, 1965.

Streeter, Floyd Benjamin. *Ben Thompson: Man with a Gun*. New York, 1957.

———. *Prairie Trails and Cow Towns.* New York, 1963.

Swayz, Nathan L. *'51 Colt Navies.* Yazoo City, Miss., 1967.

Tallent, Annie D. *The Black Hills, or Last Hunting Grounds of the Dakotas.* St. Louis, 1899.

Taylerson, A. W. F. *The Revolver (1865–1888).* London, 1966.

Thorp, Raymond W. *Spirit Gun of the West: The Story of Doc W. F. Carver.* Glendale, 1957.

Tilghman, Zoe A. *Spotlight: Bat Masterson and Wyatt Earp as U.S. Deputy Marshals.* San Antonio, 1960.

Waters, Frank. *The Earp Brothers of Tombstone.* London, 1963.

Webb, Walter Prescott. *The Great Plains.* New York, 1931.

———. *The Texas Rangers.* Austin, 1965.

Wilson, Larry R. *Bat Masterson (Colt's Firearms Lawman Series).* Hartford, 1966.

Wilstach, Frank Jenners. *Wild Bill Hickok: The Prince of Pistoleers.* New York, 1926.

Wright, Robert M. *Dodge City: The Cowboy Capital.* Wichita, 1913.

Zornow, William Frank. *Kansas: A History of the Jayhawk State.* Norman, 1957.

II. Magazines and Articles

Barnes, Lela, ed. "An Editor Looks at Early-Day Kansas—The Letters of Charles Monroe Chase," Kansas State Historical Society *Quarterly*, Vol. XXVI, No. 2 (Summer, 1960).

Bedford, R. "The Adams Dustbin Cartridge," *Guns Review*, Vol. II, No. 2 (April, 1962).

Blackmore, Howard L. "Address: Colonel Colt London," *Gun Digest* (1958).

Braddy, Haldeen. "The Birth of the Buscadero," *Guns*, Vol. VIII, Nos. 1–85 (January, 1962).

Callahan, James P. "Kansas in the American Novel and Short Story," Kansas State Historical Society *Collections*, Vol. XVII (1926–28).

Cooper, Jeff. "How Good Was Hickok?" *Guns and Ammo*, Vol. II, No. 3 (March, 1960).

Cooper, Wilbur (Jack Roban, ed.). "Hickok-Hoakum Case Goes to Jury," *The American Rifleman*, Vol. LXXIII, No. 26 (June 15, 1926).

Cushman, George L. "Abilene, First of the Kansas Cow Towns," Kansas State Historical Society *Quarterly*, Vol. IX, No. 3 (August, 1940).

Denison, William W. "Early Days in Osage County," Kansas State Historical Society *Collections*, Vol. XVII (1926–28).

Dick, Everett. "The Long Drive," Kansas State Historical Society *Collections*, Vol. XVII (1926–28).

Ducomb, Dean. "A Silent Drum Beside the Okaw," The Westerners' *Brand Book* (New York) Vol. IV, No. 1 (1957).

Dykstra, Robert R. "Ellsworth, 1869–1875: The Rise and Fall of a Kansas Cowtown," Kansas State Historical Society *Quarterly*, Vol. XXVII, No. 2 (Summer, 1961).

Gillett, James B. "The Killing of Dallas Stoudenmire," *Frontier Times* (original series), Vol. I, No. 10 (July, 1924).

Henry, Theodore C. "Two City Marshals: Thomas James Smith of Abilene," Kansas State Historical Society *Collections*, Vol. IX (1905–1906).

Kane, Robert A. "The D.A. vs. S.A. Controversy" (letter to the editor), *Outdoor Life*, Vol. XVII, No. 6 (June, 1906).

Koop, W. E. "Billy the Kid: The Trail of a Kansas Legend," *The Trail Guide*, Vol. IX, No. 3 (September, 1964).

Lewis, Col. Berkeley R. "Colt Walker-Dragoon Holsters," *Gun Digest* (1958).

Long, James A. "Julesburg—Wickedest City on the Plains," *Frontier Times*, Vol. XXXVIII, No. 2 (February–March, 1964).

McClellan, J. A. "Joseph McClellan," Kansas State Historical Society *Collections*, Vol. XVII (1926–28).

McHenry, Roy C. "In Re: Wild Bill Hickok," *The American Rifleman*, Vol. LXIII, No. 25 (June, 1926).

Mason, Frank. "What Really Happened at the O.K. Corral?" *True West*, Vol. VIII, No. 1 (September–October, 1960).

Masterson, W. B. (Bat). "Famous Gun Fighters of the Western Frontier," *Human Life*, Vol. IV (January–July, 1907).

———. "The Tenderfoot's Turn," *Guns Quarterly*, Vol. II (Summer, 1960).

Milligan, Capt. Leo. "Pistol Aces of a Past Era," *Guns Review*, Vol. III (March, 1963).

Mullin, Robert N. "The Boyhood of Billy the Kid," *Southwestern Studies*, Vol. V, No. 1 (1967).

Nichols, Col. George Ward. "Wild Bill," *Harper's New Monthly Magazine*, Vol. XXXIV, No. 201 (February, 1867).

Ornduff, Donald R. "Aristocrats in the Cattle Country," *The Trail Guide*, Vol. IX, No. 2 (June, 1964).

Osgood, Stacy. "Harry Tracy—Meanest Man, Alive or Dead," The Westerners' *Brand Book* (Chicago), Vol. XVI, No. 6 (August, 1959).

Penn, Chris. "Edward J. Masterson: Marshal of Dodge City," The English Westerners' *Brand Book*, Vol. VII, No. 4 (July, 1965); Vol. VIII, No. 1 (October, 1965).

Raymond, Henry H. (Joseph W. Snell, ed.). "Diary of a Dodge City Buffalo Hunter, 1872–73," Kansas State Historical Society *Quarterly*, Vol. XXXI, No. 4 (Winter, 1965).

Rickards, Colin W. "Vengeance: Kansas 1870's Style," The English Westerners' *Brand Book*, Vol. IV, No. 1 (October, 1961).

Roberts, Gary L. "O.K. Corral: The Fight That Never Dies!" *Frontier Times*, Vol. XXXIX, No. 6 (October–November, 1965).

Rojas, Arnold R. "The Vaquero," *The American West*, Vol. I, No. 2 (Spring, 1964).

Rosa, Joseph G. "Are These the Hickok Guns?" *Guns Quarterly*, Vol. I, No. 1 (Spring, 1960).

———. "Sam Colt Opted for British Steel," *The Gun Report*, Vol. XIV, No. 2 (July, 1968).

Smith, Duane A. "The Golden West," *Montana*, Vol. XIV, No. 3 (July, 1964).

Snell, Joseph W. "Painted Ladies of the Cowtown Frontier," *The Trail Guide*, Vol. X, No. 4 (December, 1965).

———. "The Wild and Woolly West of the Popular Writer," *Nebraska History*, Vol. XLVIII, No. 2 (Summer, 1967).

Standish, Miles. "Guns That Won the West," *The Trail Guide*, Vol. IV, No. 2 (June, 1959).

Steuart, Richard D. "The Story of the Confederate Colt," *Army Ordnance*, Vol. XV, No. 86 (September–October, 1934).

Thomas, Robert L. "Gunfight at Iron Springs," *True West*, Vol. XII, No. 3 (January–February, 1965).

Wilson, Paul E. "Law on the Frontier," *The Trail Guide*, Vol. V, No. 3 (September, 1960).

Woolem, Dee. "Fast Draw—From Six to Sixty," *Guns Quarterly*, Vol. I, (Spring, 1960).

III. Newspapers

Abilene (Kansas) *Chronicle*, 1870–71.

Atchison (Kansas) *Champion,* November 17, 1881.

Austin (Texas) *Democratic Statesman,* October 12, 26, 1871.

Austin (Texas) *Weekly State Journal,* October 26, 1871.

Boulder County (Colorado) *Miner and Farmer,* February 1, 1940.

Baltimore (Maryland) *American,* September 10–14, 1878.

Caldwell (Kansas) *Commercial,* October 14, 1880, June 29, 1882.

Cheyenne (Wyoming) *Daily Leader,* 1874–79.

Cheyenne (Wyoming) *Weekly Leader,* 1877.

Denver (Colorado) *Rocky Mountain News,* July 31, 1874.

Dodge City (Kansas) *Democrat,* July 19, 1884.

Dodge City (Kansas) *Globe Stock Journal,* August 5, 1884.

Dodge City (Kansas) *Kansas Cow Boy,* August 23, 1884.

Dodge City (Kansas) *Times,* 1877–85.

Ellsworth (Kansas) *Reporter,* 1873.

El Paso (Texas) *The Lone Star,* April 15, 1885.

El Paso (Texas) *Times,* April 15, 16, 19, 1885.

Ford County (Kansas) *Globe,* 1878–85.

Fort Scott (Kansas) *Weekly Monitor,* May 13, 1868.

Fort Worth (Texas) *Democrat-Advance,* January 27, 1882.

Hays (Kansas) *Daily News,* March 27, 1955.

Junction City (Kansas) *Union,* 1867–70.

Kansas City (Missouri) *Journal,* November 15, 1881.

Kansas City (Missouri) *Times,* 1871.

Las Vegas (New Mexico) *Daily Optic,* January 26, 1880.

Las Vegas (New Mexico) *Gazette,* November 4, 1879.

Lawrence (Kansas) *Daily Tribune,* March 3, 1869.

Leavenworth (Kansas) *Daily Commercial,* October 5, 1869.

Leavenworth (Kansas) *Times and Conservative,* June 25, 1869.

London (England) *Illustrated London News,* 1851, 1854, 1867.

London (England) *Morning Chronicle,* September 3, 1851.

Manhattan (Kansas) *Independent,* October 26, 1867.

New York *Herald,* June 15, 1836.

Oxford (Kansas) *Times,* October 21, 1871.

Rocky Mountain News, July 31, 1874.

Sacramento (California) *Daily Bee,* October 12, 1880.

St. Louis (Missouri) *Republican,* July 25, 1878.

St. Louis (Missouri) *Weekly Missouri Democrat,* 1867.

Salina County (Kansas) *Journal*, September 4, 1873.

Springfield (Missouri) *Weekly Patriot*, January 31, 1867.

Sumner County (Kansas) *Press*, July 30, 1874.

Tombstone (Arizona) *Daily Nugget*, November 17, 1881.

Topeka (Kansas) *Daily Commonwealth*, 1871–74.

Wichita (Kansas) *Beacon*, 1874–76.

Wichita (Kansas) *(Daily) Eagle*, 1873–84.

Wichita (Kansas) *Weekly Eagle*, July 30, 1874.

Yankton (Dakota Territory) *Press and Dakotaian*, December 5, 1876.

IV. Other Materials

Abilene (Kansas) Minute and Council Record Books, 1870–72 (microfilm copy). Manuscripts Division, Kansas State Historical Society, Topeka, Kansas.

Baylor, Captain George, to General W. H. King, 1881–82 correspondence, University of Texas Archives, Austin, Texas.

Connelley, William E., to Frank J. Wilstach, October 27, 1926, Wilstach Collection, New York Public Library.

Dykstra, Robert. "The Cattle Town Experience" (microfilm copy). Doctoral dissertation, University of Iowa, Iowa City, 1964. Kansas State Historical Society Library, Topeka, Kansas.

Guide Map of the Great Texas Cattle Trail, 1874, Kansas State Historical Society Collections.

Letters of Charles F. Gross to J. B. Edwards, 1922–25. Manuscripts Division, Kansas State Historical Society, Topeka, Kansas. The Edwards file also contains other communications from early Kansas residents.

Minute Books of the El Paso City Council, 1881–82, El Paso, Texas.

North, Luther, to Richard Tanner, December 31, 1930, MS1345 Tanner, Manuscripts Division, Nebraska State Historical Society, Lincoln, Nebraska.

Order Book of Thomas Firth & Sons, 1851–54, Firth, Brown, Ltd., Sheffield, England.

Police Court Dockets, Records of the City of Ellsworth, Kansas, Manuscripts Division, Kansas State Historical Society, Topeka, Kansas.

Price, Theodore F. "Newton: A Tale of the Southwest" (poem, *ca.* 1872), Snyder Collection, University of Missouri, Kansas City, Missouri.

"Recollections of Frank E. Hunter," Manuscript Collection, El Paso Public Library, El Paso, Texas.

"Recollections of George Look," an early resident of El Paso, Texas (manuscript), (copy supplied by C. L. Sonnichsen). El Paso Library, El Paso, Texas. The El Paso Public Library has a large collection of material relating to Dallas Stoudenmire and to the Rayner and Linn killings.

Records of the Ellsworth District Court, 1877, Ellsworth, Kansas.

State of Kansas vs. Joseph Lowe. Case records of the Sedgwick County District Court (microfilm copy). Manuscripts Division, Kansas State Historical Society, Topeka, Kansas.

Statistics of Agriculture, "Tenth Census Report of the United States" (Washington, 1882).

Testimony and Records in the Case of the State of Kansas vs. William Thompson, Records of the Ellsworth County District Court (microfilm copy). Manuscripts Division, Kansas State Historical Society, Topeka, Kansas.

Index

227

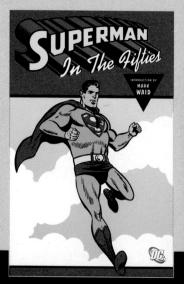

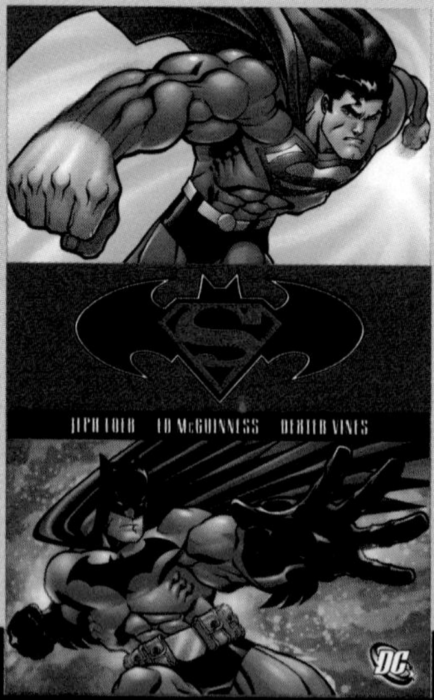

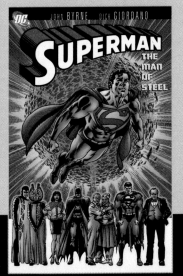
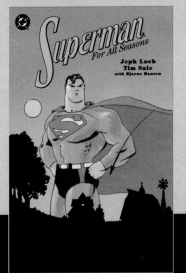